Flyfisher's Guide to™

Wyoming

including Grand Teton
and Yellowstone National Parks

TITLES AVAILABLE IN THIS SERIES

Flyfisher's Guide to Idaho

Flyfisher's Guide to Northern California

Flyfisher's Guide to Montana

Flyfisher's Guide to Colorado

Flyfisher's Guide to Oregon

Flyfisher's Guide to Washington

Flyfisher's Guide to Northern New England

Flyfisher's Guide to™

Wyoming

*including Grand Teton
and Yellowstone National Parks*

Ken Retallic

Wilderness
Adventures
Press™

Belgrade, Montana

© 1998 Ken Retallic

Cover photograph © 1998 by R. Valentine Atkinson.
Photographs contained herein © 1998 Ken Retallic or as noted.
Fish description artwork © 1998 R.D. Dye; grayling artwork © 1998 F.W. Thomas
Maps, book design, and cover design © 1998 Wilderness Adventures Press
Flyfisher's Guide to™ Wilderness Adventures Press

Published by Wilderness Adventures Press
45 Buckskin Road
Belgrade, MT 59714
800-925-3339
Website: www.wildadv.com
email: books@wildadv.com

10 9 8 7 6 5 4 3 2

Printed in the United States of America

Library of Congress Cataloging-in-Publication Data

Retallic, Ken.
  Flyfisher's guide to Wyoming / Ken Retallic.
    p.   cm.
  Includes index.
  ISBN 1-885106-37-8
  1. Fly fishing-Wyoming-Guidebooks. 2. Wyoming-Guidebooks.   I. Title.
SH565.R48   1998
799.1´757´09787-dc21

98-5197
CIP

*Dedicated with love to my mother, Mary Ralph Retallic,
and in memory of my father, Eugene K. Retallic, Sr.*

*And in heartfelt thanks and appreciation to Rob Thornberry,
a fellow writer and comrade on the stream.*

Table of Contents

Acknowledgements xi
Preface xiii
Wyoming Major Roads and Rivers (Map) xiv
Wyoming xv
Wyoming Facts xvii
Tips on Using This Book 1

Southeast Wyoming 5
  Encampment River 7
    Stream Facts 12
    Hatch Chart 13
  Upper North Platte River 14
    Stream Facts 24
    Hatch Chart 26
  Lower North Platte River 27
    Stream Facts 38
    Hatch Chart 40
  Sidebar: Miraculous Trout 41
  The Laramie Plains 47
  Southeast Hub Cities 53

Northeast Wyoming 61
  Tongue River 63
    North Tongue 66
    South Tongue 69
    Stream Facts 70
    Hatch Charts 71
  Sidebar: West's First Derby 73
  Northern Big Horns Lakes 77
  Little Bighorn River 78
  South Piney Creek 78
  Southern Big Horns Gateway 81
    Middle Fork Powder River 84
      Stream Facts 88
  Sand Creek 89
  Prairie Reservoirs 90
  Northeast Hub Cities 92

North Central Wyoming 97
  Big Horn River 99
    Stream Facts 102
    Hatch Chart 103
  Wind River 104
    Wind River Indian Reservation 104
    Upper Wind River 108
    Wind Rivers Divide 110
  Popo Agie River 113
    Alpine Roadless Area 115
    Lander Loop to the Wind River Mountains 115
  Popo Agie Wilderness 119
  North Central Hub Cities 121

Northwest Wyoming 127
  North Fork of the Shoshone River.. 129
    Stream Facts... 135
    Hatch Charts 136
  South Fork of the Shoshone River.. 139
  Shoshone River 140
  Greybull River 143
  High Desert Lakes 144
    Hatch Chart 146
  Sidebar: Home of the Monsters... 147
  Clark's Fork of the Yellowstone 151
    Stream Facts... 156
    Hatch Chart 158
  Sunlight Basin Side Trips 159
  Sidebar: State Breeds A Better Cutthroat 160
  Beartooth Wilderness Lakes.. 163
  Northwest Hub Cities 166

Yellowstone National Park 171
  Yellowstone Quick Facts... 173
  Rivers and Streams of Yellowstone 190
  Yellowstone River Drainage 193
    Yellowstone River 193
      Stream Facts... 207
      Upper Yellowstone River Hatch Charts 209
      Lower Yellowstone River Hatch Charts 211
    Lamar River 213
      Stream Facts... 218
      Lamar River/Soda Butte Creek Hatch Chart....................... 219
    Soda Butte Creek.. 221
    Pebble Creek 222
    Slough Creek 223
      Hatch Charts 227
    Gardner River.. 229
      Stream Facts... 233
      Hatch Chart 235
  Madison and Gallatin River Drainages................................. 237
    Madison River 237
      Stream Facts... 244
      Hatch Chart 246
    Firehole River.. 247
      Stream Facts... 253
      Hatch Chart 255
    Gibbon River 257
      Stream Facts... 261
      Hatch Chart 262
    Gallatin River 263
      Stream Facts... 267
      Hatch Charts 268
  Snake River Drainage 271
    Upper Snake River... 271
      Stream Facts... 274

Lewis River 275
    Stream Facts 278
    Hatch Chart 279
Cascade Corner (Bechler and Fall River Drainages) 281
    Wyoming Wilderness Lakes 282
    Bechler River 283
      Stream Facts 285
    Fall River 287
      Stream Facts 288
      Bechler and Fall Rivers Hatch Charts 289
Yellowstone's Lake Country 291
    Yellowstone Lake 294
    Lewis Lake 304
    Shoshone Lake 307
    Heart Lake 310
    Small Lakes in Yellowstone 314
Yellowstone Hub Cities 322

Close Encounters: Wildlife Observations Accentuate Fishing 331

Western Wyoming: Grand Teton National Park and Jackson Hole 339
    Snake River 341
      Stream Facts 353
      Hatch Chart 355
    Grand Teton National Park 357
      Park Lakes 359
    Bridger-Teton National Forest Lakes 364
    Teton Wilderness Lakes 364
    Upper Yellowstone River 367
    Snake River Tributaries 369
      Gros Ventre River 369
      Hoback River 370
      Spring Creeks 372
        Flat Creek 373
      Star Valley 377
        Salt River 377
          Stream Facts 379
          Hatch Chart 381
        Greys River 383
          Stream Facts 387
          Hatch Chart 388
    Western Wyoming Hub Cities 389

Southwest Wyoming 397
    Tri Basin Divide 397
    LaBarge Creek 401
    Hams Fork River 402
    Bear River 405
      Bear River Tributaries 405
    Sidebar: Cutt Slam 407
    Southwest Hub Cities 409

West Central Wyoming 413
    Green River... 414
        Stream Facts: Upper Green River 423
        Stream Facts: Lower Green River 429
        Hatch Chart 430
    New Fork River... 431
        Stream Facts... 436
        Hatch Chart 437
    Wind River Mountains 438
    West Central Hub Cities 442

Wyoming Game Fish 447

Whirling Disease.. 469

Rainbows vs. Walleyes 473

Equipment Check List and Travel Tips 475

Basic Dry Flies... 479

Food for Thought: Aquatic Insect Prey of Trout......................... 485

Catch and Release Tips 493

Wyoming Fishing Regulations 495

Grand Teton National Park General Information and Regulations................ 497

Yellowstone National Park General Information and Regulations 499

Important Phone Numbers... 507

Index.. 509

Acknowledgements

Researching this guide embellished memories of a generation ago, when my family and I made many long drives across the Midwest to the Northern Rockies, and stimulated many new campfire tales enjoyed by friends and relatives who have joined us in the Golden Circle of Trout.

Wyoming's opportunities to flyfish in pristine mountain streams and alpine lakes are so abundant they defy a single lifetime to savor them all. Those of us who heed its siren call do what we can in the time allotted and hope for more.

A book like this is not possible without the generosity of friends and experts who share a similar love for sparkling clear waters and their finned residents. At the risk of forgetting to name a few, I thank Rob Thornberry, Bruce Staples, Jerry Painter, Jimmy Gabettas, Mark Gamblin, Jack Parker, LaMoyne Hyde, and Mike Lawson, of eastern Idaho; Ron Jones, Lynn Kaeding, Glenn Boltz, and Dan Mahoney of the U.S. Fish and Wildlife Service; John Baughman, Mike Stone, Rob Gipson, Ron McKnight, and Leland McDonald of Wyoming Game and Fish; Ed Michael and Dave Nolte of Trout Unlimited's Bring Back the Natives; and the fly shop owners and guides who took the time to point a stranger in the right directions, including Bob Jacklin and John Juracek of West Yellowstone; Dave Fallon, Jim Jones, Bob Swan, and Bruce James of Jackson; Tim Wade, Chip Andrews, and Scott Aune of Cody; David Todd and Charlie Gould of Buffalo; John Ross of Pinedale; Doug and Marla Lemm of Lander; Larry and Judy Geiger of Riverside; and many more whose names I neglected to record.

Preface

Flyfisher's Guide to Wyoming including Grand Teton and Yellowstone National Parks directs anglers to excellent trout fishing in some of the most famous waters of the West.

A geological crossroads, Wyoming is where the Great Plains meet the Rocky Mountains. The Continental Divide bisects the state from the southeast to the northwest and directs its waters to four basins — the Columbia, Colorado, Missouri, and Great Basin.

Yellowstone's renowned trout fishing attracts an international clientele, but there is much more to Wyoming than the world's first national park. Among the state's 5 million visitors a year are throngs of flyfishers who find superb flyfishing in the Snake, North Platte, Wind, Shoshone, Tongue, and Green drainages. Wilderness highlands in the Wind River, Big Horn, Snowy, Grand Teton, and Sierra Madre Mountain Ranges are sprinkled with hundreds of trout-filled alpine lakes and small mountain streams. Yellowstone Park's famous waters include the Yellowstone, Madison, Firehole, Gibbon, Gardner, and Gallatin Rivers, and Yellowstone, Lewis, Shoshone, and Heart Lakes.

Wyoming has more subspecies of cutthroat trout than any other state. Its populations of the intermountain West's native trout include the Yellowstone, Snake River finespotted, westslope, Colorado River, and Bonneville cutthroat. Also found here is extraordinary fishing for imported species including rainbow, brown, brook, golden, and lake trout, as well as grayling.

MAJOR ROADS AND RIVERS OF WYOMING

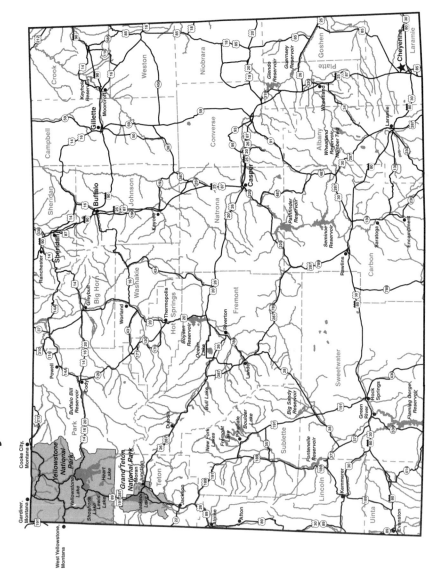

Wyoming

John Colter, who stayed behind when Lewis and Clark continued home, later regaled Easterners with the first reports of a land of steaming geysers and towering waterfalls so unusual his fellow mountain men named it "Colter's Hell." Today, Yellowstone's geological wonders are cherished worldwide.

But there is more to Wyoming than the first national park set aside in 1872. Much more.

The state's motto is "Like No Place on Earth." Less than 454,000 people live within its 96,988-square mile boundaries shaped like a picture postcard. But close to 5 million tourists a year visit Wyoming, making tourism one of the state's main industries.

Vast regions remain unchanged since the 49ers rushed to California's gold fields and stalwart pioneers made the long, arduous treks to Oregon and Utah. Indian wars and cattle wars endure as a large part of the Cowboy State's history and identity. It still retains aspects of the Old West historical fiction buffs relive through novels like *The Virginian,* and western movie fans absorb in classic films like *Shane.* Its residents remain ardently independent. Its abundant wildlife roam free in its forests and sagebrush deserts under majestic mountain vistas. Cascading alpine streams and meandering prairie rivers harbor wild trout only dreamed of in more confined environs.

In addition to Yellowstone, federally protected preserves include Grand Teton National Park, Devil's Tower National Monument, Fossil Butte National Monument, six national forests, 15 wilderness areas, one Wild and Scenic River, a national elk refuge, three national wildlife refuges, a national grassland, and a sprawling expanse of public rangelands.

State parks and historic sites at 24 locations preserve reminders of Wyoming's rich history or offer insights into its complex geology. A majority of these sites permit camping and fishing in some of the state's more scenic locales.

Geography

The Great Plains meet the Rocky Mountains in Wyoming. A high plateau, its northeast corner is rumpled by the Black Hills and Big Horn Mountains. To their south are the Laramie, Medicine Bow, and Sierra Madre Ranges. Its western highlands are crested by the Teton, Absaroka, Owl Creek, Salt, Wyoming, Gros Ventre, and Wind River Ranges. The Continental Divide bisects the state from the southeast to the northwest. Rivers east of the divide drain into the Missouri River system and eventually the Atlantic Ocean. These include the North Platte, Wind, Big Horn, Tongue, and Yellowstone Rivers. The Snake River in northwest Wyoming drains into the Columbia River and the Pacific Ocean. The Green River reaches the Pacific via the Colorado River. The waters of the Bear River remain landlocked when they become trapped by the Great Salt Lake of Utah's Great Basin.

Climate

Wyoming has the second highest mean elevation in the United States at 6,700 feet above sea level. The climate is semiarid, but because of its topographical diversity its weather is varied and unpredictable. Annual precipitation ranges from as little as 5 inches to as much as 45 inches a year, some in the form of rain but mostly as winter snow. At high elevations, it can snow any time of year.

Because of its elevation, Wyoming has a relatively cool climate. Above 6,000 feet, the temperature rarely exceeds 100 degrees Fahrenheit. Summer nights are almost invariably cool or crisp, though daytime readings may be quite high. Away from the mountains, low July temperatures range from 50 to 60 degrees. Winter temperatures often plummet to subzero extremes. The wind blows eternally.

Wyoming Facts

Ninth largest state in the union
96,998 square miles
360 miles across
280 miles north to south

Elevations: 3,099 feet on the Belle Fourche River to 13,804 feet atop Gannett Peak in the Wind River Mountains
Mean Elevation: 6,700 feet; second highest in the United States
Counties: 23
Population (1990 census): 453,588

  1 Indian Reservation (Wind River)
  2 National Parks
  2 National Monuments
  6 National Forests
  2 National Recreation Areas
  3 National Wildlife Refuges
  1 National Grassland
15 Wilderness Areas
  2 State Recreation Areas
11 State Parks

Nicknames: Cowboy State, Sagebrush State, Equality State
Primary Industries: Mineral extraction, tourism and recreation, agriculture
Capital: Cheyenne
Bird: Meadowlark
Animal: American Bison
Flower: Indian Paintbrush
Tree: Plains Cottonwood
Gemstone: Jade

Tips on Using This Book

Wyoming: So many waters, so little time.

Flyfishers will quickly discover why these waters have drawn international praise as they test their mettle against blue-ribbon trout in the myriad streams and lakes of Wyoming. At first daunting in its magnitude, the pursuit is worthy of a life-long avocation.

This guide shows you how to fish the Cowboy State's fabled waters. Its intent is not to hot-spot fishing opportunities; there is plenty of elbow room, and numerous suggestions are provided on how to get away from the madding crowds. Follow these suggestions, and your reward will be the experience of a lifetime. Even on popular streams with good road access, solitude is just around a bend or a short hike upstream from a bridge. True adventurers backpack into the wilderness to see what's on the other side of the mountain…and the next.

But anglers also must remain aware of Wyoming's strict laws against trespassing on private property, including open rangelands of ranches. The state owns the water of rivers and streams, but landowners own the banks and stream beds. Landowners are not required to post signs against trespass; it's already the law. So, if a stream or pond is not in a National Forest, on Bureau of Land Management lands, or a state school section, permission to fish must be obtained from the owner.

Still, there is good public access in farm and ranch country to fish or launch boats at scores of key sites throughout the state through easements and leases obtained by Wyoming Game and Fish. If an access site is for just one side of a river, anglers are permitted to wade out only to midstream. Anglers in boats cannot anchor in midstream or get out and wade if there is no public access along the bank.

Wyoming is a big state. Its major highways circle or cross some high mountain regions larger than New England. Most of its counties are bigger than several Eastern states. To get from one side of Wyoming to the other requires careful examination of its map. Most trips on blue highways take longer than anticipated.

On a first venture, it is best to dip into Wyoming's aquatic treasures by setting your sights on selected streams or drainages, or on specific types of fishing. Wyoming has a game fish package to suit all tastes.

To aid in planning trips to the best flyfishing waters, the state is divided into six regions. The unique fishing opportunities in Yellowstone National Park and Grand Teton National Park are treated separately. Still, the informational focus of each region and the parks is on predominant drainages, their trout, and the service hubs, communities, and resorts that cater to flyfishers. The best bets for each region and the parks are discussed in detail. Suggestions for rewarding side trips are offered.

Accommodations are identified by the rating system below. Special features—"pets allowed"—were included when that information was available.

$ – $30–$50 per night
$$ – $50 – $70 per night
$$$ – $70 per night and up

Maps to get you headed in the right direction are provided for all the top fly-fishing streams, key lowland lakes, and alpine wilderness areas. They pinpoint public access sites, boat ramps and campgrounds. Newcomers to the state are advised to pay particular attention to maps and rules posted at public access sites to avoid trespassing on private property.

Tips on fly patterns and major hatches also are given, both in the text and in hatch charts for major waters. Each hatch chart details the months when hatches occur, the time of day, and the most effective patterns. The hatch information in this book is the product of personal experience and the advice of a host of experts who have dedicated their lives to Wyoming's alluring flyfishing waters. Most of the latter are professional outfitters, guides, and fly tackle shop owners who stand ready to help you have the best possible experience on streams or lakes. Call or write for assistance in trip planning and reservations, or stop in and chat about current fishing conditions. More than a thousand phone numbers and addresses are listed.

The chapter on Wyoming's game fish details the life histories of its trout and offers additional tips on how to tackle each species. The chapter on aquatic insect prey of trout lists most of the major hatches of the Northern Rockies and provides tips on fly patterns.

Useful information at the back of the guide includes current fishing license fees. These are updated periodically, along with management regulations. Always obtain a copy of current regulations when purchasing a license.

An equipment checklist includes additional tips on trip planning and hiring a guide.

The ultimate goal of the guide is tight lines for all who use it. Good luck.

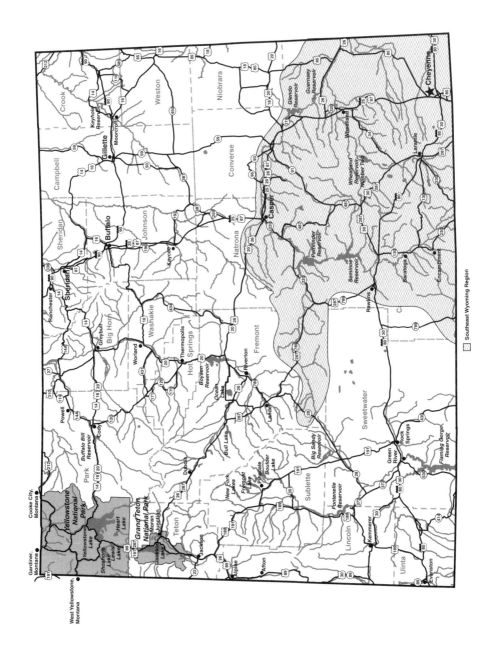

Southeast Wyoming Region

Southeast Wyoming
Prairie Meets the Rockies

The North Platte River, cutting a 300-mile loop through the mountains to the plains, defined the shape and character of Wyoming's southeastern corner. It was the route pioneers followed on their journeys west. On its upper reaches the land has changed little in this sparsely populated state.

En route from its remote mountain headwaters on the Colorado border, the North Platte collects the flows of the Encampment, Sweetwater, and Laramie Rivers, and numerous small tributaries in their relentless journeys toward the prairie. All have cut majestic canyons and gorges through cliffs and mountains And it is in these, away from the trappings of civilization, that flyfishers find the best fishing. Several of the canyons are very remote and difficult to reach. Two are protected as wilderness areas.

The popular Miracle Mile below Kortes Dam and the Seminoe Reservoir is 40 miles from the nearest town. The upper North Platte, still unchecked by a dam, offers 120 miles of blue ribbon trout waters in a mountain-prairie setting with some of the most picturesque views in the West. Only three small resort towns dot the map in this scenic corner of the state.

Downstream at Casper, the river radically changes character as it leaves the mountains and enters the Great Plains for its final run to the Nebraska border. Another string of dams harness the river as it travels through farm and ranch country, and fishing opportunities are limited. So flyfishers reaching Casper, Wyoming's second largest city, continue to look west to the upper North Platte.

The Laramie River also flows almost entirely through private rangelands with limited public access. But on the Laramie Plains is a cluster of prairie ponds that boast some of the best fishing on the Rocky Mountain Front.

Laramie, home of the University of Wyoming, is where the prairie meets the Rockies on the state's most traveled route, Interstate 80. It is the gateway to the Snowy Mountains Range and excellent alpine fishing. Just across the Snowy Range are Encampment and Saratoga, key stopovers while exploring the upper North Platte and Encampment Rivers.

Flowing off the Sierra Madre Mountains and crested by the Continental Divide, the Encampment is an excellent river to start a Rocky Mountains fishing adventure.

Outfitters and guides in Saratoga, Laramie, and Casper can help direct explorations of any of the streams and lakes in their regions or provide equipment from well-stocked fly shops.

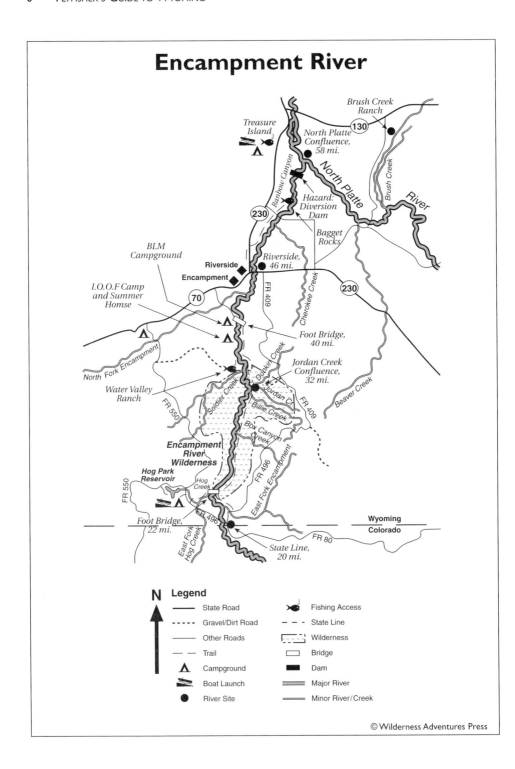

Encampment River

Brush Creek Ranch

Treasure Island

North Platte Confluence, 58 mi.

Rainbow Canyon

North Platte

Brush Creek River

(130)

(230)

Hazard: Diversion Dam

Bagget Rocks

BLM Campground

Riverside

Encampment

Riverside, 46 mi.

I.O.O.F Camp and Summer Homse

(70)

FR 409

Cherokee Creek

(230)

Foot Bridge, 40 mi.

Dunkin Creek

Jordan Creek Confluence, 32 mi.

North Fork Encampment

Water Valley Ranch

FR 550

Soldier Creek

Jordan Cr.

Billie Creek

Beaver Creek

FR 409

Box Canyon Creek

Encampment River Wilderness

Hog Park Reservoir

FR 550

Hog Creek

FR 496

East Fork Encampment

Foot Bridge, 22 mi.

FR 496

East Fork Hog Creek

State Line, 20 mi.

FR 80

Wyoming
Colorado

Legend

N

- —— State Road
- ----- Gravel/Dirt Road
- —— Other Roads
- — — Trail
- ⛺ Campground
- 🚤 Boat Launch
- ● River Site

- ✖ Fishing Access
- – – – State Line
- ⌐⌐⌐ Wilderness
- ⊏⊐ Bridge
- ▬ Dam
- ▓ Major River
- ══ Minor River/Creek

© Wilderness Adventures Press

ENCAMPMENT RIVER

Fish a river in the West, and inevitably there is a canyon to explore. Wyoming has a multitude of young mountain ranges and a host of robust rivers cutting new paths to its high desert plains. One of the most intriguing is the Encampment River. Its canyon is a great place for flatlanders to introduce themselves to the marvels of remote Rocky Mountains streams and flyfishing pocket waters in summer and autumn.

The Encampment is rated as a good river for 8- to 16-inch brown trout, with occasional catches over 20 inches. Its rainbows run a little smaller, and anglers might encounter a few cutthroat trout. Brook trout are small scrappy fighters, typically in the 6- to 10-inch range.

The Encampment rises in the shadows of the Continental Divide in Colorado and flows due north into Wyoming along the eastern shoulders of the Sierra Madre Mountains. The gentle flows of its three-mile meadow run through Commissary Park end abruptly at Entrance Falls, a Class V rapids. For the next 18 miles, it gallops down a steep, forested canyon protected as the Encampment River Wilderness Area. The first 10 miles of its plunge through the boulder-strewn channel is a back-to-back string of Class IV and III rapids and plunge pools. The pace slows slightly on the lower third of the canyon, where longer pools and shallow rock garden runs are added to the mix. The river's cascading descent falls 1,400 feet in elevation, from 8,700 to 7,300 feet.

Emerging from the canyon, the Encampment meanders another 25 miles through the rolling hills of a sagebrush desert to join the North Platte River. The pace of the lower river is still brisk, but there are more riffles, long shallow runs, and cut-bank pools.

Just south of the canyon are the sister communities of Encampment and Riverside. The two mountain villages, 20 miles south of Saratoga, mark the division of the river's passage through federal and private lands.

Upstream, public access is virtually unlimited in the Medicine Bow National Forest and on Bureau of Land Management rangelands. The best fishing for the river's feisty rainbow and brown trout is in its spectacular canyon. Its upper mountain meadow section and its tributaries also contain brook trout. Spring runoff typically peaks the first of June and rapidly diminishes by mid-July. Late summer and autumn flows are low and clear.

Below Encampment, the river flows through a string of ranches off limits to public fishing. A single public access site on state land near Baggott Rocks is difficult to reach. The primitive road into it is barely passable for 4-wheel-drive pickups. Don't even think about it in wet weather. More savvy anglers arrange shuttle services in Riverside at Lazy Acres Campground or Riverside Bait & Tackle.

Landowner permission must be obtained to launch a boat on private property below the canyon. An irrigation diversion dam below Baggott Rocks hinders float trips to the mouth. But several outfitters in Saratoga now offer float-fishing and wade-fishing trips on the lower river at least as far as Baggott Rocks.

Lower Encampment River canyon.

In the good old days there was more public access on the lower Encampment, when Ray Bergman first brought it to the public eye in his classic book *Trout*. Today's anglers who prefer freedom of movement and classic mountain stream fishing head south to the upper river. The Encampment's canyon wilderness doesn't disappoint them, although its growing popularity occasionally draws summer crowds on weekends and holidays.

Local resort owners speculate increases in anglers on the Encampment and North Platte are due to many of their southern neighbors coming over the hill because of Colorado's whirling disease problems. Wyoming Game and Fish is being pressured to impose stricter regulations on the upper Encampment. Many want a 10- to 16-inch limit and artificial flies and lures only restriction on the upper river, like the one in place below Riverside. Some advocate catch-and-release.

Autumn anglers seeking solitude essentially have the canyon to themselves. Still, they can expect to share forest roads and campgrounds with hordes of orange-capped deer and elk hunters.

An excellent green drake hatch that can start as early as late June on the lower river makes the arduous trek into Baggott Rocks a worthy adventure. The hatch lasts into July, and North Platte float-fishers also concentrate their efforts around the mouth of the Encampment. Dry fly and nymph patterns for the large drake are generally effective upstream on both rivers during this period.

Late spring dry fly action with dark stone flies is limited, although its nymph patterns are effective year round. Little yellow stones, also known as willow flies or yellow Sallies, are good producers through early summer. Caddis are the dominant hatch on the river, however. Pale morning duns are the most common mayfly through summer. Grasshoppers are another reliable summer pattern. And smaller terrestrials—beetles, crickets, and ants—work well in late summer on the upper meadows and tributaries. A few caddis linger into autumn, when the tiny fall baetis hatch becomes the dominant pattern.

But the Encampment isn't a nitty gritty, match-the-hatch stream. A variety of attractor dry fly patterns and generic nymphs, emergers, and woolly buggers are very effective on its pocket waters. These can include elk hair caddis, humpies and stimulators, royal and grizzly Wulffs, yellow and lime Trudes, grasshopper, and Adams and light Cahill patterns.

Access to the canyon mouth is located south of the village of Encampment at the end of a two-mile gravel road. Locals call this the Odd Fellows Camp, but the sign to watch for on WYO 70 is the Bureau of Land Management's campground and trailhead.

The I.O.O.F. Lodge Camp is on private land and includes a string of summer homes on the west bank. A footbridge at the BLM campground provides access to the east bank and the trail to the top of the canyon. It's best to hike at least three miles upstream to the wilderness boundary to get into better fishing waters.

To reach the Encampment's upper meadows and canyon entrance, continue south on WYO 70 to Forest Road 550. It is about 15 miles to Hog Park Reservoir, and another five miles to Commissary Park, where the Encampment crosses the state line. The river's meadows, Hog Park Reservoir and its outlet, Hog Creek, all offer good fishing.

There is a developed campground and boat launch at the dam and a picnic area and boat ramp on its western fingers. Several other Forest Service campgrounds are available in the region. Another route to Commissary Park is via Forest Roads 409 and 496. The turnoff to FR 409 is a mile east of Riverside on WYO 230.

The canyon trail is reached by a short hike down either the Encampment or Hog Creek. A footbridge provides access to both banks of the river at Entrance Falls.

For a quality fishing experience, backpack downstream and spend two or three days in the upper canyon in autumn. Flows remain steady and irrigation diversions are not a problem in the river's wilderness section.

Shuttle services to bring vehicles back to the BLM campground can be arranged in Riverside.

Hog Park Reservoir, a mountain fishery above the Encampment.

Hog Park Recreation Area

Hog Park Reservoir on the feeder stream of the same name is a principal year-round source of water for the Encampment and drinking water for residents of Cheyenne. A tunnel through the mountains from the Little Snake River drainage on the other side of the Continental Divide feeds the reservoir.

Hog Park Creek is rated as the best of the Encampment's tributaries. Brown trout in the 8- to 16-inch range are plentiful, and a few "hawgs" exceeding 20 inches can be anticipated. Smaller rainbow and brook trout also are present. Nearby beaver ponds and smaller tributaries are ready sources of additional brookies.

A small mountain meadow stream, Hog Creek is longer than it looks because of its serpentine course through the broad valley. The undercut banks and pools of its many loops and turns should be explored carefully for the creek's larger fish. It merges with the Encampment just above Entrance Falls.

The 695-acre Hog Park Reservoir is a popular family fishing destination. It holds cutthroat, rainbow and brook trout in the 8- to 12-inch range. A few rainbows that manage to overwinter a couple of years grow to line smashing proportions. Float-tubers do best in the western fingers of the lake's inlets near the picnic area and boat ramp. A campground and another boat ramp are located on the south shore above the dam.

Little Snake River

Forest Road 550 that continues west past Hog Park Reservoir is a backcountry route to Steamboat Springs, Colorado.

Several headwater branches of the Little Snake River drain the west slopes of the Sierra Madre Mountains. They are home to the rare Colorado River cutthroat, which are protected by catch-and-release regulations. Certain stream sections also are closed year round to protect the fish. But even on streams without special regulations, it's a good idea to release all Colorado River cutthroat.

The best fishing is in the higher elevations of the Little Snake's tributaries for mostly 12-inch trout which also include some brookies. Rainbows 6 to 14 inches are common in the Little Snake where it swings out of Colorado into Wyoming. But public access is very limited on the lower reaches of the river. In addition, these reaches lose a lot of water to irrigation diversions during the growing season.

Stream Facts: Encampment River

Season
- Year-round.

Regulations
- From its confluence with the North Platte River upstream to WYO 230 at Riverside, the limit on trout is 6 per day or in possession; only 1 may exceed 16 inches. All trout between 10 and 16 inches must be released. Fishing is permitted by the use of artificial flies and lures only.

Trout
- Brown trout in the 8- to 16-inch range with an occasional fish exceeding 20 inches. Rainbows are smaller, and a few cutthroat are present. Some pan-sized brook trout are found in the upper canyon, but are more common in tributaries.

Miles
- Mile 20: State line
- Mile 22: Footbridge at canyon mouth
- Mile 37: Lower boundary of wilderness
- Mile 40: BLM/I.O.O.F. footbridge
- Mile 46: WYO 230 bridge
- Mile 58: Confluence with North Platte

Character
- A high mountain stream, the Encampment meanders 2 miles through a meadow and then cascades 18 miles down a boulder-strewn canyon filled with pocket waters and pools, a few short riffles, and rock garden runs. Below the canyon, it runs through a rolling high plain in a series of longer riffles, runs, and cutbank pools.

Flows
- Spring runoff peaks in late May with flows of 780 cubic feet per second in wet years. The flow rapidly drops to 250 cfs or less by July. Fall flows are 150 cfs or less.

Access
- Full public access upstream from BLM/I.O.O.F footbridge at the lower canyon campground. State school section on the lower river near Baggott Rocks.

Camping
- BLM campground at canyon mouth
- Campgrounds in Medicine Bow National Forest and at Hog Park Recreation Area

ENCAMPMENT RIVER MAJOR HATCHES

Insect	A	M	J	J	A	S	O	N	Time	Flies
Stone Fly			█	█					A	**Dry:** Golden Stone, Orange Stimulator #6–8; **Wet:** Golden Stone Nymph, Bitch Creek Nymph, Orange and Black Bugger, Halfback #6–10
Little Yellow Stone (Willow Fly)				█	█				M//A	Yellow Sally, Yellow Humpy, Yellow Stimulator, Yellow Trude #12–14
Caddis			█	█	█	█	█		A/E	**Dry:** Elk Hair Caddis, Humpies, Goddard Caddis #12–16; **Wet:** Caddis Emerger, Soft-hackles, Prince Nymph, Squirrel Tail #14–18
Green Drake			█	█					M//A	**Dry:** Green Drake, Flav, Extended Body Green Drake #10–12; **Wet:** Green Drake Nymph #10–12
Pale Morning Dun			█	█	█	█			A	**Dry:** PMD Comparaduns, PMD, Light Cahill #14–18; Sparkle Dun #16–18; **Wet:** Hare's Ear Nymph, Pheasant Tail, Beadheads #14–18;
Baetis					█	█	█	█	A/E	Blue-winged Olive, Blue Dun, Parachute Olive Hare's Ear, Adams, Para-BWO, Para-Adams #16–22
Trico					█	█			M//A	Black and White, Trico Spinner #18–22
Midges			█	█	█	█	█		A/E	**Dry:** Griffith Gnat, Black and White, Palamino Midge #18–22; **Wet:** Sparkle Pupa, Serendipity #16–18
Terrestrials				█	█	█	█		M//A	Joe's Hopper, Dave's Hopper, Madam X, Yellow Stimulator #8–14; Foam Beetle, Black Elk Hair Caddis, Ants #14–16

HATCH TIME CODE: M = morning; A = afternoon; E = evening; D = dark; SF = spinner fall; // = continuation through periods.

UPPER NORTH PLATTE RIVER

North Platte says it all for eastern Wyoming flyfishers. Float-fishing trips down the unfettered upper river are one of the most scenic adventures in the west.

Bisecting a broad, high desert plain between the Snowy Mountains Range and Sierra Madre Mountains, the North Platte flows through a remote corner of the state little changed since the first settlers arrived more than a century ago. Its pristine mountain canyon is protected as a federally designated wilderness.

A 300-mile course through the Cowboy State—first almost due north and then southeast—makes the North Platte Wyoming's longest tributary of the Missouri River. Its total length is 600 miles from its Colorado headwaters to the confluence with the South Platte in Nebraska, where they form the Platte River. "The river effectively defines the southeast corner of Wyoming," states Rod Walinchus, author of *Flyfishing the North Platte River: An Angler's Guide*, "...about 90 miles are classified by the Wyoming Game and Fish Department as Class I, or Blue Ribbon, waters. These are defined as premium trout waters and fisheries of national importance."

Another 60 miles between the Colorado state line and Casper are classified as Class II/Red Ribbon, or very good trout waters of statewide importance. Downstream for its remaining 150 miles to the Nebraska border there are a few locally important trout waters. Numerous impoundments on the lower river also offer walleye and warm water fisheries.

Two trophy trout tailrace fisheries draw the most attention from out-of-staters: the famous Miracle Mile between Seminoe and Pathfinder Reservoirs, and the Grey Reef area below Alcova Reservoir. But the river's longest stretch of blue ribbon waters runs from its heavily forested border, down through a steep canyon, and out onto a rumpled, rolling sagebrush desert for about 10 miles below Saratoga.

Special regulations on the upper river have helped make it one of the state's premier fishing destinations, says John Baughman, Wyoming Game and Fish's new director.

From Saratoga upstream, a slot limit requires anglers to release all trout between 10 and 16 inches; only one trout may exceed 16 inches in the 6-fish bag limit. Fishing is restricted to artificial flies and lures only.

"The entire 55-mile reach offers excellent fishing and floating," notes Baughman, former state fisheries supervisor and author of *Wyoming Fishing*. "There are 2,500 to 4,000 brown and rainbow trout per mile through the stretch. Many are in the 10- to 16-inch range. Some are bigger."

The North Platte's multifaceted waters attract anglers from around the world, but their past roles as western pathways are equally remarkable. The Platte River, the North Platte, and South Pass at the headwaters of the Sweetwater River are enshrined in history through the passage of the mountain men, the Oregon Trail, and Mormon pioneers. Their phenomenal migration west might have been delayed half a century or more except for the fortunate combinations of this geological crossroads.

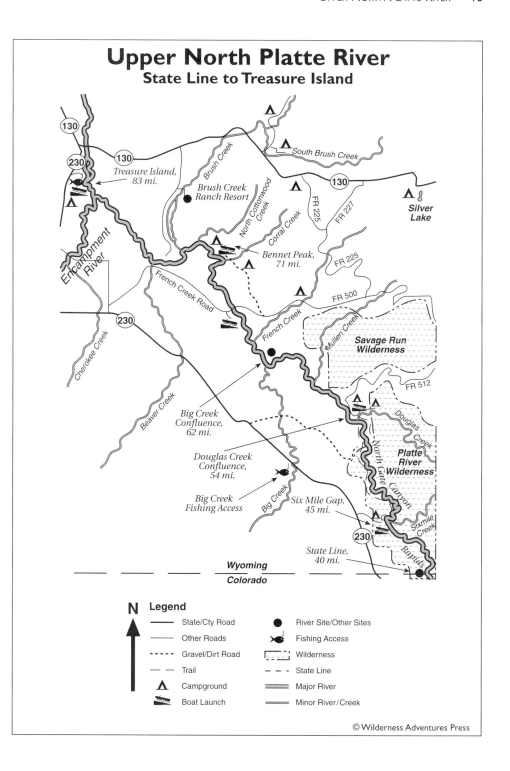

Upper North Platte River
State Line to Treasure Island

130

230

130

Treasure Island, 83 mi.

Brush Creek

South Brush Creek

130

Brush Creek Ranch Resort

North Cottonwood Creek

Corral Creek

FR 225

FR 227

Silver Lake

Encampment River

Bennet Peak, 71 mi.

FR 225

French Creek Road

FR 500

230

French Creek

Mullen Creek

Savage Run Wilderness

Cherokee Creek

FR 512

Big Creek Confluence, 62 mi.

Beaver Creek

Douglas Creek

Platte River Wilderness

Douglas Creek Confluence, 54 mi.

North Gate Canyon

Big Creek Fishing Access

Big Creek

Six Mile Gap, 45 mi.

Sixmile Creek

State Line, 40 mi.

230

Rapids

Wyoming

Colorado

N

Legend

———— State/Cty Road

——— Other Roads

- - - - - Gravel/Dirt Road

— — Trail

Λ Campground

Boat Launch

● River Site/Other Sites

🐟 Fishing Access

Wilderness

– – – State Line

Major River

Minor River/Creek

© Wilderness Adventures Press

Upper North Platte River
Treasure Island to Fort Steele

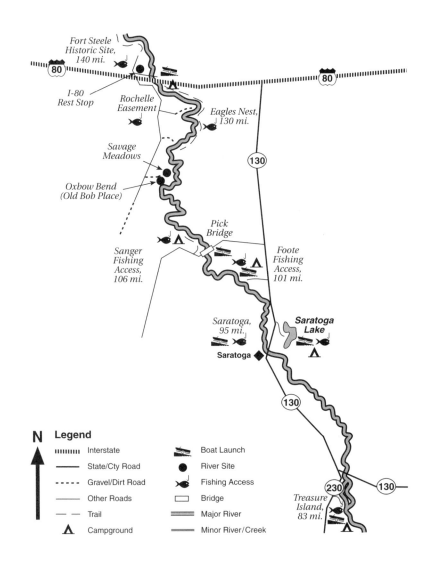

© Wilderness Adventures Press

Even today, despite numerous utilitarian roles imposed on the lower river, the North Platte retains most of its ancient characteristics. Tim Kelley, a Colorado author, likely had it in mind when he proclaimed "Fishing in Wyoming has an extra 'something.' It's more than the usual satisfaction of precious hours spent angling. It has to do with invisible things—the bigness of the country, the blueness of the sky, the contentment of enjoyment, the sense of being next to history."

To make such a journey back in time, drive southeast from Saratoga or southwest from Laramie to the Platte River Wilderness Area.

Six Mile Gap

The allure of fabled fishing waters is irresistible. A first view of the North Platte's beautiful Six Mile Gap canyon, just north of the Colorado border, immediately defines it as one of the Great Rivers of the West.

A mid-September conversation at day's end better denotes the irresistibility of this remarkable river's siren call.

"How'd you do?" I couldn't resist asking after noticing the contented smile on the incredibly sunburned face of the lone occupant in the parking lot.

"I did OK," replied Jim Widrig of Cheyenne. "Caught about a dozen rainbows and browns, a couple between 18 and 20 inches."

"What were you using?"

"Beadheads, hare's ears, pheasant tails, and other small nymphs."

"Really? I heard this is basically a dry fly stream this time of year. I stuck to blue-winged olives the short time they were hatching and did OK, but I couldn't get a thing on wet flies."

"You have to use what you're most comfortable with, but I didn't do very well my first time here, either. The river is really low this time of year. Small nymphs work best for me. I work them through the pools along the banks and in between the rocks.

"Later on, when the brown spawners start to get more active, large nymphs work pretty good, too. Caught one once at Pickaroon (Campground) that was so big that at first I thought I had snagged a log."

"Sounds great. Come here often?"

"Not as much as I would like. My car broke down about 10 miles out of Cheyenne this morning. Made a couple of calls and got a tow truck to haul it back to the garage. Soon as I got it back there, I unloaded my gear and put it in this one."

"You didn't want to give up."

"No. I didn't give up."

Even without car trouble the upper North Platte's wilderness run takes a little extra effort to reach. But those in the know can't resist its incantations. The remote 18-mile canyon remains secluded and pristine. Road access into its wilderness area, also known as the North Gate Canyon, is basically limited to two key sites.

Easiest reached is Six Mile Gap Campground on the west bank, about 35 miles southeast of Saratoga on WYO 230 at the end of a 2-mile gravel road. A 30-mile gravel road to Pickaroon Campground on the east bank drops south from the Snowy

*An angler fishes
North Gate Canyon.*

Mountains pass on WYO 130, east of Laramie. The rough road skirts the Savage Run Wilderness Area in the Medicine Bow National Forest. Autumn and late spring travelers should tune in weather reports before attempting it, as the Snowy Mountain Range lives up to its name.

At the height of spring runoff, the North Platte canyon harbors a wild and woolly river with rapids that range from Class IV to Class VII. These extremes depend on snowmelt, but most years you can leave the river to white water thrill seekers until the end of May or early June.

The majority of kayakers put in at the Routt National Forest launch site, 5 miles south of the Colorado border and run the more turbulent first 10 miles of the canyon to Six Mile Gap. Float-fishers and backpackers favor the lower canyon. A well-maintained foot trail follows the river 7.5 miles downstream from Six Mile Gap and 2 miles upstream from Pickaroon. There are plenty of good campsites above the river trail.

Mid-June through July are the best times to float fish the canyon, although the quarter-mile drag down to the Six Mile Gap put-in generally dictates the use of small water crafts like rafts, canoes, or kayaks. The canyon pullout is Pickaroon, 9 miles downstream, on the east bank. Drift boats can be more easily launched at Pickaroon but it still is a long one-day float to a vehicle, or a or two-day float to the next site.

Wyoming's strict laws against trespassing on private lands dictate pullout and launch sites below the forest boundary. The state owns the water, but landowners own the banks and streambeds. This means where Wyoming Game and Fish has obtained public access easements to just one side of a river, anglers are permitted to wade out only to midstream. Also, anglers in boats cannot anchor in midstream or get out and wade if there is no public access along a bank.

Blue signposts, placed by local fishing clubs, mark sites where float-fishers can pause to fish below the canyon. Wyoming Game and Fish also has printed a North Platte floaters map that details public access sites. It is available at local fly shops.

Developed boat ramps below the forest boundary are located at Bennett Peak, 20 miles below Pickaroon, and Treasure Island, 12 miles above Saratoga. Shuttle services can be arranged at Saratoga fly shops and the Lazy Acres Campground in Riverside. Great Rocky Mountain Outfitters in Saratoga also rents canoes and rafts.

Early season floats through the canyon are largely a case of banging the banks with woolly buggers, large nymphs and streamers on fast-sinking, sinktip lines. Slow flowing pools and eddies present occasional small wet fly opportunities. Two popular local patterns that make creative use of peacock herl are the halfback, a stonefly imitation, and the Platte River Special, a soft-hackle attractor tied with blue pheasant rump feathers. Sporadic golden stonefly hatches and the start of the caddisfly season offer some surface activity.

By late July and continuing into the golden days of autumn, the upper river is a classic western dry fly stream.

Canyon flows in summer are low and clear; the river is easily crossed by waders who tread its slick rubble bottom with care. It's textbook fishing on long riffles and pools, boulder strewn pocket waters, smooth glides and cutbank pools. The challenge is to match ever-changing hatches and spinner falls, or anticipate emergences with small nymphs, larva, and pupa patterns.

Mayflies, including darting flights of pale morning duns and smoky clouds of tricos, join fluttering swarms of caddisflies, golden stoneflies, and willow flies. The fly caster's arsenal should include elk hair caddis, stimulators, yellow Sallies, PMDs, red quills, and rusty spinners in sizes 14 to 18, and black-and-whites and trico spinners, 18 to 20. Similar-sized backup patterns can include yellow and royal humpies, Henryville specials, orange and lime Trudes, royal and grizzly Wulffs, parachute Adams, and light Cahills.

Effective wet flies include beadheads, peacock emergers, hare's ear and pheasant tail nymphs, and soft-hackles in 14 to 18, and halfbacks and woolly buggers in 10 to 14.

Anglers and floaters at Treasure Island on the North Platte.

By September, the canyon enters its autumn transition. Low water conditions require a more technical and cautious approach to trout that have moved from the riffles into protected lies behind rocks, or into the pools below large boulders and deeper runs along cutbank bends.

Tricos continue to come off in the mornings, along with a few remaining late afternoon caddis hatches. Blue-winged olives and olive parachute hare's ears, 16 to 20, are added to the dry fly arsenal. The tiny fall baetis hatch generally occurs in earnest by October.

Large nymphs, woolly buggers, Zonkers, and streamers are kept at hand for the brown trout stirring for their fall spawning runs into the upper river and its tributaries.

Solitude is almost guaranteed for late season Six Mile Gap visitors.

Days are warm and gentle; nights are crisp and cold. Twilight comes earlier and lingers with a golden butterscotch haze reflected in the rippling shallows of the river. Frostbitten cottonwoods and aspen blaze flame-yellow against the emerald backdrops of pines and firs. Early snows dust the peaks of the Snowy and Sierra Madre ranges. Piercing whistles of bugling elk signal the quickening closure of another season.

Attentions turn to the lower river.

Saratoga Valley

Spilling out of North Gate Canyon, the North Platte's channel broadens and its pace becomes more subdued on a meandering course down through arid foothills to Saratoga Valley. It enters a short canyon stretch at Bennett Peak and curves north-westerly to pick up the flows of the Encampment River. Wider and flatter, the river has more gravel bars, riffles and shallow runs, pools and undercut banks as it cuts through a cottonwood bottomland. Islands and gravel bars braid its course into numerous side channels.

Snowy Mountain tributaries worth exploring on the top end of this run are French Creek and its forks, and Brush Creek. Fish sizes are smaller, but there is excellent summer pocket water action on these tumbling mountain streams. The Brush Creek Ranch and Resort permits access to the creek's lower waters for a fee. Local fly shops also have permission to fish other private waters in the valley.

Leases or easements secured by Wyoming Game and Fish, in addition to Bureau of Land Management lands, provide public access to the river in the ranching country below Medicine Bow National Forest. Saratoga outfitters and fly shops also boast the North Platte can be fished right in town. One site is adjacent to the hot spring that inspired resort owners to name it after upstate New York's spa. Saratoga Lake, on the outskirts of town, also is popular with float-tubers casting to 8- to 18-inch rainbows and cutthroat.

Only a few of the river's access sites provide much space for wading, so the North Platte remains essentially a float-fishing river until the Miracle Mile below Kortes Reservoir. Two easily reached wading sites on the upper river's desert run are Treasure Island, 12 miles south of Saratoga, and Foote Bridge, about 5 miles north of Saratoga. The Pick Bridge site, 10 miles north of Saratoga, also was popular with campers and waders, but a 1997 lease limits its use to the parking lot and boat ramp.

Float-fishers who run unguided trips need to plan them carefully to reach intended destinations and avoid trespassing. It is against the law to stop for the night except at designated camping sites. The longest upper river float is 20 miles from Pickaroon to Bennett Peak. Others, between Bennett Peak and Picks Bridge, are spaced 12 miles or less apart. Float times increase through the season as water levels drop. In dry years, floating the river above Saratoga may not be possible by fall.

The float season on the upper river generally starts in late June. The period during the ebbing flows of spring runoff is mostly "chuck and duck" fishing with large streamers, nymphs and woolly buggers hammered into cutbanks, eddies and pools.

The valley's dry fly hatches often precede those of the canyon, as the lower river warms quicker. They erupt in earnest in July and last past October. For the persistent flyfisher, tiny baetis and midges can keep dry fly action rolling through the winter until early spring: as long as conditions permit being on the river.

Caddis are the dominant early season hatch, and sporadic hatches of golden stones and little yellow stones, or yellow Sallies, add to the mix which brings trout to the top. By July, pale morning duns are prevalent and there are scattered emergences of other mayflies, like baetis and pale evening duns. By around the Fourth of July, green drakes add a spurt of action not found in the canyon. The No. 10 and 12 drakes aren't as common as they are in the Encampment, but they draw strikes for a few weeks between Treasure Island and Bennett Peak. Grasshoppers and other terrestrials are good prospecting options through the heat of the summer.

The most anticipated hatch on the North Platte is the arrival of the tricos in August. Next in importance are the tiny fall baetis that take up the slack around mid-September as the tricos wane. PMDs and caddis linger into fall, but when temperatures plummet, baetis are the dominant species.

Crisp temperatures also spur the browns on their fall spawning runs. Effective streamers can include marabou muddlers, Zonkers, and Platte River Specials. Smaller nymphs that produce in the lower flows of autumn are beadheads, gold-ribbed hare's ears, girdlebugs, and halfbacks.

Patterns and sizes for both dry and wet flies are the same as for the canyon.

Chest waders with felt soles are recommended below the canyon because the river's cobble floor is slick and by fall usually coated with algae. Below Saratoga wading is less problematic because the gravel streambed is more stable. But be prepared to buck high winds in these wide open expanses. Short lightweight rods are not good options on the state's larger rivers. Use barbless hooks to avoid going home with an unplanned earring. Wide brimmed hats and sunglasses also help prevent injury from wind-whipped flies or errant casts of weighted nymphs and streamers.

Last Free Run

Below Saratoga, the river again changes character as it swings west from the highway and descends along eroded cliffs of a rolling high plain on its last free run. Cottonwoods and willows in the flood plain provide the only touch of green in the arid sagebrush desert. Virtually no roads in this sparsely populated rangeland reach the river's banks. About 70 miles downstream is Seminoe Reservoir, the first in a long string of impoundments to capture the North Platte's flows.

From the Pick Bridge boat ramp, 10 miles north of Saratoga, it is about 35 miles to a ramp on the east bank, just below Interstate 80 at the Fort Steele rest stop. There are several fishing access sites for about 10 miles upstream of Fort Steele, but they are not well marked. Called the Rochelle Easement, it is also a checkerboard of private and public lands.

Six miles below I-80 is the Sinclair golf course ramp. The last pullout above Seminoe Reservoir is at Dugway, a BLM site 15 miles downstream.

The oil refinery town of Sinclair, a mile west of the river's crossing under I-80, is the only dot on the map along this stretch. It has very limited services. The nearest town with full services is Rawlins, 6 miles west on I-80.

Fishing along this stretch is rated as good for trout ranging from 12 to 22 inches, and walleyes become a big part of the mix for 20 miles or more above the reservoir. All trout between 10 and 20 inches must be released, and a flies and lures only regulation exists on the five miles of river below Pick Bridge.

Foote Bridge area of the North Platte, below Saratoga.

Although this stretch gets less attention from out-of-state float-fishers, local anglers rate its dry fly action as excellent. Mayfly and caddis hatches are about the same as on the upper river, with the exception of green drakes. But it doesn't have to be approached as a match the hatch challenge. A generic set of dry flies like royal Wulffs, Adams, light Cahills, elk hair caddis, humpies, stimulators, and hoppers can be just as effective.

Float trips require more planning, however, especially as flows diminish. By fall, the only floatable stretch may be below I-80. Obtain information, maps, and shuttle services from outfitters and fly shops in Saratoga.

Stream Facts:
Upper North Platte River
(Six Mile Gap to Seminoe Reservoir)

Season
- Year-round.

Regulations
- From the state line downstream to the Saratoga Inn Bridge, the limit on trout is 6 per day or in possession; only 1 may exceed 16 inches. All trout between 10 and 16 inches must be released. Fishing is permitted by the use of artificial flies and lures only.
- From Pick Bridge (County Road 508) downstream (approximately 5 miles) to the downstream end of the old Frazier Place public fishing area, the limit on trout is 6 per day or in possession; only 1 may exceed 20 inches. All trout between 10 and 20 inches must be released. Fishing is permitted by the use of artificial flies and lures only.

Trout
- There are strong populations of 10- to 16-inch rainbows and browns, with good chances to net larger fish in both species, but especially browns. Walleye are present in the lower river to about 10 miles above I-80; trout numbers are fewer but still in 12- to 22-inch range.

Miles
- Mile 40: State line
- Mile 45: Six Mile Gap campground and trailhead
- Mile 54: Pickaroon campground and boat launch
- Mile 71: Bennett Peak campground and boat launch
- Mile 83: Treasure Island public access
- Mile 95: Saratoga
- Mile 101: Foote Bridge public access
- Mile 106: Pick Bridge public access
- Mile 140: Fort Steele/I-80 boat launch
- Mile 146: Sinclair Golf Course boat launch
- Mile 158: BLM Dugway boat launch
- Mile 160: Last pull-out
- Mile 165: Seminoe Reservoir

Character
- From 5 miles south of the state line to Six Mile Gap, the river runs down a narrow gorge filled with boulders and rapids. The canyon opens slightly at Six Mile Gap, and the river continues down the gorge in a series of rock garden runs, short riffles, and

pools to the forest boundary below Pickaroon. Below North Gate Canyon, the North Platte's channel broadens and its pace becomes more subdued on a meandering course through arid foothills. Wider and flatter, the river has more gravel bars, riffles and shallow runs, pools and undercut banks, and numerous side channels around islands. Below Saratoga, the river descends along eroded cliffs of a rolling high plain on its last free run. About 70 miles downstream, Seminoe Reservoir is the first in a long string of impoundments to capture the North Platte's flows.

Flows
- Spring runoff peaks in mid-April at extremes of 1,800 cubic feet per second in wet years and drops only a little until mid-June, when flows rapidly drop to about 500 cfs by mid-July. Fall flows drop to 250 cfs or less.

Access
- Same as river miles

Camping
- Medicine Bow National Forest and several public access sites
- Saratoga Lake

UPPER NORTH PLATTE RIVER MAJOR HATCHES

Insect	M	A	M	J	J	A	S	O	N	Time	Flies
Golden Stone										A	**Dry:** Golden Stone, Orange Stimulator, Yellow Sally #6–14; **Wet:** Bitch Creek Nymph, Halfback, Black and Orange Bugger #6–10
Caddis										A/E	**Dry:** Elk Hair Caddis, Humpies, Goddard Caddis #12–16; **Wet:** Caddis Emerger, Soft-hackles, Prince Nymph, Squirrel Tail #14–18
Green Drake										M//A	**Dry:** Green Drake, Extended Body Drake, Flav, Parachute Olive Hare's Ear #10–12; **Wet:** Green Drake Nymph #10–12
Pale Morning Dun										A	**Dry:** PMD, PMD Comparadun, Light Cahill #14–18; Sparkle Dun #16–18; **Wet:** Hare's Ear Nymph, Pheasant Tail, Beadheads #14–18
Baetis										A/E	Blue-winged Olive, Parachute BWO, Blue Dun, Adams, Para-Adams #16–22
Trico										M//A	Black and White, Trico Spinner #18–22
Midges										A/E	**Dry:** Griffith's Gnat, Palamino Midge #18–22; **Wet:** Sparkle Pupa, Serendipity #16–18
Terrestrials										M//A	Joe's Hopper, Dave's Hopper, Madam X, Yellow Stimulator #8–14; Foam Beetle, Black Elk Hair Caddis #14–16; Ants #16–18

HATCH TIME CODE: M = morning; A = afternoon; E = evening; D = dark; SF = spinner fall; // = continuation through periods.

LOWER NORTH PLATTE RIVER
MIRACLE MILE

An eon ago, when I still lived in bass country and was just learning to tie trout flies, I sent my experiments to a friend in Cheyenne. He rarely commented on the dry flies but repeatedly asked for more nymphs. They were catching trout and quite often being lost to monsters refusing the net in an obscure place called the "Miracle Mile."

Today, "The Mile" is virtually synonymous with "North Platte" for flyfishers around the world. The fishing is phenomenal, the scenery fantastic. But it rarely offers a solitary experience; even in the depths of winter there's almost a certainty someone else will be there. "Angling pressure varies depending on a variety of conditions," states John Baughman, director of Wyoming Game and Fish. "This 'miracle' area of the North Platte is, however, very popular. It gives up more fish per mile than most U.S. rivers contain."

The limit on the Miracle Mile is 2 trout per day or in possession, only 1 over 20 inches. Another regulation that may be overlooked is that night fishing is prohibited between the hours of 8 PM and 6 AM during the month of April.

Most years the so-called mile averages 5 to 8 miles from Kortes Dam, below Seminoe Reservoir, to the backwaters of Pathfinder Reservoir. In drought years it can be up to 15 miles long.

As a tailwater fishery it is a fertile environment for producing large fish. It has the added advantage of receiving upstream spawning runs of truly monstrous trout, especially browns.

Resident fish range from 10 to 24 inches, with an average size of 14 inches and a few exceeding the 2-foot mark. But during spawning runs—rainbows in spring and browns in fall—dedicated local anglers boast of "routinely" catching 24- to 30-inch fish. Measured in pounds they are even more impressive. Biologists have recorded annual catches of browns exceeding 10 pounds, and a rare few up to 20 pounds.

That's not to say every moment on The Mile guarantees a miracle. Two factors may play havoc with fishing adventures on its fabled waters—the weather and water flows. A third problem is algae buildup on the streambed that entangles hooks of nymphs and streamers.

The primary purpose of Kortes Dam is to supply irrigation waters and produce hydroelectric power. Summer flows out of Seminoe Reservoir are erratic, often high and murky, but ranging from 500 to 3,000 cubic feet per second. As a Casper fly shop owner says, "They bounce every time Denver or Phoenix switches on their air conditioners."

Most years, but not always, water levels are low and clear by late fall. Stable flows generally continue through winter to early spring. In spring, The Mile often stays fishable even when the upper Platte is blown out by runoff.

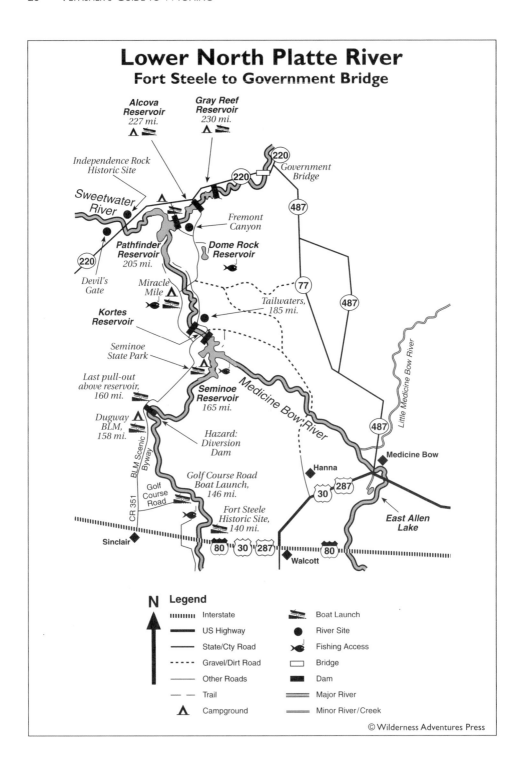

Lower North Platte River
Fort Steele to Government Bridge

Alcova Reservoir 227 mi.

Gray Reef Reservoir 230 mi.

Independence Rock Historic Site

220 Government Bridge

487

Sweetwater River

Fremont Canyon

Pathfinder Reservoir 205 mi.

Dome Rock Reservoir

Devil's Gate

220

Miracle Mile

77

Tailwaters, 185 mi.

487

Kortes Reservoir

Seminoe State Park

Last pull-out above reservoir, 160 mi.

Seminoe Reservoir 165 mi.

Medicine Bow River

Little Medicine Bow River

Dugway BLM, 158 mi.

Hazard: Diversion Dam

487

Medicine Bow

BLM Scenic Byway

Golf Course Road Boat Launch, 146 mi.

Golf Course Road

CR 351

Hanna

30 287

East Allen Lake

Fort Steele Historic Site, 140 mi.

Sinclair

80 30 287

80

Walcott

N Legend

ιιιιιιιι	Interstate		Boat Launch
▬▬	US Highway	●	River Site
▬	State/Cty Road	✖	Fishing Access
- - - -	Gravel/Dirt Road	▢	Bridge
▬	Other Roads	▬	Dam
— —	Trail		Major River
Λ	Campground		Minor River/Creek

© Wilderness Adventures Press

Lower North Platte River
Government Bridge to E.K. Wilkins State Park

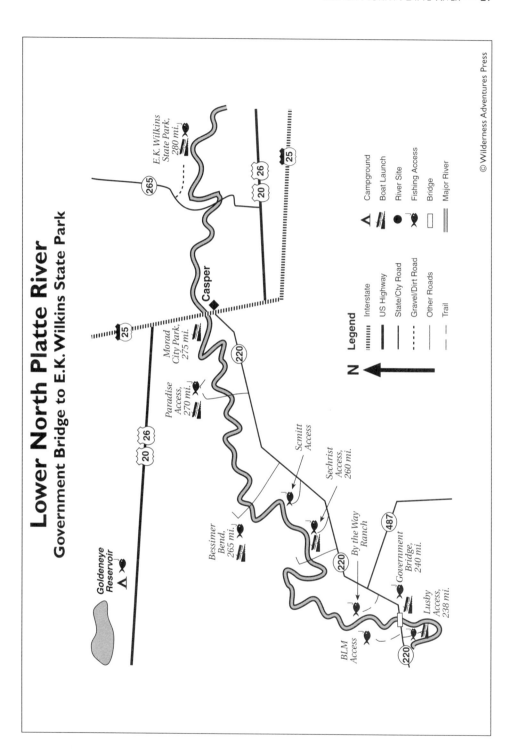

Goldeneye Reservoir

E.K. Wilkins State Park, 280 mi.

Casper

Morad City Park, 275 mi.

Paradise Access, 270 mi.

Bessimer Bend, 265 mi.

Scmitt Access

Sechrist Access, 260 mi.

By the Way Ranch

Government Bridge, 240 mi.

Lusby Access, 238 mi.

BLM Access

Legend

Interstate
US Highway
State/Cty Road
Gravel/Dirt Road
Other Roads
Trail

Campground
Boat Launch
River Site
Fishing Access
Bridge
Major River

© Wilderness Adventures Press

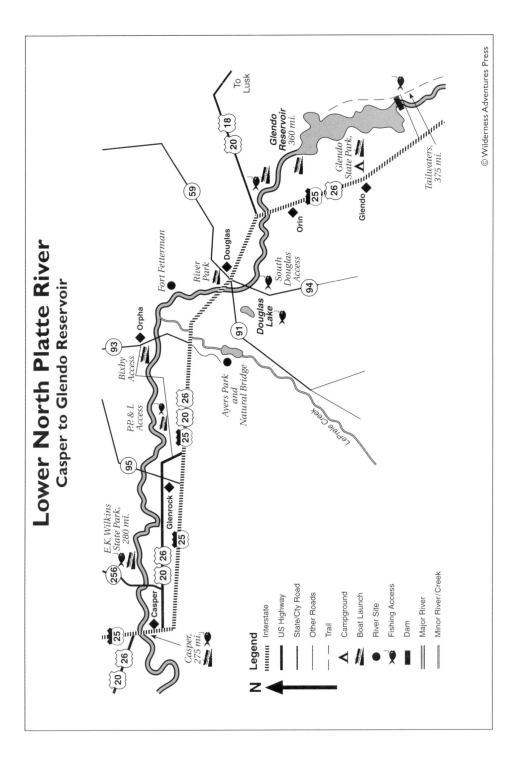

Lower North Platte River
Casper to Glendo Reservoir

© Wilderness Adventures Press

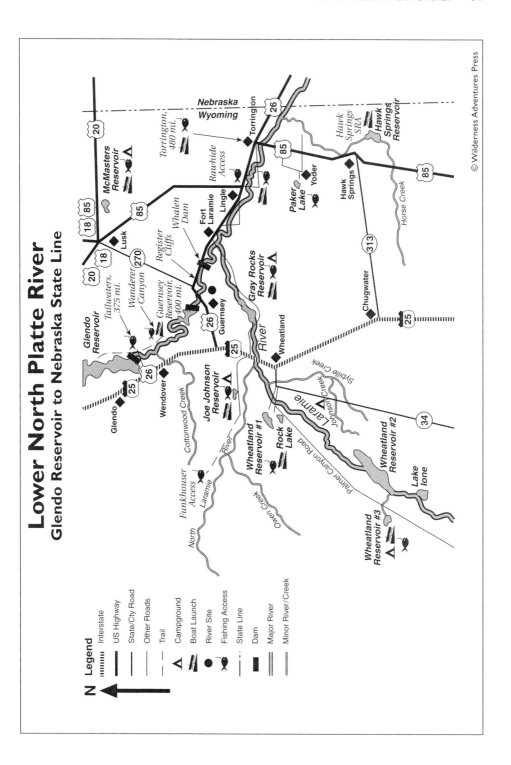

Lower North Platte River
Glendo Reservoir to Nebraska State Line

© Wilderness Adventures Press

But don't forget to check weather forecasts. Wyoming weather is unpredictable year-round, but it's a sure bet it will be nasty more than once during fall and spring spawning runs.

The fish are less troubled by either extreme. They've learned to cope with fluctuations in flows and are rarely put down by nasty weather.

Fishing techniques vary with the seasons and the quarry: resident trout or spawners.

Even on its short run the tailrace can be divided into two almost distinct fisheries. From the dam to the bridge, there's a swift running canyon stretch, followed by riffles, rocky runs and long pools, and a few side channels around islands. Below the bridge the river flattens over shallow runs, riffles and pools, and cuts long meanders along its lower banks to the slack waters of Pathfinder.

Chuck and duck casting with large nymphs, woolly buggers, and streamers, and even glo-bugs, is often the preferred option for drawing strikes from spawners. But as a tailwater fishery, The Mile presents ample opportunities for catching large fish on small wet flies. They can be fished deep or just under the surface film. Nymphs and emergers, in beadheads and unweighted, should include squirrel tails, pheasant tails, hare's ear and Prince nymphs, flashbacks, caddis larva, and midge pupa, 16 to 22, as well as halfbacks, woolly buggers, and soft-hackles, 10 to 14. Red San Juan worms, scow bugs, and rusty orange or olive scuds, 14 to 18, are common tailwater fare.

The Miracle Mile isn't known for its dry-fly fishing, and it is considered far more effective to fish it with nymphs. Also, hatches may be affected by both water fluctuations and high winds. Still, fly casters should come prepared. It's a long way back to a fly shop.

The predominant mayfly through the summer is the pale morning dun, with tricos making a late summer appearance and baetis gaining prominence in fall. Caddis and the little yellow stone compete for attention in midsummer, and midges are common in spring and late fall. Dry fly choices should include Adams, PMDs, light Cahills, BWOs, blue duns, rusty spinners, tricos, and midges, sizes 16 to 22; and elk hair caddis, willow flies and yellow sallies, 14 and 16.

There is full public access along The Mile. A dozen free campgrounds are spaced through the valley. The only resort, Miracle Mile Ranch, has 10 cabins for anglers and a small general store, but no gasoline.

Getting there is an adventure in itself. The 65-mile gravel road of the Seminoe–Alcova Scenic Byway dips and climbs along a twisting route punctuated by dramatic rock outcroppings and surrounded by forested mountains.

The southern entrance is at the Sinclair exit on Interstate 80, 6 miles east of Rawlins. It has numerous steep grades in the Haystack Mountains and a high pass through the Seminoe Mountains above the Miracle Mile. Vehicles pulling large trailers are not recommended. En route, the road skirts high, white sand dunes and the 21,000-acre Seminoe Reservoir, where camping is available at Seminoe State Park.

Middle section of the Miracle Mile.

The turnoff from the north at Alcova is 30 miles west of Casper on WYO 220. This route is flatter and traverses a high plateau after the road climbs out of the colorful, intricately eroded Fremont Canyon southwest of Alcova Reservoir. Glimpses of Pathfinder can be seen through gaps in the Pedro Mountains, and the road makes a gentle descent into the river valley.

Fill gas tanks and stock up on supplies and ice before embarking. Also take note that the scenic byway is described as a "fair weather road" in tourist literature.

Even with the long drives involved, guided fishing trips can be arranged through fly shops in both Saratoga and Casper.

North Platte Reservoirs

The North Platte's big bend swing to the east is submerged under the 22,000-acre Pathfinder Reservoir, 40 miles west of Casper. The raging torrents of its confluence with the Sweetwater River that once plunged and bucked down Fremont Canyon are reduced to a trickle. Diversions from Pathfinder are funneled through a tunnel to hydropower generators before emptying into the 2,260-acre Alcova Reservoir.

Pathfinder and the canyon are named for John C. Fremont, who mapped the route that became the Oregon Trail over South Pass near the headwaters of the Sweetwater. On the expedition's return from the Wind River Mountains in 1842,

Fremont attempted the first whitewater float down a Western river in a rubber raft. It was a short and horrific ride. The Pathfinder and his crew barely escaped with their lives, and were forced to climb out of the sheer-walled canyon.

Seminoe, Pathfinder and Alcova are excellent fisheries for both trout and walleye. Pathfinder's fishery has benefited the most from recent good waters after almost a decade of drought. Flyfishers who venture onto their waters may find some surface action at dawn and dusk in midsummer. In fall, Pathfinder's inlet arm is attractive to fly casters searching for brown trout on their spawning run up the Miracle Mile. Seminoe's upstream arm also holds larger concentrations of fish at this time.

Alcova to Casper

The North Platte's second premier tailwater fishery is below Alcova Reservoir from Grey Reef Dam to Goose Egg, just west of Casper.

Fishing is rated as good through Wyoming's second largest city and downstream past Edness K. Wilkins State Park. Cutthroat, rainbows and browns are plentiful in the 10- to 16-inch range. All offer opportunities for much larger fish, and, occasionally, browns up to 10 pounds are taken.

From Gray Reef Dam downstream to Bessemer Bend Bridge the limit is 2 trout per day or in possession; only 1 may exceed 20 inches.

The Grey Reef tailrace is the scene of excellent wild trout fishing year round. Warmer water releases keep its first few miles open even in the winter. Large trout are taken from November to March since flows are low and stable enough to permit relatively easy wading. It often remains fishable in spring when the upper river is too high and murky.

Through the heat of summer, the lower North Platte runs full to the brim, fed by high, steady flows of irrigation waters for arid rangelands and farm fields. Float-fishing is good with both dry flies and small nymphs since the river suffers few of the fluctuations common to the Miracle Mile.

This more stable environment produces prolific aquatic insect hatches of caddis, little yellow stones, pale morning duns, and tricos through summer, and baetis and midges in fall and spring. Scuds and aquatic worms common to tailwater fisheries contribute to the cornucopia of trout fodder.

Patterns and sizes for both wet and dry flies are much the same as for the Miracle Mile. That includes graduating to large nymphs and streamers to stalk spawners in fall and spring.

The river descends in a series of riffles and runs and deep cutbank pools as it meanders through the sagebrush desert. Float-fishers find dry fly action often is best toward evening on shallow channels and along the banks. Drifting small weighted nymphs through riffles and cutbank pools is effective through the day, and some fish can be tempted up with large attractors. Wade fishers obtain more access to riffles, pools and channels in late fall as water levels diminish.

Below Grey Reef, bank and wading access is provided at Wyoming Game and Fish easements and on BLM lands. Prominent road signs along WYO 220 mark loca-

*Dried-up
Fremont Canyon
on the North Platte,
below Pathfinder
Reservoir and the
Sweetwater confluence.*

tions of the WGF sites. Obtain directions locally to BLM river access points. Camping is permitted at WGF's Lusby and Sechrist sites.

There are 5 boat launch locations along the 45 miles of river between Grey Reef and Casper's Morad Park. Float distance from Grey Reef to Lusby is 9 miles; from Lusby to Government Bridge, 6 miles; from the bridge to Bessemer Bend, 18 miles; and from Bessemer Bend to Morad Park, 13 miles. Edness K. Wilkins State Park, 5 miles downstream of Casper, also has a boat ramp and permits fishing access.

Posted signs along the river banks—blue for public access and red for private property—indicate locations where boats can be anchored or anglers can get out to wade fish.

Guided float-fishing trips and shuttle services can be arranged at Casper fly shops.

North Platte below Casper

Below Glenrock, the North Platte is a marginal trout fishery because another string of impoundments slows and warms its flows. However, warmwater fishing and hatchery stocked trout in scenic surroundings are available at Glendo and Guernsey State Parks on the river's next two largest reservoirs.

Sweetwater River

The North Platte's largest tributary, the Sweetwater River, flows through wild, rugged terrain little changed since Fremont's explorations in 1842. Efforts to reach its remote canyon run are almost as difficult today as they were for Oregon Trail pioneers who followed it to the South Pass crossing of the Continental Divide.

Trips to the Sweetwater require commitment and planning. There are no towns near the river's remote first 75 miles with public access.

The Sweetwater rises northwest of South Pass in the foothills of the Wind River Mountains in Shoshone National Forest. It passes under WYO 28 at the Sweetwater Gap rest stop, midway between Farson and Lander. This mountain meadow run is the only easy access to the river. A rough gravel road, the Lander Cutoff of the Oregon Trail parallels its south bank upstream to the forest boundary.

Below the highway, the Sweetwater passes through a checkerboard of BLM lands and private property crisscrossed by a maze of primitive dirt roads and two-wheel tracks. The 8-mile canyon, once considered for Wild and Scenic River designation, is about 15 miles from the highway. To negotiate these backcountry roads, you'll need a 4-wheel-drive vehicle with high clearance; it should be in good working condition, contain emergency equipment, and carry extra gas and water. A BLM map is required to determine which roads have public rights-of-way through private property.

This is not a place to head off alone looking for a solitary experience. First time visitors are advised to explore the region with friends who know it well or with a professional guide.

One relatively easy access site to the river is Three Forks Bridge, according to *The Floater's Guide to Wyoming Rivers* by Dan Lewis. It is about 10 miles southeast of South Pass City on the Pick Axe Road. The canyon is another 5 miles downstream. The next highway, U.S. 287, is 40 miles.

The Ugly Bug Fly Shop and Kyle Wall's Trout Bum Guide Service in Casper keep tabs on the Sweetwater and its hatches. They can be consulted about guided fishing trips, as well as provide more explicit maps and directions to the river's hidden waters.

In Lander, BLM maps and advice on directions to the canyon can be obtained at The Good Place, an outdoors shop. Doug Lemm, shop owner, said getting into the high-walled canyon requires scrambling down rocky draws of tributaries. He also noted a permit to fish The Nature Conservancy's recently acquired property on the lower canyon must be obtained from its Lander office.

Below Sweetwater Station, a general store and campground west of Jeffrey City on U.S. 287, the river meanders through ranching country to Pathfinder Reservoir. Permission to fish the lower river must be obtained from landowners. Several Casper outfitters offer guided trips on this stretch.

Sweetwater River

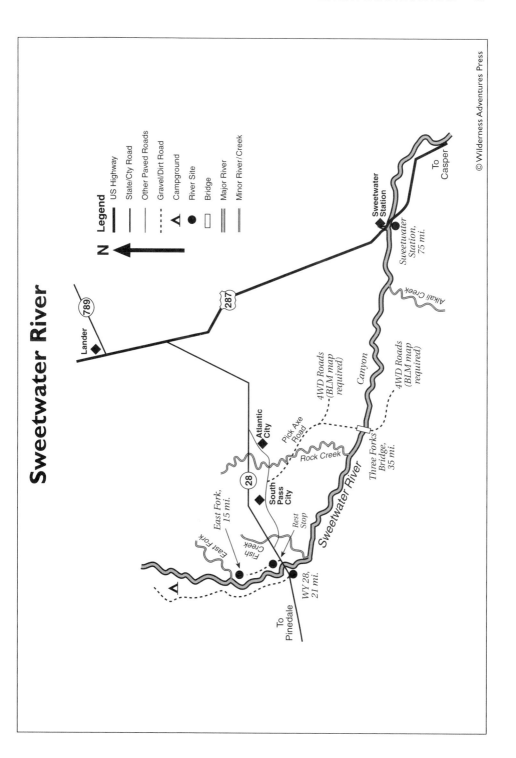

© Wilderness Adventures Press

Legend

N

- US Highway
- State/Cty Road
- Other Paved Roads
- Gravel/Dirt Road
- ▲ Campground
- ● River Site
- ▢ Bridge
- Major River
- Minor River/Creek

Stream Facts: Lower North Platte River
(Seminoe Reservoir to Casper)

Season
- Year-round.

Regulations
- From Kortes Dam downstream to Pathfinder Reservoir (Miracle Mile), the limit on trout is 2 per day or in possession; only 1 may exceed 20 inches. The Miracle Mile is closed to night fishing (8 PM – 6 AM) during the month of April.
- From Gray Reef Dam downstream to Lusby Access, the limit on trout is 1 per day or in possession.

Trout
- Rainbows and browns range from 10 to 24 inches in the Miracle Mile; upstream are spawning runs of much larger fish in the 24- to 30-inch class, as well as the occasional brown up to 10 pounds.
- Below Grey Reef Dam, rainbows, cutthroat and browns range from 10 to 16 inches, with good chances of netting much larger fish, especially browns.

Miles
- Mile 165: North Platte Arm of Seminoe Reservoir
- Mile 185: Kortes Dam–Miracle Mile tailrace
- Mile 193: Pathfinder Reservoir backwaters
- Mile 230: Grey Reef Dam
- Mile 240: Government Bridge
- Mile 265: Bessemer Bend
- Mile 275: Morad City Park
- Mile 280: E.K. Wilkins State Park

Character
- The Miracle Mile is a tailwater fishery that ranges from 5.5 to 15 miles in length, depending on levels in Pathfinder Reservoir.
- The River below Grey Reef Dam is a tailwater fishery down to about Lusby public access site. High water releases in summer make it a much bigger river than upstream as it meanders in long twists and turns through an arid sagebrush desert.

Flows
- Flows through The Mile are very erratic with fluctuations between 500 and 3,000 cubic feet per second in summer and into fall. Minimum flow in winter is 500 cfs.
- Spring and summer releases climb to 3,000 cfs or more by July and hold steady until late fall. Winter flows drop to between 500 and 250 cfs.

Access
- Grey Reef Dam
- Lusby public access
- Government bridge
- By The Way Ranch
- Sechrist fish hatchery
- Schmitt public access
- Bessemer Bridge
- Morad City Park
- E.K. Wilkins State Park

Camping
- Alcova Reservoir
- Lusby public access
- Sechrist fish hatchery

LOWER NORTH PLATTE RIVER MAJOR HATCHES

Insect	M	A	M	J	J	A	S	O	N	Time	Flies
Little Yellow Stone (Willow Fly)					X					A	**Dry:** Yellow Sally, Yellow Humpy, Yellow Stimulator #14–16; **Wet:** Halfback Nymph, Bitch Creek Nymph #10–14
Caddis			X	X						A/E	**Dry:** Elk Hair Caddis, Humpy, Yellow or Orange Stimulator #14–16; **Wet:** Squirrel Tail, Soft-hackle, Caddis Pupa, Caddis Emerger #12–16
Pale Morning Dun				X						A/E	**Dry:** PMD, Comparadun, Light Cahill #16–18; **Wet:** Hare's Ear Nymph, Pheasant Tail, Flashback Nymph, Beadheads #16–18
Baetis		X						X		M/A	**Dry:** Blue-winged Olive, Blue Dun, Adams, Para-Adams #16–18; **Wet:** Flashback Nymph, Pheasant Tail, Beadheads #16–18
Trico						X				M/A	Black and White, Trico Spinner #18–22
Midges	X						X			M/A	**Dry:** Griffith's Gnat, Palamino Midge, Disco Midge #18–22; **Wet:** Brood Midge Pupa, Brassie #18–22
Scuds	X						X				Rusty, Olive, or Tan Scud #14–18; Sow Bug, Soft-hackles #14–16
Aquatic Worms	X						X				San Juan Worm (red or orange) #14–18
Terrestrials				X							Joe's Hopper, Dave's Hopper, Yellow Stimulator #8–14; Ants #16–18; Foam Beetle, Black Elk Hair Caddis #14–16

HATCH TIME CODE: M = morning; A = afternoon; E = evening; D = dark; SF = spinner fall; // = continuation through periods.

Miraculous Trout
Famous 'Mile' Lives Up to Its Name

By Rob Thornberry

SINCLAIR, WY—It's an arrogant moniker. The Miracle Mile.

Roughly 40 miles north of the Interstate 80 turnoff at Sinclair, the Miracle Mile is a stretch of the North Platte River tucked underneath the Seminoe Mountains. It's a bitter land, especially in March when the wind rips off the mountains and straight through the layers of neoprene and polypropylene you hide behind. But still you fish, chucking well-weighted flies into the teeth of the prevailing wind.

Why? Big fish, of course, and plenty of them. Enough to make you forget I-80's hundreds of mindless miles. Enough to warrant its nickname.

"It's good enough that I don't leave to go fish in Montana or Idaho," said Rod Robinder, owner of the Ugly Bug Fly Shop in Casper. Robinder fishes the river weekly throughout the year and has high praise for the fishing. "It's probably one of the best fisheries in the United States. We fish there year round. The only thing that keeps us out of there is vicious storms that drift the roads closed."

If anglers could create the perfect trout fishery, they might come up with the Miracle Mile. Sandwiched between two huge reservoirs, The Mile has almost everything. The top reservoir—the 1 million acre-feet Seminoe Reservoir—acts like a huge settling pond, controlling the fluctuations of the river and cleaning the silt out of the water, making The Mile better than normal trout habitat. At the same time, the water temperatures are fairly consistent, with warmer than normal water in the winter and cold water in the summer.

Because of concerns about fish mortality in the 1970s, the flows from Seminoe are closely watched and always kept above 500 cubic feet per second. The downstream reservoir—the 1 million acre-feet Pathfinder Reservoir—is basically a huge hatchery, home to millions of trout, which fuel great runs of spawning trout in the spring and fall. And when Pathfinder is full, like it has been in 1996 and 1997, the stretch from the dam to the backwaters is only 5.5 miles.

"It's pretty unique," said Robinder, who has fished the river since 1964. "Of all my travels I have never run into another one. I have seen reservoirs 20 to 30 miles apart, but not six miles apart like The Mile."

During the rainbow spawning run in the spring and brown trout spawning run in the fall, the 5.5-mile stretch of river teems with huge fish.

"From St. Patrick's Day to Mother's Day and then again from Halloween to Christmas are the best," Robinder said. "That's when the runs are in and the big fish are there. If you want to catch fish over 20 inches, you have to go in those two windows. You're catching fish, consistently, between 24 and 30 inches."

Is Robinder bragging? While consistent catches may be exaggerated, the faded Polaroids at the Miracle Mile Ranch show an amazing assortment of hogs displayed by wildly happy anglers.

"It's an ideal setup," said Bill Wichers, regional fisheries supervisor for the Wyoming Game and Fish Department. "You have ideal temperatures, water quality and habitat to grow trout food and big trout."

Really big trout. "There are a few trophy-sized rainbows up there," Wichers said. "Most of the rainbows in Pathfinder max out at 18 to 19 inches. They feed mostly on zooplankton. A few of them will switch over to fish and crayfish. Some of these fish are residents in the river. Most of the big browns come out of Pathfinder. There are some fish that are up to 20 pounds. Each year, there are 10-pound plus fish caught up there."

The Mile is also a well designed fishery because of the amazing amount of public access. Both sides of the 5.5-mile reach are public property.

"It's great," Robinder said. "I can consistently catch lots of fish over 16 inches. I don't care to catch 12- and 13-inch fish. I want to go catch 20- to 26-inchers, and that river is full of them."

The Miracle Mile definitely makes fishermen cocky. Perhaps it's because of its name, whose origins remain cloaked in rumor and misinformation.

Wichers has one history. He said in the 1940s an angler from Colorado made weekly pilgrimages to the North Platte below Seminoe Dam, which was erected in the 1930s.

"He was hauling some really big trout back to Colorado," Wichers said. He was also bringing back stories of monsters that got away. Some of the stories filtered back to a Colorado outdoor writer, who didn't believe his ears.

"So the outdoor writer—some say clandestinely—followed the other angler up to the river and did a story about it," Wichers said. "He coined the phrase 'Miracle Mile.'"

But technically, it's never a mile. The Mile actually varies in length depending on the year.

"When Pathfinder is full, The Mile is about 5.5 miles long," Wichers said. "When Pathfinder is low, The Mile can be 10 to 15 miles long."

In March it was 5.5 miles long. The river starts in a tight canyon but quickly rolls into a sagebrush plain that is home to bighorn sheep, mule deer, antelope and mountain lions. You will see a lot of animals because it's the only water in this parched plain. Because it sits on a plain, the wind is a factor almost every day of the year. It can be harsh, but the locals take it in stride.

"You just have to stand on the west side of the river and lift your rod up and let the wind take your line," Robinder said. "You don't get tired from casting because the wind does it for you."

The river's flow runs between 500 and 3,000 cfs, depending on the season. Like most rivers, higher flows can greatly influence fishing. Experts say the river

Matt Thornberry lands a Miracle Mile trout. (Photo by Rob Thornberry)

only gets out of shape in June and July, when the snowpacks at the headwaters of the Platte have melted.

Every river is a riddle, with its own nuances that are waiting to be solved by the eager angler. Where is the best run? What is the best fly? The Miracle Mile is no different, especially because of the public land that surrounds the river. "It's fun to explore," Robinder said. "There is only so much river between the two reservoirs, and you can basically see and fish all of it in a couple of days. That's part of the fun."

It reminded me of the Henry's Fork between Ashton Dam and the Chester backwaters.

The monster fish caught during the spawning runs get top billing at the Miracle Mile, but the real stars of the show are the second-tier fish.

The impressive stature of the fish can be traced to the river's plentiful aquatic life. "They look like farm pond fish rather than stream fish," Wichers said. "It's because of the excellent food supply." There are large hatches of midges, baetis, and caddis at different times of the year, but, interestingly, the fish don't go crazy for them."

"There's a tremendous wealth of aquatic life," Robinder said. "The fish don't come up for the dry flies. We get clouds of caddis in the summer, but the fish stay on the bottom and gorge themselves."

On a March fishing trip, midges filled every foam line, but there was no activity on the surface. Robinder said that is common. "The fish are all eating the larva," he said. "I've seen midges so heavy in the foam line that they look like a cowpatty floating downstream."

If you want dry flies on The Mile, Robinder suggests a fall trip. "If we get dry flies, it's usually between Labor Day to Halloween, and it's usually No. 16 caddis," Robinder said.

If you don't mind using nymphs, take plenty of scuds and San Juan worms. You won't be disappointed.

While Seminoe and Pathfinder combine to make a tremendous fishery, The Mile does get help. Wicher said Game and Fish officials stock roughly 100,000 fingerlings in The Mile per year and 150,000 catchable rainbows in Pathfinder. The stocking is necessary because there is little natural reproduction in the reservoir and river.

"Our best guess is…predation, primarily by walleyes" is hurting trout reproduction, Wichers said. "We used to have pretty good recruitment on rainbows and browns. Once we got the big populations of walleyes, our stocking practices had to change."

Seminoe and Pathfinder Reservoirs have some world class walleyes, which get that way by eating the trout. "It has forced us to stock larger trout," Wichers said. "We figured the walleyes had to come from a lake that was planted years ago in Colorado," Wichers said. "They gradually move down the system in high-water years." So if you get tired of trout fishing, there is a chance to catch a record walleye in one of the reservoirs. "There are a fair number of trophy-sized walleye," Wichers said. "I'm talking about 10- to 12-pound fish. It's probably the best reservoir in Wyoming for walleye."

Because the North Platte system is heavily supplemented with hatchery fish, Game and Fish officials are conducting a major creel survey to measure the impact of the planted fish. Basically, officials are trying to figure out what type of fish get caught the most so they can stock more of that fish. Game and Fish officials are putting nose tags—similar to those used to track steelhead in the Columbia River system—in every fish stocked from Interstate 80 to Casper. That is roughly 700,000 per year since 1992.

"We're trying to find out what the contribution of wild trout is to the river sections," Wichers said. "Basically we want to know whether we should be stocking the rivers. We're also trying to find out which fish do the best in which river

Who is that masked man? Matt Thornberry with a rainbow trout . (Photo by Rob Thornberry)

sections. For example, we're stocking four strains of rainbows, and we're finding that we're getting different success from different fish in different areas. With that info, we're going to refine the stocking programs to get the best use of our hatchery fish."

Early data shows the Miracle Mile has the highest catch rates on the North Platte and the second largest fish on average at 16 inches.

The Mile has a 2-fish limit, but anglers can keep only 1 over 20 inches.

There are no gear regulations, which is a sore spot with some of the anglers. "I'm disappointed with the regulations," Robinder said. "I would rather see it be catch and release, but I'm not going to change the philosophy of the good old boy who thinks we still gather meat."

Wicher, a fishing socialist, laughs at such criticism. "We manage that stretch as a trophy fishery, and I'd rather not exclude any type of angler," he said. "Given the fishing pressure up there, we can maintain the fishery without terminal gear regulations."

It is an extremely popular fishery. The last creel survey, conducted 15 years ago, found that 25,000 angler days per year were recorded on the 5.5 mile stretch. "That's quite a bit of fishing pressure," Wichers said. "About two-thirds of that is from out of state, mostly from Colorado."

And Wichers doesn't think a great number of people know about The Mile. "It has some awfully good quality trout fishing," he said. "But it's kind of a sleeper. It hasn't had a lot of national press, but there are certainly a lot of out-of-staters that know where it is."

Brian Benson of the West Laramie Fly Store disagreed. "I think word has been out for quite a while," he said. "When you have a nice weekend, it gets pretty busy. Being as close as we are to the Front Range of Colorado, it gets hit hard."

Robinder takes the crowds in stride. "Tuesday through Thursday it's not crowded," he said. "Stay away on the weekends. By noon on Thursday, people are coming in. By noon on Sunday, they're already leaving. You can pretty much have it to yourself."

The only place to stay inside on The Mile is the Miracle Mile Ranch, a working ranch with 10 cabins for anglers. It also has a small general store but no gasoline.

If you don't want to pay, there are numerous free campgrounds along The Mile.

Should you go, I have always felt the best way to determine the quality of a fishery is to ask one simple question of the angler who has just returned from its banks: Would you go again? My answer for The Mile is yes, based on the final morning of my four-day trip.

In less than an hour, I landed four fish between 16 and 20 inches. Enough fish to make the long trip home a breeze. Enough to support the river's moniker.

(When he isn't stalking big trout, rowing a float boat or tying flies, Rob Thornberry is editor of Intermountain Hunting & Fishing *magazine published in Idaho Falls, Idaho.)*

THE LARAMIE PLAINS

Wyoming's enigmatic geology is captivatingly described in *Rising from the Plains*, by John McPhee. Long distance drivers, who endure the interminable miles of the Great Plains, appreciate the title's subtlety by the time they reach Laramie. Just about everywhere in the Cowboy State tilts toward the sky, even when it appears to be flat.

Located at the base of the 8,640-foot summit on Interstate 80, Laramie is where the prairie finally meets the Rockies. The University of Wyoming community, 50 miles west of Cheyenne, straddles a broad 7,200-foot plateau. Frosted peaks of the 12,000-foot Snowy Mountains hover on the western horizon above the forested shoulders of the 10,000-foot Medicine Bow Range.

Yet there's a touch of irony here for flyfishers rushing west with visions of sparkling mountain streams dancing in their heads. The best fishing at this cross-roads is in wind scoured bowls less than 15 miles west of town on WYO 230.

A cluster of trout rich reservoirs known as the Laramie Plains Lakes are a product of persistent efforts to preserve water in this arid environment. When it's wet enough to support burgeoning populations of trout—like it has been the past three years—fishing is phenomenal.

The largest, Lake Hattie, teems with full-bodied rainbows and lake trout, plus legendary browns of notable size. The smaller Meeboer, Twin Buttes, and Gelatt Lakes —rebounding after almost a decade of drought—produce very respectable trout, too.

These prairie ponds are the first along the Rocky Mountain Front to thaw in spring and open the fishing season in southeastern Wyoming. They fish well until late summer, when warm temperatures often force fish into deep waters. Whatever the season, expect crowds because Laramie is an easy drive from Denver. The smaller lakes ice up sooner, but Lake Hattie's reputation for big trout draws fly casters until it freezes again in December.

Be prepared for high winds. They can be fierce in these wide-open expanses, sometimes approaching gale force in winter, spring, and fall. Even almost daily summer afternoon blows kick up surf-like whitecaps that force float-tubers ashore.

Fortunately, fly casters can stick close to shore during spawning seasons. Anglers can cast from the banks or work the shallows for rainbows in spring soon after ice-out and browns in fall, starting about late September. Cooler temperatures at these times also draw lakers in closer to shore. When the wind is calm, these options present what many consider the best of stillwater opportunities: sight casting to large cruising trout.

Fly casters working weed banks and spawning beds or casting from shore can use floating lines. Float-tubers and boaters need full sink lines or sinking tips when not casting to rising trout.

The fertile alkaline waters of these lakes support a generous food base for fast growing trout. The food chain is loaded with freshwater shrimp, also called scuds, leeches, damselfly and dragonfly nymphs, and a host of plankton, water fleas, mayflies, caddis, and midges, plus forage fish, like the perch, in Hattie.

The flyfisher's arsenal covers the same spectrum.

Laramie River and Laramie Plains Lakes

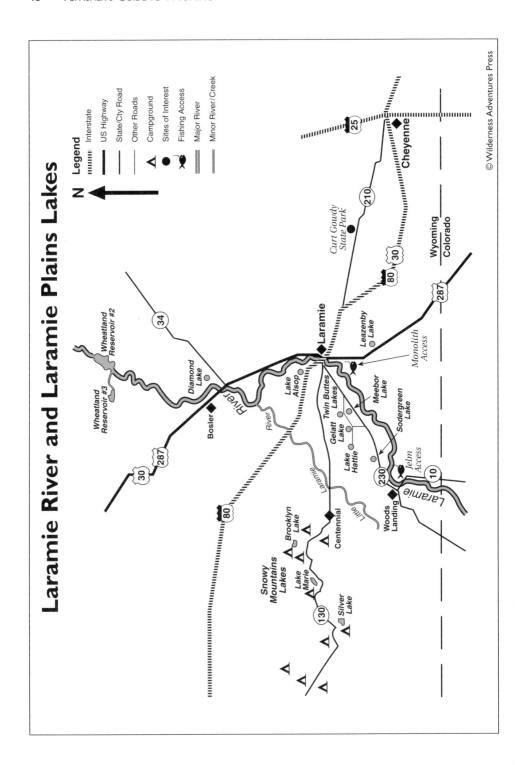

Wet flies can include muddler minnows, Matukas, Zonkers, Clouser minnows, olive or black woolly buggers, crystal buggers, and leeches, size 2 to 10; olive damsel nymphs, Zug Bugs, halfbacks, and Platte River Specials, 10 to 14; and olive or orange scuds, Prince nymphs, pheasant tail nymphs, hare's ear nymphs, soft-hackles, caddis emergers, and beadheads, 14 to 18.

Dry fly choices are light and dark elk hair caddis, light Cahill, Adams, blue duns, callibaetis, royal humpies, and royal Trudes, 14 to 18, and midges, 18 to 22. Smaller nymphs, emergers, and beadheads can be tied as dropper flies on larger dry flies.

There is a campground at Lake Hattie. Each of the lakes has picnic facilities and boat ramps.

Lake Hattie

The largest of the prairie impoundments, Lake Hattie ranges from 1,500 to 3,000 acres in size. Rainbows and browns are in the 12- to 24-inch class, with fish exceeding 5 pounds common and occasional 10-pound browns taken annually. Lake trout average 8 to 15 pounds. The reservoir also holds kokanee salmon and a few cutthroat.

It is about 15 miles west of Laramie. Make the turn north from WYO 230 at Hammony Lane and continue northwest on Hanson Lane.

Twin Buttes Lake

This 250-acre pond has benefited from both the end of the drought and a program to curb unwanted perch that tend to overpopulate smaller waters. Browns and rainbows average 12 to 15 inches, with good chances for netting fish 18 inches and larger.

It is about 2 miles east of Lake Hattie on Pahlow Lane, which intersects WYO 230 about 7 miles west of Laramie.

Gelatt Lake

At 34 acres, this is the smallest reservoir in the chain. It averages 8- to 12-inch rainbow, but fish that manage to overwinter may exceed 20 inches. It is a mile east of Twin Buttes Lake on Pahlow Lane.

Meeboer Lake

This 119-acre reservoir is noted for producing fast growing fish and fishes best in fall for 12- to 14-inch rainbows and brook trout. Reports of rainbows that overwinter one or two years exceed 24 inches.

It is south of Pahlow Lane, about 8 miles west of Laramie.

There are several other put-and-take reservoirs stocked with hatchery trout near town—Leazenby Lake, 10 miles south on U.S. 287, and Sodergreen Lake, 22 miles west on WYO 230, and Lake Alsop, 2 miles east of the Herrick Lane exit on I-80.

Diamond Lake, 40 miles northwest of Laramie, is managed as a trophy trout fishery and also has benefited from three recent good water years. Fishing is good for cutthroat and rainbows in the 15- to 18-inch class, and sizes should continue to

Prairie lakes rainbow spawner. (Photo by Jack Parker)

grow with improved over-wintering conditions. It also fishes more consistently through the heat of summer than the other prairie ponds. The limit is 2 per day or in possession, but all trout less than 16 inches must be returned to the water immediately. Fishing is permitted by the use of artificial flies and lures only.

Diamond and Little Diamond are reached by turning north from I-80 at the Cooper Cove exit, near Bosler. It is a 4-mile gravel road drive to the 200-acre reservoir and its small sister lake.

About midway between Cheyenne and Laramie on WYO 210 is Curt Gowdy State Park in the Laramie Mountains. It is a popular scenic retreat named for the state's best-known outdoorsman and sports broadcaster.

The park's Granite Springs Reservoir and Crystal Reservoir are fished hard summer and fall for medium-sized cutthroat and rainbows stocked by Wyoming Game and Fish.

Laramie River

The Laramie River, a principal tributary of the North Platte River, bisects the Laramie Plain.

Known locally as the Big Laramie, it rises in the Never Summer Mountains just south of the Wyoming/Colorado border and skirts the foothills of the Snowy Range on its northeasterly course to the high plains. There is close to 35 miles of good fishing waters along this stretch for 8- to 15-inch brown trout and a lesser number of smaller rainbows, until irrigation diversions seriously deplete the river near Laramie. But it flows almost entirely through private rangelands, and permission to fish is difficult to obtain.

Still, the upper Laramie's most scenic passage near the tiny mountain resort town of Woods Landing offers good fishing opportunities. Woods Landing is 30 miles southwest of Laramie on WYO 230, and Wyoming Game and Fish's three Jelm access sites begin a few miles south on WYO 10.

Rainbows are protected by a catch-and-release rule, and there is a slot limit to reduce harvest of the browns. All browns between 10 and 16 inches must be released, and only 1 can exceed 16 inches in the 6-fish limit. Fishing is permitted by the use of artificial flies and lures only.

Just west of Laramie on WYO 230 is the Monolith Ranch access site, but irrigation diversions often reduce the lower Laramie's flows by late summer.

The Little Laramie River emerges from the foothills of the Medicine Bows behind the village of Centennial, 20 miles west of Laramie on WYO 130. Fishing is good for 8- to 18-inch browns, but it, too, passes through private ranch property. Permission to fish is tough to get. The state school section at Millbrook Road, just east of Centennial on the highway, offers less than a mile of public access.

However, the old mining town is the gateway to the Medicine Bow and Snowy ranges. The headwater forks of the Little Laramie and other tumbling mountain streams are easily accessible from a web of gravel roads branching through the Medicine Bow National Forest.

Flyfishers don't need to burden themselves with bulging fishing vests on excursions to the rivers or their mountain tributaries. About all that's needed to match a hatch or draw rises are a few Adams, light Cahills, elk hair caddis, stimulators, humpies, and gray, yellow, or royal Wulffs in sizes 10 to 18. Small woolly buggers, Zug Bugs, soft-hackled emergers, and Prince and hare's ear nymphs can be drifted through promising pools and along cutbanks. Ignore wide, shallow flows and concentrate on log jams, riffles, undercut banks of channels and deeper pools.

The Snowy Range

Good maps and the stamina to hike alpine trails permit fly casters to roam almost at will in the national forests of the Rockies. The special bonus of the Snowy Range is its Scenic Byway that crests at a 10,847-foot pass on WYO 130, midway between Centennial and Encampment.

The mountain range lives up to its name. It was derived from the snowfields that linger throughout the summer and the fact that fresh blankets can fall any time of year. The highway is open from Memorial Day to October, or until snow closes it for the winter. Its twisting 30 mile route essentially divides the 1 million acre Medicine Bow National Forest in half. The forested alpine playground contains four wilderness areas—Platte River, Huston Park, Encampment River, and Savage Run—where no wheels are allowed.

The alpine stream angler travels light.

Fishing is good in close to 100 lakes, ponds and reservoirs and hundreds of miles of coldwater trout streams. Species present include rainbow, brook, cutthroat in the lower streams and lakes, and golden trout and splake, a hybrid between brook and lake trout, in higher, colder lakes.

A good number of the lakes and creeks are close to the highway and side roads. Many more are at the end of short day hikes or longer, more challenging treks into the wilderness that require overnight camping. Developed campgrounds are scattered along the highway, many of them on lakes or streambanks. But due to the Snowy Range's elevations, some sites may not be free of snow until the first week of July.

An information center is located just west of Centennial. Stop and pick up a copy of "Fishing the Medicine Bow National Forest Snowy Range Area." It details what trout species are present in key lakes and streams, and gives tips on trail miles and degrees of difficulty of hikes to interior waters.

For more information, stop at the forest's district office in Laramie, or write to the superintendent at Medicine Bow National Forest, 2468 Jackson Street, Laramie, WY 82070, or call 307-745-2300.

SOUTHEAST HUB CITIES
Casper
Elevation—5,129 • Population—46,800

Wyoming's second largest city, Casper is an historic crossroads community that has benefited the most from the state's past and present boom times in the oil and coal industries. Casper is where the North Platte leaves the mountains for the prairie. It was the path pioneers followed here before continuing on to Oregon and California or the gold strikes in Montana. Today, Casper is a service community for the vast arid range-lands and oil fields surrounding it, and a gateway to the Big Horn Mountains to the north and the remote central backwaters of the North Platte to the west. Savvy anglers learn the local flyfishing merits lingering delays. Fishing at Grey Reef, just upstream, is as good as it gets at the Miracle Mile and on the headwaters of the North Platte.

ACCOMMODATIONS

Westridge Motel, 955 Cy Avenue, Casper, WY 82601-4166 / 307-234-8911 / 25 units / Pets allowed / $

Bel Air Motel, 5400 West Yellowstone Hwy, Casper, WY 82604-1976 / 307-472-1930 / 10 units / Pets allowed / $

Casper Hilton Inn, 800 North Poplar Street, Casper, WY 82601-1315 / 307-266-6000 / 225 units / Pets allowed / $$

Kelly Inn, 821 North Poplar, Casper, WY 82601 / 307-266-2400 / 103 units / Pets allowed / $

Super 8 Lodge, 3838 Cy Avenue, Casper, WY 82604-4322 / 307-266-3480 / 66 units / Pets allowed / $

The Royal Inn, 440 East A Street, Casper, WY 82601-1906 / 307-234-3501 / 37 units / Pets allowed / $$

Topper Motel, 728 East A Street, Casper, WY 82601-2059 / 307-237-8407 / 19 units / Pets allowed / $

Virginian Motel, 830 East A & Jefferson, Casper, WY 82601 / 307-266-9731 / 25 units / Pets allowed / $

Yellowstone Motel, 1610 East Yellowstone Hwy, Casper, WY 82601-2245 / 307-234-9174 / 18 units / Pets allowed / $

CAMPGROUNDS AND RV PARKS

Antelope Run Campground, 1101 Prairie Lane, Casper, WY 82601 / 307-577-1664 / April 1 to October 1 / 65 RV units / Full services

Casper KOA Kampground, 2800 East Yellowstone Hwy, Casper WY 82609 / 307-237-5155 / Year-round / 71 RV and 16 tent sites / Full services

Fort Casper Campground, 4205 Fort Caspar Road, Casper, WY 82604 / 307-234-3260 / Year-round / 92 RV and 24 tent sites / Full services

Alcova Lake Campground, Alcova, WY 82620 / 307-234-6821 / April 1–Oct. 15 / 6 RV sites / Full services

RESTAURANTS
Plows Diners, 2150 East Yellowstone Hwy, Casper, WY 82609 / 307-577-1504
Thads Restaurant, 41 SE Wyoming Boulevard, Casper, WY 82609 / 307-473-1750
Chic-A-D, 601 SE Wyoming Boulevard, Casper, WY 82609 / 307-266-0151
South Sea Chinese Restaurant, 2025 East 2nd Street, Casper, WY 82609 /
    307-237-4777
Western Grill Restaurant, 2333 East Yellowstone Hwy, Casper, WY 82609 /
    307-234-7061
Viking Restaurant & Lounge, 2740 East 3rd Street, Casper, WY 82609 /
    307-234-5386

VETERINARIANS
Eastside Veterinary Hospital, 4201 Legion Lane, Casper, WY 82609 / 307-266-3737
Beverly Animal Clinic, 1411 South Beverly Street, Casper, WY 82609 / 307-237-1813
Ten Mile Veterinary Clinic, 3891 10 Mile Road, Casper, WY 82604 / 307-577-9457

OUTFITTERS
Platte River Fly Shop, 7400 Hwy 220, Box 3, Casper, WY 82604 / 307-237-5997
Ugly Bug Fly Shop, 316 West Midwest Avenue, Casper, WY 83001 / 307-234-6905
Kyle Wall's Trout Bum Guide Service, 3841 East 15th #425, Casper, WY 82609 /
    307-577-8433

FLY SHOPS AND SPORTING GOODS
Platte River Fly Shop, 7400 Hwy 220, Casper, WY 82604 / 307-237-5997
Ugly Bug Fly Shop, 316 West Midwest Avenue, Casper, WY 83001 / 307-234-6905
Wyoming River Raiders, 300 North Salt Creek Hwy, Casper, WY 82609 /
    307-235-8624
Gart Sports, 601 SE Wyoming Boulevard, Casper, WY 82609 / 307-265-8272
Bullwinkle's, 6000 Cy Avenue, Casper, WY 82604 / 307-234-7001
Timberline Sporting Goods, 4900 Cy Avenue, Casper, WY 82604 / 307-265-2903

AUTO RENTAL AND REPAIR
Big Wyoming Oldsmobile & GMC, 3250 East Yellowstone Hwy, Casper, WY 82609 /
    307-577-7252
Eastridge Autoplex, 111 SE Wyoming Boulevard, Casper, WY 82609 / 307-266-1500
Enterprise Rent-A-Car, 535 North Beverly Street, Casper, WY 82609 / 307-234-8122
Hertz Rent-A-Car, 8500 Airport Parkway #102, Casper, WY 82601 / 307-265-1355
Foss Toyota, 1415 East Yellowstone Hwy, Casper, WY 82601 / 307-237-3700

AIR SERVICE
Natrona County Airport, 8500 Airport Parkway Avenue / 307-234-3663 /
    Skywest Airlines / Charter services

MEDICAL
Casper Medical Center, 1233 East 2nd Street, Casper, WY 82609 / 800-822-7201 or
307-577-7201

FOR MORE INFORMATION
Casper Area Chamber of Commerce
500 North Center Street / P.O. Box 399
Casper, WY 82602
307-234-5311

Saratoga and Encampment
Elevation—7,000 • Population—2,500

Saratoga, once known as Warm Springs, and its sister communities of
Encampment and Riverside are nestled in a high plains bowl between the Snowy
Mountains Range and Sierra Madre Mountains. Quiet backwater communities, they
offer a sense of serenity rarely found in other Rocky Mountains resorts.
Accommodations and restaurants range from rustic to posh. The North Platte River
running through the Saratoga Valley offers some of the most scenic float-fishing trips
in the Rockies. It ranks as one of the best dry fly rivers of the West. Three wilderness
areas surround the headwater canyons of the North Platte and Encampment River in
the Medicine Bow National Forest. The fishing is phenomenal.

ACCOMMODATIONS
Hacienda Motel, Saratoga, WY 82331 / 307-326-5751 / 31 units, pets allowed /
$–$$

Hood House, 214 North 3rd, Saratoga, WY 82331 / 307-326-8901 / Host: Debora
Chastain

Riviera Lodge, 104 East Saratoga Avenue, Saratoga, WY 82331 / 307-326-5651 /
9 units / Pets allowed / $

Sage & Sand Motel, 304 South 1st, Saratoga, WY 82331 / 307-326-8339 / 18 units
/ Pets allowed / $

Saratoga Inn and Hot Springs, Saratoga, WY 82331 / 307-825-2779 / $–$$$

Silver Moon Motel, 412 East Bridge Avenue, Saratoga, WY 82331 / 307-326-5974
/ 14 units / Pets allowed / $

Hotel Wolf, 101 East Bridge Avenue, Saratoga, WY 82331 / 307-326-5525 / 9 units
/ $–$$

Far Out West Bed & Breakfast, 304 North 2nd Street, P.O. Box 1230, Saratoga, WY
82331 / 307-326-5869 / Hosts: Bill and B.J. Farr / 6 units / $$$

Riverside Cabins, 107 Riverside Avenue, Encampment, WY 82325 / 307-327-5361
/ 9 units / Pets allowed / $

Lazy Acres Campground & Motel, 110 Field Street, Encampment, WY 82325 /
307-327-5968 / 6 units / $

Medicine Bow Lodge and Guest Ranch, Star Rt. 8A, Saratoga, WY 82331 /
307-326-5439 or 800-409-5439

Big Horn Lodge, 508 McCaffrey Avenue, Encampment, WY 82325 / 307-327-5110
/ 12 units / Pets allowed / $

Elk Horn Motel, 508 McCaffrey Avenue, Encampment, WY 82325 / 307-327-5110

CAMPGROUNDS AND RV PARKS

Saratoga Inn and RV Resort, P.O. Box 869, Saratoga, WY 82331 / 307-326-5261

Lazy Acres Campground & Motel, 110 Field Street, Encampment, WY 82325 /
307-327-5968 / April 1 to November 1 / 32 RV and 5 tent sites

RESTAURANTS

River Street Deli, 106 North River Street, Saratoga, WY 82331 / 307-326-8683

Lazy River Cantina, 110 East Bridge Street, Saratoga, WY 82331 / 307-326-8472

Stumpy's Eatery, 218 North 1st, Saratoga, WY 82331 / 307-326-8132

Hotel Wolf, 101 East Bridge Street, Saratoga, WY 82331 / 307-326-5525

Bubbas Barbeque Restaurant, 119 North River Street, Saratoga, WY 82331 /
307-326-5427

Mom's Kitchen, 402 South 1st, Saratoga, WY 82331 / 307-326-5136

Corral Restaurant, 504 South Veterans, Saratoga, WY 82331 / 307-326-5046

Sugar Bowl, 706 Freeman Avenue, Encampment, WY 82325/ 307-327-5779

Bear Trap Cafe & Bar, 120 East Riverside Avenue, Encampment, WY 82325 /
307-327-5277

VETERINARIANS

Saratoga Veterinary Service, 905 South 1st Street, Saratoga, WY 82331 /
307-326-5979

Saratoga Veterinary Service, 501 6th Street, Rawlins, WY 82301 / 307-328-0317

OUTFITTERS

Hack's Tackle & Outfitters, 407 North 1st Street, Saratoga, WY 82331 / 307-326-9823

Platt's Guides & Outfitters, Rustic Mountain Lodge, Star Route, Box 49,
Encampment, WY 82325

Platte Valley Outfitters, First and Bridge, PO Box 900, Saratoga, WY 82331 /
307-326-5750

Medicine Bow Drifters, 120 East Bridge Street, Saratoga, 82331 / 307 326 8002

Brush Creek Ranch, Star Route Box 10, Saratoga, WY 82331 / 307-327-5241 or
800-726-2499

Great Rocky Mountain Outfitters, 216 East Walnut, Box 1636, Saratoga, WY 82331 /
307-326-8750

Old Baldy Club, Pic Pike Road, P.O. BOX 707, Saratoga, WY 82331 / 307-326-5222

FLY SHOPS AND SPORTING GOODS

Hack's Tackle & Outfitters, 407 North 1st Street, Saratoga, WY 82331 / 307-326-9823

Platte Valley Outfitters, First and Bridge, Saratoga, WY 82331 / 307-326-5750
Medicine Bow Drifters, 120 East Bridge Street, Saratoga, 82331 / 307-326-8002
Great Rocky Mountain Outfitters, 216 East Walnut, Box 1636, Saratoga, WY 82331 /
    307-326-8750 / Also canoe and raft rentals
Trading Post, 210 Highway 230, Encampment, WY 82325 / 307-327-5720
Bi-Rite Sporting Goods, 511 West Buffalo Street, Rawlins, WY 82301 / 307-324-3401

Auto Rental and Repair
Riverside Garage, 107 Riverside Avenue, Encampment, WY 82325 / 307-327-5361
    / Repair
Kar Kraft, 1111 Daley Street, Rawlins, WY 82301 / 307-324-6352 / Repair and
    rentals

Air Service
Shively Field, Saratoga / Charter services

Medical
Memorial Hospital—Carbon County, 2221 Elm Street, Rawlins, WY 82301 /
    307-324-2221

For More Information
Saratoga—Platte River Valley Chamber of Commerce
P.O. Box 1095
Saratoga, WY 82331
307-326-8855

Laramie
Elevation—7,165 • Population—26,000

Laramie was founded in 1868, and for many years, it typified the Old West as a major railroad and logging center and a welcome stop on long journeys westward. Historic attractions include the Territorial Prison, where the infamous Butch Cassidy was once imprisoned. Today, Laramie has a population of more than 26,000 people and is the home of the University of Wyoming. It is located at the juncture of Interstate 80 and U.S. 30 and 287. The town lies in a high mountain plain between the Laramie and Snowy ranges of the Rocky Mountains. Its best fishing is the nearby Laramie Plains Lakes and the streams and lakes of Medicine Bow National Forest in the Snowy Mountains.

Accommodations
Best Western Fosters Country Inn, 1561 Snowy Range Road, Laramie, WY 82070-
    7105 / 307-742-8371 / 112 units / Pets allowed / $
Holiday Inn, 2313 Soldier Springs Road, Laramie, WY 82070-8901 / 307-742-6611
    / 100 units / Pets allowed / $$

Laramie Inn, I-80 & US 287, Laramie, WY 82070 / 307-742-3721 / 80 units / Pets allowed / $$

Motel 6, 621 Plaza Lane, Laramie, WY 82070-8927 / 307-742-2307 / 122 units / Pets allowed / $

Super 8 Motel—Laramie, I-80 & Curtis St, Laramie, WY 82071 / 307-745-8901 / 48 units / $

Woods Landing Cabins, 9 State Hwy 10, Jelm, WY 82063 / 307-745-9638 / 6 units / Pets allowed / $$

Friendly Fly Store & Motel, Centennial, WY 82055 / 307-742-6033 / 8 units / Pets allowed / $$

The Old Corral, 2750 Hwy 130, Centennial, WY 82055 / 307-745-5918 / 16 units / Pets allowed / $$

Brooklyn Lodge Bed & Breakfast, Hwy 130, Box 292, Centennial, WY 82055 / 307-742-6916 or 307-745-7874 / Hosts: Bell Family & Corbin Family

Campgrounds and RV Parks

Laramie KOA Kampground, I-80 & Curtis Street Exit, 1271 Baker, Laramie, WY 82070 / 307-742-6553 / March 1 to November 30 / 105 RV and tent sites / Full services

Riverside Campground, 180 West Curtis Street, Laramie, WY 82070 / 307-721-7405 / Year-round / 23 RV and 7 tent sites / Full services

Snowy Range RV & Trailer Park, 404 South Taylor Street, Laramie, WY 82070 / 307-745-0297 / Year-round / 12 RV and 8 tent sites / Full services

Restaurants

3rd Street Bar & Grill, 216 East Grand Avenue, Laramie, WY 82070 / 307-742-5522

Outrider Cafe, 1952 North Banner Road, Laramie, WY 82070 / 307-745-9008

Great Wall Restaurant, 1501 South 3rd Street, Laramie, WY 82070 / 307-745-7966

Cavalryman, 4425 North 3rd Street, Laramie, WY 82070 / 307-745-5551

Chelo's, 357 West University Avenue, Laramie, WY 82070 / 307-745-5139

Veterinarians

Alpine Animal Hospital, 610 Skyline Road, Laramie WY 82070 / 307-745-7341

Animal Health Center, 4619 Bobolink Lane, Laramie, WY 82070 / 307-745-6381

All Pet Animal Clinic, 1759 North 3rd Street, Laramie, WY 82070 / 307-742-5590

Outfitters

West Laramie Fly Store, 1657 Snowy Range Road, Laramie, WY 82070 / 307-745-5425

Gary Edwards Flyfishing Adventures, Rural Route, Jelm, WY 82063 / 970-221-5066 or 800-347-4775

Old Glendevey Ranch, Glendevey Colorado Route, Jelm, WY 82063 / 970-435-5701

Steve Sheaffer Outfitters, 4506 Meadowlark Lane, Laramie, WY 82070 / 307-745-7051

FLY SHOPS AND SPORTING GOODS

West Laramie FLY Store, 1657 Snowy Range Road, Laramie, WY 82070 / 307-745-5425

Cross Country Connection, 222 South 2nd, Laramie, WY 82070 / 307-721-2851

Lou's Sport Shop, 217 East Grand Avenue, Laramie, WY 82070 / 307-745-8484

Foster's High Country Sportsman, 1561 Snowy Range Road, Laramie, WY 82070 / 307-721-7406

Friendly Fly Store & Motel, 2758 Hwy 130, Centennial, WY 82055 / 307-742-6033

Southside Tackle, 605 South Greeley Hwy, Cheyenne, WY 82007 / 307-635-4348

AUTO RENTAL AND REPAIR

N & K Rental, 1209 South 3rd Street, Laramie, WY 82070 / 307-742-6329

Burman Motors, 3600 East Grand Avenue, Laramie, WY 82070 / 307-745-8961

Laramie Ford Lincoln Mercury, 3609 East Grand Avenue, Laramie, WY 82070 / 307-745-7315

Dollar Rent-A-Car, 555 General Brees Road, Laramie, WY 82070 / 307-742-8805

AIR SERVICE

Laramie Regional Airport, 555 General Brees Road / 307-742-4164 / Charter services

MEDICAL

Ivinson Memorial Hospital, 255 North 30th Street, Laramie, WY 82070 / 307-742-2141

FOR MORE INFORMATION

Laramie Chamber of Commerce
800 South Third Street / P.O. Box 1166
Laramie WY 82070
307-745-7339

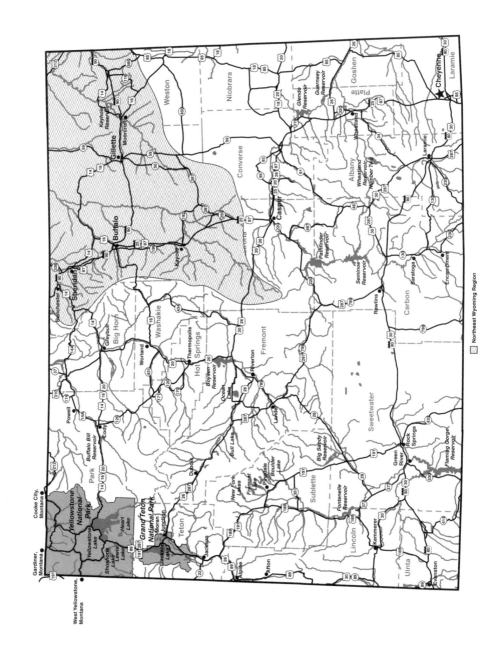

Northeast Wyoming Region

Northeast Wyoming
Gateway to the Big Horn Mountains

Continuing traditions set centuries ago, residents and visitors of northeastern Wyoming's high arid plains seek summer retreats in the alpine forests, lakes, and streams of the snowcapped Big Horn Mountains.

The region's history is as rich as its scenery—a place of cavalry troops and Indian warriors, sheepherders and cattle barons, renegades, and rustlers. Butch Cassidy and the Sundance Kid holed up here after their outlaw exploits. Miners followed the Bozeman Trail to the gold fields of Montana. The U.S. Cavalry engaged in some of the most famous Indian battles in American history. The Johnson County Cattle War left its black mark on the annals of the Old West.

Sheridan and Buffalo are the principal towns serving visitors to the Big Horn Mountains. Each offers a selection of restaurants—ranging from family fare to fine dining—hotels, motels, campgrounds and guest ranches, shops, western heritage museums, and art galleries.

Gateways to the mountains are two scenic highways encircling the 189,000 acre Cloud Peak Wilderness of the Bighorn National Forest.

The northern route, U.S. 14, northwest of Sheridan, follows the Tongue River west, bypasses its rugged canyon and climbs steeply to an 8,000-foot alpine plateau. Crisscrossing it are the North Tongue, one of Wyoming's few catch-and-release streams, and the South Tongue. There are several alpine lakes on a rugged track through the mountains called the Red Grade Road. At Burgess Junction, U.S. 14 turns south and descends scenic Shell Creek Canyon to Greybull. U.S. 14A continues west to Lovell and Cody.

The southern route, U.S. 16 out of Buffalo, crosses numerous small mountain streams lined by park-like meadows and passes several of the Big Horns' best drive-in lakes. Another lacework of side roads leads to the principal trails into hundreds of alpine lakes in the Cloud Peak Wilderness. On the west side of 9,666-foot Powder River Pass, the highway twists down picturesque Tensleep Creek Canyon to Worland.

Kaycee, at the southern edge of the Big Horns, once was on the Outlaw Trail. Back then the Middle Fork of the Powder's canyon was a winter home to outlaws. Nearby was the infamous Hole in the Wall gang's hideout. Today it is a blue ribbon trout stream with exceptional dry-fly fishing.

On the rolling prairie, three trout-filled reservoirs—Lake DeSmet, Muddy Guard No. 1 and Healy—open and end the flyfishing seasons.

For flyfishers arriving via the Black Hills, wary brown trout present a special challenge in Sand Creek, near the town of Sundance and Devils Tower National Monument.

Tongue River

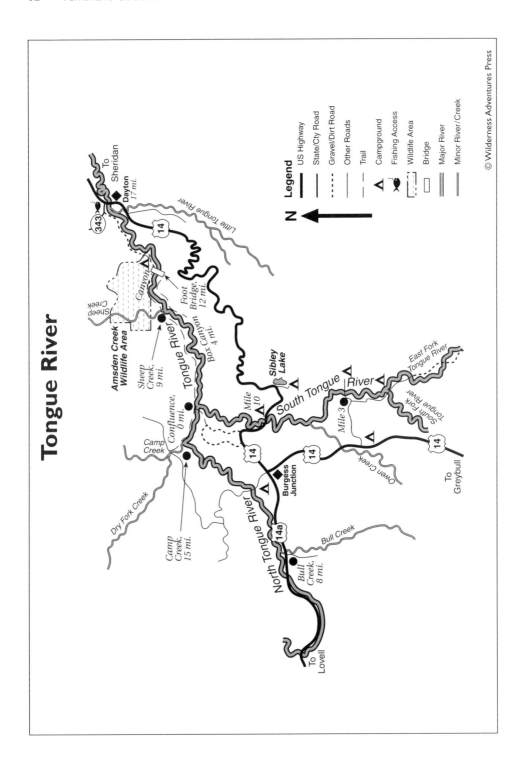

Legend

	US Highway
	State/Cty Road
	Gravel/Dirt Road
	Other Roads
	Trail
	Campground
	Fishing Access
	Wildlife Area
	Bridge
	Major River
	Minor River/Creek

N

© Wilderness Adventures Press

TONGUE RIVER

A blue ribbon trout stream, the Tongue River demands extra efforts to reach its better fishing waters. Plan at least a day to sample classic pocket water fishing for scrappy cutthroat, rainbows and browns. A two- or three-day visit delivers a fuller appreciation of the river's potential.

The 17-mile bucking bronco gallop down a deep craggy canyon is its longest run of public fishing waters. Two public access sites in the flatlands are just off U.S. 14 at the Dayton Bridge and the Conner Battlefield, a small state park at Ranchester. The remainder of the Tongue's 60-mile run through Wyoming to the Montana border, northeast of Sheridan, flows through privately owned prairie rangelands.

The upper river's cutthroat, rainbows and browns average 8 to 12 inches, with a fair number in the 14- to 16-inch range and occasionally up to 18 inches. Fall spawning runs bring up larger brown trout to the stretch above Ranchester. Downstream, the river is almost exclusively inhabited by browns, and permission to fish is required from landowners. Also check with local fly shops for guided trips.

The Tongue drops from about 7,400 feet at its head to 4,000 feet at Dayton. Spring runoff begins in April, peaks around 800 cubic feet in mid-May, and fades to about 250 cfs by July. Late summer and fall flows are approximately 150 cfs.

The lower canyon has very picturesque rock formations formed by erosion. Access to the mouth begins at the Amsden Creek Wildlife Management Area, on the north bank about 3 miles west of the Dayton Bridge. A mile upstream from the trailhead is a stock bridge at the forest boundary.

Sticking to the river in the lower canyon requires scrambling along rocky, brush-lined banks and occasional boulder hopping to make your way upstream. In mild weather, it is better to wear light chest waders that "wick" moisture, or wade wet with felt-soled wading boots. Hip waders inevitably end up being filled; neoprene chest waders restrict climbing and become sweaty.

To reach higher stretches of the river, stay on the north bank trail as it climbs to bypass a high-walled constriction in the canyon. It is a relatively moderate hike with a few steep grades, but scrambling into and out of the gorge presents a strenuous challenge. Wear hiking boots and carry waders or wading boots, equipment, water, snacks, and rain gear in a daypack.

The trail climbs in a steady uphill ascent, ranging from 75 to 300 feet above the river. About 1.5 miles above the footbridge, the canyon opens up, and massive outcroppings of the Big Horns come into view. The trail crosses rolling grassy meadows and dips into woody draws of small tributaries, but the river hugs the south cliff and remains confined to its steep gorge. Sites to climb down to the streambed should be picked with care. The only place the trail meets the river again is at Sheep Creek, about 4 miles above the bridge. It is possible to descend carefully to the river from the trail for another 4 or 5 miles. Access is impossible in the 3-mile Box Canyon section, which is 4 miles below the confluence of the North Tongue and South Tongue.

Another option to explore the river is to start from the North Tongue behind Burgess Junction and make a two- or three-day hike down the canyon. Some locals

Stair-step plunge pools on the Tongue River.

descend the canyon trail on mountain bikes. Two cars are required or a vehicle shuttle has to be arranged.

Hike and fish remote sections of the canyon with a partner. There are no easy descents or marked paths from the trail to the river. When looking for places to enter the canyon, try to pick spots that provide both upstream and downstream fishing. Mark where you reach the bank with a handkerchief or your packs so you know where to climb out again.

The river's frothy plummet down the canyon is divided by a series of deep plunge pools below boulders the size of houses intermixed with shallow rock garden runs, constricted chutes, short glides, riffles and pools, and undercut ledges. Even in low flows the pace is brisk, and the river flattens only a little as it nears the canyon mouth. More pools and pocket waters can be reached as spring runoff wanes and flows recede from the rough, boulder-laden floodplain. The river fishes best in July through autumn.

Rock formations at the canyon mouth of the Tongue River.

Be prepared to lose flies, both to snags and fish that flee downstream into fast water. And practice your roll cast. For the most part it is very close-quarters for casting although the need for long ones are rarely necessary on pocket waters. Far sides of pools and runs may be reached by finding places to make quartering casts up and across a channel. Wade carefully since the rough cobble bed is laced with irregular sized boulders. Don't go in over your hips or put yourself at risk attempting to cross the river.

Cutthroat and rainbows share the swifter waters and pools of the upper canyon. The cutthroat favor slower waters more than the rainbows and have a preference for quiet pools with long downstream glides. The mix in the lower canyon consists mostly of rainbows and brown trout, and the browns tend to hug banks or lurk in deeper pools and runs.

Dry fly action can be good through the summer with large attractors, elk hair caddis, stimulators, and grasshoppers. Watch for fish keying on mayfly and caddis hatches in the afternoon and at dusk. Heavy nymphs, rubberlegs, woolly buggers, and streamers can be dredged through pockets behind boulders, pools and eddies, and along cutbanks. In flatter rock garden runs and channels at pool heads, a small nymph or emerger tied on a larger dry fly as a dropper fly increases chances for a strike. In fall during the brown spawning run, larger woolly buggers and streamers come into play.

When fish start hitting, explore the spot well since the trout tend to congregate in preferred habitats, especially cutthroat.

North Tongue

The North Tongue rises at 8,000 feet on the bowl-like slopes of a broad plateau traversing the northern tip of the Big Horn Mountains. A narrow twisting stream, it forms at the confluence of Wallrock and Trail Creeks within sight of U.S. 14A. About 20 miles downstream it merges with the South Tongue to form the Tongue River above its plunge into a steep, dramatic canyon.

The North Tongue is a captivating, gentle brook filled with a healthy population of Yellowstone cutthroat and lesser numbers of rainbow and brook trout. Its channel rarely exceeds 15 or 20 feet as it gains strength from spring seeps and small tributaries like Bull Creek. It can be easily waded, except in deeper pools below riffles or along cutbank bends.

On the upper 15-mile valley run, it bends and twists through pockets of brushy swamps and a series of willow-lined channels and short grassy meadows. Crystal clear flows of the serpentine river shunt through meanders with undercut banks, occasional deep pools, shallow riffles and runs, and a few braided channels. Behind Burgess Junction, the stream enters a conifer forest as its descent grows steeper. This 4-mile run is swifter and rumpled by rocky pocket waters as it rushes to join the South Tongue.

Few could imagine a better stream for teaching children to flyfish or for novices to hone their skills.

On a July afternoon while eating a late lunch, I watched a teenager studiously cast to an outside bend of the river. Intently watching his fly, he paid little notice to a cowboy riding by on a horse.

"Doing any good?" the horseman called out.

"Yeah, I caught 25," the youth replied.

"That's fun."

"Yeah…," the youth agreed as his response dissolved into a chuckle.

By coincidence I met the boy that evening at a crowded U.S. Forest Service campground. From southern California, he was spending the summer with his grandparents in Denver. They had been coming to the Big Horns for decades. He was having the time of his life and was full of advice after three days of fishing. "I fish the tails of the riffles…at 2 o'clock there's a boil (of blue-winged olives), and I use 16 and 18 parachute Adams…I've been getting 25 to 30 fish a day…There may be larger fish in the pools but they spook real easy…," Jason Dees said, his rambling dissertation punctuated by more chuckles.

North Tongue angler Jason Dees.

The river's trout are mostly in the 7- to 12-inch class, although there are enough 14- and 15-inch fish to keep things interesting. A rare trout 18 inches or longer may be found lurking in a hidden pool. But a lot of the cutthroat have mangled jaws from being repeatedly caught and released.

Because of its easy access from U.S. 14A and its popularity, there's a danger of "hot spotting" on the North Tongue, said Mike Stone, assistant director of Wyoming Game and Fish. "There's a lot of pressure because it is a catch-and-release stream," he explained. Special regulations were "put in place because of angler desire to have larger fish, which is OK, but recruitment is still not certain…We're still not done with the North Tongue River."

From its headwaters down to Bull Creek, cutthroat, rainbows and browns are protected by the catch-and-release rule. Fishing is permitted with only flies or lures. Bull Creek—an excellent dry fly stream for cutthroat that may go to 16 inches—has the same restrictions.

Only brook trout can be kept on Bull Creek or the upper North Tongue for a campfire meal. General regulations apply on the lower North Tongue, South Tongue and Tongue Rivers.

Stunted willows lining sections of the North Tongue's bank present problems in casting and force continual maneuvering back and forth across the stream or short roll casts. Due to the clarity of the water, downstream or down and across presentations are most effective. Faster riffles require less finesse. Strikes are light, so it's also best to pause before setting the hook.

Alpine streams aren't worrisome fisheries. Their growing seasons are short and trout rise eagerly to flies passing through feeding lanes. This is why they appeal to novices and family fishing parties.

Anglers—young and old—often can get strikes with larger flies than the sometimes microscopic patterns needed on lower elevation waters. High floating attractors and generic mayfly imitations in sizes 12 and 14 work in most situations. When large flies are on the water, like golden stoneflies in late spring and grasshoppers in late summer, sizes can graduate from 8 to 14.

Still, mountain trout can be fussy enough at times to key in on specific stages of hatches—the emerger of nymphs or larvae, the adult flying insects, or a spinner fall. It pays as skill levels advance to carry a compliment of match-the-hatch patterns, plus smaller sizes in generic patterns and attractors.

Generic dry fly choices include Adams, parachute Adams, and light Cahills, sizes 12 to 20; renegades, 12 to 16; red, royal, and yellow humpies, 10 to 18; gray, yellow, and royal Wulffs, 12 to 18; tan, brown, and olive or peacock elk hair caddis, 12 to 18; yellow Sallies and willow flies, 14 to 16; yellow and green Trudes, and orange and yellow stimulators, 10 to 14; Joe's Hopper, Dave's hopper, and parachute hopper, 8 to 14; ants and beetles, 14 to 18.

Wet flies choices include caddis pupa, emergers, and soft-hackles, 14 to 18; Prince, hare's ear, and pheasant tail nymphs, 12 to 20; black, olive, and brown woolly buggers, halfbacks, Zug Bugs, black rubberlegs, girdlebugs, Bitch Creek nymphs, and Montana stones, 2 to 8; and muddler minnows, spruce flies, and other streamers, 4 to 10.

The Fly Shop of the Big Horns, Big Horn Mountain Sports and Ritz Sporting Goods in Sheridan keep track of hatches on the Tongue River, its two forks, and other mountain streams. Inquiries also can be made at Sports Lure and Just Gone Fishing in Buffalo.

Hatches to watch for in the Tongue River drainage are baetis, midges, and caddis in early spring before runoff, and golden stones and little yellow stones as runoff wanes in late June and into July. Caddis hatches continue through most of the season, along with pale morning duns starting in early July. Short-lived hatches are green and brown drakes in mid-July and tricos in mid-August. The reign of the terrestrials is from mid-July until a hard freeze around mid-October. Baetis and midges return in fall to close the season.

To match hatches, pack golden stones, Bird's stone, orange stimulators, and orange bucktails, 8 to 12; blue-winged olives and blue duns, 14 to 22; pale morning duns, 16 to 18; rusty spinners, 14 to 18; green drakes, Flavs, and slate-wing western drakes, 12 to 16; gray drakes, gray sparkle duns, and callibaetis, 12 to 16; tricos and black-and-whites, 18 to 22, and Griffith's gnat, black or cream midges, and Palomino midges, 16 to 22.

Short, lightweight rods and hip boots work well on small mountain streams and meadow runs. But even if you decide to wade wet, it is best to wear wading boots with felt soles rather than tennis shoes or hiking boots. Wear polarized sunglasses so you can watch where you are going. The clarity of high mountain streams makes it difficult to gauge water depth. Avoid going in over your hips in swift channels or at the tops of deep pools.

On longer hikes into backcountry waters, fish with a partner and tell family or friends when you expect to return. Always carry a water bottle or canteen. Pack snacks, warm clothing and rain gear in a backpack or fanny pack for protection against inclement weather.

Burgess Junction, 50 miles northwest of Sheridan at the intersection of U.S. 14 and U.S. 14A, is in the center of the North and South Tongue drainages of the Bighorn National Forest. It is one of the few points on the scenic highways where supplies and lodging are available. There are national forest campgrounds scattered throughout the area. Lovell is west on U.S. 14A, and Greybull is southwest on U.S. 14.

South Tongue

The South Tongue tumbles for about 15 miles down the rocky, forested slopes of the Big Horns to join the North Tongue at the mouth of a narrow gorge and create the Tongue River.

A small, cascading stream, the South Tongue heads at the merger of its East Fork and West Fork, just south of Dead Swede Campground. Three miles downstream is the scenic Tie Flume Campground. Their names reflect the region's turn-of-the-century logging history when spring floods flushed logs downstream to the prairie. The timber was used for railroad ties.

Access to the upper river is about 5 miles south of Burgess Junction, where the gravel Red Grade Road turns east into the forest at Owen Creek Campground on U.S. 14. It also flows briefly along U.S. 14, about 5 miles east of Burgess Junction at Prune Creek Campground, and then it cuts north through a steep rocky canyon with very difficult access.

The South Tongue's best fishing is along its 7-mile descent between Tie Flume and Prune Creek for 6- to 12-inch rainbow and brook trout. Unmarked footpaths follow the stream from both campgrounds. Pan-sized trout also are found in its headwater tributaries.

High floating dry flies work well in the cascading pocket waters, and swift riffles and rocky runs of small mountain streams like the South Tongue. Look for bigger fish hiding under logjams and behind midstream boulders, or along undercut banks of short meadow flats and in hard-to-reach pools and eddies. On slower stretches, a small nymph or emerger can be tied on a larger dry fly as a dropper fly to increase chances for a strike.

There's rarely much room to maneuver, and landing larger fish may be a challenge in swift, rocky runs. Use leaders strong enough to end a fight quickly and not exhaust the fish. Pan-sized trout make an excellent campfire meal, but don't waste any that you keep.

Stream Facts: Tongue River

Season
- Year-round.

Regulations
- On the North Tongue, from Bull Creek upstream, catch-and-release for cutthroat and rainbows, flies or lures only. General regulations and limits on South Tongue and Tongue River.

Trout
- Cutthroat and rainbow are found in the North Tongue in the 8- to 16-inch range, as are pan-sized brook trout. Rainbow in the South Tongue range from 6 to 14 inches. The Tongue River's cutthroat, rainbow, and brown trout average 8 to 12 inches, with fair numbers in the 14- to 16-inch class, and occasional larger browns.

Miles

North Tongue:
- Mile 8: Bull Creek
- Mile 15: Burgess bridge
- Mile 20: Confluence with South Tongue

South Tongue:
- Mile 3: Tie Flume Campground
- Mile 10: Prune Creek Campground
- Mile 15: Confluence with North Tongue

Tongue River:
- Mile 0: Head of Tongue River
- Mile 4: Box Canyon
- Mile 9: Sheep Creek
- Mile 14: Stock bridge
- Mile 15: Amsden WMA campground
- Mile 19: Dayton bridge
- Mile 25: Ranchester

Character
- The North Tongue is a gentle mountain meadow stream for most of its run across a high plateau in the Big Horn Mountains. The South Tongue is a swift, small mountain stream laced with pocket waters. The Tongue River tumbles down a steep narrow canyon filled with cascading drops, plunge pools, long runs of pocket waters and shallow rock gardens, and short riffles and pools. The river exits the canyon above Dayton and flows across a high rolling plain to the Montana border.

Flows
- Spring runoff begins in April, peaks by May and rapidly wanes by July. Stable late summer and fall flows may be roiled by mountain storms.

Access
- The Tongue River canyon and both forks are in the Bighorn National Forest. Public access sites are located at the mouth of the canyon, the Dayton Bridge and at a small park in Ranchester. The lower river flows through farm and ranch land, where permission to fish is required.

Camping
- Numerous campgrounds in the Bighorn National Forest and an undeveloped Wyoming Game and Fish campground at the canyon mouth.
- Commercial campground at Dayton Bridge.

TONGUE RIVER MAJOR HATCHES

Insect	M	A	M	J	J	A	S	O	N	Time	Flies
Golden Stone				▮	▮					A	**Dry:** Golden Stone, Bird's Stone, Orange Bucktail, Orange Stimulator #8–12; **Wet:** Halfback Nymph, Bitch Creek Nymph, Montana Stone, Rubberlegs, Woolly Bugger #8–14
Little Yellow Stone (Willow Fly)					▮	▮				A/E	Yellow Sally, Blonde Humpy, Yellow Stimulator, Yellow Trude #12–14
Caddis			▮	▮	▮	▮	▮			M/E	**Dry:** Elk Hair Caddis (tan, brown, or olive), Hemingway Caddis, Renegade, Yellow and Royal Humpy #10–14; **Wet:** Soft-hackles, Caddis Emerger, Peacock Caddis, Prince Nymph, Squirrel Tail #10–16
Baetis		▮					▮	▮		A/E	**Dry:** Blue-winged Olive, Blue Dun, Olive Dun, Adams, Parachute Adams #14–16; **Wet:** Pheasant Tail, Beadheads #14–16
Green Drake					▮	▮				M/A	**Dry:** Green Drake, Flav, Parachute Olive Drake, Slate-wing Western Drake #10–14; **Wet:** Zug Bug, Marabou Olive Nymph, Prince Nymph #10–14

HATCH TIME CODE: M = morning; A = afternoon; E = evening; D = dark; SF = spinner fall; // = continuation through periods.

TONGUE RIVER MAJOR HATCHES, CONT.

Insect	M	A	M	J	J	A	S	O	N	Time	Flies
Trico										M/A	**Dry:** Trico, Black and White, Para-Adams #18–22; **Wet:** Pheasant Tail #18–22
Brown Drake										D	**Dry:** Brown Sparkle Dun, Brown Drake Spinner, Rusty Spinner #10–12; **Wet:** Hare's Ear Nymph #10–12
Pale Morning Dun										A/E	**Dry:** PMD, Compara-dun, Sparkle Dun, Light Cahill, Sulphur #14–16; **Wet:** Hare's Ear Nymph, Pheasant Tail, Beadheads #14–18
Terrestrials										A	Dave's Hopper, Joe's Hopper, Parachute Hopper, Yellow Humpy, Yellow Trude, Yellow Stimulator #8–14; Foam Beetle, Disc O'Beetle, Black Elk Hair Caddis #10–16; Black Ant, Rusty Ant #14–18
Midges										M/E	**Dry:** Griffith's Gnat, Black Midge, Cream Midge, Palamino Midge #16–22; **Wet:** Brassie, Blood Midge, San Juan Worm, Midge Pupa #16–22

HATCH TIME CODE: M = morning; A = afternoon; E = evening; D = dark; SF = spinner fall; // = continuation through periods.

West's First Derby
Crook Fished the Day Custer Died

Gen. George Armstrong Custer's Seventh Cavalry could have used some help June 25, 1876, when it attacked Sitting Bull's camp at the Little Bighorn.

It didn't come because the general leading a reinforcement column was fishing on the Tongue River in Wyoming. A third column was wandering around to the north along the Yellowstone River.

Ultimately, Custer's fate was sealed eight days before the Battle of the Little Bighorn.

Gen. George Crook's Second Cavalry and infantry forces fought a fierce running battle June 17 with Crazy Horse's Sioux and Northern Cheyenne warriors. The 6-hour battle raged along Rosebud Creek, about 60 miles south of the Little Bighorn. Both sides claimed victory. Quixotically, Crook didn't advance and failed to send a warning about the tribes' strength to Custer.

The Battle of the Rosebud was overshadowed by Custer's Last Stand, but it's more than a footnote in the Summer Wars of 1876. Except for an aide's journals, details of Crook's retreat likely would be lost to history. His 6-week sojourn at the present site of Sheridan ranks as one of the strangest episodes in the annals of the U.S. Army.

"The merits of Tongue River and its tributaries as great trout streams were not long without proper recognition at the hands of our anglers," states Lt. John Bourke in *On the Border with Crook*. "Under the influence of the warm weather the fish had begun to bite voraciously, in spite of the fact that there were always squads of men bathing in the limpid waters or mules slaking their thirst. The first afternoon 95 were caught and brought into camp."

The first Yellowstone cutthroat trout taken from Big Goose and Little Goose Creeks were meant to supplement the Army's monotonous field rations. But fishing quickly became an obsession. As word passed down the creeks that the trout were taking grasshoppers, virtually the whole battalion got in on the action. It turned into the West's first fishing derby.

"My notebooks about this time seem to be almost the chronicle of a sporting club, so filled are they with the numbers of trout brought by different fishermen into camp," Bourke continues. "Mills started in with a record of over 100 caught by himself and two soldiers in one short afternoon. On the 28th of June the same party has another record of 146. On the 29th of same month, Bulb is credited with 56, while the total brought into camp during the 28th ran over 500."

"Three Stars," as the general was known among Indians, apparently was more of a hunter than fisherman. Not a model cavalryman, Crook rode a sturdy mule rather than a horse. His claim to fame was in subduing the Apache in

Arizona. He also quelled a Shoshone uprising in Idaho. In 1883, he returned to Arizona to capture Geronimo.

"General Crook started out to catch a mess (of fish), but met with poor luck," Bourke states. "He saw bear tracks and followed them, bringing in a good-sized 'cinnamon' (black bear), so it was agreed not to refer to his small number of trout."

It takes a lot of fish to feed 1,100 soldiers, not to mention the many mule packers accompanying the column. Bourke notes that "Buffalo and elk meat were both plenty, and with the trout kept the men well fed."

Bourke says the cavalry was kept busy mornings practicing maneuvers, but troopers and soldiers were permitted to roam the countryside in the afternoons, hunting and fishing. The packers also organized a mule race. "It was estimated by conservative judges that fully 5 dollars had changed hands in 10-cent bets."

Amid this holiday atmosphere the general's aide said little about the Rosebud battle and nothing about an earlier skirmish on the Tongue River. On June 9, the column had traded potshots with about 200 Sioux and Cheyenne who fired into their camp from the river's bluffs.

"Up to the end of June no news of any kind, from any sources excepting Crow Indians [scouts], had been received from General [Alfred] Terry and his command, and much comment, not unmixed with uneasiness, was occasioned thereby," Bourke states.

Terry was commander of the column that had set out from Fort Abraham Lincoln in North Dakota. Custer was his point man. Custer was supposed to lead the way to the Sioux for Crook, moving north from Fort Fetterman, with Col. John Gibbon coming from the northwest from Bozeman. Custer found the huge Indian encampment first but didn't wait for reinforcements. And the rest is history, as the saying goes.

Crook grew impatient with the lack of news. On July 1, he set out with a small detachment for the summit of the Big Horns to look out over the plains. He spied no smoke from campfires nor dust plumes from Indian ponies or cavalry columns. So the general went deer hunting.

Bourke's journals wax poetic over the rugged beauty of the Big Horns. He admired the snow-capped dome of Cloud Peak towering a thousand feet above timberline, and willow-choked meadows laced by translucent mountain streams and dotted with pristine lakes.

"On the 'divide' was a lake, not over 500 yards long, which supplied water to the Big Horn (River) on the west and the Tongue on the east side of the range. Large cakes and floes of black ice, over a foot in thickness, floated on its waters. Each of these was covered with snow and regelated ice," he reports.

Later they were intrigued when they found "the snow in one place was 60 to 70 feet deep and had not been disturbed for years, because there were five or six strata of grasshoppers frozen stiff, each representing one season."

Bourke complained that trout leaping for early mayflies ignored bait tossed by anglers in the party. The keen, rarefied air of the mountains had "aggravated" already hearty appetites. But the general's venison would make "epicures" sigh "in vain for the pleasure with which it was devoured." Bighorn sheep and mountain bison also fed their voracious appetites during the alpine trek.

Crook returned to the flatlands July 4, still unaware of the Custer catastrophe. But not even the nation's centennial intruded on Bourke's notations of the wilderness wonders of his surroundings.

Sheridan is where the prairie meets the Rocky Mountains. To the east are the high plains, dry rolling hills dotted with clumps of short grass and sagebrush. To the west are the thickly timbered foothills of the Big Horns, capped by the range's snowy peaks. Streams flowing out of the mountains spill onto the plains from the mouths of narrow steep-walled canyons. Picturesquely eroded rock formations rim the canyons, and huge boulders and swirling pools pocket the tumbling streams.

In addition to the gluttony of his troops, Crook had to feed the more than 2,000 horses and mules of the cavalry, wagon trains, pack trains, Indian scouts and soldiers. Camp was moved repeatedly to the mouth of another Tongue tributary for new grazing grounds. The battalion's fishing bonanza was renewed at each new camp.

"The credulity of the reader will be taxed to the utmost limit if he follows my record of the catches of trout made in all these streams," Bourke declares. "What these catches would have amounted to had there been no herds of horses and mules…I am unable to say; but the hundreds and thousands of fine fish taken from that set of creeks by officers and soldiers, who had nothing but the rudest of appliances, speaks of the wonderful resources of the country in game at that time."

But even with the bounty of the frontier, numbers alone were not enough. The "big fish" syndrome took over. Quiet reports of "hidden fish far greater in size and weight than those caught closer to camp" enticed Bourke to explore "beautiful deep pools farther up the mountain."

Gaudy handtied flies of the period didn't phase the suspicious mountain trout, but native grasshoppers were irresistible. Bourke's party was soon plucking trout "from all sorts of unexpected places—from the edge of the rapids below us, from under gloomy blocks of granite, from amid the gnarly roots of almost amphibious trees."

Still, Bourke wanted bigger fish to fry. An Irish teamster, born and bred in the salmon districts of Ireland, steered him in the right direction. He even loaned the lieutenant his willow rod.

The cutthroat trout that rose to Bourke's grasshopper "was noble, heavy, and gorgeous in his dress of silver and gold and black and red." A spirited but brief tussle ended with the 3-pound fish flopping in the grasses of the creek bank.

Bourke hurried off to dinner, pleased to return with "the largest specimen reaching camp that week."

The battalion's final angling honors went to Major Noyes, one of its most earnest fishermen. When he failed to return to camp during a heavy thunderstorm, a search party was launched.

"Noyes was found fast asleep under a tree, completely exhausted by his hard work," Bourke reports. "He was afoot and unable to reach camp with his great haul of fish, over one hundred and ten in number; he had played himself out, but had broken the record, and was snoring serenely."

In all, Bourke estimated the battalion captured more than 15,000 trout from the Tongue River and its tributaries. To their credit, Crook and his officers insisted there be no waste. All the fish had to be eaten in camp or dried for later use.

Their party came to a sobering halt July 10 when messengers brought word Custer and 263 troopers of the Seventh Cavalry had been overwhelmed at the Little Bighorn. "The shock was so great that men and officers could hardly speak when the tale slowly circulated from lip to lip," Bourke reports.

The same day the Sioux returned and tried to burn out the Army camp by setting fire to the prairie. They continued to harass the column for two weeks "by trying to stampede stock, burn grass, annoy pickets, and devil the command generally."

The Second Cavalry was back in the war, but the column still didn't return to the field until the end of July.

Crook declared, "I am at a loss what to do," in a letter to Gen. Philip Sheridan, commander of the Army's western forces. The comment is indicative of the malaise that paralyzed the field commanders in the wake of the campaign's major battles. But not even the Sioux recorded ultimate victory. Their summer of glory was short-lived.

NORTHERN BIG HORNS LAKES

Sibley Lake is adjacent to U.S. 14 midway between Dayton and Burgess Junction. A popular alpine fishery, it has a picturesque campground overlooking the lake and a picnic area at its inlet. Stocked with hatchery rainbow, it also contains a few cutthroat and brook trout and is rated as good fishing for 8- to 12-inch fish.

Southeast of Dead Swede, the Red Grade Road parallels the East Fork of the Tongue en route to Sawmill Lakes and Twin Lakes, and trails into the northern tip of the Cloud Peak Wilderness at Park Reservoir. Its terminus—or starting point—is at the small village of Big Horn, about 5 miles southwest of Sheridan.

Vehicles with high clearance are recommend for this rough gravel road, especially on its steep twisting climb up the east slopes of the mountains from Big Horn. Cars pulling trailers are not recommended. Several Forest Service campgrounds are located near the lakes.

The smaller Sawmill and Twin Lakes are rated as good to fair fishing for 8- to 14-inch cutthroat, rainbow and brook trout. The 1- to 2-mile hikes into these lakes are short enough to carry float tubes.

The larger Park Reservoir has 10- to 14-inch cutthroat and rainbows, as well as lake trout.

Fly choices for alpine lakes are as basic as they are for mountain streams, but dry fly action is much more limited in midsummer. Plan on working lakes mostly with wet flies. In addition to wet flies and streamers previously mentioned, a lake fishing assortment should include tan, olive, and orange scuds, Carey specials, and olive marabou damsel nymphs, sizes 10 to 14, and olive, black, and brown leeches, 4 to 8.

The most common dry flies occurring on lakes are midges and the callibaetis mayfly, although pale morning duns and baetis often hatch in tributaries and float into inlets. Flying ants and windblown grasshoppers and beetles also draw lusty strikes.

Concentrate on shorelines and shallows, ledges and tributary inlets when stripping in wet flies or casting dry flies and attractors. Use a small dropper fly on both wet and dry flies to speed up prospecting. During quiet spells without a hatch, a very slow, twitch-and-pause retrieve of a dry fly sometimes draws rises.

Rod choices depend on conditions or length of the hike into a lake. A three-piece, 8-foot, 5- or 6-weight travel rod with a weight-forward or floating line and medium sinking tip is handy on longer trips. Big lakes or windy conditions may require a 9-foot, 6- or 7-weight rod.

At high elevations snow occurs in all seasons. Even on midsummer day hikes into remote forest lakes or the wilderness, be prepared for early spring or fall-like conditions. Rain gear, a sweater, wool socks, knit cap and gloves should be carried in a daypack, with a water bottle and snacks. Don't forget maps, camera, insect repellent and sunglasses.

LITTLE BIGHORN RIVER

A smaller version of the Tongue requiring a duplication of hiking and climbing efforts is the Little Bighorn River in the remote northwest corner of the Big Horns.

Its canyon mouth is at the end of a rough 15-mile gravel road west of Parkman near the Montana border. To reach the Pass Creek Road to the Kerns Wildlife Management Area, take the County 144 exit about 3 miles north of Parkman on Interstate 90. Access to the lower Little Bighorn is on the smaller, western unit of the Kerns habitat preserve. The upper canyon and headwaters are in the Bighorn National Forest.

High clearance vehicles in good running condition are recommend for back-country roads like this, far from a major town. Carry extra water and supplies even when a camping trip is not planned.

An excellent dry fly stream, the Little Bighorn canyon is rated as good fishing for 8- to 12-inch rainbows and a few cutthroat. The cutthroat are protected by a catch-and-release rule. Pan-sized brook trout are more common in the upper river and tributaries like Dry Creek.

Good small stream fishing is also available on the large eastern unit of Kerns Wildlife Management Area in West Pass Creek and Elkhorn Creek. Keep an eye out for rattlesnakes.

Camping is permitted at undeveloped campgrounds on the Wyoming Game and Fish preserve, but you have to bring water and pack out trash.

SOUTH PINEY CREEK

Nestled in the eastern foothills of the Big Horns, midway between Sheridan and Buffalo, is the village of Story. It presents three incentives for getting off the beaten path—history, aquaculture, and, of course, fly casting.

From 1866 to 1868, Fort Phil Kearny was the epicenter of battles fought by Red Cloud and Crazy Horse against the U.S. Cavalry to close the Bozeman Trail to the Montana goldfields. Fort Phil Kearny State Historic Site and Museum and the Wagon Box and Fetterman battlefields record the tumultuous events of the Sioux Indian Wars.

Story Fish Hatchery is located on South Piney Creek, which flows through the center of town. A tour of its visitor center and holding ponds provides a cool interlude on a hot summer day. A nearby trail offers easy access to the foothills and the stream's tumbling waters with excellent pocket water fishing.

South Piney Creek is a small mirror image of the Tongue River, canyon and all, but its broad floodplain allows a bit more casting room than the Tongue's. To reach it, turn south off Hatchery Road onto Thornerider Road. After about a half mile park on the county side of the road at a green gate.

It is a pleasant 1-mile hike to the forest boundary, and another half-mile to the canyon mouth above a diversion dam that divides the creek in two. Fishing can commence at the bottom of the canyon, or you can climb the trail above the north bank to explore pools, pocket waters and rock garden runs higher upstream. Despite its

South Piney Creek at Story.

brisk pace, top water action is good on high-riding dry flies for pan-sized rainbows, browns and brookies.

Piney Creek, which loops northeast around Story, is another good side trip. Check locally on where to park or obtain permission to cross private lands to reach the forest boundary. Below town along WYO 193, Piney Creek flows through a state school section, but its boundaries are not marked. Again, check where it is permitted to park and fish.

Piney Creek and its tributaries are rated as good fishing for 8- to 14-inch rainbows and browns, and pan-sized brook trout.

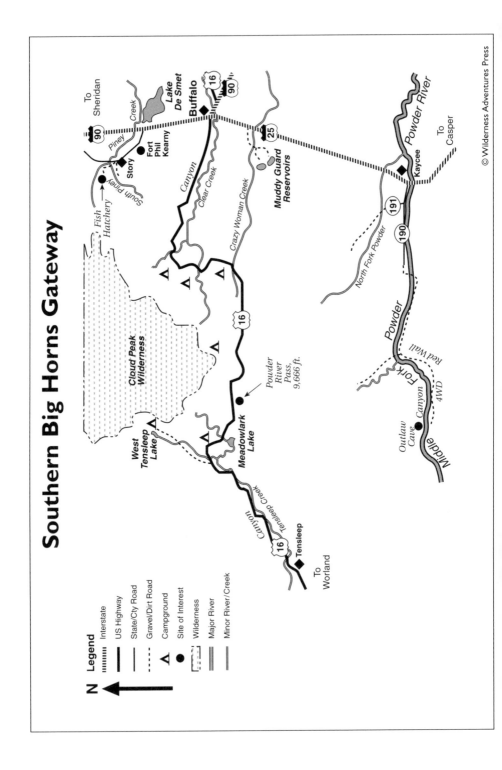

Southern Big Horns Gateway

© Wilderness Adventures Press

SOUTHERN BIG HORNS GATEWAY

The southern route into the Big Horn Mountains is the Cloud Peak Skyway along U.S. 16. It begins in Buffalo at the intersection of I-90 and I-25 .

Clear Creek runs through the center of the Old West resort community and can be fished right in town or just upstream along an extensive green belt tail system. The scenic highway parallels Clear Creek canyon to the Bighorn National Forest and a mountain plateau. It provides access to the Clear Creek's three forks and several other mountain brooks such as Doyle Creek and Crazy Woman Creek and its tributaries. A web of gravel roads connects campgrounds to the upper reaches of the creeks lined by stunted willows in park-like meadows.

Fishing is good for 6- to 10-inch rainbow, brown and brook trout, with chances to net a few old-timers of 12 inches. Flies recommended for the Tongue River drainage work equally well in the southern Big Horns. Hatches to watch for are similar, and action can be found throughout most days with standard attractors and generic mayfly and caddis patterns.

Cloud Peak Wilderness

A lacework of side roads along U.S. 16 leads to starting points for hikes into the Cloud Peak Wilderness.

The 189,000 acre wilderness stretches along the backbone of the Big Horns, with Cloud Peak towering to 13,175 feet. More than 200 trout-filled lakes dot the mountain range, and numerous feeder streams and outlets crisscross its forested slopes.

Trout in the lakes are larger than those found in streams, ranging from 8 to 16 inches. In addition to rainbows and brookies, cutthroat or grayling are present in some lakes. Lake trout in a few lakes may go to 24 inches. Some of the alpine lakes are at elevations of 10,000 feet or higher, and hikers should be in good physical condition.

There are many loop trails in the wilderness, and some trail combinations can result in hikes lasting a week or longer. More than 70 percent of the Cloud Peak's hikers enter its alpine backcountry via trailheads off U.S. 16. These trailheads are located at Hunter Corral and Circle Park on the east side of the highway's pass and at West Tensleep and Battle Park on the west side.

Popular hiking and fishing destinations for day hikes or loop trips from the Hunter Corral trailhead are the Seven Brothers Lakes, Lake Angeline and Willow Park Reservoir. Lake Solitude is a focal point of hikes from the Battle Park trailhead and also can be reached from the West Tensleep Lake trailhead.

For more solitary wilderness experiences, the Wilderness Watch Chapter suggests trips be planned using alternate routes. However, most of the less popular trailheads require 4-wheel-drive vehicles with high clearance to reach them.

Registration is mandatory when entering the wilderness. Campfires within 300 feet of lakes, streams and designated trails are prohibited, and camping within 100 feet of any water is prohibited.

Meadowlark Lake.

Brochures about the Big Horns, information on trail lengths and conditions, and descriptions of lakes and fish species can be obtained at U.S. Forest Service offices, visitor centers and fly shops in Sheridan and Buffalo.

Guided trips can be arranged with local outfitters, who also pack in supplies and camping equipment on horses or mules for parties that want to hike on their own in comfort.

For more information, contact Bighorn National Forest, 1969 South Sheridan Avenue., Sheridan, WY 82801, 307-672-0751; or Cloud Peak Wilderness Coordinator, Buffalo Ranger District, Buffalo, WY 82834, 307-684-7981.

West Slopes

West of the 9,666-foot Powder River Pass, U.S. 16 enters the Tensleep Creek drainage with its many mountain meadow tributaries. Another collection of Forest Service campgrounds invites stopovers and alpine explorations. Two of the Big Horns' better drive-in lakes also are west of the pass.

Tensleep Creek and its east and west forks hold excellent populations of 6- to 12-inch rainbows, browns and brookies, plus a few cutthroat in each creek.

Meadowlark Lake, a large reservoir on Tensleep Creek, is right next to the highway. It holds 9- to 14-inch rainbow, cutthroat and brook trout. There are several Forest Service campgrounds on or near the lake. Meadowlark Lake Resort provides accommodations, supplies and boat rentals.

Canyon of Tensleep Creek.

The scenic West Tensleep Lake is 8 miles north of the highway at the edge of the wilderness. The little lake holds 6- to 10-inch brook trout. The gravel road into the lake follows West Tensleep Creek.

About 5 miles west of Meadowlark Lake, U.S. 16 swings down a string of dramatic switch backs through the picturesque Tensleep Creek Canyon to the small town of Tensleep and continues west to Worland in the Big Horn River basin. Tensleep gets its name from Indian folk lore that it was 10 nights distance from Fort Laramie on the North Platte River to the Yellowstone River.

The best way to fish Tensleep Creek Canyon is to drive to the bottom of the foothills and backtrack into it on a gravel road along the west bank. There is a campground in the cottonwood floodplain of the lower canyon.

Lower Tensleep Creek offers a shot at some larger rainbows and browns than those found in its mountain meadow runs. Another 3.5 miles of public access to the creek is located at the Wigwam Rearing Station below the U.S. 16 bridge.

Tensleep Creek flows into the Nowood River. It has no public access, but anglers interested in a loop trip back to the Big Horns can take a paved country road north along the river to WYO 31. This route offers interesting side trips to Medicine Lodge or Paint Rock Creeks in the foothills near the farming hamlet of Hyattville.

There is a beautiful little park, campground and museum at the Medicine Lodge State Archaeological Site. A mural of ancient Indian petroglyphs and pictographs on a sandstone cliff is slowing dissolving into oblivion.

Fishing for 8- to 14-inch browns in Medicine Lodge Creek is excellent. The shallow, rocky stream provides a refreshing interlude in the arid Big Horn Basin.

Paint Rock Creek is harder to reach since a change in ownership caused a public access site at its canyon mouth to be closed. The grueling hike in is on BLM land across hot, dry slick rock. "Unless you're in good shape, don't try it," said the manager of the Medicine Lodge Archaeological Site. He'll give you directions, if you are.

The other option is to continue northwest on WYO 31 to U.S. 20/16 and take U.S. 14 east at Greybull to the Tongue River drainage at Burgess Junction. The scenic U.S. 14 climbs the Shell Creek Canyon, a gorge as dramatic and picturesque as the Tensleep's.

Shell Creek's wild brown and brook trout are in the 8- to 12-inch range, and occasionally a 14- to 20-inch brown is taken. There are lesser numbers of rainbows in the drainage. Climbs into its canyon are more strenuous than the Tensleep's because there is no public access on Shell Creek's lower run.

It also should be noted that rattlesnakes are present at lower elevations on the west slopes of the Big Horns and in the Big Horn Basin.

Middle Fork Powder River

The idea to pay a visit to Hole in the Wall Country popped to mind whenever Newman and Redford's epic Western film *Butch Cassidy and the Sundance Kid* appeared on late-night TV. Glowing reports of the Middle Fork of the Powder as a blue ribbon trout stream finally clinched it. Here was a chance to capture myths of the Old West and cast to trout as exquisite as surrounding vistas.

Both eventually happened, but the adventure almost ended before it started.

Public access to the Middle Fork canyon is about 20 miles southwest of the little town of Kaycee, 45 miles south of Buffalo, on I-25. The first 18 miles are on well-maintained roads into the Red Wall Country and along Buffalo Creek. But the bumpy, deeply rutted road to Outlaw Cave Canyon is a white-knuckle escapade in a vehicle with not quite enough clearance. It's one of a few places I broke my 4-wheel-drive rule—don't use it until you're in trouble.

Almost immediately after the final turnoff to the canyon, I started straddling deep ruts in the two-track "road" climbing a ridge. Blithely bypassing the first pullout for a trail into the canyon, I put the car in 4-wheel-drive when it bogged down in a soft, crumbly spot on the next ridge. As I topped it, the deep ruts in a narrow cut through the next hump came into view. It presented a definite potential for a high-center catastrophe. I chickened out and made a tight turnaround in the saddle between the ridges.

Red Wall Country along the Middle Fork Powder River.

The 4-wheel-drive mode of a barely moving vehicle puts a lot of strain on an engine. Pausing to let it cool down, I climbed up the slope to admire the view.

Red Wall Country is named for the ruby sandstone escarpments of the high plains encircling the southern tip of the Big Horn Mountains. The panoramic view of forested slopes and craggy peaks on the north and endless cloudy skies south and east over the red cliffs and west above arid sagebrush foothills was breathtaking.

Perfect country for horsemen, it was easy to imagine Butch and Sundance loping along Buffalo Creek in the valley below. Cassidy would be plotting the next train robbery or bank heist. Awaiting his return would be the Hole in the Wall gang in its notorious hideout in another canyon to the south.

Idle daydreams are amusing, but trout finning in a nearby river are more seductive. I returned to the first trail into the Middle Fork's gorge to get to the fish.

For properly equipped drivers, the Outlaw Cave trail is 1.75 miles west of the first access. The cave is named for another band of desperadoes who holed up in it one winter in the 1880s. There are five other primitive trails into the canyon, including one to another cave with Indian pictographs.

A first view of the river far below is spectacular. Its silvery thread courses down a narrow channel hugging richly colored cliffs of 800 to 1,000 feet on the north. Terraces of chalky cliffs, 700 to 800 feet in height and dotted with stunted trees and sagebrush, tower above the south bank.

The Middle Fork canyon is managed as a wild trout fishery protected by a slot limit to reduce harvest. Rainbows and browns range from 9 to 16 inches, with an average size of 12 inches. A few larger fish, 18 to 20 inches, lurk in deep pools. Pan-sized brook trout also reside in the upper river.

All trout between 10 and 16 inches must be released, and fishing is permitted with flies and lures only. The limit is 6 per day or in possession; only 1 can exceed 16 inches.

Approximately 10 miles of public access are available to flyfishers in the gorge. The strenuous hike into it is on treacherous loose-rock trails that branch in different directions, but the only way is down. Wear hiking boots, not tennis shoes, take your time, and watch your step. Carry extra water and be sure to save enough for the climb out. It is even tougher, and savvy anglers start the climb at least an hour before dark.

The best routine is to hike into the canyon in the morning, fish through the heat of the day and hike out when it cools again at dusk. In mild weather the river can be waded wet with felt-soled wading boots or light, stocking-foot waders that "wick" moisture. The rough cobble floor, coated with algae, is slippery, and anglers wearing tennis shoes or river sandals may end up with bruised feet.

The river descends a relatively moderate incline through the canyon. There are a few low waterfalls and rapids and numerous shallow rocky runs and riffles, deep pools and undercut ledges. The channel is only 10 to 15 feet in width and lined with thick underbrush in places. It can be easily crossed to maneuver up and downstream.

Spring runoff peaks in late May, fades through June and stabilizes by July. Summer and fall flows are low and clear, but still brisk through stair-step runs.

The Middle Fork is an excellent dry fly stream, but matching the hatch is not a major concern. A basic assortment of attractor patterns, generic mayflies, elk hair caddis, stimulators and grasshoppers handle most situations for good top water action. A typical August report from local fly shops states, "Any dry flies 16 to 18 will catch fish…more and more caddis are showing up." But small weighted nymphs and beadheads drifted through deeper pools tend to score larger fish.

Although some flyfishers feel naked without a fishing vest, remember that it adds to the load going in and coming out. All that's needed is a fanny pack stocked with an assortment of leaders and tippets, fly floatant and strike indicators, clippers and forceps, and a few boxes for dry flies and nymphs.

Dry fly boxes can hold tan, olive, or peacock elk hair caddis, yellow and royal humpies, yellow and orange stimulators, and grasshoppers, 10 to 14; Adams, parachute Adams, light Cahills, and blue-winged olives, 14 to 18. Wet fly boxes can contain halfbacks, Bitch Creek nymphs, or Montana stones, 6 to 10; hare's ear, Prince, and pheasant tail nymphs, soft-hackles, emergers, and beadheads, 12 to 18.

Still, not all the trout roll over like puppies and ask to be scratched on their bellies. The river's principal guide, Charlie Gould of Just Gone Fishing in Buffalo, notes Middle Fork trout present ample challenges to discerning flyfishers.

The narrow channel and clarity of the water demand finesse in presentations and occasional hide and stalk situations. Gould says drift-free downstream presentations work best with dry flies. When using nymphs and emergers, strike indicators improve hook ups on subtle hits.

Canyon of the Middle Fork Powder River.

It takes a little extra effort to reach the Middle Fork's trout, but the rewards are many. Their brilliant, sparkling colors match picture postcard environs.

Pick an evening with a rising full moon for the drive back to civilization, and the beauty and serenity of Red Wall Country is exquisite.

How to get there:
- Turn west at the Kaycee interchange on I-25 and drive 1 mile to Barnum Road (WYO 190).
- Follow Barnum Road 17 miles west to the Bar C Ranch Road, marked by sign for the Middle Fork Management Area, and turn left.
- Follow the Bar C Ranch Road southwest 4 miles to the Outlaw Cave sign and drive west 2 miles to its trail. Road maintenance ends at the Outlaw Cave/BLM sign. High clearance vehicles with 4-wheel-drive are required to continue to the canyon rim. Wet weather makes the two-track road virtually impassable.
- Outlaw Cave Road is closed to travel from Nov. 15 to April 15.

Stream Facts: Middle Fork Powder River

Season
- Year-round.

Regulations
- All trout between 10 and 16 inches must be released, and fishing is permitted with flies and lures only. The limit is 6 per day or in possession; only 1 may exceed 16 inches.

Trout
- Rainbows and browns range from 9 to 16 inches, with a few 18 to 20 inches; pan-sized brook trout are in upper river.

Miles
- Approximately 10 miles of public access in the deep, narrow Outlaw Cave Canyon. Hikes into the canyon are on seven primitive trails that are strenuous, and climbs out are tougher.

Character
- River stair-steps down narrow rocky canyon between sheer cliffs of 800 to 1,000 feet on north wall and 700 to 800 feet on south wall in shallow rocky runs and riffles, deep pools, and undercut ledges. Channel is only 10 to 15 feet in width and lined in some sections with thick underbrush.

Flows
- Spring runoff peaks in late May, fades through June and stabilizes by July. Summer and fall flows are low and clear, but still brisk.

Access
- Public access to canyon is 20 miles southwest of Kaycee via the Barnum Road and Bar C Ranch road to Outlaw Cave Road. High clearance vehicles with 4-wheel-drive are required to continue past BLM boundary, where road maintenance ends. Outlaw Cave trail is 2 miles west. There are six other primitive trails into the canyon.

Camping
- Undeveloped BLM campground at Outlaw Cave trail is accessible only with high clearance 4-wheel-drive vehicles; must bring own water and pack out trash.
- Hole in the Wall Campground and Guest Ranch on Barnum Road, 17 miles west of Kaycee.

SAND CREEK

Don't let the name fool you; Sand Creek is loaded to the brim with trout. The spring creek flows through a grassy valley in the eastern foothills of the Wyoming Black Hills and crosses the border into South Dakota at the village of Beulah on I-90. It harbors so many small brown trout a generous bag limit begs anglers to keep fish. The caveat is, "Catch 'em if you can."

An axiom often quoted by fisheries biologists asserts 10 percent of anglers catch 90 percent of the fish. And browns rank as the most wary of trout and the hardest to net. They make fishing on Sand Creek a challenge. "It's a real productive stream and its biomass, pound per pound, is about the best in the state," said Mike Stone, Wyoming Game and Fish's assistant director. "But there's no big fish habitat and a lot of little fish people can't catch."

Stream counts of the dense population of 8- to 12-inch browns show there are 4,000 to 6,000 trout per mile in Sand Creek. A few browns top 16 inches, and there are remnant populations of cutthroat and brook trout.

Flyfishers can tackle 4.5 miles of public waters on Sand Creek, including the Ranch A unit and a second unit downstream from a housing development. Signs along the gravel road from Beulah indicate where anglers must park to fish.

From I-90 upstream through Ranch A to the national forest boundary, the limit on brown trout is 12 per day or in possession, only 1 over 12 inches. All other trout must be returned to the water immediately. Also, on the Ranch A public access area near the hatchery, fishing is permitted with flies and lures only.

If the brown trout weren't enough of a challenge, the creek's terrain makes it difficult to fish. As it meanders down the valley, Sand Creek cuts deeply into its loamy soil. Overhanging cutbanks rise 3 to 6 feet above the narrow channel, which rarely exceeds 20 feet in width. But the creek is easily waded. Its slow, crystal clear flows are relatively shallow, except for holes 4 feet or more in depth. Summer growth of weed beds provides additional cover for the trout.

The clarity of the water dictates downstream presentations with long, delicate leaders. Small Adams, pale morning dun, blue-winged olive, midge, caddis, and grasshopper patterns draw top water action. Wet flies can include small nymphs, emergers, beadheads, scuds, and muddler minnows.

The historic Ranch A was owned and developed by Chicago publishing tycoon Moe Annenburg in the 1930s. U.S. Fish and Wildlife purchased the ranch in 1968 and conducted trout genetics research at a hatchery until 1980. State lease agreements have permitted public access since then, and in 1996 Wyoming agreed to take over management when USFWS said it no longer wanted the ranch.

Federal legislation granting the ranch to the state preserves access to the fishery and protects public rights-of-way to Black Hills National Forest, Stone said.

The Black Hills are an isolated eastern extension of the Rocky Mountains, and the region is a transition zone between prairie and mountains for wildlife and plants.

White-tailed deer, wild turkey and other wildlife are common on the ranch. It has one of the most varied populations of birds in the state.

Food, services, accommodations, and campgrounds are available at Sundance, 12 miles southwest of Beulah. Two miles west of Sundance, U.S. 14 branches north to the mystical Devils Tower, a National Monument. Scenic forested campgrounds are located at Keyhole State Park, about 15 miles west of Sundance. Its large reservoir on the Belle Fourche River is a popular fishery for walleye and northern pike.

Prairie Reservoirs

Four reservoirs in the high plains around Buffalo entice anglers year-round. They often open and close the seasons for fly casters when mountain streams are blown out by spring floods or closed down by freezing autumn temperatures.

Public access is good for shoreline casting in spring and fall, and float-tubers find good action when trout go deeper in summer.

Three of the reservoirs have special regulations to reduce harvest.

Lake DeSmet

This 3,220-acre reservoir, just north of Buffalo on I-90, has a healthy population of Eagle Lake rainbow in the 12- to 18-inch range, with a few going to 20 inches. Yellowstone cutthroat fingerlings were stocked in the lake in 1996. A few large brown trout also are present.

The Eagle Lake rainbow, native to California, does especially well in highly alkaline waters such as Lake DeSmet. The cutthroat are expected to take advantage of the lake's abundant zooplankton. However, illegally stocked walleye pose a threat to the fishery. Biologists are closely monitoring the situation.

DeSmet is the most popular of the region's prairie ponds and the scene of an annual fishing derby on Memorial Day weekend. Ice-out is in late April, and the lake fishes well until summer temperatures push trout to deeper waters. Fall fishing is excellent. The best float-tubing is along the south and southeast shores and along the cliffs near the center of the west bank.

The trout limit is 4 per day or in possession; only 1 may exceed 15 inches. There is some private property around the lake, so be sure to follow posted rules at parking lots.

Muddy Guard Reservoir No. I

A 17-acre reservoir 11 miles southeast of Buffalo, Muddy Guard No. 1 is managed as a trophy fishery for rainbows that range from 12 to 25 inches. A few browns also are present. Fishing is rated as good, particularly in spring and fall.

The trout limit is 2 per day or in possession. All trout less than 18 inches must be returned to the water immediately. Fishing is permitted with flies and lures only.

Muddy Guard Reservoir No. 2

A 36-acre reservoir, Muddy Guard No. 2 is just north of its sister pond. It holds 12- to 16-inch rainbows and browns that also respond best in spring and fall.

There are no special regulations, and general trout limits apply.

Healy Reservoir

This 200-acre reservoir, just east of Buffalo, is a popular fishery and receives a fair amount of pressure. It fishes best in spring and fall for 10- to 18-inch rainbow and cutthroat trout.

The trout limit is 4 per day or in possession; only 1 may exceed 18 inches. Motor boats are not permitted.

Recommended dry fly patterns for the prairie ponds include: palomino midges and Griffith's gnats, 18 to 22; Adams, para-Adams, blue-winged olives, 16 to 20; callibaetis spinners and Adams, 14 to 16; beetles and flying ants, 14 to 16, and grasshoppers and stimulators, 8 to 14.

Wet flies include olive Matukas, muddler minnows, Mickey Finns, and other streamers, 2 to 8; halfbacks, olive marabou nymphs, and damsel nymphs, Carey's Special, black or brown leeches, olive, black, and brown woolly buggers, and crystal buggers, 8 to 12; Prince, hare's ear, foxtail, and beadhead nymphs, 14 to 18; and midge larva, blood midge, and brassies, 18 to 22.

NORTHEAST HUB CITIES
Buffalo/Story/Kaycee
Elevation—4,645 • Population—3,560

Buffalo is the quintessential Old West town, rich in Cowboy and Indian lore and the turbulent history of the 19th century. It is located at the intersection of I-25 and I-90, and U.S. 16, the scenic route through the southern half of the Big Horn Mountains and gateway to the Cloud Peak Wilderness. Visit its museums or fish right in town on the Clear Creek green belt before continuing on to the mountains. Nearby, you'll also find the towns of Story and Kaycee. Story, a village of less than 250 approximately 15 miles north on I-90, is the location of the Fort Phil Keary State Historic Museum, Sioux Indian battle grounds and the Story Fish Hatchery on Piney Creek. Kaycee, a town of 250 approximately 45 miles south on I-25, is the gateway to blue ribbon fishing in the Middle Fork of the Powder River's Hole in the Wall canyon.

ACCOMMODATIONS
Arrowhead Motel, 749 Fort Street, Buffalo, WY 82834-2316 / 307-684-9453 / 13 units / Pets allowed / $

Big Horn Motel, 209 North Main Street, Buffalo, WY 82834-1728 / 307-684-7822 / 18 units / $

Comfort Inn, 65 U.S. Hwy 16 East, Buffalo, WY 82834-9347 / 307-684-9564 / 41 units / Pets allowed / $$

Econo Lodge, 333 East Hart Street, Buffalo, WY 82834-1762 / 307-684-2219 / 43 units / Pets allowed / $

Mansion House Inn, 313 North Main Buffalo, Buffalo, WY 82834 / 307-684-2218 / 19 units / Pets allowed / $

Mountain View Motel, 585 Fort Street, Buffalo, WY 82834-1856 / 307-684-2881 / 13 units / Pets allowed / $

Super 8 Motel, 655 East Hart Street, Buffalo, WY 82834-9349 / 307-684-2531 / 48 units / Pets allowed / $

Wyoming Motel, 610 East Hart Street, Buffalo, WY 82834-9349 / 307-684-5505 / 27 units / Pets allowed / $$

Meadowlark Lake Resort, U.S. 16, Big Horn Mountains, P.O. Box 86, Ten Sleep, WY 82441 / 307-366-2424 or 800-858-5672

Siesta Motel, 255 Nolan Avenue, Kaycee, WY 82639 / 307-738-2291 / 13 units / Pets allowed / $

Cassidy Inn Motel, 346 Nolan Avenue, Kaycee, WY 82639 / 307-738-2250 / 18 units / Pets allowed / $

CAMPGROUNDS AND RV PARKS
Deer Park Campground, 146 U.S. Hwy 16 East, Buffalo, WY 82834 / 307-684-5722 / May 1 to October 31 / 80 RV and 20 tent sites / Full services

Indian Campground, 660 East Hart, Buffalo, WY 82834 / 307-684-9601 / April 1 to October 31 / 80 RV and 40 tent sites / Full services

Wagonbox Campground & Cabins, Hatchery Road, Box 248, Story, WY 82842 / 307-683-2444 or 800-308-2444

Hole in the Wall Campground, 1601 Barnum Road, Kaycee, WY 82639 / 307-738-2340 / Guest ranch 17 miles west of Kaycee

RESTAURANTS

Tom's Main Street Diner, 41 North Main Street, Buffalo, WY 82834 / 307-684-7444

Breadboard, 190 East Hart Street, Buffalo, WY 82834 / 307-684-2318

Dash Inn, 620 East Hart Street, Buffalo, WY 82834 / 307-684-7930

Colonel Bozeman's, 675 East Hart Street, Buffalo, WY / 307-684-5555

Stagecoach Inn, 845 Fort Street, Buffalo, WY; 307-684-2507

Pistol Pete's, 800 North Main Street, Buffalo, WY 82834 / 307-684-7172

Wagonbox Restaurant, Hatchery Road, Story, WY 82842

VETERINARIANS

Big Horn Veterinary Hospital, 145 US Hwy 16 East, Buffalo, WY 82834 / 307-684-5310

Buffalo Veterinary Clinic, 120 US Hwy 16 East, Buffalo, WY 82834 / 307-684-2851

OUTFITTERS

Sports Lure, 66 South Main Street, Buffalo, WY 82834 / 307-684-7682

Just Gone Fishing, 777 Fort Street, Buffalo, WY 82834 / 307-684-2755

Bear Track, 8885 U.S. 16 West, Buffalo, WY 82834 / 307-684-2528 / Guest lodge

Hole in the Wall Country Tours, P.O. Box 228, Kaycee, WY 82630 / 307-738-2243

FLY SHOPS AND SPORTING GOODS

Alabam's, 421 Fork Street, Buffalo, WY 82834 / 307-684-7452

Cowboy Sports, 171 U.S. Hwy. 16 East, Buffalo, WY 82834 / 307-684-0922

Beutlers, 59 North Lobban Avenue., Buffalo, WY 82834 / 307-684-7931

Sports Lure, 66 South Main Street, Buffalo, WY 82834 / 307-684-7682

Just Gone Fishing, 777 Fort Street, Buffalo, WY 82834 / 307-684-2755

AUTO RENTAL AND REPAIR

AAA Emergency Towing, 70 Tw Road, Buffalo, WY 82834 / 307-684-2274

East & West Quality Towing Service, I-25 & Hwy 16 East, Buffalo, WY 82834 / 307-684-5158

AIR SERVICE

No airline service.

MEDICAL

Johnson County Memorial Hospital, 497 West Lott Street; Buffalo, WY 82834 / 307-684-5521

FOR MORE INFORMATION

Buffalo Chamber of Commerce
55 North Main Street / P.O. Box 927
Buffalo, WY 82834
307-684-5544

Sheridan

Elevation—3,745 • Population—13,900

Sheridan shares Buffalo's roles in the events that shaped the Old West, and is a good place to pause and explore the region's history and modern day charms. Sheridan is located on I-90, 15 miles south of its interchange with U.S. 14, the scenic route through the northern half of the Big Horn Mountains. Story is 15 miles south on I-25. Dayton, a town of 560, is 25 miles northwest of Sheridan on U.S. 14, at the mouth of the Tongue River Canyon and en route to the Big Horns.

Sheridan's zip code is 82801.

ACCOMMODATIONS

Bramble Motel, 2366 North Main Street / 307-674-4902 / 15 units / Pets allowed / $

Days Inn, 1104 Brundage Lane / 307-672-2888 / 46 units / $$$

Evergreen Inn, 580 East 5th Street / 307-672-9757 / 40 units / Pets allowed / $

Triangle Motel, 540 Coffeen Avenue / 307-674-8031

Guest House Motel, 2007 North Main Street / 307-674-7496 / 43 units / Pets allowed / $

Sheridan Center Motor Inn, 612 North Main Street / 307-674-7421 / 40 units / Pets allowed / $

Parkway Motel, 2112 Coffeen Avenue / 307-674-7259 / 14 units / Pets allowed / $

Arrowhead Lodge—Big Horn Mountains, U.S. Hwy 14, Dayton, WY 82836 / 307-655-2388 / Resort, RVs, tents

Bear Lodge, Burgess Junction & Hwy 14A, Dayton, WY 82836 / 307-655-2444 / Resort, RVs, tents

CAMPGROUNDS AND RV PARKS

Big Horn Mountains KOA, 307-674-8766 / May 1 to October 31 / 80 RV sites / Full services

Foothills Motel & Campground, 101 North Main Street, Dayton, WY 82836 / 307-655-2547 / May 1 to October 31 / 50 RV or tent sites / Full services

RESTAURANTS
Sheridan Palace & Passio, 138 North Main Street / 307-672-2391
Sugarland Fine Dining, 1809 Sugarland Drive / 307-672-8931
Overland, 612 North Main Street / 307-674-7421
Greenery, 1809 Sugarland Drive / 307-672-8931
Ciao, 120 North Main Street / 307-672-2838
Coffee House, 123 North Main Street / 307-674-8619
Country Kitchen, 2617 North Main Street / 307-672-8144
Grinnell Street Cafe, 24 East Grinnell Street / 307-672-0421

VETERINARIANS
Big Horn Animal Clinic, 2417 Coffeen Avenue / 307-674-7133
Big Goose Animal Hospital, 241 Centennial Lane / 307-674-4111

OUTFITTER
Fly Shop of the Big Horns, 227 North Main Street / 307-672-5866

FLY SHOPS AND SPORTING GOODS
Fly Shop of the Big Horns, 227 North Main Street / 307-672-5866
Big Horn Mountain Sports, 334 North Main Street / 307-672-6866
Ritz Sporting Goods, 135 North Main Street / 307-674-4101

AUTO RENTAL AND REPAIR
AAA Authorized Towing, 584 East 8th Street / 307-672-5382
Ted's Towing, 584 East 8th Street / 307-672-5382

AIR SERVICE
No airline services.

MEDICAL
Sheridan County Memorial Hospital, 1401 West 5th Street / 307-672-1000

FOR MORE INFORMATION
Sheridan County Chamber of Commerce
I-90 and East 5th / P.O. Box 707
Sheridan, WY 82801
307-672-2485

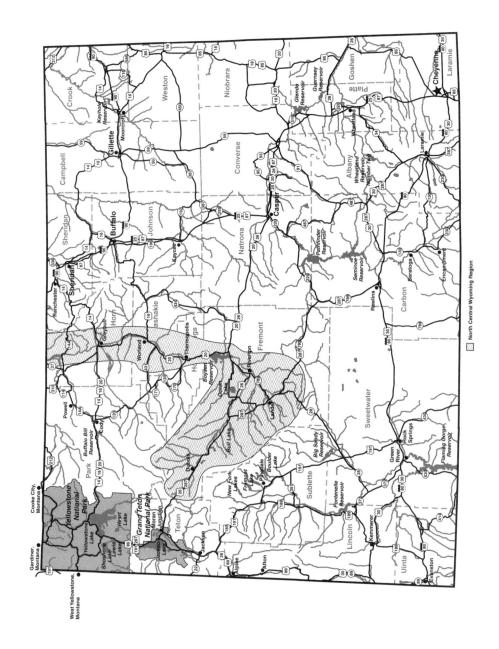

North Central Wyoming
Wedding of the Waters

Birth of the Big Horn River at the Wedding of the Waters, south of Thermopolis, is an anomaly on modern maps that preserves the history and folklore of northcentral Wyoming.

Dramatic differences in direction and character between the Wind River and the Big Horn were reflected in the descriptive languages of the region's Indian tribes. The unique aspects of the basin later convinced 19th-century mountain men and mapmakers they were separate rivers.

Individual names for segments of one river further reflect the difficulties even today in traveling through Wyoming's rugged terrain. Massive mountain ranges that shaped the Wind River–Big Horn drainage rumple the region in two directions. The Wind River Range extends southeast to northwest along the Continental Divide, from South Pass below Lander to Union Pass above Dubois. The Big Horn Range erupts against the horizon east of Shoshoni and curves north to the Montana border above Lovell.

The Wind River and the Big Horn followed courses dictated by the mountains, and today's highways parallel the same routes. There are no short cuts through the vast interior of the region. So, for flyfishers, the territory centered on the Wedding of the Waters necessitates a skipping stone approach to pursue its distinct variety of fishing options.

Changes in landowners somewhat complicate access to valley streams and alpine lakes, but the purchase of two licenses broadens admission to the basin's full diversity. A tribal permit is needed to fish two sections of the Wind River flowing through the Wind River Indian Reservation and its alpine lakes. A state fishing license is required for waters outside the reservation on both private and public lands.

The Big Horn's slow meandering flows through the arid sagebrush desert, above and below Thermopolis, are a float-fisher's dream. It fishes best from the mouth of the Wind River Canyon down to Black Mountain Road, where good public access ends and the river's cold water fishery begins to wane.

Just upstream, the surging waters of the Wind River coursing down its dramatic sheer-walled canyon clearly demonstrate the distinctions between desert and mountain streams. A tribal permit is required to plunk large nymphs and streamers into the raging pocket waters of the canyon for robust trout.

Focal points for exploring the drainage's mountain waters are Lander, the Wind River Indian Reservation and Dubois.

Lander is the southeast gateway to the Wind River Mountains and the lattice of streamlets forming the Popo Agie, largest tributary of the Wind River. The 115-mile middle reach of the Wind flows through the reservation, which opens a less traveled doorway into the alpine wilderness. At the top of Wyoming's longest mountain range is Dubois, northern entrance to the mountains and headwaters of the basin.

In the desert between Thermopolis and Lander, the Wind River's flows are trapped and held in reserve by Boysen Reservoir, a mixed fishery noted for producing large walleye and moderate sized trout. Boysen State Park sprawls along the lake's banks.

It is one of three in the region. The therapeutic waters of the largest mineral hot spring in the world are a popular attraction at Hot Springs State Park in Thermopolis. Sinks Canyon State Park, south of Lander, is where the Popo Agie vanishes into a cavern and reappears downstream at The Rise, a trout filled pool.

BIG HORN RIVER

The Big Horn's superb cold water fishery centered on the resort town of Thermopolis extends for nearly 20 miles below the Wind River Canyon. The remainder of its 130-mile course through an arid sagebrush desert to another canyon near the Montana border is too warm to support trout.

It rises as the Wind River in the mountains above Dubois, about 200 miles to the southwest, and plunges from the mouth of the canyon at the Wedding of the Waters historic site that marks its name change. The abrupt flattening of the terrain stalls the Big Horn's flows only a little. It is still a swift river, but it is well suited for float-fishing in drift boats, John boats, rafts and canoes. A dozen public access sites offer excellent opportunities for floaters to pause and wade fish with care and shore anglers to reach the river.

The fertile waters of this stretch produce good fishing for fast growing rainbow, brown and cutthroat trout in the 1- to 5-pound range as the river rebounds from the effects of a prolonged drought. Also, Wyoming Game and Fish is working on improvements to decrease the fishery's reliance on supplemental stocking. It is anticipated flushing flows from the reservoir will scour silt from the streambed and improve spawning conditions for wild trout.

From the Wedding of the Waters downstream to the Black Mountain Road at the WYO 172 bridge, the trout limit is 3 per day or in possession, only 1 over 18 inches.

The river fishes best in late spring, fall and winter when its waters are cooler and clearer. Often the best times occur as the trout begin to stir for spawning seasons— rainbows and cutthroat in spring and browns in autumn. Aquatic vegetation and algae are notoriously thick in summer, but the fish keep feeding. Also, when floating algae permeates flows from Boysen Reservoir, fly casters have the advantage over spin casters.

Dead drifting mayfly nymphs, caddis emergers, scuds, San Juan worms, or leech patterns is more effective than stripping streamers or large nymphs. Backwater sloughs and quiet eddies of the river make damselfly nymphs and crane fly larva prime patterns to include in a day's fishing strategies.

The Big Horn presents limited match-the-hatch situations through summer, and a basic set of generic dry flies, attractors, and terrestrial patterns covers the bases. One hatch to watch for is the green drake in May. Caddis are present from spring into autumn, and pale morning dun flights erupt sporadically throughout summer. In late summer hoppers, beetles and ants can be tossed along grassy banks. The best top water action occurs in September through November with tiny baetis and midge patterns. Midge activity continues through the winter and the baetis return in spring.

The warmer flows out of Boysen Reservoir keep the Big Horn ice free, and the basin's winters are relatively mild.

Reggie Treese of Big Horn River Outfitters is the resident flyfishing expert. For a change in pace ask him about "cast and blast" outings during waterfowl seasons. If you never heard of one, that means dividing a day between casting to trout and

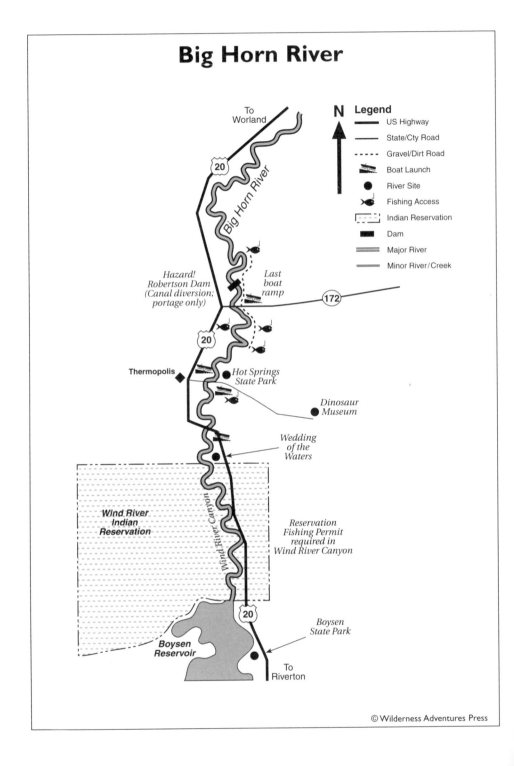

Big Horn River

shooting at ducks and geese. Pete and Darren Calhoun of Wind River Canyon Whitewater, who have the only float-fishing permit for the canyon, also offer guided trips on the Big Horn.

The Big Horn differs from most tailwater fisheries since its flows remain fairly constant through summer, around 1,000 cubic feet per second, as Boysen Reservoir is drained for irrigation waters. Flows are bumped up a little in September to help flood alfalfa fields and pastures, then drop again and remain steady through winter. Spring anglers can expect releases accommodating runoff to begin around late April and steadily climb into June to 3,000 cfs or more. After the peak runoff, flows fall rapidly; by mid-July there are steady summer flows again.

There are few rapids in the river, but float-fishers need to remain aware of several obstacles, primarily irrigation diversions and bridge abutments. Two rocky diversion dams just below Thermopolis effectively divide the river into two optimum floats.

The upper float begins at the Wedding of the Waters boat ramp, 7 miles south of town on U.S. 20. There are three pullouts right in town at the Eight Street Bridge, Broadway Bridge and Rainbow Terrace at Hot Springs State Park. The last pullout on the upper river is at the Kirby Ditch Dam, about 1.5 miles below the park. The Lucerne Dam is another boating hazard immediately below the Kirby diversion.

All the boat ramps are on the east bank. They also are access sites for shore anglers.

The lower float typically begins at the McCarthy access site, 4.5 miles below the park, on the east bank. The last set of pullouts is about 8 miles downstream at the Black Mountain Road Bridge on WYO 172. There are three ramps above and below the bridge on the east bank. In between Thermopolis and the bridge, there are three other access sites off U.S. 20 to the river's west bank. They offer shore access and places for floaters to pause and wade. Check with local fly shops and sporting goods stores for landmarks to watch for when floating this stretch, or to arrange shuttles.

The last public boat ramp is about a mile below the WYO 172 bridge. The Big Horn's trout fishery effectively ends at this point. Below it the river is a catfish and bass fishery, although it holds a few brown trout.

For the next 28 miles the river flows through private property to Worland's Riverside Park. There are two dangerous boating hazards, the Robinson Dam and the Lower Hanover Canal Dam, that must be portaged.

From Worland the Big Horn continues 85 miles north past Basin and Greybull to Lovell, where its flows are trapped by the backwaters of the Yellowtail Dam, about 80 miles downstream, in Montana.

The river skirts the Big Horn Mountains and slices a deep picturesque gorge through the Pryor Mountains, now inundated by the dam. Big Horn Canyon National Recreation Area is a worthwhile side trip. Anglers bent on continuing to the fabulous tailwater fishing for monster browns below Yellowtail need to look again at the map. There is no road continuing north into Montana from Lovell to Fort Smith. The quickest route is U.S. 14A up over the Big Horns to Ranchester on I-90, north of Sheridan.

Stream Facts: Big Horn River

Season
- Year-round.

Regulations
- From the Wedding of the Waters downstream to the Black Mountain Road at the WYO 172 bridge, the trout limit is 3 per day or in possession, only 1 over 18 inches.

Trout
- Rainbow, brown and cutthroat trout in the 1- to 5-pound range.

Miles
- Mile 0: Wedding of the Waters
- Mile 7: Thermopolis
- Mile 9: Kirby Ditch water hazard
- Mile 10: Lucerne Dam water hazard
- Mile 11: McCarthy boat ramp
- Mile 13: Wakely boat ramp
- Mile 14.5: Shaffer boat ramp
- Mile 15.5: Longwell boat ramp
- Mile 18: Mario boat ramp (Black Mountain Road)
- Mile 19: Skelton boat ramp
- Mile 19.5: Sorenson boat ramp (last pull out)

Character
- Large, swift, desert river with few rapids, but float-fishers need to remain aware of several obstacles, primarily irrigation diversions and bridge abutments. Two rocky diversion dams just below Thermopolis effectively divide the river into two optimum floats. The top 20 miles of the river are a superb trout fishery, but the remainder of its 130 mile run to the Big Horn Lake created by Yellowtail Dam in Montana is too warm to support trout.

Flows
- Spring releases from Boysen Reservoir to accommodate runoff begin around late April and steadily climb into June to 3,000 cubic feet per second or more. After the peak, flows fall rapidly by mid-July to steady summer flows around 1,000 cfs. Flows are bumped up a little in September, but then drop to 1,000 cfs and remain steady through winter.

Access
- Same as river miles.

Camping
- Boysen State Park
- Thermopolis

BIG HORN RIVER MAJOR HATCHES

Insect	M	A	M	J	J	A	S	O	N	Time	Flies
Caddis			▮	▮	▮	▮				M/D	**Dry:** Elk Hair Caddis, Red or Yellow Humpy, Renegade, Hemingway Caddis #12–16; **Wet:** Prince Nymph, Peacock Emerger, Soft-hackles #12–14
Little Yellow Stone (Willow Fly)				▮	▮					M/A	**Dry:** Yellow Sally, Blonde Humpy, Yellow Stimulator #12–14 **Wet:** Halfbacks, Soft-hackles #10–14
Green Drake				▮						A	**Dry:** Green Drake, Olive Wulff, Olive Sparkle Dun, Para-BWO #10–12; **Wet:** Prince Nymph, Zug Bug #10–14
Baetis		▮					▮			A/E	**Dry:** Blue-winged Olive, Para-BWO, Blue Dun, Para-Adams #16–22; **Wet:** Pheasant Tail, Baetis Nymph #16–18
Pale Morning Dun				▮		▮				A/E	**Dry:** PMD, Para-Adams, Yellow Sparkle Dun, Light Cahill #16–18; **Wet:** Hare's Ear Nymph, Pheasant Tail #14–18
Damselfly (nymphs)						▮				M/E	Olive Damsel Nymph, Swimming Damsel, Olive or Brown Leech #8–14
Scuds		▮	▮	▮	▮	▮	▮	▮	▮	M/E	Tan or Green Scud, San Juan Worm #14–18
Midge		▮			▮		▮			A/E	**Dry:** Griffith's Gnat, Palomino Midge, Black and White Midge, Para-Adams #16–22; **Wet:** Blood Midge Pupa, Brassies, Serendipity #14–18
Terrestrials					▮	▮				M/A	Para-hoppers, Joe's Hopper #8–14; Foam Beetle, Sparkle Beetle, Dave's Cricket #14–16; Ants #16–18

HATCH TIME CODE: M = morning; A = afternoon; E = evening; D = dark; SF = spinner fall; // = continuation through periods.

WIND RIVER

Wind River Indian Reservation

The Wind River Indian Reservation is the home of the Eastern Shoshone and Northern Arapahoe Indian Tribes. Established by the Fort Bridger Treaties of 1863 and 1868, it is the only Indian reservation in Wyoming.

At 2.3 million acres, the reservation is nearly the size of Yellowstone National Park. It is bounded on the north by the Owl Creek Mountains, on the west by the East Fork of the Wind River, on the south by the Wind River Mountains, and on the east by the Popo Agie and Wind River. The Bridger-Teton National Forest is southwest of the reservation, and the Shoshone National Forest is on the north and southeast.

It receives very little angling pressure, but fishing opportunities on the reservation rank among the best in the West.

Since the 1970s, when fishing was banned for about four years to stimulate growth and reproduction, numerous habitat and conservation projects have enhanced the reservation's fisheries. The tribes and the U.S. Fish and Wildlife Service continue to work on improvements.

In 1990, a federal court awarded the Shoshone and Arapahoe Tribes a senior water right of 500,000 acre-feet for the Wind River. The hitch is they haven't been allowed to use the water for nonagricultural purposes. They also are trying to repair channelization and limit siltation caused by nontribal entities with irrigation diversion rights. The tribes would like to leave some of the water in the river to support a better trout fishery and attract more tourism to the impoverished reservation.

Nontribal members are required to obtain a recreation permit to fish, hike or camp on the reservation in designated open areas.

The fishing season on the upper Wind River, and most other waters south of the river, is April 1 to September 30. The Wind River Canyon is open to fishing year-round to anglers on foot. Fishing from private boats or rafts is not allowed on streams in the reservation.

Wind River Canyon Whitewater, based in Thermopolis and at Crowheart on the reservation, has the only tribal permit to provide guided float-fishing trips on the Wind River, both in the canyon and on the upper river. It also offers rapids running whitewater trips in the canyon.

Permits for noncommercial rafting and kayaking in Wind River Canyon are available only in August and September, when flows are between 1,000 and 1,500 cubic feet per second. The fee is $40 per day or $100 for a two-month permit.

Recreation permits are available at Fort Washakie and Crowheart on the reservation and sporting goods stores in Thermopolis, Riverton, Shoshoni, Lander, Dubois, and Pinedale. A $5 recreation stamp was required with the purchase of a permit in 1997:

- One-day permit: $7 for Wyoming residents and $15 for nonresidents.
- Seven-day permit: $25 resident / $35 nonresident.
- Season permit: $35 resident / $60 nonresident.

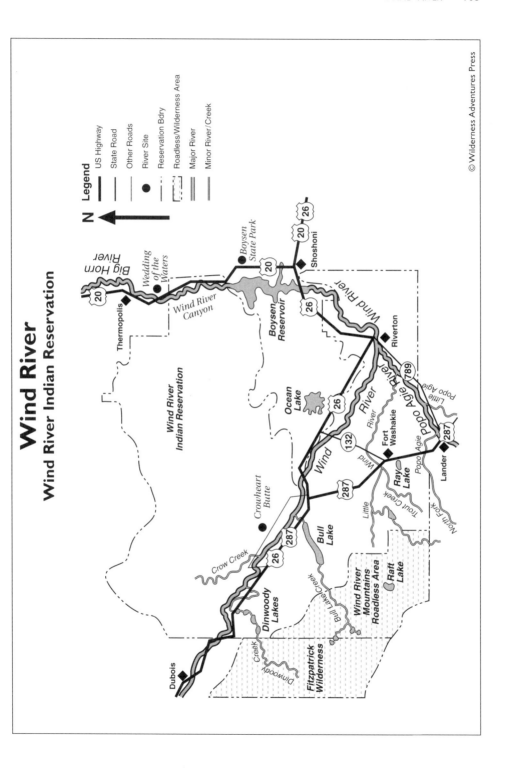

Wind River
Wind River Indian Reservation

Legend

— US Highway
— State Road
— Other Roads
● River Site
–·– Reservation Bdry
Roadless/Wilderness Area
Major River
Minor River/Creek

N

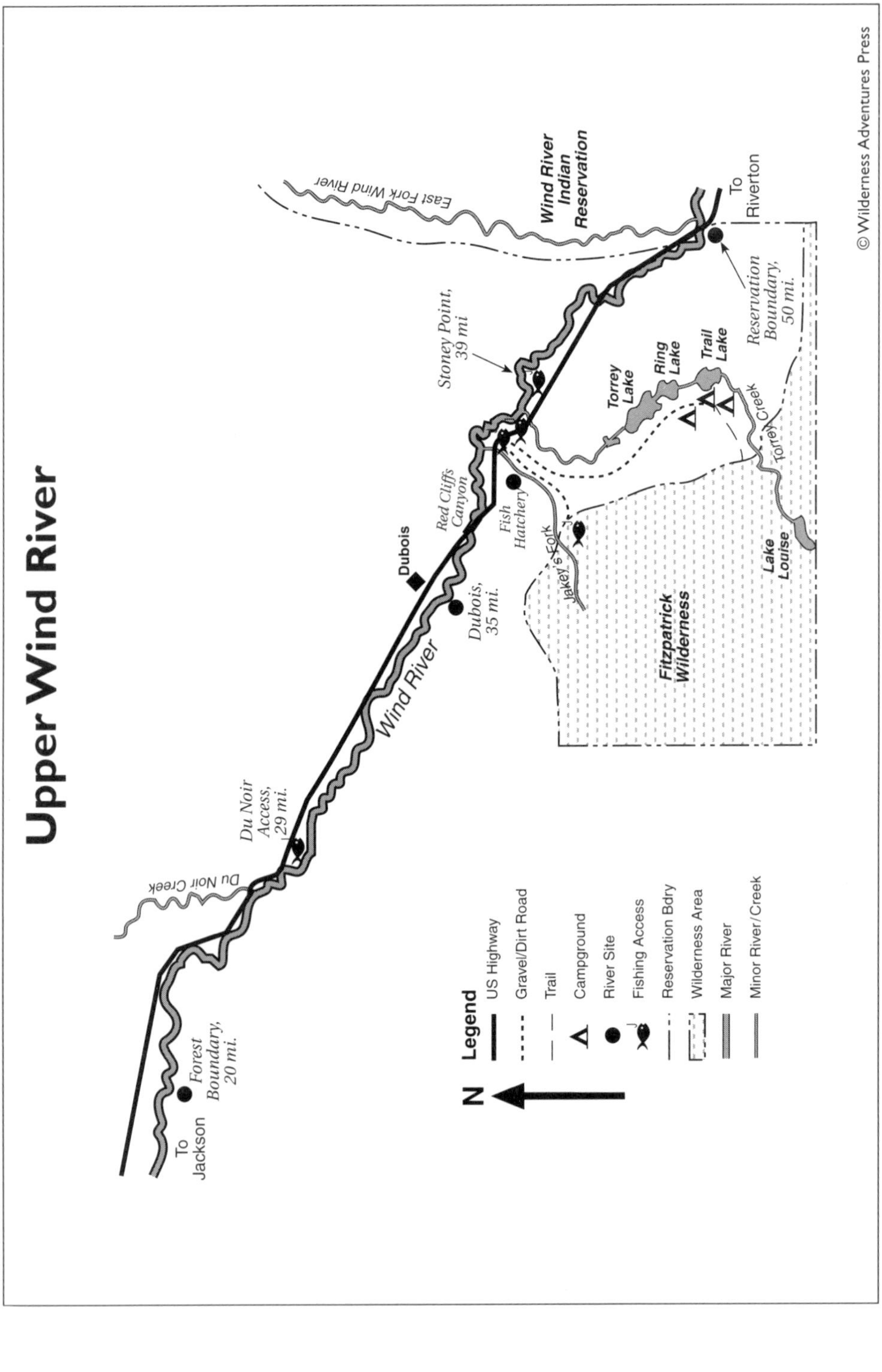

Upper Wind River

To Jackson

Forest Boundary, 20 mi.

Du Noir Creek

Du Noir Access, 29 mi.

Wind River

Dubois, 35 mi.

Dubois

Red Cliffs Canyon

Fish Hatchery

Stoney Point, 39 mi.

East Fork Wind River

Wind River Indian Reservation

To Riverton

Reservation Boundary, 50 mi.

Torrey Lake

Ring Lake

Trail Lake

Jakey's Fork

Torrey Creek

Fitzpatrick Wilderness

Lake Louise

© Wilderness Adventures Press

Legend

N

	US Highway
	Gravel/Dirt Road
	Trail
△	Campground
●	River Site
⚲	Fishing Access
	Reservation Bdry
	Wilderness Area
	Major River
	Minor River/Creek

Also check on discounts for youths, 14 through 18, and senior citizens, 60 or older.

The Wind River trout limit is 8 per day, only 1 over 20 inches. Check regulations for closed waters and special bag limits for some waters south of the Wind River on the reservation.

Small parties of hikers are permitted to fish alpine lakes in the Wind River Mountains on their own. A guide must accompany parties entering the wilderness on horseback. Groups larger than 10 require permission from the tribal council. A guide must accompany both hikers and horseback riders entering the Owl Creek Mountains north of the Wind River.

For a list of licensed guides for the reservation write the Shoshone and Arapahoe Tribes Game and Fish Department, Wind River Indian Reservation, P.O. Box 217, Fort Washakie, WY 82514, or call 307-332-7207.

Wind River Canyon

The Wind River's last wild plunge under its own name cuts a dramatically picturesque gorge through a billion years of geology.

At its head below the Boysen Dam, the Wind River Canyon is narrow and constricted, its walls rising 2,500 feet above the streambed. Signs along U.S. 20 point out the geological formations the river sliced through the Owl Creek Mountains. The canyon widens only a little on the river's rocky descent to the desert at the Wedding of the Waters, where it becomes the Big Horn River.

For flyfishers, the canyon is one of the West's best kept secrets. It harbors good to excellent pocketwater fishing along its entire 15-mile run. "The Wind River (Canyon) is known to many as a trophy style river, where the fish caught frequently range in size between 18 inches and 26 inches," states Pete Calhoun of Wind River Canyon Whitewater. "We have had catches of 30-plus-inch brown trout. Rainbow and brown trout are predominant, and catches of Snake River cutthroat also occur frequently." There are good populations of 14- to 16-inch fish as well, and occasional 10-pound browns are netted.

The outfitter's permit for guided float-fishing trips through the canyon covers the period from April 1 to September 30. The canyon is open to shore anglers year-round.

Wading is not a safe option during spring runoff and throughout the high flows caused by summer irrigation releases. More pockets waters and some wading opportunities become available as flows slacken in fall and hold steady through winter.

The river descends the canyon in a series of Class II and III rapids, a few low drops and plunge pools, and strings of long rock garden flats. The heaviest whitewater, or strongest pocket water stretches, are at the top of the canyon and near its mouth.

There are three sheer wall bends on the east bank, where U.S. 20 passes through tunnels, and several others on the west bank where tunnels were cut for a railroad

High summer flows flatten pocket waters in the Wind River Canyon.

line. Numerous pullouts along the highway allow anglers to park and scramble down to the river.

Fishing is best in spring before runoff, and in fall and winter. Floating algae occasionally flushed out of Boysen Reservoir during summer can be a problem. For the most part it is chuck-and-duck pocketwater fishing with large weighted nymphs and streamers, or drifting beadheads, scuds, woolly buggers, and leeches through quieter pools and rock garden runs. Check with local fly shops and sports stores on which patterns are working and possible top water opportunities.

Camping is available at Boysen State Park above and below the reservoir. Below the dam there is a two-mile tailwater fishery that can be fished with a state license.

Accommodations, supplies and sports shops are available at Thermopolis, 4 miles below the Wedding of the Waters.

Upper Wind River

The Wind River crosses into the reservation at the confluence of its East Fork, about 35 miles below its headwaters above Dubois. It meanders in a southeasterly direction for nearly 75 miles to Riverton, where it turns abruptly north. About 20 miles downstream its flows are captured by Boysen Reservoir, which is outside the reservation's boundaries.

Du Noir Access of the Wind River at the top of its forest run.

The broad, high plain of the Wind River Valley is lined on the north by the Owl Creek Mountains and to the south and east by the Wind River Range. Prevailing strong currents of wind funneled down the valley from the northwest by the mountains gave the river its name.

The top third of the river above the intersection of U.S. 287 with U.S. 26 is of most interest to flyfishers. Below a dam at the U.S. 26 bridge, fishing is spotty due to reduced flows from irrigation diversions, and there are some problems with siltation and unstable banks. But where habitat remains good, trout are available.

Flows on the upper river fluctuate during the growing season due to irrigation releases from tributary lakes. Heavy summer storms also occasionally muddy the river's flows. Best fishing on the Wind River is in early spring before runoff and in August as irrigation demands decrease. Its season is from April 1 to September 30.

Fishing is good for rainbows, browns and cutthroat in the 12- to 16-inch range, with a fair number of larger fish.

Hatches are sporadic, but the river can be fished effectively with basic mayfly and caddis patterns, attractors, and terrestrials.

A full-sized river, the Wind is stronger and swifter than expected on first appearance. Its rough cobble floor can be waded with care in waders with felt-sole boots. A 9-foot, 6- or 7-weight rod is recommended due to the wind.

Access is along U.S. 26/287 on the south bank. Bridges at Crowheart and Dinwoody Creek lead to a gravel road that skirts the river's north bank.

Fishing is good in Dinwoody and Bull Lake Creeks, although it can be more tricky than in the river, said Bruce Tadeyeske of Rocky Mountain Dubbing in Lander. "There's a lot of good fishing on the reservation that people often overlook because they don't want to pay the fee," Tadeyeske said. "Most of the tribal residents don't fish, so you are often alone."

However, Bull Lake and Dinwoody Lake are popular fisheries for boaters and float-tubers. Bull Lake has 14- to 20-inch rainbows, plus lake trout. Dinwoody has fair sized rainbows and some large browns, plus lake trout.

The Little Wind River is closed to fishing year-round.

Wind Rivers Divide

At the top of the Wind River valley is Dubois, a resort town that has played many roles in the history of western Wyoming.

To the west over 9,658-foot Togwotee Pass on U.S. 26/287 are Jackson Hole, Grand Teton National Park and Yellowstone National Park. John Colter, the first of the mountain men, pioneered the route in 1807. A monument to Colter and the fur trapper era is on 9,210-foot Union Pass. The pass divides the Wind River Range and the Absaroka Mountains, which define the Yellowstone River drainage northwest into Montana.

Noted for its alpine fishing and big game hunting, Dubois is the social center for recreation in the northern Wind Rivers and eastern Absarokas.

Wind River Headwaters

The source of the Wind River is tiny Wind River Lake at the base of Togwotee Pass on the divide, northwest of Dubois.

For its first 10 miles it is barely more than a trickle as it courses down the mountain slopes. About 15 miles above Dubois, it doubles in size as it merges with Sheridan Creek and a cluster of small feeder streams. Another 3 miles downstream at the Shoshone National Forest boundary, the valley flattens and the river meanders through a broad meadow. Du Noir Creek joins it at a bridge on U.S. 26/287, and just downstream is a small public fishing site, 6 miles west of Dubois.

The terrain to the north changes dramatically above and behind the resort town as the sculptured cliffs and rock formations of the arid badlands come into view. The river loops around the town and cuts a deep canyon through a colorful cliff banded with layers of red, yellow and tan stone.

The river continues to play tag with the stony face of the badlands for about 15 miles as it picks up the Jakeys Fork from the south and the East Fork from the north, and enters the Wind River Indian Reservation.

There is a half-mile of public access at Jakeys Fork, 3 miles east of Dubois, which also permits fishing in the creek. About a mile downstream there are 5 miles of public access dispersed along the river at a series of parking lots along U.S. 26/287.

This reach of the river is called the Stony Point section, and fishing is rated as good to excellent for 8- to 16-inch rainbows, browns and cutthroat. Whitefish also are present in the river.

It meanders through a few grassy meadows and cuts along red cliffs as it descends in a series of riffles and runs along the highway. Its pace is brisk, but the river is relatively easy to wade and can be crossed at the heads of shallow riffles.

Hatches are sporadic, but the river can be fished effectively with basic mayfly and caddis patterns, attractors and terrestrials. Fishing is best from July into autumn, and dry fly action can be especially good in August and September with terrestrials. In October and November spawning brown trout run up the Jakeys Fork.

Upstream at the Du Noir Access site and in the headwaters of the Wind River, fishing is rated as fair for small rainbows and brook trout.

Tributaries worth exploring are the Jakey's Fork and the East Fork of the Wind River.

The Jakey's Fork fishes well from spring through summer, and it gets a strong brown spawning run in late fall. A classic small mountain stream, it passes through some state land sections near the fish hatchery.

The East Fork and its tributaries, the Wiggins Fork and Bear Creek, hold cutthroat mostly in the 8- to 12-inch range, with some larger fish. Rainbows and brookies also are present.

There are two special regulation sections on the East Fork to reduce harvest of cutthroat. It passes through several state lands sections below the forest boundary, but you need a map to find them. The stream's east bank is on the Wind River Indian Reservation, and a tribal recreation permit is required to fish past the middle of the channel.

Fitzpatrick Wilderness

The 191,103-acre Fitzpatrick Wilderness is the most remote corner of the Wind River Mountains, but it doesn't lack attention.

On the east side of the Continental Divide, it covers the northern half of the range. To the south are the Wind River Indian Reservation and Popo Agie Wilderness above Lander. West across the divide is the Bridger Wilderness above Pinedale.

The Fitzpatrick Wilderness was named for Tom Fitzpatrick, a partner of Jim Bridger, the King of the Mountain Men. It is known for numerous glaciers and high mountain peaks. There are 44 active glaciers, and 13,804-foot Gannett Peak, Wyoming's highest summit, straddles the divide. About 60 lakes and more than 75 miles of fishing streams offer angling opportunities for fly casters.

The main trailhead into the wilderness is on the same road that leads to two other popular destinations in the area—Whiskey Mountain and the Torrey Lakes. Even so, it's a rough dirt road and not kind to vehicles with low clearance. Vehicles pulling trailers are not recommended.

The turnoff to the road is about 4 miles east of Dubois on U.S. 26/287 at the Whiskey Mountain Wildlife Management Area sign. At the parking lot there are several routes into the mountains. The longest and most heavily traveled is Glacier Trail to the base of Gannett Peak and the largest glacier in the Lower 48 States. The Whiskey Mountain trail has no fish at the end, but its slopes are home to the largest herd of Rocky Mountain bighorn sheep in the West.

A few lakes along other trails into the wilderness also lack fish. A good reference to consult for the best fishing opportunities and trails to them is *Walking The Winds*, by Rebecca Woods. Topographic hiking maps are available in Dubois. Also consult local fly shops and outfitters about alpine lakes and streams to fish in the wilderness and elsewhere in the national forest.

For more information contact, Shoshone National Forest, 808 Meadow Lane, Cody, WY 82414 / 307-527-6241, or the Wind River Ranger District, Box 186, Dubois, WY 82513 / 307-455-2466.

Recommendations for equipment, fishing strategies and fly patterns are the same as those detailed in discussions of the Popo Agie Wilderness above Lander, and the Big Horn Mountains.

Foothill Lakes

There are three lakes along the road leading to the Whiskey Mountain Wildlife Management Area, about 4 miles east of Dubois. The largest is 231-acre Torrey Lake. Ring Lake is 108 acres, and Trail Lake is 120 acres.

Torrey Lake is mostly surrounded by private property, but there is good public access and campgrounds at Ring and Trail Lakes.

All three hold a mix of rainbow, brown, and lake trout, and splake, a hybrid between lake and brook trout. The lake trout range from 16 to 30 inches, and the other trout are mostly 12 to 16 inches. The lakes fish best in spring and autumn.

About 25 miles northwest of Dubois in the foothills of the Absaroka Mountains is Brooks Lake. It is one of the most scenic panoramas in western Wyoming.

Nestled in a grassy, high mountain meadow, the lake reflects the sheer face of the rugged Absarokas. In the forest at its back are two excellent campgrounds, and the Brooks Lake Lodge is on its southeast shore.

A perfect canoe outing, Brooks Lake offers good fishing for 9- to 14-inch rainbows and splake. It also hold large lake trout. Fishing is best shortly after ice out and in autumn.

Short hikes to the north are four small mountain ponds below the rim of the Absarokas—Upper and Lower Jade Lakes, Upper Brooks Lake, and Rainbow Lake.

POPO AGIE RIVER

The Popo Agie forms at Lander, but it is most accessible from the reservation side of the river. The North Fork of the Popo Agie also is part of the reservation's boundary.

Local residents weed out tourists in their midst by hearing their pronunciation of this beautiful little river's name. In the Crow Indian language, it's pronounced *Po-Po-Zshuh* and means Tall Grass River.

After collecting the flows of its mountain tributaries, the Popo Agie's desert run is barely 30 miles to its merger with the Wind River at Riverton. Its swift shallow flows meander through the arid valley in a series of riffles and runs, short glides, and deeper pools and runs. Undercut banks line its bends and braided channels. Its lush floodplain is lined with thick ranks of cottonwoods and willows. Wading may become tricky in late summer as algae growth accumulates.

The Popo Agie is full of plump medium-sized rainbows and browns. "They are fat little guys; they're just good looking," Tadeyeske said. Larger browns run upstream from Boysen Reservoir to spawn in autumn, and walleye also are present in the river.

Irrigation diversions are not a problem on the Popo Agie, but aquatic vegetation builds up and it's too warm to fish in August. The river fishes best in late June through July, and again in late September and October after water temperatures cool. Dry-fly fishing can be excellent in the fall.

The river has a golden stonefly hatch, so medium-sized Bitch Creek nymphs, rubberlegs, and woolly buggers are effective wet flies, along with small hare's ear, Prince, and pheasant tail nymphs, Tadeyeske said. Generic mayflies, like the slate-wing Coachman and Adams, plus elk hair caddis, PMDs, and BWOs, provide top water action.

The North Fork and upper Popo Agie are open to fishing year-round and managed under Wyoming Game and Fish regulations since the state and the tribes share these waters. About 15 miles below Lander on WYO 789, the Popo Agie reenters the reservation at Hudson.

There are only two access points to the river from the highway. About 7 miles below Lander there is an unmarked bridge to oil fields on the reservation. Shore fishing is permitted here, although there is no public easement. The other site is at the Nicole Bridge, at the confluence of the Little Popo Agie, and it is open to fishing with permission.

There is a small Wyoming Game and Fish access site on the North Fork, a mile northwest of Lander on the Milford Road.

The river can be floated in small boats, rafts or canoes, but anglers have to keep to the right side of the channel. Water craft are not permitted on streams in the reservation. Boats can be launched at the access site on the North Fork. The pullout is at the Nicole Bridge, where permission to land must be obtained before setting out, or when arranging vehicle shuttles.

Popo Agie River

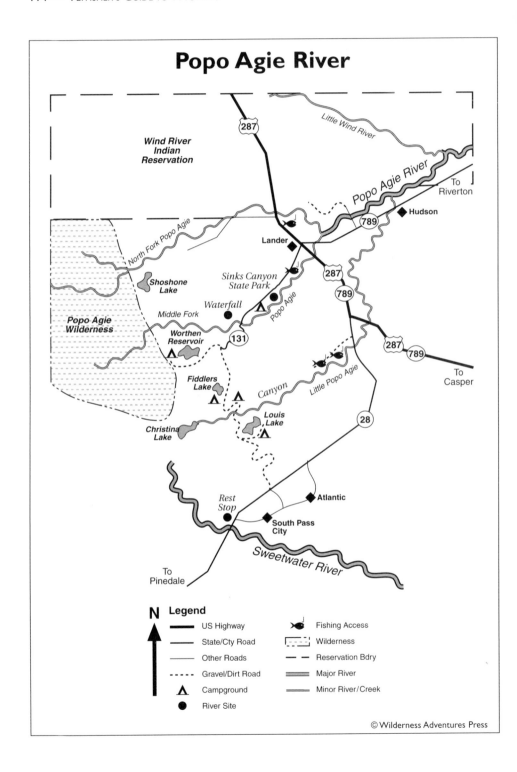

Legend

N

- US Highway
- State/Cty Road
- Other Roads
- Gravel/Dirt Road
- ⋀ Campground
- ● River Site
- 🐟 Fishing Access
- Wilderness
- Reservation Bdry
- Major River
- Minor River/Creek

© Wilderness Adventures Press

Alpine Roadless Area

The least traveled fishing paths on the reservation lead to its alpine lakes on the shoulders of the Continental Divide. Hikes to the high country aren't easy, which further explains why the fishing is rated as excellent.

There are more than 250 lakes in the Wind River Roadless Area, with about 100 filled with trout. A thousand miles of fishing streams interconnect the lakes.

Those who make the trek into the mountains report the fishing is fast and the trout are big. The lakes are noted for producing large cutthroat and golden trout. Rainbow and brook trout also are common, a few lakes have lake trout, and one has Dolly Varden. The latter is a char species, like the lake trout, and also is known as bull trout.

Many of the lake are above 10,000 feet. Most are unnamed and recorded on maps only with numbers. Topographic trail maps can be obtained at Lander or Dubois.

For recommendations on which lakes to fish, contact the reservation's Fish and Game Department. In some areas, the lakes are clustered together and can be fished on day hikes from a base camp. The department also provides a list of licensed guides for those who prefer to enter the wilderness on horseback.

Trails on the reservation are marked with large blaze marks cut into trees or rock cairns. There are no written signs like those found in national parks or forests. Topographic hiking maps are available in Lander and Dubois. Also be aware that ice-out on some lakes is not until July, when some trails may still be blocked with snow.

A basic box of flies to carry into the alpine lakes can include small tan or gray elk hair caddis, Adams and para-Adams, gray Wulffs and a few other small attractors, and small black midges. Small grasshopper, ant, and spider patterns also work when windblown terrestrials are on the water.

Lander Loop to the Wind River Mountains

The Popo Agie River, which forms at the confluence of the North Fork and Middle Fork in Lander, was a favorite gathering place for the mountain men of the 19th century. Lander annually celebrates its early history with the Popo Agie Rendezvous the second weekend of June.

Fishing on the Lander side of the Popo Agie is limited by its passage through private property; however, a Wind River Indian Reservation recreation permit grants full access to the river on its side. Small tributaries with state access sites are the Little Popo Agie, 10 miles south of Lander, and the Middle Fork Popo Agie, 3 miles southwest of town.

Other fishing sites in the flatlands below Lander are mostly warm water fisheries, including the 21-mile Boysen Reservoir on the Wind River, Lake Cameahwait, which is also known as Bass Lake, and Ocean Lake.

Most fly casters approaching Lander have high mountain trout fishing on their minds. The small resort town is the eastern gateway to the Popo Agie Wilderness of the Wind River Mountains. Dubois is the northern entrance to the Wind River Range and, across the Continental Divide, Pinedale is the western gateway.

The route from Lander follows the Middle Fork upstream, via WYO 131, to a Shoshone National Forest road that loops through the foothills to WYO 28 at South

Little Popo Agie in Red Canyon, south of Lander.

Pass. A Scenic Byway, the 28-mile gravel road is well maintained and offers excellent fishing in foothill lakes and streams. Campgrounds are located at most of the lakes, and spur roads lead to trailheads into the Wind River Range. Just east of the forest boundary is Sinks Canyon State Park on the Middle Fork.

A good side trip from Lander is the public access site on the lower Little Popo Agie. It is on the Red Canyon Road, another Scenic Byway connected to WYO 28.

Little Popo Agie

The Little Popo Agie is a pleasant diversion in a scenic pastoral valley about 10 miles south of Lander.

It is reached by driving southeast from town on U.S. 287 and turning south on WYO 28. About a mile below the intersection turn west onto the Red Canyon Road, and continue about 2 miles to the first of two access sites. The next parking lot is another 2 miles south. The gravel road continues south about 10 miles to WYO 28.

The tiny river meanders through lush irrigated meadows edged by fiery red cliffs of eroded sandstone. Fishing is good for 8- to 14-inch rainbows and browns. There are a few larger browns, although the majority of the fish seem to have been cut from a 12-inch cookie mold.

With pastures and alfalfa fields lining most of its south bank, it doesn't take a rocket scientist to pick fly patterns for the Little Popo Agie. Dry fly action is excellent in August

Louis Lake on the Lander Loop Road.

and September with terrestrial patterns, including hoppers and beetles, and small attractors, humpies, and stimulators. Small nymphs or emergers tied as droppers improve chances for strikes. Look for caddis or mayfly hatches toward dusk.

The swift narrow stream is easily waded, although care has to be taken not to trip over small boulders on its rough cobble floor. There are a few deep pools on cutbank bends and some deeper channels along the cliffs.

Fish it wet with felt-sole wading boots and cool off after a long hot day in central Wyoming's sagebrush desert.

Lander–South Pass Scenic Byway

The first stop on the Lander's loop road to the mountains is Sinks Canyon State Park, 6 miles southwest on WYO 131.

Sinks Canyon gets its name from the vanishing act of the Middle Fork Popo Agie. About halfway down the canyon the river abruptly turns into a large limestone cavern, and the crashing water "sinks" into fissures and cracks at the back of the cave. The river flows underground for a quarter-mile and emerges in a large calm pool called "The Rise." Huge rainbow trout flourish in The Rise, but they are off limits to anglers.

There are two campgrounds at the park, and anglers can fish for 8- to 12-inch rainbow, brown and brook trout. It's tough fishing in tumbling, cascading plunge pools and roaring pocket waters in the canyon. More subdued pocketwater fishing is available upstream in Shoshone National Forest, below the scenic Popo Agie Falls.

Also, a public access site in the valley, 3 miles south of Lander, offers quieter waters and good dry-fly fishing in late summer with terrestrial patterns.

The forest boundary starts at the top of the park, and the paved road ends at the parking lot for the trail to the waterfall. A steep gravel road climbs in tight switch backs up the south cliff to the foothills of the Wind River Range.

The two most popular lakes on the 28-mile loop road to South Pass are Louis Lake and Christina Lake. Both offer fair fishing for 8- to 12-inch rainbow. There is a developed campground at Louis Lake, which is on the road. Most people hike 4.5 miles into Christina, but some drive its two-track jeep trail in 4-wheel-drive, high-clearance vehicles.

Also on the loop road are Frye Lake, Fiddlers Lake, and Worthen Reservoir, and the foothills are dotted with smaller mountain lakes. The best stream fishing along the road is the Little Popo Agie, which flows out of Christina Lake. It fishes best after a hike away from the road for 8- to 12-inch rainbows and brookies.

The main trailheads into the Popo Agie Wilderness of the Wind River Range are at Christina Lake and Worthen Reservoir. A rough gravel road to the Sweetwater Gap trailhead is southwest of the South Pass rest stop on WYO 28.

Another route into the wilderness is the Dickinson Park Entrance, northwest of Lander. The rough gravel road to Dickinson Park enters the mountains behind Fort Washakie on the Wind River Indian Reservation. Hikers who intend to cross into the reservation's alpine wilderness must purchase a tribal recreation permit.

POPO AGIE WILDERNESS

For many, the Wind River Range is the quintessential vacation site to flyfish for trout in crystal clear alpine lakes. The massive range, extending 100 miles from Union Pass above Dubois to South Pass below Lander, is dotted with thousands of lakes surrounded by scenery that rivals the Swiss Alps.

The range is topped by 15 of Wyoming's 16 highest peaks. On the east side of the Continental Divide, 13,255-foot Wind River Peak is the highest summit in the Popo Agie Wilderness that extends 25 miles along the southern end of the range. More than 20 summits above 12,000 feet are in the wilderness. Its lowest point is 8,400 feet, where the eastern boundary crosses the Middle Fork Popo Agie River.

The 101,991-acre Popo Agie is noted for its scenic vistas of high, jagged peaks towering above deep, narrow valleys and canyons cut by cascading streams. Sheer granite walls are prevalent, and several permanent snowfields cap the divide. More than 300 lakes and ponds are dispersed through the wilderness, which are the head-waters of the Middle Fork Popo Agie, North Fork Popo Agie, and Little Popo Agie.

Most lakes below 10,500 feet hold cutthroat, rainbow or brook trout. Lakes around 10,500 feet hold grayling, and lakes around 11,000 feet hold golden trout. Some may contain more that one species and some only one.

Golden trout are the goal of many flyfishers heading into the high country, but the pursuit of any of the range's trout is not a casual endeavor. Most of the lakes with big-ger fish are above 10,000 feet, so being physically fit is a prerequisite to starting out.

At these elevations, summer temperatures rarely exceed 80 degrees. There is no frost free period, and snow can be expected during any month. Average annual precip-itation is between 25 and 30 inches and occurs chiefly in the form of snow. Occasional heavy rains occur during the summer, and light thunderstorms are common during the afternoons. During lightning storms it is best to avoid open areas such as meadows, ridges, lone trees, and mountain tops. Find safer shelter in dense stands of trees or boulder fields.

Winter snows generally do not leave the high mountain passes and highest trails until mid-July. Stream flows are high and swift during spring runoff in June and July when some stream crossings can be hazardous. August is the best month to hike the Wind Rivers.

Pack for early spring- or fall-like conditions even in midsummer. On day hikes always include rain gear, a sweater, wool socks, knit cap and gloves or mittens in a backpack. Don't forget insect repellent, since mosquitoes, deerflies and horseflies are plentiful most of the summer.

Plan a minimum of three days to fish high or remote lakes. Topographical hiking maps are available at Lander fly shops and sports stores, where you can check on trail conditions and which lakes are fishing best. A new guidebook with good hiking sug-gestions is *Walking the Winds* by Rebecca Woods. It details the current status of trout species in the 2.25 million-acre mountain range's thousands of lakes.

For more information contact, Shoshone National Forest, 808 Meadow Lane, Cody, WY 82414, 307-527-6241, or the Washakie Ranger District, 333 Highway 789, South, Lander, WY 82520, 307-332-5460.

Fishing in alpine lakes usually is best in early morning and late in the day, while action in streams continues throughout the day. Many anglers save the streams for afternoon and hit the lakes first thing in the morning and late in the day.

Fly choices are very basic for high mountain lakes and streams. Dry fly action is limited in midsummer, so plan on mostly working the lakes with wet flies. Concentrate on shorelines and shallows and use a dropper fly to speed up prospecting. Dry flies include the standard mayfly, caddis, and small terrestrial patterns. The most common mayfly in lower lakes is the callibaetis, but tiny baetis and midges are common at higher elevation lake inlets. Attractor patterns include Adams, renegades, ants, beetles, humpies, stimulators, royal Wulffs, and Coachmans. Wet flies for high lakes range from leech patterns, small streamers, and woolly buggers to beadhead nymphs, chironomid or green midge pupa, soft-hackle nymphs, Carey's Special, Prince nymph, hare's ear nymph, green caddis emerger, peacock emerger, and pheasant tail to green scud and gray or green shrimp patterns.

Rod choices depend on conditions or length of the hike into a lake. A three-piece, 8-foot, 5- or 6-weight travel rod with a weight-forward or floating line and medium sinking tip is handy on longer trips. Big lakes or windy conditions may require a 9-foot, 6- or 7-weight rod.

NORTH CENTRAL HUB CITIES
Thermopolis
Elevation—4,326 • Population—3,500

Thermopolis is named for the therapeutic hot springs that have attracted visitors through the ages and from around the world. Hot Springs State Park preserves the largest single mineral hot spring in the world. The Wyoming Dinosaur Center & Dig Site also is located here. Just south of town is the Wedding of the Waters where the Wind River's name changes to the Big Horn River. Boysen State Park is 14 miles south at the head of the scenic Wind River Canyon. Fishing is excellent through town, in the canyon, and at Boysen Reservoir.

Thermopolis' zip code is 82443.

ACCOMMODATIONS
Bah Gue Wana Hot Springs Motel, 401 Park Street / 307-864-2303
Best Western Moonlighter Motel, 600 Broadway Street / 307-864-2321 / 26 units / Pets allowed / $
Cactus Inn, 605 South 6th Street / 307-864-3155 / 10 units / Pets allowed / $
Coachman Motel, 112 Highway 20 South / 307-864-3141 / 19 units / Pets allowed / $
El Rancho Motel, 924 Shoshoni Street / 307-864-2341 / 13 units / Pets allowed / $
Holiday Inn, 115 East Park Street / 307-864-3131 / 80 units / Pets allowed / $$
Jurassic Inn, 501 South 6th Street / 307-864-2325 / 16 units / Pets allowed / $
Super 8 Hot Springs Hotel, Lane 5, South Hwy 20 / 307-864-5515 / 52 units / $–$$

CAMPGROUNDS AND RV PARKS
Fountain Of Youth RV Park, 250 Hwy 20 North / 307-864-9977 / March 1 to October 31 / 52 RV and 10 tent sites / Full services
Grandview Mobile & RV Park, 122 Highway 20 South, Thermopolis, WY 82443-9403 / 307-864-3463 / May 1 to October 15 / 21 RV sites / Full services
Latch String Campground, 204 South U S Hwy 20 / 307-864-5262 / March 1 to October 31 / 50 RV and 30 tent sites / Full services

RESTAURANTS
Pumpernicks, 512 Broadway Street / 307-864-5151
Sideboard Cafe, 109 South 6th Street / 307-864-5335
Spatol's Delicatessen, 500 Broadway Street / 307-864-3960
Manhattan Inn, 526 Broadway Street / 307-864-2501
Log Cabin Cafe, 706 South 6th Street / 307-864-9219
Big T Rex Drive In, 800 Shoshoni Street / 307-864-5460

VETERINARIANS
Hot Springs Veterinary Clinic, 827 South 6th Street / 307-864-5553

OUTFITTERS
Big Horn River Outfitters, Hwy 20 South, P.O. Box 1216, Thermopolis, WY 82443 /
307-864-5309 or 800-828-7102
Wind River Canyon Whitewater, 210 Hwy 20 South, Suite 5 / 307-864-9343 /
Off-season Bookings: 307-486-2253, P.O. Box 592, Crowheart, WY 82512
High Island Ranch, 25 miles NW of Thermopolis; Box 71, Hamilton Dome, WY
82427 / 307-867-2374

FLY SHOPS AND SPORTING GOODS
Big Horn River Outfitters, Hwy 20 South / 307-864-5309 or 800-828-7102
Wind River Canyon Whitewater, 210 Hwy 20 South, Suite 5 / 307-864-9343
Canyon Sporting Goods, 1002 Shoshoni Street / 307-864-2815
Coast To Coast Store, 502 Arapahoe Street / 307-864-3672

AUTO RENTAL AND REPAIR
Auto & RV Specialties, 144 North 6th Street / 307-864-3681

AIR SERVICE
Nearest airline service is Riverton.

MEDICAL
Hot Springs County Memorial Hospital, 150 East Arapahoe Street / 307-864-3121

FOR MORE INFORMATION
Thermopolis Chamber of Commerce
111 North 5th Street / P.O. Box 768
Thermopolis WY 82443
307-864-3192

Lander
Elevation—5,357 • Population—7,050

One of the oldest communities in Wyoming, Lander was a favorite gathering place for the Mountain Men Rendezvous on the banks of the Popo Agie River. Just south of the Wind River Indian Reservation, it is the southern gateway to the Wind River Valley and the eastern entrance to the Wind River Mountains. Sinks Canyon State Park is on the nearby loop road through the Wind River Mountains.

Lander's zip code is 82520.

ACCOMMODATIONS
Horseshoe Motel/One Shot Lounge, 685 Main Street / 307-332-4915 / 15 units / $
Pronghorn Lodge—Budget Host, 150 East Main Street / 800-BUD-HOST /
54 units / Pets allowed / $
Downtown Motel, 569 Main Street / 307-332-3171 / 16 units / Pets allowed / $
The Western Motel, 151 North 9th / 307-332-4270 / 13 units / $
Silver Spur Inn, 1240 Main Street / 800-922-7831 / 25 units / Pets allowed / $
Holiday Lodge, Jct. Hwy 287/789 / 800-624-1974 / 40 units, pets allowed / $

Maverick Motel and Restaurant, 808 Main Street / 307-332-2821 / 31 units /
Pets allowed / $
Inn At Lander, Best Western, 260 Grand View Drive / 800-528-1234 / 46 units /
Pets allowed / $$
Edna's Bed & Breakfast, 53 North Fork Road / 307-332-3175
Blue Spruce Inn Bed & Breakfast, 677 South 3rd Street / 888-503-3311
The Outlaw Bed & Breakfast, 2411 Squaw Creek Road / 888-668-8529
Whispering Winds Bed & Breakfast, 695 Canyon Street / 307-332-9735

CAMPGROUNDS AND RV PARKS
Lander City Park, 405 Freemont Street / 307-332-4647 / Free
River Campground, 4181 Wyoming Hwy 789 / 307-544-9319
Rocky Acres Campground, 5700 Wyoming Hwy 287 / 307-332-6953 / May 1 to
September 30 / 13 RV and 23 tent sites / Full services
K-Bar Ranch, 7192 Wyoming Hwy 789 / 307-332-3836 / February 1 to November
11 / 68 RV and 20 tent sites / Full services
Louis Lake Lodge, 28 miles SW of Lander / 888-422-2246
Atlantic City Mercantile, 100 East Main, Atlantic City, WY 82520 / 30 miles SW
of Lander / 888-257-0215

RESTAURANTS
Pronghorn Lodge, 150 East Main Street / 307-332-3940
Judd's Grub, 634 West Main Street / 307-332-9680
Bread Board, 125 East Main Street / 307-332-6090
Magpie, 159 North 2nd Street / 307-332-5565
Highwayman Cafe, 974 Wyoming Hwy 789 / 307-332-4628
Sweetwater Grille, 148 Main Street / 307-332-7388
Hitching Rack, Hwy 287 South / 307-332-4322

VETERINARIANS
Wind River Veterinary Service, 108 Tweed Lane / 307-332-5512
Table Mountain Veterinary Clinic, 266 Tulip Street / 307-332-5424

OUTFITTERS
Rocky Mountain Dubbing, 115 Poppy / 307-332-2989
Allen's Diamond Four Wilderness Ranch, Box 243, Lander, WY 82520 /
307-332-2995
Lander Llama Co., 2024 Mortimore Lane / 307-332-5624
The Nature Conservancy, 258 Main Street / 307-332-2971

FLY SHOPS AND SPORTING GOODS
Rocky Mountain Dubbing, 115 Poppy / 307-332-2989
Good Place, 155 Main Street / 307-332-3158
Pamida, Hwy 287

AUTO RENTAL AND REPAIR
F & S Rent A Wreck, 323 North 2nd Street / 307-332-9965
Ford Rent-A-Car, 555 East Main Street / 307-332-4355

D & S Truck & Auto Repair, 976 Hwy 789 / 307-332-3609
Bailey Tire & Auto Service, 401 West Hwy 287 / 307-332-5307

AIR SERVICE
Nearest airline service is Riverton.

MEDICAL
Lander Valley Medical Center, 1320 Bishop Randall Drive / 307-332-4420

FOR MORE INFORMATION
Lander Area Chamber of Commerce
160 North First Street
Lander, WY 82520
307-332-3892

Dubois
Elevation—6,197 • Population—895

Found in the northern foothills of the Wind River Mountains and seated on the Wind River, Dubois is in one of the most scenic areas in the state. A ranching and logging community and Old West resort, it is also the northern gateway to the Fitzpatrick Wilderness. The National Bighorn Sheep Interpretive Center is in Dubois, and the largest herd of bighorn sheep in North America roams Whiskey Mountain southeast of town.

Dubois' zip code is 82513.

ACCOMMODATIONS
Black Bear Country Inn, 505 West Ramshorn / 307-455-2344 / 16 units / Pets allowed / $
Branding Iron Motel, 401 West Ramshorn / 307-455-2893 / 23 units / Pets allowed / $
Chinook Winds Motel, 640 South 1st / 307-455-2987 / 16 units / Pets allowed / $
Stagecoach Motor Inn, 103 East Ramshorn / 307-455-2303 / 16 units / Pets allowed / $
Super 8 Motel, 1414 Warm Springs Dr / 307-455-3694 / 32 units / Pets allowed / $
Trail's End Motel, 511 West Ramshorn / 307-455-2540 / 20 units / $
Twin Pines Lodge & Cabins, 218 West Ramshorn / 307-455-2600 / 16 units / $
Wind River Motel, 519 West Ramshorn / 307-455-2611 / 12 units / Pets allowed / $
Dunloggin Bed & Breakfast, 305 South 1st / 307-455-2445
Brooks Lake Lodge, 458 Brooks Lake Road / 307-455-21210
Red Rock Lodge, 7026 U.S. Hwy 26, Dubois, WY 82513-9523 / 307-455-2944

CAMPGROUNDS AND RV PARKS
Circle Up Camper Court, 225 West Welty / 307-455-2238 / May 11 to November 15 / 66 RV and 35 tent sites / Full services

Lakes' Lodge, 1 Union Pass Road / 307-455-2171 / June 15 to October 1 / 9 RV and 6 tent sites / Full services

Pinnacle Buttes Lodge & Campground, 3577 West Hwy 26 / 307-455-2506 / 15 RV and 6 tent sites / Full services

RESTAURANTS

Roadrunner Restaurant, 712 West Ramshorn Street / 307-455-3638

Line Shack, 448 Union Pass Road / 307-455-3232

Cowboy Cafe, 115 East Ramshorn Street / 307-455-2595

Ramshorn Inn, 202 East Ramshorn Street / 307-455-2400

Lakes' Lodge, 1 Union Pass Road / 307-455-2171

Village Cafe, 515 West Ramshorn Street / 307-455-2122

Old Yellowstone Garage, 112 East Ramshorn / 307-455-3666

Wild West Deli, 206 West Ramshorn Street / 307-455-3354

Hangout, 151 Bald Mountain Road / 307-455-3800

Wild Bunch Cafe, 3577 U.S. Hwy 26 / 307-455-3873

VETERINARIANS

Dubois Veterinary Clinic, 408 Ramshorn Ranch Road / 307-455-3434

East Fork Veterinary Service, 31 Gilliland Avenue / 307-455-2538

OUTFITTERS

Whiskey Mountain Tackle Shop, 102 West Ramshorn Street / 307-455-2587

Wind River Productions, 211 West Ramshorn / 307-455-2140

Wind River Mountain Outfitters, P.O. Box 5, Dubois, WY 82513 / 307-455-2464

Lazy L & B River Co., 1072 East Fork Road / 307-455-2839, 800-453-9488

George H. Hunker, Box 612, Crowheart, WY 82512 / 307-486-2266; in winter, call 307-332-3986

Double Bar J Guest Ranch, 3609 U.S. Hwy 26 / 307-455-2681

DT Outfitting, 19 Dutch Ed Lane / 307-332-4502, 800-408-9149

FLY SHOPS AND SPORTING GOODS

Whiskey Mountain Tackle Shop, 102 West Ramshorn Street / 307-455-2587

AUTO RENTAL AND REPAIR

Grand Teton Towing, 307-455-2764

AIR SERVICE

Nearest airline services are in Jackson and Riverton.

MEDICAL

Dubois Medical Clinic, 706 Meckem Street / 307-455-2516

FOR MORE INFORMATION

Dubois Chamber of Commerce
P.O. Box 632
Dubois, WY 82513
307-455-2556

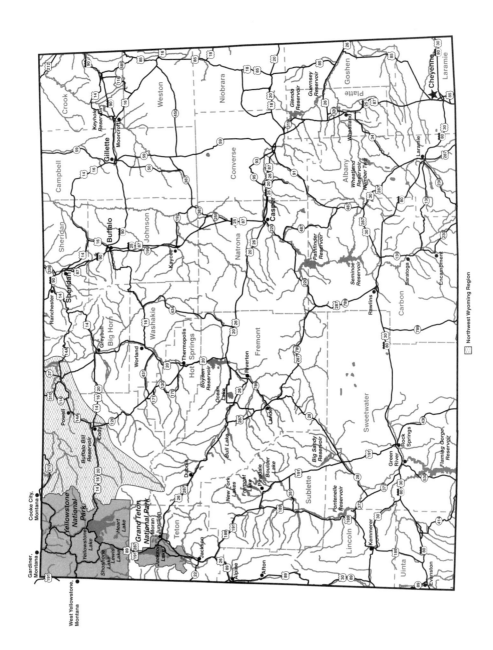

Northwest Wyoming
Mirror Image of the Nation's First Park

Park County's bounty of mountain trout streams offers flyfishers all they ever dreamed about in the waters of its famous neighbor, Yellowstone National Park, only without the crowds. The bonus for fishing this gateway to the nation's first park is towering snowcapped peaks and a host of jewel-like alpine lakes.

In a state of many firsts, Park County also has the oldest federal forest in the nation and its first ranger station. Shoshone National Forest was set aside in 1891 as the Yellowstone Timberland Reserve. In 1907 it joined the national forest system established by President Theodore Roosevelt. Wapiti Ranger Station is located on the banks of the North Fork of the Shoshone River, midway between the Park's eastern gate and Cody.

Wapiti Valley was a favorite playground of William "Buffalo Bill" Cody and the Rough Rider president, Theodore Roosevelt, who described its road as "the most scenic 50 miles in the world." Thousands of acres of their former haunts are preserved as the Beartooth, Absaroka, and Washakie Wilderness Areas. These pristine highlands sprawl across one of the largest contiguous roadless areas in the West.

Dominated by the Absaroka and Beartooth mountains, the Big Horn Basin's alpine scenery matches the Swiss Alps. Their forested lower slopes are etched by cascading blue-ribbon trout streams. The Clark's Fork of the Yellowstone, Wyoming's only Wild and Scenic River, plunges through one of the deepest, most picturesque gorges in North America. Above and below timberline are hundreds of emerald green lakes harboring trout and grayling. Access to the lakes on the Wyoming side of the Beartooth Wilderness starts from trailheads along the scenic Beartooth Highway. But those planning to venture into the challenging Absaroka and Washakie Wilderness Areas might want to consider guided horseback trips.

The basin's premier flyfishing streams are the North Fork of the Shoshone and Clark's Fork of the Yellowstone. But the region's rolling sagebrush desert holds secret charms, too; several high desert lakes are managed as trophy fisheries. Paralleled by the highway to the park's East Entrance, the North Fork tends to be crowded at the height of the tourist season. Fishing is superb, and the atmosphere is more serene after Labor Day. The Clark's Fork, on the road to Yellowstone's northeast entrance, is off the beaten track and allows chances for solitude even during the busy season. In autumn, it is a scenic wonderland with awesome dry-fly fishing.

Opportunities to view a multitude of wildlife is guaranteed, especially for moose, mule deer, elk, and coyote. Sighting a grizzly bear is very possible. Wolves are back, too, since their reintroduction into the Greater Yellowstone Ecosystem. Mountain lions also inhabit the forest and share the high country with mountain goats and bighorn sheep.

The frontier resort town of Cody is the main service hub for the region and the eastern gateway community for Yellowstone. Be sure to visit its fascinating Old West museums at the Buffalo Bill Historical Center or catch the action at the Cody Nite Rodeo, a summer-long hoedown.

North Fork Shoshone River

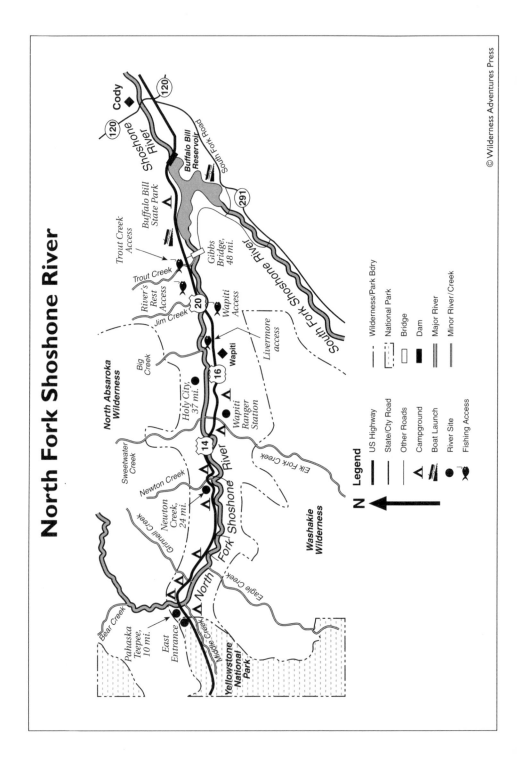

© Wilderness Adventures Press

Legend

US Highway	
State/Cty Road	
Other Roads	
Campground	
Boat Launch	
River Site	
Fishing Access	
Wilderness/Park Bdry	
National Park	
Bridge	
Dam	
Major River	
Minor River/Creek	

N

NORTH FORK OF THE SHOSHONE RIVER

Cascading along the scenic Wapiti Valley Highway to Yellowstone National Park's East Entrance, the North Fork of the Shoshone is irresistible to family fishing parties during the summer tourist season. More savvy anglers bide their time to savor the North Fork's stellar early autumn dry-fly fishing or stalk the browns of October running upstream from Buffalo Bill Reservoir.

The North Fork is managed as a wild trout fishery. It hasn't been stocked by Wyoming Game and Fish since 1989, and holds strong populations of Yellowstone cutthroat and rainbows. Hybrids, or cuttbows, are relatively few in number, unlike in many other western streams where native cutthroat have been virtually eliminated by the more aggressive rainbow, a West Coast species.

North Fork cutthroat and rainbows are mostly in the 10- to 14-inch class, with chances for souvenir photographs of fish exceeding 20 inches. Some brown trout roam the lower river year-round, but the best opportunity for a trophy is after fall's frosty nights cool the water and spark their annual spawning migration. By late autumn rainbow and cutthroat also drop down through the system to winter in the lower third of the river or Buffalo Bill Reservoir. Pan-sized brook trout reside in the tumbling upper reaches, and whitefish can be enticed to rise to dry flies in quieter sections of the river.

The North Fork rises at an elevation of 8,184 feet at the merger of Hughes and Silvertip Creeks below Hughes Basin on the crest of the Absaroka Wilderness. This is remote, rugged country and the realm of grizzly bears. Don't hike or fish it alone. Parties of three or more are recommended. First-time visitors should explore it with a professional guide or friends who know the terrain.

The North Fork emerges from the wilderness behind Pahaska Teepee as a classic small mountain stream. It stair-steps down the narrow valley in a series of rocky rapids, shallow riffles, slick glides and runs, and intermittent cutbank pools. Thick ranks of pine and fir carpet the slopes, and sheer rocky outcroppings funnel the river through its swiftest runs. A few flats slow the stream and braid it into meandering channels. Additional pocket waters and gravel bars are exposed as spring runoff wanes.

On its descent, the North Fork grows in strength as it collects the flows of numerous creeks spilling off the mountains. But its channels rarely exceed 40 or 60 feet in width.

Above the Wapiti Ranger Station, the North Fork changes character as the valley widens and the river enters a high sagebrush desert. Conifer forests of the upper slopes retreat as cottonwoods and willows line the floodplain. Barren, wind-sculptured cliffs and quaint rock formations dominate the northern skyline. The river ends its descent at an elevation of 5,400 feet, where the Buffalo Bill Reservoir traps its flows.

The lower river meanders in broader sweeps, and flows are heavier from the accumulated contributions of its tributaries. But it follows the same pattern of riffles and runs, cutbank pools and occasional braided channels. Recent high water years have blown out some favorite fishing holes local residents enjoyed during a prolonged drought, but change is part of the cyclical nature of the mountains. Exploring these alterations after a flood adds to the challenge, as well as the charm, of fishing unfettered streams.

Public access is excellent for nearly 30 miles along U.S. 20/16/14 in the Shoshone National Forest. The last 8 miles of the river flow through private property, and fishing is confined to Wyoming Game and Fish access sites or streamside resorts. The upper river is open to fishing year-round. From Gibbs Bridge upstream to Newton Creek it is closed April 1 through June 30.

The closure has been in place for almost a decade to protect the native cutthroat, which evolved to migrate upstream and spawn during spring floods. Due to increased fishing pressure, the daily bag and possession limit was reduced in 1996 to three trout, only one over 20 inches.

Coincidentally, fishing is most difficult during the closed period. Like other streams of the Northern Rockies, the North Fork is a high, off-color torrent when winter snows are melting. Spring runoff begins in April, peaks in June and usually extends into July. In many years the best fishing doesn't kick in until mid- or late July. Then the river runs clear and cool, and sight fishing is a pleasant prospect.

Its size and character make the North Fork of the Shoshone a good introduction to western streams for beginners. It is less intimidating than large rivers like the North Platte, Yellowstone or Snake. Wading is relatively easy throughout its course, although its cobble floor is slippery in places. To be safe, wear waders with felt soles and avoid wading too deep in swifter runs or near pools.

The North Fork's limited float fishing opportunities can be rollicking affairs in some stretches. Some local outfitters offer this option in small, three-man rafts. Cody's fly shops also are excellent sources for updates on river conditions and advice on what the fish are hitting.

Tim Wade and Chip Andrews at North Fork Anglers and Scott Aune at Aune's Absaroka Angler are the resident gurus of flyfishing. Matthew Cruikshank recently acquired Yellowstone Troutfitters. Stop in to chat and check out their chalkboards listing current hatches before hitting the river. Wade advises, "take several days to get an appreciation for what trout fishing used to be like before crowds and whirling disease."

Matching the Hatch

One of the most amiable features of the North Fork is that it is a big fly stream throughout its seasons. Golden stoneflies, green drakes, grasshoppers, gray drakes, and the large fall caddis entice fish to look up from late June to October. Robust caddis and mayfly hatches spawn evening feeding frenzies and keep surface action going through the dog days of summer. Attractor patterns often draw strikes as effectively as dry flies for specific hatches. They are a good way to pound up fish throughout the day when there are few naturals on the water.

But you don't have to wait until trout start porpoising for floating flies. As spring runoff wanes, woolly buggers, rubberleg patterns, large nymphs, and emergers bring trout to the net until warmer water temperatures start producing

Anglers and guide float the North Fork of the Shoshone.

hatches. Double your prospecting chances by tying on smaller beadhead nymphs or emergers as tandem flies.

Woolly buggers, yuk bugs, girdlebugs, Bitch Creek nymphs, or Montana stones, sizes 2 to 8, are good choices. Smaller wet patterns can include soft-hackles, half-backs, beadhead Prince nymphs, or hare's ear nymphs, Zug Bugs, and golden stone nymphs in sizes 6 to 12.

Later, when big flies or grasshoppers are out, it is equally effective to trail an emerger or beadhead nymph on a dropper line from a large dry fly or attractor pattern. The usual method to fish the North Fork during summer is to nymph fish the riffles in the morning, or toss large nymphs or woolly buggers against the banks and into pools while waiting for an afternoon or evening hatch. As temperatures peak and begin to drop again in autumn, most hatches come off progressively later in the day or not until dusk. Some spinner falls follow a similar pattern.

Golden stones and early caddis kick off the dry fly season in late June and early July. Small yellow stones, also known as willow flies or yellow Sallies, often are a tandem hatch. Yellow or orange stimulators, golden stones, orange bucktails, yellow Sallies, olive- or tan-bodied elk hair caddis, and yellow humpies, 8 to 14, mimic these flies.

Green drakes start the mayfly season in early July, followed in mid-month by western green drakes, or Flavs, and the ever popular pale morning duns. Baetis, or

*Holy City
rock formations
above the North Fork.*

blue-winged olives, are among the hardiest of mayflies and show up just about any time of year on western streams. They also linger the longest in fall. The same goes for midges.

Green drake Wulffs, Flavs, and olive parachute hare's ears, 10 to 14, and PMDs, BWOs, olive or cream sparkle duns, and elk hair caddis, 14 to 18, are part of the arsenal now. Generic mayflies like light Cahills, Adams and para-Adams, as well as attractors like yellow or royal humpies, yellow, gray or lime Wulffs, and royal Trudes, 8 to 18, also are effective. A Griffith's gnat, black midge spinner, or even a trico spinner, 16 to 20, may nab a picky, quiet water feeder.

The reign of the terrestrials can begin any time after mid-July and linger after the first hard frost. Dave's or Joe's hoppers, para-hoppers, Madam Xs, yellow stimulators, 4 to 10, fit the bill during "hoppertunity time." But don't forget the ant, beetle, and cricket patterns tucked away in virtually every flyfisher's vest.

Gray drakes are a special late summer treat on the North Fork. The large fall caddis, or sedge, adds a new dimension to the stream after Labor Day. Gray Wulffs, gray drake spinners, Adams and para-Adams, 10 to 14, and tan elk hair caddis and orange bucktails, 12 to 14, fit these scenarios.

Flows are usually quite low during the North Fork's limited fall brown trout spawning run. But cutthroat and rainbows come out of the reservoir at this time and are on the prowl, too. Dead drifting large nymphs and rubberlegs may draw surprising strikes. Keep tiny BWO or midge patterns handy for when rising trout offer a chance to switch gears.

In the fall, reaching the river from the west is occasionally difficult. Late September or October snows may temporarily block Sylvan Pass in the park. By November, vehicle travel through the East Entrance is closed and doesn't open again until late April. This is a time of rest for the North Fork as local anglers focus their attention on the tailwater fishery of the Shoshone River below Cody, or the South Fork's stronger brown trout run.

Tributaries of the North Fork

Good fishing tributaries of the North Fork of the Shoshone include Grinnell, Eagle, Fishhawk, Sweetwater, Clearwater and Elk Fork Creeks. Flyfishers who plan to follow them to their wilderness headwaters should go with professional guides or friends familiar with the country. In any event, remember Mr. Grizz. Don't fish alone.

All six creeks hold good populations of pan-sized brook, rainbow, and cutthroat trout. A 12-inch fish in these tumbling waters is a virtual monster as challenging to land as the big guys in large streams. But whatever their size, these alpine gems are strong and feisty. They often hit bouncing dry flies with suicidal abandon. Use terminal tackle strong enough to end battles quickly and not exhaust the fish. Save a few for a campfire meal, if you like, but don't waste any that you keep.

Stiff-hackled, high-floating dry flies work best in the cascading pocket waters and swift riffles and runs of high mountain creeks. Try elk hair caddis, yellow or red humpies, grasshoppers, yellow Sallies, royal Trudes, and gray, yellow, or lime Wulffs in sizes 10 to 16. Wet flies of about the same sizes can include weighted and unweighted rubberlegs, Bitch Creek nymphs, soft-hackles, hare's ear and Prince nymphs. Meadow runs and a few quiet pools offer chances for mayflies. Again, stick to the basics with Adams, light Cahills, PMDs, and BWOs in sizes 14 to 18.

Look for bigger fish hiding under logjams, behind midstream boulders or in hidden pools.

Forest Service campgrounds are located at the mouths of all but Fishhawk Creek, and bridges cross the North Fork to trails up Eagle and Elk Fork Creeks. To reach the Fishhawk, cross the river at the Buffalo Bill Boy Scouts of America Camp bridge and walk downstream to the creek.

Here's an idea of what to expect:

- Grinnell Creek rises northeast of Pahaska Teepee and enters the North Fork just downstream of the historic landmark. It is rated as fair fishing for 6- to 10-inch brookies, cutthroat, and rainbows.

- Eagle Creek enters the river from the south about 4 miles below Pahaska. It is rated as good fishing for 6- to 12-inch brookies and cutthroat.
- Fishhawk Creek also enters from the south, a mile downstream from the BSA bridge. It is rated as fair fishing for 6- to 12-inch brookies, cutthroat, and rainbows.
- The other three creeks are midway down the valley, just upstream from Wapiti Ranger Station.
- Clearwater Creek enters the river from the north. It is rated as good fishing for 6- to 14-inch cutthroat and rainbows.
- Sweetwater Creek also enters from the north and has a road part way upstream. It is rated as fair fishing for 6- to 8-inch cutthroat and rainbows.
- Elk Fork Creek enters the North Fork from the south. It is rated as fair fishing for 6- to 12-inch brookies, cutthroat, and rainbows.

Buffalo Bill Reservoir

The 8,500-acre Buffalo Bill Reservoir is the most popular fishery in Park County. It gets a lot of pressure, but draws little attention from flyfishers. One clue why is its advertised designation as the Wind Surfing Capitol of Wyoming.

Most anglers use big water tactics, such as trolling, for 12- to 18-inch cutthroat and rainbows. Lake trout are reported to reach 15 pounds.

General regulations bag and possession limits apply on the reservoir. It's open to fishing year-round, except for one restriction. The upper arm of the reservoir from the mouths of Rattlesnake Creek and Sheep Creek, also known as Spring Creek, up to Gibbs Bridge is closed from April 1 through July 14.

Buffalo Bill State Park is located at the reservoir. It has two campgrounds and a boat launch site on the north shore. Another boat launch and picnic area are just off the South Fork Road.

Stream Facts: North Fork Shoshone River

Season
- Upper river is open year-round. Lower river and its tributaries from Gibbs Bridge upstream to Newton Creek are closed to fishing April 1 through June 30.

Regulations
- In the North Fork and its tributaries, the limit is 3 trout per day or in possession, only 1 over 20 inches. In Buffalo Bill Reservoir, the limit is 4 trout per day or in possession, only 1 over 20 inches.

Trout
- Yellowstone cutthroat and rainbows are in the 10- to 14-inch class, with a good chance for larger fish; brown trout are found on the lower end and brook trout are found in the upper reaches. Whitefish also are present, and a few lake trout may come out of the reservoir in fall during the brown spawning run.

Miles
- Mile 10: Pahaska Teepee
- Mile 24: Newton Creek
- Mile 37: Holy City
- Mile 40: Shoshone National Forest boundary
- Mile 48: Buffalo Bill Reservoir

Character
- The North Fork emerges from the remote Absaroka Wilderness east of Yellowstone Park as a small mountain stream and builds into a narrow rushing river as it collects flows of numerous tributaries. The upper river descends through a heavily wooded valley in shallow, rocky glides, pools, riffles, and runs, and a few braided channels to Wapiti. The lower river follows a similar pattern through the high plains desert along picturesque cliffs and rock formations to Buffalo Bill Reservoir. Its shallow stretches provide easy wading, but its cobble floor can be slippery. Occasional float-fishers run the river in small, three-man rafts.

Flows
- Spring runoff begins in April and peaks in June. In exceptionally wet years, high flows can extend well into July. Best fishing is in late summer and autumn.

Access
- Shoshone National Forest boundary is 10 miles upstream from the reservoir. Except for a few private resorts, public access is unrestricted on forest and in wilderness areas. Four Wyoming Game and Fish access sites are located between Gibbs Bridge and Wapiti.

Camping
- Buffalo Bill State Park has camp sites on the north and southeast shores.
- Shoshone National Forest has 8 campgrounds located along the river.
- Commercial campgrounds for RVs and tents are located in Cody.

NORTH FORK SHOSHONE RIVER MAJOR HATCHES

Insect	A	M	J	J	A	S	O	N	Time	Flies
Golden Stone				▮	▮				A	**Dry:** Golden Stone, Bird's Stone, Orange Stimulator #8–10; **Wet:** Black Rubberlegs, Woolly Bugger, Girdlebug, Bitch Creek Nymph #2–8
Little Yellow Stone (Willow Fly)				▮	▮				M//A	Yellow Sally, Willow Fly, Yellow Humpy, Yellow Stimulator #12–14
Caddis				▮	▮	▮			M//D	**Dry:** Elk Hair Caddis, Red or Yellow Humpy, Gray Wulff, Royal Trude #12–16; **Wet:** Caddis Emerger, Soft-hackles, Prince Nymph, Halfback #12–14
Large Fall Caddis (sedge)							▮		A	Dark Elk Hair Caddis, Orange Bucktail, Stimulators #10–14
Pale Morning Dun					▮	▮	▮		A/E	**Dry:** PMD, Light Cahill, Para-Adams, Rusty Spinner, Sparkle Dun #16–18; **Wet:** Hare's Ear Nymph, Pheasant Tail, Beadheads #14–18
Pale Evening Dun					▮	▮	▮		A/D	Pale Evening Dun, Light Cahill, PMD #16–18

HATCH TIME CODE: M = morning; A = afternoon; E = evening; D = dark; SF = spinner fall; // = continuation through periods.

NORTH FORK SHOSHONE RIVER MAJOR HATCHES, CONT.

Insect	A	M	J	J	A	S	O	N	Time	Flies
Baetis	■	■				■	■	■	A/E	Blue-winged Olive, Blue Dun, Para-Adams, Olive Parachute Hare's Ear #16–22
Green Drake			■	■					A	**Dry:** Green Drake, Extended Body Drake, Olive Parachute Hare's Ear #10–12; **Wet:** Zug Bug, Olive Marabou Nymph #10–12
Western Green Drake				■	■				A/E	Flav, Green Wulff, Blue-winged Olive, Olive Parachute Hare's Ear #12–14
Gray Drake					■	■			M//A	Adams, Gray Drake, Gray Wulff #10–12
Midge	■	■	■	■	■	■	■	■	A/E	**Dry:** Griffith's Gnat, Trico, Black Midge #18–22; **Wet:** Blood Midge Pupa, Brassie #18–22
Terrestrials				■	■	■	■		A/E	Joe's Hopper, Dave's Hopper, Yellow Stimulator; Double Humpy, Madam X #8–14; Ants #16–18; Foam Beetle, Disc O'Beetle, Black Elk Hair Caddis #14–16

HATCH TIME CODE: M = morning; A = afternoon; E = evening; D = dark; SF = spinner fall; // = continuation through periods.

South Fork Shoshone River

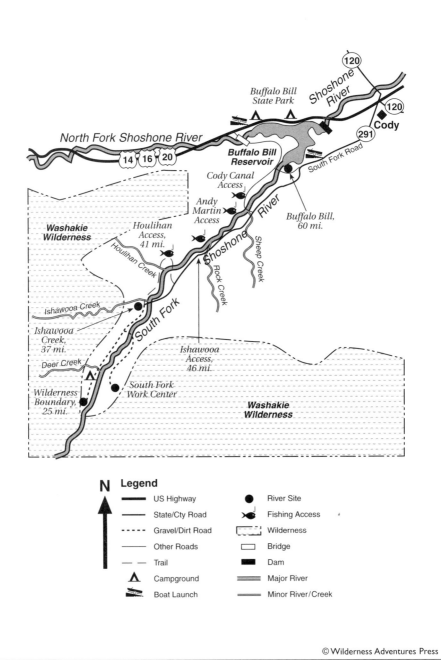

SOUTH FORK OF THE SHOSHONE RIVER

The South Fork of the Shoshone River is a smaller carbon copy of the North Fork. One difference is that it flattens out sooner and divides into more numerous, shallow channels on its flow through a wide pastoral valley. The scenery is just as spectacular.

But its tempting waters are for the most part off limits to casual flyfishers. This is unfortunate, because its undercut banks, snags, boulders, and pools provide classic brown trout habitat. The lower river is rated as good fishing for browns in the 12- to 16-inch range through the summer. Its fall spawning run is much stronger than the North Fork's.

The bottom 35 miles of the river, upstream to the Shoshone National Forest, flows through private property. Permission to fish is difficult to obtain. Four access sites managed by Wyoming Game and Fish offer less than 5 miles of public fishing on this stretch of the South Fork. After mid-September, a local fly shop guide suggested, it is worth the effort to go to the top end of the Game and Fish access sites to tackle fall-running browns.

But another Cody fly shop guide warned that first time anglers need to be certain that they are on public land. Some landowners are more than ready to "question the fine points of Wyoming's riparian laws" when a trespass dispute occurs. He added another note of caution after persistent questions about going into the upper reaches alone. "The valley section of the South Fork is one of the most beautiful in the country, but you might meet a lot of hairy guys up there."

"You talking about grizzly bears?"

"Yep."

A paved road follows the river upstream to the Guard Station at Ishawooa Creek, and a gravel road continues another 10 miles to the forest boundary at Cabin Creek. A Forest Service campground is downstream at Deer Creek.

At this point, 25 miles of stream is open to public access. A Wyoming Game and Fish biologist advises hiking at least 2 or 3 miles upstream to get past shallow, unproductive waters. The reward for the extra effort is "bigger-than-average brook trout" and "an occasional 16-inch cutthroat." But don't make the hike alone.

Be Cautious in Grizzly Bear Country

"You are in Bear Country."

The warning is one of the first signs visitors see when they enter the park or national forests surrounding Yellowstone.

The range of the great bear has expanded since the park booted roadside panhandlers into the backcountry and weaned garbage dump feeders in the 1970s. At first the population boom expanded into remote wilderness areas adjacent to Yellowstone. Now, grizzlies are venturing into popular forest playgrounds near Cody, Jackson and Pinedale. "Grizzly bears are expanding their range south, and campers and hunters need to assume some responsibility to help prevent conflicts," said Dave Moody, chief bear biologist for the Wyoming Game and Fish Department. Anglers and hikers should follow the same advice.

Most times, the bears lose in adverse encounters. In six recorded incidents in 1997, seven bears died. Five were killed by hunters, including a sow and its three cubs, during two attacks. Another hunter escaped after being mauled. And two park rangers were able to thwart two attacking bears by using pepper spray.

Two other bears were killed after they refused to give up their taste for human food items at Green River campgrounds. A fed bear is a dead bear.

Yellowstone officials encourage the use of pepper spray as a last resort in a bear encounter. But Wyoming Game and Fish and other federal wildlife agencies adamantly urge guides and hunters to carry bear repellent spray to help reduce the chances of additional grizzly bear deaths. The jury is still out on whether hikers and fishers need to follow the same advice. But they should be aware of the option.

Using spray to repel a charge prevents possible death of another bear and delivers a dose of "aversive conditioning to humans," Moody said. Case histories and research also show there is less chance the human will be injured. "In dozens of human grizzly encounters in the last 15 years in the Yellowstone area, only once has a grizzly bear come through the spray and knocked down or injured the sprayer," Moody said. "The spray has repelled the bear and protected the person 99 percent of the time."

If you're going to pack pepper spray, carry it where you can reach it, he said. Two proven brand names are Counter Assault and Bear Prepared. The sprays cost from $30 to $50 and are available in most northwest Wyoming communities. The sprays also are available through outdoor equipment catalogs.

Moody further recommends practicing the "normal precautions." Hike in groups of three or more when in remote areas. Make noise on a routine basis—talking to each other, wearing bear bells or tapping metal items. Most importantly, keep a clean camp. Store supplies and utensils, including game and fish as well as pet food, 10 feet off the ground and 100 yards away from sleeping areas. Cooking should also be done 100 yards away from tents. In developed campgrounds, store food and coolers in locked vehicles.

Literature on camping and traveling in grizzly country is available from Game and Fish and Forest Service offices or by calling 800-842-1934 or 307-777-4600.

SHOSHONE RIVER

The Shoshone River, formed by the confluence of the North and South Forks, is what's known in the West as a working river. In 1910, the massive Buffalo Bill Dam captured its flows to provide irrigation waters for the Big Horn Basin's farmers and ranchers. In 1993 another 25 feet was added to the 325-foot dam to store more water.

Downstream from Cody are six additional dams. These are called diversion dams that retain upstream releases and divert water to crop fields and pastures during the growing season. "The Shoshone below Cody is not worth the effort (to fish) through summer because of its erratic flows," said Scott Aune, of Aune's Absaroka Angler.

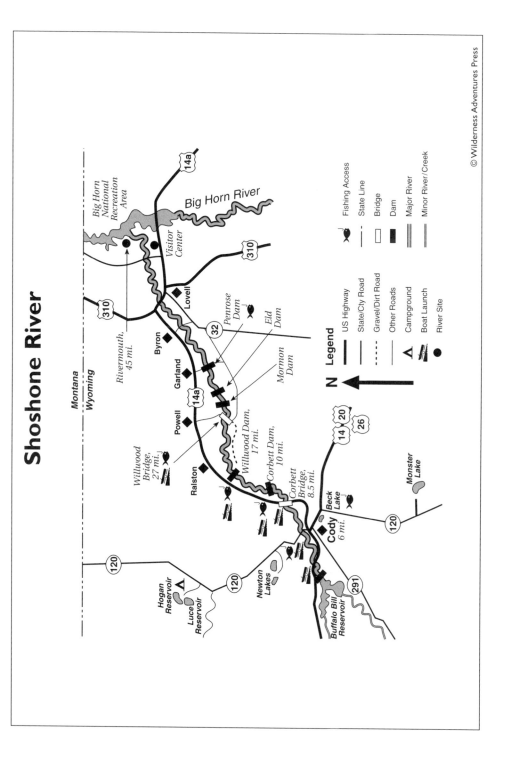

Shoshone River

© Wilderness Adventures Press

Legend

N

US Highway
State/Cty Road
Gravel/Dirt Road
Other Roads
Campground
Boat Launch
River Site

Fishing Access
State Line
Bridge
Dam
Major River
Minor River/Creek

Montana
Wyoming

Big Horn National Recreation Area

Big Horn River

Visitor Center

Rivermouth, 45 mi.

Lovell

Byron

Garland

Powell

Ralston

Willwood Bridge, 27 mi.

Penrose Dam

Eld Dam

Mormon Dam

Willwood Dam, 17 mi.

Corbett Dam, 10 mi.

Corbett Bridge, 8.5 mi.

Cody

Beck Lake

6 mi.

Monster Lake

Newton Lakes

Hogan Reservoir

Luce Reservoir

Buffalo Bill Reservoir

"The river holds some very good fish, though. In past years, in late winter and early spring, it's had some amazingly excellent fishing."

Releases from the reservoir stabilize after October and are kept low to store water for the next season. This is when boats are launched and the banks are pounded for brown trout ranging from 12 to 20 inches. On a good day, a trophy brown up to 25 inches might even be netted. The river also holds 10- to 14-inch cutthroat and rainbow, plus some topping the 16-inch mark.

So, while most people are content to toast their toes in front of a fireplace, a hard core group of Cody fly casters fish the river right through the winter, even under the worst of conditions. The more sane bide their time and greet a chinook with open arms. The warming winds that can melt huge snowbanks in an afternoon are a uniquely western phenomenon. Even with the high winds casting is possible, and its a more pleasant way to cure cabin fever blues.

The river fishes best through the 10 miles from Corbett Dam down to Willwood Dam. The next 10 miles down to Willwood Bridge, south of Powell, also is considered good fishing. Below Mormon Dam, just below the bridge, the Shoshone is not considered much of a fishery any time of year.

Big river tactics is the name of the game. It is mostly "chuck and duck" casting with large weighted woolly buggers and rubberleg nymphs, streamers, muddler or marabou minnows, and Clouser minnows. Pound the banks and strip them in fast or drift them along the edges.

Hatches of tiny blue-winged olives and midges sometimes offer a change of pace and are a lot easier on the arm. Casting caddis or small nymphs and emergers also are options when fish are feeding.

If iced-up rod guides are your thing, or you want to visit Monster Lake and need another excuse to do it, contact Aune or Tim Wade at North Fork Anglers. They can arrange float trips or tell you where to launch your own boat.

After May the Shoshone returns to the irrigators.

GREYBULL RIVER

The Greybull River is the third prominent trout stream flowing off the eastern slopes of the Absaroka Mountains.

On its meandering lowland course, the narrow, shallow river bisects the center of the Big Horn Basin's high desert plateau. There is little other running water until it reaches the Big Horn River.

The sprawling expanse of rangeland traversed by the Greybull is home to more cattle than people. Roads are few, and trespassers aren't welcome. Permission to fish the lower river is difficult to obtain, so it's best to head for the mountains.

Meeteetse, population 370, is the only dot on the map in this quiet backwater corner of Park County. The ranching community is 30 miles south of Cody on WYO 120.

The upper waters of the river are due west of Meeteetse on WYO 290. About midway on the 20-mile drive, the road turns to gravel. At its end is Jack Creek Campground in the Shoshone National Forest.

West of the campground is the Washakie Wilderness. It's beautiful country defined by deep, narrow valleys and steep, rugged slopes with volcanic outcroppings. The broad, flat-topped peaks of the Absarokas soar to 13,000 feet or more. To the east, across the oblong bowl of the basin, the massive upthrusts of the Big Horn Mountains dominate the horizon.

The Greybull's 25-mile northerly course down its V-shaped valley turns abruptly east at Jack Creek as it exits the mountains. Its headwaters flow off the slopes of 13,153-foot Franks Peak and 12,449-foot Mount Crosby.

A good foot trail skirts the river upstream. This is grizzly bear country, so take the usual precautions.

Yellowstone cutthroat in the 6- to 16-inch range make scrappy rises to dry flies after hatches start in earnest in mid-July. A few old timers topping 18 inches may be lurking in hidden pools. And a few pan-sized brook trout compete with the cutts for high floating flies.

Flyfishers don't need to burden themselves with bulging fishing vests on a day hike up the river. About all that's needed to match a hatch or draw rises are a few Adams, light Cahills, elk hair caddis, or humpies and royal Wulffs in sizes 10 to 18. Small soft-hackled emergers and Prince and hare's ear nymphs also can be drifted through promising pools. Ignore wide, shallow sections of the river and concentrate on log jams, the undercut banks of its channels, and deeper pools.

Mountain cutthroat are very accommodating and too easily netted for their own good. Have fun, but refrain from taking more than needed if a camp fire meal is planned.

South of Greybull Pass is the headwaters of the Wood River, which joins the Greybull 7 miles west of Meeteetse. Obtaining permission to fish its lower levels is very difficult. The Wood's mountain course holds pan-sized cutthroat and brook trout, but its fishing is rated as poor. A small, shallow stream, its flows may be reduced to trickles in low water years.

High Desert Lakes

Water is precious on the windswept, semi-arid plains of the Big Horn Basin. Small dams trap many small feeder streams trickling off the Absaroka Mountains onto the sagebrush desert. The impoundments preserve water for cattle through the dry summers and supply irrigation for alfalfa meadows.

Several of these nutrient-rich reservoirs produce big, fast-growing trout. One, Monster Lake, is named for the size of its gargantuan trout. It's a private pond, and the privilege to fish it commands a pricey reservation fee. Two other reservoirs are public waters managed by Wyoming Game and Fish as trophy fisheries. A third set a record in 1997 for splake, a hybrid trout.

That's not to say all the trout in the high desert lakes around Cody are trophies. They hold fish of all age classes, and anglers often have to work hard for their rewards.

"East Newton Lake is fishing like it always does," Chip Andrew, of North Fork Anglers, said in response to a caller's questions. "You can go out there and score really big time—or you can end up having a truly intellectual experience. You can end up tossing 20 different patterns at a fish, and he won't take a one."

Flyfishers can stalk fish cruising the shores just after ice-out and again in fall as temperatures plummet. Most of the season, though, fishing is best from canoes, small boats and float tubes in early morning, or late afternoon and evening. Generally the desert lakes thaw in late April or early May and remain ice-free well into November.

The trout feed on a smorgasbord of aquatic and terrestrial insects, nymphs and larvae, freshwater scuds, leeches, and chubs.

During hatches or swarms, fly pattern selections can range from callibaetis, baetis and *Tricorythodes* mayflies to damselflies and dragonflies to caddis and sedges, as well as midges, flying ants, and beetles. A host of wet flies are effective through the seasons. Nymphs, larvae, and pupae of the aquatic insects are year-round residents along with the scuds, or freshwater fairy shrimp, and leeches and minnows.

Check with the folks at Cody's fly shops for updates on which lakes are producing best and what the fish are taking. Give the lakes a break in late summer if water temperatures rise to a point that they cause stress for the fish.

Here's what to expect on the high desert lakes:

East Newton Lake

East Newton Lake is 5 miles north of Cody. Watch for the sign on WYO 120 and turn left onto a good gravel road.

The secret is out of the bag for this 30-acre pond's strong, full-bodied rainbow and brown trout. When rivers are blown out by spring runoff it's a good choice to pursue rainbows that often exceed 20 inches and browns surpassing the two-foot mark. It also holds above average brook trout.

Managed as a trophy fishery, East Newton Lake has a limit of one trout per day or in possession. All trout less than 20 inches must be returned to the water immediately. Fishing is permitted by the use of artificial flies and lures only.

Just upstream is West Newton Lake, which has no special regulations. It holds 10- to 16-inch cutthroat and brook trout.

Luce Reservoir

Luce Reservoir, which was poisoned in 1994 to eliminate an illegal stocking of perch, is one of Wyoming's best success stories. Today, it is a catch-and-release trophy fishery for Kamloops, as well as the primary source of eggs to stock other lakes with the giant rainbow. Only flies and artificial lures are permitted to fish the 30-acre reservoir, 25 miles north of Cody.

To reach it drive north on WYO 120, continue about a mile past the turn off to the Chief Joseph Scenic Highway and watch for the Luce-Hogan Reservoirs sign on the left. Following hard rains, anglers driving small compact sedans should check on the condition of the unpaved road to the lakes before setting out.

The 3-mile road ends at the Hogan Reservoir campground. Luce Reservoir is a quarter-mile walk upstream.

The Kamloops, native to British Columbia, is a landlocked steelhead or ana-dromous rainbow. It grows big fast and is a strong fighter. Luce's Kamloops range from 13 inches to more than 24. Float-tubers do best at the lake since shrubs and trees line its shore.

Hogan Reservoir holds Snake River fine-spotted cutthroat trout and is open to all fishing, except with live bait. It is intended as an easy-to-reach family fishery, said Steve Yekel, a fisheries biologist.

Upper and Lower Sunshine Reservoirs

Upper and Lower Sunshine Reservoirs are west of Meeteetse, south of WYO 290 which parallels the Greybull River. The 600-acre Upper Sunshine is a 10-mile drive, and the 250-acre Lower Sunshine is at the next turnoff 5 miles down the road. Both are popular fisheries for 10- to 18-inch cutthroat.

In 1997, Cody angler Jeremy Rose put Upper Sunshine on the map with a new breed of fish that's been stocked in the lake. He set a state record for splake, a cross between a male brook trout and female lake trout. The 23-inch, 5.61-pound hybrid bested the old record by more than a pound-and-a-half.

Monster Lake

Monster Lake is a private reservoir on the Desert Ranch, located 10 miles south of Cody on WYO 120. With a moniker like that it better produce big fish. It does.

It advertises "Alaska-size" rainbows and cutthroat that "start at 7 pounds." Anglers report that 10- to 14-pound trout are caught on a regular basis and most fish average about 8 pounds. One of the ranch's rules is that no rods less than 5-weight are allowed. Fishing is strictly by reservation, and flyfishers must be accompanied by guides.

For information write Monster Lake Fly Fishing, 1558 RD. 9 1/2, Lovell, WY 82431, or call 800-840-5137 for reservations.

HIGH DESERT LAKES MAJOR HATCHES

Insect	A	M	J	J	A	S	O	N	Time	Flies
Callibaetis				X	X	X			A/E	**Dry:** Adams, Para-Adams, Sparkle Dun #10–14; **Wet:** Hare's Ear Nymph #10–14
Damsel Fly (nymphs)				X	X				M/A	Olive Marabou Damsel Nymph, Swimming Damsel, Olive Crystal Bugger; Woolly Bugger #8–12
Dragonfly (nymphs)				X	X					Assam Dragon, Olive or Brown Woolly Bugger; Crystal Bugger #6–10
Baetis			X	X	X	X	X			Blue-winged Olive, Blue Dun, Parachute Olive Hare's Ear, Olive Sparkle Dun #14–18; Pheasant Tail #16–18
Midge	X	X	X	X	X	X	X	X	A/E	**Dry:** Griffith's Gnat, Para-Adams, Palamino Midge #16–20; **Wet:** Chironomid, Serendipity #16–20
Trico				X	X	X			M/A	**Dry:** Black and White, Trico Spinner #18–22; **Wet:** Pheasant Tail #18–22
Caddis			X	X	X	X			A/E	**Dry:** Elk Hair Caddis, Hemingway Caddis, Stimulators #12–16; **Wet:** Hare's Ear Nymph, Soft-hackles #10–14
Flying Ant				X	X				M	Black Flying Ant, Black Elk Hair Caddis #14–18
Beetle			X	X	X	X			M/E	Foam Beetle, Disc O'Beetle, Olive Beetle, Black Elk Hair Caddis #12–16
Scud	X	X	X	X	X	X	X	X		Green, Pink, or Tan Scud #14–16
Leech	X	X	X	X	X	X	X	X		Mohair Leech, Marabou Leech, Swimming Leech (olive, black, or brown) #2–8
Chub	X	X	X	X	X	X	X	X		Muddler Minnow, Clouser Minnow, Girdlebug, Halfback, Woolly Bugger #2–10

HATCH TIME CODE: M = morning; A = afternoon; E = evening; D = dark; SF = spinner fall; // = continuation through periods.

Home of the Monsters
Cody Lake Harbors Gargantuan Trout

by Jack Parker

The name caught my eye. Monster Lake. While traveling the flyfishing show circuit, I heard stories of this trout heaven pop up. People, over and over, said Monster Lake was home to maybe the biggest rainbows in the United States. I also saw the brochures touting Alaska-sized rainbows just a few hours from Idaho Falls, Idaho. They boasted of 10- to 14-pound trout being caught on a regular basis and most fish averaging roughly 8 pounds.

Needless to say, I was hooked.

Monster Lake is a private reservoir on a ranch just 10 miles south of Cody, one of my favorite places to visit. Cody is the essence of the Old West, with a professional rodeo every night all summer long. In addition, huge herds of deer, elk, bighorn sheep, and buffalo can be seen between Cody and Yellowstone National Park, depending on the time of year.

But as much as I like Cody, I never associated it with fishing. I thought the closest fishing was Yellowstone National Park or the Big Horn River in Montana. Boy, was I wrong. Cody has at least three full time flyfishing shops selling great gear and booking trips. And where there are shops there has to be fishable water in the area to support them. And I soon learned that a short drive in any direction from Cody will get an angler to likely water.

My sights, however, were set on Monster Lake. This 150-acre lake is private, and a rod fee is required. I know that a lot of folks don't like or won't pay access fees, but it's getting more popular as anglers try to avoid crowds and catch quality fish.

Ted Rasmussen and I met Dick Brenkerfoff, the assistant ranch manager, for breakfast, and he filled us with food and coffee. We also met up with another friend from Idaho Falls, Steve Birrer, and his fishing partner, Arnie, who was visiting from Saudi Arabia.

We were prepared for the worst Mother Nature has to offer. You see, any time I've ever fished in Wyoming, the wind did not blow—it howled. This seemed to be the pattern as we drove to Cody. Flags, at least what was left of them, snapped in the wind, dust storms blew and tumbleweeds tumbled.

But the morning we met Dick seemed to be too good to be true. We had bright blue, cloudless skies, mild temperatures and no wind. We all agreed it couldn't last and just wondered when the wind would start.

At the lake, our host gave us a quick rundown of the areas to fish and told us about the best fly patterns. The food in Monster Lake had to be amazing to grow the huge trout it was producing. Fresh water shrimp were so abundant they clung to our waders while we waded. Leeches, damsels, dragonflies, mayflies, caddisflies and lots of minnows also fuel the amazing fishery.

It was suggested that we try big minnow and leech imitations to start. This was fine with me; I'd rather hook a big fish on a big fly than on a small one anytime. It was also recommended that we fish 10-pound tippet to handle the monsters.

As is my custom, I was the first one in the water and started with a No. 4 Zonker and a No. 6 black leech. The others soon joined me and tied on similar patterns.

Ted hooked the first fish, a beautiful rainbow of several pounds, but lost him at the net while I was trying to get a picture. Just then Arnie hooked his first. I tubed over to him for some pictures and to admire his trophy of almost 8 pounds. Before releasing him, I took a stomach sample to see what they were feeding on. I found tiny scuds and midge larva. Two fish within the first 10 minutes, so we ignored the telltale sign and none of us switched to smaller flies.

Three of the four of us had fish finders on our float tubes and we spotted lots of fish. However, getting them to hit was another story. After about an hour with no fish and bruised egos, we changed flies to change our luck.

Dick went to the east end of the lake and took a walk along the dam.

The fish were past spawning, and we assumed they were leaving the shallows and returning to deeper water, but Dick saw a number of fish in the shallows. So I abandoned my tube and switched techniques. But in my haste to get on the water, I left my floating line in the truck. I was fishing a No. 2, full-sink line that was not what I needed. But once I got my gear in order the switch worked.

Using a No. 14 beadhead nymph and a No. 16 midge, I started sight fishing to the big cruisers. Within the next few minutes, three great trout were caught and released. Stomach samples showed they were gorging themselves on midge pupa.

All of the fish were swimming in the same area and depth. Rigging a long leader with beadhead pupa, for weight to get down quick, as well as another pupa, I placed a strike indicator about 5 feet above the flies. The indicator held the flies in the zone where the fish were cruising, so they spotted them easily.

Over the next couple of hours, a dozen of the biggest rainbows and cutthroat I've ever seen were caught on this method. Some folks don't like "bobber" fishing, but those fish would make converts of even the most ardent purists.

Meanwhile, Ted stuck with dredging the depths with the big flies, and he caught rainbows that looked like they were on steroids.

As evening approached, more fish moved into the shore areas and fed aggressively in the surface film. We wanted to fish later into the evening, but we knew we had a five-hour drive ahead of us to get home.

While our float tubes were being loaded into the truck and our gear was stowed, the last two remaining fishermen on the lake shouted with joy as they hooked up with more huge trout. When I hit the truck seat, I finally realized how tired I was from the long day of fishing. It was a good tired, not the weariness of a day's work or lawn mowing. It was a satisfied feeling from fishing new water and catching some of the biggest and nicest trout of my life.

From now on, any time I visit Cody, I'll head to Monster Lake for another chance to catch the biggest trout of my life. With all of our local rivers being high and muddy in spring, it sounds pretty inviting.

Want to go?

Jack Parker, who has hugged monster trout in both the Northern and Southern Hemispheres, lives in Idaho Falls, Idaho.

A Monster rainbow taken off Monster Lake. (Photo by Jack Parker)

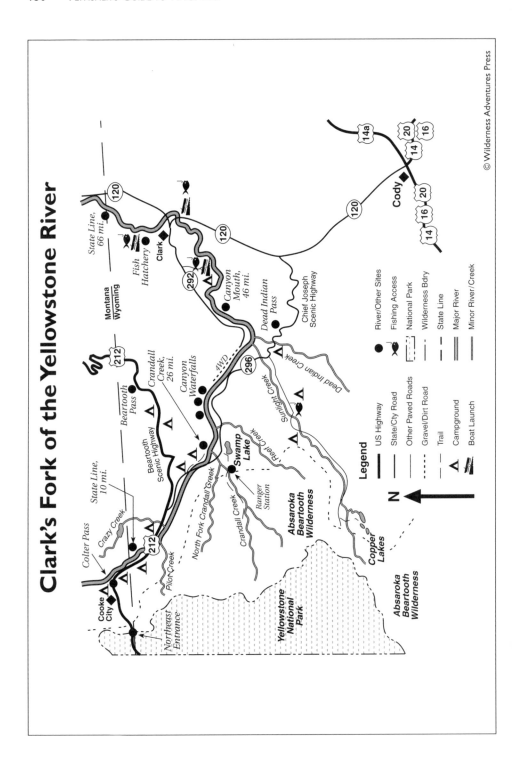

Clark's Fork of the Yellowstone River

© Wilderness Adventures Press

Legend

▬▬	US Highway	
──	State/Cty Road	
──	Other Paved Roads	
──	Gravel/Dirt Road	
····	Trail	
△	Campground	

●	River/Other Sites	
🐟	Fishing Access	
	National Park	
- -	Wilderness Bdry	
— —	State Line	
══	Major River	
──	Minor River/Creek	

N

CLARK'S FORK OF THE YELLOWSTONE

Clark's Fork of the Yellowstone is the arterial nucleus of one of the West's most remote and scenic getaways. Flyfishers who cast over its crystalline waters reap a sense of solitude lost amidst the madding crowds of nearby Yellowstone National Park. Their quarry is three species of wild trout.

Wyoming's only Wild and Scenic River, the Clark's Fork enters Wyoming from Montana through a rift in the rugged, glaciated Absaroka Mountains. To the northeast are the craggy, snow-capped peaks of the Beartooth Mountains, and to the southeast are the jagged Sawtooth Mountains. The dagger-point of Pilot Peak thrusts 11,708 feet into the sky above the northwest lip of the Sunlight Basin.

The river's 66-mile run through Wyoming promises good fishing for Yellowstone cutthroat, rainbow and brook trout in the upper half of the river. Grayling and brown trout add to the selection below the canyon on the river's desert run back to Montana.

But native Yellowstone cutthroat are having a tough time holding out against the rainbows, says Steve Yekel, a fisheries biologist for Wyoming Game and Fish in Cody. The department stopped stocking hatchery cutthroat in the upper river in 1988 because the restoration program wasn't working. That means most of the angling action in this section is now with wild rainbows. There is still a small population of cutthroats in the river and several tributaries. Brook trout are more common in the highest reaches of the river.

The canyon's waterfalls prevented brown trout from migrating upstream. The brookies, stocked by Montana, migrated into the upper Clark's Fork drainage from tributary streams in the Beartooth Plateau.

Good populations of 12- to 14-inch rainbows, with an occasional 16-incher, reside in the upper valley. Special regulations are giving the fish time to increase in size. The middle section through the 1,200-foot high walled gorge also contains all wild fish, mostly in the 12- to 14-inch class, with an occasional 18-incher.

The lower, slow-water section offers the potential for 20-inch browns. It receives hatchery plants of 8- to 12-inch rainbow and cutthroat, as well as grayling. Whitefish also are present.

Cessation of a prolonged drought has benefited a growing population of wild cutthroat in the lower river, according to Leland McDonald, Clark Fish Hatchery superintendent. Mountain cutthroat drop down to lower elevations as water levels recede in fall and return upstream to spawn on the spring floods. He said, "I suspect there are even some cutthroat coming up out of the Yellowstone River in these high-water years."

The Clark's Fork is most remembered as the daring escape route Chief Joseph and his fleeing bands of Nez Perce took out of Yellowstone for their ill-fated dash across Montana to Canada. The scenic byway, WYO 296, through the basin was named for Joseph. It wasn't paved until 1994.

To reach Sunlight Basin from Cody take WYO 120 north to WYO 296. The major hump on the Chief Joseph Scenic Highway is 8,060-foot Dead Indian Pass. From the north, the basin is reached by driving east through Yellowstone to Cooke City, Montana, and over 8,000-foot Colter Pass via U.S. 212. The other option is to take U.S.

212 south from Red Lodge, Montana, over the Beartooth Scenic Highway and its 10,947-foot pass.

The Clark's Fork is open year-round to fishing, but Colter and Beartooth passes are blocked by snow until late May. All three routes are worth the scenery alone. But the main objective is wild and uninhibited trout, incredible fly hatches, and unprecedented solitude.

A Wyoming fishing license can be purchased in Cooke City or Cody. Also gas up your vehicle and replenish supplies as there are no towns and few resorts between Cooke City and Cody. The Forest Service provides a dozen campgrounds along the scenic routes.

The Clark's Fork descends from 8,500 feet at its headwaters in the Absaroka Mountains behind Cooke City to 3,000 feet at its northeastern crossing of the state line. The most dramatic loss of elevation is nearly 3,000 feet in its gallop down the gorge. Three waterfalls and sheer cliffs make the middle of the canyon inaccessible.

From the state line to Crandall Creek, the river meanders 15 miles in a moderate descent down a high-mountain, forested valley. Most of this stretch is easily waded, except for several low-walled canyon runs. To be safe, resist going in up to your waist in swift runs and pocket waters.

At Crandall Creek, the river cascades into the canyon and hurls 20 miles through boulder-strewn pocket waters, deep plunge pools and swirling eddies. It's challenging fishing, but doable if you're into boulder-hopping and bank-hugging. Don't wear waders; wear shorts and sneakers. Don't even think about wading or swimming in the canyon.

The canyon is the Wild and Scenic River section of this rollicking stream, and it is very popular with kayakers, too. Trailheads into it are at Reef, Russell, Crandall and Dead Indian Creeks.

Emerging from the canyon, the Clark Fork's flows slowly, meandering 25 miles across a sagebrush-dotted high desert back to the Montana border. From there, it flows another 72 miles to its confluence with the Yellowstone River.

Public access is excellent. Highways parallel most of the upper Clark's Fork, where for about 25 miles the river passes through the Shoshone National Forest. Anglers can stop to fish anywhere along the road, except at a few housing developments and ranches. The highway leaves the canyon at Sunlight Creek, but its mouth can be reached via a rough, gravel road (WYO 292). The turnoff from WYO 120 is just south of Clark. At the forest boundary a 4-wheel-drive trail continues upstream.

The lower river runs through private land, but there are four public access sites managed by Wyoming Game and Fish. It also offers the only safe option to float-fish the Clark's Fork. Float-boaters who continue past the Clark Fish Hatchery need to obtain permission to pull out downstream. Waders also must follow the rules posted at access sites.

Spring runoff can extend through June, possibly into mid-July. Flows usually remain steady through late summer to September, when they may pick up again from autumn storms. "It makes for pretty good wading," Yekel said.

*Pilot Peak
above the Clark's Fork.*

The best places to get off alone on the Clark's Fork are found in the canyon. For a less strenuous approach to solitude on the upper waters, wait until after Labor Day. "It's pretty busy (in summer) anymore, except for the canyon," Yekel said.

Chip Andrews of North Fork Anglers in Cody agreed. "The Clark's Fork canyon can be a little difficult to get into, but that's part of its charm."

Autumn fishing can be phenomenal, Andrews said. "There's excellent dry fly action in the fall, September to October, and it's less crowded."

The lower river at the mouth of the canyon also fishes best after Labor Day.

A standard set of dry flies and attractors for the Clark's Fork is much the same as for the North Fork of the Shoshone. Its hatches also mirror its sister river.

Golden stones and early caddis announce the dry fly season in late June and early July. Green drakes arrive in July, too, followed by western green drakes, or

An angler on the Clark's Fork.

Flavs, and pale morning duns, and in August by pale evening duns. Swarms of baetis, or blue-winged olives, and midges can occur on western rivers just about any time in a season.

Before embarking for the Clark's Fork, check your fishing vest pockets for these flies: tan- and olive-bodied elk hair caddis; yellow and red humpies; orange and yellow stimulators; Adams; gray and yellow Wulffs; pale morning duns; blue-winged olives and western green drakes, or Flavs; and olive parachute hare's ear patterns in sizes 12 to 18. Larger attractors also should include golden stone patterns, orange bucktails, and yellow Sallies, 8 to 14.

Small emergers and nymphs like soft-hackles, halfbacks, beadhead Prince and hare's ear nymphs, 12 to 16, are effective dropper flies to trail behind bigger dry flies. Large woolly buggers, yuk bugs, girdlebugs or black rubberlegs, Bitch Creek nymphs, or Montana stones, 2 to 10, and Zug Bugs and golden stone nymphs, 6 to 14, can be fished alone or in tandem with nymphs and emergers.

The grasshopper action in the upper reach is best in August and September, and may kick in as early as late July in a warm year. Dave's or Joe's hoppers, parahoppers, Madam Xs, and Turk's tarantulas, 2 to 10, are standard fare here, and just about anywhere in the West at this time.

View of the Clark's Fork Canyon from Dead Indian Pass.

Andrews' boss, Tim Wade, has taken the Turk's concept a step further by designing a rubberleg hopper specifically for pounding up trout on the Clark's Fork and its tributaries. A spade-is-a-spade kind of guy, Wade calls it "The Whore."

Big buggy patterns that don't drown in the violent waters of its canyon and pocket water stretches are a hallmark of fishing the Clark's Fork. Another aspect of its charm appears when tiny mayflies shimmering in the fading light of day demand delicate flies and exquisite presentation.

Mayflies become their most microscopic by fall, when the river's best "match the hatch" challenges occur at dusk. But the lower river also gets a gray drake hatch that can be matched with gray Wulffs, gray drake spinners, Adams, and para-Adams, 10 to 14.

The choices this fertile river presents keep anglers hopping just like its wild trout. Its generosity makes it an excellent choice for a family trip or for beginners. Yet it provides enough challenges to satisfy even the most dedicated of dry fly purists.

And the scenery is spectacular.

Stream Facts:
Clark's Fork of the Yellowstone River

Season
- River is open to fishing year-round.

Regulations
- From state line to Reef Creek limit is 6 trout per day or in possession, none over 8 inches; artificial flies and lures only. From Reef Creek through canyon to Shoshone National Forest boundary, 3 trout per day or in possession, only 1 over 12 inches. From forest boundary to state line, 6 trout per day or in possession, no size restrictions.

Trout
- Rainbows are in 10- to 14-inch range in upper reaches, plus a few 16-inchers; also a few cutthroat and brook trout. In the canyon, rainbows are in the 10- to 14-inch class with chances for 18-inch or larger fish. Lower stretch below canyon holds bigger fish, including brown trout, and is one of few streams in the West with grayling. Crandall Creek harbors a healthy cutthroat population. Sunlight Creek has larger than average brook trout.

Miles
- Mile 10: Wyoming–Montana state line
- Mile 26: Crandall Creek
- Mile 46: Canyon mouth
- Mile 66: Wyoming–Montana state line

Character
- Wyoming's only Wild and Scenic River, the Clark's Fork meanders from the state line to Crandall Creek through a high-mountain, forested valley. Flows descend in a series of riffles and glides, scattered pocket waters, and occasional deep runs, pools, and braided channels. At Crandall Creek, it plunges into a deep, scenic canyon and dashes 20 miles through boulder-strewn pocket waters, deep pools and strong eddies. Waterfalls in the middle of the 1,200-foot canyon make it inaccessible. At the canyon mouth, the river flows onto a high sagebrush desert and meanders to the state line.

Flows
- Spring runoff begins in April and peaks in June. In exceptionally wet years, high flows can extend into July. Best fishing is in late summer and autumn. Steady late season flows may rise briefly after autumn storms.

Access

- Upper river and tributaries flow almost entirely through Shoshone National Forest along U.S. 212 and WYO 296. A few private inholdings and ranches, particularly along Sunlight Creek, are the only restrictions to public access. It is mostly easy wading in top stretches, but do not go in above your knees in deeper runs. Do not wear waders or attempt to wade anywhere in the canyon. On the lower river, below the canyon, there is public access at the Clark Fish Hatchery and three other Wyoming Game and Fish sites near the town of Clark. The lower end of the canyon is at the end of a rough gravel road (WYO 292) southwest of Clark

Camping

- There are 10 national forest campgrounds located along Chief Joseph Scenic Highway between Cody and Cooke City.
- Commercial campgrounds for RVs and tents are located in Cody and Cooke City.

CLARK'S FORK OF THE YELLOWSTONE MAJOR HATCHES

Insect	A	M	J	J	A	S	O	N	Time	Flies
Golden Stone									A	**Dry:** Golden Stone, Orange Stimulator, Yellow Sally #8–10; **Wet:** Halfback Nymph, Black Rubberlegs, Girdlebug, Bitch Creek Nymph #6–10
Baetis									A/E	Blue-winged Olive, Blue Dun, Adams, Parachute Olive Hare's Ear #16–18
Green Drake									A	Green Drake, Flav, Extended Body Drake #10–12
Western Green Drake (Flav)									A	Flav, Olive Parachute Hare's Ear, Blue-winged Olive, Adams #12–14
Caddis									M/D	**Dry:** Elk Hair Caddis, Yellow or Royal Humpy, Yellow Sally #12–16; **Wet:** Caddis Emerger, Soft-hackles, Prince Nymph #12–16
Pale Morning Dun									M/A	**Dry:** PMD, Light Cahill, Sparkle Dun #16–18; **Wet:** Hare's Ear Nymph, Pheasant Tail, Beadheads #14–18
Pale Evening Dun									A/E	Pale Evening Dun, PMD, Sparkle Dun, Light Cahill #16–18
Gray Drake									M/A	Gray Drake, Adams, Para-Adams, Gray Wulff #10–12
Midge									A/E	Griffith's Gnat, Black and White Midge #18–22
Terrestrials									A/E	Joe's Hopper, Dave's Hopper, Madam X, Parachute Hopper #8–14; Ants #16–18; Foam Beetle, Disc O'Beetle, Black Elk Hair Caddis #14–16

HATCH TIME CODE: M = morning; A = afternoon; E = evening; D = dark; SF = spinner fall; // = continuation through periods.

SUNLIGHT BASIN SIDE TRIPS

Three tributaries of the Clark's Fork—Sunlight, Crandall and Dead Indian Creeks—offer excellent fishing for alpine cutthroat, rainbow and brook trout of respectable size. For information on what's happening on the tributaries, check with the North Fork Anglers fly shop in Cody.

The Sunlight Basin also has a trophy brook trout lake and a chain of three alpine lakes harboring the rare golden trout.

"Each of these are separate fisheries and deserve at least one day of fishing each," said Tim Wade, owner of North Fork Anglers. "Although the trout aren't huge in these tributaries, every once in a while a 16-, even a 19-incher, shows up in a long pool behind a log jam. Enough so to keep one fishing upstream."

Wade's partner, Chip Andrews, bragged of curing a case of cabin fever by netting a 20-inch cutthroat in Crandall Creek several years ago in early spring before the runoff.

All three creeks are rated by Wyoming Game and Fish as good fishing for Yellowstone cutthroat, rainbow, and brook trout. Crandall and Dead Indian's fish average 8 to 12 inches. Sunlight's fish average 8 to 14 inches, and it is noted for holding above average brookies.

Public access is unrestricted on Crandall and Dead Indian, which flow through Shoshone National Forest. Lower Sunlight Creek is lined by ranches. Wyoming Game and Fish provides an access site about half-way up this stretch. At the forest boundary a gravel road continues another 6 miles upstream. There also is a Forest Service campground on the upper waters of the creek.

"Sunlight Creek has good fishing with brook trout down low and cutthroat up above," said Ron McKnight, Region 2 fisheries manager.

Above its headwaters are the three Copper Lakes nestled below the crest of the Absaroka Wilderness. The department is looking at the Copper Lakes as a source of golden trout eggs for its stocking program, but heavy winter snows and ice in 1996 and 1997 made it impossible to get into the lakes during the spawn, McKnight said. A new source of eggs is needed because a wild brood stock in Surprise Lake near Pinedale was lost in a forest fire in 1995.

The Copper Lakes' golden trout average 9 to 10 inches, with some going up to 16 inches. Copper 1 is 35 acres and holds the largest fish of the three lakes. "They could take some (fishing) pressure," McKnight said. The trailhead is 2 miles up a 4-wheel-drive road that continues up Sunlight Creek from the Forest Service gravel road. The 1.5-mile climb up to Copper 1 is a steep climb, McKnight warned. "Golden trout reside only in high alpine lakes," he said. "They're tough to get into but I guess that's the reward of golden trout fishing."

An easier proposition is Swamp Lake, a drive-in lake managed as a trophy brook trout fishery. The 10-acre lake on Corral Creek is 2 miles southeast of the Crandall Ranger Station. It can be reached via Forest Road 128.

Fishing at Swamp Lake is flyfishing or lures only. The limit is 2 fish per day or in possession, only 1 over 12 inches.

State Breeds
A Better Cutthroat

Native trout devotees can take heart. The Clark Fish Hatchery is developing a new brood stock of Yellowstone cutthroat.

A visit to the hatchery north of Cody was prompted by the startling sight of a young man with a long-handled net dipping trout out of Yellowstone River's LeHardy's Rapids.

Wyoming went to the park to collect eggs and milt, or fish sperm, because of the poor performance of its previous brood stocks in streams. The state's first brood stock came from Paint Rock Creek, a tributary of the Big Horn River, in 1972. The advantage of making collections at LeHardy's Rapids is the park's large population of pure Yellowstone cutthroat and the dual nature of the river's fishery, said Mike Stone, Wyoming's chief of fisheries. "It's definitely better than just having a lake (dwelling) fish."

The second brood stock was acquired from Montana, which had developed it from cutthroat in McBride Lake in Yellowstone Park. Leland McDonald, hatchery superintendent, also stressed that while many of the cutthroat in the upper Yellowstone are lake dwellers that run out of the lake to spawn, there are year-round resident trout in the river, too.

Only a portion of the eggs and milt were collected from each cutthroat caught at the rapids so that the fish could still spawn naturally. Collections ended in 1996 after four years of netting. The project's goal is to develop a 250-pair brood stock.

"We're making the switch because we feel it will do better in running water and won't do any worse than the McBride (stock) in lakes," McDonald said. "Generally, fish that do well in streams also perform well in lakes, but the reverse doesn't always pan out."

McDonald noted there are obvious differences between the LeHardy brood stock and the "very domesticated" McBride stock. The LeHardy stock has more wild characteristics, like fewer, smaller eggs. The survival rate is lower, too, but the spawning period is longer. Its progeny "probably will do real well in the wild," McDonald added.

The cutthroat will be stocked in about 20 waters, including a few streams unable to fulfill the state's wild trout management policy. Most will be within the fish's native range "unless there's a compelling reason we stock (a stream or lake) with only Yellowstone cutthroat," McDonald added

Like a doting father, McDonald suggested a tour of the spring-fed pond holding the progenitors of the new brood stock. True to their nature, the cutthroat were not overly bashful. As we approached, they made a short dash to deeper water but many soon reappeared, swimming in lazy figure-eights in search of their next meal.

McDonald obliged. Snaring a grasshopper from a nearby reed, he tossed it onto the pond. The wriggling insect disappeared in an instant. The rise form was a classic-gentle ripples of undulating water flaring out toward the bank in a widening circle of rings.

Fish netting for Yellowstone cutthroat on the LeHardy Rapids of the Yellowstone. The eggs and milt collected from the fish will provide a more viable brood stock for Wyoming's waters.

Beartooth Wilderness Lakes

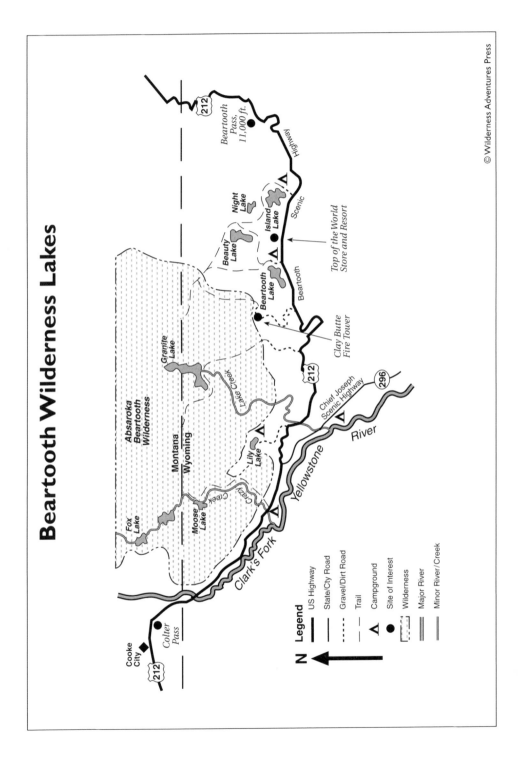

Legend

N

— US Highway

⋮ State/Cty Road

--- Gravel/Dirt Road

— — Trail

△ Campground

● Site of Interest

▨ Wilderness

Major River

Minor River/Creek

© Wilderness Adventures Press

Beartooth Wilderness Lakes

The Beartooth Wilderness straddles the Montana–Wyoming border east and north of Yellowstone National Park. The Big Sky state calls the Beartooth Plateau "The Roof of Montana." Not to be outdone, Wyoming declares it is "The Top of the World."

Scattered like pearls across this high, broad plateau are 1,000 lakes; more than 430 hold trout or grayling. Most are above timberline at 8,500 feet or higher. Granite peaks surrounding the plateau soar to more than 11,000 feet.

The Beartooths' fabulous alpine scenery draws hundreds of adventurous souls with iron lungs and steel thighs. For flyfishers, brilliant iridescent trout in a lake at trail's end make all the huffing and puffing worth the effort. For a fortunate few, the ultimate reward is a lake with a hatch in progress, dimpled with hundreds of concentric circles from the rise-forms of feeding fish. But windows of opportunity are short on alpine lakes. Above timberline, ice break up occurs most years in late June or early July, and snowfall threatens again by September or early October.

The species list for the multitude of lakes and streams ranges from native Yellowstone cutthroat to brook, rainbow, and golden trout, splake and lake trout to grayling.

Sizes vary with lake conditions and fish populations. Most are filled with pan-sized brookies begging to be caught. Wyoming encourages harvest with a 10-fish bonus on brook trout 8 inches or smaller.

Anglers who haven't visited the Beartooths for a few years can expect to be surprised. A variety of new species are being stocked in winterkilled lakes and previously barren waters. Cutthroat have been added to Native, Elk, and Long Lakes. Sterile lake trout have gone to T, Granite, and Twin Lakes, and splake—a cross between lake and brook trout—to Claw and Horseshoe Lakes. Golden trout now reside in Snyder Lake. "Our intention is to get as much diversity as we can," said Ron McKnight, Region 2 fisheries manager for Wyoming Game and Fish.

The department manages 108 Beartooth lakes as fisheries. Only one—Little Moose Lake east of Crazy Creek—has restricted regulations. It is managed as a trophy fishery for Yellowstone cutthroat. "You can start in June along the highway (on Beartooth, Island and Long Lakes) and can fish into October—if you are tough," McKnight said.

Fly choices are very basic for high mountain lakes and streams. Dry fly action is limited in midsummer, so plan on mostly working the lakes with wet flies. Concentrate on shorelines and shallows and use a dropper fly to speed up prospecting. Dry flies include the standard mayfly, caddis, midge, and small terrestrial patterns. The most common mayfly in lakes is the callibaetis. Attractor patterns include Adams, renegades, ants, beetles, humpies, stimulators, royal Wulffs, and Coachmans. Wet flies for high lakes range from leech patterns, small streamers, and woolly buggers to beadhead nymphs, chironomid or green midge pupa, soft-hackle nymphs, Carey's Special, Prince nymph, hare's ear nymph, green caddis

The Beartooth.

emerger, peacock emerger, and pheasant tail nymph to green scud and gray or green shrimp patterns.

Rod choices depend on conditions or length of the hike into a lake. A three-piece, 8-foot, 5- or 6-weight travel rod with a weight-forward or floating line and medium sinking tip is handy on longer trips. Big lakes or windy conditions may require a 9-foot 6- or 7-weight rod.

At these elevations snow can occur any time of the year. Pack for early spring or fall-like conditions even in midsummer. Summer squalls, sometimes accompanied by intense lightning, are common and can drop the temperature by 20 degrees. Always include rain gear, a sweater, wool socks, knit cap and gloves or mittens in your daypack. Don't forget insect repellent. Take note, too, that this is grizzly bear country. Never hike alone—groups of three or four are recommended—and keep a clean camp.

Anglers drift on Island Lake in the Beartooth Mountains.

Plan a minimum of three days for really high or remote lakes. If you intend to cross the border, a Montana fishing license is needed.

Maps are available from the Shoshone and Gallatin national forests. Topographical maps help to plan extended hikes or determine elevation gains of shorter ones. Wyoming trailheads are the starting points of many routes recommended by Bill Schneider in *The Trail Guide to the Beartooths.*

The lowest principal trailhead is at Crazy Creek in the Clark's Fork valley. Four higher ones en route to the Beartooth Pass are at Muddy Creek, Clay Butte, Beartooth Lake, and Island Lake.

To reach the top of the Beartooth Wilderness fast, take U.S. 212 east from Cooke City over the Beartooth Scenic Highway. An equally picturesque route is north out of Cody on WYO 120 to WYO 296. The Chief Joseph Scenic Highway follows the Clark's Fork of the Yellowstone northwest to U.S. 212

NORTHWEST HUB CITIES
Cody
Elevation—5,016 • Population—7,900

Founded by William F. "Buffalo Bill" Cody in 1896, Cody is the quintessential Old West tourist town. The Cody Nite Rodeo has been a summer feature since 1938. The Buffalo Bill Historical Center has a vast collection of western exhibits in its four museums—the Buffalo Bill Museum, the Plains Indian Museum, the Cody Firearms Museum, and the Whitney Gallery of Western Art. Only an hour's drive to the west is Yellowstone National Park via the Wapiti Valley of the North Fork of the Shoshone River. President Teddy Roosevelt called it the most scenic 50 miles in North America. Just two miles from the park is Buffalo Bill's original hunting lodge, Pahaska Teepee. And The Irma, the hotel named for his daughter, is still the town's favorite watering hole. An hour northwest of town is Sunlight Basin and Wyoming's only Wild and Scenic River, the Clark's Fork of the Yellowstone. Both the Clark's Fork and North Fork are rated as two of the best dry fly streams in the West. Their feeder streams flowing down the Absaroka Mountains in the Shoshone National Forest further entice flyfishers to the highlands. Down on the sagebrush flats, float-tubers find trophy trout in the High Desert Lakes north and south of town. Cody stands ready to serve and entertain tourists and anglers, alike.

Cody's zip code is 82414.

Accommodations

Big Bear Motel, 139 West Yellowstone Avenue / 307-587-3117 / 42 rooms / Pets allowed / $

Buffalo Bill Village, 1701 Sheridan Avenue / 307-587-5555 / 83 rooms / $$

Frontier Motel, 1801 Mountain View Drive / 307-527-7119 / 28 rooms / $$

The Irma Hotel, 1192 Sheridan Avenue / 307-587-4221 / 40 rooms / $$

Western 6 Gun Motel, 423 West Yellowstone Avenue / 307-587-4835 / 40 rooms / Pets allowed / $$

Buffalo Bill Cody House (B&B), 101 Robertson Street / 307-587-2528 / Hosts: Mr. & Mrs. Philip W. Robertson

The Bunkhouse Bed & Breakfast, 410 West Yellowstone Avenue / 307-527-5132 / Hosts: Lloyd Tice and George Steadham

Wind Chimes Cottage Bed & Breakfast, 1501 Beck Avenue / 307-527-5310 / Host: Hardy Stucki

Pahaska Teepee, 183 Yellowstone Hwy / 307-527-7701 or 800-628-7791 / Cabins, restaurant and lounge, and grocery/gas station

Crossed Sabres Ranch, Wapiti, WY 82450 / 307-587-3750 / Guest ranch

The Lodge at June Creek, 1710 Yellowstone Hwy, P.O. Box 110, Wapiti, WY 82450 / 307-587-2143 / Guest ranch

Rimrock Ranch, 2728 North Fork Route / 307-587-3970 / Guest ranch

Campgrounds and RV Parks

Cody KOA Kampground, 5561 Greybull Highway / 307-587-2369 / Open May 1 to October 1 / 100 RV and 90 tent sites / Full services

Gateway Motel & Campground, 203 Yellowstone Avenue / 307-587-2561 / Open April 1 to October 1 / 74 RV and tent sites / Full services

Parkway Village & RV Campground, 132 West Yellowstone Avenue / 307-527-5927 / Open May 1 to October 30 / 25 RV sites / Full services

Camp Cody RV Park, 415 Yellowstone Avenue / 307-587-9730 / Open year-round / 83 RV sites / Full services

Restaurants

Cary Inn Restaurant, 3946 Crandall Road / 307-527-5510

Franca's Italian Dining, 421 Rumsey Avenue / 307-587-5354

Granny's Restaurant, 1550 Sheridan Avenue / 307-587-4829

The Irma Hotel, 1192 Sheridan Avenue / 307-587-4221

The Proud Cut Saloon, 1227 Sheridan Avenue / 307-527-6905

Zapatas, 325 West Yellowstone Hwy / 307-587-3961

Veterinarians

Blessing Animal Hospital, 2627 Big Horn Avenue / 307-587-4324

Cody Veterinary Hospital, 5524 Greybull Highway (U.S. 14/16/20) / 307-587-3151

Outfitters

Aune's Absaroka Angler, 754 Yellowstone Avenue / 307-587-5105

North Fork Anglers, 1438 Sheridan Avenue / 307-527-7274

Yellowstone Troutfitters, 239A Yellowstone Avenue / 307-587-8240

Yellowstone Outfitters, Cody, WY / Contact Dennis Williams, 307-754-2496, or Ed Conkle, 307-754-6709

Monster Lake, Desert Ranch 10 miles south of Cody on WYO 120 / For reservations, write Monster Lake Fly Fishing, 1558 RD. 9½, Lovell, WY 82431; or call 800-840-5137

Fly Shops

Aune's Absaroka Angler, 754 Yellowstone Avenue / 307-587-5105

North Fork Anglers, 1438 Sheridan Avenue / 307-527-7274

Yellowstone Troutfitters, 239A Yellowstone Avenue / 307-587-8240

Rocky Mountain Discount Sports, 1820 Sheridan Avenue / 307-527-6071

Auto Rental and Repair

Free Spirit Car Rental, 2130 Big Horn Avenue / 307-587-8538

Hertz Rent-A-Car, Box 847, Cody, WY 82414 / 307-587-2914

Rent-A-Wreck of Cody, 2515 Greybull Hill / 307-527-5549

Graham Motor Co., 2226 Big Horn Avenue / 307-587-6211

LA Service, 2830 Big Horn Avenue / 307-587-8464
Mobile Service, 2517 Frank Court / 307-527-6531

Air Service
Yellowstone Regional Airport, 1 mile south of Cody / Served by Skywest–Delta Connection via Salt Lake and United Express via Denver / Charter services available / 307-587-5096

Medical
West Park Hospital, 707 Sheridan Avenue / 307-527-7501 or 800-654-9447

For More Information
Cody Chamber of Commerce
836 Sheridan Avenue
P.O. Box 2777
Cody, WY 82414
307-587-2777 or 307-527-6228

Cooke City, Montana
Elevation—7,500 • Population—300

Cooke City and its sister community, Silver Gate, are rustic mountain hamlets retaining elements of their gold mining history that preceded the founding of Yellowstone National Park. Yellowstone's Northeast Entrance is 4 miles west of Cooke City at the end of the two most picturesque drives to the park: The Beartooth Scenic Highway via U.S. 212 from Red Lodge, Montana, and the Chief Joseph Scenic Highway via WYO 296 from Cody. Soda Butte Creek flows through the two hamlets and leads anglers to the Lamar River and Yellowstone's superb fishing. Just over Colter Pass and east of Cooke City, you will find the headwaters of the Clark's Fork of the Yellowstone, an unforgettable invitation to Wyoming's blue ribbon trout streams. Beartooth Pass (11,000 feet) and Colter Pass (8,000 feet) on U.S. 212 are blocked by snow until late May. The road from Gardiner, Montana, via Mammoth and the Park's Lamar Valley is open year-round.
Cooke City's zip code is 59020.

Accommodations
Alpine Motel, Main Street, Box 1030, Cooke City, MT 59020 / 406-838-2262 / 25 rooms / $$
Antlers Lodge, U.S. 212 / 406-838-2432 / 18 rooms / $
Elkhorn Lodge, 208 Main Street / 406-838-2332 / 6 rooms / Pets allowed / $$$
Grizzly Lodge, U.S. 212, Box 9, Silver Gate, MT 59081 / 406-838-2219 / 17 rooms / $$

Park View Cabins and Motel, U.S. 212, Box 19, Silver Gate, MT 59081 / 406-838-2371 / 14 rooms / Pets allowed / $
Range Rider's Lodge, U.S. 212, Silver Gate, MT 59081 / 406-838-2359 / 18 rooms / $$

Campgrounds and RV Parks
Big Moose Resort, 3 miles east of Cooke City on U.S. 212 / 406-838-2393 / Open June 1 to September 30 / 10 tent and 6 RV sites / 7 cabins / Store / Pets allowed

Restaurants
Beartooth Cafe, Highway 212
Pine Tree Cafe & Cabins, 315 Main Street

Veterinarians
None.

Outfitters
Beartooth Plateau Outfitters, Main Street (P.O. Box 1127), Cooke City, MT 59020 / 406-838-2328 or 800-253-8545
Greater Yellowstone Flyfishers, 211 W. Main (P.O. Box 1150), Cooke City, MT 59020 / 406-838-2468
Skyline Guide Service, Box 507, Cooke City, MT 59020 / 406-838-2380

Fly Shops and Sporting Goods
Beartooth Plateau Outfitters, Main Street (P.O. Box 1127), Cooke City, MT 59020 / 406-838-2328 or 800-253-8545

Auto Rental and Repair
No auto rental.
Nearest repair shop and wrecker service is Yellowstone National Park at Canyon Village.

Air Service
None.

Medical
Yellowstone National Park's Lake Hospital, 307-242-7241
Mammoth Clinic, 307-344-7965

For More Information
Call Town Hall at 838-2495.

Yellowstone National Park

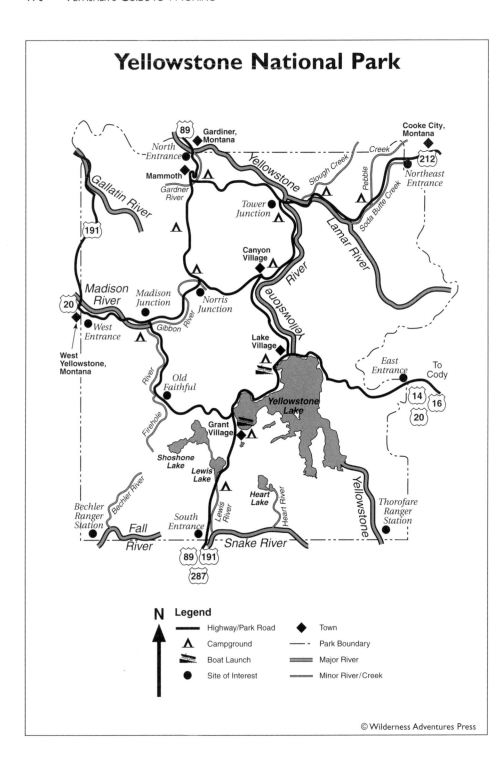

© Wilderness Adventures Press

Yellowstone National Park

Yellowstone National Park was "dedicated and set apart as a public park or pleasuring ground for the benefit and enjoyment of the people" and "for the preservation, from injury or spoilation, of all timber, mineral deposits, natural curiosities, or wonders...and their retention in their natural condition," by Congress on March 1, 1872.

Yellowstone is the first and oldest national park in the world. The commanding features that initially attracted interest and led to the preservation of Yellowstone are its geological wonders. There are more geysers and hot springs in the park than in the rest of the world combined. The colorful Grand Canyon of the Yellowstone River, fossil forests, and the size and elevation of Yellowstone Lake also make it unique.

Today, the park is famous for its unique concentrations of wildlife, including elk, bison, moose, deer, grizzly bears, black bears, wolves, coyotes, trumpeter swans, and bald eagles. The park's native trout, the Yellowstone cutthroat, is a prime attraction to both wildlife watchers and anglers.

Cultural sites dating back 12,000 years are evidence of the park's human history. More recent history can be seen in structures and sites that represent the various periods of park administration and visitor facilities development.

Ninety-nine percent of the park's 3,400 square miles (2.2 million acres) remain undeveloped, providing a wide range of habitat types that support one of the continent's largest and most varied large mammal populations. Yellowstone is a true wilderness, one of the few large, natural areas remaining in the Lower 48.

Visitors meet nature here on its own terms. Park regulations exist for visitor safety and for the protection of natural and cultural resources. Please obey all park rules and regulations.

Summer days are in the 70s and 80s with cool nights in the 40s. Summer thunderstorms are common. Mild to cool temperatures linger through September and October. Rain gear is recommended during spring, summer, and fall. The first heavy snows fall by November 1 and continue through March, with snow and frost possible during any month.

Coping with the Crowds

More than 3 million tourists visit Yellowstone annually, primarily between Memorial Day and September 30, but it is almost always crowded when roads are open. Traffic through the park's loop roads is slow and delays occur often. Anticipate these delays and don't expect to arrive at planned destinations at highway speeds.

The five entrances to the park are reached from the following gateway communities: North Entrance—Gardiner, Montana; Northeast Entrance—Cooke City, Montana; East Entrance—Cody, Wyoming; South Entrance—Jackson Hole, Wyoming; and West Entrance—West Yellowstone, Montana. In addition, the park's southwest corner —Cascade Corner, home of the Fall and Bechler River drainages—can be accessed from Ashton, Idaho, but has no connecting roads to the rest of the park.

Park roads open in May as early as conditions permit and close after the first Sunday in November. The only road open year-round is from Gardiner to Cooke City.

A visit to Yellowstone requires advance planning and timing. During the summer season, lodging and camping facilities in the park and its gateway communities generally fill by early afternoon. Reservations are essential for main season stays at the park's lodges and inns, and equally important for gateway communities. Some reservations for park accommodations are made as much as a year in advance.

All reservations for accommodations and designated campgrounds in the park are handled by Amfac Resorts, which operates lodges in Yellowstone and other parks. The number for Yellowstone is 307-344-7311. There is no toll-free number.

Accommodations are available on a seasonal basis at the following locations:
- Mammoth Hot Springs: Mammoth Hot Springs Hotel and cabins.
- Tower Junction: Roosevelt Lodge and cabins
- Canyon Village: Canyon Village Lodge
- Lake Village: Lake Hotel and cabins, Lake Lodge and cabins
- Grant Village: Grant Village Motel
- Old Faithful Village: Old Faithful Inn, Old Faithful Lodge, Snow Lodge

Camping in the park opens May 1 and ends November 3, except at Mammoth, which is open year-round.

Seasonal campground reservations can be made for the following sites in the southern half of the park: Bridge Bay, Canyon Village, Fishing Bridge recreational vehicle area (hard-sided vehicles only), Grant Village, and Madison Junction.

Park campgrounds not available for reservations are located at Mammoth, Norris, Indian Creek, Slough Creek, Pebble Creek, and Tower Falls in the northern half of the park, and Lewis Lake Campground near the South Entrance. They frequently fill by noon. Arrive early, plan carefully, and seek information at visitor centers.

Yellowstone's headquarters are located at Mammoth, and visitor centers are located at each of the villages on the park's loop road. Shaped like a figure 8, the loop road parallels most of the park's major rivers.

A park permit is required to fish in Yellowstone's waters, and the park has its own set of fishing regulations. Advance reservations are required for backcountry campsites. Other activities such as boating, canoeing, and snowmobiling also require registration, permits, or licenses. Special regulations may apply, so take the time to become informed at any visitor center or ranger station.

For more information write, Yellowstone National Park, Attn: Visitor's Service, P.O. Box 168, Yellowstone National Park, Wyoming 82190-0168; or call 307-344-7381 or 307-344-2386.

Additional information on permits, fees, and reservations is in the appendix of this guide.

Yellowstone Quick Facts

Size
- 3,472 square miles (8,987 square km), 2,219,823 acres (898,714 hectares)
- 63 miles north to south (102km), 54 miles east to west (87km). It is larger than Rhode Island and Delaware combined, with 91 percent located in Wyoming, 7.6 percent in Montana, and 1.4 percent in Idaho.

Topography
- Highest point: 11,358 ft (3462m)—Eagle Peak
- Lowest point: 5,282 ft (1610m)—Reese Creek
- Tallest waterfall: 308 feet (94m) at Lower Falls of the Yellowstone River.
- Approximately 5 percent is covered by water; 15 percent is meadow and grassland, and 80 percent is forested.

Weather
- Precipitation ranges from 10 inches (26 cm) at north boundary to 80 inches (205 cm) in the southwest corner. Temperatures range from 10°F (–12°C) mean in January, to 55°F (13°C) mean in July at Lake Yellowstone in the center of the park.

Flora
- 8 species of conifers, with approximately 80 percent of the forests comprised of lodgepole pine. Approximately 1,050 species of native vascular plants and 168 species of exotic (nonnative) plants .

Wildlife
- Largest concentration of free-roaming wildlife in the Lower 48 states and the global temperate zone. There are 7 species of native ungulates (hoofed mammals), 2 species of bears, and approximately 49 species of other mammals, 290 species of birds, 18 species of fish (5 nonnative), 6 species of reptiles, 4 species of amphibians. Five species are protected as threatened or endangered.

Ecology
- Approximately 10,000 thermal features and approximately 200–250 active geysers. The park has one of the world's largest calderas (volcanic explosion crater). It measures 28 miles by 47 miles (45km by 75km).

Yellowstone Lake
- 136 square miles surface area (35,400 hectares), 110 miles of shoreline (177km), 20 miles north to south (32km), and 14 miles east to west (23km). Average depth is 139 feet (42m), and maximum depth is 390 feet (119m).

Roads and trails
- 370 miles of paved roads and approximately 1,200 miles of trails, with 97 trailheads. There are 300 backcountry campsites.

As early as 1903, tourism promotions for the park, like this Northern Pacific Railroad poster, extolled the park's fishing paradise comprised of five different species of trout. Prior to 1889, there was only one species, the native cutthroat.

Legends and Follies: A Century of Fishing in Yellowstone

Everyone has a favorite Yellowstone fishing story. Mine is the day clouds of deer-flies drove a horde of faint-hearted flyfishers out of Slough Creek's First Meadow. A 23-inch cutthroat was a handsome reward for the price of a few insect bites.

Yellowstone National Park's hallmark on its 125th anniversary is its legendary fishing. The *pas de deux* between angler and trout is performed on a stage of stunning beauty and dramatic variety.

Majestic backdrops feature fountain-spewing geysers and sulfurous mudpots, snow-capped mountains and rainbow-colored canyons. Vying for star roles in crystalline streams and emerald green lakes are cutthroat, rainbow, brown, brook, and lake trout, as well as grayling and whitefish. Quick to steal a scene are elk, deer, moose, grizzly bears, black bears, coyotes, wolves, eagles, ospreys, and pelicans.

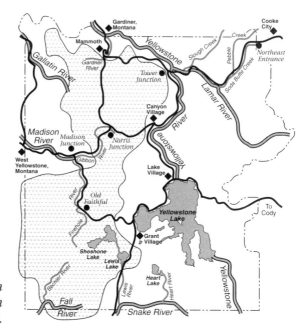

Shaded area shows region in park that had no fish prior to 1889.

Today's campfire yarns and magazine articles rival the tall tales of early explorers and tourists. Sooner or later there comes a time in Yellowstone "when a dry fly fisherman thinks he's died and gone to heaven," says Tim Wade of North Fork Anglers in Cody.

Slough Creek is a popular wilderness getaway in late summer and autumn. Even with occasional overcrowding, it is still possible to sense an escape in time in the stream's alpine meadows. Surrounded by the Absaroka Mountains' volcanic ramparts, the meandering flows of First Meadow are a comfortable hike from the campground road. Second and Third Meadows are just up the trail.

Former President Jimmy Carter hiked to First Meadows in 1993. Unlike VIPs of the past, he fished the park without fanfare. His Volunteer Angler Report details the bounty of a pristine stream. In three days, Carter caught and released 25 Yellowstone cutthroat. Four were 10 to 12 inches; two, 12 to 14 inches; three, 14 to 16 inches; seven, 16 to 18 inches; eight, 18 to 20 inches, and one over 20 inches.

"Fished caddis hatch size 16–18. *Tricorythodes* size 22–24, and size 12 muddlers and hoppers," Carter noted on his report.

Albert McClane, author of *McClane's Game Fish of North America*, was captivated by Slough Creek's scenery and the marvel of 30-fish days. "However, it's not the quality of the angling that is so compelling as the feeling, I suppose, of being transposed to a valley that was chronologically bypassed."

The allure of wilderness retreats also draws anglers to the headwaters of the Yellowstone River, Bechler Meadows, the upper Lamar River, Heart Lake, and Shoshone Lake.

Owen Wister, author of *The Virginian*, marveled in an 1887 journal entry that he could look back across the broad expanse of Yellowstone Lake and see the distant Grand Teton and its sister peaks looming above the Continental Divide.

A less traveled trail, even today, is into the Grand Canyon of the Yellowstone, where its rumbling flows drown all sounds of civilization. Wister couldn't resist its depths. "The canyon seems so deep that the sky comes close to the tops of the trees," he wrote in his journal.

But Wister's diary notations were more prosaic a short four years later.

"We came down the (Yellowstone) river and camped on an island near the mud geysers where we had originally intended to ford. Good fishing, but some of the trout wormy. Lots of outfits and people passing on the road and children screaming," he wrote on August 11, 1891. "This park is an immense thing for the American bourgeoisie. Popper takes mommer and children in a very big wagon with two mules and their kitchen and beds, and forth they march hundreds of miles and summer in the park. Nothing like this ever existed before, I think."

Grumbling about crowds is easy to appreciate today. Harder to fathom was the incredible abundance of 19th-century Yellowstone's cutthroat trout—or the gluttony of its visitors. Living off the land was the order of the day. Give a boy a fishing rod, and he could help feed a party of 40 dignitaries and cavalry troopers.

At age 15, Edward Hewitt fulfilled his camp duty with single-minded zeal in 1877. He landed 50 or more cutthroat a day from the mouth of Yellowstone Lake. On the party's way out of the park, an officer enlisted the youth to help feed another, even larger cavalry troop. In a single afternoon, Hewitt said he hooked 450 to 500 pounds of cutthroat from a stream he called Boulder Creek. From his description, it must be the South Fork of the Madison River.

Impossible? Not if you can picture Rocky Mountain flying fish. Gen. W. F. Strong described the technique in an 1887 diary entry. Stout poles and heavy lines were used so that when fish were hooked, they "could be immediately jerked clear of the moving water and flung to men waiting on the grassy banks."

Hewitt returned to the park in 1914. In *A Trout and Salmon Fisherman for 75 Years*, he bragged about a fishing duel on the Madison River. The contest was between his dry flies and a commercial fisherman's wet flies. Hewitt lost 165 to 162, but said he was way ahead until high winds hindered his fly casting.

More noteworthy than his embellishments is Hewitt's notation that his catch was comprised of browns and a few rainbows.

Brown trout, a European fish, were introduced into the Madison in 1890, and in less than a quarter century it was a dominant species. Rainbow and brook trout also made their way into the river. Native westslope cutthroat trout and fluvial Arctic grayling of the Madison drainage have been struggling for survival ever since. It's a story that's been repeated throughout the West.

Park Ranger DuPuir and two helpers plant fish in a small lake
in Yellowstone National Park in 1922. (NPS Photo/YNP)

Fortunately, it did not happen in the park's Yellowstone drainage. The star player in Yellowstone's legendary fishing is still a cutthroat. In the last citadel of intermountain West native trout, the Yellowstone cutthroat still reigns in Yellowstone Lake and the Yellowstone River.

But it has had a bumpy ride during a century of tinkering with paradise. Today, it faces its greatest threat, the unauthorized invasion of predatory lake trout in Yellowstone Lake.

Johnny Appleseed Era

Early explorers found nearly 40 percent of Yellowstone's waters barren of fish. In streams of the Lower Geyser and Norris Geyser Basins, the absence of fish was attributed to thermally heated and chemically impregnated waters. Actually, waterfalls were the most common barriers to upstream migration.

Barren streams included the upper Firehole and Gibbon Rivers in the Madison drainage; the Gardner River in the Yellowstone drainage; and the Bechler, Fall, and Lewis Rivers in the Snake drainage. Only 17 of the park's 150 lakes were known to hold fish. Lewis and Shoshone Lakes were not among them.

Park rangers drove a truck to the bank of the Bechler River to stock fish in the secluded stream in 1936. Proposals in 1920 and 1926 to dam the Bechler to create an irrigation reservoir were rejected by park officials. (NPS Photo/YNP)

The first formal survey of park waters was conducted in 1889. David Starr Jordan found 11 native fish. Four are game fish: Yellowstone cutthroat, westslope cutthroat, fluvial Arctic grayling, and whitefish. Seven suckers and minnows and the mottled sculpin are also natives.

Today, biologists note that Snake River finespotted cutthroat occur in small numbers in the upper river. Also, while it is genetically the same as Yellowstone cutthroat, park biologists say Heart Lake cutthroat have different characteristics, including that of a predator. A small, isolated population of Sedge Creek cutthroat is considered to be on the evolutionary fast track to subspecies status.

But even as Jordan conducted his survey, fishery biologists rushed in to fill vacant waters under the park's original mandate "for the benefit and enjoyment of the people."

The fledgling U.S. Fish Commission was eager to take the job because it needed "a proper outdoor laboratory in which to exercise its science," states park historian Aubrey L. Haines in *The Yellowstone Story*. The park offered "an opportunity to broaden the commission's activities…(to include)…the development of a sport fishery in what was then the only area of wild land under federal management."

Its "grand experiment" left an indelible imprint on Yellowstone's lakes and streams.

In 1889, brook trout were introduced into the upper Firehole and Gardner Rivers, as well as Glenn Creek. The upper Gardner also received Yellowstone cutthroat, and the upper Firehole received brown trout. Rainbows were planted in the upper Gibbon River.

The following year, lake and brown trout were introduced into Shoshone and Lewis Lakes. Brown trout were stocked in Madison River, and mountain whitefish were planted in Yellowstone River above its falls. Only the whitefish did not take.

Rainbow stocked in tributaries of Shoshone Lake in 1893 also did not survive, but the brook trout planted in 1895 did.

Yellowstone has no warmwater game fish, but not for lack of trying. In 1895, black bass were planted in the Gibbon River and several lakes with outlets to the Firehole River in Lower Geyser Basin. None survived.

Rainbow were planted in the Yellowstone River above the falls in 1902. They disappeared, presumably genetically swamped by the dominant Yellowstone cutthroat.

Five years later, park officials began to display mixed feelings about the Johnny Appleseed philosophies of the U.S. Fish Commission.

David C. Booth, a fisheries employee, was reprimanded in 1907 for an unauthorized stocking of rainbow into Yellowstone Lake. The next year, transplants of landlocked Atlantic salmon were sanctioned in Yellowstone and Duck Lakes, but a request to plant smelt in Yellowstone and Shoshone Lakes was rejected. The rainbow and salmon did not survive.

A lake-dwelling subspecies of Montana grayling was transplanted to Grebe Lake, headwaters of the Gibbon River, in 1921.

Not until 1936 was stocking of nonnative fish in native fish waters banned by the National Park Service.

However, yellow perch in Goose Lake had to be poisoned in 1938. No one knows how they got there. In 1967, brown trout were poisoned in Duck Lake. Brook trout discovered in Arnica Creek, a tributary of Yellowstone Lake, were poisoned in 1985.

The park's worst nightmare erupted in 1994 when lake trout were officially recorded in Yellowstone Lake. Former Superintendent Bob Barbee called illegal stocking of the voracious predator in the lake "environmental vandalism." Yellowstone declared a war of attrition against the threat to the last stronghold of inland cutthroat.

Another perspective on the transplantation debate, according to John Varley, chief of Yellowstone research, and others, is that some park waters contain "museum quality" trout from single or limited plants in the past. Lake trout eggs collected from Lewis Lake were used to establish brood stocks to replenish Lake Michigan, where lake trout were decimated by the sea lamprey and pollution. Isolated populations of rainbow may provide answers to the whirling disease threat that has descended on Western streams—perhaps even a future broodstock.

The Hatchery Era

Turn-of-the-century efforts to improve nature did not stop with importing game fish to the park. During its 50-year hatchery period, starting in 1901, Yellowstone Lake became the largest exporter of inland cutthroat eggs to the world. Its hatcheries also stocked several park waters and, supposedly, made more cutthroat available for Yellowstone Lake's sport fishery.

In 1921, a rainbow hatchery was established on Trout Lake to maintain stocks of "catchable size" fish in park streams, including the Firehole, Madison, Gallatin, Gardner, Bechler, Snake, lower Yellowstone, and lower Lamar. Internal and external grayling exports were added to the park's cottage industry in 1931 with a hatchery at Grebe Lake.

Most of the park's small lakes also were stocked with a variety of trout. Many did not take, but the number of lakes with fish increased from 17 in the past to 40 today. Two of the latter include Wolf and Cascade Lakes, which accepted grayling transplants.

Of the park's hatcheries, only the one for grayling appears to have had a redeeming value. Today, "most Western grayling stocks can be traced back there," states Mary Anne Franke in *Yellowstone Science*.

The article's headline is "A Grand Experiment: 100 Years of Fisheries Management in Yellowstone." But no amount of spin doctoring can obscure the sins of the past. Most manipulations of Yellowstone cutthroat populations were misguided and decidedly unprofitable.

"Between 1903 and 1953, 818 million trout eggs were exported from Yellowstone," Franke said. "All together, more than 50 federal, state, and private hatcheries received eggs from Yellowstone.... The Yellowstone cutthroat has survived in seven Western states and two Canadian provinces in which it was planted...."

A more pernicious impact of the Yellowstone cutthroat follies was on the mother lake. The abstract of a 1988 report to an American Fisheries Society symposium is succinct but revealing:

"Although egg-taking and hatchery operations (on Yellowstone Lake) were terminated over 30 years ago, it is now apparent egg removal, genetic mixing, and greatly reduced natural spawner escapement led to a gradual reduction in reproductive potential and undermined the complex mosaic of reproduction and recruitment. Angler harvest also had a negative impact as it became excessive," state Varley and Robert Gresswell, a former U.S. Fish and Wildlife Service researcher.

Correcting Past Sins

The cutthroat is a colorful fish. It has evolved into as many as 15 subspecies, including the three present in the greater Yellowstone ecosystem. But in a trout fishing contest, cutthroat win the Miss Congeniality title.

During the last Ice Age, cutthroat took the lead in migrations up the Columbia River system. They beat out their Pacific Coast cousin, the rainbow, and became the only native trout in the vast intermountain interior of the West. Cutthroat even man-

Early day-tourists flocked to Fishing Bridge over the Yellowstone River at the mouth of the lake. On a single day in June 1954, U.S. Fish and Wildlife Service biologists recorded more than 700 cutthroat creeled by anglers on the bridge. It was closed to fishing in 1973, and cutthroat were restricted to catch-and-release fishing on the majority of park streams. (NPS Photo/YNP)

aged to cross the Continental Divide; however, later barriers, such as Shoshone Falls on the Snake River in Idaho, halted the rainbow's upstream migrations.

To share their limited resources and make the best of short growing seasons, accommodation became the cutthroat's forte. They don't compete well with introduced trout. Also, when hybridization with rainbows occurs, rainbow characteristics usually become dominant.

"The cutthroat trout appears to be more social and less territorial than the introduced salmonids," reports Varley. "In unexploited or lightly exploited streams, pools seem to have cutthroat of various sizes schooled together which exhibit no territorial or antagonistic behavior towards each other."

They also are highly susceptible to overharvest. In a catch-and-release experiment, "wild cutthroat trout were twice as catchable as wild brook trout and 18 times more vulnerable than wild brown trout," Varley said.

But it was not until after Yellowstone celebrated its centennial that the park's cutthroat were guaranteed protection. In 1973, cutthroat were declared catch-and-release on almost all park streams. The creel limit on Yellowstone Lake and its tributaries was set at two fish under 13 inches. Fishing Bridge was closed. The upper river and the mouths of the lake's creeks were declared off-limits until spawning runs end.

Anglers readily accepted the regulations. Many were already proponents of catch-and-release fishing for all trout.

Cutthroat numbers in Yellowstone Lake and the upper river bounced back to historical levels. Fish size increased dramatically and age distributions reflect healthy populations.

An Idaho State University study in 1980 showed that, on average, each cutthroat in the upper Yellowstone River was caught nearly 10 times during its short season. The catch-and-release mortality rate was estimated at 3 percent.

In another study of the upper river, "85 percent of the fishermen catch one or more wild cutthroat trout in an average daily trip," Varley said. "Excellent fishing is provided despite enormous pressure, in the recent annual range of 2,800 anglers per stream mile…. The fishery remains excellent only because all cutthroats caught are returned alive to the stream to be caught again." It is perhaps the park's greatest success story.

Yellowstone has been the proving ground for numerous transitions in wildlife management, including the natural regulation concept. Pivotal events in protection of the park's trout include:

- 1908: First angler creel limit set at 20 fish per day; decreased to 10 fish in 1921, to 5 fish in 1949, to 3 fish in 1954, and to 2 fish in 1973.
- 1919: Commercial fishing banned.
- 1936: Introduction of nonnative fish in native fish waters banned.
- 1950: Madison, Firehole, and lower Gibbon Rivers restricted to flyfishing only.
- 1953: Cutthroat hatcheries closed; grayling and rainbow hatcheries closed in 1956.
- 1968: National Park Service implemented natural regulation of wildlife, including fish.
- 1969: Bait fishing banned in park.
- 1973: Cutthroat restricted to catch-and-release angling, except in Yellowstone Lake and the river above the lake.
- 1994: Anglers required to kill lake trout in Yellowstone Lake as part of efforts to curb the predator's threat to cutthroat.
- 1997: Native Fish Restoration Plan submitted for public review.
- 1998: Yellowstone Lake opened to fishing June 1 to give anglers a better chance to take more lake trout.

Curse of the Aliens: Guardians Still Tinkering with Paradise

Few believed a century ago there was a lake in the Rocky Mountains where a fisherman could easily catch a trout, turn around, and immediately cook it on the line in the boiling waters of a geyser. He didn't have to move a foot.

Today, this former highlight of fishing trips to Yellowstone Lake is preserved only on grainy photographs and faded postcards. Casting to cruising trout from Fishing Cone is *verboten*.

In 1900, a U.S. Cavalry trooper demonstrates the unique practice of catching a Yellowstone cutthroat trout from Yellowstone Lake and cooking it on the spot at Fishing Cone in West Thumb Geyser Basin. Current park rules prohibit fishing from the cone or from shore in this area. (NPS Postcard/YNP)

Fishing Cone is symbolic of the transitions in attitudes and policies during Yellowstone National Park's 125-year history.

Millions of tourists view West Thumb Geyser Basin as just another geological marvel to squeeze into their whirlwind tours. Those who read the boardwalk sign at Fishing Cone see it as an historical footnote. Most anglers view it differently. Its off-limits status reflects more than a lost opportunity. Fishing in Yellowstone is no longer a novelty. It is serious business.

Once the primary exporter of cutthroat eggs to the world, the park is now the strongest proponent for conservation of inland cutthroat. The single native trout in the intermountain West occurs in only 10 to 15 percent of its historic range. Ninety percent of the Yellowstone cutthroat's current range is within the park's boundaries. Westslope cutthroat are virtually gone from the Madison drainage.

But changes in management perceptions and goals were slow to come following the casual introductions of exotic, or nonnative, game fish into the park's lakes and streams in the late 1880s and early 1900s. Not until 1936 was stocking of nonnative fish banned in the home waters of cutthroat trout and fluvial, or river dwelling, Arctic grayling. The hatcheries were closed in the late 1950s, and put-and-take stocking of fish ended. Stricter fishing regulations imposed in the 1970s and mid-1990s were directed at restoring Yellowstone cutthroat populations to historic levels, first in Yellowstone Lake and later in the lower river's tributaries.

Both cutthroat and anglers reaped tremendous benefits from the stricter regulations. But even as fisheries managers patted themselves on the back, another storm cloud spilled over the Continental Divide into Yellowstone Lake. In 1994, the park declared a no-prisoners-taken war against illegally transplanted lake trout threatening the largest bastion of Yellowstone cutthroat. Few deny the voracious predators have to go.

Current Park Service policies reflect another morality play driving modern fisheries management. Natural regulation concepts stress protection of native fish where they still remain and encourage their return to vacated waters. In Yellowstone, the emphasis is on restoring westslope cutthroat and fluvial grayling to the Madison and Gallatin drainages. But many anglers are not happy with continued tinkering in paradise.

Yellowstone's lightning rod in the politically charged debate is Superintendent Mike Finley. In addition to two highly publicized quandaries—finding a way to halt the slaughter of migrating bison and justifying reintroduction of gray wolves—he tries to smooth troubled waters on the fishing front.

In a 1996 report to the Federation of Fly Fishers, he made key commitments to preserving Yellowstone's fishing traditions. Moreover, he acknowledged Park Service mandates to restore native fish "is not practical in all waters" in Yellowstone.

"At the same time, we have no plans to change the way we manage fish in waters that were originally fishless but where nonnatives have been stocked," Finley stated. Shoshone and Lewis Lakes were cited as examples.

"Our goal during the next few years is to move cautiously toward protecting, enhancing, and restoring native fish and mitigating the effect of nonnatives on natives while continuing to provide recreational angling."

Finley said the park's primary goal is to suppress the lake trout threat to cutthroat in Yellowstone Lake. Heart Lake's lake trout were added to the list of enemies to be consistent with the concept of protecting "native fish in waters where they are clearly threatened by nonnatives." Anglers are obliged to join the battle. All lake trout caught in either lake must be killed.

"Our second priority is to mitigate the effects of nonnative fish in waters where they are suppressing native fish (such as brook trout in several cutthroat drainages), and to protect native species where they exist currently without threats from nonnatives (such as the cutthroat in the upper Yellowstone River)," Finley said.

"Finally, we plan to restore some native fish where this is feasible," such as grayling in Cougar Creek, a Madison tributary, and westslope cutthroat in Canyon Creek, a Gibbon tributary below its falls.

Finley's report to the 1996 FFF conclave went almost unnoticed. Not until the park formally announced a native species restoration proposal the following January did some anglers hoist storm warning flags.

The goal of the restoration plan is to stock westslope cutthroat and fluvial Arctic grayling in tributaries where competition from exotic species can be eliminated and further upstream migration blocked by barriers. If approved, it would begin at Canyon Creek. After evaluating the pilot project, the park said it might consider restoration sites on Maple, Duck, and Grayling Creeks in the Madison drainage, and the headwaters of the Gallatin River, including two of its tributaries, Fan and Specimen Creeks.

So far, the park has a checkered track record in restoration efforts.

Canyon Creek was poisoned in 1976 in an attempt to reintroduce grayling. The fish didn't take. A man-made barrier prevented upstream migration of rainbows and browns, but the grayling slipped downstream.

Also, grayling in Cougar Creek are struggling after being stocked in the Madison tributary between 1993 and 1996.

"The fluvial grayling don't seem to be very fond of Cougar Creek," said John Varley, chief of park research, in *Yellowstone Science*. "They're a big river fish. But we'll probably get them back in the park someday."

Adding confusion to this part of the restoration debate are well-established populations of grayling in Grebe, Wolf, and Cascade Lakes. They are a lake-dwelling Montana subspecies, but in high-water years, grayling often make their way into the Gibbon and Madison Rivers. The state of Montana also has stocked grayling in the Gallatin River.

But the vagueness of the stream restoration proposal is the biggest concern of outfitters and anglers. They are skeptical it won't have downstream impacts on the brown and rainbow fisheries in the Madison and Gallatin Rivers. It also is seen by some as the opening salvo in a future war of attrition against all nonnative fish in the park.

The plan endangers two of the park's best fisheries, says Bob Jacklin, a West Yellowstone outfitter. He feels brown, rainbow, and brook trout deserve naturalized citizenship. Their roles in Yellowstone's legendary fishing cover nearly a century, too.

Jacklin said he is not opposed to saving westslope cutthroat and fluvial grayling from extinction, "but not at the expense of killing all nonnative or 'exotic' salmonids." He favors nonlethal measures to remove exotics from native fish refuges established in Yellowstone's backcountry. A majority of other comments on the plan also stress restoration efforts should be confined to headwater tributaries.

"Introduced species such as the brook, brown, lake, and rainbow trout have, in fact, become 'native' and are self-propagating, and I might add a very large reason why Yellowstone has become the Mecca and home of quality trout fishing in the United States," Jacklin said in a letter to Finley. "Yellowstone, like no other place in the world, shares this unique title."

Continued experimentation with the park's fisheries is unwarranted, Jacklin says. He described natural regulation as a "cancer" fostered by the U.S. Fish and Wildlife Service. The agency's tinkering at Montana's Red Rock Lakes National Wildlife Refuge decimated its trophy rainbow and brook trout fisheries, Jacklin said.

Ryan Jordan, of J&J Flies in Bozeman, was one of many who joined the debate through an internet survey by *Fly Fisherman* magazine. "The quality of Yellowstone's fishing lies in its diversity of species and varied opportunities for anglers of all skill levels and fishing preferences," Jordan said. "The Madison's heritage lies in its trophy browns and opportunity to fish challenging water and fish without fear of a smaller cutt chasing your fly. The Gallatin, although absent of 'trophy' size fish, is a well-balanced river in terms of its species. I love fishing the park sections, and commonly catch everything in a single stretch of water, including rainbows, cutts, whitefish, and the occasional brown and grayling. I find this chance for a 'surprise at the end of my line' one of the Gallatin's most attractive features."

Jacklin says local interests want a more direct say in park policies. He also wants an end to the good trout vs. bad trout debate. "A steering committee should be established to help the Park Service make sound judgments in the rules and regulations regarding the fisheries," he told Finley. Yellowstone needs to "adopt a catch-and-release, fish for fun concept for all species except for lake trout in Yellowstone Lake.... Mr. Superintendent, it is time for this in Yellowstone. I am opposed to a species regulation which favors one species over another."

After receiving a barrage of comments on two versions of the native fish restoration proposal, "the consensus is that it's an all-right idea—but not in my stream," said Dan Mahoney, a Yellowstone fisheries biologist. He said park officials would revise the proposal and submit it for public comment again in early 1998.

But it is doubtful the debate will end there. Even if the conceptual aspects of the proposal are approved, the dialogue is sure to continue into the next century, and each individual stream restoration project closely scrutinized.

Yellowstone's Fishing Rules

Anglers may play a role in Yellowstone's annual war against the lake trout invasion now that Yellowstone Lake opens two weeks earlier under new fishing rules implemented in 1998. Fishing on Yellowstone Lake opens June 1, and, in another major switch, Yellowstone cutthroat trout in the lake are protected for six weeks by a catch-and-release rule, from June 1 to July 15.

"We want to take advantage of the chance to catch lake trout that show up close to shore at that time," said Dan Mahoney, a fisheries biologist with the National Park Service. All lake trout caught by anglers in Yellowstone Lake must be killed.

First officially recorded in 1994, the illegal transplant of the predatory nonnative species could seriously decimate the cutthroat fisheries in the lake and upper Yellowstone River. Park biologists are trying to find solutions to the peril, including extensive gillnetting, and want anglers to assist them as much as possible.

Angler catches accounted for about a quarter of the 2,050 lake trout taken from the lake in the first four years of the battle, Mahoney said. It's all right to keep the lake trout for a meal, but anglers are required to take them to a visitor's center or ranger station for inspection by a biologist. A mandatory kill order for lake trout in Heart Lake was imposed in 1996.

Flyfishers who have not visited the park in recent years should note several other changes in the rules. One of the most significant was dropping catch-and-release protection for rainbows in lakes and streams, except for four flyfishing-only rivers. The nine-year hiatus as a protected species ended in 1996 as part of the increased emphasis on protecting native cutthroat.

Other key aspects to note in current fishing regulations include:

- Cutthroat are catch-and-release on virtually all park waters, including the Soda Butte Creek drainage and Pebble Creek. The only exceptions are on the upper Lamar River drainage, including Calfee Creek and higher tributaries, two cutthroat any size; and, after July 14, on Yellowstone Lake and its headwaters tributaries, including the upper Yellowstone River, two cutthroat under 13 inches.
- The lake trout limit remains two fish, any size, in Lewis and Shoshone Lakes and tributaries.
- Daily creel limit on rainbow trout is two fish, any size, except for the continued catch-and-release requirement on the Madison River, Firehole River and its tributaries, Gibbon River below Gibbon Falls, and Bechler River and its tributaries.
- Creel limit for brook trout is five fish, any size, except in Richard's Pond, Fawn Lake, and Blacktail Ponds, where it is five brookies under 13 inches. Brook trout netted in Pocket Lake, above Shoshone Lake, must be killed to protect Heart Lake cutthroat transplanted to the small lake to maintain a reserve population.
- Brown trout creel limit is two fish under 13 inches on the Madison, Firehole, and Gibbon, below its falls. Elsewhere in the park, the brown limit is two fish, any size, except for a catch-and-release rule that still applies on Lewis River below its waterfall to its canyon.

Yellowstone's guardians also upped the ante for the privilege to fish in the park in 1996. The price of fishing is $10 for a 10-day permit (16 years of age or older), and $20 for a season permit. Children 12 to 15 continue to fish free but need a personal permit. Children 11 or younger do not need a permit when supervised by an adult.

The park's annual fishing season begins on the Saturday of Memorial Day weekend and continues through the first Sunday in November, with a few exceptions. Waters with later opening dates include:

- Yellowstone Lake opens on June 1 with a catch-and-release rule that protects cutthroat until July 15.
- Streams flowing into Yellowstone Lake, including the upper Yellowstone River, open July 15.
- Yellowstone River, between the lake and the upper falls, opens July 15.
- Heart Lake opens July 1.

Night fishing is not permitted on park waters, which are open daily from 5 AM to 10 PM.

Be sure to sign the fishing permit and read all the park's regulations before fishing. For example, another rule to remember is that Yellowstone implemented a nontoxic fishing policy in 1994. Fishing tackle, such as lead split-shot or sinkers, weighted jigs (lead molded to a hook), and soft, lead-weighted ribbon for flyfishing nymphs, are no longer allowed. Only nontoxic alternatives are permitted for these types of fishing tackle to prevent lead poisoning of waterfowl.

"These changes are intended to help the park meet its fisheries management objectives which include: managing aquatic resources as an important part of the park ecosystem; preserving and restoring native fishes and their habitats; and providing recreational fishing opportunities for the enjoyment of park visitors when consistent with the first two objectives," state Yellowstone's guardians.

Several trends were cited as cause and effect for the new regulations:

- Monitoring of the Soda Butte Creek drainage and upper Lamar River indicates too many large cutthroat were harvested under the old regulations that permitted a limited take of cutthroat and rainbow. Brook trout also have been found in the headwaters of Soda Butte Creek, outside the park. "The new (catch-and-release) regulation will allow the larger cutthroat trout to compete better with brook trout."
- The limited creel limit on rainbows "will help preserve and restore native (cutthroat) in waters where they compete with rainbow trout (Yellowstone River drainage) while protecting and enhancing some outstanding angling opportunities in areas that no longer contain native fish (Madison River drainage)."
- Anglers who decide to keep a rainbow where permitted in waters where cutthroat-rainbow hybrids may occur should make sure the fish has no orange-red slash marks under its jaws—no matter how faint the color of the slash marks. The distinctive slash mark classifies even hybrids as cutthroat under the new rules.
- The expanded brook trout bag limit permits anglers to creel larger brook trout where they occur in most park waters. The under 13-inch limit on Blacktail Ponds, Richard's Pond, and Fawn Lake protects fishing on popular isolated lakes without cutthroat that contain trophy brookies.
- Expanding the mandatory kill requirement of lake trout to Heart Lake continues the all-out war on the fish-eating species in the park's cutthroat citadels.

The latter also was an attempt to simplify the regulations, Mahoney said. While Heart Lake's cutthroat have a longer history of coexisting with lake trout, there are indications their numbers are declining. Also, they are considered a unique subspecies, more closely related to the Snake River finespotted cutthroat, he said.

Few disagree with the mandatory kill requirement for lake trout in Yellowstone Lake, but the open season on rainbows received mixed reviews.

Bob Jacklin, of Jacklin's Fly Shop and Outfitters in West Yellowstone, Montana, saw removal of catch-and-release protection of rainbows as a step back in Yellowstone fisheries management. "I think we're following the wrong path here, and I'm not happy with the taking of rainbows," he said. While Jacklin is for restoration of native cutthroat fisheries, he promotes preservation of all trout species in the park as equally important to maintaining its internationally acclaimed stature as a fishing destination. He opposes any improper efforts to eradicate nonnative species. Human intervention has made its indelible imprint on Yellowstone's fisheries and attempts to bring it back to its historic nature would be unrealistic, according to Jacklin. "Treat the park as a living thing and let it evolve."

A colleague on the Yellowstone River side of the park viewed the regulation changes as less draconian. Richard Parks, of Parks' Fly Shop and Outfitters in Gardiner, Montana, saw the new regulations as a process of rationalization and simplification that present minor changes in previous policy. Permitting the take of rainbows on waters where cutthroat populations are still strong "seems to make reasonable sense.... It will buy us toward cutthroat, which is the intent," Parks said. "Protection of cutthroat on Soda Butte Creek is long overdue. It should have been done 15 years ago."

Flyfishers who traditionally pursue rainbows on the other side of the park will see no change in the rules, Parks added. Catch-and-release protection of rainbows continues on the Madison, Firehole, lower Gibbon, and the Bechler and its tributaries.

The fishing permit fee, introduced in 1994, has not been a commercial problem, Parks said. Traffic through the region's flyfishing shops did not decrease the first two years. However, he said, the 1996 fee increase may mean more anglers will buy a 10-day permit and fewer will buy a season permit.

"It's still cheap entertainment" compared to resident license fees for Montana, Wyoming, or Idaho anglers, and nonresident weekly fees charged by the three states.

Rivers and Streams of Yellowstone

Winter snows in Yellowstone fall on a gargantuan, percolating sponge. The broad plateau crisscrossed by the Continental Divide's wandering course is the fountainhead of the West's two preeminent networks of flyfishing streams.

The Madison and Gallatin exit the park from its northwest corner and flow to their confluence with the Jefferson to form the Missouri River at Three Forks in Montana. The Madison rises at the confluence of the Firehole and Gibbon Rivers. Carving its ancient course through the park's colossal caldera is the Yellowstone, the Missouri's largest tributary. The Yellowstone's principal tributaries in the park are the Lamar and Gardner Rivers.

The Snake River, largest tributary of the Columbia, rises in the park's southernmost highlands and flows through western Wyoming into Idaho. Its flows are augmented by the Lewis and Heart Rivers in the park. The Fall River picks up the Bechler River and exits the park into Idaho to join the Henry's Fork, or North Fork, of the Snake.

The Yellowstone is the longest freeflowing river in the contiguous United States. But from the park's earliest days, the Yellowstone and other streams were the focus of schemes that would dam them for flood control or divert their flows for irrigation and hydroelectric power. These assaults on its waters were called the Second Yellowstone War by park historian Aubrey Haines in *The Yellowstone Story*. The first war denied the invasion of Yellowstone by railroads.

In 1893, an Idaho senator launched a counterattack with a proposal to set aside two unnamed waterfalls to produce power for an electric train loop. A generation later, both the Idaho and Montana congressional delegations attempted to tap the park's bounty in the 1920s: Montana proposed a dam on the Yellowstone three miles below the lake and Idaho proposed to dam the Fall and Bechler Rivers; Idaho even tried to remove the Bechler Basin from the park. The most grandiose resolution was a product of the Dust Bowl drought of the 1930s. Its improbable scheme was to tunnel through the Continental Divide from Yellowstone Lake to Shoshone Lake and through the Pitchstone Plateau to the Fall River to divert irrigation waters to the Henry's Fork.

"Though it was but a war of words, Yellowstone Park stood in grave jeopardy, and with it the integrity of the entire national park system," Haines said. "However, it was a fight in which the park found staunch allies who saved the day."

Yet, like a phoenix, attempts to tame the Yellowstone as a "working river" continued over the years, both in the park and downstream. The most bitterly fought battle was in the 1970s against plans to dam it south of Livingston, Montana, and flood the beautiful Paradise Valley. Later, a hydropower entrepreneur's filing of a claim to dam the mouth of Yellowstone Lake in the mid-1990s resulted only in a rolling-of-the-eyes at his audacity.

Past transgressions in the addition of nonnative trout and manipulation of the park's native cutthroat were not considered problematic at the time. However, significant changes in modern fishing attitudes and management practices have revealed the errors, and today managers and anglers work to ameliorate these past sins. Fishing today in Yellowstone rivals its historic heyday.

"While we can never return to pristine conditions, Yellowstone still sustains one of the least impacted areas of the Lower 48 States," said John Varley, chief of research for Yellowstone. In a *Trout* magazine report, Varley and his colleague, Paul Schullery, dispelled concerns about the effects of the forest fires of 1988 on streams and fish. Their short answer that the trout are doing "just fine" was based on 20 years of U.S. Fish and Wildlife Service surveys.

"We know, for example, that the landing rate has not changed—about a fish an hour—that the average size of the fish caught has actually increased some, and that fishermen are fishing longer and landing more fish than in the 1970s or 1980s. How many trout regions can claim that? We also know that in 1993, both the index of angler satisfaction with the fishing experience and the size of fish caught were the highest since the surveys began."

Anglers embraced efforts to protect cutthroat, Varley said in another report. "The old campfire meal tradition is now rare, more by angler choice than federal regulations."

Yellowstone cutthroat trout are still the principal quarry in the park's waters, primarily on Yellowstone Lake, Yellowstone River, and its tributaries, the Lamar River, Slough Creek, Soda Butte Creek, and the lower Gardner River. At the opposite end of the park, the Fall River is also an excellent cutthroat stream.

The most crowded fishing area in the park is the Yellowstone River between the lake and its Grand Canyon. This short stretch sees 90 percent of the river's nearly 11,000 annual anglers. Still, U.S. Fish and Wildlife surveys indicate that more than 70 percent of the Yellowstone's one-day anglers land one or more cutthroat. The caveat is that both the cutthroat and the catch rate decline dramatically after August.

If crowds are a concern, dip into the Yellowstone's canyon stretches. To get completely off the beaten track, explore the river's headwaters above the lake. This corner of the park and the Snake River basin offer the most remote fishing waters in the park. The lower Fall River and Bechler Meadows are also good choices; trailheads to the basin are reached by road only from Idaho.

If cutthroat are considered too tame, brown trout in the Gibbon, Firehole, and Madison offer the park's most challenging fishing. Its finest rainbow trout waters are in the Firehole and Bechler Meadows. The rare grayling is present in Cougar Creek, a tributary of the Madison, and is flushed into the Gibbon and Madison in high runoff years from Grebe Lake.

A reserved treat for children are the brook trout of Panther, Obsidian, and Indian Creeks, as well as the Gardner River meadows. The Gardner and its upper tributaries are the only park steams open to worm fishing by children 11 years old or younger. Joffe Lake, near Mammoth, also is open to worm fishing by children.

On the other end of the spectrum, the Madison, Firehole, and the Gibbon below its waterfall are all mandated as flyfishing only.

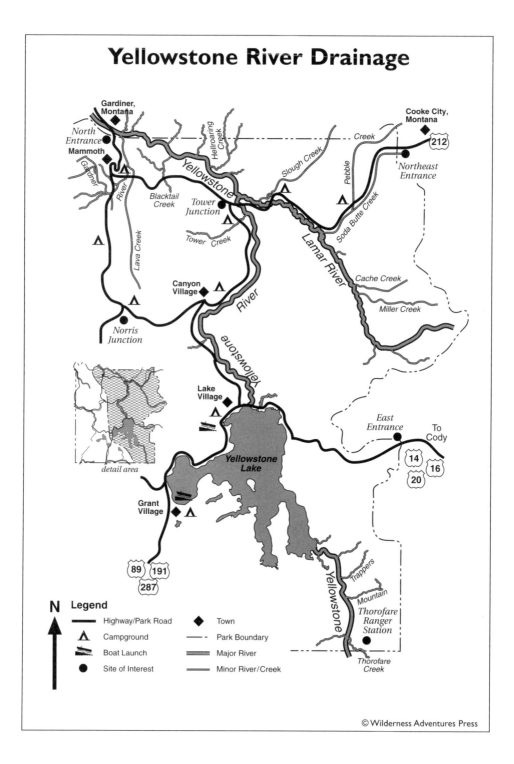

Yellowstone River Drainage

YELLOWSTONE RIVER DRAINAGE

The Yellowstone River drains 60 percent of the park's collected waters. The basin's broad arc from the southeast corner to the North Entrance rigorously erodes two-thirds of the park. Yet prime sections of the river and its tributaries are easily fished along loop roads.

Hardest to reach are the headwaters of the Yellowstone, found in the most remote wilderness in the Lower 48 States. Hikes or horse rides to fish the Yellowstone delta and Thorofare region above the huge Yellowstone Lake require a minimum of five days, and a week is better. The trip is easier by boat, but time commitments are about the same.

The loop road closely follows the most heavily fished sections of the river between Fishing Bridge and the Grand Canyon of the Yellowstone. Ventures into the Grand Canyon and Black Canyon are down steep trails with lots of switchbacks.

The two principal tributaries of the Yellowstone, the Lamar and Gardner Rivers, are also closely followed by the loop roads. The Yellowstone and Gardner merge at the park's North Entrance and the gateway community of Gardiner, Montana. The scenic U.S. 89 ascends the Yellowstone from Livingston to Gardiner through Paradise Valley. The loop road then follows the Gardner to Mammoth Hot Springs, the park's headquarters. Soda Butte Creek and the beautiful Lamar Valley are followed by the loop road from the Northeast Entrance at Cooke City, Montana, to Tower Junction.

Two eastern routes to Cooke City traverse some of the most remote and beautiful alpine landscapes in the West. Starting at Red Lodge, Montana, the Beartooth Scenic Highway crosses a 10,950-foot pass via U.S. 212 to Cooke City. The Chief Joseph Scenic Highway, starting about 20 miles north of Cody, Wyoming, follows the Clark's Fork of the Yellowstone through Sunlight Basin to U.S. 212 and Cooke City.

Visitors arriving from Cody by way of Wapiti Valley and the East Entrance first greet the Yellowstone at the famous Fishing Bridge over Yellowstone Lake's outlet. It is also the first view of the river for visitors arriving from Jackson and Grand Teton National Park through the South Entrance.

Yellowstone River

Renowned for its legendary trout fishing, the Yellowstone River ranks among the most famous landmarks on Earth. Its sense of place embodies a significance far beyond its role as a river or a name. Yellowstone encompasses the concept of wilderness and is synonymous with the principles of the national park idea that radiated from its environs in 1872.

The earliest known appearance of the name occurred on John Evans' manuscript map of 1797. Evans, a Welshman employed by Spaniards to record the Missouri River drainage, showed a tributary stream as River Yellow Rock. The park's first historian, Hiram Chittenden, considered the name an earlier translation of the Minnetaree Indian expression *Mi tsi a-da-zi* by French explorers as *Roches Jaunes*, or 'Rocks Yellow.' In 1798, the French name was anglicized by Canadian geographer David Thompson to 'Yellow Stone.'

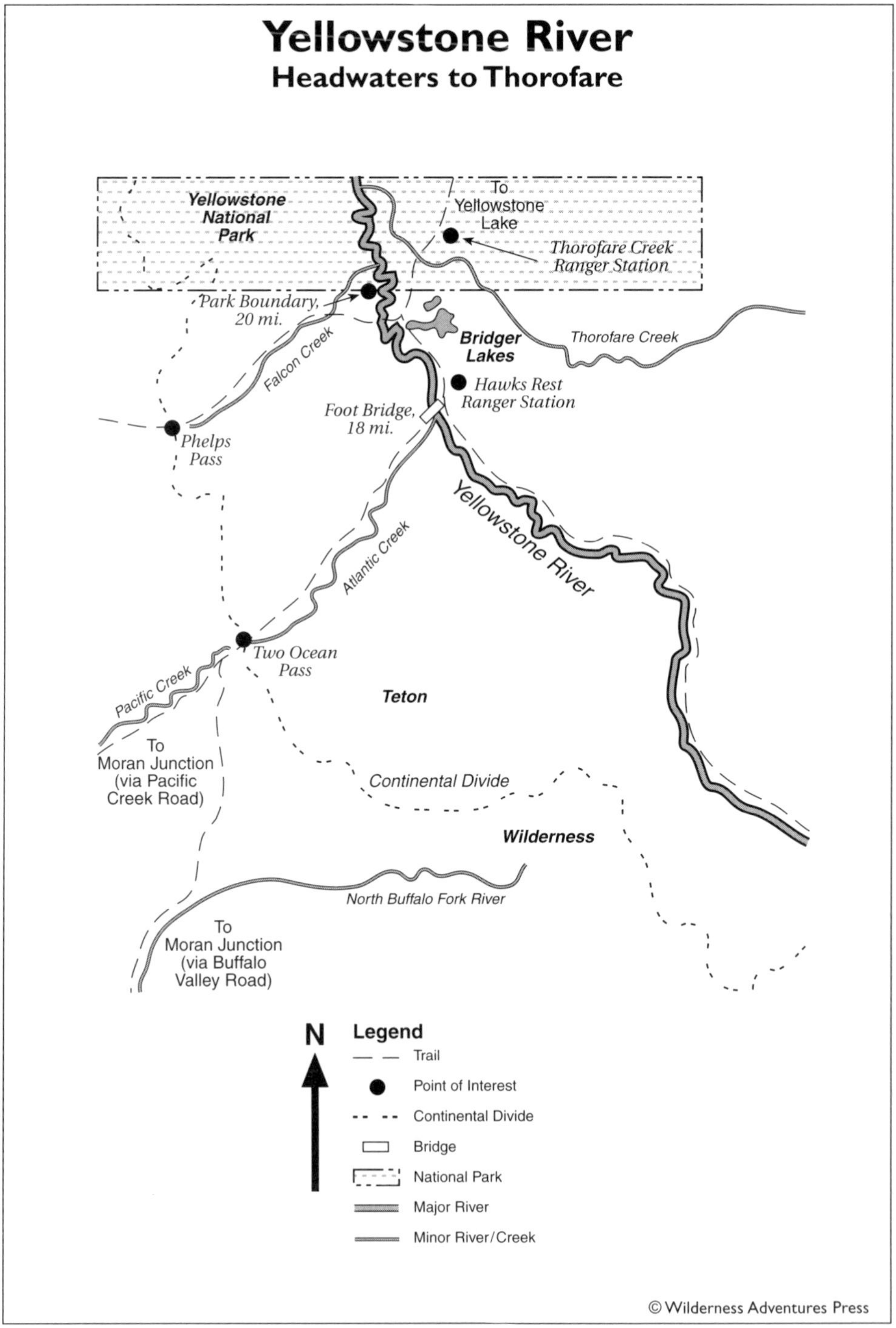

Yellowstone River
Headwaters to Thorofare

Yellowstone National Park

To Yellowstone Lake

Thorofare Creek Ranger Station

Park Boundary, 20 mi.

Falcon Creek

Bridger Lakes

Thorofare Creek

Hawks Rest Ranger Station

Foot Bridge, 18 mi.

Phelps Pass

Yellowstone River

Atlantic Creek

Two Ocean Pass

Teton

Pacific Creek

To Moran Junction (via Pacific Creek Road)

Continental Divide

Wilderness

North Buffalo Fork River

To Moran Junction (via Buffalo Valley Road)

N

Legend
— — Trail
● Point of Interest
-- -- Continental Divide
▭ Bridge
National Park
Major River
Minor River/Creek

© Wilderness Adventures Press

Yellowstone River
Thorofare to Yellowstone Lake

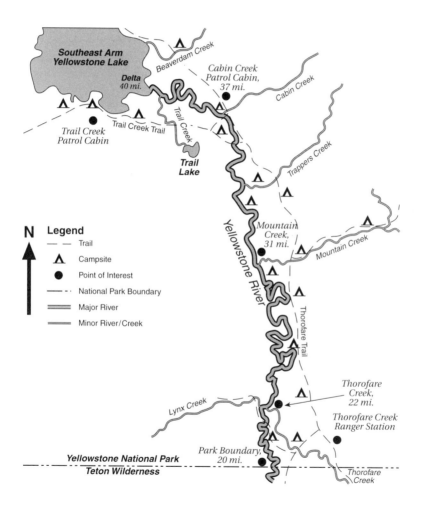

© Wilderness Adventures Press

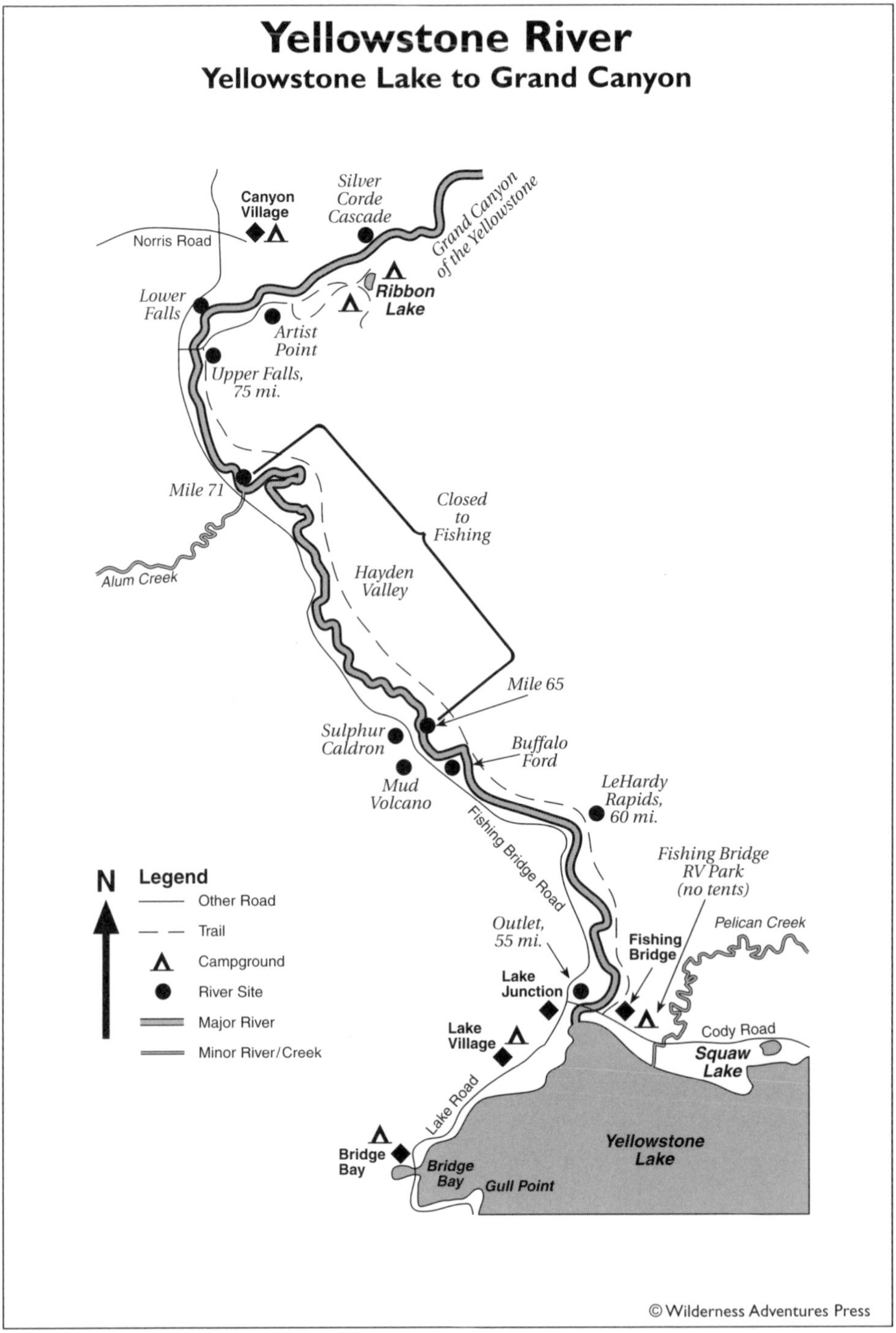

Yellowstone River
Yellowstone Lake to Grand Canyon

Canyon Village

Norris Road

Silver Corde Cascade

Grand Canyon of the Yellowstone

Lower Falls

Ribbon Lake

Artist Point

Upper Falls, 75 mi.

Mile 71

Closed to Fishing

Alum Creek

Hayden Valley

Mile 65

Sulphur Caldron

Buffalo Ford

Mud Volcano

LeHardy Rapids, 60 mi.

Fishing Bridge Road

Fishing Bridge RV Park (no tents)

Pelican Creek

N

Legend
— Other Road
- - Trail
Λ Campground
● River Site
═ Major River
═ Minor River/Creek

Outlet, 55 mi.

Fishing Bridge

Lake Junction

Lake Village

Cody Road

Squaw Lake

Lake Road

Bridge Bay

Bridge Bay

Gull Point

Yellowstone Lake

© Wilderness Adventures Press

Yellowstone River
Grand Canyon to Lamar River Confluence

Legend

N

——	Other Road
-----	Gravel/Dirt Road
– – –	Trail
⛺	Campground
●	River Site/Point of Interest
═══	Major River
══	Minor River/Creek

Mammoth Road

Mile 90

Slough Creek

Lamar River

Tower Junction

The Narrows

Cooke City Road

Roosevelt Lodge

Specimen Ridge Trail

Tower Falls

Bannock Ford, 85 mi.

Tower Creek

Tower Junction Road

● *Dunraven Pass*

Cascade Lake

Grebe Lake

Seven Mile Hole Trail

Grand Canyon of the Yellowstone

Cascade Creek

Canyon Village

Norris Road

Fishing Bridge Road

● *Silver Corde Cascade, 78 mi.*

© Wilderness Adventures Press

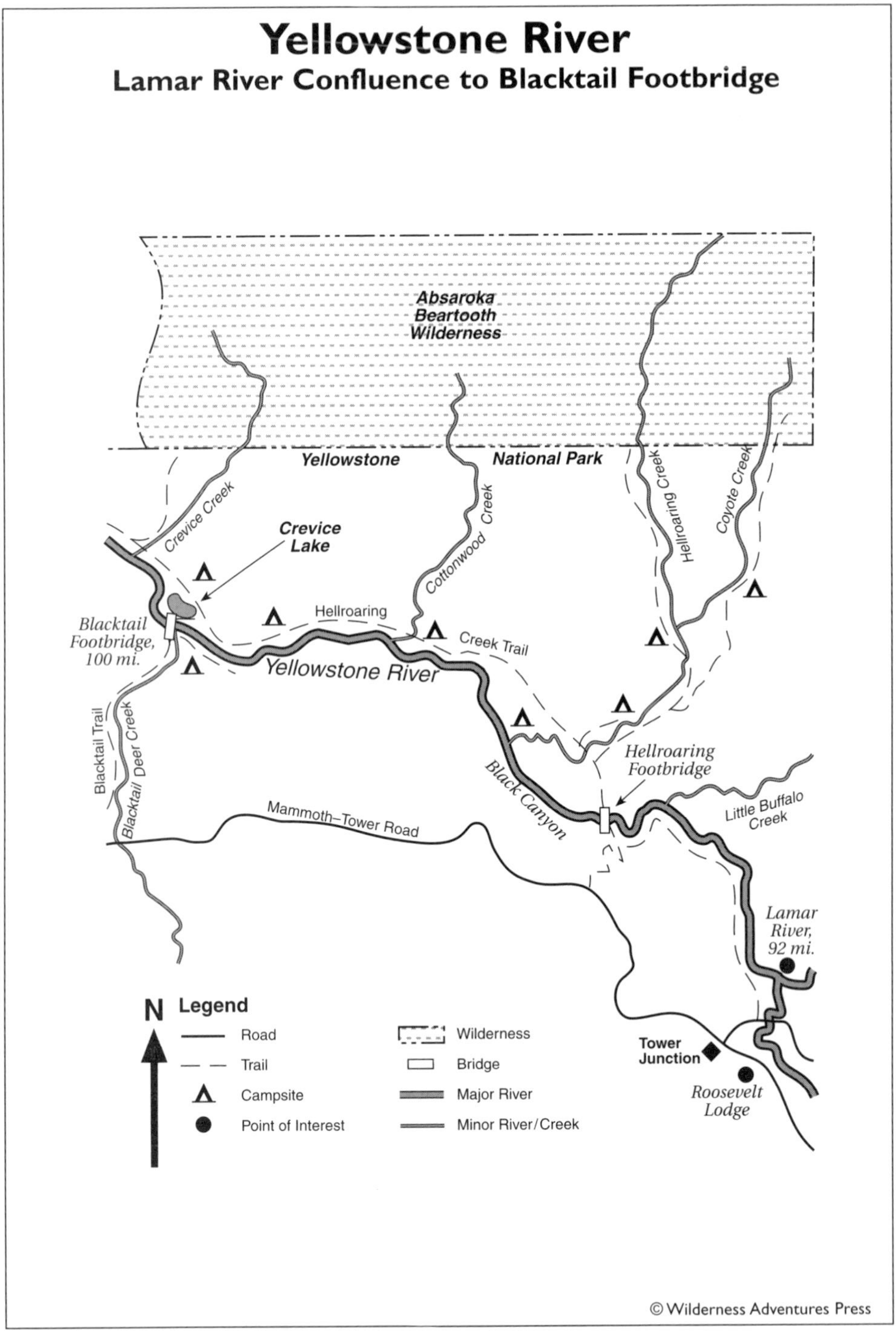

Yellowstone River
Lamar River Confluence to Blacktail Footbridge

Absaroka Beartooth Wilderness

Yellowstone   **National Park**

Crevice Creek

Cottonwood Creek

Hellroaring Creek

Coyote Creek

Crevice Lake

Hellroaring   Creek Trail

Blacktail Footbridge, 100 mi.

Yellowstone River

Blacktail Trail

Blacktail Deer Creek

Mammoth–Tower Road

Black Canyon

Hellroaring Footbridge

Little Buffalo Creek

Lamar River, 92 mi.

N

Legend
— Road
– – Trail
Δ Campsite
● Point of Interest

▢ Wilderness
▭ Bridge
━ Major River
═ Minor River/Creek

Tower Junction ◆

Roosevelt Lodge ●

© Wilderness Adventures Press

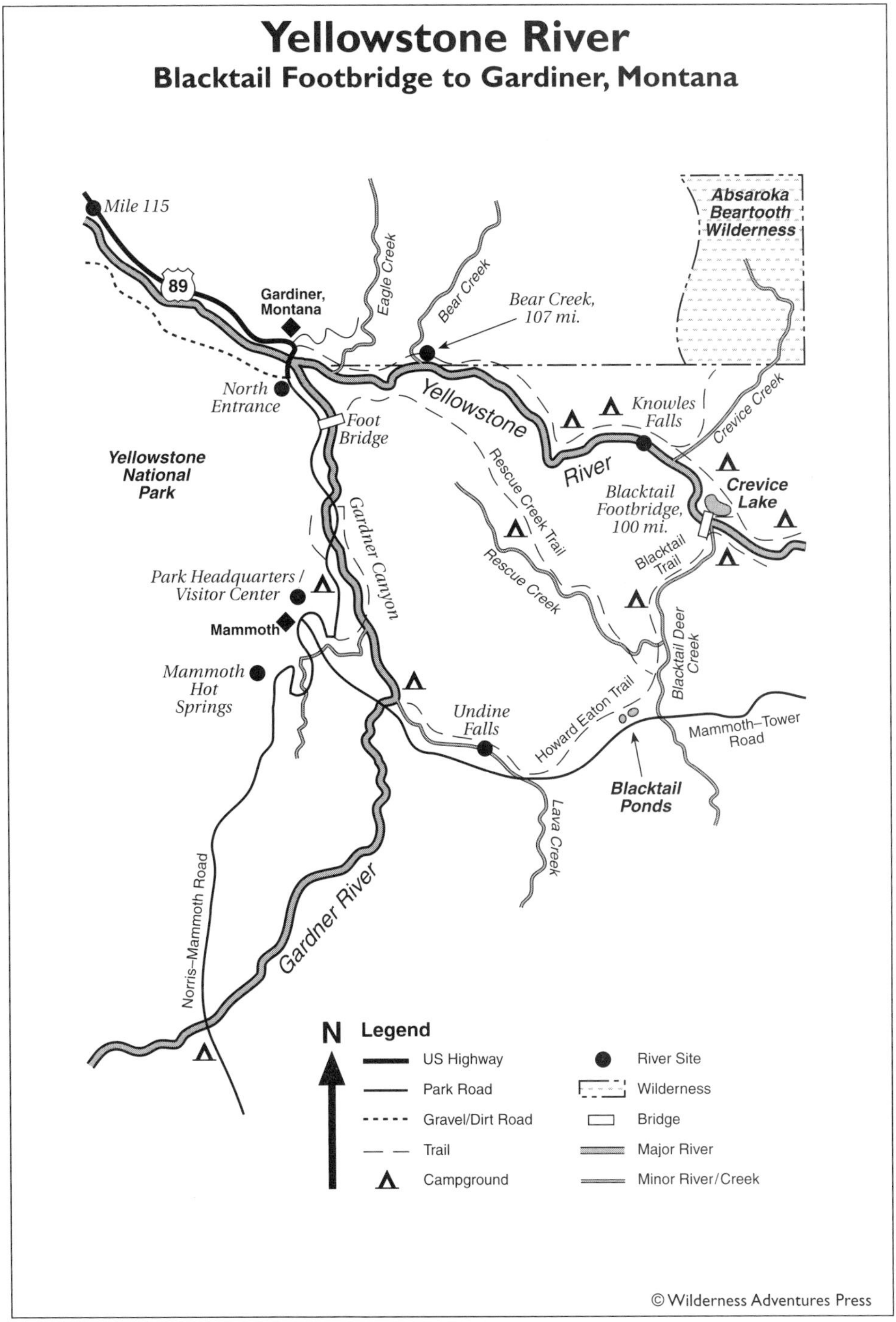

Yellowstone River
Blacktail Footbridge to Gardiner, Montana

Absaroka
Beartooth
Wilderness

Mile 115

89

Eagle Creek

Bear Creek

Bear Creek,
107 mi.

Gardiner,
Montana

Yellowstone

River

Knowles
Falls

Crevice Creek

North
Entrance

Foot
Bridge

Yellowstone
National
Park

Blacktail
Footbridge,
100 mi.

Crevice
Lake

Rescue Creek Trail

Blacktail
Trail

Gardiner Canyon

Rescue Creek

Park Headquarters /
Visitor Center

Blacktail Deer Creek

Mammoth

Mammoth
Hot
Springs

Undine
Falls

Howard Eaton Trail

Mammoth–Tower
Road

Blacktail
Ponds

Norris–Mammoth Road

Gardner River

Lava Creek

N

Legend

—— US Highway	●	River Site
—— Park Road	⌐⋯⌐	Wilderness
----- Gravel/Dirt Road	▭	Bridge
— — Trail	≡≡≡	Major River
▲ Campground	===	Minor River/Creek

© Wilderness Adventures Press

Although Chittenden believed the name Yellowstone originated from the color-ful walls of the Grand Canyon of the Yellowstone, most modern historians do not agree. They think historic uses of the name referred to the yellowish sandstone bluffs that border the river for about 100 miles near Billings, Montana. It is unlikely the Minnetaree Indians or early explorers knew of the now famous canyon below Yellowstone Lake.

The Yellowstone rises on the slopes of Yount's Peak, about 20 miles south of the park in the Teton Wilderness. Geologist Arnold Hague traveled to the Absaroka Mountains in 1887 and reported the source of the river "in a long snowbank lying in a large ampihitheater on the north side of the peak." The mountain was named for Harry S. Yount, Yellowstone's first gamekeeper, or park ranger.

From its source, the Yellowstone flows 671 miles to the Missouri at Williston, North Dakota. It pauses once—at Yellowstone Lake, the largest natural freshwater lake above 7,000 feet in the Lower 48 States.

On its 115-mile passage through the park, the river meanders through two extensions of the ancient lake, the delta and meadows above the lake, and Hayden Valley above the Upper Falls. Floods from melting glaciers carved the Grand Canyon of the Yellowstone during the last Ice Age, and the river was ultimately redirected by resurgent ice caps into the Missouri and the Atlantic Basin.

In all, four major canyons line its course from the mountains to the plains. The Grand Canyon features the dramatic 109-foot Upper Falls and 308-foot Lower Falls. At its deepest point, the multi-hued cliffs tower 1,200 feet above the river. The canyon is 4,000 feet wide at its broadest point. Downstream, the Black Canyon extends from Tower Junction to Gardiner. North of the park are Yankee Jim Canyon, north of Gardiner; and Rock Canyon, south of Livingston.

Sometime before or after the river carved its exit to the north, its celebrated Yellowstone cutthroat trout arrived through the basin's back door. Cutthroat began their migration up the Columbia and Snake Rivers about 1 million years ago and crossed the Continental Divide during the last Ice Age. The Yellowstone cutthroat's crossing was made by climbing Pacific Creek to the 8,200-foot Two Ocean Pass, north of Jackson Hole. From the pass, Atlantic Creek flows northeast to the Yellowstone River.

Biologists presume occasional movements of fish across the unique pass occur even today. But until the 19th century, the cutthroat was the only trout on the Atlantic side of the Northern Rockies. The Yellowstone cutthroat, which also inhabits eastern Idaho lakes and streams, expanded its range to include the headwaters of the Sho-shone, Big Horn, and Tongue Rivers. A subspecies, the westslope cutthroat, crossed the divide by a northern route south of Glacier National Park to reach several west-ern headwaters of the Missouri, including the Madison and Gallatin Rivers.

The Yellowstone's Lower Falls prevented upstream migration of rainbows to the upper river and the lake. First planted in the late 1880s in Montana, the West Coast species is now found in the lower canyon and its tributaries, including the Lamar River. The 40-foot Knowles Falls, 4 miles east of Gardiner in the Black Canyon, halted the migration of brown trout, a European species. Mountain whitefish also are com-mon in the Yellowstone's canyon waters.

Bottom of the open area below the Yellowstone Lake outlet.

Attempts to establish nonnative game fish in the upper river and lake during the park's early days fortunately failed. But the world famous fisheries face their greatest threat from the illegal introduction of lake trout, a northeastern U.S. and Canadian species, in Yellowstone Lake. Cutthroat anglers will suffer irrevocable losses in both the lake and upper river if the battle against the predatory lake trout is lost.

Flyfishers who flock to Buffalo Ford and other popular stretches of the upper Yellowstone marvel at the size of the cutthroat. Many assume they are year-round residents of this quintessential trout stream, although the majority are not. Joining the much fewer resident cutthroat in the river in spring and summer are huge swarms of adults that migrate out of the lake to spawn. The same is true of the headwaters.

Cutthroat caught in the upper Yellowstone are the same size as those hooked in the lake. Averaging 15 inches in length, they range from 14 to 18 inches, with a few rare trout exceeding 20 inches.

Smaller cutthroat are absent from the river and upper tributaries because they migrate to the lake. For about three years, young cutthroat ply its depths feeding almost exclusively on zooplankton filtered from the water with specially developed gill rackers. At 13 to 14 inches in size they switch to feeding on larger invertebrates and join the schools of adults cruising the lake shore.

The trout make their first migration into the river at 14 to 16 inches in size. Larger trout in the river have survived another two years in the lake to make a second migration.

Resurrection of these massive migrations is the park's greatest success story. Today's superb fishing is the product of a series of strict restrictions to reverse previously unsustainable harvests and prevent future exploitation of the cutthroat's "dumb gene."

"The cutthroat is more vulnerable to being caught by anglers than any other species of trout. It exhibits a general lack of wariness and can be readily caught on a wide variety of flies, lures, and baits," notes Albert McClane, author of *McClane's Game Fish of North America*. "Studies show it can be easily over-exploited by anglers. Even with light fishing pressure, up to half of the legal-sized cutthroat are often caught in a stream. However, it responds well to special regulations, such as size or bag limits, or catch-and-release restrictions."

Park guardians initiated their efforts to save Yellowstone cutthroat in the 1960s and made a series of changes in regulations before finding the right formula. In 1973, a catch-and-release rule protecting cutthroat in the river was imposed and fishing was delayed until July 15 from a mile below Fishing Bridge to the Upper Falls. That same year, Fishing Bridge was closed to anglers and the bag limit was reduced to 2 cutthroat under 13 inches on Yellowstone lake. The under 13-inches rule and delayed opening date were extended to the lake's tributary streams, including the Yellowstone delta, in 1978. A catch-and-release restriction for cutthroat in the lower basin and its tributaries and rainbows in all but a few park streams followed in 1987. But, in 1996, a 2-fish bag limit was reinstated for rainbows in the lower Yellowstone drainage. A ban against fishing the 6 miles of river from Sulphur Cauldron to Alum Creek created an additional sanctuary for the cutthroat.

"This prohibition was a good deal for everyone," M.R. Montgomery says in *Many Rivers to Cross*. "The undisturbed spawning beds and loitering pools in the Hayden Valley assure a reservoir of very large fish that will amble upstream and down into fishable waters for the amusement of flyfishers."

Seasons of the Yellowstone

Spring runoff in the Yellowstone drainage is stupendous, but the end to a decade of drought dramatically demonstrated the full power of the river.

It set a record in June 1997 with 22,540 cubic-feet-per-second mean flows at Corwin Springs, just below its exit from the park north of Gardiner. The river's flows were 195 percent of the previous median. It had been above normal in the eight months before spring runoff broke the record set in 1996.

Back-to-back record flows must be viewed as an anomaly, but it always pays to check on the previous winter's snowpack and late spring conditions before heading to high elevation rivers like the Yellowstone.

Its canyons, which open Memorial Day weekend, present few fishing opportunities before late June or early July. The bonus is that this period announces the vanguard of its excellent stonefly hatch and the best excuse to clamber into the rugged canyons.

Runoff above the delta also is problematic around its July 15 opener. It fishes best in August for those who accept the river's biggest commitment in time and effort.

LeHardy Rapids of the Yellowstone River.

For the majority of the Yellowstone's anglers, the huge lake acts as a buffer to the upper river. Most years it settles into its best fishing by the July 15 opening day. The date is circled on calendars around the world, so expect to share Buffalo Ford and other popular stretches with hordes of flyfishers.

The nine miles of open river below Fishing Bridge are the most heavily fished waters in the park. First-timers need to be aware, however, that the season of plenty is short-lived. After spawning on the spring flood, the cutthroat linger only briefly to rest and feed. They start returning to the lake in August, and by September the river is a different ball game. Autumn trout are scattered, fewer in number, and never as accommodating as those in midsummer.

The cutthroat's gullibility results in many anglers catching the same trout. A 1980–1981 Idaho State University study revealed each cutthroat tagged was caught an average of 9.7 times per season above the Upper Falls. Nevertheless, these remarkable trout are not a sure bet against being skunked. Even in the earliest days of a season, they often selectively feed on only one insect species or stage of a hatch. Late summer and autumn anglers are guaranteed challenges to match hatches.

The upper Yellowstone produces the most complex series of overlapping hatches in the park. Summer fly choices range from size 4 stoneflies and size 8 golden stones to size 14 little yellow stones and caddis, to size 12 or 14 green drakes and flavs, to size 16 or 18 pale morning duns and blue-winged olives. Fly casters also score bonuses with gray drake, pink lady, and trico patterns during sporadic hatches.

Evening spinner falls of mayflies in August at Buffalo Ford can be as exquisite as they are daunting. But on many days caddis outnumber mayflies, and the trout take just about any pattern in the right size during blizzard hatches. An elk hair caddis, small humpy, or stimulator is generally the best choice during quiet periods. Grasshoppers and other terrestrials are reliable in drawing up trout and linger until the first hard frosts. In September and October, fly choices are mostly restricted to microscopic caddis and tiny fall baetis—and gossamer leaders and tippets.

Beadheads, or nontoxic weights, are required to get small nymphs and emergers or moderate-sized woolly buggers down to bottom lies of the trout in summer. Small nymphs and emergers also are effective as dropper flies.

Wear chest waders, but don't overestimate your strength. Although the upper river runs flat, it is deceptively strong and very difficult to cross. One of the very few places it can be done safely—in low water—is above Buffalo Ford. Avoid unstable gravel bars along cutbank channels, and keep an eye out for hidden holes and deep pools. There are a few braided channels around small islands. Swift riffles are above and below LeHardy Rapids and above Sulphur Cauldron.

Access to the west bank is available at numerous parking lots along the loop road. For your own safety and that of other drivers, use them. The Howard Eaton Trail follows the river's east bank downstream from Fishing Bridge. It is rarely crowded, but solitary excursions are not recommended since grizzly bear sightings may occur.

Another factor to keep in mind is that the bison breeding season peaks in August. Buffalo Ford lives up to its name. Give all bison a wide berth, but most importantly bulls escorting cows. A mature bull may weight up to 1,800 pounds and can run 35 miles per hour.

The river between Alum Creek and the canyon runs deeper over a broad, weedy flat. Wading this stretch is difficult and it is dangerous near the Upper Falls. However, it offers good chances to sight fish for rising trout along the bank. The key hatch to watch for on or around opening day—and to avoid the circus at Buffalo Ford—is the green drake.

Forest-lined stretches away from the road offer better chances for solitude at both ends of the upper river.

Canyons of the Yellowstone

Delving into remote sections of the Yellowstone's canyon waters customarily results in more hiking than fishing, but it is a true wilderness experience. The canyon waters are deep, swift, and a milky green color as the river churns down a boulder-strewn bottom filled with swirling pocket waters and dangerous eddies. Cutthroat range from 10 to 18 inches, with a few going longer. Whitefish join the mix, along with rainbows above Knowles Falls and browns below it. Don't even think about wading; the only safe fishing is from the banks. Leave waders in the car and wear hiking boots.

A well-documented route to the canyon waters is Seven Mile Trail on the west bank at the top of the Grand Canyon. The first two miles are flat and offer great views of Silver Corde Cascade. The next five miles drop 1,300 feet to the river, where there

Grand Canyon of the Yellowstone at Tower Falls.

is little room to maneuver. The climb out is brutal. Think twice before attempting this one, although for the hardy there are reserved campsites at the bottom.

The best route for a day hike is found at the scenic Tower Falls. A popular trail with easy switchbacks leads to an overlook of the waterfall. Continue the descent to the river, and you are virtually alone. The broad floodplain and forested banks permit safe fishing for two miles or more upstream. The mouth of Tower Creek also offers good fishing.

Downstream at the Tower Junction Bridge, east of Roosevelt, several foot paths provide access for day hikes into the lower river and to the mouth of the Lamar River. More rock scrambling is required in these areas, so take care along unstable cliffs.

Maintained trails to Black Canyon start at the Hellroaring and Blacktail Deer Creek trailheads on the Tower–Mammoth Road. Foot bridges across the Yellowstone are located at the bottom of the trails. These trails are steep, 5 miles or longer in length, and better suited for overnight trips. Hellroaring, Coyote, and Cottonwood Creeks increase the fishing options for smaller cutthroat. Reservations are required for backcountry campsites.

The most exciting fishing in the canyons is during the stonefly hatch in late June or early July. Golden stones and little yellow stones, or willow flies, follow through July. Sofa pillows, salmonflies, Bird's stones, and smaller attractor patterns such as stimulators, double humpies, and yellow Sallies, draw full-charge strikes. Throughout the summer, elk hair caddis, humpies, attractors like Trudes and Wulffs, and grasshoppers are effective in quieter pocket waters, along current seams.

Pocket waters and holes can be explored with large dark stone nymphs and woolly buggers in early spring and summer. Moderate-sized wet flies and streamers are more effective in autumn.

Muddy flows from the Lamar River roil the waters of the Black Canyon after intense summer storms and temporarily shut down the fishing. Check on conditions before heading out.

Yellowstone Headwaters

Flowing out of the Teton Wilderness south of the park, the Yellowstone's Thorofare region above the lake's delta is the trip of a lifetime. It requires a major commitment since the long hikes in and out take a minimum of four days. Outfitters throughout the region specialize in horseback trips into this pristine area. Many anglers also go in on their own horses, but it still requires about the same amount of time. Reservations are required for backcountry campsites.

Mosquitoes are fierce to pesky in marshy meadows all summer. The region is prime grizzly bear country, so it is safer to hike in parties of three or more and absolutely necessary to keep clean camps.

The Thorofare Trail to the delta is 20 miles along the lake's east shore, starting from Lake Butte Drive. It continues another 20 miles along the river to the park's southern boundary. A foot bridge, 2 miles south of the park border, is the only one on the upper river.

The other route to the delta is 35 miles from the South Entrance, starting from the Heart Lake trailhead and continuing east along the Trail Creek trail. Crossings the delta east of Trail Creek can be dangerous in high water years.

Fishing is incredible for trout in the 14- to 18-inch range. It's also great in the many tributaries to the delta and the lake along its east shore. It is usually best in August, but runoff varies year to year. Check on conditions and forecasts before making the trip.

The Yellowstone Thorofare is a classic meadow stream, with numerous braided channels, riffles and runs, and large pools. The tributaries, like the highly rated Thorofare Creek, are tumbling mountain streams with pocket waters.

After the spawn, the cutthroat rest in quiet pools and runs of the river and feed throughout the day. Good hatches in early July are golden stones, caddis, and little yellow stones. Pale morning duns and green drakes also are on the water in mid-July and August. The cutthroat readily take generic mayfly and attractor patterns, too, like Adams, Cahills, stimulators, renegades, humpies, and elk hair caddis.

In dry years, anglers who enter the river south of Yellowstone's border can fish earlier than the park's July 15 opener. Reservations for designated campsites are not required.

Trails from Jackson Hole to the Yellowstone's headwaters are up Pacific Creek, west of Moose Junction, and up the North Fork of Buffalo Fork River, starting from Turpin Meadows east of Moose Junction. Both routes are about 30 miles long, and the trails meet at Two Ocean Pass to continue down Atlantic Creek to the Yellowstone River.

Stream Facts: Yellowstone River

Season
- Grand Canyon and Black Canyon: Memorial Day weekend through the first Sunday in November.
- Yellowstone Delta and Fishing Bridge to Grand Canyon: July 15 through the first Sunday in November.

Regulations
- No fishing for 1 mile below Fishing Bridge, and for 6 miles between Sulphur Cauldron and Alum Creek in Hayden Valley.
- Cutthroat are catch and release. Individual bag limits in the canyons for rainbows and browns is 2 fish, any size.

Trout
- Cutthroat above and below Yellowstone Lake average 15 inches in length and range from 14 to 18 inches, with a few rare trout exceeding 20 inches. Cutthroat in the canyons range from 10 to 18 inches. A few rainbows and browns are present in the canyons, as are mountain whitefish. Angler report cards give the Yellowstone an 84 percent satisfaction rating for its .9 fish per hour catch rate for trout averaging 15.3 inches.

Miles
- Mile 20: Park's southeast boundary
- Mile 25: Thorofare Creek Confluence
- Mile 31: Trail Creek trail crossing
- Mile 40: Yellowstone delta
- Mile 55: Yellowstone Lake outlet
- Mile 60: LeHardy Rapids
- Mile 65: Sulphur Cauldron
- Mile 71: Alum Creek
- Mile 75: Upper Falls
- Mile 85: Tower Creek
- Mile 90: Tower–Cooke City road bridge
- Mile 92: Confluence of Lamar River
- Mile 95: Hellroaring Creek
- Mile 105: Blacktail Deer Creek
- Mile 110: Knowles Falls
- Mile 115: Gardiner
- Mile 118: Park's northwest boundary

Character
- The Yellowstone delta and Thorofare region is a high mountain meadows run with numerous braided channels, riffles and runs, and cutbank pools.
- Fishing Bridge to Sulphur Cauldron is a long flat run with a pushy current through long meandering glides, riffles and runs, cutbank pools, and a few braided channels. The river below Alum creek is deep and unsafe to wade.
- Canyon waters are deep and swift as the river churns down a boulder-strewn bottom filled with swirling pocket waters and dangerous eddies. Wear hiking boots and fish from the banks; it is unsafe to wade at any time.

Flows
- The river runs high though June and clears in July in the canyons. Muddy flows from the Lamar River roil the waters of Black Canyon after intense summer storms and temporarily shut down fishing.
- Yellowstone Lake acts as a buffer for the upper river and generally fishes best around its July 15 opener.
- The Yellowstone delta runs high through June and begins to clear in July. It fishes best in August.

Access
- Loop road between Fishing Bridge and Upper Falls bridge.
- Trailheads to the canyons and the Yellowstone delta are located along the loop roads.

Camping
- Canyon Village Campground
- Fishing Bridge RV campground (no tents)
- Mammoth Campground

UPPER YELLOWSTONE RIVER MAJOR HATCHES (ABOVE LAKE)

Insect	A	M	J	J	A	S	O	N	Time	Flies
Golden Stone				X					A	**Dry:** Golden Stone, Yellow or Orange Stimulator, Bird's Stone #6–10; **Wet:** Bitch Creek Nymph, Montana Stone, Girdlebug, Woolly Bugger #6–10
Little Yellow Stone (Willow Fly)				X	X				A/E	Yellow Sally, Willow Fly, Blonde Humpy, Yellow Stimulator #10–14
Caddis				X	X	X			A/E	**Dry:** Tan and Olive Elk Hair Caddis, Goddard Caddis, Renegade, Hemingway Caddis #14–16; **Wet:** Beadhead Emerger, Soft-hackles, Squirrel Tail #14–16
Baetis					X	X	X		A/E	**Dry:** Blue-winged Olive, Blue Dun, Para-Adams, Para-Olive Hare's Ear #16–18; **Wet:** Pheasant Tail, Baetis Nymph #16–18
Pale Morning Dun				X	X	X			M/E	**Dry:** PMD, PMD Cripple, Yellow Sparkle Dun, Rusty Spinner #14–18; **Wet:** Hare's Ear Nymph, Pheasant Tail, Beadheads #14–16

HATCH TIME CODE: M = morning; A = afternoon; E = evening; D = dark; SF = spinner fall; // = continuation through periods.

UPPER YELLOWSTONE RIVER MAJOR HATCHES (ABOVE LAKE), CONT.

Insect	A	M	J	J	A	S	O	N	Time	Flies
Green Drake			▓	▓					A	**Dry:** Green Drake, Olive Extended Body Drake, Olive Wulff #10–12; **Wet:** Ida Mae, Prince Nymph, Zug Bug #10–12
Gray Drake				▓					A/E	**Dry:** Adams, Gray Wulff, Gray Sparkle Dun, Spinner #10–12; **Wet:** Hare's Ear Nymph #10–12
Trico					▓	▓			A	Black and White, Trico Spinner, Para-Adams #14–18
Callibaetis					▓	▓			A	Thorax Callibaetis, Crystal Spinner, Para-Adams #14–16
Midges				▓	▓	▓			E	Griffith's Gnat, Black and White Midge, Cream Midge, Palomino Midge #18–22
Terrestrials				▓	▓	▓			M/E	Joe's Hopper, Dave's Hopper, Parachute Hopper #8–14; Foam Beetle, Black Elk Hair Caddis #14–16; Black Ant, Rusty Ant #14–18

HATCH TIME CODE: M = morning; A = afternoon; E = evening; D = dark; SF = spinner fall; // = continuation through periods.

LOWER YELLOWSTONE RIVER MAJOR HATCHES (BELOW LAKE)

Insect	A	M	J	J	A	S	O	N	Time	Flies
Stonefly				■					A	**Dry:** Sofa Pillow, Bird's Stone, Orange Stimulator, Salmonfly #2–8; **Wet:** Black Stone Nymphs, Girdlebug, Woolly Bugger #2–6
Golden Stone					■		■		A	**Dry:** Golden Stone, Yellow or Orange Stimulator, Willow Fly #6–8; **Wet:** Bitch Creek Nymph, Montana Stone, Rubberlegs, Woolly Bugger #6–10
Caddis				■	■	■			A/E	**Dry:** Olive or Tan Elk Hair Caddis, X Caddis, Blonde Humpy, Yellow Sally, Stimulators, Renegade, Dark Deer Hair Caddis #14–18; **Wet:** Beadhead Emerger, Soft-hackles, Squirrel Tail #14–16
Baetis				■	■	■	■		A/E	**Dry:** Blue-winged Olive, Blue Dun, Olive Sparkle Dun, Para-Olive Hare's Ear, Para-Adams #16–22; **Wet:** Pheasant Tail, Baetis Nymph #18–20
Pale Morning Dun					■	■			M/E	**Dry:** PMD, Rusty Spinner, PMD Cripple, Yellow Sparkle Dun, Para-Adams #14–18; **Wet:** Hare's Ear Nymph, Pheasant Tail, Beadheads #14–16

HATCH TIME CODE: M = morning; A = afternoon; E = evening; D = dark; SF = spinner fall; // = continuation through periods.

LOWER YELLOWSTONE RIVER MAJOR HATCHES (BELOW LAKE), CONT.

Insect	A	M	J	J	A	S	O	N	Time	Flies
Green Drake				█					A	**Dry:** Green Drake, Olive Extended Body Drake, Olive Wulff, Para-Olive Hare's Ear #10–12; **Wet:** Ida Mae, Prince Nymph, Zug Bug #10–12
Flav (Small Western Green Drake)					█				A	**Dry:** Flav, Para-BWO, Slate Wing Western Drake, Coachman #14–16; **Wet:** Ida Mae, Prince Nymph, Zug Bug #12–14
Gray Drake				█	█	█			A/E	**Dry:** Adams, Gray Wulff, Gray Sparkle Dun, Spinner #10–12; **Wet:** Hare's Ear Nymph #10–12
Pink Lady				█	█	█			A	Prince Albert, Pink Lady, Pink Cahill #14–18; Pink Lady Spinner #14–16
Trico						█	█		A	Black and White, Trico Spinner, Para-Adams #18–22
Midges				█	█	█	█		E	Griffith's Gnat, Black and White Midge, Cream Midge, Palomino Midge #18–22
Terrestrials					█	█			M/A	Joe's Hopper, Dave's Hopper, Parachute Hopper, Madam X #8–14; Foam Beetle, Black Elk Hair Caddis #14–16; Flying Ant, Black Ant, Rusty Ant #14–18

HATCH TIME CODE: M = morning; A = afternoon; E = evening; D = dark; SF = spinner fall; // = continuation through periods.

Lamar River

The Lamar Basin is idyllic and serene through most of its short fishing season, but it no longer offers a solitary experience. The reputations of the Lamar River and Soda Butte Creek for producing large cutthroat trout annually captures the attention of growing numbers of flyfishers. Slough Creek's extraordinary fishing is no longer a secret in Yellowstone. Still, there is plenty of elbowroom, and anglers willing to hike a bit find solitude in secluded valleys and behind gently sloping hills.

The Lamar was named for Lucius Lamar in 1885 when he became Secretary of the Interior for President Grover Cleveland. Lamar is credited with keeping railroads and other developments out of the park. The first written mention of the beautiful Lamar Valley was 50 years earlier by Osborne Russell. His *Journal of a Trapper* is filled with intriguing descriptions of the waning days of the mountain men and the matchless wilderness of the greater Yellowstone region. Awed by the tranquility of the Lamar, Russell called it "Secluded Valley" and hoped its peace would never be disturbed. Earlier maps listed the Lamar as Beaver Creek and East Fork of the Yellowstone.

Today, the big sky expanses of the broad glacial bowl dwarf huge bison herds grazing on its sagebrush plain. Smaller herds of elk and bands of antelope roam the range. And the rolling hills and mountains of the Lamar again echo the howls of Rocky Mountain grey wolves.

The Mammoth–Tower–Cooke City Road bisecting the Northern Range is the only year-round road in the park.

Geographically, the Lamar Valley extends from Cache Creek to the Lamar Canyon, but most visitors to the basin also embrace the Soda Butte Creek and Slough Creek Valleys.

Soda Butte Creek, largest tributary of the Lamar, is the first stream to tempt flyfishers entering the park through the Northeast Entrance. A smaller carbon copy of the Lamar, it parallels the loop road to its confluence with the Lamar at the base of Druid Peak.

One of the few park streams with no road along its banks, Slough Creek's alpine meadows offer scenic backcountry fishing adventures. Charles Brooks, author of *Fishing Yellowstone Waters*, encouraged visitors to savor the creek's unique charms with the words, "You are in the most beautiful part of the largest angler's paradise in the world. Take time to enjoy it."

Cutthroat in the lower Lamar, Soda Butte Creek, Pebble Creek, and Slough Creek are catch-and-release only. On the upper Lamar, starting from and including Calfee Creek and all other tributaries, the limit is 2 fish, any size. The limit on rainbows in the Lamar drainage is 2 fish, any size.

Seasons of the Lamar

The Lamar drains the largest and most rugged mountains in Yellowstone, the Absaroka Range. A rushing torrent in spring, it pumps tons of mud and silt into the Yellowstone River long past June. Its runoff surge usually begins to wane by mid-July,

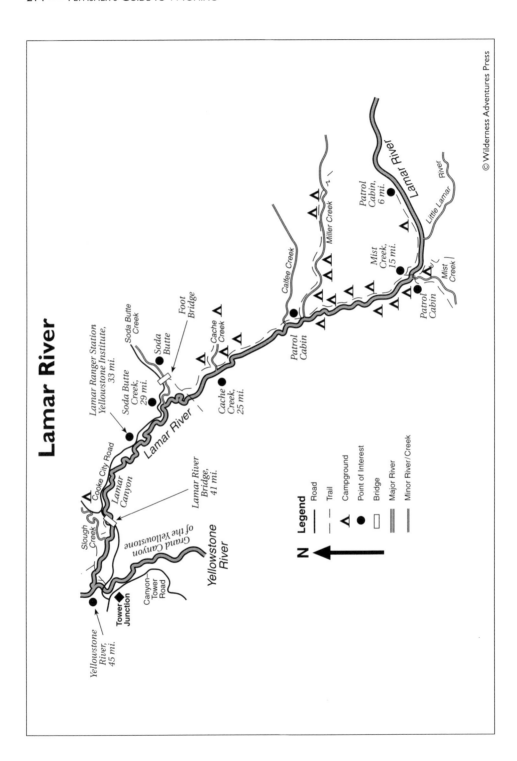

Lamar River

© Wilderness Adventures Press

Lamar River

Little Lamar River

Patrol Cabin, 6 mi.

Miller Creek

Mist Creek, 15 mi.

Mist Creek

Patrol Cabin

Caffee Creek

Patrol Cabin

Cache Creek

Soda Butte Creek

Soda Butte

Foot Bridge

Lamar Ranger Station
Yellowstone Institute,
33 mi.

Soda Butte Creek, 29 mi.

Cache Creek, 25 mi.

Lamar River

Cooke City Road

Lamar Canyon

Slough Creek

Lamar River Bridge, 41 mi.

Grand Canyon of the Yellowstone

Yellowstone River

Canyon-Tower Road

Tower Junction

Yellowstone River, 45 mi.

Legend

N

Road

Trail

Campground

Point of Interest

Bridge

Major River

Minor River/Creek

but dry fly action often doesn't start in earnest until the end of the month, and sometimes even later. After the Lamar calms down, much of the broad floodplain dries and the river retreats to its main channel; its numerous side channels are then relatively easy to wade. Still, its summer moods can change as quickly as a flash of lightning. Intense storms periodically muddy the river for days.

The Lamar rises at 8,000 feet in the Hoodoo Basin on the shoulder of Lamar Mountain and flows west and then northwesterly for about 45 miles to the Yellowstone. It tumbles in swift runs down a descent of almost 3,000 feet in 25 miles from the western slopes of the Absarokas to top of the Lamar Valley at Cache Creek. En route it grows in strength as it picks up the Little Lamar River and Mist Creek near the top, and Miller and Calfee Creeks above Cache Creek. Four miles downstream, it doubles in size as it merges with Soda Butte Creek. From Junction Pool, at the confluence with Soda Butte Creek, the Lamar plays tag with the loop road for more than 6 miles to the mouth of a sheer-walled canyon and another 2 miles to the Lamar Bridge above the confluence with Slough Creek. At the bridge, the river cuts away to the northwest through a shallow canyon for 4 miles to its plunge into the Yellowstone.

The valley or meadow run is marked by many serpentine turns through eroded glacial till in long riffles and runs, cutbank pools, and braided channels. Hikes into the river are short and relatively easy, except where the floodplain is marshy. This section receives the most pressure from anglers, with good reason. The canyon run is fast-paced and filled with large boulders, cascades, and pocket waters. Below the bridge, the river is essentially a long, continuous riffle, with smaller boulders, pools, and pocket waters.

The trail to the upper Lamar begins from a footbridge over Soda Butte Creek. A good day trip is the 4-mile hike to Cache Creek. It has the best fishing of the upper tributaries, and holds small cutthroat that go to 12 inches. Hikes to Calfee and Miller Creeks or the river's headwaters are better suited for overnight stays. The cutthroat are mostly under 10 inches. Backcountry campsites must be reserved in advance.

Bison in more remote areas of the park are more easily spooked than those seen along the loop roads. Stay alert when a herd comes down to a stream to drink. Grizzly bears are also present in the Lamar Valley, so take the usual precautions.

When the Lamar is clear, the fishing is often hot. Cutthroat in the valley range from 12 to 18 inches, and fish going 20 to 24 inches are occasionally reported. It also holds a few rainbow and cutthroat-rainbow hybrids. Cutthroat above the confluence of Soda Butte Creek are smaller on average and approach pan-size in the Lamar's high canyon runs and tributaries.

The Lamar fishes best in August and September, but finding the trout may be more difficult than catching them. They routinely change holding lies as river conditions and clarity alternate and flows create or expose secure shelter areas.

Hatches are random and scattered up and down the river, so large attractors and terrestrials are generally the most effective patterns. It is a classic dry fly stream.

Anglers on the scenic Lamar.

Some anglers don't even bother to pack nymphs, but they work, too, particularly in the canyon's pocket waters and holes.

Sporadic stonefly and golden stone hatches occur in July, but the river may be too out of shape to take advantage of the big bugs. Caddis and little yellow stones, or willow flies, are better summer options. Pale morning duns appear through summer and baetis linger longest into autumn. The key mayfly hatch to watch for is the green drake in late August or September, which is also prime time for terrestrials. The Lamar is the best grasshopper stream in the park.

Elk hair caddis, stimulators, humpies, yellow Sallies, and other high-riding attractor patterns like renegades, Trudes, and Wulffs work through the season. Generic mayfly patterns like blue duns, Adams, and light Cahill match most hatch situations, but don't forget a selection of green drakes. Grasshopper and beetle patterns should be large and bushy.

If the action remains slow, tie on a tag-along fly, like an ant or beetle, behind a larger terrestrial or attractor pattern. It could be the one the trout hit the hardest.

A low water year provides angling opportunities in the Lamar Canyon.

Searching forays up and down the river are a prerequisite on the Lamar. Ignore shallow riffles and work the logjams, undercut banks, and the holes and deeper runs below side channel riffles.

Be prepared to buck high winds in these wide-open expanses. They will kick terrestrials onto the water, but fishing with a short lightweight rod is not a good option. Use barbless hooks to avoid going home with an unwanted earring. Wide-brimmed hats and sunglasses also help prevent injury from wind-whipped flies.

When a lightning storm boils over Specimen Ridge, south of the valley, head for cover.

Stream Facts: Lamar River

Season
- Memorial Day weekend through the first Sunday in November.

Regulations
- Cutthroat in the lower Lamar, Soda Butte Creek, Pebble Creek, and Slough Creek are catch-and-release. On the upper Lamar, starting from and including Calfee Creek and all other tributaries, the limit is 2 fish, any size. The limit on rainbows in the Lamar drainage is 2 fish, any size.

Trout
- Cutthroat in the Lamar Valley range from 12 to 18 inches, and some exceed 20 inches; a few rainbow and cutthroat-rainbow hybrids are also present in this area. Cutthroat above the confluence of Soda Butte Creek range from 6 to 12 inches. Angler report cards give the Lamar an 81 percent satisfaction rating for its 1.14 fish per hour catch rate for trout averaging 11.7 inches.

Miles
- Mile 6: Upper Lamar Patrol Cabin
- Mile 15: Mist Creek
- Mile 25: Cache Creek
- Mile 29: Soda Butte Creek
- Mile 33: Lamar Ranger Station
- Mile 41: Lamar Bridge
- Mile 42: Slough Creek
- Mile 45: Confluence with Yellowstone

Character
- The upper river tumbles down a steep narrow valley to Cache Creek. The valley run is marked by many serpentine turns through eroded glacial till in long riffles and runs, cutbank pools, and braided channels. The canyon run is fast-paced and filled with large boulders, cascades, and pocket waters. Below Lamar Bridge, the river is essentially a long, continuous riffle with smaller boulders, pools, and pocket waters.

Flows
- Spring runoff surges through June and usually begins to wane by mid-July, but the river may not fully clear until the end of the month, and sometimes even later. Periodic summer storms muddy flows for several days.

Access
- Tower–Cooke City Road
- Footbridge across Soda Butte Creek, a mile east of Junction Pool, is the trailhead to the upper river

Camping
- Slough Creek Campground
- Pebble Creek Campground
- Cooke City
- Gallatin National Forest

LAMAR RIVER/SODA BUTTE CREEK MAJOR HATCHES

Insect	A	M	J	J	A	S	O	N	Time	Flies
Stonefly			█	█					A	**Dry:** Sofa Pillow, Salmonfly, Bird's Stone, Orange Stimulator #4–8; **Wet:** Black Rubberlegs, Woolly Bugger #2–8
Golden Stone			█	█					A	**Dry:** Golden Stone, Orange Zonker, Yellow Stimulator #6–10; **Wet:** Bitch Creek Nymph, Montana Stone, Girdlebug #6–10
Caddis				█	█	█			A/E	**Dry:** Tan or Olive Elk Hair Caddis, Blonde Humpy, Goddard Caddis #14–18; **Wet:** Caddis Emerger, Soft-hackles, Beadheads #14–16; Prince Nymph #16–18
Baetis						█	█		A/E	**Dry:** Blue Dun, Blue-winged Olive, Para-Adams #14–18; **Wet:** Pheasant Tail, Baetis Nymph #16–18
Pale Morning Dun				█	█				M/E	**Dry:** PMD, PMD Cripple, Rusty Spinner, Yellow Sparkle Dun #14–18; **Wet:** Hare's Ear Nymph, Pheasant Tail, Beadheads #16–18
Green Drake					█				A	**Dry:** Green Drake, Olive Wulff, Lime Trude #10–12; **Wet:** Prince Nymph, Zug Bug #10–12
Gray Drake					█	█			A/E	**Dry:** Gray Wulff, Para-Adams, Gray Sparkle Dun, Spinner #10–14; **Wet:** Hare's Ear Nymph #10–14
Callibaetis						█			A	Thorax Callibaetis, Crystal Spinner, Para-Adams #14–16
Midges							█	█	E	Griffith's Gnat, Black and White Midge #18–22
Terrestrials						█	█		M/A	Joe's Hopper, Dave's Hopper, Parachute Hopper #8–14; Foam Beetle, Disc O'Beetle #14–16; Ants #14–18

HATCH TIME CODE: M = morning; A = afternoon; E = evening; D = dark; SF = spinner fall; // = continuation through periods.

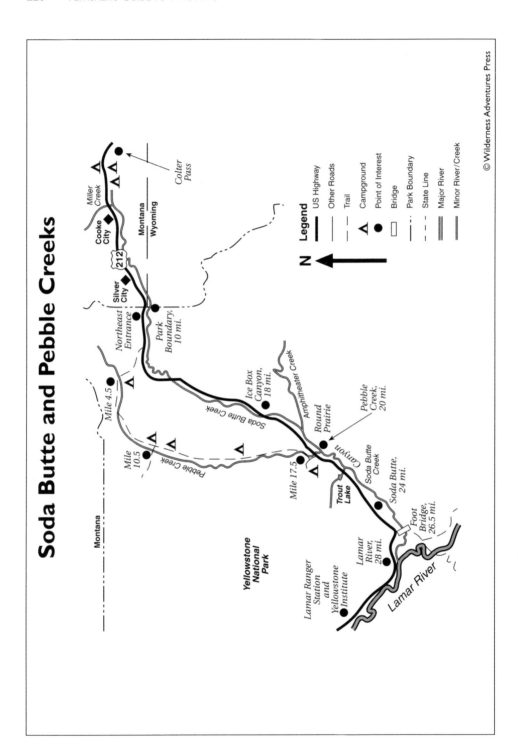

Soda Butte Creek

Soda Butte Creek, largest of the Lamar River's tributaries, rises in the Beartooth Mountains behind Cooke City, Montana. It skirts the highway as it enters the park at the Northeast Entrance and plays tag with the Tower Junction Road for more than 15 miles en route to its merger with the Lamar. From a small, bubbling brook, Soda Butte Creek grows in strength on its dash through a thickly forested valley, disappears briefly into Icebox Canyon, and bursts into view again at Round Prairie where it picks up Pebble Creek. After dipping into another short canyon, Soda Butte meanders down a broad, sloping sagebrush plain as it braids into numerous channels and flirts with the road again. Its lower valley run is a smaller, mirror image of the beautiful Lamar it joins at the face of Druid Peak.

Like the Lamar, the creek runs high through June and sometimes is muddied by intense storms in summer. It fishes best from mid-July to October. In fact, Soda Butte Creek boasts the third highest catch rate in the park. Angler report cards give it an 83 percent satisfaction rating for landing trout averaging 10.3 inches at a pace of 1.53 fish per hour.

Cutthroat in the 12- to 14-inch range inhabit the riffles and runs, pools, and braided channels of the meadows. But trout going 18 inches or better are occasionally netted from deeper pools and sheltered lies by persistent fly casters who explore remoter waters. A few rainbows also are found in the creek, and there are reports that brook trout have invaded its headwaters. Cutthroat above Round Prairie average 10 to 12 inches, but, again, occasional surprises are found in the pocket waters and long, deep pools of the forest run and lower end of Icebox Canyon.

The meadows are heavily fished near Soda Butte's confluence with the Lamar and in Round Prairie. To seek solitude, park north of Soda Butte, the travertine core of an extinct hot spring, and hike across the sagebrush flats to the creek. A footbridge crosses the creek about a mile south of Soda Butte.

The stream is easily waded, but a better tactic is to fish it from shore. Stalk the banks, channels, and tops of riffle pools in search of rising trout or explore grassy undercuts and logjams with terrestrials or attractors. When necessary, cross the creek at unproductive shallows to avoid disturbing fish downstream.

Hatches mimic those of the Lamar. Baetis, pale morning duns, and caddis make sporadic appearances through summer. Gray drakes in August and green drakes in August and September spur top water action. The high, semi-arid plain of Soda Butte Valley produces good crops of grasshoppers, beetles, and ants. But the stream also fishes well with attractors and generic mayfly patterns and small nymphs and emergers.

Bison are common in the meadows and should be given the right-of-way to avoid problems. A lucky few might sight wolves at dawn or dusk since the Druid Pack, the most active in the park, has claimed the eastern end of the Northern Range for its home territory. Grizzly bears may be sighted in the upper reaches of the creek. Fish the forested area only with at least two or three partners.

Upper Soda Butte Creek.

Pebble Creek

Pebble Creek joins Soda Butte Creek at Round Prairie on the Tower–Cooke City Road, about 10 miles southwest of the Northeast Entrance. It is one of the most scenic small mountain streams in Yellowstone and is as popular as a hiking destination as it is for fishing.

The creek's best fishing is in its meadow run through a forested valley near the top of the drainage; cutthroat averaging 10 inches, with some going 14 to 16 inches inhabit the run. A few deep pools and numerous logjams shelter the cutthroat in the crystal clear flows of the upper valley. Trout in the lower half of the 13-mile stream are smaller and very difficult to reach as Pebble Creek tumbles down a narrow rocky canyon. Its last mile is flatter, but swift and quite shallow after spring runoff wanes.

The easiest route for a day hike into Pebble Creek is from the top of its loop trail that begins at a picnic site about a mile west of the Northeast Entrance. It is a 2-mile hike to the stream from the road. Another trail climbs up and around the canyon starting from the footbridge at the campground above the stream's mouth. It is a steep, 7-mile hike to the creek's upper meadow fishery. A half-dozen backcountry campsites along the stream must be reserved in advance for longer visits.

This also is grizzly bear country, so it is best to explore the region in groups of three or more. Keep a clean camp, both at developed campgrounds and backcountry sites. Pebble Creek Campground often is one of the last ones in the park to fill. It is a good second choice base camp for anglers who can't find a site at the smaller and more popular Slough Creek Campground.

Slough Creek

A hike to Slough Creek's fabled alpine meadows is a rite of passage for many first-time flyfishers in Yellowstone. For those who return, the trek into the mountains is a pilgrimage of renewal. But both pilgrims and acolytes must anticipate crowds in July and August.

Surrounded by the towering Absaroka Mountains, the creek's meandering course through three high meadows is a setting virtually unrivaled for wilderness splendor. But it is the sight of large cutthroat cruising limpid pools as clear as aquariums that most haunts the memories of anglers.

Tied for third in sending home happy flyfishers, Slough Creek is given an 89 percent satisfaction rating by those who complete the park's fishing report cards. Its landing rate is 1.10 fish per hour for trout averaging 13.3 inches. One of the Volunteer Angler Reports confirming the pristine stream's bounty was filled out by former President Jimmy Carter. On a three-day visit to First Meadow in 1993, Carter caught and released 25 cutthroat. Eight were 18 to 20 inches and one was over 20 inches.

The cutthroat in all three meadows above the campground are thick-bodied and robust, compared to the long, slender cutthroat in the Yellowstone River. Cutthroat in the creek's final meander to the Lamar below the campground are alluring and strapping, too, and a fair number of rainbows and cutthroat-rainbow hybrids up the ante in size-classes. One of the most fertile streams in the park, Slough Creek's hatches are rich and complex.

Fly selections in the meadows range from midges, blue-winged olives, pale morning duns, and caddis that become progressively minute as the season advances, to jumbo gray drakes and green drakes that are surprisingly available well into September. Grasshoppers, beetles, and ants, including flying ants, are standard fare as in all meadow fisheries. But low-profile patterns are more productive. Stoneflies, golden stones, and little golden stones, or willow flies, are early season options in the creek's few large riffles and canyon waters.

Feeding frenzies occur, but just as often the trout key on specific stages of a hatch and are super selective. The gentle flows and clarity of the water give them ample opportunity to window shop. The larger trout cruise at will in long, glassy glides along deeply undercut bends. About the only structure in the meadows is scattered clumps of the banks calved into the stream by spring floods. Short, shallow riffles leading into the bends as well as the inside lies of pools typically hold smaller trout.

Slough Creek

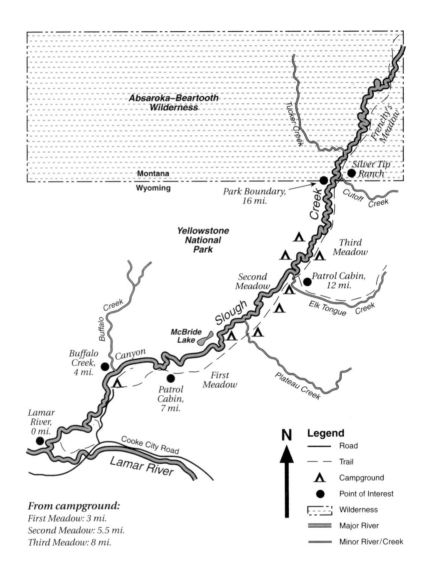

Absaroka–Beartooth
Wilderness

Tucker Creek

French's Meadow

Silver Tip Ranch

Montana
Wyoming

Park Boundary,
16 mi.

Creek

Cutoff Creek

Yellowstone
National
Park

Third
Meadow

Second
Meadow

Patrol Cabin,
12 mi.

Elk Tongue Creek

Buffalo Creek

Slough

McBride
Lake

Buffalo
Creek,
4 mi.

Canyon

First
Meadow

Plateau Creek

Patrol
Cabin,
7 mi.

Lamar
River,
0 mi.

Cooke City Road

Lamar River

N

Legend

——— Road
– – – Trail
Λ Campground
● Point of Interest
⌇⌇ Wilderness
▬▬ Major River
▬▬ Minor River/Creek

From campground:
First Meadow: 3 mi.
Second Meadow: 5.5 mi.
Third Meadow: 8 mi.

© Wilderness Adventures Press

Spring creek tactics are required to stalk the trout, and downstream presentations are generally the most effective. As flows diminish through the summer, it becomes even more prudent to keep a low profile when pursuing rising trout.

There is no need to lug chest waders to the upper meadows; a change of boots or hip waders suffice to make stream crossing at the tops of shallow riffles and to get across marshy flats.

Runoff on Slough Creek normally begins to subside by late June, and it fishes best from mid-July through September. But like the rest of the Yellowstone drainage following the end of a protracted drought in 1995, a string of exceptionally high water years has wreaked havoc with fishing agendas. Still, it is often ready earlier then the Lamar and Soda Butte Creek, and clears quicker after summer storms.

Slough Creek rises in the Beartooth Mountains near the famous Grasshopper Glacier behind Cooke City. It follows a meandering course down a forested valley between the Beartooths and Absarokas to Frenchy's Meadow and the Silver Tip Ranch at the Montana border.

The two-track trail from the Slough Creek Campground to the ranch is the only backcountry wagon road in the park. It also is the best route into the stream's three high meadows since the canyon above the campground is virtually impassable.

At the top of Slough Creek's 16-mile run through the park is Third Meadow. It extends about 5 miles to Elk Tongue Creek and the top of Second Meadow. About 2 miles through second meadow, the creek dips and romps through a short forest-lined stretch of riffles and pocket waters to First Meadow, where it flattens out again. The creek then cuts another long string of meanders for nearly 3 miles to the lip of its steep canyon.

The trail from the campground below First Meadow climbs about 3 miles up and around the canyon. The first half-mile or so is steep, but the rest of the route to First Meadow is relatively flat, with another short drop as the trail returns to the creek. Moose are often seen along this part of the trail.

First Meadow is a comfortable, hour-long hike and is often crowded. Second and Third Meadows are 5.5 and 8 miles from the campground, respectively, and are better suited for overnight visits but close enough for spry and fit hikers seeking solitude. Advance reservations are required for the seven backcountry campsites along the creek, as they remain solidly booked throughout the summer season.

The meadows are notorious for their pesky mosquitoes and deer flies. Don't forget bug spray, carry extra water for the hike out, and depart early enough to get back before dark. This last point is particularly important since grizzly bear sightings are very common in this valley. Heed posted warnings, both at the campground and in the backcountry, and don't hike alone. Keep a clean camp.

Finding a site at Slough Creek Campground is always tough, but high spring runoff in 1996 and 1997 made it even more difficult. Several sites were flooded and the park announced it may move up to 18 sites out of the flood plain to new locations; however, there are no plans to add more sites. The number available will

Canyon mouth below First Meadow on Slough Creek.

remain a meager 29 after completion of the reconstruction project. Arrive very early in the day to nab one.

The next park campground, about 5 miles east at Pebble Creek, often doesn't fill until late afternoon or early evening. Large public campgrounds are available a few miles east of Cooke City in the Gallatin National Forest.

From the campground, the creek meanders through the lower meadow for about 3 miles and drops down a short cascade into the Lamar. It has a few brief stretches of pocket waters and long deep holes, glassy glides, and oxbows. The trout are especially wary because they get even more pressure than the high meadows.

A number of turnouts to trails are spaced along the gravel road to the campground. The bottom of the creek also can be reached from the Lamar Bridge on the loop road.

SLOUGH CREEK MAJOR HATCHES

Insect	A	M	J	J	A	S	O	N	Time	Flies
Stonefly			▮						A	**Dry:** Salmonfly, Sofa Pillow, Orange Stimulator #2–8; **Wet:** Brook's Stone Nymph, Black Rubberlegs, Girdlebug, Woolly Bugger #2–10
Golden Stone				▮					A	**Dry:** Golden Stone, Orange Zonker, Yellow Stimulator, Bird's Stone #6–10; **Wet:** Bitch Creek Nymph, Montana Stone, Girdlebug #6–10
Little Yellow Stone (Willow Fly)					▮				A/E	Yellow Sally, Blonde Humpy, Yellow Stimulator, Willow Fly #10–14
Caddis						▮			A/E	**Dry:** Olive or Tan Elk Hair Caddis, X Caddis, Hemingway Caddis, Partridge Caddis, Renegade #14–20; **Wet:** Prince Nymph, Soft-hackles, Emergers, Squirrel Tail #14–18
Baetis							▮		A/E	**Dry:** Blue-winged Olive, Blue Dun, Para-BWO, Flav, Para-Olive Hare's Ear #14–20; **Wet:** Pheasant Tail #16–18

HATCH TIME CODE: M = morning; A = afternoon; E = evening; D = dark; SF = spinner fall; // = continuation through periods.

SLOUGH CREEK MAJOR HATCHES, CONT.

Insect	A	M	J	J	A	S	O	N	Time	Flies
Pale Morning Dun			█						M/E	**Dry:** PMD, Thorax PMD, PMD Cripple, Sparkle Dun, Rusty Spinner #16–18; **Wet:** Hare's Ear Nymph, Pheasant Tail #14–18
Green Drake					█				A	**Dry:** Green Drake, Olive Extended Body Drake, Parachute Olive Drake #10–12; **Wet:** Olive Sparkle Dun, Prince Nymph #10–14
Gray Drake				█	█				A/E	**Dry:** Para-Adams, Gray Wulff, Gray Sparkle Dun, Spinner #10–12; **Wet:** Hare's Ear Nymph #10–12
Midges			█	█	█	█	█		E	Griffith's Gnat, Cream Midge, Palomino Midge #18–22; Black and White Midge #16–20
Terrestrials			█	█	█	█	█		M/A	Joe's Hopper, Dave's Hopper, Parachute Hopper, Foam Beetle, Crystal Beetle, Dave's Cricket #12–14; Flying Ant, Black Ant, Rusty Ant #14–18

HATCH TIME CODE: M = morning; A = afternoon; E = evening; D = dark; SF = spinner fall; // = continuation through periods.

Gardner River

The Gardner River cuts a steep rocky course on its final sprint to merge with the Yellowstone River before it leaves the park. Joining the Yellowstone in the deep canyon bisecting the gateway community of Gardiner, the Gardner is the first stream to tempt many visitors who come to the North Entrance.

The river was named for Johnson Gardner, one of the first fur trappers to explore the upper Yellowstone region in the 1830s. Its upper meadow, or "hole," was a favorite mountain man rendezvous site during their heyday.

Divided in half by a deep impassable canyon, the bottom third of the river holds moderate-sized cutthroat, rainbow, and brown trout, as well as whitefish. Brown spawners running out of the Yellowstone in late fall draw the most attention of anglers. The river's upper mountain meadow run is a haven for small brook trout.

The Gardner River and three of its tributaries, Panther, Obsidian, and Indian Creeks, are the only streams in the park open to worm fishing by children 11 years old or younger. Joffe Lake, a tiny pond east of Mammoth, also can be fished with worms by children.

Cutthroat in the river are protected by a catch-and-release rule. Individual limits on browns, rainbows, and whitefish are 2 fish, any size. The brook trout limit is 5 fish, any size.

Seasons of the Gardner

The Gardner rises at 7,500 feet below Cache Lake in the shadows of the park's highest mountain, the 10,992-foot Electric Peak, west of Mammoth. It trickles east off the shoulders of the Gallatin Range into a broad bowl and lazily meanders through the marshy Gardner Meadow in a southeasterly direction. At the confluence of its three large tributaries at Indian Creek Campground, it doubles in size. It then swings north, and its pace quickens as it passes the Sheepeater Cliff Picnic Area and plunges into a deep narrow canyon to Osprey Falls.

Emerging from Sheepeater Canyon just above the Mammoth–Tower Road bridge, the river immediately enters the Gardner Canyon and picks up Lava Creek on its remaining 8-mile run to the Yellowstone.

The top 3 miles of the canyon are fairly wide on the south bank as the river cuts a northwesterly course around the barren, sun-baked slopes of Mount Everts. The river descends its narrow channel in a series of riffles and runs, long rock garden glides, and a few lava chutes. Near the end of this stretch, the steaming waters of Boiling River create a hot plume in the Gardner. This is the only hot spring in the park where bathing is permitted.

Just downstream at the 45th Parallel Bridge on the Mammoth–Gardiner Road, the river swings through a short oxbow bend and down a sloping riffle to enter a narrow rapids. The river's final 3 miles is a gallop down a constricted, boulder-strewn channel to its confluence with the Yellowstone.

The Gardner River is a torrent of muddy foam-flicked water in May and June. Most years it begins to clear by late June, but in exceptional runoff years it may not

Gardner River

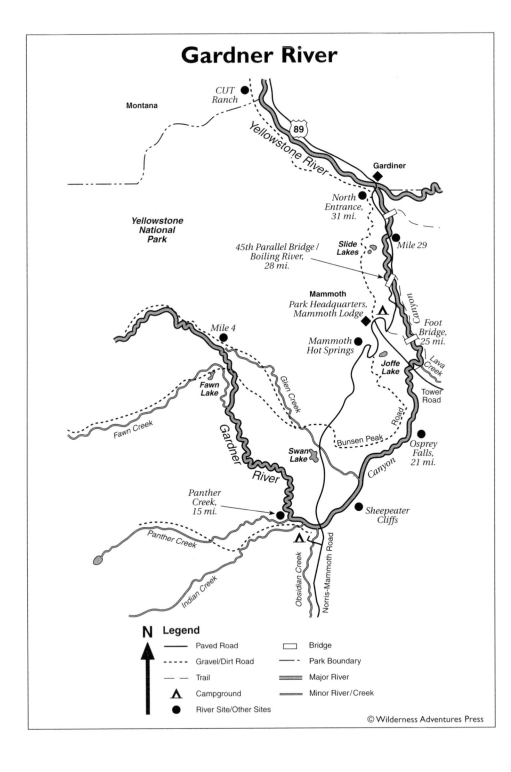

Montana

Yellowstone Ri ver

89

CUT Ranch

Gardiner

Yellowstone National Park

North Entrance, 31 mi.

45th Parallel Bridge / Boiling River, 28 mi.

Slide Lakes

Mile 29

Mammoth
Park Headquarters, Mammoth Lodge

Mile 4

Canyon

Foot Bridge, 25 mi.

Mammoth Hot Springs

Joffe Lake

Lava Creek

Fawn Lake

Glen Creek

Tower Road

Fawn Creek

Gardner River

Bunsen Peak

Osprey Falls, 21 mi.

Road

Swan Lake

Canyon

Panther Creek, 15 mi.

Panther Creek

Sheepeater Cliffs

Indian Creek

Obsidian Creek

Norris-Mammoth Road

N Legend

——— Paved Road   ▭ Bridge

- - - - Gravel/Dirt Road   — - Park Boundary

— — Trail   ▰▰▰ Major River

▲ Campground   ▰▰ Minor River/Creek

● River Site/Other Sites

© Wilderness Adventures Press

fish well with dry flies until mid-July. Summer flows are occasionally clouded by intense storms, but in autumn they are low and crystal clear.

Pan-sized brook trout in the river's headwaters—Gardner Meadow and its three key tributaries, Panther, Indian, and Obsidian Creeks—offer pleasant diversions for children and adults, alike. Visitors staying at the scenic Indian Creek Campground often keep a few of the chubby, brightly colored char for campfire meals.

There are a few small trout in the steep, narrow Sheepeater Canyon, but it is too dangerous to pursue them. In the middle of the canyon, the river plunges 150 feet over Osprey Falls.

Resident cutthroat, rainbow, and brown trout in the Gardner Canyon, below the Mammoth–Tower Road bridge, range from 8 to 14 inches, with a few larger browns. Lava Creek, which enters the river just below the bridge, adds more cutthroat to the mix, and both streams hold whitefish. In late fall, big browns run upstream from the Yellowstone to spawn, which makes the Gardner an important nursery stream for its larger sister.

The Gardner Canyon is an excellent dry fly stream. Effective patterns include high-riding attractors, like the royal Wulff or Coachman Trude, plus elk hair caddis, humpies, Goddard caddis, stimulators, and generic mayflies, like Adams and light Cahill. Hoppers and beetles draw slashing strikes in late summer. Similar patterns in smaller sizes work on the brookies in the upper meadow and its tributaries.

Stonefly nymphs, beadhead nymphs, caddis emergers, and soft-hackles dredge resident trout out of the canyon's pocket waters throughout the season. Larger nymphs, woolly buggers, and streamers come into play during the fall migration of brown spawners.

A prolific dark stonefly hatch in late June and early July, overlapped by hatches of golden stones and little yellow stones, or willow flies, kicks off the dry fly season in Gardner Canyon. Mayfly hatches, primarily baetis and pale morning duns, are sporadic in the canyon, but summer evening hatches entice the brookies into dimpling the waters of the meadows until after dark. Caddis hatches are good throughout summer into autumn. The milder climate of the park's northern range awakens terrestrials early in July and permits them to remain active into October.

Flyfishing is difficult in the narrow canyon below the 45th Parallel riffle due to extremes in water velocity and lack of room to maneuver. Fishing is good upstream to Lava Creek and in the lower end of the tributary's canyon. Only a few small fish are in the river above the Mammoth–Tower Road bridge.

There is a steep scramble down to the river at the bridge. A better route into the top of Gardner Canyon is a trail from the lower Mammoth residence area, east of Mammoth Campground, that starts from behind the elementary school. The parking lot at the 45th Parallel Bridge is often crowded, but the majority of the people using it wear bathing suits, not waders.

A pleasant approach to fishing the canyon is to hike slowly upstream hitting its riffles and runs, pocket waters, and pools with dry flies and attractors. Then, on the way back, search the same waters with nymphs, caddis emergers, or soft-hackles.

*Upper Gardner River,
near Mammoth.*

Autumns are often mild in the Gardner Canyon and fall brown hunters rarely are forced off the river before the season's closing day in November.

The upper meadows are easily reached from the Indian Creek Campground and the Fawn Pass-Electric Peak trailhead at the top of Swan Lake Flats, where Glen Creek crosses the loop road.

The park's Northern Range is home to one of the largest elk herds in North America. Moose are common in the Gardner's upper meadows and along its tributaries. Bull elk and moose in velvet are fairly docile in summer, but give them a wide berth when they polish their antlers for the fall rut. Also don't get in between a cow moose and her calves.

Black bears and grizzly bears are found in this region. Hike in groups when entering the upper meadows, and keep clean camps at both developed campgrounds and backcountry sites.

Stream Facts: Gardner River

Season
- Memorial Day weekend through the first Sunday of November.

Regulations
- Cutthroat are catch-and-release. Individual limits on browns, rainbows, and whitefish are 2 fish, any size. Brook trout limit is 5 fish, any size.
- Children 11 years of age or younger may fish with worms as bait in the Gardner River, Obsidian, Indian, and Panther Creeks, and Joffe Lake.

Trout
- Pan-sized brook trout are found in both the headwaters and meadow run to Sheepeater Canyon. Resident cutthroat, rainbow, and brown trout in the lower canyon range from 8 to 14 inches, with a few larger fish. Large browns run upstream from the Yellowstone River in late fall to spawn. Angler report cards give the Gardner an 85 percent satisfaction for its 1 fish per hour landing rate for trout averaging 8.5 inches.

Miles
- Mile 4: Glen Creek trail
- Mile 5: Fawn Pass trail
- Mile 7: Gardner Meadows
- Mile 15: Panther Creek
- Mile 21: Osprey Falls
- Mile 24.5: Mammoth–Tower Road bridge
- Mile 28: Boiling River hot springs
- Mile 29: 45th Parallel Bridge
- Mile 32: Confluence with Yellowstone River

Character
- The top half of the river cuts a narrow winding course across the marshy flats of Gardner Meadows to its confluence with Panther, Indian, and Obsidian Creeks at the Mammoth–Norris Road. About a half-mile downstream, it passes under Sheepeater Cliffs and plunges into a steep narrow canyon and over 150-foot Osprey Falls. Sheepeater Canyon is impassible, but the lower canyon below the Mammoth–Tower Road bridge is wider, and its shallow riffles and runs and pocket waters are easily fished. Below the 45th Parallel Bridge on the Mammoth–Gardiner Road, the river gallops down a constricted, boulder-strewn course to its confluence with the Yellowstone River in a deep canyon at the town of Gardiner.

Flows
- The Gardner flows high and muddy through June and starts to clear by late month or in early July. Summer flows may be clouded by intense storms, but autumn flows are low and crystal clear.

Access
- Mammoth–Gardiner Road
- Mammoth–Norris Road

Camping
- Mammoth Campground
- Indian Creek Campground
- Gardiner

GARDNER RIVER MAJOR HATCHES

Insect	A	M	J	J	A	S	O	N	Time	Flies
Stonefly			▓	▓					A	Dry: Sofa Pillow, Salmonfly, Bird's Stone, Orange Stimulator #2–8; Wet: Black Stone Nymph, Brook's Stone, Girdlebug, Rubberlegs, Woolly Bugger #2–6
Golden Stone				▓	▓				A	Dry: Golden Stone, Yellow or Orange Stimulator #6–8; Wet: Bitch Creek Nymph, Montana Stone, Girdlebug, Woolly Bugger #6–10
Little Yellow Stone (Willow Fly)					▓				A/E	Yellow Sally, Willow Fly, Blonde Humpy, Yellow Stimulator #14–16
Caddis						▓	▓		A/E	Dry: Elk Hair Caddis (tan, olive, or peacock), Renegade, Yellow or Royal Humpy #10–14; Wet: Caddis Emerger, Soft-hackles, Squirrel Tail #14–16
Baetis							▓		A/E	Dry: Blue-winged Olive, Blue Dun, Olive Sparkle Dun #14–18; Adams, Para-Adams #16–18; Wet: Pheasant Tail #16–18
Pale Morning Dun						▓			M/E	Dry: PMD, Thorax PMD, Yellow Sparkle Dun, PMD Cripple, Rusty Spinner #14–18; Wet: Hare's Ear Nymph, Pheasant Tail, Beadheads #14–18
Terrestrials						▓	▓		M/A	Joe's Hopper, Dave's Hopper, Parachute Hopper #8–14; Yellow Humpy, Yellow Trude, Yellow Stimulator #12–14; Madam X #8–10; Disc O'Beetle, Black Elk Hair Caddis #14–16; Ants #14–18

HATCH TIME CODE: M = morning; A = afternoon; E = evening; D = dark; SF = spinner fall; // = continuation through periods.

Madison and Gallatin River Drainages

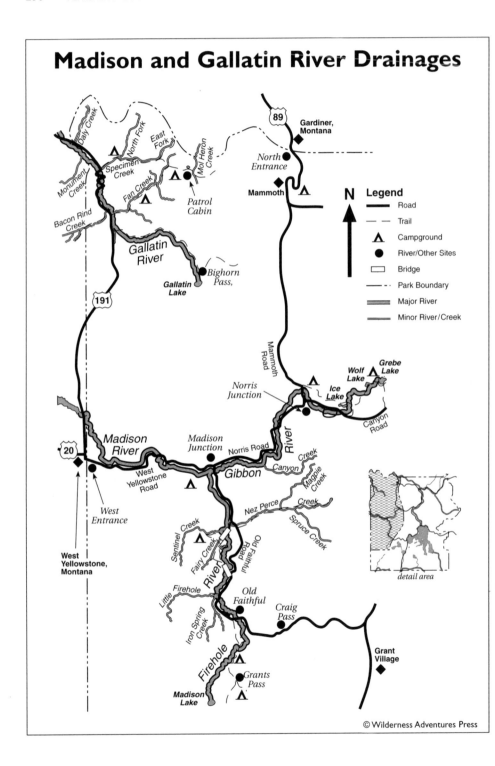

© Wilderness Adventures Press

MADISON AND GALLATIN RIVER DRAINAGES

The Madison and Gallatin Rivers, draining the northwestern highlands of Yellowstone, exit the park through separate valleys outlining Montana's Madison Mountain Range. Downstream at the tiny town of Three Forks, west of Bozeman, the Madison and Gallatin merge with the Jefferson to form the Missouri River.

Both the Madison and Gallatin course along two scenic highways to the park's West Entrance at the gateway community of West Yellowstone.

The road that follows the Gallatin upstream from I-90 at Bozeman is U.S. 191. It is the only major highway that passes through the park and offers more than 15 miles of direct access to the river.

Scenic U.S. 287 ascends the Madison from I-90 at Three Forks to West Yellowstone. The southern route to the popular resort town is U.S. 20 through eastern Idaho.

After passing through the West Entrance, anglers find the upper Madison fully accessible for nearly 10 miles of the park's loop road. A gravel side-road a half mile inside the entrance provides access to the lower half of the river.

At Madison Junction, the loop road provides the park's next two choices for easily reached fishing waters. The road to the south closely follows the Firehole River to Old Faithful and the Upper Geyser Basin. The road to the north parallels the Gibbon River to Norris Geyser Basin.

Madison River

The Madison River is the first of Yellowstone's fabled waters seen by the hordes of flyfishers who flock to the gateway community of West Yellowstone. Paralleled by the loop road to Madison Junction, it entices anglers to park, unpack rods, and delve into its mysteries.

The Madison is a moody river, difficult to fish, and gives up its secrets reluctantly; despite these characteristics, it is the second most renowned river in the park. It is the river Charles Brooks used to research and write his seminal books, *Nymph Fishing For Larger Trout*, *The Living River*, and *The Trout and the Stream*. Classics in flyfishing literature, they are textbooks for complex streams just about anywhere, not only the Madison. Brooks claimed it as his home river but never said it was easy.

The river has a good mix of moderate-sized brown and rainbow trout, with the browns going to trophy proportions during fall spawning runs out of Hebgen Lake in Montana. It is loaded with whitefish, and a few grayling make their way down the Gibbon from Grebe Lake.

One of the largest bison herds in Yellowstone inhabits the Madison Valley. Elk numbers rival bison, especially in autumn. The river is also home to the rare trumpeter swan; other waterfowl, as well as bald eagles and osprey, are common.

The Madison is formed by the confluence of the Firehole and Gibbon Rivers at National Park Meadow. It was named for James Madison, fourth president of the United States.

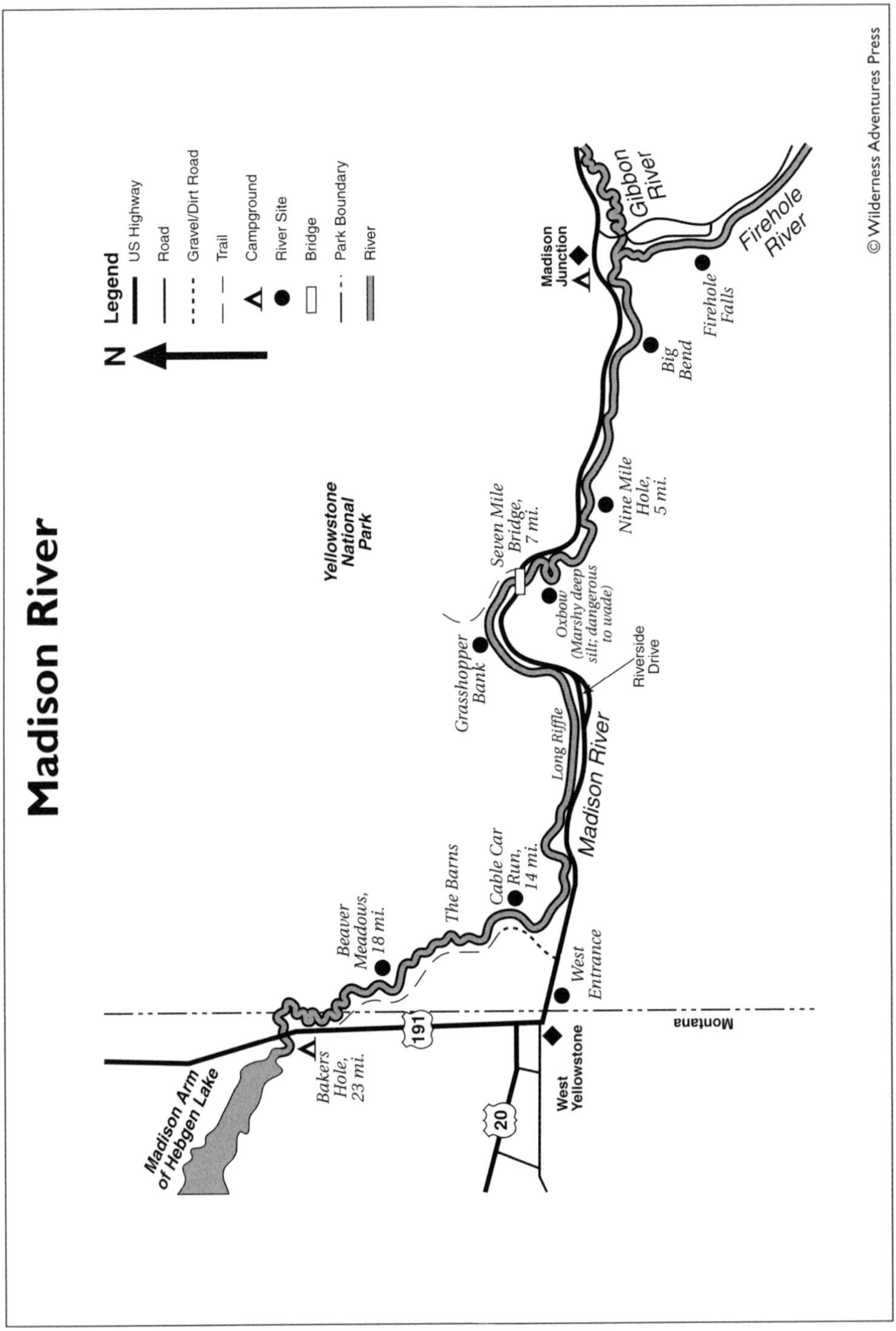

Madison River

Legend

US Highway	
Road	
Gravel/Dirt Road	
Trail	
▲	Campground
●	River Site
▢	Bridge
	Park Boundary
	River

N

Yellowstone National Park

Madison Arm of Hebgen Lake

Bakers Hole, 23 mi.

Beaver Meadows, 18 mi.

The Barns

Cable Car Run, 14 mi.

West Entrance

West Yellowstone

191

20

Montana

Grasshopper Bank

Seven Mile Bridge, 7 mi.

Oxbow (Marshy deep silt; dangerous to wade)

Long Riffle

Riverside Drive

Madison River

Nine Mile Hole, 5 mi.

Big Bend

Firehole Falls

Madison Junction

Gibbon River

Firehole River

© Wilderness Adventures Press

When the Lewis and Clark Expedition reached Three Forks in 1805 in present-day Montana, the captains found two streams so close in size and appearance that they could not decide which was the real Missouri. "We called the S.W. fork, that which we meant to ascend, Jefferson's River in honor of that illustrious personage (President) Thomas Jefferson. The Middle fork we called Madison's River in honor of James Madison (secretary of State), and the S.E. Fork we called Gallatin's River in honor of Albert Gallatin (secretary of the Treasury)," Meriwether Lewis wrote in his journal.

The Madison is restricted to flyfishing only. Rainbows and grayling are protected by a catch-and-release rule. The limit on browns is 2 fish under 13 inches.

Seasons of the Madison

Winter releases its grasp on the park earlier in the Madison Basin than in other areas of Yellowstone. It is the best wet fly option for opening day anglers, although the only guarantee about springtime in the Rockies is that it is capricious.

Runoff on the Madison is dictated by the Firehole and Gibbon Rivers, and most years it is fairly moderate. It peaks by June and begins to clear thereafter. In wet years, the river may run out of its banks and recede more slowly. Muddy flows from the Gibbon occasionally keep it off-color into July.

The warmer flows of the Firehole cause a summer doldrums on the Madison in low water years. It is less of a factor in cool, wet summers with good flows.

Rainbows and browns are in the 10- to 16-inch range, with a few browns exceeding 20 inches. The larger fish are most often found in the bottom half of the river away from the loop road.

Late autumn spawning runs by browns extend to the waterfalls on the Gibbon and Firehole, and all three waters are important nursery streams. Good numbers of the brown spawners exceed 24 inches. Larger rainbows follow the runs upstream from Hebgen Lake to nab eggs drifting out of the brown redds.

The Madison's hatches are not overly complex, but when they occur, they make a difference. Through summer, the river fishes best early and late in the day. Overcast days, and even rain, are most productive. Attractor patterns also work in riffle sections of the river.

A stonefly hatch on a few segments of the river draws top water action in early June into July, although it is difficult to time. It is most productive in the heavier waters above and below Cable Car Run, and sporadic activity occurs near the mouth of the Firehole Canyon. More important are the dark stone nymphs, rubberlegs, and woolly buggers critical to a flyfisher's arsenal throughout the year.

Little yellow stones, or willow flies, join caddis in June and July, and the caddis outnumber mayflies until late autumn. A short green drake hatch joins baetis and pale morning duns in mid-June or early July, but the key mayfly hatch to watch for is the trico hatch in August and September. The drakes and tiny tricos are found on quieter stretches of the river.

The Madison's meadow runs make terrestrials important components of fly boxes from early July to the first hard frosts of October. Low-profile hoppers are generally more effective.

Kathy Harris of Aiken, South Carolina, casts on the Madison.

Small nymphs, emergers, and beadheads take as many whitefish as trout, and quite often more. Anglers who follow the advice of Brooks on *Nymph Fishing For Larger Trout* need to remember that Yellowstone is a lead-free zone. Nontoxic materials must be used for weighted flies, split shot, and leader wraps.

The loop road follows the Madison from its birth to about 10 miles downstream, where it cuts away to the northwest to circle behind West Yellowstone. The lower river is reached from a gravel road about a half-mile east of the West Entrance. It leads to the famous Cable Car Run and Barns Holes. The trail into the bottom of the Madison's 20-mile run through the park starts from Bakers Hole Campground, a couple of miles north of West Yellowstone. This is the quickest route to Beaver Meadows.

Wading the Madison is tricky in some areas as its character changes. Its gradient is moderate and currents are subtle, but it flows with the full force of a river. Some channels are deeper than they appear, especially through boulder-filled runs and weed beds and around logjams.

The main place to stay out of is the long meandering bend between Seven Mile Bridge and Nine Mile Hole. It is marshy, and the deep silt in the channel is dangerous. Areas near the bridge may be closed in spring to protect nesting trumpeter swans.

Another set of obstacles to tread lightly around are the "beaver holes" of the lower meadow. These are actually channels cut into stream banks by beavers to

*Fish with big nymphs, ala Charles Brooks, pictured here,
when on the Cable Car Run of the Madison*

reach willows and other shrubs in the marshes. The murky water in the channels hides their depth. Unwary anglers may end up face down in the grass with one leg buried in the muck. Circle above the channels when they are too wide to step across easily.

Collecting the flows of the Firehole and Gibbon, the Madison swings west through Elk Meadow below Madison Campground and rambles though grassy flats past Big Bend down to a wooded run above Nine Mile Hole. The meanders are marked by series of undercut banks, long glides and pools, short swift runs, and weedy channels.

Below Seven Mile Bridge, the river's pace quickens and swings through a shallow weedy bend to the riffles and runs along Grasshopper Bank. From Riverside Drive, a short byway off the loop road, the river is a long shallow riffle that offers poor fishing until it reaches the Barns Holes and Cable Car Run. This area is a series of rumpled rocky runs, swift riffles above long, deep holes, and intermittent gravel bar channels.

About 3 miles downstream, the river flattens and meanders through the marshy Beaver Meadows in long pool-like glides divided by side channels, broad riffles, and narrow runs. It exits the park just above Bakers Hole Campground in the Gallatin National Forest.

The meadows are prime grizzly bear country, and no tents are permitted in the campground.

In fall, the undercut banks, deeper side channels, and pools of Beaver Meadows are holding areas in the first stage of the brown spawning run out of Hebgen Lake. Browns start showing up in the meadows as early as late August, but most wait until autumn storms cool water temperatures in late September or October. The colder the weather, the faster the run surges upstream to Madison Junction and the lower Firehole and Gibbon. And the nastier the weather, the better the fishing.

In cold weather, big weighted nymphs and woolly buggers are most effective, along with larger streamers, like Clousers, spruce flies, double bunnies, and Zonkers. During warmer weather, moderate-sized soft-hackles and beadheads such as Prince nymphs work, and even dry flies occasionally bring up a fish. Egg patterns may nab both rainbows and browns.

The window of opportunity to attack the spawning run is short. The season ends for the winter after the first Sunday in November. Park roads close sooner if early snows are heavy.

Madison Tributaries

Three small tributaries of the Madison flow out of the park north of Beaver Meadows to join the river in the backwaters of Hebgen Lake. A Montana fishing license is needed to fish the creeks west of the park boundary.

The first two, Cougar and Duck Creeks, join just west of U.S. 191, about 8 miles north of West Yellowstone. Short side roads to the east from the highway lead to parking lots and access to the creeks in the park. The third, Grayling Creek, runs parallel to U.S. 191 for more than 5 miles inside the park before it cuts west to reach the reservoir.

Moose and bison are common in the meadows around Cougar and Duck Creeks, and the region is prime grizzly bear country.

Cougar Creek: Cougar Creek meanders through a marshy meadow dotted by thick clumps of willows and shrubs and scattered beaver ponds. The turnoff to the park boundary, 7 miles north of West Yellowstone, is a gravel road south of the highway bridge.

The creek holds moderate-sized rainbow, brown, and brook trout that average about 10 inches, with occasional surprises. There are reports of westslope cutthroat in its higher reaches. Grayling were planted in the creek between 1993 and 1996, but the restoration project has had limited success.

Attractors and generic mayflies work in Cougar Creek, but it fishes best in late summer and fall with terrestrials and streamers. Also search carefully for large browns and rainbows in the beaver ponds. They are wary and difficult to hook.

Duck Creek: Duck Creek is a challenging mountain meadow fishery flowing through a broad, grassy flat with islands of lodgepole pine. The side road to the park boundary, 8 miles north of West Yellowstone, starts at the Highway Department shed south of the U.S. 191 and U.S. 287 intersection.

Formed by the confluence of Campanula, Richards, and Gneiss Creeks, Duck Creek offers about 3 miles of excellent fishing along its meadow run in the park. Like the Madison, it benefits from spawning runs of rainbows and browns from Hebgen Lake that average 16 inches. Brook trout also are present.

Low profile, spring creek tactics are required to stalk the wary trout in Duck Creek's open waters. Cautiously presented drag-free drifts of dry flies are critical. Mayflies in early summer include pale morning duns and green drakes, and terrestrials are most effective in late summer and fall. Its grassy undercut banks also can be explored with moderate-sized leeches and woolly buggers.

Gneiss Creek presents a side trip option for browns and rainbows averaging 10 inches, and occasional larger fish. Richards and Campanula Creeks hold tiny brookies.

Grayling Creek: A shallow, tumbling mountain stream, Grayling Creek gambols along U.S. 191 in an intermittent series of pocket waters, riffles and runs, cutbanks, and deeper pools. It exits the park at the point U.S. 191 enters it, 11 miles north of West Yellowstone. Anglers can pull over to fish it just about anywhere for the next 6 miles upstream. Northeast of the highway, the creek flows out of a rugged, steep valley not worth the effort to enter.

Grayling Creek holds westslope cutthroat, browns, and rainbows that average about 12 inches. Look for larger trout in deeper pools, sheltered lies, and around logjams.

Spring hatches include golden stones, little yellow stones, and caddis; pale morning duns are the predominant mayfly in summer. The creek also fishes well with attractors like humpies, stimulators, irresistibles, Wullfs, and Trudes, and generic mayflies like Adams and light Cahill.

Stream Facts: Madison River

Season
- Memorial Day weekend through the first Sunday in November.

Regulations
- The Madison is restricted to flyfishing only. Rainbows and grayling are protected by a catch-and-release rule. The limit on browns is 2 fish under 13 inches.

Trout
- Rainbows and browns are in the 10- to 16-inch range, with a few browns exceeding 20 inches. Larger fish are most often found in the bottom half of the river away from the loop road. Late autumn spawning runs by large browns extend to the waterfalls on the Gibbon and Firehole. Large rainbows follow browns out of Hebgen Lake. Whitefish are plentiful, and a few grayling are washed down the Gibbon from Grebe Lake. Angler report cards give the Madison a 62 percent satisfaction rating for its .51 fish per hour landing rate for trout averaging 13 inches.

Miles
- Mile 0: Madison Junction
- Mile 5: Nine Mile Hole
- Mile 7: Seven Mile Bridge
- Mile 10: Riverside Drive
- Mile 14: Barns Holes and Cable Car Run
- Mile 18: Beaver Meadows
- Mile 22: Park boundary
- Mile 22.5: Bakers Hole Campground

Character
- The Madison manifests as a quintessential trout stream with the confluence of the Firehole and Gibbon Rivers. From Elk Meadow below Madison Campground down through Nine Mile Hole, the river twists and turns in long, sweeping curves, undercut banks, deeper pools, intermittent riffles and runs, and channels. The marshy area extending above Seven Mile Bridge to Nine Mile hole is hazardous to wade. Flow quickens below the bridge, where a weedy channel descends to the riffles and runs of Grasshopper Bank. At Riverside Drive, the river turns into long shallow riffle as it veers away from the loop road. Downstream at Barns Holes and Cable Car Run, it runs through a series of rumpled rocky runs, short swift riffles, and long, deep pools. The final run flattens and meanders through the marshy Beaver Meadows in long, pool-like glides divided by side channels, broad riffles, and narrow runs to the park's boundary.

Flows
- Spring runoff peaks by June and begins to clear thereafter. In wet years, the river may run out of its banks and recede more slowly. Muddy flows from the Gibbon occasionally keep it off-color into July.

Access
- Madison Junction Road
- Cable Car Road, half mile east of West Yellowstone
- Bakers Hole Campground, north of West Yellowstone

Camping
- Madison Campground
- West Yellowstone
- Gallatin National Forest

MADISON RIVER MAJOR HATCHES

Insect	A	M	J	J	A	S	O	N	Time	Flies
Stonefly			█						A	**Dry:** Sofa Pillow, Salmonfly, Orange Bucktail, Orange Stimulator #4–8; **Wet:** Brook's Stone Nymph, Black Rubberlegs, Woolly Bugger #2–6
Little Yellow Stone (Willow Fly)			█	█					A/E	Yellow Sally, Yellow Stimulator, Blonde Humpy, Willow Fly #10–14
Caddis					█	█			A/E	**Dry:** Tan or Olive Elk Hair Caddis, X Caddis, Yellow or Royal Humpy, Hemingway Caddis #12–16; **Wet:** Beadhead Emerger, Soft-hackles, Prince Nymph, Squirrel Tail #14–18
Pale Morning Dun				█	█				M/E	**Dry:** PMD, PMD Cripple, Sparkle Dun, Rusty Spinner #14–18; **Wet:** Beadhead Hare's Ear, Pheasant Tail #16–18
Green Drake			█	█					A	**Dry:** Green Drake, Olive Wulff, Para-BWO #10–12; **Wet:** Ida Mae, Prince Nymph, Zug Bug #10–12
Baetis			█	█			█	█	A/E	**Dry:** Blue-winged Olive, Para-BWO, Olive Sparkle Dun, Blue Dun, Para-Adams #14–18; Tiny BWO #18–22; **Wet:** Pheasant Tail #16–18
Trico					█	█			A	**Dry:** Black and White, Trico Spinner, Para-Adams #18–22; **Wet:** Pheasant Tail #18–22
Midges							█	█	E	Griffith's Gnat, Para-Adams #18
Terrestrials					█	█	█		M/A	Joe's Hopper, Dave's Hopper, Parachute Hopper, Madam X #8–14; Foam Beetle, Dave's Cricket #14–16; Flying Ant, Black Ant, Rusty Ant #14–18

HATCH TIME CODE: M = morning; A = afternoon; E = evening; D = dark; SF = spinner fall; // = continuation through periods.

Firehole River

The most exotic trout stream in the world, the Firehole has mystified and captivated the outside world since its discovery by 19th century fur trappers.

Its name is often attributed to one of the tall tales of Jim Bridger, the king of the mountain men. However, it more likely derived from first being associated with a nearby valley gutted by a forest fire, and later with its geysers and hot springs. Fur traders and trappers often called open mountain valleys "holes," as in Jackson Hole.

The Firehole's modern fame as an extraordinary dry fly stream springs as much from the wariness of its brown and rainbow trout as from the privilege to cast a line in such a spellbinding amphitheater of nature. Puffs of steam and sulfurous vapors drift on the winds across an arena carpeted with spouting geysers, hissing fumaroles, and bubbling mud pots linked by the most genial of Yellowstone's streams. Lush meadows and verdant pine forests lining its banks harbor large herds of bison and scattered bands of elk, occasionally spooked by roaming coyotes, grizzly bears, and wolves.

The Firehole's character and trout are greatly influenced by voluminous geothermal outflows of the large geyser basins it bisects. But while it is commonly assumed that trout cannot live and reproduce in warm waters, they thrive in the Firehole. It is doubly amazing since the river held no fish prior to Yellowstone becoming a park. In 1889, brook trout were introduced into the upper Firehole, and the lower river received brown trout. Rainbows came later, and the river received supplemental plantings until park officials ended its hatchery programs in the mid-1950s.

The tiny cold mountain stream rises at an elevation of 8,670 feet from Madison Lake, 17 miles southwest of Old Faithful Village; later, it is dramatically warmed by the Upper Geyser Basin. Continuing to grow in size, it collects the steaming runoffs of Black Sands Geyser Basin and smaller thermal areas. The boiling outwellings of Excelsior Geyser Crater alone increase the temperature of the river by 5 to 7 degrees as it passes the Midway Geyser Basin. By the time it reaches the 40-foot Firehole Falls below the Lower Geyser Basin, the river's temperature has risen almost 27 degrees.

Seasonal temperatures and cold water tributaries like Iron Spring Creek, the Little Firehole River, and Sentinel and Nez Perce Creeks help moderate the Firehole's temperatures. However, summer flows routinely approach 70 degrees. In hot, dry years they may become lethal to trout as water temperatures approach 80 degrees.

As water temperatures increase in July and August, the trout bail out of the river into its tributaries. Conversely, in cold, wet summers, larger trout often remain in the river where there is more food and shelter.

The hot, mineralized waters of the geysers and hot springs contribute to winter production of aquatic insects and year-round growth of trout, said Lynn Kaeding, former Yellowstone research director for the U.S. Fish and Wildlife Service. But summer temperatures are high enough to inhibit brown trout maturity and kill rainbows.

"They grow fast—an 8- or 10-inch fish is only a year or a year and half old, but the high seasonal temperatures may limit growth after that initial burst," Kaeding said. The Firehole's rainbows and browns average 8 to 10 inches. "You'll get some 14 to 16 inches, and even fewer in the 18- to 20-inch range."

Firehole River

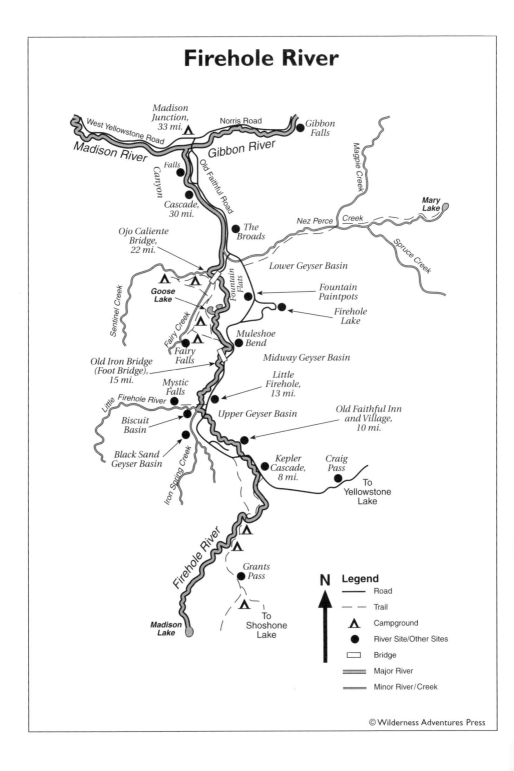

Madison Junction, 33 mi.

West Yellowstone Road

Norris Road

Gibbon Falls

Madison River

Gibbon River

Magpie Creek

Mary Lake

Falls

Canyon

Old Faithful Road

Cascade, 30 mi.

Nez Perce Creek

Spruce Creek

Ojo Caliente Bridge, 22 mi.

The Broads

Lower Geyser Basin

Sentinel Creek

Goose Lake

Fountain Flats

Fountain Paintpots

Firehole Lake

Fairy Creek

Muleshoe Bend

Midway Geyser Basin

Old Iron Bridge (Foot Bridge), 15 mi.

Fairy Falls

Mystic Falls

Little Firehole, 13 mi.

Little Firehole River

Upper Geyser Basin

Old Faithful Inn and Village, 10 mi.

Biscuit Basin

Black Sand Geyser Basin

Iron Spring Creek

Kepler Cascade, 8 mi.

Craig Pass

To Yellowstone Lake

Firehole River

Grants Pass

To Shoshone Lake

Madison Lake

N Legend

Road

Trail

Λ Campground

● River Site/Other Sites

▭ Bridge

Major River

Minor River/Creek

© Wilderness Adventures Press

A four-year study by Kaeding in the mid-1990s documented the exodus from the Firehole. "The numbers of fish in tributaries increased exponentially in relation to nearby Firehole River temperatures that ultimately exceeded incipient upper lethal levels for rainbow and brown trout," he stated in his report. But it is not a total evacuation from the river. "Periodic forays from tributaries were made, perhaps in response to food availability and competition for other resources," noted Kaeding. He speculated the trout take advantage of cooler water temperatures at night and in the first hours of daylight to forage in the river. Some trout also linger in cool water plumes below tributaries.

Electroshocking samples by Kaeding's crew found migrating rainbows in the tributaries averaged 10 inches and browns averaged 11.5 inches. The largest rainbow tagged was 19 inches and the largest brown was 22 inches.

But the two deans of flyfishing literature, Charles Brooks and Ernest Schwiebert, often fondly recalled days of yore when the "Queen of Yellowstone" held many more large trout and a richer aquatic insect population. They contended that a series of minor earthquakes in the 1970s raised its temperature and flushed toxic silt into the river.

Park biologists, on the other hand, note that significant changes in the river's trout populations occurred after the closure of its hatchery programs. It is now functioning as a wild trout fishery, but it also has had to cope with prolonged droughts.

But the answer to who is right might be moot. Kaeding raises an even direr specter. "Rainbow and brown trout in the middle and lower Firehole River in summer live near their upper lethal temperatures, an existence made more tenuous by climate warming," he stated. "As the river warms, use of cool water tributaries will increase, along with agonistic behaviors, predation, disease, and competition among fish in its tributaries. Moreover, the capacity for the cool water tributaries to hold fish could be reduced as ground water, the source of the summer flows in the tributaries, is warmed by climate warming."

A flyfishing only stream, the Firehole is closed to fishing in the Upper Geyser Basin. Its rainbows are protected by a catch-and-release rule. The limit on brown trout is 2 fish under 13 inches and the brook trout limit is 5 fish, any size.

Seasons of the Firehole

The Firehole sets the pace for Yellowstone's fishing season. Its spring runoff is the earliest in the park, it warms more quickly, and its hatches occur sooner.

Mostly flat along its meandering course through the long valley above its canyon, runoff is usually minor. But when the Firehole runs high and off-color into June, expect the rest of the park's streams to be filled to the brim or even out of their banks.

Generally, the Firehole is at its best in June for all brands of flyfishers. The trout show an interest in a great variety of flies they maddeningly ignore later in the season. Local flyfishers flock to it in spring, explore other waters in midsummer, and return in autumn for its most challenging dry-fly fishing.

Mayflies and caddis are small at the start of the season and truly microscopic as autumn descends into winter. Caddis species outnumber mayflies, but it is not a place for bushy, high-profile flies or attractor patterns. Neither is fair weather a blessing on the Firehole. It fishes best during cool, heavily overcast days.

Try thorax, sidewinder, and parachute patterns for mayflies, along with spinners and sparkle duns. The only consistent large mayfly in the river is the flav, or small western green drake. Dark flat-wing caddis patterns and sparsely tied elk hair caddis are most effective. But small yellow Sallies, blonde humpies, and stimulators work when little yellow stones, or willow flies, are on the water. Grasshopper choices rarely exceed size 12 and also require slim silhouettes, like parachute hoppers, Jacklin's hopper, or Joe's hopper. Tiny ants and small foam or fur beetles round out the terrestrial options.

During spring runoff, small beadhead nymphs or emergers and moderate-sized woolly buggers or soft-hackles are most effective in exploring the river. They also can be used to prospect for trout after it clears and top water action slows through midday. When making quartering casts with wet flies, pause and let the fly dangle at the end of the swing before retrieving it. This tactic often draws slashing strikes.

During hatches, or when using them as dropper flies, nymphs and emergers diminish in sizes like the adult insects as the season progresses.

Early day and evening hatches in June include baetis, or blue-winged olives, and pale morning duns, along with midges on quiet back waters. PMDs linger the longest into July, and tiny BWOs and midges return in force in late September to close out the season on the upper Firehole. Small western green drakes make their brief appearances around mid-June, and a few gray drakes may be encountered on quieter sections of the river about the same time.

Caddis options are good in early season; a few even emerge through the summer doldrums, and a new burst of activity in September and October lasts until hard frosts shut it down. Terrestrial activity is best in late August and September.

The Firehole is easily waded, although it has some deceptively deep channels in its lava rock floor, around weed beds, and along undercut banks. There also are a few marshy areas that present difficulties in approaching the banks without waders.

But wading usually is a second choice on the Firehole. The larger trout hang tight to the banks, which can have deep undercuts even along rocky ledges and along openings in weed beds. Except when fishing its few braided channels, the outside bends of wide meanders, or channelized weed beds, it is best to stay out of the water as much as possible. Stream crossings should be made at shallow riffles to avoid disturbing trout downstream.

The river is best suited to sneak and stalk fishing approaches from the banks, and offers good lessons in spring creek tactics found on other challenging waters. Precise, delicate casts with good slack in long, light leaders and slender tippets are required to dead drift flies through the subtle swirls of its currents.

The Firehole's Biscuit Basin Run starts at the loop road bridge just north of the exit to Old Faithful Village. The narrow river loops around the Black Sand Geyser Basin in a series of long slick glides and channels, with deep strong currents, as it gains strength from the flows of Iron Spring Creek and Little Firehole River.

It then rambles down a narrow rocky channel lined by forests and marshy meadows to the Old Iron Bridge and makes a short rocky turn north to the broad meanders

Mike Retallick,
of Cambellcroft, Canada,
fishes the Firehole.

of the famous Muleshoe Bend. This broad S-shaped loop of the Firehole is popular for sight-fishing to rising trout and often is the most crowded section of the river.

Fishing effectively ends as the stream dashes past the Middle Geyser Basin. It picks up again in the meadow and forest runs below Goose Lake in the Fountain Flats. There are some interesting pools and channels in this area, but fishing is often poor in the swift pocket waters above the Ojo Caliente hot spring.

The river then cuts a long loop past the mouth of Sentinel Creek, where there are some deep weedy runs, pools, and long undercut banks through the grassy meadow down to Nez Perce Creek.

From here downstream to the Firehole Cascade, the river rambles down a forest-lined flat paralleled by the Madison–Old Faithful Road. This short section, called The Broads, is essentially a long riffle, with weedy channels and braided gravel bars, and some deeper pools and pocket waters above the canyon lip.

The pocket waters of the canyon below Firehole Falls receive the most attention in early spring and late autumn, but are worth exploring throughout the park's season. Care should be taken in wading the rough cobble floor of the canyon run, which also requires some rock scrambling.

The middle of the canyon is reached by a one-way spur that begins just south of the loop road bridge below Madison Junction.

This is the one place on the river where big flies come into play. Sporadic hatches of small stoneflies and golden stones around mid-June open the canyon's season. Caddis, generic mayfly and attractor patterns, and moderate-sized stonefly nymphs and woolly buggers are effective year-round. In late fall the lower canyon is a large nymph and streamer fishery for big brown trout spawners that migrate up the Madison River from Hebgen Lake. Good-sized rainbows tag along to feed on eggs.

Even if your only visit to the park is at the height of summer, don't forego the otherworldly experience of fishing the Firehole. Dawn or dusk visits generally are more productive at this time. The shaded, swift runs through the forests below Biscuit Basin and behind Goose Lake often keep trout active through summer. Trout in the riffles and runs between Nez Perce Creek and the river's canyon often are less picky and continue to feed through summer.

The upper river above Old Faithful presents opportunities for another summer diversion. Rarely crowded, the riffles and runs of its meadow meanders below Kepler Cascade hold small brook trout and a few browns.

Remarkable rainbows and browns find refuge in late summer in cooler tributaries like the Little Firehole River, but they are incredibly shy and selective. Crystal clear flows and tangles of fallen lodgepole pine confound the challenges to net easily startled large trout. The most accommodating of the Firehole's feeder streams, Nez Perce Creek requires a 2-mile hike from the loop road to reach its best fishing in the meadow above the Culex Basin thermal area.

Anglers returning to the Firehole after long absences will find slightly longer hikes to portions of the river. New construction on the Madison–Old Faithful Road turned it away from several portions of the river. Also, the old Fountain Flat Freight Road was closed to motor traffic below the Ojo Caliente Bridge, south of the Nez Perce Picnic Area. The road, which once permitted anglers to drive to Goose Lake and the middle section of the river, is restricted to foot or mountain bike traffic. The southern route into the river above Fountain Flats is the Iron Bridge trailhead, below Biscuit Basin.

Thermal zones along the river should be approached with caution. Stick to clearly defined footpaths when entering these areas and walking along the banks. Don't attempt to cross chalky, unstable soils around geysers, hot springs, and mud pots.

Some backcountry areas and tributaries of the river, like Fountain Flats south of Ojo Caliente, are periodically closed to entry because of grizzly bear or bison activity. Check on restrictions at local fly shops or the Old Faithful Visitor Center when planning trips into more remote areas.

Stream Facts: Firehole River

Season
- Memorial Day Weekend through the first Sunday in November. Upper Geyser Basin, from Old Faithful to Biscuit Basin, is closed to fishing.

Regulations
- The entire river is restricted to flyfishing only. Rainbows are catch-and-release only. The brown trout limit is 2 fish under 13 inches. The brook trout limit is 5 fish any size.

Trout
- Rainbows average 10 inches and browns average 11.5 inches, with fair numbers of both species 14 to 16 inches, and a few in the 18- to 20-inch range. Anglers who fill out the park's report cards give the Firehole a 76 percent satisfaction rating for its .8 fish per hour landing rate and trout that average 9.7 inches.

Miles
- Mile 0: Madison Lake
- Mile 10: Old Faithful Village
- Mile 13: Little Firehole River
- Mile 15: Old Iron Bridge
- Mile 16: Muleshoe Bend
- Mile 21: Trail from Goose Lake
- Mile 23: Sentinel Creek
- Mile 24.5: Nez Perce Creek
- Mile 31: Firehole Cascade
- Mile 31.5: Firehole Falls
- Mile 34: Confluence with Gibbon

Character
- A small mountain stream from its source at Madison Lake on the north slope of the Continental Divide to the Upper Geyser Basin. Below Old Faithful Village, the river drops through riffle-filled runs into the broader, meandering flows of Biscuit Basin and continues to twist and turn through Midway Geyser Basin and behind Fountain Paint Pot Flats to Nez Perce Creek. Serpentine meadow runs hold occasional shallow riffles, numerous cutbanks, deeper pools, and long glides. Below Nez Perce Creek, the river's pace quickens through The Broads, a string of riffles and swift rocky runs above the Firehole Cascade and Firehole Falls. The short canyon is filled with swift channels, pocket waters, and deeper pools above the Firehole's confluence with the Gibbon at Madison Junction.

Flows
- Spring runoff is not a major factor most years, and flows during the remainder of the year are relatively moderate and stable, except in drought years. The Firehole may flow high and off-color through June after exceptionally wet winters.

Access
- The Madison–Old Faithful road skirts the east bank of the river with ample pull-outs. Trails to the west side start at Old Iron Bridge, north of Black Sand Geyser Basin, and from Ojo Caliente Bridge, on a deadend side road south of Nez Perce Creek Picnic Area.

Camping
- Madison Junction
- Gallatin National Forest
- West Yellowstone

FIREHOLE RIVER MAJOR HATCHES

Insect	A	M	J	J	A	S	O	N	Time	Flies
Stonefly			▓						A	**Dry:** Sofa Pillow, Bird's Stone, Orange Bucktail #4–8; **Wet:** Brook's Stone Nymph, Black Rubberlegs, Girdlebug, Woolly Bugger #2–8
Golden Stone			▓						A	**Dry:** Golden Stone, Yellow or Orange Stimulator, Yellow Sally #6–10; **Wet:** Bitch Creek Nymph, Montana Stone #6–10
Caddis			▓			▓			A/E	**Dry:** Elk Hair Caddis, Partridge Caddis, X Caddis, Yellow or Blonde Humpy, Dark Deer Hair Caddis #14–20; **Wet:** Caddis Emerger, Caddis Pupa, Prince Nymph #14–18
Little Yellow Stone (Willow Fly)			▓						A/E	Yellow Sally, Yellow Stimulator, Yellow or Lime Trude, Willow Fly #14–16
Baetis			▓				▓		A/E	Blue-winged Olive, Blue Dun, Blue Quill, Para-Adams #16–22; Tiny BWO #20–24
Pale Morning Dun			▓						M/E	**Dry:** PMD, Thorax PMD, PMD Cripple, Sparkle Dun, Pale Evening Dun, #16–20; **Wet:** Hare's Ear Nymph, Pheasant Tail #16–18
Flav (Small Western Green Drake)				▓					A	Flav, Slate-winged Western Drake, Para-BWO #14–16
Gray Drake			▓						A	Gray Drake Sparkle Dun, Spinner #10–12
Midges			▓				▓		E	Griffith's Gnat, Black and White Midge, Cream Midge #18–22
Terrestrials			▓				▓		M/A	Parachute Hopper, Jacklin's Hopper, Henry's Fork Hopper #10–14; Flying Ant, Black Ant, Rusty Ant #16–18; Foam Beetle, Disc O'Beetle #14–18

HATCH TIME CODE: M = morning; A = afternoon; E = evening; D = dark; SF = spinner fall; // = continuation through periods.

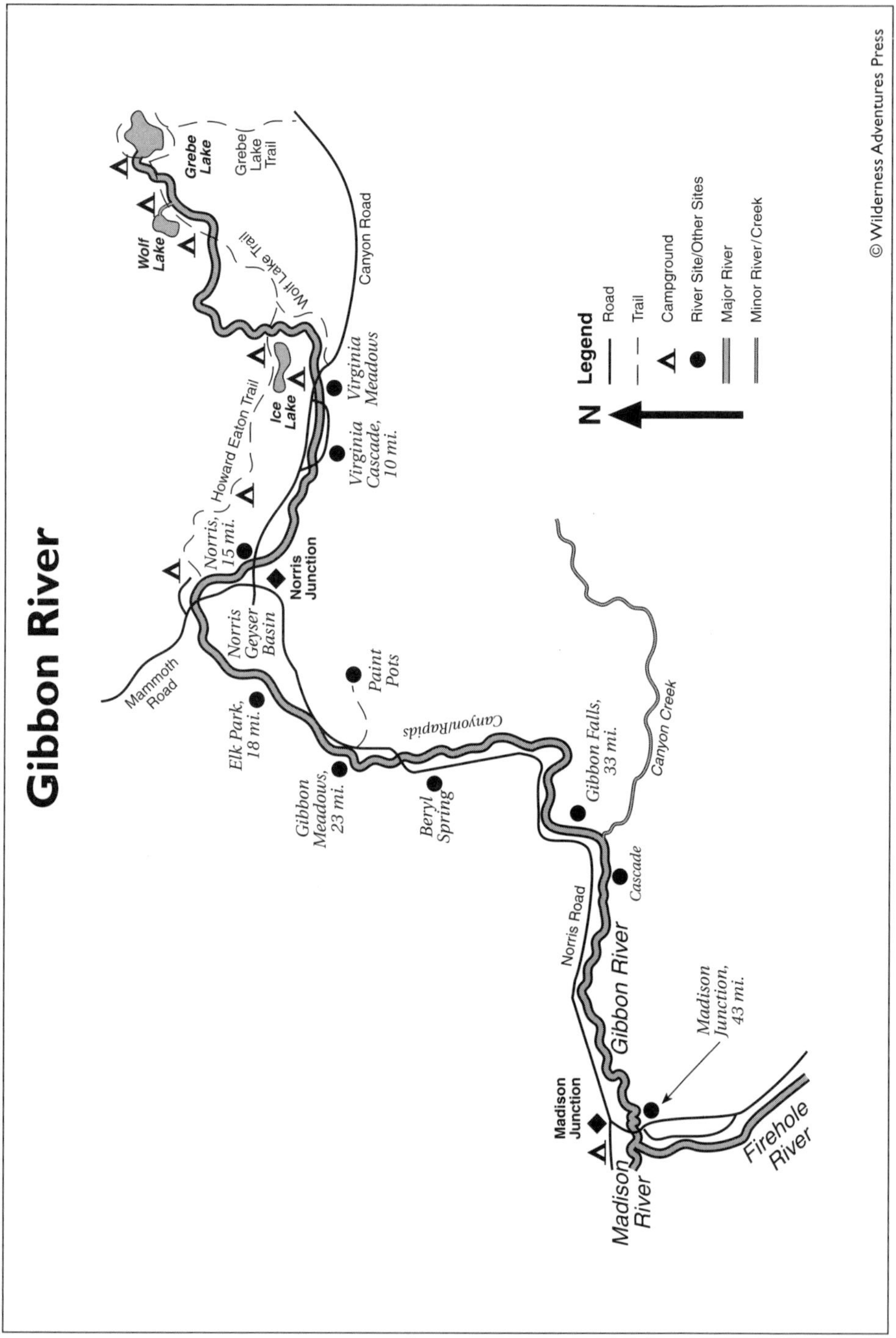

Gibbon River

Grebe
Lake

Grebe
Lake
Trail

Canyon Road

Wolf
Lake

Wolf Lake Trail

Howard Eaton Trail

Ice
Lake

Virginia
Meadows

Virginia
Cascade, Meadows
10 mi.

Norris,
15 mi.

Norris
Junction

Norris
Geyser
Basin

Mammoth
Road

Paint
Pots

Canyon/Rapids

Elk Park,
18 mi.

Gibbon
Meadows,
23 mi.

Beryl
Spring

Gibbon Falls,
33 mi.

Canyon Creek

Cascade

Norris Road

Gibbon River

Madison
Junction,
43 mi.

Madison
Junction

Madison
River

Firehole
River

Legend

N

— Road
- - - Trail
◬ Campground
● River Site/Other Sites
▬ Major River
— Minor River/Creek

© Wilderness Adventures Press

Gibbon River

The Gibbon River's generous variety in fishing alternatives reflects its transformations in character and trout populations.

Its fish range from pan-sized brook trout in the narrow headwaters and short meadow above Virginia Cascade to small rainbows and browns down through Norris Geyser Basin, to large wary browns in the long, meandering glides of Elk Park and Gibbon Meadows, to feisty rainbows and more brookies in the cascading, foam-flicked pocket waters of its canyon. Grayling in Grebe Lake, the river's source, often are flushed into the Gibbon. Late fall migrations of brown spawners run up the Madison River from Hebgen Lake to the face of Gibbon Falls.

Following the Gibbon from top to bottom is like opening a textbook on the evolution of a quintessential small mountain stream. Its passage through Norris Geyser Basin adds a uniquely Yellowstone chapter on geothermal dynamics. The 84-foot Gibbon Falls in the middle of the canyon is the most photographed waterfall in the park.

The river was originally named Gibbon's Fork of the Madison for Gen. Frank Gibbon, commander of Fort Ellis at present-day Bozeman in 1877. His forces joined the pursuit of northern Idaho's Nez Perce Indians on their ill-fated flight through western Montana and southeastern Idaho en route through Yellowstone to northern Montana. The Gibbon also was briefly known as the East Fork of the Madison and as the Hoppin River.

The Gibbon has the park's most complex set of regulations. It is restricted to fly-fishing only below Gibbon Falls. Rainbows below the waterfall are protected by a catch-and-release rule, and the limit above it is 2 fish, any size. The limit on brown trout below Gibbon Falls is 2 fish under 13 inches, and above it the limit is 2 fish, any size. The brook trout limit is 5 fish, any size. Grayling are catch-and-release only.

Seasons of the Gibbon

Spring comes earlier to the west side of the park, and in normal years, flyfishers can look for the Gibbon's runoff to start waning by mid-June. When winter snowpack is exceptionally high, Elk Park and Gibbon Meadows look like small lakes until late in the month.

Matching the hatch is not overly critical on the Gibbon, and generic mayflies, caddis patterns, stimulators, attractors, and terrestrials often fit the bill on most of its runs. The pocket waters, pools, and riffles and runs above and below the waterfall are perfect for wet fly anglers using beadheads, soft-hackles, and small woolly buggers. The river's most challenging fishing is for elusive browns in the high meadows.

A golden stone hatch in June jump starts the season in the canyon below Gibbon Falls, and fluttering flights of little yellow stones, or willow flies, draw fish to the top in late June and July. Caddis are a standard bearer throughout the year. A sporadic gray drake hatch also occurs in mid-June or early July in the meadow above Madison Junction.

The emergence of brown drakes is the principal mayfly hatch local anglers watch for in the upper meadows around the end of June. It is difficult to connect with these Big Mac drakes since both the emergence and spinner fall typically occur after dark. Still, when the weather man forecasts a dark, brooding, heavily overcast day, head for the backwaters of Elk Park or Gibbon Meadows.

Baetis and midges make short appearances in spring, but return in stronger numbers in autumn. Sporadic hatches of pale morning duns occur in July and August, and mahogany duns are worth watching for around mid-July.

August and September are the time to fish terrestrials, and hoppers offer the best chances to bring up large browns in the meadows.

Brown spawners, their autumn migration blocked by the waterfall, draw the most concentrated fishing efforts on the Gibbon. Dedicated local anglers routinely brave early winter snowstorms to get a last shot at the lower canyon before the park's roads close for the year. Moderate-sized woolly buggers and large nymphs generally work best at this time.

The only reason to journey to the Gibbon's headwaters—and it's a superb one—is to visit Grebe and Wolf Lakes. Among the prettiest backcountry ponds in the park, both hold the rare grayling and moderate-sized rainbows. Grebe Lake boasts the highest catch rate in Yellowstone, with 1.94 fish per hour, according to angler report cards. Sitting above 8,000 feet on the Solfatara Plateau, the lakes fish best after late June. The hike into Grebe Lake from the Norris–Canyon Road is 3.5 miles. Wolf Lake is about a mile west of Grebe.

Fishing starts in earnest on the Gibbon where it exits the forest at the Norris–Canyon Road and tumbles into Virginia Meadows. A picnic area offers a good site for family outings and fishing for pan-sized brookies. To reach it take the byway to the scenic Virginia Cascade and follow the road to the meadow.

Below the cascade, the river loops down to the Norris Junction Picnic Area and passes Norris Campground to circle behind the large geyser basin and enter Elk Park. The pocket waters, pools, and meandering, undercut glides between the cascade and the campground harbor more brookies and small to medium-sized rainbows and browns. High-floating generic mayflies, caddis, stimulators, and attractor patterns are the order of the day on this stretch. It is an excellent place for novices to hone their dry fly skills or help older children gain confidence and appreciation of flyfishing.

Elk Park, just south of the impressive Norris Geyser Basin, is where the Gibbon displays its status as a small mountain river. The collected flows of Solfatara Creek and geothermal runoffs from geysers and hot springs add strength and nutrients to the stream. But its long glassy glides and undercut banks are spring creek in nature, and the trout, almost exclusively browns, are correspondingly more wary. The meadow waters also hold a few brookies and rainbows.

A short quick drop through unproductive pine-lined riffles along the Madison–Norris Road connects Elk Park to the longer Gibbon Meadows and its equally challenging twists and turns across a high grassy plain. The river comes within 100 yards of the road at both meadows, but fishing is better in the interior of the two broad

Randall Vanhoof fishes the Gibbon Meadows.

bowls. The river is easily waded, but it is best to cross the stream at shallow runs to avoid disturbing trout downstream.

Browns in the 10- to 16-inch range meet the expectations of most visitors to the meadows, but seasonal reports of trophies exceeding 24 inches haunt the thoughts of serious trout stalkers. Sight-fishing to rising trout requires low-profile approaches to get into casting range. Stalking inside banks helps avoid lining and spooking the trout, and downstream presentations are generally more effective.

Hatches are sporadic and sometimes short-lived. It pays to keep moving in search of rising trout, but tread the banks lightly. Exploring grassy undercuts with hoppers and drifting ants or beetles down the inside lies of channels are often the best options to bring up browns in late summer and early fall.

Few have waxed so eloquently on the challenges of the Gibbon than Howard Back. Author of *The Waters of Yellowstone With Rod and Fly*, he wrote "... your fly must fall like down upon the water, for this is *kittle* fishing, no work for a novice or a bungler." *Kittle* is Scottish for tricky. Back, who fished the Gibbon in the 1930s, always packed an extra sandwich in his lunch. He knew he would have to apologize to his wife for not returning in time for dinner.

In autumn, the Gibbon's high meadows are hauntingly serene. The fishing is slower, but the days are pleasant and peaceful. Bull elk jealously guard their harems, and their bugling challenges announce the waning days of another season. A few giant bull bison plod stolidly along the river in lonesome forays across the flats. Prowling coyotes freeze in midstep, perk their ears, and nosedive into the amber, sun-cured grasses in pursuit of scampering field mice.

But don't become too beguiled by the wonders of nature unraveling around you. Give each elk boss, his harem, and the bachelors challenging him wide berths to maneuver.

The Madison–Norris Road closely parallels the Gibbon through its canyon run, and there are several narrow turnoffs to park and fish between the meadows and Gibbon Falls. The dramatic forest fires in 1988 generally had little impact on Yellowstone's fisheries, but this is one place where they did. Massive mudslides the following year temporarily blocked the road, and silt smothered some key trout rearing and holding areas.

Still, this is one of the most heavily fished parts of the river simply because it is so visible. Moderate-sized rainbows and brookies are scattered throughout the canyon, so it takes some extra effort to explore pocket waters, deeper pools below rocky riffles and sheltered lies under logjams. Embark on the search with high-floating attractors, caddis, and humpies and generic mayflies, or small nymphs and woolly buggers.

Similar options are presented by the river below the waterfall where there are longer riffles and runs, grassy cutbanks, and intermittent pocket waters. The channel is less confined than the upper reaches, and short hikes from the road easily reach its waters. They are rarely crowded until the browns of October run upstream. The same goes for the short meadow above the Gibbon's confluence with the Firehole to form the Madison. Grasshopper season is a good time to explore its grassy undercut banks, but keep an eye out for bison when entering the lower river.

Stream Facts: Gibbon River

Season
- Memorial Day weekend through the first Sunday in November.

Regulations
- Restricted to flyfishing only below Gibbon Falls. Rainbows below the waterfall are protected by a catch-and-release rule, and the limit above it is 2 fish, any size. The limit on brown trout below Gibbon Falls is 2 fish under 13 inches and above it the limit is 2 fish, any size. The brook trout limit is 5 fish, any size. Grayling are catch-and-release only.

Trout
- Pan-sized brookies are found in the headwaters and Virginia Meadows. Brookies and 8- to 12-inch rainbows and browns are found above Norris Geyser Basin to Virginia Cascade. In Elk Park and Gibbon Meadows, you'll find mostly 10- to 16-inch browns, with a few much larger fish. Brookies and 8- to 12-inch rainbows are found in the canyon runs. Brown spawners migrate up Madison River to the face of Gibbon Falls in late fall. Grayling are flushed out of Grebe and Wolf Lakes in high runoff years. Angler report cards give the Gibbon a 67 percent satisfaction rating for its 1.02 fish per hour catch rate for trout averaging 7.7 inches.

Miles
- Mile 0: Grebe Lake
- Mile 1: Wolf Lake outlet
- Mile 10: Virginia Cascade
- Mile 15: Norris Picnic Area
- Mile 18: Top of Elk Park
- Mile 23: Bottom of Gibbon Meadows
- Mile 33: Gibbon Falls
- Mile 43: Confluence with Firehole

Character
- A small, narrow, mountain stream to Norris Geyser Basin, where flows increase and the river cuts a shallow meandering course through Elk Park and Gibbon Meadows and enters a steep narrow canyon. It then cascades in swift runs and rocky pocket waters to 84-foot Gibbon Falls and plunges down a wider canyon with longer riffles and runs to a short meadow above Madison Junction.

Flows
- Spring floods normally drop in mid-June, and the river clears by July; runoff may remain high into July after exceptionally wet winters.

Access
- Madison–Norris Road
- Norris–Canyon Road

Camping
- Norris Campground
- Madison Campground
- West Yellowstone

GIBBON RIVER MAJOR HATCHES

Insect	A	M	J	J	A	S	O	N	Time	Flies
Golden Stone			▮						A	**Dry:** Golden Stone, Yellow or Orange Stimulator, Bird's Stone #6–10; **Wet:** Bitch Creek Nymph, Girdlebug, Woolly Bugger #6–10
Little Yellow Stone (Willow Fly)				▮					A/E	Yellow Sally, Willow Fly, Yellow Stimulator; Blonde Humpy, Yellow Wulff #10–14
Caddis					▮				A/E	**Dry:** Olive or Tan Elk Hair Caddis, X Caddis, Yellow or Royal Humpy, Renegade, Hemingway Caddis #14–16; **Wet:** Prince Nymph, Caddis Emerger, Soft-hackles #12–16
Baetis			▮		▮		▮		A/E	**Dry:** Blue-winged Olive, Blue Dun, Para-Adams #16–20; **Wet:** Pheasant Tail, Baetis Nymph #16–18
Pale Morning Dun					▮				M/E	**Dry:** PMD, PMD Cripple, Rusty Spinner, Sparkle Dun, Pale Evening Dun #14–18; **Wet:** Hare's Ear Nymph, Pheasant Tail, Beadheads #14–18
Brown Drake			▮						D	**Dry:** Brown Sparkle Dun, Spinner #10–12; **Wet:** Hare's Ear Nymph, Brown Emerger #10–12
Gray Drake			▮						A/E	**Dry:** Para-Adams, Gray Wulff, Sparkle Dun, Spinner #10–12; **Wet:** Hare's Ear Nymph #10–12
Mahogany Dun				▮					A	Mahogany Dun, Sparkle Dun, #16
Terrestrials				▮			▮		M/A	Parachute Hopper, Jacklin's Hopper #10–14; Foam Beetle, Disc O'Beetle, Dave's Cricket #12–14; Black Ant, Rusty Ant #16–18

HATCH TIME CODE: M = morning; A = afternoon; E = evening; D = dark; SF = spinner fall; // = continuation through periods.

Gallatin River

Coursing down a high mountain valley, the steep incline of the Gallatin River is an evident and lively aspect of its scamper to join the Missouri River. Yet, by Western river standards, it is a small and gentle stream along its run through Yellowstone.

The Gallatin is a popular diversion for travelers along U.S. 191, the only major highway through the park. Its best drawing cards are rare westslope cutthroat trout and grayling. It also holds rainbows, cutthroat-rainbow hybrids, and browns, as well as whitefish. Hook-ups on the Gallatin always possess elements of surprise in genial surroundings. Several key tributaries offer interesting side trips into remote, rarely explored waters.

The Gallatin was named for Albert Gallatin, Secretary of State in the Cabinet of President Thomas Jefferson. First documented by the Lewis and Clark Expedition, it is the eastern tributary of the three forks that merge to form the Missouri.

Cutthroat and grayling in the Gallatin are protected by a catch-and-release rule. Individual limits on rainbows and browns are 2 fish, any size.

Seasons of the Gallatin

The Gallatin is not a major runoff stream, but it may run high in June and not fully clear until early July. Fishing is good from July into October, except when periodic storms cloud the river and cause temporary doldrums.

Trout in the Gallatin range from 8 to 18 inches and average 11.5 inches. Tributary trout are generally smaller but offer occasional surprises. Grayling were planted in the lower river by the state of Montana and occasionally are found in the park's waters.

Matching hatches usually is not a problem even though the river has a good mix of small stoneflies, golden stones, caddis, and mayflies to play with when fish are rising. Generic mayflies and high-riding caddis, stimulators, and attractors answer most situations. Terrestrials are dynamite in late summer and early fall.

Caddis are prolific throughout the river's season. Small dark stoneflies and golden stones appear in late June and into July, and little yellow stones, or willow flies, linger to the end of July.

Green drakes and flavs, or small western green drakes, draw top water action in late June or early July. Baetis and pale morning duns appear through summer, with the blue-winged olives lasting into late fall. Cool, overcast days produce the best mayfly and caddis hatches, which occur progressively later in the day as the season advances.

August and early September are the prime grasshopper periods, but attractors produce on swifter waters from spring to fall. A popular tactic with Montana fly-fishers for drawing more strikes is to tie on a tag-along fly, like an ant, beetle, or generic mayfly behind a larger terrestrial or attractor pattern. When trout start hitting one more than the other, that's the time to fish in earnest with the primary target.

Access to the Gallatin is continuous for about 15 miles along U.S. 191, from just below the fishless Divide Lake to the park boundary. On the bottom end of the river in the park, anglers must stay within posted boundaries of the Black Butte Ranch on the west bank.

Gallatin River

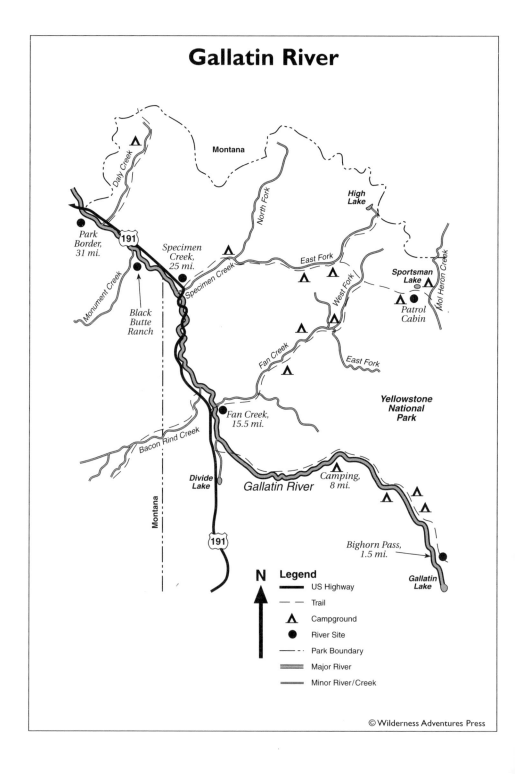

Montana

High
Lake

Daly Creek

North Fork

Park
Border,
31 mi.

191

Specimen
Creek,
25 mi.

East Fork

Sportsman
Lake

Mol Heron Creek

Monument Creek

Specimen Creek

West Fork

Patrol
Cabin

Black
Butte
Ranch

Fan Creek

East Fork

Yellowstone
National
Park

Fan Creek,
15.5 mi.

Bacon Rind Creek

Divide
Lake

Gallatin River

Camping,
8 mi.

Montana

191

Bighorn Pass,
1.5 mi.

Gallatin
Lake

N

Legend

———	US Highway
– – –	Trail
Λ	Campground
●	River Site
–··–	Park Boundary
▨▨▨	Major River
———	Minor River/Creek

© Wilderness Adventures Press

A father and son explore the Gallatin.

The Gallatin rises from the mouth of fishless Gallatin Lake at 8,500 feet on the north shoulders of Three Rivers Peak in the Gallatin Range. It remains a small trout mountain stream for its first 15 miles until it gains strength from the flows of Bacon Rind and Fan Creeks, 2 to 3 miles below Divide Lake. The next key tributary is Specimen Creek, about 5 miles down the valley.

Each of the tributaries offer an interesting, short hike to less crowded waters, and fishing for smaller but respectable cutthroat and cutthroat-rainbow hybrids in a pleasant meadow run. The scenery is great.

Fan Creek has its confluence with the Gallatin off of U.S. 191 22 miles north of West Yellowstone. It has populations of rainbow, cutthroat, and brown trout; some cutthroat in this stream are in the 12-inch range. To reach the fishable stretches of Fan, take the Fawn Pass Trail and then take the Sportsman Lake Trail as it follows Fan.

Bacon Rind Creek is found only a half-mile further north on U.S. 191. It contains cutthroat and rainbow trout in the 9-inch range, but receives heavy pressure right after snowmelt. Specimen Creek is found 27 miles north of West Yellowstone and offers fishing for cutthroat, rainbows, and cutthroat-rainbow hybrids in the 9-inch range. Fishing is best from the trailhead to the confluence of the East and North Forks 2 miles upstream.

It also should be noted that this is prime bear country. Generally, black bears are more often sighted than grizzlies, but it is always a good idea to travel in groups and keep a clean camp in remote areas.

The Gallatin's romp down the valley along the highway is essentially a continuous riffle. There are a few deep pools and braided channels. The trout hold tight to undercut banks and in sheltered lies along current seams.

The river is easily waded and there is no need for chest waders. Narrow channels permit casts from one bank to the other. Its size and basic fly choices make the Gallatin good for beginner flyfishers. Charles Brooks, author of *Fishing Yellowstone Waters*, saw the Gallatin in the park as "one of the friendliest rivers in the West ... The fish are where you think they are, and you fish it as you think you should. No stream can be more honest."

Downstream, the Gallatin dramatically changes character as it gathers larger tributaries, plunges through a narrow whitewater canyon, and spills onto a high plain for its final run to Three Forks, Montana. A very popular river, it is a great late summer and fall fishery. Its winter fishing ranks among the best in the West.

The Gallatin's wild and free romp through the canyon made it the obvious choice as a realistic setting for the popular film *A River Runs Through It*, based on Norman Maclean's classic autobiography.

Stream Facts: Gallatin River

Season
- Memorial Day weekend through the first Sunday of November.

Regulations
- Cutthroat and grayling are protected by a catch-and-release rule. Limits on rainbows and browns are 2 fish, any size.

Trout
- A mix of trout, mostly cutthroat and fewer rainbows and browns, range from 8 to 18 inches and average 11.5 inches. Tributary trout are generally smaller but offer occasional surprises. Grayling and whitefish are also present in the river. Angler report cards give the Gallatin a 79 percent satisfaction rating for its .92 fish per hour catch rate and trout averaging 11.5 inches.

Miles
- Mile 0: Gallatin Lake
- Mile 1.5: Big Horn Pass trail
- Mile 15.5: U.S. 191
- Mile 19: Bacon Rind Creek
- Mile 25: Specimen Creek
- Mile 27: Black Butte Ranch
- Mile 31: Park boundary

Character
- A gentle, mountain meadow stream with swift shallow runs, occasional deep pools and braided channels, and undercut banks along its many twists and turns down a sloping valley. It is easily waded.

Flows
- Spring runoff falls in June, and the river clears by early July. Periodic storms sometimes cloud the river and cause temporary doldrums.

Access
- U.S. 191

Camping
- Gallatin National Forest
- West Yellowstone

GALLATIN RIVER MAJOR HATCHES

Insect	A	M	J	J	A	S	O	N	Time	Flies
Stonefly			▮						A	**Dry:** Sofa Pillow, Salmonfly, Orange Stimulator #2–8; **Wet:** Black Rubberlegs, Brook's Stone Nymph, Girdlebug #2–10
Golden Stone			▮						A	**Dry:** Golden Stone, Yellow or Orange Stimulator #6–8; **Wet:** Bitch Creek Nymph, Montana Stone, Girdlebug #6–10
Little Yellow Stone (Willow Fly)									A/E	Yellow Sally, Willow Fly, Blonde Humpy, Yellow Trude, Yellow Wulff #14–16
Caddis					▮		▮		A/E	**Dry:** Elk Hair Caddis, Goddard Caddis, X Caddis, Hemingway Caddis, Humpies #14–16; **Wet:** Beadhead Emergers, Soft-hackles, Squirrel Tail #14–16
Pale Morning Dun			▮			▮			M/E	**Dry:** PMD, Yellow Sparkle Dun, PMD Cripple #14–18; **Wet:** Hare's Ear Nymph, Pheasant Tail, Beadheads #14–16
Baetis			▮				▮		A/E	**Dry:** Blue-winged Olive, Blue Dun, Olive Sparkle Dun, Para-Adams #14–18; **Wet:** Pheasant Tail, Baetis Nymph #16–18

HATCH TIME CODE: M = morning; A = afternoon; E = evening; D = dark; SF = spinner fall; // = continuation through periods.

GALLATIN RIVER MAJOR HATCHES, CONT.

Insect	A	M	J	J	A	S	O	N	Time	Flies
Green Drake				▮					A	**Dry:** Green Drake, Olive Extended Body Drake, Olive Wulff #10–12; **Wet:** Prince Nymph, Zug Bug #10–12
Flav (Small Western Green Drake)				▮					A	Flav, Para-BWO, Slate Wing Western Drake, Coachman #12–14; Lime Trude #10–12
Pink Lady					▮				A	Prince Albert, Pink Lady, Pink Cahill #14–18; Pink Lady Spinner #14–16
Midges							▮		E	Griffith's Gnat, Para-Adams, Black and White Midge #18–22
Terrestrials						▮			M/A	Joe's Hopper, Dave's Hopper, Parachute Hopper, Madam X #8–14; Foam Beetle, Disc O'Beetle #14–16; Ants #16–18

HATCH TIME CODE: M = morning; A = afternoon; E = evening; D = dark; SF = spinner fall; // = continuation through periods.

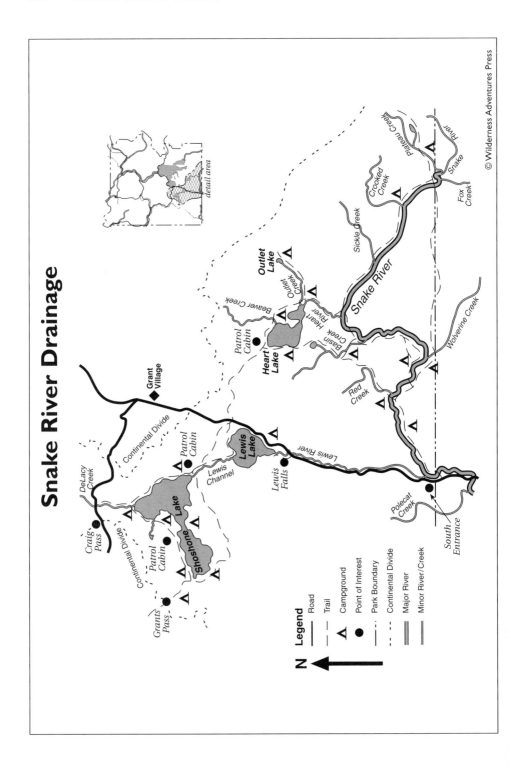

Snake River Drainage

SNAKE RIVER DRAINAGE

Some of the park's most remote fishing waters are located in its Snake River Basin southwest of the Continental Divide bisecting the southern third of Yellowstone.

The Snake River briefly skirts the South Entrance–West Thumb Road before it exits the park en route to Jackson Lake and its run through Grand Teton National Park. The south road also offers access to the Lewis River and Lewis Lake. Shoshone and Heart Lakes are at the end of relatively short hikes from the loop road.

But other routes into the eastern regions of this broad basin are strictly by foot or astride a horse. Extensive trip planning is required to reach the upper Snake River. It is a turbulent and often unpredictable river that offers better fishing to the south in Jackson Hole. The Snake also offers an alternate route to Heart Lake via its outlet, but both the lake and better fishing in Heart River are more easily reached by the Heart Lake Trail, northeast of Lewis Lake on the loop road.

Flyfishers looking for more rewarding streams off the beaten path in this basin find the best options in the Fall and Bechler Rivers. To reach them, you have to start from another state, Idaho. Located in the park's little explored southwest corner, hiking trails to the lower Fall River and Bechler Meadows are at the end of a short drive east from Ashton to the Cave Falls Road.

Another route to the upper and lower Fall River, along with Beula Lake, the Fall's source, is a very primitive road that parallels the park's southern boundary from Flagg Ranch, just south of the South Entrance, to Ashton.

Upper Snake River

The Snake River rises at about 9,000 feet on the shoulders of the high, rumpled Two Ocean Plateau defining Yellowstone's southeast corner and the Teton Wilderness Area north of Jackson Hole.

Beginning as a humble trickle south of Mariposa Lake, the Snake makes a brief loop south into the Teton Wilderness and turns north to return to the park. It collects small tributaries as it cuts a steep northwesterly course along the face of Big Game Ridge in a rapid descent of nearly 1,000 feet in 10 miles to pick up the Heart River in a short valley. It then turns abruptly south through a narrow 10-mile canyon that loops north again until the Red Mountains bounce its course to the southwest. The river's final 5-mile run in the park is through a broad valley above the South Entrance, where it turns almost due south and exits the park.

Few anglers venture very far upstream afoot from the park boundary to fish the Snake's banks during its early season. Spring runoff is often high and turbulent, and very murky. Later hikes upstream are along trails that dip and climb along the river and circle its canyon. Several stream crossings can be treacherous well into July in high water years. A few Jackson outfitters offer horseback trips into the upper Snake and to Heart Lake and other sites on the plateau.

Most years, the lower Snake fishes best after late July but it still must be approached with caution in swift runs or deep channels. Unstable gravel bars and undercut banks along the main channel of the braided river should be avoided. River

Upper Snake River

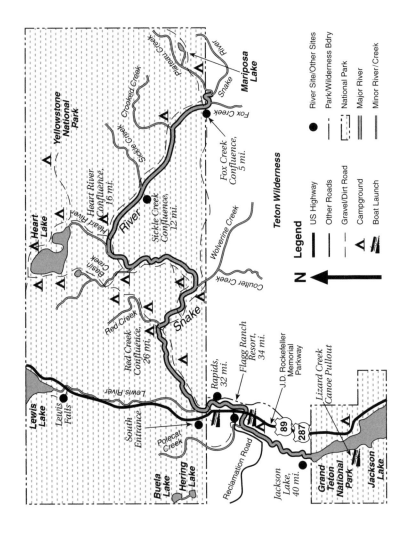

Legend

N

	US Highway
	Other Roads
	Gravel/Dirt Road
▲	Campground
	Boat Launch

●	River Site/Other Sites
	Park/Wilderness Bdry
	National Park
	Major River
	Minor River/Creek

Teton Wilderness

Yellowstone National Park

Heart Lake

Mariposa Lake

Pelican Creek

Crooked Creek

Sickle Creek

Snake River

Fox Creek

Fox Creek Confluence, 5 mi.

Heart River Confluence, 16 mi.

Heart River

Sickle Creek Confluence, 12 mi.

Basin Creek

Wolverine Creek

Coulter Creek

River

Snake

Red Creek

Red Creek Confluence, 26 mi.

Lewis Lake

Lewis Falls

Lewis River

South Entrance

Polecat Creek

Buela Lake

Hering Lake

Flagg Ranch Resort, 34 mi.

Rapids, 32 mi.

J.D. Rockefeller Memorial Parkway

Reclamation Road

89

287

Lizard Creek Canoe Pullout

Jackson Lake, 40 mi.

Grand Teton National Park

Jackson Lake

crossings should be made only at the tops of shallow riffles. Care also must be taken when exploring deep pools, swift runs, and pocket waters in the canyon between Red Creek and Heart River.

Yellowstone cutthroat are the dominant species, ranging from 8 to 16 inches. A few Snake River finespotted cutthroat are still present in the upper river. Whitefish are numerous and, occasionally, quite large. Brown trout increase in number and size in fall as spawners run upstream from Jackson Lake. A few brook trout and lake trout, washed out of Lewis Lake, also are hooked by anglers.

Fishing is fairly straightforward with basic mayfly, caddis, and attractor patterns, as well as terrestrials in late summer. Moderate-sized stonefly nymphs and leeches are wet fly prospecting options. Beadhead nymphs, emergers, and soft-hackles tied as dropper flies on larger dry flies increase chances for hits. Streamers and large nymphs are the flies of choice when hunting brown trout spawners in late fall.

A mystical river of the West, the mighty Snake unfortunately demands more effort at its headwaters then most anglers are willing to expend knowing that they'll find better fishing up the road in the park. Still, the lower river and its canyon present quiet backwater options to explore with surprising results by those who time it right. But don't venture into this region alone; grizzly bears may be present. Keep a clean camp when staying overnight.

Heart River

The Heart River descends a steep, 4-mile course to its merger with the Snake, about 15 miles east of the park's South Entrance.

Although it is the Snake's largest tributary in the park, the river's only good fishing access is along its half-mile outlet from Heart Lake. A boggy marsh at the confluence and a deep canyon in between the outlet and the Snake make fishing the lower river difficult.

The most direct route to the outlet is a 12-mile hike via the Heart Lake Trail, northwest of Lewis Lake on the loop road. The lake and its outlet don't open to fishing until July 1 due to restrictions against entering prime grizzly bear country in early season.

The outlet meadow is a popular side trip for those who camp at the lake, especially during cool, late springs. The river's canyon produces a prolific stonefly hatch in late June that wafts upstream on the winds and draws robust, savvy cutthroat from the lake to the feast.

Callibaetis and smaller mayflies offer top water action in summer, along with small terrestrials, for 8- to 14-inch cutthroat.

Stream Facts: Upper Snake River

Season
• Memorial Day weekend through first Sunday in November.

Regulations
• Cutthroat are catch and release. Limit on brown trout is 2 fish, any size.

Trout
• Mostly moderate-sized cutthroat and smaller numbers of brown trout in the 8- to 16-inch range. Brown trout increase in numbers and size with their fall spawning run out of Jackson Lake. Numerous whitefish are present, along with a few brook and lake trout.

Miles
• Mile 0: Source on Two Ocean Plateau, south of Mariposa Lake
• Mile 5: Park boundary
• Mile 12: Confluence of Sickle Creek
• Mile 16: Confluence of Heart River
• Mile 26: Mouth of canyon
• Mile 32: Park boundary at South Entrance

Character
• The river descends a steep narrow course from its source down a high valley for about 15 miles to its confluence with the Heart River, where it almost doubles in size and enters a high walled canyon. Its canyon stretch is a series of swift runs, rapids, and deep pools. The river braids into channels, riffles and runs, and undercut banks on its final run through a broad valley to the South Entrance.

Flows
• Spring runoff is high and off-color from late May into July. Most years the river isn't fishable until mid-July or later. In dry years, flows can be quite low in autumn.

Access
• South Boundary Trail and Snake River Trail, starting from South Entrance.

Camping
• Lewis Lake Campground
• Flagg Ranch
• Snake River Campground in Bridger-Teton National Forest

Lewis River

Divided into four distinct sections almost like a jigsaw puzzle, the Lewis River is the most quixotic stream in Yellowstone.

It rises at the mouth of Shoshone Lake and meanders 4 miles through a picturesque meadow to Lewis Lake. Exiting the lake, it rambles for 2 miles down a low-walled canyon to cascade over one of the park's most scenic waterfalls and spills out onto a broad marshy valley. At the lip of the 4-mile meadow the river plunges into a deep narrow canyon and gallops 10 miles to its confluence with the Snake.

Closely linked to its two lakes, the Lewis River's mixed bag of fishing options draws the most attention from flyfishers during its fall spawning runs by brown trout.

In late September and October, browns in the 14- to 26-inch range migrating from both lakes into the channel are followed by large lake trout. A similar migration occurs at the outlet from Lewis Lake into the upper canyon.

Fishing for fall spawners and lake trout with large streamers and nymphs is intense but smaller beadhead nymphs also can be effective. This is about the only time the river is crowded, although the window of opportunity is short. Fishing ends after the first weekend of November.

The river's other seasons are equally rewarding for anglers with different agendas.

After ice-out on Lewis Lake in late May or early June, look for brown and lake trout congregating at the mouth of the Lewis River Channel, or explore the lower meadow run of the channel as it warms and hatches erupt.

Mayflies in the channel include green drakes in late June and pale morning duns and baetis in July and August. Caddis and attractor patterns also are effective through the season, along with small terrestrials in late summer. Midges and tiny baetis provide some top water action in late fall.

In early summer, good-sized brown trout take up feeding lies at the outlet of Lewis Lake and in downstream shelter areas for about a half-mile of the river's upper run. The trout lie in wait for caddis, midges, and callibaetis and other mayfly spinners flushed out of the lake. The short canyon above the waterfall also produces a prolific overlapping hatch of small dark stoneflies, golden stones, and little yellow stones, or willow flies, around the Fourth of July.

The browns attack the smorgasbord with abandon, although they can be as selective in their feeding patterns as rainbows. The bonus is that they offer a tussle as acrobatic as the rainbow's.

The riffles and runs of the canyon immediately above the waterfall offer a pleasant diversion for smaller browns and an occasional large trout that may have over-wintered in a deep pool or under a logjam. The plunge pool below the waterfall also gives up occasional surprises and in high water years is sometimes full of lake trout flushed out of Lewis Lake.

The Lewis River's most challenging fishing is in the long deep channels of the meadow above its second canyon. It is full of 8- to 12-inch browns but also harbors a good population of wily adults in the 16- to 20-inch range.

An angler fishes the meadow section of the Lewis River.

A spring creek in nature, this stretch requires long, delicate leaders and precise presentations to score on its larger browns. Wading can be a bit difficult in silty areas, and in high water years marshes and flooded flats hinder hiking into some parts of the meadow. But anglers who make the effort to get away from easy access sites along the road generally find better fishing.

A mid-June green drake hatch offers early season top water action, along with stoneflies blown out of the canyons in early July. Tiny baetis and pale morning duns and small caddis patterns are the most common options through most of the summer when casting to rising trout. In late season, terrestrials sometimes pound up large fish. And prospecting undercut banks and pools with moderate-sized woolly buggers or leeches may be effective during quiet periods.

Attempting to fish the upper Lewis Canyon is dangerous and not worth the effort for the small trout it holds. But the flatter riffles and runs in its mouth above the Snake offer another interesting diversion for still another trout in this complex stream. Cutthroat join the browns in the lower river, and even here an occasional lake trout may be encountered in cool waters of tributaries like Moose Creek.

The Lewis River's name derives from Lewis Lake. It was named for Meriwether Lewis, a captain of the Lewis and Clark Expedition. Ironically, the closest the Corps of Discovery got to the park was when William Clark and a small party of men descended the Yellowstone River from present-day Livingston, Montana.

The South Entrance–West Thumb Road parallels the river's lower meadow for about 2 miles. Other access routes to the river are by trails above and below Lewis Lake or by boat or canoe from the boat ramp at the Lewis Lake Campground.

A 1.5-mile footpath near the campground leads to the outlet and the upper canyon. Trying to take a short cut through the forest is virtually impossible because of numerous barriers created by downed timber. The lower end of the canyon can be reached from a footpath that loops south around the waterfall from a parking lot on the loop road.

Two trails into the Lewis River Channel start from a trailhead at the north end of Lewis Lake. The Doghead Trail, which goes directly to the top of the channel, is 4 miles long. The Lewis Channel Trail is 3 miles along the top of the lake to the inlet and then 4 miles to the top of the channel.

A short trail from the South Entrance leads to the river's confluence with the Snake and provides access to the mouth of the Lewis Canyon.

The Lewis River Channel is the only stream in the park that can be floated in hand-propelled watercraft. The top .75 miles of the channel is a shallow rapids and has to be portaged.

Boats and canoes are not permitted past a posted line on the outlet bay of Lewis Lake.

The Lewis Lake Campground is an excellent base for exploring the river. It is one of the few in the park that doesn't require reservations. Camping also is available at Flagg Ranch and the Snake River Campground, just south of the park's South Entrance.

Boat permits are available at the ranger stations at the campground and South Entrance.

Stream Facts: Lewis River

Season
- Memorial Day weekend through first Sunday in November.

Regulations
- Limit on brown trout and lake trout is 2 fish, any size, above Lewis Falls. Below the waterfall, brown trout are catch and release. Cutthroat in the lower canyon are also catch and release.

Trout
- Good populations of brown trout in 10- to 18-inch range. Brown trout increase in numbers and size with fall spawning runs into the Lewis River Channel and the Lewis Lake outlet. Large lake trout follow the migrations and also occur in the lower river when flushed out of Lewis Lake. Yellowstone cutthroat join the browns in the mouth of the Lewis Canyon. The Lewis River Channel's 91 percent satisfaction rating is the highest reported by park anglers. Its catch rate is .91 fish per hour for trout averaging 14.5 inches.

Miles
- Mile 0: Outlet of Shoshone Lake
- Mile 4: Inlet of Lewis Lake
- Mile 6: Lewis Falls below Lewis Lake outlet
- Mile 10: Top of Lewis Canyon
- Mile 20: Mouth of canyon and confluence with Snake River

Character
- The river is divided into four distinct sections: A meadow run through the Lewis River Channel between Shoshone and Lewis Lakes; a short canyon and waterfall below Lewis Lake; a marshy meadow run below the waterfall; and a long steep canyon above its confluence with the Snake River.

Flows
- Spring runoff is somewhat moderated by outflows from Shoshone and Lewis Lakes, although runoff from tributaries can muddy the lower river. Most years the river fishes well in late June and through the remainder of the season.

Access
- South Entrance–West Thumb Road.
- Trailheads above and below Lewis Lake, and the Lewis Lake Campground boat ramp.

Camping
- Lewis Lake Campground
- Flagg Ranch
- Snake River Campground in Bridger-Teton National Forest

LEWIS RIVER MAJOR HATCHES

Insect	A	M	J	J	A	S	O	N	Time	Flies
Stonefly			█						A	**Dry:** Bird's Stone, Orange Stimulator, Salmonfly #4–8; **Wet:** Black Rubberleg, Girdlebug, Woolly Bugger #2–6
Golden Stone				█					A	**Dry:** Golden Stone, Yellow Stimulator #6–10; **Wet:** Bitch Creek Nymph, Montana Stone #4–10
Little Yellow Stone (Willow Fly)				█					A/E	Yellow Sally, Blonde Humpy, Yellow Stimulator #10–14
Green Drake			█						A/E	Green Drake, Olive Wulff, Flav, Para-BWO #10–12
Pale Morning Dun				█	█				M/E	**Dry:** PMD, Light Cahill, Rusty Spinner, Yellow Sparkle Dun #14–18; **Wet:** Hare's Ear Nymph, Pheasant Tail #14–20
Baetis			█	█	█	█	█		A/E	**Dry:** Blue-winged Olive, Blue Dun, Olive Sparkle Dun, Para-Adams #16–22; **Wet:** Pheasant Tail, Baetis Nymph #16–18
Caddis			█	█	█	█	█		A/E	**Dry:** Elk Hair Caddis, Renegade, Yellow or Royal Humpy #12–16; **Wet:** Soft-hackles, Squirrel Tail #14–16
Terrestrials				█	█	█			M/A/E	Joe's Hopper, Jacklin's Hopper, Para-Hopper #12–14; Dave's Cricket #14–16; Ants #16–18
Callibaetis					█	█			A	Thorax Callibaetis, Crystal Spinner, Para-Adams, Rusty Spinner #12–14

HATCH TIME CODE: M = morning; A = afternoon; E = evening; D = dark; SF = spinner fall; // = continuation through periods.

Cascade Corner: Fall and Bechler River Drainages

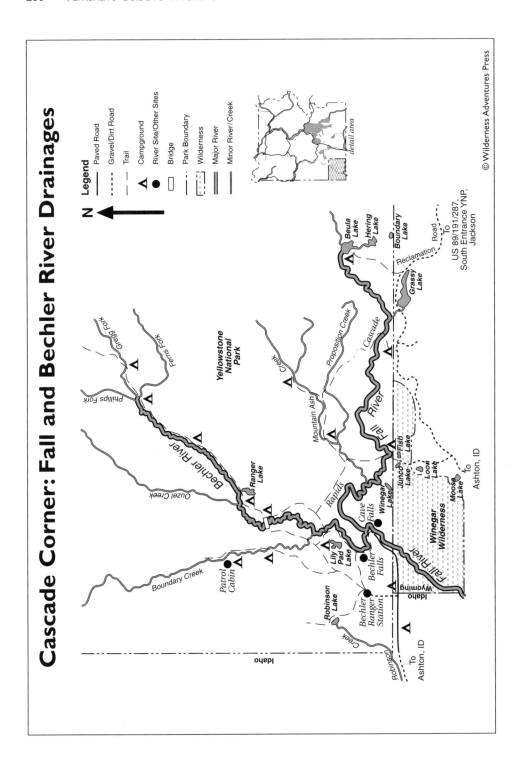

Legend

Paved Road
Gravel/Dirt Road
Trail
Campground
River Site/Other Sites
Bridge
Park Boundary
Wilderness
Major River
Minor River/Creek

N

© Wilderness Adventures Press

detail area

Gregg Fork

Ferris Fork

Phillips Fork

Yellowstone National Park

Bechler River

Ouzel Creek

Ranger Lake

Rapids

Mountain Ash Creek

Proposition Creek

Beula Lake

Hering Lake

Boundary Lake

Grassy Lake

Reclamation Road

To US 89/191/287, South Entrance YNP, Jackson

Cascade

Fall River

Junco Lake
Fish Lake
Loon Lake
Moose Lake

Winegar Wilderness

to Ashton, ID

Cave Falls

Winegar Lake

Lily Pad Lake

Bechler Falls

Patrol Cabin

Boundary Creek

Robinson Lake

Bechler Ranger Station

Idaho
Wyoming

Fall River

To Ashton, ID

Robinson Creek

Idaho

CASCADE CORNER:
IDAHO'S ENTRANCE TO YELLOWSTONE

The little explored southwest corner of Yellowstone is Idaho's only entry into the park. Called Cascade Corner, the Fall and Bechler Rivers and their tributaries flowing off the slopes of the Pitchstone Plateau are adorned with 21 of the park's 40 waterfalls.

Scholarly rainbows in the Bechler River's meadows are among the most challenging in Greater Yellowstone's golden circle of trout. The Bechler canyon, the upper Fall River, and Beula Lake harbor healthy populations of Yellowstone cutthroat.

Rainbows in the Bechler and its tributaries are protected by a special catch-and-release regulation, as are all cutthroat in this corner of the park. However, several lakes south of Yellowstone's boundary permit a chance to broil a brace of trout over a campfire in the John D. Rockefeller Memorial Parkway and Wyoming's section of the Targhee National Forest. The "parkway" is a wilderness area linking Grand Teton and Yellowstone National Parks. The Targhee's tiny Winegar Wilderness Area is southwest of the park on the Idaho border.

To get to the Bechler and lower Fall Rivers from Idaho turn east off U.S. 20 at Ashton, 60 miles north of Idaho Falls and 65 south of West Yellowstone. At Ashton, drive east about 6 miles on Idaho Highway 47 to the Cave Falls Road. A 10-mile gravel forest ends at the scenic falls and the Bechler Ranger Station.

From the east, Cascade Corner is reached via the primitive Reclamation Road that runs from Flagg Ranch, south of the park's South Entrance and 60 miles north of Jackson, to Ashton. The western end of its 35-mile course parallels the south rim of the Fall River. Turn north at the first bridge in Idaho to reach the Cave Falls Road and Bechler Ranger Station. Four-wheel-drive vehicles with good clearance are strongly advised for travel over the Reclamation Road. Trailers are prohibited on the unmaintained, deeply rutted, one-way stretch between Calf Creek and Gibson Meadows.

Good references for trip planning are Targhee National Forest's Island Park-Ashton Ranger Districts map and Bridger-Teton National Forest's Buffalo-Jackson Ranger Districts map. Topographic trail maps include Trails Illustrated's SW Yellowstone map and American Adventures Association's South Yellowstone Park map.

Snow or flooded meadows may make two-track sections of the Reclamation Road impassible in late spring. Late fall visitors to this remote region should check weather forecasts before setting out. Snow storms can occur as early as mid-October.

A park fishing permit can be purchased at Flagg Ranch or the Bechler Ranger Station. Reservations are required to camp overnight at designated backcountry campsites in the park. A Forest Service campground is located at Cave Falls. It fills fast in midsummer, so get there early. In fall, it is largely deserted. Also, numerous undeveloped campgrounds are available in the national forests.

One of Yellowstone's wettest regions, Cascade Corner fishes best in late summer and early fall. Mosquitoes are thick in spring and early summer until marshes start to dry. This is also grizzly bear country. It is best to hike in parties of three or more and to keep a clean camp.

Some of the more interesting fishing requires longer hikes or rock scrambling into canyons. Carry topographic maps and a compass, and know how to use them. At the end of the rainbow are wild trout in spectacular mountain forest country. Views of the Teton Mountains pop up to the south as you come out of a canyon or crest a rise in the trail.

Fishing these waters is a fairly straightforward proposition. Backcountry trout are less wary than those pounded unmercifully on better known streams.

For top water action, elk hair caddis, stimulators, humpies, and other high-riding attractor patterns like renegades, Trudes, and Wulffs work through the season, along with generic mayfly patterns like Adams and light Cahill. Don't forget grasshoppers, ants, and beetles.

Best choices in wet flies are stonefly and golden stone nymphs, woolly buggers, and smaller nymph and larva patterns like hare's ears, pheasant tails, soft-hackle nymphs, and caddis emergers. Beadhead patterns also are best since Yellowstone bans the use of lead jigs, split-shot, wires, or ribbon twist-ons. Non-toxic options are available for the latter.

The Fall River Flasher, in green or brown, is a popular variation on the woolly bugger theme. It has a chenille body and rainbow crystal strands tied along the sides of its marabou tail. The matching-color saddle hackle is wrapped only on the head of the fly. It is a good pattern on other fast-water streams.

Some mayfly hatches may arrive latter than expected in high water years, but this quiet backwater has them all.

The real nitty-gritty, match-the-hatch situations likely to be encountered are in Bechler Meadows. Choices may include midges, tricos, callibaetis, or green drakes in summer and, in fall, the gray drake and mahogany dun. Always hope for overcast days and carry a selection of pale morning duns and blue-winged olives.

Wyoming Wilderness Lakes

Float-tubers or canoers who want to buy only a Wyoming fishing license can stick to the Reclamation Road, west of Flagg Ranch, and tackle Grassy Lake, Tillery Lake, Lake in the Woods, Fish Lake, and Indian Lake. Lake trout and brook trout are added to the mix of opportunities.

Grassy Lake—346 acres; 9- to 20-inch cutthroat and lake trout, a few cutthroat-rainbow hybrids. Rated by Wyoming Game and Fish as good fishing.

Tillery Lake—15 acres; 6- to 18-inch rainbow; rated as fair.

Lake in the Woods—245 acres; 8- to 16-inch rainbow; rated as good.

Fish Lake—20 acres; 8- to 16-inch brook trout; rated as good.

Indian Lake — 40 acres; moderate-sized cutthroat; not rated.

Several other lakes in the region—South Boundary, Tanager, Loon, and Winegar —are fishless.

Be sure to check current state or park regulations wherever you plan to fish.

Bechler River

The Bechler rises at 8,000 feet at the confluence of the Phillips, Gregg, and Ferris Forks and flows about 20 miles to its merger with the Fall River at Cave Falls.

Waterfalls on each of the headwater tributaries set the pace for the Bechler's dash down its narrow canyon in a series of waterfalls, cascades, and roaring pocket waters. Mostly pan-sized cutthroat reside in its canyon pocket waters.

At the canyon mouth, the Bechler plunges over two-tiered, 100-foot Colonnade Falls to enter its 4-mile meadow run. Crystal-clear waters of the meadow meander through a broad, marshy flat. The final couple miles of river gallop down a lava rock cascade to the Fall River.

Bechler Meadow holds good numbers of 9- to 14-inch rainbows, with a fair amount in the 16- to 20-inch range. Tributaries of the Bechler hold mostly 9- to 12-inch rainbow and cutthroat, with chances for occasional larger fish. Rainbows in the tributaries are protected by the catch-and-release rule since they are wild trout and contribute to the Bechler's pristine fishery.

Channels in Bechler Meadow are usually too deep to wade, and the trout are extremely skittish. If you can see them, they can see you.

Fish cautiously from the banks as you would on a spring creek with delicate leader tippets and refined presentations. Surface swirls frustrate attempts at drag-free floats. It's best to work to rising fish, early and late in the day, or hope for a heavy overcast. Grassy overhangs along banks and deep pools may harbor large trout and offer nymphing prospects. Prospecting in late summer with grasshoppers can be fruitful.

The 5-mile relatively flat trail to the meadows starts from the Bechler Ranger Station. A suspension bridge crosses the river at top end of the meadow near Ouzel Creek. Rocky Ford, on the Union Falls Trail, at the bottom end of the meadow has to be waded.

For day hikes into the meadows, set up a base camp at the Targhee National Forest campground below Cave Falls.

Bechler River

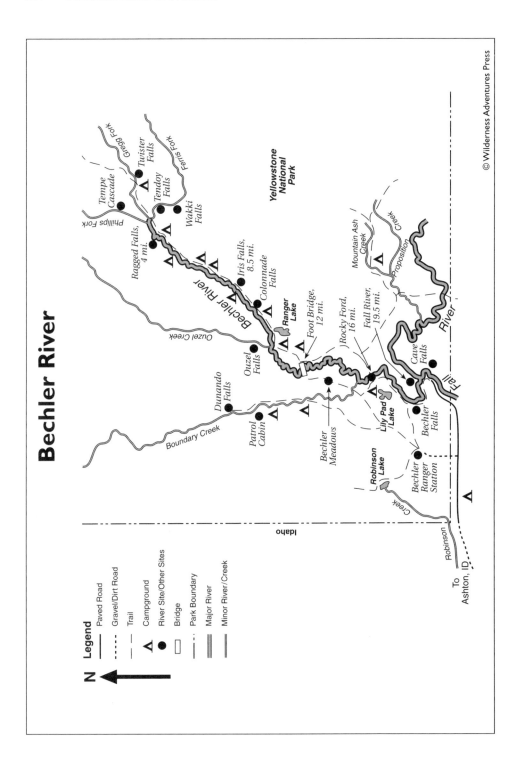

Stream Facts: Bechler River

Season
- Memorial Day weekend through the first Sunday in November.

Regulations
- Cutthroat, rainbows, and cutthroat-rainbow hybrids are catch-and-release, including in tributaries (such as Boundary and Ouzel Creeks).

Trout
- Bechler Meadow holds a strong population of 10- to 14-inch rainbows, with a fair number in the 16- to 18-inch range and a few larger fish. Numerous pan-sized cutthroat are found above Colonade Falls in the canyon run. Anglers report 61 percent satisfaction with a .63 fish per hour catch rate for fish averaging 10.7 inches.

Miles
- Mile 0: Confluence of Phillips, Gregg, and Ferris Forks
- Mile 4: Ragged Falls
- Mile 8.5: Iris Falls
- Mile 10.5: Colonnade Falls
- Mile 12: Foot bridge at top of Bechler Meadows
- Mile 16: Rocky Ford trail crossing
- Mile 19.5: Confluence with Fall River

Character
- The upper pocket water stretch of the Bechler cascades down a narrow canyon and plunges over a series of waterfalls to the 100-foot Colonnade Falls at its mouth. The crystal clear waters of its 4-mile meadow run below the falls meander through a marshy flat. The final couple miles of river are a shallow gallop down a lava rock cascade to the Fall River. Channels in the meadow are usually too deep to wade. Fish cautiously as you would on a spring creek. There are grassy overhangs along the banks, and the deep pools of cutbanks harbor larger trout. A suspension bridge crosses the river at the top end of the meadow. Marshes in this corner of park are often mosquito-infested into August. It is also grizzly bear country. Hike in groups of 3 or more and keep clean camps.

Flows
- Spring runoff on Bechler usually peaks in late June, but may extend into July. It fishes best in late summer and early fall.

Access
- Cave Falls road east of Ashton, Idaho
- Reclamation Road, which connects Ashton with Flagg Ranch, at Yellowstone's South Entrance, north of Jackson

Camping
- Targhee National Forest
- Bridger-Teton National Forest
- Flagg Ranch resort

Fall River

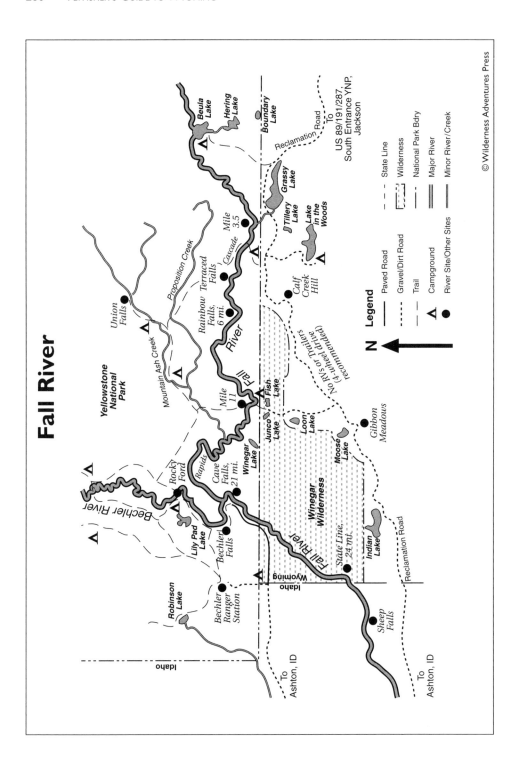

© Wilderness Adventures Press

Legend

N

Paved Road ——— State Line
Gravel/Dirt Road ------- Wilderness
Trail ——— National Park Bdry
△ Campground ——— Major River
● River Site/Other Sites ——— Minor River/Creek

Fall River

The Cave Falls Campground offers an excellent opportunity to tackle the lower Fall River, at the plunge pool below Cave Falls and in the rocky pocket waters of its lower canyon. The two best options to hike into the upper river and its tributaries are at trailheads on the Reclamation Road at Grassy Lake Reservoir, on the east side of the road, or Fish Lake, on the west side.

Headwaters of the Fall rise at 8,500 feet on the south slopes of the Pitchstone Plateau. It meanders across meadow and forest below Beula Lake, the Fall's official source, and then drops dramatically down a string of swift cascades and over a series of water falls to scenic Cave Falls. Interspersed along its swift course are a series of long meandering forested runs. Its 50-mile southwesterly run ends at the Henry's Fork of the Snake in eastern Idaho. The average rate of descent is more than 50 feet per mile. Its canyons are often deep and picturesque.

While it is listed on most maps as the Falls River, its name was officially changed to Fall River by the U.S. Geological Service. The alteration in the mid-1980s was made to agree with the name local residents use for the river.

The many waterfalls along its course are the source of its original name. For the flyfisher, the name reflects the chance he might take a tumble in its refreshing waters. It is tough wading, more difficult than Box Canyon on the Henry's Fork. Felt-bottomed boots are needed to negotiate its slick basalt lava streamed carpeted with slippery cobblestones.

The upper river holds mostly cutthroat and its lower reaches hold rainbows and a few cutthroat-rainbow hybrids. Most are in the 9- to 15-inch range, with a few exceeding 20 inches. Its tributaries are loaded with cutthroat in similar sizes.

The two most popular hikes into the Fall River Basin are to Beula Lake and its outlet, and to 260-foot Union Falls on Ash Mountain Creek. Both can be reached from trails starting from the eastern tip of Grassy Lake, 10 miles west of Flagg Ranch. Another Union Falls trail starts from Fish Lake, about midway along Reclamation Road.

The 2.5-mile jaunt into 107-acre Beula Lake is most productive for float-tubers. Hering Lake, 60 acres, is just upstream. There's a minor climb at the start but the rest of the route is flat.

The 7-mile hike to Union Falls is more of a workout, with more ups and downs, but you get a chance to fish three of the Fall's better cutthroat tributaries, Cascade, Proposition, and Ash Mountain Creeks. The hike from Fish Lake is slightly longer. Pools below waterfalls and at stream confluences often harbor larger fish.

The general rule of thumb on cutthroat waters is that if the fish aren't hitting, move on. If it still isn't happening, move on again. Remember, this is get-away-from-it-all country. Keep exploring. Have fun. Take a post card photograph.

Stream Facts: Fall River

Season
- Memorial Day weekend through the first Sunday in November.

Regulations
- Cutthroat and cutthroat-rainbow hybrids are catch and release; limit on rainbows is 2 fish any size.

Trout
- Moderate-sized rainbows outnumber cutthroat in lower section of river. Mostly moderate-sized Yellowstone cutthroat in upstream pocket waters of the Fall and in Beula Lake, its source. Most are in the 9- to 15-inch range, with a few exceeding 20 inches. Its tributaries are loaded with cutthroat in similar sizes. Anglers report 86 percent satisfaction with a 1.38 fish per hour catch rate for fish averaging 8.3 inches.

Miles
- Mile 0: Beula Lake
- Mile 3.5: Cascades trail crossing, west of Grassy Lake
- Mile 6: Rainbow Falls
- Mile 12: Fish Lake trail crossing
- Mile 21: Cave Falls
- Mile 24: Idaho border
- Mile 50: Confluence with Henry's Fork River

Character
- The river meanders a few miles through meadows and forest below Beula Lake to its canyon runs over the Cascades, Terrace Falls, and Rainbow Falls. It continues to drop dramatically down a string of swift cascading runs to scenic Cave Falls, interspersed with long riffles and runs and pocket waters. Flows increase significantly with mergers of Mountain Ash Creek and Bechler River. Meadow marshes in this corner of park are often mosquito-infested into August. It is also grizzly bear country. Hike in groups of 3 or more and keep clean camps.

Flows
- Spring runoff on the Fall usually peaks in late June, but may extend into July. It fishes best in late summer and early fall.

Access
- Cave Falls road east of Ashton, Idaho
- Reclamation Road, which connects Ashton with Flagg Ranch, at Yellowstone's South Entrance, north of Jackson

Camping
- Targhee National Forest
- Bridger-Teton National Forest
- Flagg Ranch resort

BECHLER AND FALL RIVERS MAJOR HATCHES

Insect	A	M	J	J	A	S	O	N	Time	Flies
Stonefly			▓						A	**Dry:** Sofa Pillow, Salmonfly, Orange Stimulator #2–8; **Wet:** Brook's Stone Nymph, Black Rubberlegs, Woolly Bugger, Fall River Flasher #2–8
Golden Stone				▓					A	**Dry:** Golden Stone, Yellow or Orange Stimulator, Yellow Sally #6–10; **Wet:** Bitch Creek Nymph, Montana Stone, Girdlebug, Woolly Bugger #6–10
Caddis				▓	▓	▓	▓		A/E	**Dry:** Olive or Tan Elk Hair Caddis, Goddard Caddis, Yellow, Royal, or Blonde Humpy, Renegade #12–16; **Wet:** Prince Nymph, Beadhead Emerger, Caddis Pupa, Soft-hackles #14–16
Fall Caddis						▓	▓		A	Orange Stimulator, Orange Bucktail #10–12
Baetis					▓	▓			A/E	Blue-winged Olive, Para-BWO, Para-Adams, Blue Dun #14–18; Tiny BWO #18–22
Pale Morning Dun				▓	▓				M/E	**Dry:** PMD, Thorax PMD, PMD Cripple, Sparkle Dun, Rusty Spinner #14–18; **Wet:** Hare's Ear Nymph, Pheasant Tail, Beadheads #14–16

HATCH TIME CODE: M = morning; A = afternoon; E = evening; D = dark; SF = spinner fall; // = continuation through periods.

BECHLER AND FALL RIVERS MAJOR HATCHES, CONT.

Insect	A	M	J	J	A	S	O	N	Time	Flies
Green Drake			▓						A/E	**Dry:** Green Drake, Olive Wulff, Olive Extended Body Drake #10–12; **Wet:** Ida Mae, Prince Nymph, Zug Bug #10–12
Gray Drake						▓			A/E	Gray Sparkle Dun, Spinner, Para-Adams #10–12
Mahogany Dun						▓			A	Mahogany Dun, Sparkle Dun #16
Trico					▓	▓			A	**Dry:** Black and White, Trico Spinner, Para-Adams #18–22; **Wet:** Pheasant Tail #18–22
Callibaetis						▓			A	Thorax Callibaetis, Crystal Spinner, Para-Adams #14–16
Terrestrials				▓	▓	▓			M/A	Joe's Hopper, Dave's Hopper, Henry's Fork Hopper, Parachute Hopper #8–14; Foam Beetle, Disc O'Beetle, Dave's Cricket #14–16; Black Ant, Rusty Ant #14–18

HATCH TIME CODE: M = morning; A = afternoon; E = evening; D = dark; SF = spinner fall; // = continuation through periods.

YELLOWSTONE'S LAKE COUNTRY

The breathtaking scenery of Yellowstone Lake and its grand expanses, tinctured by its brooding power, have fascinated visitors through the ages.

In 1869, Charles Cook, David Folsom, and William Peterson of Helena, Montana Territory, were the first to visit the wilderness with the express purpose of confirming Yellowstone's wonders. The vast lake was at the top of their agenda. They were not disappointed. Reports of their ebullient Yellowstone observations in the press spurred further exploration parties and eventually led to the creation of the first national park.

"As we were about departing on our homeward trip we ascended the summit of a neighboring hill and took a final look at Yellowstone Lake," Folsom wrote. "Nestled among the forest crowned hills which bounded our vision, lay this inland sea, its crystal waves dancing and sparkling in the sunlight as if laughing with joy for their wild freedom. It is a scene of transcendent beauty which has been viewed by few white men, and we felt glad to have looked upon it before its primeval solitude should be broken by the crowds of pleasure seekers which at no distant day will throng its shores."

A year later Nathaniel Langford with the Washburn Expedition gave a more prosaic picture of the lake's awesome strength.

"How can I sum up its wonderful attractions! It is dotted with islands of great beauty...The winds from the mountain gorges roll its placid waters into a furious sea, and crest its billows with foam."

The throngs eventually came to the lake, but more often for its spectacular fishing than the scenery. Yellowstone Lake is home to the largest inland cutthroat trout population in the world. Its Yellowstone cutthroat survived decades of exploitation and rebounded to historic proportions under strict regulations to limit harvest. Now, unfortunately, it faces its greatest challenge, the illegal presence of lake trout, a voracious predator.

Yellowstone Lake is the largest natural freshwater lake above 7,000 feet elevation in the United States. Shaped like a giant hand with two fingers pointed south and a thumb extended to the west, it is 20 miles long and 14 miles wide. Its 110-mile shoreline encircles a surface area of 196 square miles. The lake's average depth is 140 feet and its maximum depth is at least 320 feet.

Following its creation 600,000 years ago, when a cataclysmic volcanic explosion carved out the Yellowstone caldera, the lake was 300 feet higher and covered an area twice its present size. West Thumb was formed about 150,000 years ago in the region's last major volcanic eruption.

Yellowstone River first flowed south to the Snake and the Pacific. Floods from melting glaciers carved the Grand Canyon of the Yellowstone during the last Ice Age and the river was ultimately directed by resurgent ice caps into the Missouri and the Atlantic. At 671 miles, it is the longest undammed river in the Lower 48 States.

The park's three other big lakes are significantly smaller and across the Continental Divide in the Snake drainage. Lewis Lake is easily reached from the loop

Yellowstone's Lake Country

© Wilderness Adventures Press

Legend

N

Road
Trail
Campground
Boat Launch
Point of Interest
Continental Divide
Major River
Minor River/Creek

Yellowstone Lake
West Thumb
Geyser Basin
Delusion Lake
Grant Village
Solution Creek
Riddle Lake
Continental Divide
Patrol Cabin
Lewis Lake
Lewis Channel
Lewis Falls
Lewis River
Heart Lake
Patrol Cabin
Beaver Creek
Outlet Lake
Outlet Creek
Heart River
Snake River
DeLacy Creek
Craig Pass
Kepler Cascade
Continental Divide
Pocket Lake
Grants Pass
Patrol Cabin
Shoshone Lake
Lake
Old Faithful
Firehole River

road. Relatively short hikes to Shoshone and Heart Lakes offer two of Yellowstone's best wilderness fishing destinations.

Shoshone Lake, at 8,050 acres, is the largest backcountry lake in the Lower 48 States. It is connected to the 2,716-acre Lewis Lake by the Lewis River Channel and both offer excellent fishing for brown and lake trout. The two nonnative trout species were established in the previously fishless lakes in 1890.

Heart Lake is the most fertile body of water in the park and holds more species, including forage fish, than any other. This remote 2,150-acre gem established unofficial park records for lake trout and Yellowstone cutthroat.

Boating and Canoeing Dangers

An abiding feature of the four big lakes is that they can be fished exceptionally well from shore, wading their shallows, or float-tubing. Boats really aren't necessary to fish them. But those who venture away from shore need to be aware of almost daily high winds and the threat of sudden storms. The lakes' chilly waters can become death traps for capsized boaters.

Yellowstone Lake harbors a malevolent beauty, states park historian Lee Whittlesey. "All things considered, no body of water in Yellowstone Park and probably in all of the United States is more potentially dangerous," Whittlesey writes in *Death in Yellowstone: Accidents and Foolhardiness in the First National Park.*

Despite its macabre topic, the book is a fascinating read. Among other points, it refutes an often held misconception that geysers have killed the most Yellowstone visitors. Cold water has slain six times more people than hot water. Of the approximately 300 deaths caused by natural phenomena, 115 people have died from drowning compared to 19 falling into hot springs. Yellowstone Lake is the biggest killer, with 41 deaths, followed by the Yellowstone River's 29 fatalities.

Fed by melting snows, Yellowstone Lake barely gets to 60 degrees in summer. Its average year-round temperature is 45 degrees. Prevailing winds from the southwest routinely kick up 4- to 5-foot waves, and storms push crests to 6 feet or more. The winds begin to stir around 11 AM almost daily. Storms are most likely to occur between 1 and 6 PM. Squalls may occur at any time.

The same combinations of cold temperatures, prevailing winds and sudden storms occur on Lewis and Shoshone lakes. Anglers in small boats and canoes are cautioned to hug the shorelines on all three. Lewis Lake has recorded seven deaths and Shoshone Lake has tallied four.

The majority of accidents on the lakes occur when small boats capsize or canoes tip over in sudden squalls or when larger boat are caught in the open by storms, states Whittlesey. The water is so cold people can't hold onto capsized vessels as hypothermia takes its toll in as little as 20 minutes.

Russ Pollard of the Wyoming Game and Fish Department encourages anglers and floaters to keep the 50-50-50 rule in mind on cold water lakes. "If you fall in 50-degree water, and stay in the water for 50 minutes, your chances of survival are about 50 percent."

Boating Regulations and Fees

A permit is required for all motorized and non-motorized vessels, including float tubes. Permits can be purchased at the South Entrance Ranger Station, Lewis Lake Campground, Grant Village Visitor Center, Bridge Bay Ranger Station, or Lake Ranger Station. At Canyon and Mammoth Visitor Centers, only non-motorized boating permits are available. The fee is $20 for an annual permit or $10 for a week for motorized vessels and $10 annual or $5 for a week for non-motorized vessels. A Coast Guard approved, wearable personal flotation device is required for each person boating, including float-tubers.

Grand Teton National Park's boat permits are honored as a one-time, 7-day permit, or can be applied toward a Yellowstone annual permit.

All vessels are prohibited on park rivers and streams except the channel between Lewis and Shoshone lakes, where only hand-propelled vessels are permitted. Only hand-propelled vessels are permitted at the tips of Yellowstone Lake's South and Southeast arms and Flat Mountain Arm.

Outboards and rowboats may be rented at Bridge Bay Marina on Yellowstone Lake. It also provides guided fishing boats which may be reserved in advance by calling 307-344-7311. Numerous other commercial businesses have permits to offer guided services for canoeing, kayaking, and motorized boating.

Yellowstone Lake

Yellowstone Lake, which opens to fishing June 1, is the most popular fishery in the Greater Yellowstone region. Almost 30,000 anglers a year, or 33 percent of the park's fishers, are lured to its waters. Even after a 100-year history of overfishing, including commercial exploitation, and a half-century of hatchery meddling, the lake endures as the finest citadel of inland cutthroat in North America. Its fishing is legendary.

A series of increasingly stricter fishing regulations imposed in the 1970s and 1990s on Yellowstone Lake, Yellowstone River, and their tributaries, brought the Yellowstone cutthroat back from a disconcerting downward spiral. But now the lake's native trout are engaged in mortal combat with their deadliest nemesis, illegally introduced lake trout. One must hope the intricate mix of subpopulations in the enormous lake and varied spawning and rearing strategies will enable the cutthroat to survive the alien invasion.

A 14-inch minimum catch size imposed in 1970 helped curb the intense overfishing of the 1950s and 1960s, but still allowed too many adult cutthroat to be taken from the lake. The two fish under 13 inches limit imposed in 1973 was designed to improve the population's age structure and gain an increased number of older, larger trout. It was hoped this would provide additional stability and productivity that would more closely resemble historic cutthroat populations. The under-13 inch limit worked, along with the closure of Fishing Bridge and delayed openings of the upper river and spawning tributaries until July 15.

Before the lake trout invasion, biologists were highly encouraged by the lake's comeback, said Lynn Kaeding, former Yellowstone research director for U.S. Fish

Yellowstone Lake

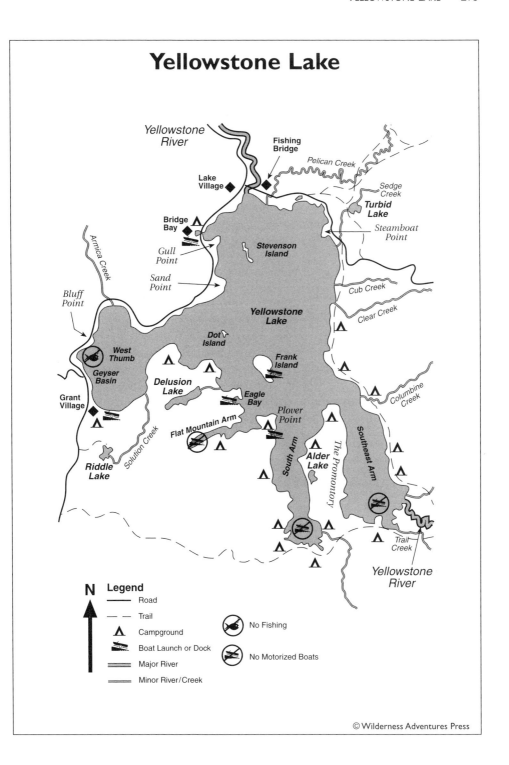

Yellowstone River

Fishing Bridge

Pelican Creek

Lake Village

Sedge Creek

Turbid Lake

Bridge Bay

Steamboat Point

Gull Point

Stevenson Island

Sand Point

Arnica Creek

Bluff Point

Cub Creek

Clear Creek

Yellowstone Lake

Dot Island

West Thumb

Frank Island

Geyser Basin

Delusion Lake

Eagle Bay

Columbine Creek

Grant Village

Plover Point

Flat Mountain Arm

Solution Creek

South Arm

Alder Lake

The Promontory

Southeast Arm

Riddle Lake

Trail Creek

Yellowstone River

N

Legend

—— Road

– – – Trail

⚐ Campground

🚤 Boat Launch or Dock

▦ Major River

══ Minor River/Creek

🚫🐟 No Fishing

🚫 No Motorized Boats

© Wilderness Adventures Press

and Wildlife Service. "We were very close, if not there, to correcting the adverse human activity."

Population estimates for the sport fishery of catchable-sized fish, 8 to 10 inches and larger, is 2.5 million cutthroat. Total population, including immature cutthroat, is 4 million or more.

Gill net surveys by Fish and Wildlife show the cutthroat population's size structure was approaching equilibrium, with an average size of 15 inches. Capture of a 10-year old cutthroat in 1994 indicated the population was approaching its historical age structure.

Anglers report 24 percent of landed trout exceed 16 inches. The catch rate is .8 fish per hour from shore and 1.4 per hour from a boat.

"Currently five large trout (14–18 inches) are captured and released for each trout under (13 inches) creeled," states a Fish and Wildlife report. "Over two-thirds of all anglers catch one or more trout, and one-third creel one or more. Excellent landing rates, often associated with 'no kill' regulations...have been sustained (with the) privilege of harvesting trout for a campfire meal."

But, today, park officials much prefer that the meal be a lake trout.

All lake trout caught by anglers in Yellowstone Lake must be killed under an order imposed in 1994. The June 1 opening day implemented in 1998 allows anglers to join the war against the invaders two weeks earlier. However, a catch-and-release rule protects cutthroat in the lake for six weeks, from June 1 to July 15.

"We want to take advantage of the chance to catch lake trout that show up close to shore at that time," said Dan Mahoney, a fisheries biologist with the park's aquatic resource center.

First officially recorded in 1994, illegal transplant of the predatory nonnative species was described as an "appalling act of environmental vandalism" by former Superintendent Bob Barbee. "The potential consequences of this thoughtless act are enormous," he said. "It could mean the destruction of the last major stronghold of inland cutthroat. Yellowstone Lake has been an almost museum-pure home of these fish for thousands of years, and it would be a tragic loss to Yellowstone's wilderness quality, to anglers and to science."

Barbee said other wildlife could be seriously harmed if lake trout succeed in taking over the lake. "If lake trout make serious inroads on the cutthroat trout population, many animals will suffer, including eagles, osprey, otters, and bears." Unlike cutthroat, which spawn in streams, lake trout spend almost all their time in deep waters, out of reach of other predators. "Many grizzly bears feed heavily on stream-spawning cutthroat trout and could simply lose that important food source," Barbee said.

Park biologists are trying to perfect gill-netting techniques to capture large lake trout, which are the prime spawners. Most of their efforts have been focused on West Thumb where adult lake trout congregate. However, anglers have taken lake trout from numerous places around the lake, and they are asked to continue to assist in the battle as much as possible.

Angler catches accounted for about a quarter of the 2,000 lake trout taken from the lake in the first four years after their discovery, Mahoney said. Even if they don't want to keep them, anglers are required to first take captured lake trout to a visitor's center or ranger station for inspection by a biologist.

Fishing Yellowstone Lake

Nearly 35 miles of the park's loop roads offer easy access to the lake's west and north shores. Anglers can fish virtually anywhere they want, but the most popular areas are the banks north of Bridge Bay and to the south at Gull Point, Sand Point, and Rock Point. West Thumb is a favorite with float-tubers because the warm waters around its thermal features are prime feeding grounds for cruising trout.

Boat ramps are located at Bridge Bay and Grant Village, although the latter may be closed in early season during high water years.

The best hiking route is the Thorofare Trail, which starts from Lake Butte Drive on the northeast corner of the lake. It follows the east shore for about 20 miles to the Yellowstone River delta. The Trail Creek Trail, from the delta to Heart Lake, skirts the tips of the lake's two southern arms. Otherwise, the only access to the lake's south shore east of Grant Village is by boat or canoe.

Cub Creek and Clear Creek, on the Thorofare Trail, are closed to fishing until August 11 because of grizzly bear activity. Areas near Lake Lodge, Grant Village, and Fishing Bridge often are closed for the same reason. Tributaries, including the upper Yellowstone River, don't open to fishing until July 15, and a 100-yard zone around their mouths also are closed. Fishing is not permitted in posted areas of the outlet above and below Fishing Bridge. Anglers who elect to keep two cutthroat under 13 inches after July 15 are not permitted to continue catch-and-release fishing.

Yellowstone Lake's 7,728-foot elevation means ice-out occurs in late May or early June.

Adult cutthroat cruise the shorelines to feed in 4 to 10 feet of water in shallow bays, along sandbars and near points and inlets. Spring spawning migrations often keep the trout close enough to banks and land points to be reached by fly casters without boats or float tubes. The lake fishes best in morning and evening because of its prevailing winds.

Anglers in float tubes cover more water, but need to hug the shore and dress warmly to avoid hypothermia. Boaters who embark for the shoals around the lake's few islands or its southern arms should be wary of high winds and sudden intense storms.

The most prudent option for canoers headed to the South or Southeast Arms is to arrange ferry shuttles to The Promontory. In addition to being safer, it saves a great deal of time and effort that could be better spent fishing. Advance reservations are required for backcountry campsites.

Early spring float-tubers often do best slowly stripping small woolly buggers or leech patterns, size 4 to 6, or medium-sized nymphs, size 10 to 14, with a fullsink line or sinking tip and short leader. Hits are often subtle, so be prepared to set the hook at the first hint of a strike.

Wet fly choices include green or black woolly buggers, dark leeches, stonefly nymphs, damselfly nymphs, Zug Bugs, marabou muddlers, spruce flies, and beadhead nymphs (such as Prince, hare's ear, and pheasant tail), soft-hackles, and scuds. The same patterns also are most effective in autumn.

The best top water action is usually sight casting to cruising cutthroat as the lake warms and clears. Shoreline casters find fishing improves by early July. Present dry flies on a long leader with a shooting head floating line.

When prospecting, try elk hair caddis, terrestrial, or attractor patterns, such as Adams or royal Wulffs, size 10 to 14; also try giving them an occasional twitch. Callibaetis are the principal mayfly hatch on late July and August mornings. Try callibaetis cripples, parachute Adams, and gray sparkle duns, size 12 to 16. Sporadic mayfly hatches and spinner falls include gray drakes, baetis, and tricos, and usually occur near inlets. Midges often are a good option in quiet bays and near inlets.

Lake trout hunters lobbing large colorful streamers, size 2 to 6, are most likely to find them closest to shore from ice-out until early July and again in late autumn as they migrate and congregate near spawning reefs. Tiny Carrington Island in West Thumb was the first documented spawning site. Others have been found along the southeast shore of the bay and near Breeze Channel.

Spinning rod anglers do well with Rooster Tail, Dare Devil and Mepps spinners, small flat fish, and Rappela lures, in a variety of colors. Bait fishing is prohibited.

Some anglers complain Yellowstone Lake's cutthroat are cookie cutter fish all about the same size. The trout average 15 to 18 inches, and maximum size rarely exceeds 20 inches. However, it is reasonable to expect the lake's most exceptional trout to be in spawning tributaries at the height of the fishing season.

Small cutthroat are uncommon near shorelines because of their different feeding requirements. Young cutthroat in the lake ply its deeper reaches, feeding almost exclusively on zooplankton, like water fleas and copepods. The tiny crustaceans are filtered from the water with specially developed gill rackers. There also are indications that subpopulations remain in perennial tributaries like Pelican Creek, Arnica Creek, and Beaverdam Creek until they approach adult age.

But perhaps the lake's most unique feature is its dramatic spawning runs out of the outlet. It is a mirror image of other lake tributaries, notes Robert Gresswell, a U.S. Forest Service biologist. The adults go downstream to spawn and their fry swim upstream to the lake. Moreover, there are populations of robust resident cutthroat in the upper and lower river often overlooked in the dynamics of the basin.

When the lake's cutthroat reach 13 to 14 inches in size, they move to its warmer and shallower littoral zones, where they switch to eating invertebrates, like leeches, larvae, and nymphs, and larger crustaceans, like scuds and snails. But, unlike other Yellowstone cutthroat races, the lake's large trout do not switch to being predators as is common in Heart Lake and eastern Idaho waters.

Yellowstone Lake's water level reached 20-year highs due to winter snowpacks far above normal in 1996 and 1997. Shorelines were flooded, and caused bank erosion and difficulties for wading anglers. But the high water bodes well for the trout.

An angler off-shore on Yellowstone Lake.

"Cutthroat spawn better during wet years," Kaeding said. "There tends to be more fish five years later coming back (to the tributaries) as adults. So there is a definite positive relationship."

Mahoney noted the high water brought spawners back to 17 tributaries for the first time in decades.

He was cautious about foretelling the future of the lake's native trout population, but after two decades or more into the assault by lake trout it appears to be holding its own. "I don't see any evidence the cutthroat are dropping off the deep end," Mahoney said.

Lake Trout War

The escalating numbers and increased sizes of lake trout captured in gill nets in 1996 and 1997 in Yellowstone Lake terrify Yellowstone's guardians. The predator is well established and has been in the lake much longer than first believed.

"It's a beautiful fish, but it doesn't belong here," said Glenn Boltz of the U.S. Fish and Wildlife Service. "The numbers showing up this year are scary." And a 10-inch jump in a single year for the largest lake trout netted meant older than expected fish were in the lake. "Even with the (exceptionally prolific) feed base, the growth can't be expected from that alone."

In the first two weeks of the 1996 gill-netting season, his crew captured a 13-pound lake trout and a 12.5-pounder, both more than 30 inches in length. By year's end, a total catch of 580 in nets and 206 by anglers included lake trout ranging from 17 to 21 pounds. The larger fish were estimated to be 20 to 25 years old. By comparison, the 204 fish captured in 1994 and 1995 had been in the 8- to 22-inch range.

The pattern was repeated in 1997 when 1,056 lake trout were taken from the lake, including 240 by anglers. The largest was 16 pounds, said Dan Mahoney, fisheries biologist for the park's aquatic resource center.

The age of the lake trout debunks a theory that they got into the lake when helicopters were used to dip huge buckets of water from Lewis Lake to fight forest fires in 1988, Mahoney said. One of the hardest fought battles saved Grant Village on Yellowstone Lake's West Thumb, where most of the lake trout have been netted.

The older age classes also cast a questioning light on doomsday predictions for the ultimate fate of the lake's cutthroat.

The consensus of a group of experts brought to the park in 1995 was that if no action was taken to fight the invasion, Yellowstone Lake would lose 80 percent of the 2.5 million cutthroat in its sport fishery in 20 years, and in a century, all the cutthroat would be gone. Drastic measures to reduce lake trout populations, they said, would reduce losses to 30 percent in 20 years and, in 100 years, to 60 percent.

The experts agreed it would be virtually impossible to eradicate lake trout from the vast lake. But Upper Midwest scientists offered some hope expansion of its population might be contained through an aggressive gillnetting program such as the one used by commercial fishing operations in the Great Lakes.

The dire warnings were based on assumptions lake trout had been present for only about eight to 10 years when first discovered in 1994. But even if their tenure has been longer and the impact much less, there is no cause for jubilation. It just means a lot more information is needed.

Nor can there be any doubt the lake trout aren't making a dent in the cutthroat population. Annual consumption estimates range from 40 to 90 cutthroat per lake trout, depending on the size of an adult predator.

Capture ratios indicate the lake trout population is in the tens of thousands and larger sizes mean more are sexually mature then previously expected. Sonar studies of the lake currently under way may give biologists a better picture of population dynamics, including how well the cutthroat are faring. Until then it is a guessing game.

Once the information is gathered and analyzed, biologists will have a better idea of their options, said Stu Coleman, the park's chief of natural resources. Until then, the park hesitates to do more than net lake trout and ask anglers to keep all they catch.

Weeding out sexually mature adults with gill nets is the focus of current suppression efforts, Mahoney said. Discovery of a key spawning area near Carrington Island in West Thumb enabled biologists to take 165 spawners in 1996 and 235 in 1997. Another 168 spawners were taken from Breeze Channel between West Thumb and the main lake, and 80 were caught along the southeast shore of West Thumb in 1997.

Radio-tagged "Judas fish" led the gillnetters to concentrations of adults.

"That was our biggest contribution" in the war against the lake trout, said Jim Risch, a University of Utah graduate student. "We found spawners as soon as the surface temperature of the water dropped below 50 degrees. It was classic."

But, while they can take adults any time they want in West Thumb, the juveniles are dispersed throughout the lake where they compete with young cutthroat for zooplankton, their principal food source. Biologists also are concerned about the large numbers of 12-inch lake trout in the lake, Risch said. But using small-mesh nets to take them results in a currently unacceptable loss of cutthroat, an almost 1-to-1 ratio.

Lake trout switch to a fish diet at about 12 inches and rapidly grow in size. Males become sexually mature at about 16 inches and females at 17 or 18 inches. When they surpass 20 inches, their appetite skyrockets.

Biological analysis shows lake trout are doing better in Yellowstone Lake than in Lewis Lake, said Boltz.

"The head size to body size ratio shows fast growth. They all have really good body fat. Scale studies show they have the fastest growth after they reach 20 inches," he said. "They surpass the cutthroat in reaching that size by as much as two years earlier."

Lake trout have an amazingly large mouth for a salmonid species.

"A large lake trout can easily take a fish one-half its own body weight," Boltz said. "Smaller ones can easily take fish one-third their body weight. The 12.5-pound lake trout we caught had the remains of a 20-inch cutthroat in its stomach."

It's particularly disconcerting the lake trout are hitting cutthroat rather than other prey species in the lake, including longnose dace, longnose sucker, redside shiner, and lake chub.

"What we have learned is that fish predation is keyed on cutthroat," Boltz said. "The longnosed sucker is abundant but is found only in shallow, warm water. Predation on cutthroat is occurring because their habitat overlaps."

Growth potential for lake trout in Yellowstone Lake is phenomenal, considering the histories of the park's other lakes. Unofficial trophy fish records from the three range from 50 pounds in Heart Lake to 40 pounds in Shoshone Lake and 30 pounds in Lewis Lake.

The record angler catch was a 63-pound, 51.5-inch lake trout from Lake Superior in 1952. The largest one ever netted was a 121-pound gargantuan from a Canadian lake.

Some lake trout hunters may champ at the bit to pursue trophies in the lake, but it isn't going to happen if park officials can prevent it. A lake trout sport fishery in no way would equal Yellowstone Lake's cutthroat fishery—ecologically, economically or morally.

Lake Trout Mysteries

The lake trout bombshell ticking ominously in Yellowstone Lake was almost inevitable considering previous attempts—both official and unofficial—to fill supposed voids in its waters. Previous fish transplants in the upper Yellowstone drainage fizzled, but it will take a Herculean effort to defuse today's lake trout fiasco.

"Landlocked salmon planted in Yellowstone and Duck Lakes in 1908 have not been recorded since," F. Phillip Sharpe stated in a Yellowstone Library and Museum Association pamphlet from the 1960s. "Mountain whitefish were introduced above Yellowstone Falls in 1889, but none survived. Rainbow trout first planted above the falls in 1908 probably survived but were subsequently hybridized into the dominant cutthroat trout population."

By then a philosophical trend toward natural management was evolving. The U.S. Fish Commission employee who made an unauthorized transplant of rainbows into Yellowstone Lake in 1907 was reprimanded. A proposed transplant of smelt into Lewis Lake was rejected.

Still, at least one more attempt was made to establish rainbows in the upper river in 1929, according to records uncovered by Steve Pierce, author of *The Lakes of Yellowstone.*

Also, redside shiner, lake chub, and longnose sucker found their way into Yellowstone Lake, probably from the dumping of baitfish buckets.

"The only other exotic species in the (Yellowstone) lake drainage were brown trout in Duck Lake, and those were eradicated in 1967," stated Sharpe.

But two decades later brook trout showed up in Arnica Creek, a tributary of Yellowstone Lake's West Thumb. U.S. Fish and Wildlife, the modern successor of the U.S. Fish Commission, struck hard and fast. Arnica was poisoned in 1985 and 1986 to eliminate the nonnative species, which could have flourished in the lake.

Ironically, West Thumb is the star player in the riddle of how lake trout got into Yellowstone Lake.

"Fish Story," published in 1991 by *Gray's Sporting Journal,* might be the title of just another tall tale or a clue to solving the mystery. An intriguing piece of fiction, it revolves around the search for a park ranger who drowned in West Thumb. According to the story, he was fishing for lake trout planted in the lake in the 1960s to produce trophy-sized fish. A sonar search for his body reveals monster fish in the lake, but the story ends with a plot to keep them secret.

Law enforcement authorities talked extensively with the author, Gary Parks, a former Yellowstone Lake fishing guide. They concluded there is no basis to the story, said Cheryl Matthews, a Yellowstone spokeswoman. "It was just pure fiction, there was nothing to it."

Investigation of the illegal transplant of lake trout continues. There is a $10,000 reward for information leading to the arrest and conviction of those involved.

"We have had no solid leads, which leads us to conclude that lake trout have been in the lake longer than we previously anticipated," Matthews said.

Still, the magazine story is intriguing to Lynn Kaeding, former research director of Yellowstone fisheries for U.S. Fish and Wildlife. "I don't know if we will ever get to the bottom of it. There are some elements of fact in it, and there are some elements of barroom talk.

"I would say that whoever did it was a misdirected lake trout enthusiast."

There's strong evidence more than one unwarranted transplant of lake trout has occurred in Yellowstone Lake, Kaeding said.

Glenn Boltz, a colleague, agreed.

"If I were to guess, the West Thumb area was planted years ago," he said. The large number of lake trout being captured there would seem to be more than coincidence. Boltz suspects many small lake trout were slipped into the lake several times. "It's not human nature to give up a trophy fish" to produce a brood stock.

DNA analysis may determine the origin of the lake trout, Boltz said. Most assume they came from Lewis Lake. Lake trout planted in Lewis Lake and Shoshone Lake in 1890 are the Bear Island strain from the northwest shore of Lake Michigan. They migrated to Heart Lake and Jackson Lake. Heart Lake's cutthroat have been holding their own, but Jackson Lake's population was decimated. Snake River finespotted cutthroat, fortunately, still reign in the river below the lake.

Lewis and Shoshone Lakes, which also hold brown trout from the 1890 transplants, were previously barren of fish. They were stocked with nonnative species because they are across the Continental Divide from Yellowstone Lake. The danger of infiltration was considered impossible.

Famous last thoughts.

Lewis Lake

Lewis Lake offers a mixed-bag of fishing opportunities that deserve more attention than they receive. Despite its easy access from the South Entrance–West Thumb Road, it is rarely crowded.

The lake's reputation for big trout is often associated with the channel linking it to its larger sister, Shoshone Lake. Anglers who only visit Lewis Lake during brown trout spawning runs into the Lewis River Channel in late fall are missing the boat. The lake fishes well with streamers and nymphs throughout its seasons and offers good top water action in midsummer. But it is difficult to separate the lake from the river running through it, and the outlet is another positive link to its dynamic fishery.

The bottom line is that each of the lake's many options need to be explored to appreciate fully its rewards. It has one of the prettiest campgrounds in the park, and it is one of the few that doesn't fill early.

Lewis Lake is loaded with smaller than average lake trout in the 14- to 18-inch range because of its limited prey base. However, those that succeed in making the conversion to full-sized predators may exceed 36 inches in length and 25 pounds in weight. The unofficial record for the lake was a 30-pound lake trout.

Brown trout fare better in Lewis Lake, and plump, acrobatic fish in the 12- to 20-inch range are common, with a fair number exceeding 26 inches.

Anglers also take an occasional brook trout, and a few report cutthroat in the lake. The latter apparently have worked their way down from Pocket Lake, a small pond above Shoshone Lake. Heart Lake cutthroat were planted in it in the 1970s as a safeguard against losing the unique race of Yellowstone cutthroat.

Angler reports give Lewis Lake a 74 percent satisfaction rating for its .49 fish per hour catch rate and fish averaging 14.5 inches.

More than a century ago, Lewis Lake and Shoshone Lake had no fish in their pristine waters. The Lewis River waterfall blocked upstream migration of Yellowstone cutthroat. In 1890, lake trout from the Bear Island area of Lake Michigan and Loch Leven brown trout from Scotland were planted in the lakes, where they quickly took hold and were reproducing within a decade. Lewis Lake also received a transplant of lake trout in 1941.

In a unique switch in roles in the 1980s, lake trout from Lewis Lake returned to their natal waters. Brood stocks created from eggs collected from the lake helped reestablish Lake Michigan's lake trout fishery that had been decimated by sea lampreys in the 1960s. However, pollution in the second-largest of the Great Lakes has thwarted attempts to accomplish natural reproduction by Lewis Lake progeny.

Efforts to establish cutthroat and graylings in Lewis Lake in the 1930s failed, as did rainbow transplants in tributary streams. The few brook trout in tributaries are holdovers from fish stocked in 1893.

Shaped like a crudely drawn valentine, Lewis Lake is about 5 miles long and 3.5 miles wide at the top. The third largest of the park's lakes, it rests at 7,779 feet in a pine-rimmed bowl on the Pacific side of the Continental Divide. Puffs of steam rising from small thermal features at its outlet remind visitors it also is on the southern rim of the Yellowstone Caldera.

The lake opens to fishing Memorial Day weekend but it often isn't completely free of ice until mid-June.

Motorized boats are permitted, although small boats and canoes should hug its shores and avoid the center of the lake. Prevailing winds kick up a heavy chop or white capped waves almost daily in midafternoon. Sudden storms can capsize small craft without warning and the lake has claimed seven lives over the years.

Its high elevation means the water never has time to warm much above 50 degrees and hypothermia is an acute danger. Float-tubers should dress warmly to avoid becoming too chilled.

Spring and autumn anglers do best searching the lake's in-shore ledges, shallows, points, and coves with moderate-sized streamers and black or olive woolly buggers and dark leech patterns. A floating line with a long stout leader can be used in shallow waters and around weed beds, but a sinking tip or fullsink line is needed for deeper waters off ledges and points.

Actually, two reels are better than one in midsummer. A second reel loaded with a floating line comes in handy as the waters warm and cruising trout sipping callibaetis or caddis draw attention away from the lake's depths.

After ice-out, also look for brown and lake trout congregating at the mouth of the Lewis River Channel, or explore the lower meadow run of the inlet as it warms and hatches start to erupt. The channel between Lewis and Shoshone Lakes is the only stream in the park that can be floated in hand-propelled watercraft.

Hatches in the channel, which are often flushed into the inlet bay, include green drakes in late June and PMDs and BWOs in July. Small terrestrial patterns are effective in late summer. Midges and tiny BWOs also provide some top water action in late fall.

In late June and July, good-sized brown trout also take up feeding lies at the outlet of the lake and in downstream shelter areas for about a half mile of the river's upper run to its scenic waterfall. The trout lie in wait for caddis, midges, callibaetis, and other mayfly spinners being flushed out of the lake. And, in the afternoon, this is the one place on the lake where the winds work to an angler's advantage. The short canyon between the waterfall and the lake produces a prolific overlapping hatch of small dark stoneflies, golden stones, and little yellow stones, or willow flies, in early July.

The browns attack the smorgasbord with abandon, although they can be as selective in their feeding as rainbows. The bonus is that they offer a tussle as acrobatic as the rainbow's.

Unlike the inlet channel, boats or canoes are not permitted past a posted line on the outlet bay. Boaters can either anchor near the top of the outlet or land their craft and work the outlet bay and upper river from the banks.

In late September, lake trout start to follow brown trout into both the channel and the outlet on their fall spawning runs. Fishing with larger streamers can be intense, but beadhead nymphs also may be effective. This is about the only time the lake is crowded, but the window of opportunity is short. Fishing ends the first weekend of November.

Outlet of Lewis Lake. Boats are not permitted to enter the river.

There is an excellent boat ramp at the campground on the south end of the lake. Canoes and float tubes also can be bank launched at several coves along the South Entrance–West Thumb Road, which parallels the lake for about 2.5 miles.

It is shallow enough in a few places near the campground for wading anglers, although float-tubers cover more water. Shore anglers also can find a few places along coves and points, as well as shallows and bays near the outlet and inlet, to cast to cruising or rising fish. Fishing is best in early morning and on warm summer evenings since afternoon winds blow from the southwest.

Footpaths skirt much of the east shore near the campground and the loop road. Stick to the path on the 1.5-mile hike to the outlet. Trying to take a shortcut through the forest is virtually impossible because of numerous barriers created by downed timber.

Two trails into the Lewis River Channel start from a trailhead at the north end of the lake. The Doghead Trail, which goes directly to the top of the channel, is 4 miles long. The Lewis Channel Trail is 3 miles along the top of the lake to the inlet and then 4 miles to the top of the channel.

The Lewis Lake Campground is one of the few in the park that doesn't require reservations. Camping also is available at Flagg Ranch and the Snake River Campground, just south of the park's South Entrance.

Boat permits are available at the ranger stations at the campground and South Entrance.

Yellowstone's Hidden Gem: Avoid Crowds at Shoshone Lake

By Bruce Staples

Open any angling magazine and you can expect an article on a famous stream or lake. The Henry's Fork, Henry's Lake, the Madison River, and the South Fork are common subjects. It's nice to see these fisheries gain the attention they deserve, but the fanfare can crowd rivers and, for some people, diminish the experiences touted in the articles.

On the other end of the spectrum, there are waters that deserve attention and can absorb a few more anglers without destroying the experience. One such place is Yellowstone's Shoshone Lake.

If the huge lake was located next to a highway, it would receive the same fanfare. But even though it is hidden in the shadows of the region's other angling heavyweights, Shoshone still shines. Fish it and you'll experience a true wilderness adventure. At 12 square miles, it is the largest lake in the Lower 48 without a road to its doorstep.

A little more than 100 years ago, Shoshone Lake didn't have trout. The same was true for its sister, Lewis Lake, and all the waters above Lewis Falls in the river's drainage. In 1890, brown trout and lake trout were released into Shoshone Lake. A bit later, brook trout were released into its tributaries.

Shoshone Lake is so fertile that in the 1920s it sustained a commercial fishery. Anglers got the idea to fish the lake after being served some of its trout at eateries in the park. The result was four decades of degradation. Powerboats roared up and down the lake, and anglers camped indiscriminately on its shores. Garbage and human waste littered the shores and polluted its waters. Bag limits were not enforced and often scoffed at by many anglers. Complaints finally brought the Park Service to the rescue.

In the early 1960s, bag limits were enforced, and powerboats were removed despite howls of protest. Later, bag limits were rolled back to compensate for the increasing number of visitors. At the same time, backcountry camping permits were required and the number of visitors per campsite was limited.

Shoshone Lake has a surprising mix of trout.

The result of the new regulations is Yellowstone Park's greatest population of brown trout. That may come as a surprise to many anglers, particularly those who frequent the Madison River. But it is certain that Shoshone Lake hosts more brown trout than the entire Madison River drainage within the park.

Shoshone Lake's other major salmonid resident is lake trout. The lake trout, which received a black eye because of its illegal introduction into Yellowstone Lake, are doing well in Shoshone Lake. In fact, the park's largest population of lake trout is in Shoshone Lake.

The lake's brown trout can range up to 8 pounds, while its lake trout tip the scales at 30 pounds. Brook trout make up a minor part of the fish population and can run up to 3 pounds. Brook trout-lake trout hybrids, known as splake, are also present and achieve the same size as the brookies.

Another resident is the Heart Lake strain of Yellowstone cutthroat trout. In the 1970s, these were planted in nearby Pocket Lake after its brook trout population was eradicated. Some Pocket Lake cutthroat descended to Shoshone Lake and grew large. I can verify this. In 1985, I caught and released a 20-inch cutthroat in Moose Creek Bay on the other side of Shoshone Lake from Pocket Lake's outlet.

Shoshone Lake's climate is as harsh as you would expect to find in northern Alberta or the Northwest Territories. Because it sits at nearly 8,000 feet, winter stays late and comes early. As a result, lake waters are cold.

The elevation also means the angling season is short, beginning with a late May to early June ice-out. Wintry weather usually closes the lake to angling in mid-October.

Another thing to consider are the storms that can lash the lake's surface without warning, turning it from glass to 4-foot whitecaps in minutes. Over the years, a number of people have drowned or died of hypothermia after being pitched into the lake.

The fishing experience reveals that Shoshone Lake is best early in the season. As if celebrating spring, the fish feed to the point of gorging right after ice-out.

Any streamer, nymph, or attractor pattern allowed to sink to near bottom around dropoffs, shoals, inlets, submerged hot springs, or weed beds will bring action from juvenile browns and lake trout that range in size from 15 to 23 inches. Find one of these natural features and enjoy the action. Use a fullsink or sinktip line depending on depth. A long-tapered leader is a must in Shoshone Lake's ultra-clear waters.

As the surface water warms in June, midge and speckled dun mayfly emergences grab the attention of cruising browns. If you rise early, you can experience the lake's best dry-fly fishing during these emergences. Again, it is important to use a long-tapered leader.

The results can be acrobatic and beautiful browns that take several minutes to subdue. Once in a while, a brookie or juvenile lake trout will respond to these tactics. Midmorning winds usually end this action, but when winds die down in the evening, it repeats.

By early July, waters in the shallows warm to the point where the trout move to deeper water. So the tactics mentioned above become increasingly less effective. In a sense, fishing on Shoshone Lake "takes a nap" during midsummer, and I recommend that you seek better action elsewhere.

Fishing improves again after Labor Day. The cool weather makes the fish more active and signals the upcoming spawning season. Throughout September and early October, both browns and lake trout move to shallower waters. The lake trout head toward rocky shoals and the browns move toward the lake's outlet.

During the fall, use large, colorful streamers to explore waters around the shoals and outlet. The fish that respond will be the largest the lake has to offer.

Fall is the best time of year for flyfishers to encounter the huge lake trout in Shoshone lake. The rest of the year they reside in the lake's depths, which range to 300 feet.

There are two fundamental approaches to Shoshone Lake: by water and by land. For the more adventurous, a float trip starting from the boat ramp at Lewis Lake campground is the choice. By this route, visitors travel across Lewis Lake to the out-

A lake trout is released by a successful angler on Shoshone Lake.

let of the Lewis River Channel. From there, motors are not allowed. Visitors must paddle up the river, which runs through a beautiful meadow. Above the meadow, the river changes to a riffle and run stream. This demands a .75-mile portage to the outlet bay of Shoshone Lake.

If you prefer to backpack, here are the three routes to consider:

The shortest starts from a trailhead near DeLacey Creek on the Old Faithful–West Thumb road. The trail follows the creek for about 3 miles to the lake. It is a flat walk, and is the best choice for carrying a float tube.

The next most convenient route starts at the trailhead just north of Lewis Lake and off the South Entrance–West Thumb road. This is a 5-mile walk over easy terrain to the outlet bay of the lake. This is a good choice in the autumn when the brown trout are migrating to spawning redds in the channel.

If you wish to see the west end of Shoshone Lake, which hosts a large and beautiful geyser basin and very few anglers, then take the Lone Star Geyser Trail, which begins just a few miles east of Old Faithful. This choice is an 8-mile walk, but it lets you explore very lightly fished Shoshone Creek and its brook and brown trout.

No matter how you reach it, Shoshone Lake offers a wilderness angling experience of high quality and more difficult to achieve as time goes by.

(Bruce Staples is the author of Yellowstone Park: A River Journal *and* Snake River Country: Flies and Waters.*)*

Park's Wild Soul: Heart Lake Is Cutthroat Bonanza

By Bruce Staples

Where would you fish if you could only fish one place? My choice is Yellowstone's Heart Lake Basin, without hesitation.

Its primary quarry—Yellowstone cutthroat—are found elsewhere in the region, but nowhere else will you find a stronger and more beautiful race of this native trout. Hefty lake trout are prime drawing cards, too, and whitefish complete the basin's salmonid options.

Many anglers are not familiar with Heart Lake Basin for a good reason: It's 8 miles from the nearest highway. But its remoteness assures exceptional water quality and all other requirements for excellent trout populations. The long hike guarantees a wilderness angling experience because it keeps all but the most hardy away.

The most direct route is the Heart Lake trailhead a few hundred yards north of Lewis Lake, on the east side of the South Entrance–West Thumb road. A longer trail from the South Entrance along the Snake River requires stream crossings not always safe in wet years.

The Heart Lake Trail winds through a monotonous pine forest for the first 5 miles, but then the sulfide aroma of hot springs wafts through the trees and a sight of rare beauty meets the eyes. At the top of Heart Lake Geyser Basin, known as Paycheck Pass, the trees part to reveal Heart Lake three miles in the distance and 500 feet below. At the east end of the lake, the outlet to the Snake River can be seen. Traces of Outlet and Surprise Creeks are visible. On the horizon is the Absaroka Mountain Range, the park's east boundary.

As you get closer, you can guess the course of Beaver Creek through its picturesque meadow. Right at your feet, Witch Creek gurgles. It traverses the geyser basin and ends in the lake below. At certain times of the year, all these streams host cutthroat trout.

The entire vista is dominated by Mount Sheridan, which towers over the basin at 10,308 feet. Its impressive figure is graced by snow throughout the year. Its numerous springs feed the lake. Mount Sheridan appears to be an enormous ice cream sundae slipping into Heart Lake, an illusion brought about by the faults that ripped at its eastern flank.

The basin is hugely impressive in stature, especially since you know that you are already five miles from the closest road.

But it hasn't always been that way. Until 1960, a primitive road coursed the easy grade from the trailhead to the top of Paycheck Pass. Anglers would park at the top of the pass and portage boats down the 3-mile trail through the geyser basin to the lake. Damage to the habitat—garbage—was collecting in alarming amounts, so the Park Service closed the road. Lazy anglers complained, but the rewards were quickly apparent to those who hiked to the improved fishery.

My first visits to the Heart Lake Basin were in the early 1970s, not long after my love of flyfishing began. In those days, my fishing efforts were focused on the park's

Looking west to Heart Lake. (Photo by Bruce Staples)

fourth largest lake. Elegant cutthroat could be caught on dry or wet flies from shore right under Sheridan's heights or at the mouth of Witch Creek. Occasionally a lake trout could be lured from the depths, especially early in the season.

In time I began to explore the basin's other waters.

I first discovered Heart River during a Fourth of July weekend. Its first half-mile is as beautiful as a trout stream can be. It meanders through a beautiful meadow and its crystal clear water allows visitors to watch schools of cutthroat search for food. After the first half-mile, the river drops downstairs into a brawling canyon.

A thick, giant stonefly emergence was in full stride and windborne adults were wafting up the river to the lake. The catching was fabulously easy. In addition to the river's residents, trout from the lake were partaking of the giant bugs. It was an unforgettable experience. I exhausted my supply of floating imitations and was left to encourage my companions as they spotted, fooled, and released all the largest trout in sight.

On another trip, I fished the river in June, only to discover that its trout ravenously accepted anything offered, from PMDs to caddis patterns to woolly worms. It was on that trip that I noticed the giant grizzly bear tracks that had obliterated the tracks I made that morning. It is something I will never forget.

In the early 1980s, I discovered cutthroat and occasional lake trout would be in Witch and Beaver Creeks in June. They were feasting on roe from spawning suckers. They would fatten to the point of being grotesque, yet still remained wary. The slightest hint of danger triggered a dash to the lake below. They were great sport and remain the prettiest and strongest cutthroats I have ever encountered. Fish up to 8 pounds could be fooled with almost any large, brightly colored wet fly and, occasionally, with a dry fly.

The only problem was they were not the only ones who fed off the suckers. For grizzlies, both the suckers and the trout were the main course. As a result, fishing required vigilance. Bears and man in such close proximity worried the Park Service, especially since bear habitat was diminishing while the basin was becoming more popular.

Over time, I discovered the remainder of the basin. During one trip, I ventured up Outlet and Surprise Creeks, where I was greeted by small, but eager, cutthroat. I received the same greeting in Outlet Lake. Torrential rains drove me back to camp before I could really enjoy this remote gem, so it remains a personal goal to return to it and systematically test its waters.

It was during a four-day stay in June 1985 that we learned our Heart Lake fishing patterns were going to be interrupted. The ranger at the Heart Lake Patrol Cabin told us the Park Service had determined the basin was critical grizzly bear habitat in June when they were still in the lower country. She told us the basin would no longer be open in June in order to lessen conflicts and help the grizzlies survive.

The rule eliminated a month of great fishing, a pain I have found hard to endure. I still go to the basin today, but I've had to learn the nuances of its other seasons.

The forest fires of 1988 scarred the face of Heart Lake Basin, but they didn't impact the fishing. In the years after the fires, I learned the basin was not just a springtime fishery.

One of my angling friends from Jackson Hole invited me on a float-tubing trip during the second week of September to look for spawning lake trout. It taught me the best tactic for lake trout is to pitch big streamers and let them sink close to the rocky bottom and then vary the retrieve until the right combination is found. The result is huge lake trout and superb cutthroats that follow the lake trout to snitch eggs as they do from the suckers in June in the basin's creeks.

Float-tubing provides the most mobility, but also the biggest chance of a back ache after a 16-mile round trip. Chest waders can get you out deep enough to take part in the action.

Since June is closed, pick early July for a trip. Float tube or wade around the creek confluences using leeches and streamers. There are some caddis and speckle dun hatches, so be prepared for everything. There is also the stonefly hatch on the river just below the lake. To enjoy it, a 24-mile round trip is required, and camping is a must. It is important to make reservations in advance and to know and follow all the park rules in bear country.

An angler gets a strike on Beaver Creek, ½ mile north of Heart Lake.
(Photo by Bruce Staples)

One of the newest rules is the Park Service's requirement that anglers keep all lake trout they catch to help protect the lake's unique race of cutthroat. And, since you can't effectively carry them out, be prepared for a lake trout dinner. Again, beware of the bears. That may sound like a lot to consider, but the extra planning is worth the effort.

If you go, remember Heart Lake Basin is a rare resource. It offers a total wilderness with scenic surroundings and waters inhabited by perhaps the world's best cutthroat trout. Take care of it.

(Bruce Staples is the author of Yellowstone Park: A River Journal *and* Snake River Country: Flies and Waters.*)*

Small Lakes in Yellowstone

Less than 35 of Yellowstone's 140 small lakes and ponds contain trout today. However, only 17 lakes were inhabited with fish in 1872 when the park was founded.

Stocking and hatchery programs that began in the late 1880s attempted to establish native or nonnative fish in all the big lakes and the majority of the smaller ones. Yellowstone's put-and-take philosophy ended in the mid-1950s, but many of the transplants never took hold or were only briefly sustained through supplemental stockings. Others dwindled into oblivion due to inadequate spawning habitat, a fate still facing several small lakes.

Small backcountry lakes in the Yellowstone drainage contain cutthroat, except for a few isolated waters with brook trout. Some lakes in the Snake, Madison, and Gallatin drainages hold cutthroat, but most are rainbow or brook trout fisheries. Only three backcountry lakes—Grebe, Wolf, and Cascade—hold grayling.

A few ponds with trout are located near the park's loop roads, and several of the most popular fisheries are reached by hikes of 5 miles or less. Fishing in some remote lakes is not worth the hike if that is the only purpose for venturing off the beaten path. Still, they are in scenic locations and many have backcountry campsites.

Topographic hiking maps are recommended for trips into the backcountry, including day hikes. An excellent hiking guide, with notes on fish transplant attempts, is Steve Pierce's *The Lakes of Yellowstone*. Hikers may cross paths with grizzly bears anywhere in the park; it is safer to hike in groups of three or more. Campers, who must make reservations in advance, need to follow rules for keeping a clean camp and campfire restrictions. Float-tubers must purchase boating permits and wear a life vest when on the water.

Park biologists rarely get enough time to sample remote lakes. Completing angler report cards greatly assists data collection on the health of Yellowstone's fisheries.

The following list details locations of small lakes and ponds by principal drainages in the park. Lakes without fish are named to help avoid confusion in making trip plans.

Upper Yellowstone Drainage

Fishless lakes in the upper Yellowstone drainage include Glade, Aster, and Forest Lakes.

Indian Pond

- Location: 3 miles east of Fishing Bridge on East Entrance Road; Indian Pond is named Squaw Lake on older maps.
- Access: Just south of loop road.
- Topography: 24 acres / maximum depth 72 feet / 7,780 elevation.
- Trout: Marginal fishery for small cutthroat.
- Comments: Most people just give it a glance when walking along a scenic nature trail to a point on Yellowstone Lake.

Eleanor Lake

- Location: 7 miles west of East Entrance; 17 miles west of Fishing Bridge.
- Access: Just south of loop road.

- Topography: 2.5 acres / maximum depth 13 feet / 8,450 elevation.
- Trout: Cutthroat average 10 inches.
- Comments: It gets a lot of pressure, but there is better fishing down the road.

Sylvan Lake
- Location: 10 miles west of East Entrance; 16 miles east of Fishing Bridge.
- Access: Just south of loop road.
- Topography: 28 acres / very shallow with maximum depth of 21 feet / 8,410 elevation.
- Trout: Cutthroat in 10- to 14-inch range.
- Comments: It gets a lot of pressure after it opens to fishing on July 15. Lake's outlet flows into Clear Creek, a principal spawning stream on Yellowstone Lake.

Riddle Lake
- Location: Southeast of Yellowstone Lake.
- Access: Trailhead is 2.5 miles south of Grant Village Junction on South Entrance Road; 2.5 mile hike, flat terrain.
- Topography: 274 acres / maximum depth 27 feet / 7,913 elevation.
- Trout: cutthroat mostly in 14-inch range, possibilities for a larger fish.
- Comments: This lake is often closed in the early season due to grizzly bear activity in the area. Check at Grant Village or Lewis Lake Ranger Stations before setting out. Solution Creek flowing out of the lake is closed to fishing until July 15.

Trail Lake
- Location: South of South Arm of Yellowstone Lake.
- Access: 2 miles south of Trail Creek Trail to Yellowstone River delta; Trail Creek Trail connects Heart Lake Trail and Thorofare Trail to delta; total length from either direction is 25 miles or more; terrain is more extreme along Heart Lake route. Another option is to canoe to the bottom of the South Arm of Yellowstone Lake.
- Topography: 55 acres / maximum depth is 12 feet / 7,748 elevation.
- Trout: Cutthroat in 14- to 18-inch range.
- Comments: This lake could be the icing on the cake during a backcountry trip of a lifetime to the upper Yellowstone. To fish it requires adding an extra overnight camp to an itinerary that involves a minimum of four days just to hike into and out of the delta. Canoers might find it a more attractive option.

Alder Lake
- Location: West side of Promontory point separating the South and Southeast Arms of Yellowstone Lake.
- Access: Boat or canoe to the South Arm, hike about a half-mile to the lake; 4-mile crosscountry bushwhack hike from Trail Creek Trail.
- Topography: 123 acres / maximum depth 20 feet / 7,752 elevation
- Trout: Cutthroat in 10- to 14-inch range.
- Comments: Effort involved to reach this lake makes it a questionable fishing destination for hikers.

Middle Yellowstone Drainage

Fishless lakes in the middle Yellowstone drainage include Beach Springs, Turbid, Wrangler, Dewdrop, Wapiti, Mirror, Tern, and Clear.

Cascade Lake
- Location: Northwest of Canyon Village.
- Access: 2.5 mile hike up Cascade Creek from trailhead on Norris–Canyon road, just west of junction; 2.5 mile hike from first picnic area on Canyon–Tower road, north of junction; 4.5 miles west of Grebe Lake on loop hike; moderate climbs on all trails.
- Topography: 36 acres / maximum depth 27 feet / 7,980 elevation.
- Trout: Grayling, mostly in the 10-inch range; cutthroat in the 12-inch range.
- Comments: Cascade Lake contains the only grayling in the Yellowstone drainage of the park. Cascade Creek also is a pleasant diversion for small cutthroat when Yellowstone is running high or before the upper river opens.

Ribbon Lake
- Location: Northeast of Yellowstone's waterfalls.
- Access: 2-mile hike from the trailhead near the scenic Artist Point, flat terrain.
- Topography: 11 acres / maximum depth 19 feet / 7,820 elevation.
- Trout: Marginal fishery for small rainbow.
- Comments: Marsh and thick water lily growth around lake's edges make fishing very difficult. Basically a nice hiking or camping site.

Fern Lake
- Location: North of Pelican Valley.
- Access: 12-mile hike via Pelican Creek Trail to Broad Creek Trail; moderate terrain.
- Topography: 90 acres / maximum depth 25 feet / 8,245 elevation.
- Trout: Marginal fishery for a few, small cutthroat.
- Comments: Not worth the hike. Fish upper Pelican Creek instead.

White Lakes
- Location: North of Pelican Valley.
- Access: 9-mile hike via Tern Lake Trail; moderate terrain.
- Topography: 90 acres / maximum depth of 25 feet / 8,245 elevation.
- Trout: Marginal fishery for few small cutthroat.
- Comments: Not worth the hike. Fish upper Pelican Creek instead.

Lamar Drainage

Fishless lakes in the Lamar drainage include Buck, Shrimp, Trumpeter, Foster, and Rainey Lakes.

Trout Lake
- Location: 1.5 miles west of Pebble Creek Campground.
- Access: half-mile steep climb from unmarked parking lot on Tower–Cooke City road.
- Topography: 12 acres / maximum depth of 17 feet / 6,900 elevation
- Trout: Rainbows in the 14- to 20- inch range; a few go to 30 inches.

- Comments: Trout Lake was once the park's hatchery site for rainbows. It gets hit hard the first weeks after its June 15 opening day, especially by park employees and the region's residents, and it rarely offers a solitary experience. If there are more than a half-dozen cars in the tiny parking lot, look for better fishing experiences elsewhere. Nearby Shrimp and Buck Lakes are fishless. Inlet to Trout Lake is closed to fishing until July 15.

This is basically a nymph fishery with small leech and damselfly patterns, woolly buggers, scuds, soft-hackles, and beadheads. Callibaetis is the principal hatch in July and August, but sporadic hatches of other mayflies, midges, and terrestrials draw top water action. Fishing from float tubes is the best option, but many anglers patrol its banks to sight-cast to cruising trout. Trout Lake's 90 percent satisfaction rating is the second highest in the park reported by anglers, who record a .74 fish per hour catch rate for fish averaging 14.3 inches.

McBride Lake
- Location: Above First Meadow of Slough Creek.
- Access: 3-mile hike up Slough Creek trail, and 2-mile crosscountry bushwhack to lake; moderate climbs on both routes.
- Topography: 23 acres / maximum depth 22 feet / 6,560 elevation.
- Trout: Cutthroat in the 10- to 14-inch range; a few larger fish.
- Comments: Mosquitoes and deerflies are fierce in marshes above Slough Creek. It also is prime grizzly bear country. Carry spray repellents for both contingencies, and don't hike it alone. A topo map is recommended whenever a hike departs from a groomed trail.

McBride Lake was the source of Montana's brood stock for Yellowstone cutthroat. Wyoming developed one of its brood stocks from Montana's McBride cutthroat, but currently is developing a new brood stock from eggs collected at the LeHardy Rapids of the Yellowstone River.

Lower Yellowstone / Gardner Drainages
Fishless lakes in lower Yellowstone and Gardner drainages include Mammoth Beaver Ponds, Rainbow, Cache, Twin, Swan, Crevice, Geode, Nymph, Beaver, Phantom, Floating Island, Lake of the Woods, and Obsidian.

Blacktail Ponds
- Location: 7 miles east of Mammoth on Mammoth–Tower Road.
- Access: Near loop road.
- Topography: 11 acres / shallow with maximum depth of 26 feet / 6,600 elevation.
- Trout: Cutthroat and brook trout average 14 inches.
- Special regulations: Limit on brook trout is 5 under 13 inches.
- Comments: In early season, the lakes are often closed to protect nesting trumpeter swans or sandhill cranes.

A very popular fishery, it is called "Shaky Lake" by some because of marsh and spongy banks surrounding it, plus mudsucking flats as levels diminish. Basically a small nymph, leech, damselfly, and scud fishery. Callibaetis is the main mayfly hatch; small terrestrials may bring top water action in late summer.

Fawn Lake
- Location: Southwest of Mammoth above Gardner Meadows.
- Access: 5 mile hike via Glenn Creek–Fawn Pass Trail; moderate terrain.
- Topography: 5 acres / shallow lake with maximum depth of 18 feet / 7,800 elevation.
- Trout: brook trout in 10- to 14-inch range.
- Special regulations: Brook trout limit on Fawn Lake is 5 under 13 inches.
- Comments: This is a possible side trip on a popular hiking and horseback riding trail in the scenic northwest corner of Yellowstone.

Joffe Lake
- Location: 1 mile southeast of Mammoth.
- Access: Just off the bottom of Bunsen Peak road that passes through employee housing area east of Mammoth–Norris loop road.
- Topography: 1.5 acres / maximum depth 9 feet / 6,500 elevation.
- Trout: Pan-sized brook trout.
- Comments: Great spot to teach a child to fly cast to eagerly rising trout.

Slide Lakes
- Location: 2 miles northwest of Mammoth.
- Access: Gravel road behind Mammoth Inn that goes to North Entrance; no trail to lower lake, which holds rainbow.
- Topography: 1 acre / maximum depth 43 feet / 5,170 elevation.
- Trout: Sparse population of rainbows.
- Comments: Good chances to see antelope and other wildlife up close are the better prospect on this road, which is usually closed during wet weather.

Grizzly Lake
- Location: 6 miles northwest of Norris Campground on Norris–Mammoth Road.
- Access: 2 mile steep climb from trailhead; easier route in is to follow Straight Creek upstream from Apollinaris Springs trailhead, mile or so north on loop road.
- Topography: 136 acres / maximum depth 36 feet / 7,508 elevation.
- Trout: Pan-sized brook trout.
- Comments: Grizzly Lake is a popular day hike, although campsites on Straight Creek are available for a loop trip. Brookies are a little bigger in Straight Creek.

Madison Drainage
Fishless lakes in Madison drainage include Ice, Feather, Harlequin, Nymph, Lower Basin, Mary, Nuthatch, Isa, Scaup, and Mallard.

Grebe Lake
- Location: Northeast of Virginia Cascade on Gibbon River.
- Access: 3.5 mile hike from trailhead on Norris–Canyon road; relatively flat terrain.
- Topography: 156 acres / maximum depth of 32 feet / 8,000 elevation.
- Trout: Rainbows, mostly in 14-inch range; grayling around 11 inches.
- Comments: Grebe Lake is the source of the Gibbon River. By far the most popular small backcountry lake in the park, it sees relatively heavy pressure early in the

season when grayling spawn at the outlet in mid-June. Hike along old grayling hatchery road crosses marshy areas in wet years, and mosquitoes can be fierce. Region also is prime grizzly bear country and should not be entered alone.

Best option is to pack in a float tube. Small nymphs and emergers work very well for grayling, along with medium-sized black or purple woolly buggers, damsel nymphs, leeches, and Zug Bugs. Watch for sporadic caddis and mayfly hatches, primarily callibaetis, and terrestrials as the summer progresses. Rainbows help keep fishing hopping. Grebe Lake has the highest catch rate in the park—1.94 fish per hour—and anglers give it an 89 percent satisfaction rating for fish averaging 9.9 inches.

Grayling spill out of the lake in wet years into the Gibbon and down into the upper Madison River.

Wolf Lake
- Location: 2 miles southwest of Grebe Lake outlet.
- Access: 5 mile hike from Ice Lake trailhead on Norris–Canyon road, or backtrack from Grebe Lake trail.
- Topography: 5 acres / maximum depth of 32 feet / 7,998 elevation.
- Trout: Grayling and rainbows average 10 inches.
- Comments: Wolf Lake is a stopping point on the Gibbon River's course downstream. Spawning habitat is sparse and grayling and rainbows are smaller than in Grebe Lake.

  There are no fish in nearby Ice Lake.

Goose Lake
- Location: Fountain Flats south of Firehole River.
- Access: 2-mile hike from Fairy Falls trailhead south of Nez Perce bridge on Madison–Old Faithful road; 3-mile hike from Steel Bridge trailhead, west of Black Sand Basin; flat terrain.
- Topography: 34 acres / maximum depth of 31 feet / 7,170 elevation.
- Trout: Very marginal fishery for rainbow.
- Comments: Rarely fished, Goose Lake was poisoned in 1937 to eliminate the unauthorized transplant of yellow perch. Attempts to establish browns failed, and the rainbow population continues to dwindle.

Gallatin Drainage

Fishless lakes in the Gallatin Drainage include Gallatin, Divide, Shelf, Crescent, and Crag.

High Lake
- Location: On park's northwest boundary in the Gallatin Mountains .
- Access: 10-mile hike via north spur off Sportsman Lake trail, which starts from mouth of Bacon Rind Creek on Gallatin River, on U.S. 191; rugged terrain.
- Topography: 7 acres / maximum depth of 18 feet / 8,774 elevation.
- Trout: Cutthroat in the 8- to 11-inch range.

- Comments: Remote location of this lake makes it more a hiking destination or an overnight camping site.

Sportsman Lake
- Location: 5 miles west of Electric Peak in Gallatin Mountains.
- Access: 12-mile hike from trailhead at mouth of Specimen Creek on Gallatin River, on U.S. 191, or 14 mile hike from south of Mammoth via the Glenn Creek Trail to Sportsman Lake Trail; eastern route much more extreme.
- Topography: 7 acres / shallow lake with maximum depth of 26 feet / 7,730 elevation.
- Trout: Cutthroat in the 8- to 11-inch range.
- Comments: Remote location of this lake makes it more a hiking destination or an overnight camping site. The Mammoth route crosses a high, steep pass south of 10,992-foot Electric Peak, the highest point in Yellowstone.

Snake Drainage
Fishless lakes in the Snake drainage are mostly in the Fall River Basin. They include Lilypad, Winegar, Robinson, Wyodaho, Buffalo, South Boundary, and Summit.

Sheridan Lake
- Location: Southwest of Heart Lake.
- Access: 12-mile hike via Heart Lake trailhead on South Entrance road.
- Topography: 15 acres / very shallow lake / 7,378; rugged terrain.
- Trout: Small population of pan-sized cutthroat.
- Comments: There is much better fishing in Heart Lake.

Basin Creek Lake
- Location: Southwest of Heart Lake.
- Access: 2.5 miles southwest of Heart Lake; or 11-mile hike via Southern Boundary Trail, starting at South Entrance, and Heart Lake Trail from Snake River; rugged terrain.
- Topography: 8 acres / maximum depth of 17 feet / 7,390 elevation.
- Trout: Pan-sized cutthroat.
- Comments: There is much better fishing in Heart Lake.

Outlet Lake
- Location: East of Heart Lake below rim of Continental Divide.
- Access: 4-mile hike from Heart Lake on Trail Creek Trail; rugged terrain.
- Topography: 16 acres / very shallow lake / 7,749 elevation.
- Trout: Pan-sized cutthroat.
- Comments: Possible overnight campsite on hike into or out of upper Yellowstone delta.

Mariposa Lake
- Location: On Two Ocean Plateau northeast of headwaters of Snake River.
- Access: 30 mile hike from Southern Boundary trailhead at South Entrance; very rugged terrain.
- Topography: 12 acres / very shallow / 8,950 elevation.
- Trout: Cutthroat and cutthroat-rainbow hybrids in the 8- to 12-inch range.

- Comments: This is the highest and most remote backcountry lake in Yellowstone. It is also in the heart of grizzly bear country. Campsites offer possible stopovers on the longest route to the upper Yellowstone River, across the Continental Divide.

Pocket Lake
- Location: Above Shoshone Lake.
- Access: Half-mile steep climb from northwest corner of Shoshone Lake; easiest route in is the 3-mile hike on DeLacy Creek trail from Old Faithful–West Thumb road, and 2-mile hike to mouth of lake's outlet.
- Topography: 14 acres / maximum depth of 24 feet / 8,100 elevation.
- Trout: Cutthroat average 14 inches, with a few in the 18- to 20-inch range.
- Comments: Heart Lake cutthroat were planted in Pocket Lake in the mid-1980s to establish a second population as a hedge against anything happening to the unique strain of Yellowstone cutthroat. Brook trout in the lake were poisoned but have returned. In 1998, the park issued a mandatory kill order for brook trout hooked by anglers in Pocket Lake. The cutthroat, which occasionally show up in Shoshone Lake, are protected by a catch-and-release rule.

Beula Lake
- Location: West of South Entrance and Flagg Ranch.
- Access: 2.5-mile hike from trailhead at Grassy Lake, 9 miles west of Flagg Ranch on rough gravel road that skirts southern boundary of the park; relatively flat terrain.
- Topography: 107 acres / maximum depth of 36 feet / 7,377 elevation.
- Trout: Cutthroat in the 10- to 14-inch range, with some larger fish.
- Comments: Beula Lake is the source of the Fall River. It fishes best in late summer and fall with a float tube. Sporadic caddis and mayfly hatches and small terrestrials offer top water options. Moderate-sized leeches, woolly buggers, small nymphs, emergers and beadheads, and scuds are all effective for prospecting with wet flies. Hering Lake is just upstream. Grizzly bears are common, so don't enter this little-explored corner of the park alone, and keep a clean camp on overnight stays.

Hering Lake
- Location: Half-mile southeast of Beula Lake.
- Access: Backtrack from Beula Lake Trail by following outlet channel.
- Topography: 60 acres / maximum depth of 44 feet / 7,381 elevation.
- Trout: Cutthroat average about 12 inches.
- Comments: Good side trip from Beula Lake if trip allows enough time to explore.

Ranger Lake
- Location: East of Bechler River.
- Access: Half-mile hike from northeast side of Bechler Meadows; no trail, moderate climb.
- Topography: 58 acres / maximum depth of 38 feet / 6,980 elevation.
- Trout: Rainbows in the 8- to 10-inch range.
- Comments: This lake offers minor reward for a lot of extra effort.

YELLOWSTONE HUB CITIES

Below, you'll find some of the gateway cities of the nation's first national park. The park's northeast entrance, Cooke City, Montana, and the park's east entrance, Cody, Wyoming, are covered in the previous chapter on Northwest Wyoming.

West Yellowstone, Montana
Elevation–6,666 • Population–1,000

West Yellowstone rests on the western edge of Yellowstone National Park and it is an ideal location for flyfishers to call home for as long as they want. You should not have any trouble finding a nice spot to stay, whether in a plush hotel or an improved campground. West also hosts excellent eateries, lively bars and some nice bookstores. There are many flyshops, well-stocked, waiting for your visit.

West Yellowstone's zip code is 59758.

ACCOMMODATIONS
Alpine Motel, 120 Madison Avenue / 406-646-7544 / $
Best Western, 201 Firehole Lane / 406-646-9557 Hwy 2 West / 406-293-8831 / $$
Best Western, 103 Gibbon Lane / 406-646-7373 / $$
Campfire Lodge, 8500 Hebgen Lake Road / 406-646-7258 / $$
Lakeview Cabins, Hebgen Lake Road / 406-646-7257 / $$

CAMPGROUNDS AND RV PARKS
KOA Campground, West of West Yellowstone / 406-646-7606 / $$
Hebgen Lake Lodge, motel and tent campground, Highway 287, West Yellowstone / 406-646-9250 / $$
Hideaway RV Camp, Corner of Gibbon Avenue / 406-646-9049 / $

OUTFITTERS
Beartrap Outfitters, 19 Madison Avenue / 406-646-9642
Madison River Outfitters, 125 Canyon / 406-646-9644

RESTAURANTS
Alice's Restaurant, 1545 Targhee Pass Road / 406-646-7296
Cappy's Bistro, 104 Canyon Road / 406-646-9537

FLY SHOPS AND SPORTING GOODS
Bud Lilly's Trout Shop, 39 Madison Avenue / 406-646-7801
Blue Ribbon Flies, 315 Canyon Road / 406-646-7642
Arricks Fishing Flies, 128 Madison Avenue / 406-646-7290
Jacklin's Fly Shop, 105 Yellowstone Avenue / 406-646-7336

AUTO REPAIR
Budget Rent-A-Car, 131 Dunraven / 406-646-7882
Big Sky Car Rentals, 415 Yellowstone Avenue / 406-646-9564

AIR SERVICE
West Yellowstone Airport (SkyWest Airlines, a Delta subsidiary) / 406-646-7351

FOR MORE INFORMATION:
West Yellowstone Chamber of Commerce
40 Yellowstone Avenue
West Yellowstone, MT 59758
406-646-7701

Island Park, Idaho
Elevation—6,380 • Population—winter, 143; summer, 20,000

Island Park, located by Island Park Reservoir on the Henry's Fork of the Snake, is an easy drive from West Yellowstone and the West Entrance of the park. From here, you can also drive south to Ashton and the park's Cascade Corner to fish on the Fall and Bechler Rivers. Also nearby are the famed waters of the Henry's Fork, Henry's Lake, Island Park Reservoir, and Silver Creek.

Island Park and its surrounding areas share the zip code 83429.

ACCOMMODATIONS
Henry's Fork Lodge, 4 miles south of Last Chance on U.S. 20 in Pinehaven / 208-558-7953
A-Bar Motel, Last Chance, ID / 208-558-7358 / Allows pets
Mack's Inn, U.S. 20 / 208-558-7272
Phillips Lodge, 208-558-9939
Aspen Lodge, 4 miles north of Mack's Inn / 208-558-7407
Pond's Lodge, 5 miles north of Last Chance on U.S. 20 / 208-558-7221
Staley Springs Resort, Henry's Lake / 208-558-7471
Wild Rose Ranch, Henry's Lake / 208-558-7201
Last Chance Lodge, Last Chance, ID / 208-558-7068
Island Park Lodge, U.S. 20, North / 208-558-7281
Edgewater Inn and Resort, Last Chance, ID / 208-558-9555

CAMPGROUNDS
Redrock RV & Camping Park, 5 miles west on Red Rock Road from U.S. 20 / 208-558-7442
Sawtelle Mountain Resort, 1 block west on Sawtelle Peak Road from U.S. 20 / 800-574-0404
Valley View Trailer Park, ¼ mile south from U.S. 287/U.S. 20 junction / 208-558-7443

RESTAURANTS
A-Bar Motel & Supper Club, Last Chance / 208-558-7358
Henry's Fork Lodge, 208-558-7953
Ponds Lodge, 208-558-7221
Lucky Dog Retreat, Big Springs Rd. / 208-558-7455
Edgewater Inn and Resort, Last Chance / 208-558-9555

FLY SHOPS AND SPORTING GOODS
Henry's Fork Anglers, 208-558-7525 / Owner: Mike Lawson
Island Park Liquor & Sports, Elk Creek / 208-558-7448
Last Chance Outfitters, HC 66, Box 482, Island Park, ID 83492 / 800-428-8338 /
    Owners: Lynn & Melanie Sessions / 7AM–10PM, 7 days, May–Sept

HOSPITALS
Closest is in Rexburg, ID, or West Yellowstone, MT

AIRPORT
Idaho Falls, ID, 75 miles south

AUTO RENTAL
Closest is in Idaho Falls, ID, or West Yellowstone, MT

AUTO SERVICE
Elk Creek Service, Elk Creek / 208-558-7571

FOR MORE INFORMATION
Island Park Chamber
Elk Creek, ID 83429
208-558-7755

Livingston, Montana
Elevation–4,503 • Population–6,700

Livingston is located in south central Montana, on a big bend of the Yellowstone River, 53 miles north of Yellowstone National Park and 25 miles east of Bozeman. It sits in the lovely Paradise Valley, surrounded by the Absaroka-Beartooth Wilderness, and the Gallatin, Bridger, and Crazy Mountain Ranges. Livingston is a hospitable Western town, with over 600 rooms in its hotels, motels, and bed and breakfasts. It offers excellent eateries and it is considered by many seasoned flyfishers the king of western trout fishing towns. Campgrounds, scenic areas, and fishing access sites are readily available.

Livingston's zip code is 59047.

ACCOMMODATIONS
The Murray Hotel, 201 West Park / 406-222-1350 / Located downtown, next to
    Dan Bailey's Fly Shop / Newly renovated, deluxe, turn-of-the century hotel /

40 charming guest rooms with or without adjoining baths / The Winchester Cafe, The Murray Bar, and a large lounge are adjoining / Dogs allowed / $$

Paradise Inn, P.O. Box 684 / 800-437-6291 / Off Interstate 90, Exit 333 / 42 rooms, all ground floor / Lounge, indoor pool, jacuzzi, and restaurant / Dogs allowed, some restrictions / $$

Parkway Motel—Budget Host, 1124 West Park Street / 406-222-3840 / Reservations: 800-727-7217 / Interstate 90, Exit 333 / 28 rooms, 8 kitchenettes, 3 two-bedroom rooms / Dogs allowed, $3 charge / $$

Livingston Inn and Campground, Box 3053-A, Rogers Lane / Motel: 406-222-3600 / Interstate 90, Exit 333, ½ block north / 16 rooms / Campground: 406-222-1122 / 26 hook-ups / Pull-through spaces, showers, and laundry / $

Chico Hot Springs Lodge, Pray, Montana / 406-333-4933 / Located 23 miles south of Livingston on route 89 / Inn has 50 Rooms / Motel has 24 rooms, 4 cabins, 3 cottages with kitchens, log house with kitchen, 2 condos with kitchens / Mineral hot springs pool / Chico Inn gourmet dining room / Poolside Grill, Saloon / Dogs allowed, $2 charge / $$

RESTAURANTS

Winchester Cafe and Murray Bar, 201 West Park / 406-222-1350 / Downtown Livingston / Full-service—breakfast, lunch, dinner, Sunday brunch / Home-made desserts, espresso, fine wine selection

Chico Inn, Pray / 406-333-4933 / 23 miles south of Livingston on Route 89 / Fine dining, reservations recommended / Great wine list / Poolside Grill has great homemade food, bar

Stockman, 118 North Main Street / 406-222-8455 / Bar and restaurant / Lunch and dinner—steaks, prime rib, seafood, and burgers

Livingston Bar and Grill, 130 North Main Street / 406-222-7909 / Antique bar / Steak, seafood, and buffalo burgers

The Sport, 114 South Main Street / 406-222-3533 / Barbecue ribs, chicken, burgers, cocktails, and wine

Martin's Cafe, 108 West Park Street / 406-222-2110 / Open 24 hours, 7 days / Carry-out, breakfast specials, smorgasbord on Sundays

Uncle Looie's, 119 West Park Street / 406-222-7177 / Good Italian cuisine

VETERINARIANS

Colmey Veterinary Hospital, P.O. Box 521 / 406-222-1700 / Duane Colmey, DVM / ½ mile south of Livingston on Rt 89 / Pet food, supplies, grooming, kennel

Shields Valley Veterinary Service, Rt 85, Box 4321 / 406-222-6171 / Donald Smith, DVM

FLY SHOPS AND SPORTING GOODS

Dan Bailey's Fly Shop, 209 West Park Street / 406-222-1673 or 800-356-4052 / Flies, fishing equipment, clothing, and accessories

George Anderson's Yellowstone Angler, Rt 89 South, P.O. Box 660 / 406-222-7130. / Flyfishing specialties, outdoor clothing

Wilderness Outfitters, 1 mile south of town on Rt 89 / 406-222-6933 / Guns, shells, clothing, and accessories
Montana's Master Angler, 107 South Main / 406-222-7437
Big Sky Flies and Guides, Highway 89, Emigrant, MT 59027 / 406-333-4401

AIR SERVICE
Mission Field, east of Livingston / 406-222-6504

AUTO RENTAL AND REPAIR
Livingston Ford-Lincoln-Mercury, 1415 West Park Street / 406-222-7200 / All models, 4-wheel-drive, and vans

MEDICAL
Livingston Memorial Hospital, 504 South 13th Street / 406-222-3541

FOR MORE INFORMATION
Livingston Area Chamber of Commerce
Depot Center, Baggage Room
212 West Park Street
Livingston, MT 59047
406-222-0850

Gardiner, Montana
Elevation—5,286 • Population—800

Gardiner sits on the confluence of the Gardner and Yellowstone Rivers at the Park's north entrance. Named for a fur trapper, Gardiner was founded in 1880 and was originally a mining boomtown. It is the only year-round entrance to the park, and the only year-round road through the park runs through the Lamar Valley from Gardiner to Cooke City, Montana. Its situation in a canyon of the Yellowstone between the Gallatin and Absaroka Mountain Ranges provides incredible scenery as well as access to excellent fishing.
Gardiner's zip code is 59030.

ACCOMMODATIONS
Absaroka Lodge, Hwy 89 / 406-874-7414, 800-755-7414 / On the Yellowstone River / 41 rooms / $$$
Yellowstone Village Inn, Hwy 89 / 800-228-8158 / 43 rooms, 3 family condos / email: yellowstoneinn@gomontana.com / $–$$
Super 8 Motel—Gardiner, Hwy 89 / 406-878-7401 / $

CAMPING
Rocky Mountain Campground, Hwy 89 / 406-848-7251

Yellowstone RV Park and Camp Ground, west of Gardiner on U.S. 89 / 406-848-7496

RESTAURANTS
Town Cafe, downtown Gardiner / 406-848-7322
Sawtooth Deli, downtown Gardiner / 406-848-7600
Bear Country Restaurant, 232 Park Street / 406-848-7188

FLY SHOP
Park's Fly Shop, P.O. Box 196 / 406-848-7314 / Licenses / Flyfishing guides and instructors / Full-service fly shop

AIR SERVICE
Nearest is Mission Field, east of Livingston, Montana / 406-222-6504

AUTO RENTAL AND REPAIR
Nearest is in Livingston, Montana.

MEDICAL
Nearest is **Livingston Memorial Hospital,** 504 South 13th Street, Livingston, MT 59047 / 406-222-3541

FOR MORE INFORMATION
Gardiner Chamber of Commerce
233 Main Street
Gardiner, MT 59030
406-848-7971

Bozeman, Montana
Elevation–4,793 • Population–25,000

Known for its blue-ribbon trout fishing and great skiing, Bozeman is a rapidly growing resort and college town. There has been a recent population boom, resulting in crowded conditions and high prices. However, Bozeman has a lot to offer the fly-fisher. There is still a small town atmosphere with big city amenities: good air service, shopping, fine restaurants, and outdoor activities.

Bozeman's zip code is 59715.

ACCOMMODATIONS
Days Inn, 1321 North 7th Avenue / 406-587-5251 / 80 rooms / Cable, continental breakfast / Dogs allowed, $25 deposit / $$
Fairfield Inn, 828 Wheat Drive / 406-587-2222 / 57 rooms, 12 suites with kitchenettes / Continental breakfast, pool, and jacuzzi / Dogs allowed, no restrictions / $$–$$$

Holiday Inn, 5 Baxter Lane / 406-587-4561 / 178 units / Restaurant, bar, pool and jacuzzi, cable / Dogs allowed, but not unattended in rooms / $$$

Super 8, 800 Wheat Drive / 406-586-1521 / 108 rooms, cable / Dogs allowed, no restrictions / $

The Bozeman Inn, 1235 North 7th Avenue / 406-587-3176 / 45 rooms / Outdoor pool, sauna, cable / Mexican restaurant and lounge / Dogs allowed for a $5 fee / $$

Wild Rose Bed & Breakfast, 1285 Upper Tom Burke Road, Gallatin Gateway, MT 59730 / 406-763-4692 / Hosts: Dennis and Diane Bauer

CAMPGROUNDS AND RV PARKS

Bozeman KOA, 8 miles west on U.S. 91 / 406-587-3030 / Open year–round / 50 tent and 100 RV spaces / Full services, including laundry and store

RESTAURANTS

Bacchus Pub and Rocky Mountain Pasta Co., 105 East Main / 406-586-1314 / Breakfast, lunch, dinner / *Bacchus* 7AM–10PM / Sandwiches, burgers, salads, soups, and daily special entrees / $$ / *Pasta Company*, 5:30PM–10PM / Fine dining, pasta and seafood

John Bozeman's Bistro, 125 West Main / 406-587-4100 / International and regional specialties

Mackenzie River Pizza Company, 232 East Main / 406-587-0055 / M–F 11:30AM–10PM, Sun 5–9PM / Fancy pizzas, pasta, salad

Mint Bar and Grill, 27 East Main Street, Belgrade, MT 59714 / 406-388-1100 / Great steaks and seafood / Good selection of single malt scotches

O'Brien's, 312 East Main / 406-587-3973 / M–Sun 5PM–9PM / Continental cuisine

Crystal Bar, 123 East Main / 406-587-2888 / Open every day / Beer Garden / Will pack lunches

Spanish Peaks Brewery, 120 North 19th / 406-585-2296 / Italian cuisine, micro-brewed ales

VETERINARIANS

All West Veterinary Hospital, 81770 Gallatin Road / 406-586-4919 / Gary Cook, Honor Nesbet, David E. Catlin, DVMs / 24-hour emergency service

Animal Medical Center, 216 North 8th Avenue (behind Kentucky Fried Chicken) / 406-587-2946 / Sue Barrows, DVM / Emergency service

FLY SHOPS AND SPORTING GOODS

Bob Ward and Sons, 2320 West Main, Bozeman, MT 59718 / 406-586-4381

Powder Horn Sportsman's Supply, 35 East Main / 406-587-7373

The River's Edge, 2012 North 7th Avenue / 406-586-5373

Montana Troutfitters, 1716 West Main, Suite 4 / 406-587-4707

R.J. Cain, 24 East Main / 406-587-9111

AUTO RENTAL AND REPAIR
Budget Rent-A-Car of Bozeman, Gallatin Field Airport / 406-388-4091
Avis Rent-A-Car, Gallatin Field Airport / 406-388-6414
Hertz Rent-A-Car, Gallatin Field Airport / 406-388-6939
College Exxon Service, 723 South 8th Avenue / 406-587-4453
Frank Manseau Auto Clinic, 715 East Mendenhall / 406-586-4480
E.J. Miller Service and Towing, 28373 Norris Road / 406-587-0507

AIR SERVICE
Gallatin Field Airport, 8 miles west of Bozeman / 406-388-6632 / Served by Delta, Horizon, Northwest, and Aspen Airlines / Charter service available

MEDICAL
Bozeman Deaconess Hospital, 915 Highland Boulevard / 406-585-5000

FOR MORE INFORMATION
Bozeman Chamber of Commerce
1205 East Main
P.O. Box B
Bozeman, MT 59715
800-228-4224

Close Encounters
Wildlife Observations Accentuate Fishing

An enthralling aspect of fishing in Yellowstone and its wild environs is the privilege of sharing each river's moods and whims with an abundant array of wildlife.

Even if the trout don't cooperate, I'm satisfied it's been a good day when an antelope comes to a stream bank to drink or a great blue heron remains fixated on spearing dinner as I quietly wade upstream.

Wildlife observations are recorded as faithfully in my journals as the trout and mayfly hatches. Large fish brought to the net are measured and released. Ones that get away are listed as "LDRs" for Long Distance Releases. Wildlife captured on film rate "stars" in my notes. And, most years, autumn "stars" outnumber those of other seasons.

Fall is the favorite time of western anglers. Tourist crowds depart for home; hunters abandon the streams for the woods. A renewed sense of quiet and solitude prevails. Rivers and lakes reflect the shimmering gold of frost-nipped cottonwoods and the salmon-orange blush of lingering sunsets. Yearlings entering these beguiling times embark on their first adventures a tad too inquisitive. Their peregrinations almost guarantee an unplanned rendezvous.

Juvenile predators often ignore or don't worry about solitary anglers because finding dinner is a major preoccupation. Such was the case with a coyote on the Yellowstone River.

Coyotes spotted in farm and ranch country rarely pause for a second glance back. But in a sanctuary like Yellowstone National Park they are less skittish. Juveniles often prowl throughout the day. Grassy meadows and knolls in the upper Lamar, Gibbon, and Yellowstone valleys are prime hunting grounds for coyotes stalking deer mice and meadow voles.

The tans and golden browns of a coyote's new winter coat blend perfectly into the autumn colors of sun bleached grasses, wilted wildflowers and dusty sagebrush along the Yellowstone. Fishing a sheltered alcove in the river, I almost missed seeing a small coyote exploring the bank a short distance downstream.

This time I was prepared, my camera set up nearby on a tripod. Wading back to shore, I slowly eased into position behind it. I was just in time as the coyote froze, cocked her head and peered at a clump of grass. Her back curled catlike as she leaped into the air and dived headfirst into the bunch grass. She came up empty mouthed and, probably, with a bruised nose.

A classic moment in coyote mouse hunting, it was over in seconds. But the cumbersome, sometimes frustrating, exertions involved in lugging a camera and tripod on fishing jaunts paid off again.

A telephoto lens—400 mm at minimum—is best for bringing in small animals and birds close enough to be more than a dot on a slide or print. Long lenses also provide an element of security when photographing big game or large predators.

Coyote pouncing on a hillside above the Yellowstone River.

I have yet to confirm this axiom with a grizzly bear test, although I have spotted a few disturbingly fresh saber-clawed paw prints on gravel bars. A pair of two-year-olds on Mount Washburn a few years ago was photographed in the safety of a crowd and two pistol-packing rangerettes. Still, the overgrown cubs provided a better appreciation of the great bear's formidable size. I no longer hike or fish alone in grizzly country.

It's also wise to stay back when moose and elk start polishing the velvet from their antlers. And bison are unpredictable and dangerous year-round.

Remember the song "You Can't Roller Skate in a Buffalo Herd"? Well, it's no picnic to fly fish in one, either. But the day the bison crashed the party at Buffalo Ford on the Yellowstone River was fairly comical.

A horde of flyfishers there for opening day was forced to retreat to the parking lot. About a dozen walked around the milling bison to get to the river, and four dumb-and-dumber types waltzed back through a split in the herd. Another guy declared with much bravado that he was going to eat his lunch at a picnic table.

The dude contentedly chomped on a sandwich until a buddy sneaked up and bumped the table. His sandwich flew in the air as the dude executed a long jump that probably set a world record from a sitting start.

Yellowstone's elk may seem docile, but they aren't shy about sticking to their appointed rounds, either.

Bull elk in Gardner River Meadows.

Last year I closed the park's season by searching for migrating brown trout in the Gardner River. A narrow, boulder-strewn stream, its swift current drowns out virtually all other sounds. So the herd of cow elk and fawns suddenly scrambling down a rocky cliff into my fishing hole took me by surprise. I backed up onto a gravel bar to give them room to drink and to retrieve my camera.

The herd boss was not far behind his harem. He sauntered down the slope with the stately cadence of a monarch. But it was a hot, dusty day. Plunging into the water up to the dark brown bib on his neck, the bull greedily stuck his snout into the river.

My picture complete, I savored the moment until the inevitable gaggle of photographers showed up. They made the elk nervous, and I retreated to a footpath along the cliff.

Two times I have seen photographers charged by elk. Each was when a bull was approached too closely. Both men had small point-and-shoot cameras. Once, though, I beat a hasty retreat from the Gibbon River when a herd boss decided his cows had strayed too far and went on a rampaging roundup.

Moose are less common in Yellowstone, and sightings are guaranteed traffic stoppers. Western Wyoming, however, has one of the largest moose populations in the West. Encounters along the Snake River below Jackson Lake or at Green River Lakes north of Pinedale dramatically enhance a day's fishing.

Bull Moose
on the Snake River.

Incredible swimmers and waders, moose range back and forth across even the largest of rivers. I once watched a bull plunge into the Snake directly across from me, swim the river and climb up the bank only 40 yards downstream. The flow was more than 15,000 cubic feet per second. Another time, a young bull labored up through the deep water of a cutbank and waded into my fishing hole within 20 feet of me. Up to my waist in a side channel, I couldn't believe he kept coming. I froze and we warily eyed each other as he waded through the eddy to an island and disappeared into the willows.

Bulls still in velvet are relatively stoic about human interlopers. Cows with calves remain sanguine as long as they aren't separated. But when a bull starts making that loony gurgling sound and his antlers are polished tawny white, admire him from a distance. Lovestruck bulls cut and wheel in any direction when escorting cows.

Late one evening at the tip of a gravel bar island I stood entranced on the far side of a log for a half-hour. Vying for the attention of a cow in the inside channel was an amorous but frustrated bull. Much of his worrying and fussing was directed at trying to drive off the cow's calf. But mother and son finally bolted up the far bank and clattered off through the cottonwoods. The grumbling bull trailed the pair into the darkness.

Don't be like these flyfishers at Buffalo Ford in Yellowstone National Park.
Bison are dangerous; keep your distance.

Grizzly at Dunraven Pass, Yellowstone National Park.

American White Pelicans on the Yellowstone.

Osprey perch above the Snake River.

Such moments are intriguing, but legions of two-legged characters also are princely players in daily dramas on nature's stage. Birdwatchers and anglers can learn a lot from each other.

An incredible array of birding hot spots accentuates the interconnected waterways of the Northern Rockies. Sometimes you can get quite close, especially when fishing from a boat. In autumn, young birds appear almost tame in how closely they can be approached.

On rare occasions, a fish struggling at the end of a line may be too much to resist. That was the case one day on the Yellowstone River in the park. A young pelican was eager to share its bonanza with numerous flyfishers. He followed splashing cutthroat trout almost to the nets of several successful anglers.

Monitoring the fledging of generations of cygnets by a pair of trumpeter swans is as compelling a reason for me to return annually to the Madison River as its wily rainbow and brown trout. An osprey hovering over a shallow run instantly causes my flyline to go slack. It drifts unattended until the fish hawk plummets into the stream. When it struggles aloft with a wriggling whitefish or trout in its talons, I salute the master angler.

To me, osprey, bald eagles, pelicans, cormorants, mergansers, egrets and herons are signs of healthy fisheries. Their shares of the bounty are not begrudged.

Many outfitters are expanding their services to include birding and photography. Guides are spending a lot of extra time rowing against the current to give clients time to identify or photograph streamside birds. It makes for a fuller day on the stream.

Rivers never rest; their residents are ever busy. Birds amplify a stream's idyllic moods as flows of avian chatter wash through reeds and brush. But, just as often, the whims of nature catapult their prosaic pastimes into dynamic melodramas.

A strident chattering announces the flight of a kingfisher from one snag overhanging a river to another. It's a brief and welcoming background noise on a stream as the tiny indigo dive-bomber flies to a perch over a new fishing site. But one day an incessant clamor echoing off the walls of a canyon caused me to take a longer look around.

I spotted the screeching kingfisher darting and wheeling along the far bank, barely skimming the surface of the river. Splashes marked its flight as it weaved and bobbed in frantic maneuvers to escape a goshawk. Silence descended on the canyon when the kingfisher darted into a tangle of willows. The tumult irrupted again when the patrolling raptor flushed his prey. Their whirling aerial combat coursed up and down the river for another five minutes until the ghostly gray marauder gave up the chase.

It was just another electrifying day in paradise.

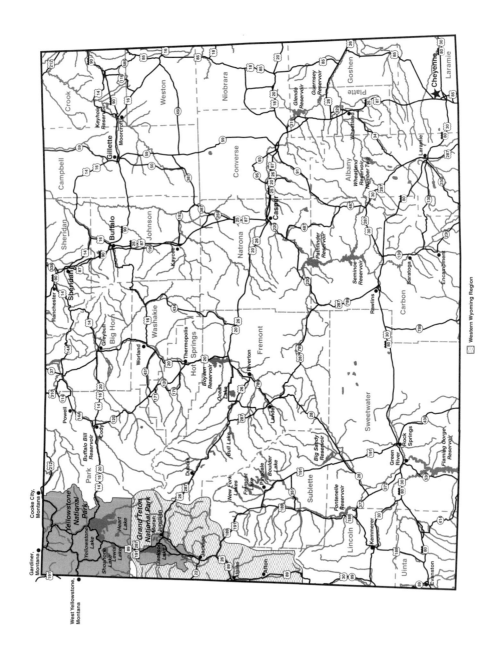

Western Wyoming
Grand Teton National Park and Jackson Hole

The majestic Teton Mountains dominating the horizon above Jackson Hole in western Wyoming attract more than 3 million visitors a year to Grand Teton National Park. It is an incredible playground of sagebrush flats, forested foothills, snowcapped peaks, and sparkling clear waters.

The Snake River, flowing through the center of the vast wilderness, is the connecting link between Grand Teton and Yellowstone National Parks.

It was the route followed by fur trappers and Indian tribes during the region's Fur Trade Era in the 19th century. Jackson Lake's Colter Bay is named for John Colter, a member of the Lewis and Clark Expedition who stayed on in the West when the Corps returned from the Pacific. The first of the mountain men, he explored the Teton–Yellowstone country during the winter of 1807–1808. Jackson Hole is named for David Jackson, a partner of Jim Bridger, who pioneered many other routes through the Northern Rockies. The Bridger-Teton National Forest surrounding Jackson Hole and the Bridger Wilderness in the Wind River Mountains are named for the king of the mountain men.

The fur trappers stripped the mountain streams of beaver by the late 1840s. Later explorers, like John Fremont and Benjamin Bonneville, charted pathways to the West Coast. Pioneer settlers followed, and many dropped off to stay in places like Jackson Hole and Star Valley.

This is where western Wyoming's waters separate on their journeys to the sea. The parting of the waters occurs at a springfed trickle that splits and spills off Two Ocean Pass on the Continental Divide above Jackson. Atlantic Creek flows northeast to join the Yellowstone River, the largest tributary of the Missouri. Pacific Creek flows southwest to join the Snake River, the largest tributary of the Columbia.

The Snake River finespotted cutthroat is the predominant trout on the Pacific side of the mountains. Its first cousin, the Yellowstone cutthroat, inhabits some of these waters, but its realm of dominance is in the park on the Atlantic side of the divide. A subspecies still being studied by biologists, the Snake River finespotted is unique in its ability to coexist with a related species. Its spotting pattern is heavier with many more smaller spots than the Yellowstone cutthroat. Many consider it less gullible and a stronger fighter than its cousin. Also present in the basin streams, in varying populations, are brown, rainbow, and brook trout, and lake trout inhabit Jackson Lake and a few other lakes. Whitefish are plentiful throughout the basin.

The Snake is a big, brawling river and demands respect. It fishes best from a boat, but newcomers or inexperienced boaters are advised to make their first floats with guides or friends who know the river. Fly casters who prefer to wade should stick to quiet, shallow sections of the river and side channels. Good access is found near boat ramps and bridges. Spring runoff is often late, so plan to fish the Snake in late summer or autumn.

More accommodating to wading and virtually undiscovered are the fine mountain streams flowing into the Snake. Good prospects closest to Jackson are the upper Gros Ventre River and Flat Creek, a challenging spring creek fishery flowing through the National Elk Refuge. South of Jackson, the Salt and Greys Rivers flow into Palisades Reservoir at Alpine. The Salt's most productive fishing is from a small boat or canoe. The Greys is a perfect camping getaway for family fishing parties or neophyte flyfishers who want to hone their skills in relative solitude. In between Jackson and Alpine, the Hoback River enters the Snake. Granite Creek, a tributary of the Hoback, is a classic, small mountain stream.

North of Jackson is the Teton Wilderness. Its most tempting cutthroat fishing—a long hike over the divide—is the upper meadow section of the Yellowstone River and Thorofare Creek. On the west slopes of the divide, good streams to consider are Pacific Creek and the Buffalo Fork River.

One of the West's most popular summer and ski resorts, reservations are often needed in advance for accommodations or guided fishing trips in the Jackson Hole area. Jackson has a host of well stocked fly shops, outfitters, and guides available to fill equipment needs or help guide explorations.

The Star Valley communities of Afton and Alpine are the recreation centers for the Salt and Greys Rivers and the backcountry lakes and streams of the Salt and Wyoming mountain ranges.

SNAKE RIVER

Tourists headed for Grand Teton National Park envision the Snake River as a silvery thread in the foreground of Ansel Adam's brooding portrait of the Tetons shrouded by storm clouds. Flyfishers intent on snapping their own pictures—ones with trout in them—head for Jackson Hole.

Both views are intertwined in the history and compellingly beautiful scenery of the region. The Teton Range sets the stage, but the Snake is the common link between the park and Jackson Hole.

The most heavily fished waters of the river's run through western Wyoming are the 35 miles in the park below Jackson Dam and the remaining 17 miles flowing through Jackson Hole. It ranks as one of the best dry fly streams in the West.

The soaring cathedrals of the Tetons and Mount Moran are elegant distractions, but both the river and its trout demand attention from anglers. The Snake is a wild and woolly river. It punishes those who drop their guard but rewards prudent fly-fishers with feisty native trout that inhale large easy-to-see dry flies like popcorn.

As remarkable as the scenery is the river's personal race of native trout. The home range of the Snake River finespotted cutthroat is Jackson Hole and its environs. A beautiful fish, it is unique in a breed that was once the only trout in the interior of the West, evolving into 14 subspecies. Many feel the taxonomy list should be expanded to 15.

Cutthroat won the race up the Snake against rainbow trout and crossed the Continental Divide during the last Ice Age. The crossing was made at 8,200-foot Two Ocean Pass, north of Jackson. From the pass, Atlantic Creek flows northeast to the Yellowstone River. Pacific Creek flows southwest to the Snake. The rainbow were then confined to the lower Snake and Columbia drainages when a massive flood created southern Idaho's Shoshone Falls about 50,000 years ago.

The Yellowstone cutthroat, which still inhabits eastern Idaho waters, is the only native trout on the Atlantic side of the divide. It expanded throughout the head-waters of its drainage, including the Shoshone, Big Horn, and Tongue Rivers. Evolving separately, or staying behind, in the Jackson Hole area, was the Snake River finespotted cutthroat. Its native range is confined to the upper river from Heart Lake to Palisades Reservoir.

The Snake River cutthroat is unique in its ability to coexist with a species of its own genus. Its spotting pattern is heavier with many smaller spots than the Yellowstone cutthroat has, and it is considered less gullible and a stronger fighter. But while some argue otherwise, genetic studies indicate it is not a separate subspecies.

The most vocal proponent for reclassifying the Snake River cutthroat is Colorado State University professor Robert Behnke. "They are visually different but genetically the same—but the trout know, they don't mix," he said. "They also are the least sus-ceptible of the cutthroat to harvest."

Disputes over its genetics won't be settled soon, but Behnke maintains the Snake River cutthroat is hard to beat as a game fish. "It, to my mind, fights better than the

Snake River
Source to Jackson Lake

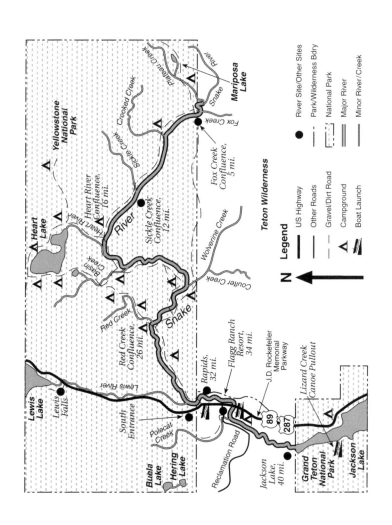

Yellowstone National Park

Heart Lake

Heart River

Basin Creek

Red Creek

Lewis Lake

Lewis Falls

Lewis River

South Entrance

Buela Lake

Hering Lake

Polecat Creek

Reclamation Road

Red Creek Confluence, 26 mi.

Snake River

Snake

Rapids, 32 mi.

Flagg Ranch Resort, 34 mi.

J.D. Rockefeller Memorial Parkway

Sickle Creek Confluence, 12 mi.

Heart River Confluence, 16 mi.

Coulter Creek

Wolverine Creek

Snake River

Fox Creek

Fox Creek Confluence, 5 mi.

Crooked Creek

Plateau Creek

Stoke Creek

Mariposa Lake

Teton Wilderness

Lizard Creek Canoe Pullout

Jackson Lake, 40 mi.

Grand Teton National Park

Jackson Lake

Legend

N

US Highway

Other Roads

Gravel/Dirt Road

Campground

Boat Launch

● River Site/Other Sites

Park/Wilderness Bdry

National Park

Major River

Minor River/Creek

89

287

Snake River
Jackson Lake to Moose

Jackson Lake

Elk Island

Bear Claw Lake

Donoho Point

Spaulding Bay

Oxbow Bend

89 191 287

Pacific Creek

Cattleman's Bridge (Foot Bridge)

Moran Junction

26 287

Jackson Lake Dam, 57 mi.

Pacific Creek, 62 mi.

26

89

191

Buffalo Fork River

Leigh Lake

(canoes only)

Grand Teton National Park

Jenny Lake Lodge

Spread Creek

Cunningham Cabin

Jenny Lake

Deadmans Bar, 73 mi.

Snake River

Topping Lakes

Cottonwood Creek

Triangle X Ranch Resort

Bar BC Creek

Schwabacher's Landing (High water only), 78 mi.

Bar BC Ranch

26

89

191

Antelope Flats

The Maze (Numerous side channels)

Moose

Black Tail Ponds

Park Entrance Gate

Moose, 85 mi.

Gros Ventre Road

Kelly

N

Legend

▬▬▬ US Highway	● River/Other Sites
── Other Roads	▭ Bridge
···· Gravel/Dirt Road	▬ Dam
— — Trail	—·— Park Boundary
▲ Campground	▬▬ Major River
Boat Launch	══ Minor River/Creek

© Wilderness Adventures Press

Snake River
Moose to Jackson

Legend
N

— US Highway	Boat Launch
— State/Cty Road	● River Site/Other Sites
Other Roads	National Park
– – Trail	Bridge
✈ Air Service	Major River
⛺ Campground	Minor River/Creek
🐟 Fishing Access	

© Wilderness Adventures Press

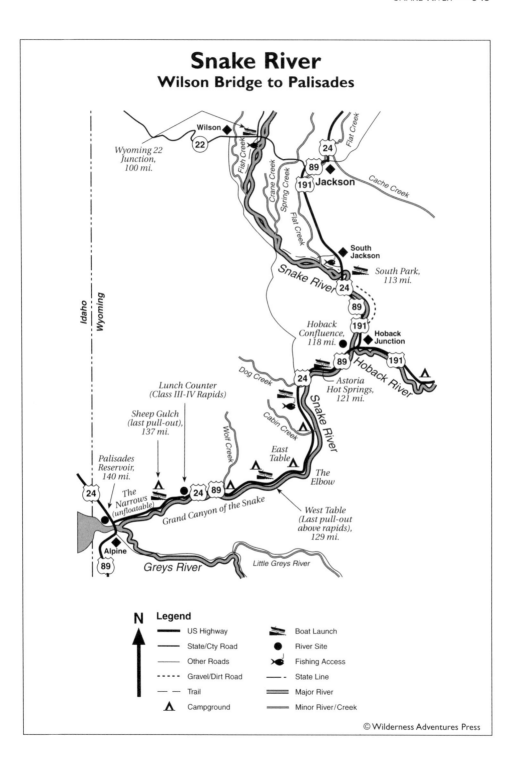

Snake River
Wilson Bridge to Palisades

Wilson

22

Wyoming 22
Junction,
100 mi.

Flat Creek

24

89

191 Jackson

Cache Creek

Fish Creek

Crane Creek

Spring Creek

Flat Creek

Snake River

South
Jackson

South Park,
113 mi.

24

89

191

Hoback
Confluence,
118 mi.

Hoback
Junction

Idaho

Wyoming

89

24

Dog Creek

191

Hoback River

Astoria
Hot Springs,
121 mi.

Lunch Counter
(Class III-IV Rapids)

Sheep Gulch
(last pull-out),
137 mi.

Cabin Creek

Snake River

Wolf Creek

East
Table

The
Elbow

Palisades
Reservoir,
140 mi.

24

The
Narrows
(unfloatable)

24

89

Grand Canyon of the Snake

West Table
(Last pull-out
above rapids),
129 mi.

Alpine

89

Greys River

Little Greys River

N

Legend

US Highway	Boat Launch
State/Cty Road	River Site
Other Roads	Fishing Access
Gravel/Dirt Road	State Line
Trail	Major River
Campground	Minor River/Creek

© Wilderness Adventures Press

Yellowstone cutthroat. It is the champion of cutthroat—but for the same reason: genetic quality. It can only be seen by the eye and at the end of your fly rod."

The trout's aggressive nature has evolved from its need to cope with a big, brawling river like the Snake. It eats just about anything: mostly aquatic insects and windblown terrestrials as juveniles, and forage fish and large aquatic invertebrates as adults.

The Snake River cutthroat has a well-deserved reputation as an excellent dry-fly fish, but large streamers and nymphs are standard fare on the river, too. The cutthroat hits both hard. Large dry flies continue to be effective into late autumn on the Snake, unlike many other rivers.

Once spring runoff releases abate and top water action kicks off in late July, fishing can be incredible with large attractors like royal Trudes or Wulffs, stimulators, Madam Xs, and terrestrial patterns. The average dry fly in summer is often size 12, and in early fall an effective strategy is to graduate to size 8 or larger patterns.

Two locally perfected patterns are Turk's tarantula and the Chernobyl ant. Both have wiggling, antenna-like rubberlegs to help entice strikes. Another Jackson production, Joe Allen's double humpy, ups the ante for hits on one of the West's best gifts to pocket water fly casters. All three incorporate provocative body colors like red, yellow, and green to further draw the attention of fish.

Snake River cutthroat are not total pushovers. While they often hit skating flies early in the season, as flows stabilize and the water clears the cutthroat start window shopping. Proper presentation to feeding lanes and lies and long dead drifts are critical in late summer and autumn.

One of the few places on the Snake where match-the-hatch challenges occur with standard flies is on the quieter waters of the Oxbow Bend stretch between Jackson Dam and Pacific Creek. There also are some quiet backwaters between Pacific Creek and Deadman's Bar for boaters. And waders who make the effort to hike into braided channels in the floodplain find smaller waters with rising trout.

Hatches to watch for are stoneflies and golden stones soon after runoff wanes in July, along with caddis and yellow Sallies. Pale morning duns appear in midsummer and gray drakes may be August options. September is the time to watch for mahogany duns. Still, the prime candidates for good late summer fishing are grasshoppers.

Small mayfly nymphs and caddis emergers are effective dropper flies in many sections of the river throughout the season. Beadhead patterns or small split shot on tag lines keep droppers down.

Good wet flies in the murky waters of early season are woolly buggers, leeches, Zonkers, black rubberlegs, JJ's special, Double Bunny, and other streamers.

A short-lived, fast-growing fish, the Snake River cutthroat reaches a maximum size of about 22 inches; a rare fish may go to 24 inches. Generally, trout in the upper river average 12 to 14 inches, but there are enough in the 16-inch range to keep things interesting. In the deeper channels below Hoback, there are fewer cutthroat, but the fish are larger.

Brown trout also are found in the river above Jackson Dam, and whitefish are plentiful throughout the drainage.

The native trout has been hard pressed to survive radical changes in its home range this century. It's taken a licking but keeps on ticking.

Improved numbers and sizes of cutthroat in the Snake are largely the success of special regulations to restrict harvest, extraordinary efforts to rejuvenate spawning streams, and aggressive measures taken to maintain minimum winter flows.

A 1990 agreement with the Bureau of Reclamation guarantees a minimum winter flow of 280 cubic feet per second to provide cover for more age classes of trout.

In 1996, several regulations were refined to further protect the native trout:

- The creel limit from Yellowstone National Park to the West Table boat ramp was reduced to 3 fish.
- The slot limit from 1,000 feet below Jackson Lake dam to the Wilson Bridge was modified to require the release of all trout between 12 and 18 inches.
- The size restriction from Wilson Bridge to the West Table boat ramp was changed to only 1 fish exceeding 12 inches.

Spawning runs in some restored spring creeks have been tripled since the 1970s, said John Kiefling, Wyoming Game and Fish's fisheries supervisor in Jackson.

The renovation project started by his predecessor, Jon Erickson, involved a lot of work aided by the cooperation of landowners and volunteer assistance of local sportsmen and organizations such as Trout Unlimited. Hundreds of tons of clean gravel were trucked in to the spring creeks to recreate spawning redds and riffles. Silt was removed from key areas and pools, and overhead structures were created to give trout places to hide.

Some of the spring creeks also are being stocked with eyed eggs to restore spawning runs. The trout will imprint on the streams, and future generations will continue to return to their natal waters, Kiefling said.

Funds to assist rejuvenation of the spring creeks and other conservation projects on the river are garnered by Jackson's annual One Fly Contest and, in 1997, by hosting the 17th Annual World Fly Fishing Championship.

Basically, the department and local anglers are trying to protect what they have left, Kiefling said. The river has radically changed over the years since Jackson Dam was built in 1911, and dikes started going up after a devastating flood in 1950.

Summer-long high flows to funnel irrigation water downstream broke the natural rhythm of the river and disrupted spawning by inundating river channels and creek mouths. The dikes, which now extend 40 miles to protect the expensive homes of Jackson Hole, cause channelization and aggradation, or buildup, of the streambed. In some places the river flows higher than the floodplain behind the dikes. Instream structure has been lost and, by blocking natural meanders through side channels, cottonwood regeneration is prevented in riparian areas.

But while downstream irrigation demands mostly dictate flows below Jackson Lake, Mother Nature still calls the shots.

The highest flows since 1895 were recorded in 1997 along the Snake from the park to Palisades Reservoir at the Idaho–Wyoming state line. The U.S. Geological Survey reported record flows occurred June 11 and ranged from greater than 24,000 cubic feet per second at Moose to about 32,000 cfs near Jackson to over 38,000 cfs upstream of Palisades.

The previous record at Moose was 22,000 cfs on June 16, 1996. Average annual maximum flows are about 16,000 cfs at Jackson and 19,000 cfs upstream of Palisades. Back-to-back high water years, hopefully, caused only temporary setbacks on this great river. In most years, they are much less extreme.

Runoff usually begins in late May, peaks around 15,000 cfs in June and drops to around 5,000 cfs in July. But even August through September flows can fluctuate between 2,000 and 5,000 cfs. Winter and early spring flows are 1,000 cfs or less, but in high snowpack years, they may be bumped significantly. The minimum winter flow on the river is 280 cfs.

Still, spring runoff may be late, so it's best to plan trips to the Snake in late summer or autumn. The river is closed to fishing from November 1 to March 31.

Floating the Snake

To say the Snake demands respect cannot be overstated. It fishes best from a boat, but beginner or inexperienced boaters are advised to make their first floats with guides or friends who know the river. Even people familiar with the Snake need to check on current conditions before setting out. It can change overnight, and flows vary greatly through the summer. Reports posted at the park's boat launch sites are updated weekly or whenever significant changes in the river occur.

Motorized watercraft are not permitted on the river in Grand Teton National Park, and floating is not permitted on other streams in the park. A guide on "Floating the Snake River," as well as permits required for float boats, rafts, and canoes, is available at visitor centers and ranger stations. The fees are $5 for a week permit and $10 for an annual permit. For river information, call 307-739-3602.

For additional information on how to safely float the river, contact the Jackson Game and Fish Office at 307-733-2321 or 800-423-4113, or the Bridger Teton National Forest at 307-739-5400. Also consult guides and outfitters at Jackson fly shops.

The two most dangerous stretches of the river are Deadman's Bar to Moose Landing and Moose to Wilson Bridge. Both park officials and Jackson outfitters stress that only people with advanced boating or rafting skills should enter these runs.

Most of the river's accidents occur on the 10-mile reach from Deadman's Bar to Moose, which is the most challenging on the river. The river drops more steeply and has swifter flows than other stretches. "Complex braiding obscures the main channel. Strong current can sweep boaters into side channels blocked by logjams," states the park's floating guide.

The Schwabacher boat landing, midway between Deadman's Bar and Moose, requires a tight turn into a narrow channel on the east bank. However, it can't be used during low flows.

Driftboat on the Snake in Grand Teton National Park.

The 12-mile Moose to Wilson Bridge run is as difficult as the Deadman's Bar stretch. It also has numerous braided channels and obstructions that require careful choice of route by experienced boaters and rafters. The park's south boundary is halfway down this stretch.

Park officials also caution that the 10.5-mile run from Pacific Creek to Deadman's Bar is not for beginners. Intermediate boating or rafting skills are required because this is the first significant drop in the river, and its channel is braided. "Boating experience on lakes has proven to be of little help to river runners on the Snake," states the park's floating guide.

The only beginner stretch on the river, and one of its prettiest with Mount Moran in the background, is from Jackson Dam to Pacific Creek. Called the Oxbow Bend for

Rafters run the Lunch Counter Rapids of the Snake.

its big looping curve, the 5-mile run is suitable even for canoes. Watercraft also can be launched from Cattleman's Bridge, 2 miles below the dam boat ramp.

The Oxbow Bend run offers the earliest shot at the river. It is less affected by spring runoff and remains clearer. Pacific Creek and the Buffalo Fork River are where runoff's most dramatic effects on the river begin.

Two other runs on the river above Jackson Lake receive much less attention.

The 3-mile stretch from the Yellowstone boundary to Flagg Ranch is an advanced run because it has the only whitewater on the upper river. Its rapids are Class III to IV during spring runoff.

The 10-mile run from Flagg Ranch to Lizard Creek Campground on Jackson Lake is an intermediate run because of the many channels that cut through the marshy flats above the lake. The last 4 miles is a long row or paddle on the lake, which can be made even harder by stiff winds.

Jackson outfitters caution that the channel between Wilson Bridge and the South Park landing, 13 miles downstream at the U.S. 26/89 bridge, also was significantly changed by the floods of 1996 and 1997. Below South Park, the river runs through an 8-mile canyon with strong currents and eddies past Hoback to Astoria Hot Springs. The next 8 miles to West Table is flatter but does have some channels and logjams.

West Table is the last pull out for float-fishers. Below it is the famous whitewater run in the Grand Canyon of the Snake. At peak use during the summer, up to 600 boats and 4,000 people per day run the Class III to V rapids in the canyon.

Because the river is so crowded, motorized watercraft, including Jet Skis and other personal watercraft, are banned on the 8-mile stretch from the West Table Boat Ramp to Sheep Gulch.

Wading the Snake

Proceed with caution around the Snake, even when walking the banks. The current is treacherous along undercut banks and where the river spills around logjams and plunges down deep, narrow side channels. Keep back from the river when hiking through heavy brush or deadfall.

Fly casters who wade fish must stick to quiet, shallow sections of the river and side channels. Take care not to get too far into channels on unstable gravel bars. The Snake is deceptive, and its rumpled flows disguise a strong, swift undercurrent.

Unlike the case with boaters, experience as a wader can lull the unwary into a false sense of confidence. A good rule of thumb is to not go in over the knees near the main channel of the river. If the river or a side channel is murky and the bottom can't be seen, stay out of it.

Waders can take advantage of the Snake's meandering runs and quieter back-waters where the floodplain is braided into side channels.

Working side channels and the banks essentially reduces the Snake to small stream fishing. There's more time to pursue rising fish, and fly choices may be more critical. But just as often, tossing out an attractor pattern or generic mayfly is as effective for wading fly casters as it is for those zipping past hot spots in float boats.

Don't linger over unproductive waters. Generally, if you're cutthroat fishing and nothing happens within an hour, it is best to move on. When fish start hitting, work the spot fully. Where there's one cutthroat, there's sure to be another.

The best access to the river's east bank from U.S. 26/89 is found near boat ramps, bridges, and the mouths of tributaries, like Pelican Creek and the Buffalo Fork River near Moran Junction, and below the dam. An often-overlooked access site to the middle section of the river is the Schwabacher boat landing. The turn-off down a steep gravel road is just north of the Glacier View scenic turnout on the highway.

Another route to the river not shown on small maps handed out by the Park Service is a dirt road that parallels much of its west bank. It is shown on topographic trail maps and the Buffalo and Jackson Ranger Districts map of the Bridger-Teton National Forest.

The southern turnoff to the road is at a sign for the Bar BC Ranch on Cottonwood Creek, just north of the Taggart Lake parking lot on the park's loop road. The north-ern turnoff, near Jackson Lake, is unmarked and easily missed.

The upper river in the Flagg Ranch area also offers good access. It fishes well after runoff subsides through summer into autumn. Large brown trout run upstream from

*Braided channels of the Snake along west bank gravel road
in Grand Teton National Park.*

the lake on their fall spawning runs. An excellent tributary on this section is Polecat Creek that flows out of Yellowstone.

South of the park, the best access sites closest to Jackson are at the Wilson Bridge on WYO 22 and at the South Park Bridge on U.S. 26/89. The bonus at South Park is the chance to fish the bottom of Flat Creek.

Below Astoria Hot Springs, the river reenters the national forest. Generally, wherever you can walk to it from the highway it is legal to fish without fear of trespass.

Because of the size of the river and the need to punch flies to the banks and log-jams where fish are lurking, a 9-foot 5- or 6-weight rod is recommended.

Stream Facts: Snake River

Seasons
- Snake River proper upstream from Palisades Reservoir is closed to trout fishing November 1 through March 31.
- Snake River for a distance of 150 feet below the downstream face of Jackson Lake Dam in Grand Teton National Park is closed all year.

Regulations
- Snake River proper from Yellowstone National Park boundary to Jackson Lake. The limit on trout shall be 3 per day or in possession. Only 1 may exceed 20 inches.
- Snake River proper from 150 feet below Jackson Lake dam to the gauging station 1,000 feet below Jackson Lake dam. The limit on trout shall be 3 per day or in possession. Only 1 may exceed 20 inches. The use or possession of fish, parts thereof, or fish eggs for bait is prohibited.
- Snake River proper from 1,000 feet below Jackson Lake dam (at gauging station) to the Highway 22 bridge (Wilson bridge). The limit on trout shall be 3 per day or in possession. Only 1 may exceed 18 inches. All trout between 12 and 18 inches (inclusive) must be returned to the water immediately. Fishing is permitted by the use of artificial flies and lures only.
- Snake River proper from the Highway 22 bridge (Wilson bridge) to West Table boat ramp and Buffalo Fork River downstream of the wilderness boundary. The limit on trout shall be 3 per day or in possession. Only 1 may exceed 12 inches.

Trout
- Snake River cutthroat trout average 12 to 14 inches, with good numbers in the 16- to 18-inch range, and a rare fish going to 22 inches. Some brown trout are in the river above Jackson Dam in the 14- to 18-inch range, as are some larger fall spawners from the lake.

Miles
- Mile 32: Yellowstone Park boundary
- Mile 40: Jackson Lake
- Mile 57: Jackson Lake Dam
- Mile 62: Pacific Creek
- Mile 73: Deadman's Bar
- Mile 85: Moose Landing
- Mile 95: Wilson Bridge
- Mile 121: Astoria Hot Springs
- Mile 129: West Table landing (last pullout above whitewater canyon)
- Mile 137: Sheep Gulch landing
- Mile 140: Palisades Reservoir (state line)

Character

- Big strong river with treacherous flows and undercurrents, numerous braided channels and logjams in stretch between Deadman's Bar and South Park. Very dangerous to wade around main channel in all parts of the river; waders should stick to shallow side channels or banks. Best suited for float fishing but should not be attempted without advanced boating skills. Float trips with outfitters or guides recommended for river runners with intermediate or beginner boating skills.

Flows

- Runoff usually begins in late May, peaks around 15,000 cfs in June and drops to around 5,000 cfs in July. August through September flows can fluctuate between 2,000 and 5,000 cfs. In extreme wet years, flows are dramatically higher.

Access

- Grand Teton National Park on upper river
- Wyoming Game and Fish access sites in Jackson Hole
- Bridger-Teton National Forest below Hoback

Camping

- Grand Teton National Park
- Bridger-Teton National Forest
- Jackson

The Snake River finespotted cutthroat.

SNAKE RIVER MAJOR HATCHES

Insect	M	A	M	J	J	A	S	O	N	Time	Flies
Stonefly				█						A	**Dry:** Sofa Pillow, Salmonfly, Chernobyl Ant, Turk's Tarantula, Yellow or Red Double Humpy #2–8; **Wet:** Black Stone Nymph, Rubberlegs, Woolly Bugger #2–10
Golden Stone				█	█					A	**Dry:** Golden Stone, Bird's Stone, Yellow or Orange Stimulator, Yellow Double Humpy #8–10; **Wet:** Bitch Creek Nymph, JJ's Special, Woolly Bugger #4–12
Little Yellow Stone (Willow Fly)				█	█	█				A/E	Yellow Sally, Blonde Humpy, Willow Fly, Yellow Stimulator #10–14; Yellow Wulff, Yellow or Royal Trude #10–12
Caddis					█	█	█	█		M/D	**Dry:** Elk Hair Caddis, Yellow or Royal Humpy, X Caddis, Goddard Caddis, Renegade #10–14; **Wet:** Beadhead Prince Nymph, Soft-hackles, Halfback #10–16
Baetis		█	█				█	█		A/E	**Dry:** Blue-winged Olive, Para-BWO, Adams, Para-Adams #14–18; **Wet:** Beadhead Pheasant Tail, Baetis Emerger #16–18
Pale Morning Dun				█	█	█				A/E	**Dry:** PMD, Light Cahill, Rusty Spinner, Sparkle Dun #16–18; **Wet:** Beadhead Hare's Ear, Beadhead Pheasant Tail #14–18
Gray Drake					█	█				A	Adams, Para-Adams, Gray Wulff #10–12; Para-BWO, Flav #10–14
Trico						█	█			A	Black and White, Trico Spinner, Para-Adams #18–20
Mahogany Dun							█				Mahogany Dun, Sparkle Dun #16
Midge		█	█				█	█		M/E	Griffith's Gnat, Black Midge, Trico Spinner, Para-Adams #18–22
Terrestrials					█	█	█	█		M/A	Dave's Hopper, Madam X, Turk's Tarantula, Yellow or Red Double Humpy, Chernobyl Ant #6–12; Dave's Cricket, Disc O'Beetle #10–14

HATCH TIME CODE: M = morning; A = afternoon; E = evening; D = dark; SF = spinner fall; // = continuation through periods.

Grand Teton National Park

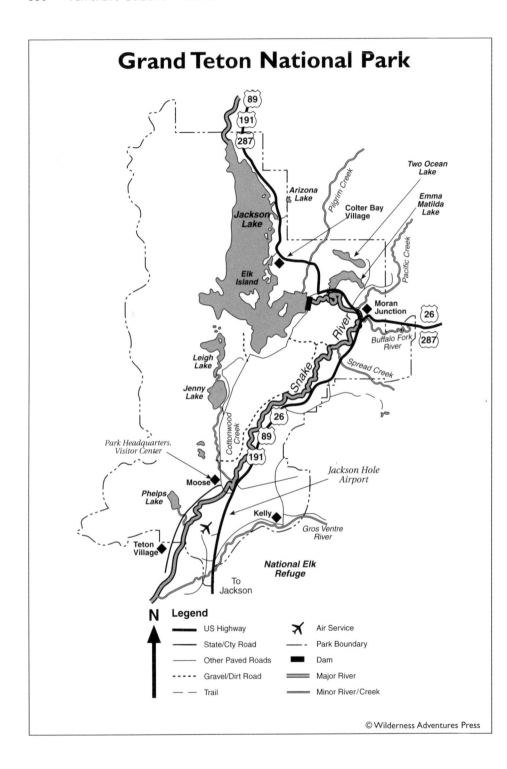

89
191
287

Two Ocean
Lake

Arizona
Lake

Pilgrim Creek

Colter Bay
Village

Emma
Matilda
Lake

Jackson
Lake

Pacific Creek

Elk
Island

Moran
Junction

26

River

287

Buffalo Fork
River

Snake

Leigh
Lake

Spread Creek

Jenny
Lake

Cottonwood Creek

26

89

191

Park Headquarters,
Visitor Center

Jackson Hole
Airport

Moose

Phelps
Lake

Kelly

Gros Ventre
River

Teton
Village

National Elk
Refuge

To
Jackson

N

Legend

▬▬ US Highway	✈ Air Service
─── State/Cty Road	─ ─ Park Boundary
─── Other Paved Roads	▰ Dam
····· Gravel/Dirt Road	▰▰ Major River
─ ─ Trail	▰▰ Minor River/Creek

© Wilderness Adventures Press

GRAND TETON NATIONAL PARK

Towering more than a mile above Jackson Hole, the Grand Teton rises to 13,770 feet. It is the second highest peak in Wyoming. Twelve Teton peaks reach above 12,000 feet, high enough to support a dozen mountain glaciers. Many of the most dramatic views of the Teton's jagged peaks are mirrored in large glacial lakes and the Snake River.

The park's varied terrain is carpeted by ribbons of cottonwoods and willows bordering rivers and streams; sagebrush flats, lodgepole pine and spruce forests, subalpine meadows, and alpine stone fields checker the valleys and mountains. Wildflowers bloom everywhere throughout spring and summer. Wildlife viewing opportunities in the park, Jackson Hole, and the Teton Wilderness rival the numbers and variety more commonly associated with Yellowstone National Park. The most diverse animal and plant communities are along the Snake River. Visitors are advised to keep their distance from big game animals like elk, moose, and bison. Black or grizzly bears may be encountered on park trails or in the backcountry.

Humans have visited Jackson Hole and used its abundant resources for approximately 11,000 years. Early residents occupied the valley during the short spring, summer, and fall seasons. During the other eight months of the year, they moved to lower elevations and warmer winter climates.

Beginning in the late 1800s, homesteaders, ranchers, and later dude ranchers moved into the valley, bringing the technologies of irrigation and insulation to allow them to stay through the long, harsh winter. With the establishment of Grand Teton National Park in 1929 and later additions in 1950, culminating in today's park, a wide variety of resources are protected for future generations in an area covering 485 square miles.

Because more than 3.1 million tourists annually visit the park, primarily between Memorial Day and September 30, a visit requires some measure of planning and timing. During the summer season, all lodging and camping facilities throughout Yellowstone and Grand Teton national parks fill by early afternoon, including overnight lodging in Jackson. Many dining establishments recommend or require reservations during summer. Waiting lists often exceed one hour.

Some basic services such as rental cars, rental equipment, and lodging are sold out every day. Reservations should be considered essential for main season visits. Campgrounds are frequently filled by noon, with the possible exception of Gros Ventre Campground near the park's south boundary, west of Kelly. Arrive early, plan carefully, and seek information at park visitor centers and ranger stations.

The Moose Visitor Center is 12 miles north of Jackson on Highway 89/191/287 and a half-mile west of Moose Junction on the Teton Park Road. The Jenny Lake Visitor Center is 8 miles north of the Moose Visitor Center on the Teton Park Road. The Colter Bay Visitor Center is 30 miles north of Jackson on Highway 89/191/287 and a half-mile west of Colter Bay Junction. The Flagg Ranch Information Station is 15 miles north of Colter Bay Junction on Highway 89/191/287.

The Grand Tetons.

The distance from Yellowstone's south boundary to Grand Teton's south boundary is 56 miles. The approximate driving time with no stops is 1.5 hours. Always consider driving time and distance to your next destination before setting out.

There are approximately 100 miles of park roads and 200 miles of trails throughout the park. Most park trails are rough rock or dirt and are not accessible to visitors with disabilities. There are many asphalt trails in the Jenny Lake area, some of which are accessible. Some trails may begin as asphalt and deteriorate to dirt or gravel shortly thereafter. Hikes into the park's alpine backcountry range from moderate to strenuous.

Summer days are in the 70s and 80s, with cool nights in the 40s. Summer thunderstorms are common. Mild to cool temperatures linger through September and October. Raingear is recommended during spring, summer, and fall. The first heavy snows fall by November 1 and continue through March, and snow and frost are possible during any month.

Grand Teton National Park and the John D. Rockefeller, Jr., Memorial Parkway offer a variety of activities from traditional mountain hiking, walking, wildlife viewing, photography, backpacking, camping, climbing, and fishing to swimming, boating, floating, canoeing, biking, and skiing, snowshoeing, and snowmobiling in the winter. Some activities such as overnight backpacking, boating, floating, canoeing, fishing, and snowmobiling require fee permits, licenses or registration. Special regulations may also apply, so take the time to become informed at any visitor center or ranger station.

A Wyoming fishing license is required to fish in Grand Teton National Park. Seasons, regulations, and bag limits for the Snake River and the park's lakes are set by the Wyoming Game and Fish Department in cooperation with the National Park Service. A park boating permit is required to float the Snake within its boundaries, both above and below Jackson Lake.

Permits are available at Grand Teton visitor centers. Fishing licenses may be purchased in fishing tackle stores in Jackson and Wilson, Dornan's at Moose Village, and at park marinas.

For more information write Grand Teton National Park, P.O. Drawer 170, Moose, WY 83012; or call 307-739-3300. Free printed publications are available for backcountry camping, hiking, mountaineering, fishing, boating, floating the Snake, bicycling, skiing, and snowmobiling.

Additional information on park permits, fees, and reservations are in the appendix of this guide.

Park Lakes

A string of deep glacial lakes mirroring the towering peaks of Grand Teton National Park are popular with stillwater anglers in Jackson Hole.

The largest, Jackson Lake, is a deep water fishery best suited for trolling for cutthroat, brown and lake trout from large watercraft. More intimate waters favored by hikers, canoers, and float-tubers are Jenny and Leigh Lakes. Several lakes on the lower slopes of the Tetons, like Phelps, Taggart, and Bradley, are favorite day hikes. Savvy hikers tote fly rods. High alpine tarns, like Lake Solitude, may or may not hold trout, depending on the last time they were stocked. Check with the Wyoming Game and Fish office in Jackson before packing a rod to the high country.

A Wyoming fishing license is required in the park. The following waters are closed to fishing: Christian Ponds, Hedrick's Pond, Moose Pond, Sawmill Pond, and Swan Lake.

Jackson Lake

Jackson Lake is a large natural lake in a deep glacial and structural depression at the base of Mount Moran and the northern Tetons. The Snake River flows into the lake from Yellowstone and exits the lake about 30 miles north of Jackson.

Jackson Lake Dam was built at the outlet in 1911 and raised the lake level 40 feet. It now covers about 25,730 acres. In 1991, the dam was modified and strengthened against potential damage from earthquakes.

The lake routinely gives up 14- to 18-inch cutthroat and lake trout, and a few browns. Occasional trophy lake trout are caught, and it set the state lake trout record with a 50-pound fish in the 1980s.

The Lakes of Grand Teton National Park

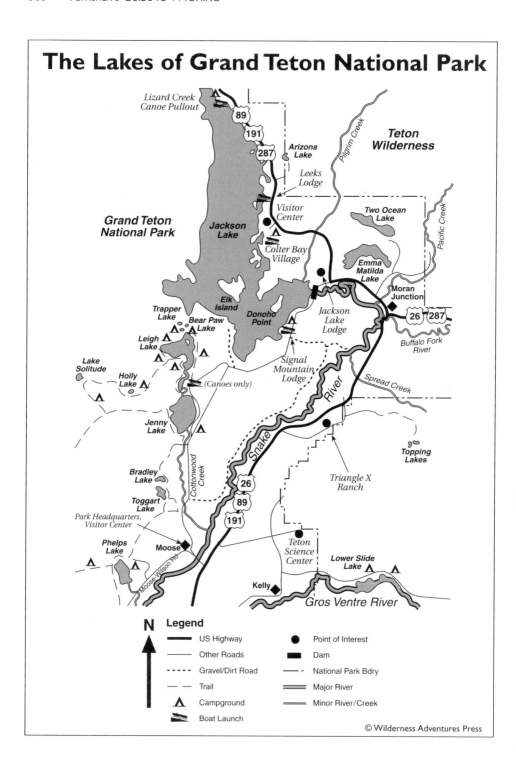

Lizard Creek
Canoe Pullout

89
191
287

Arizona
Lake

Pilgrim Creek

**Teton
Wilderness**

Leeks
Lodge

Visitor
Center

Two Ocean
Lake

Pacific Creek

**Grand Teton
National Park**

**Jackson
Lake**

Colter Bay
Village

Emma
Matilda
Lake

Moran
Junction

Trapper
Lake

Bear Paw
Lake

Elk
Island

Donoho
Point

Jackson
Lake
Lodge

26 **287**

Buffalo Fork
River

Leigh
Lake

Lake
Solitude

Holly
Lake

(Canoes only)

Signal
Mountain
Lodge

Snake River

Spread Creek

Jenny
Lake

Cottonwood Creek

Topping
Lakes

Bradley
Lake

26

89

Triangle X
Ranch

Toggart
Lake

Park Headquarters,
Visitor Center

191

Phelps
Lake

Moose

Moose-Wilson Rd.

Teton
Science
Center

Lower Slide
Lake

Kelly

Gros Ventre River

N

Legend

— US Highway
— Other Roads
- - - - Gravel/Dirt Road
— — Trail
Λ Campground
Boat Launch

● Point of Interest
▬ Dam
— National Park Bdry
Major River
Minor River/Creek

© Wilderness Adventures Press

Leigh Canyon inlet on Leigh Lake.

Most anglers troll with jigs or bait, or use spinning rods from shore. It gets only moderate attention from fly casters. Deep water rigs are used when lake trout escape warm temperatures in summer.

Jackson Lake is closed to fishing in the month of October. The limit on trout is 6 per day or in possession. Only 1 trout may exceed 24 inches.

Canoe Lakes

Jenny and Leigh Lakes are popular with canoers as well as flyfishers. Anglers also share Jenny's waters with a shuttle boat that takes hikers to Hidden Falls and the scenic Cascade Canyon. Jenny Lake is most popular with float-tubers because it is directly off the loop road.

In between the two larger lakes is a long, river-like depression called String Lake. It is a marginal fishery because it is shallow and warms early.

In any other mountain range, these would be called foothills lakes. There are no foothills in the Tetons, and the mountains thrust against the sky right over the glacial ponds. Jenny Lake is at the base of Mount Owen, and Leigh Lake is at the base of Mount Moran. String Lake offers great views of the Grand Teton.

Fishing is good in Jenny and Leigh Lakes for 14- to 18-inch cutthroat and lake trout, and a few small brook trout. Each occasionally gives up a trophy lake trout, a surprise to some float-tubers taken for an unexpected ride.

The trout limit in the two lakes is 6 per day or in possession. Only one trout may exceed 24 inches.

Fishing is best after ice-out in spring and again in fall, but both lakes produce in early summer. Floattube or canoe the shallows for cruising fish in early morning. Also cast to fish lurking around underwater logs and look for fish hanging out at the inlets of mountain streams.

Jenny Lake is fairly deep at the center but has lots of waterlogged deadfall in the shallows and along the edges of dropoffs. It is circled by trails and has a boat ramp at the mouth of Cottonwood Creek. The inlet from String Lake is at the top of Jenny Lake.

Leigh Lake is reached by a 3-mile trail along String Lake. Canoers must put in at the String Lake parking lot, paddle to the top of the narrow lake and portage about 250 yards to Leigh Lake's landing. Leigh Lake is deep and wide, with incredible views of Mount Moran at its north end. There are a few small islands in the lake and broad shallows along its east shore. A jaunt back into the large bay on the west side can be productive at the inlets of Leigh and Paintbrush canyons.

Backcountry campsites on Leigh Lake require reservations in advance.

Top water action on the lakes is limited to basically fly black ants in July and sporadic hatches of large caddis and callibaetis through the season. Underwater fishing with full sinking lines is best with woolly buggers, leeches, double bunny, Kiwi muddlers, and other streamers. Beadhead nymphs, emergers, and soft-hackles are effective at inlets.

Hike-in Lakes

A pair of low lakes about 2 miles north of Leigh Lake offers a pleasant hike with dramatic scenery and good fishing at the end of the trail.

The lower lake, Bear Paw, holds 10- to 14-inch cutthroat, and Trapper Lake has 8- to 14-inch cutthroat. Backcountry campsites are located at both lakes. The trail to Bear Paw is flat, and there is a moderate climb to Trapper Lake.

The most popular mountain lakes are 2- to 4-miles hikes with moderate climbs on the south end of the park. The lakes are in glacial depressions on the shoulders of the mountains with wide-open views of the Teton Range.

Taggart and Bradley Lakes are reached by the same trailhead a couple miles north of the Moose Visitor Center. Taggart has 8- to 18-inch cutthroat and brook trout, and Bradley's fish are a little smaller.

Phelps Lake is reached from the Death Canyon trailhead on the Moose-Wilson Road. It offers 14- to 18-inch cutthroat and lake trout.

Fishing is best on the higher lakes in early morning and late in the day for cruising trout in the shallows. The lakes are especially productive when flying black ants are swarming.

*String Lake,
with Mount Owens and
the tip of Grand Teton
in the background.*

Boating Permits
- Permits required for motorized and nonmotorized watercraft are available at visitor centers and ranger stations. Non-motorized boat fees are $5 for a week permit or $10 annual permit. Motorized boat fees are $10 for a week permit, and $20 for annual permit.

Backcountry Camping Permits
- To obtain reservation forms for backcountry camping permits call 307-739-3602.

BRIDGER-TETON NATIONAL FOREST LAKES

Four lakes in the Gros Ventre foothills northeast of Jackson are popular fisheries. An historic landslide that blocked the Gros Ventre River created lower Slide Lake. The Topping Lakes are the only ones in the area with grayling.

The map for the Buffalo and Jackson Ranger Districts of the Bridger-Teton National Forest includes the Teton Wilderness Area.

Lower Slide Lake

This 1,123-acre lake is about 5 miles northwest of Kelly via the Gros Ventre Road, and also is popular with canoers and wind surfers.

It is rated as good fishing for 14- to 18-inch cutthroat and lake trout.

The 1925 landslide that created Lower Slide Lake blocked the river for two years, when it broke during a spring flood. The little town of Kelly, 3.5 miles downstream, was inundated by the torrent rushing down the river, and six people were killed.

A dam was later constructed at the break to regulate the lower river for irrigation diversions.

Soda Lake

This small lake is about 3 miles southeast of Upper Slide Lake on the Gros Ventre Road. At the lake, take the south fork about 2 miles to the trail. It is a 2-mile hike to the lake.

Fishing is rated as good for 12- to 18-inch cutthroat, and it is managed as a trophy fishery. The limit is 1 per day or in possession. All trout less than 20 inches in length must be released, and fishing is permitted with flies and lures only.

Toppings Lakes

At Cunningham Cabin parking lot in park on U.S. 26/89, turn east on forest service road. First lake is an hour's hike from trailhead with a steep climb. It is rated as excellent for 8- to 16-inch grayling. The second lake is tougher fishing for 12- to 16-inch grayling.

TETON WILDERNESS LAKES

Several small lakes in the Teton Wilderness Area northeast of the park at the end of relatively short hikes include:

Gravel Lake

Start at Pacific Creek trailhead, west of Moran Junction. The small lake is an 8-mile hike via Pacific Creek Trail and Gravel Creek Fork. It is rated as good fishing for 10- to 13-inch cutthroat. Both creeks also offer good cutthroat fishing.

Lower Slide Lake on the Gros Ventre River; the scar from the 1925 landslide is visible on the mountain in the background.

Enos Lake

The largest lake in the wilderness, it is reached by a 12-mile hike from Box Creek trailhead in Buffalo Fork Valley, east of Moran Junction, on U.S. 26/287. It is rated as good fishing for 12- to 14-inch cutthroat.

Arizona Lake

A small lake that drains into Arizona Creek, a tributary of Jackson Lake, it is a 2-mile hike from the trailhead near the picnic site north of Leeks Marina on U.S 26/89. It is rated as good fishing for 8- to 14-inch cutthroat and brook trout.

Upper Yellowstone River

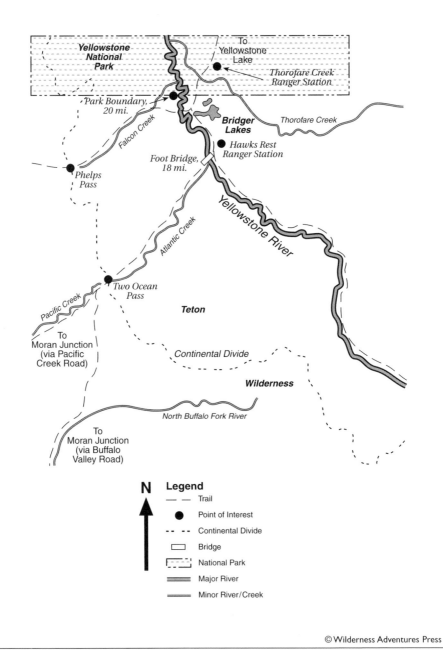

Yellowstone National Park

To Yellowstone Lake

Thorofare Creek Ranger Station

Park Boundary, 20 mi.

Falcon Creek

Bridger Lakes

Thorofare Creek

Hawks Rest Ranger Station

Foot Bridge, 18 mi.

Phelps Pass

Atlantic Creek

Yellowstone River

Two Ocean Pass

Pacific Creek

Teton

To Moran Junction (via Pacific Creek Road)

Continental Divide

Wilderness

North Buffalo Fork River

To Moran Junction (via Buffalo Valley Road)

N

Legend
— — Trail
● Point of Interest
- - - Continental Divide
▭ Bridge
National Park
Major River
Minor River/Creek

© Wilderness Adventures Press

UPPER YELLOWSTONE RIVER

Jackson is the southern gateway to the upper Yellowstone River and the best cutthroat fishing in the West. Located in the Teton Wilderness, the upper river is a long 30-mile hike or horse ride, but fishing is incredible for Yellowstone cutthroat in the 14- to 18-inch range. It's also great in Atlantic and Thorofare Creeks in the Hawks Rest area.

Cutthroat spawning runs out of Yellowstone Lake, peaks with spring runoff in late June or early July, and then tapers off. The spawners linger awhile before quickly dropping out of the upper river in August. Some heavy-bodied resident cutthroat reside in the upper river, and fishing is good in nearby Bridger Lake. The window of opportunity is short, but by staying south of Yellowstone's border, anglers can fish earlier than the park's July 15 opener. Also, they don't have to make reservations for designated campsites as the park requires.

Wilderness trails to the Yellowstone's headwaters are up Pacific Creek, west of Moose Junction, and up the North Fork of Buffalo Fork River, starting from Turpin Meadows east of Moose Junction. Both trails meet at 8,200-foot Two Ocean Pass to continue down Atlantic Creek to the Yellowstone River. The Forest Service's Buffalo and Jackson Ranger District map and the USGS topographic map for Two Ocean Pass, which shows the meadows and Hawks Rest, are available in Jackson.

A footbridge, 2 miles south of the park border, is the only one on the upper river. The only other access to this section of river is via two park trails that meet at the river's delta at Yellowstone Lake, 20 miles downstream. One follows the lake's east shore and is 20 miles in reaching the delta; the Heart Lake Trail begins at the South Entrance and traverses 35 miles to reach the delta.

The upper Yellowstone in the Teton Wilderness is a classic meadow stream, with riffles and runs, and large pools and glides. The tributaries are tumbling mountain streams with riffles and runs, pools and pocketwaters.

After the spawn, the cutthroat rest in quiet pools and runs meandering through the meadows and feed throughout the day. Good hatches in late June and July are golden stones, caddis, and little yellow stones. Pale morning duns and green drakes also are on the water in mid-July and August. Cutthroat readily take generic mayfly and attractor patterns, too, like Adams, Cahills, stimulators, renegades, humpies, and elk hair caddis.

The best fishing is after runoff wanes, which can vary year to year. Check on conditions before planning a trip. Outfitters and guest ranches based in Jackson specialize in horseback trips into this pristine area. Many anglers also go in on their own horses. There are corrals and a loading ramp at the Turpin Meadows parking lot.

Mosquitoes can be very pesky in marshy meadows, and the region is prime grizzly bear country. Hike in parties of three or more, and keep a clean camp.

Pacific Creek on the western access route into the wilderness has good fishing for 10- to 16-inch cutthroat, as well as brook trout. Buffalo Fork River and its North Fork above the Turpin Meadow Campground offer good fishing for 8- to 16-inch cutthroat and rainbows and also contain brook trout.

The bag and possession limit in the wilderness is 2 cutthroat, only 1 over 20 inches.

Gros Ventre River

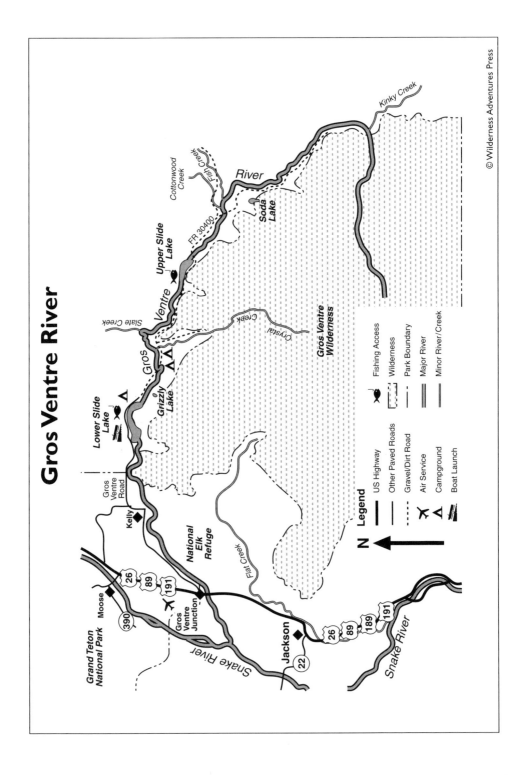

© Wilderness Adventures Press

SNAKE RIVER TRIBUTARIES

Two Snake River tributaries above and below Jackson offer pleasant day trips. Campgrounds in Bridger-Teton National Forest invite longer stays.

The lower Gros Ventre River shapes the southern border of the park and the northern boundary of the National Elk Refuge. Its name is another Wyoming tongue twister. Pronounced "Gro Vont," it means "big belly" in French. It was the name fur trappers gave to an Indian tribe that often traveled the region with the Blackfeet.

The Hoback River is the southern boundary of Teton County and Jackson Hole.

Gros Ventre River

The Gros Ventre rises in the Gros Ventre Mountains in the wilderness area behind Jackson and flows about 50 miles to the Snake.

Lower Slide Lake on the Gros Ventre was created in 1925 when one of the largest landslides in modern geologic history blocked the river. The dam burst two years later and flooded the little town of Kelly, 3.5 miles downstream. Six people were killed. A dam at the outlet now regulates the lower river for irrigation diversions.

Upper Slide Lake is a string of pools and marshes where the Gros Ventre's head-waters and small tributaries collect to form the main stem of the river. The semi-arid terrain is very rugged, with steep ridges and colorful rock outcroppings and sheer cliffs eroded from a variety of formations tinted with layers of red, tan, yellow or gray-green stone.

A road northeast of Kelly hugs the upper river's passage through the steep narrow valley, and up, down, and around a series of short canyons. Rainy weather turns the unpaved portion of the road above Crystal Creek into a muddy mess that is treacherous. Check on weather forecasts before venturing past the two campgrounds near the creek.

Snake River finespotted cutthroat are the dominant fish in this small mountain stream, and it has lesser populations of rainbows. Fishing is good for 10- to 16-inch fish, with a few going 22 inches. Most of the bigger cutthroat are in the upper river where it gets the least pressure. Pocket waters in a deep canyon below Lower Slide Lake offer the best rainbow fishing.

The Gros Ventre is a late summer, early fall fishery that fishes well until water flows drop too low. Public access is good throughout the park and the national forest, but there are several ranches on the river, where anglers are warned against trespassing. The section running along the north end of the National Elk Refuge is closed to fishing from October 31 to May 20.

The upper river is easily waded in most places after spring runoff subsides, but late summer storms can muddy the water and raise levels temporarily. It descends in a series of riffles and runs, long glides, undercut banks, and deep runs and pools, with some pocket waters on steeper pitches.

In dry years, the river below Kelly, where the park's largest campground is located, can be seriously depleted due to irrigation diversions.

A stonefly hatch around the second week of July draws the most attention from local anglers, but the river is rarely crowded above the campgrounds at Crystal Creek and Red Hills. Even though mayfly hatches are sporadic, it fishes well with small generic mayfly patterns, caddis patterns, attractors, and terrestrials, plus small nymphs and emergers.

Flows in late summer usually are low and clear and require more delicate leaders and finesse in presentation than other rivers in Jackson Hole.

Where the road loops around the canyons, flyfishers find the best chances for solitude in serene surroundings. The weather during late summer and early fall is often pleasant and mild.

Hoback River

The Hoback River merges with the Snake River 17 miles south of Jackson at Hoback Junction on U.S. 26/89.

Public access and good wading opportunities are best along U.S. 191 above the canyon at its mouth. The river is a popular destination during the stone fly hatch in early July, but it fishes better in late summer and fall.

Fishing is good for Snake River finespotted cutthroat in the 8- to 14-inch range. Some larger cutthroat are found in deeper pools and runs, and a few brook trout lurk in the upper river.

Nearly 55 miles long, the Hoback rises in the Wyoming Range southeast of Hoback Junction and almost due south of the village of Bondurant. It emerges from the mountains onto a heavily braided floodplain at U.S. 191 and loops around the village through a marshy flat. Picking up the flows of several tributaries, it returns to the highway and sharply turns northwest on a 20-mile run through a narrow valley to the high-walled canyon above the Snake. The valley descent is mostly riffles and runs, with intermittent pocket waters and cutbank pools, and some deep pools and rock gardens.

The canyon and a short stretch above it are private land, and permission is required to cross it. Otherwise, public access is excellent, and there are two Forest Service campgrounds on the highway.

A gravel road to its headwaters climbs about 6 miles through ranch lands and continues 6 miles into the national forest. Fishing in the headwaters is mostly for pan-sized trout.

Granite Creek enters the Hoback midway between Bondurant and the Snake. A classic, small mountain stream, it holds 8- to 12-inch cutthroat and occasional pleasant surprises. It is a principal access route into the south side of the Gros Ventre Wilderness Area. Granite Hot Springs Resort is at the end of the road.

The Hoback's runoff is high and often turbulent from May into July. Summer storms can muddy the water and raise water levels, but late summer and fall flows are mostly gentle and clear.

Both wet and dry stonefly patterns are most effective in early July. Later in the season, traditional high-floating dry flies, grasshoppers, small nymphs, and emergers work best. Like most higher-elevation streams, caddis outnumber mayflies.

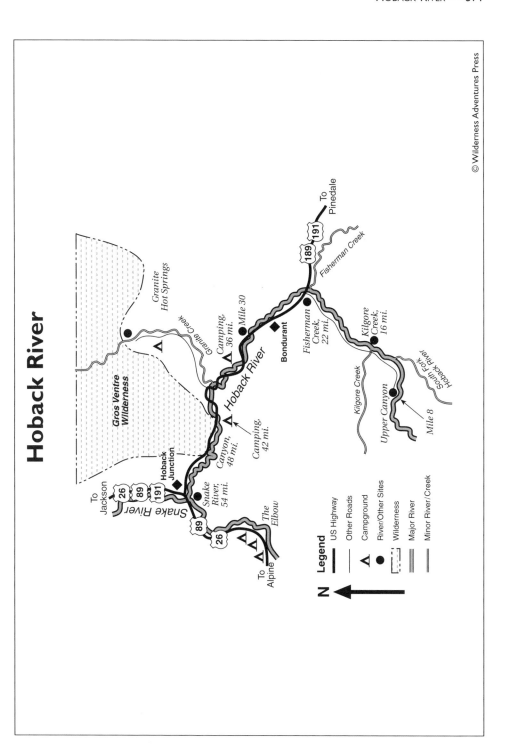

Hoback River

Gros Ventre Wilderness

Granite Hot Springs

Granite Creek

Camping, 36 mi.

Mile 30

Hoback River

Bondurant

Fisherman Creek, 22 mi.

Kilgore Creek, 16 mi.

Kilgore Creek

South Fork Hoback River

Upper Canyon

Mile 8

189 191

Fisherman Creek

To Pinedale

Camping, 42 mi.

Canyon, 48 mi.

Hoback Junction

Snake River, 54 mi.

Snake River

To Jackson

26 89 191

89

26

The Elbow

To Alpine

Legend
— US Highway
| Other Roads
△ Campground
● River/Other Sites
Wilderness
Major River
Minor River/Creek

N

© Wilderness Adventures Press

*A Hoback River angler
fishes a riffle.*

Spring Creeks

The clear, cool spring creeks of Jackson Hole are critical spawning grounds for Snake River finespotted cutthroat trout. The majority meander through private property and are closely guarded against trespass.

In recent years, the creeks have been the focus of cooperative projects to return them to their full potential for spawners running out of the Snake River. The landowners opened their gates to Wyoming Game and Fish biologists and local volunteers working on stream renovations crucial to the preservation of the Snake's unique native trout. The rest of the year, most of the spring creeks remain closed.

Unless you are a friend of an owner the chances of fishing one of these ultra exclusive waters are virtually nil. If you have to ask the cost, you probably can't afford the privilege on a few where limited access is granted. Two in Wilson that advertise accommodations and fishing rights are Fish Creek Ranch, on Fish Creek, and Crescent H Ranch, on Fall Creek. Several other private creeks are available through special arrangements with Jackson fly shops.

The few public spring creeks in Jackson Hole draw little attention because they are closed most of the year to protect spawning cutthroat. Blacktail Spring Creek, Cottonwood Creek, and Upper Bar BC Spring Creek, in Grand Teton National Park, and Lower Bar BC Spring Creek do not open to fishing until August 1. After the larger spawners return to the Snake River, the creeks hold 6- to 14-inch cutthroat.

But don't despair; Jackson Hole does offer an incredible window of opportunity for quiet water fishing over super wary cutthroat. It's called Flat Creek.

Lower Flat Creek

While technically not a spring creek, Flat Creek on the National Elk Refuge is the best meadow fishery in western Wyoming. Its special charm is that it fishes like a spring creek, complete with graduate school lessons from selectively rising trout.

Its fame precedes it, so expect hordes of flyfishers from the August 1 opener through Labor Day. Even then the numbers of anglers diminish only when bad weather weeds out the less hardy. There is rarely a solitary moment on the creek right up to closing day on October 31.

Flat Creek tumbles out of the Gros Ventre foothills onto the grassy flats of the preserve at Jackson's back door to begin its slow serpentine course to the city line. The remainder of its run down the valley is through private property, except for a short stretch above the Snake River at the South Park access site.

Through spring and most of summer on the refuge below McBride Bridge, Flat Creek is host to spawning Snake River cutthroat and broods of trumpeter swans, ducks, and geese. In winter, it harbors migrating swans and other waterfowl, and the refuge is a sanctuary for the largest elk herd in the world. Coyotes and bald eagles prowl year-round on their own missions of mischief, but only in August, September, and October are people on foot allowed to enter this mystical realm.

Flyfishers are permitted to roam along 3 miles of Flat Creek but nowhere else on the refuge.

Many come looking for a fish of a lifetime—the proverbial 22-inch trout caught on a size 22 dry fly. It may happen, but it won't come easy. The bigger the fish, the smarter the fish is another proverb worth noting on Flat Creek.

Its cutthroat range from 14 to 27 inches, with the majority of the fish caught in the 14- to 18-inch class. The really big guys wise up fast.

But whatever size fish you see or hear rising, stalk it with care. The deeply undercut banks of Flat Creek are spongy sounding boards that telegraph the approach of heavy-footed anglers. Also, the water is crystal clear, and the trout flash away to cover at the first hint of danger. Downstream presentations are often the rule.

Long rods with lightweight lines and long, slender leaders and delicate tippets are needed for precise presentations demanded by the stream. A good selection of tiny dry flies completes a flyfisher's arsenal. Jackson outfitters recommend spring

Flat Creek

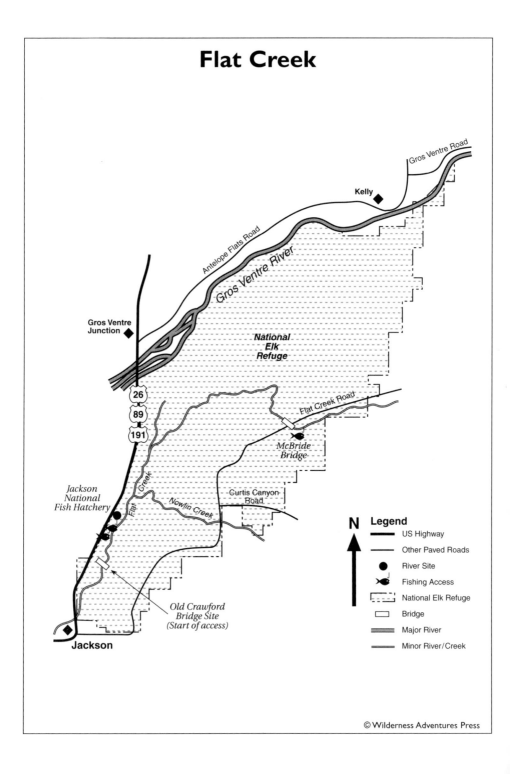

Gros Ventre Road

Kelly

Antelope Flats Road

Gros Ventre River

Gros Ventre
Junction

National
Elk
Refuge

26
89
191

Flat Creek Road

McBride
Bridge

Jackson
National
Fish Hatchery

Flat Creek

Nowlin Creek

Curtis Canyon
Road

Old Crawford
Bridge Site
(Start of access)

Jackson

N

Legend

———— US Highway

———— Other Paved Roads

● River Site

Fishing Access

National Elk Refuge

□ Bridge

Major River

Minor River/Creek

© Wilderness Adventures Press

creek type flies, like thorax patterns, comparaduns, and hairwing duns, as well as midges and ants.

Hatches to watch for in August are pale morning duns, size 16–18, and tiny dark caddis, size 18. September is a good month for mahogany duns, size 16, and as October begins to huff and puff with hints of winter, tiny fall baetis, size 20–22, come out to play

Most of the fishing will be to rising trout, but you don't have to spend all day trying to be a dry fly wizard to catch one special fish. After all, these are cutthroat and quite often accommodate less expert tactics and techniques.

There are ample options to prospect opposite banks and have fun with large dries, like grasshoppers and craneflies, or search undercut banks with large nymphs and streamers, like woolly buggers and muddlers.

By either choice, studious or adventurous, Flat Creek is a special place. Savor its window of opportunity when it opens, and leave the trout for the next students and adventurers.

Fishing Regulations
- Lower Flat Creek is open to fishing August 1 through October 31 from the Old Crawford bridge site upstream to McBride bridge, and on the mouth of Nowlin Creek, up to the closed area signs a quarter mile upstream.
- Fishing is permitted with flies only.
- Fishing at night is not permitted.
- Below Old Crawford Bridge, Flat Creek is closed year-round.
- Above McBride Bridge, the season on Upper Flat Creeks is May 21 through October 31.
- The limit on cutthroat in Lower Flat Creek is 1 per day or in possession. All trout less than 20 inches in length must be returned to the water immediately.

Kids-Only Waters
Children under the age of 14 have exclusive rights to fish Flat Creek between the west boundary of the National Elk Refuge and U.S. 191 bridge adjacent to the Sagebrush Motel and on the Elk Park Pond in Jackson. Teenagers 14 or older and adults are not permitted to fish these waters.

Salt River

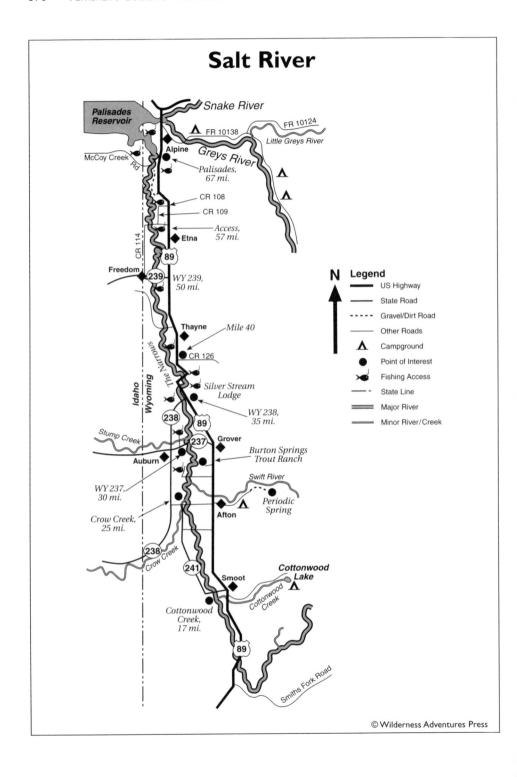

© Wilderness Adventures Press

Star Valley

The last two tributaries of the Snake in Wyoming, the Salt and Greys Rivers, rush to meet it at the border as it exits into Idaho. The confluence occurs at the little resort town of Alpine, the northern gateway to Star Valley and the lower Greys River.

Known as the "Little Switzerland of America," Star Valley's broad bowl is dotted with dairy farms and small hamlets and rimmed by rugged mountains on both sides. The Salt River flows almost due north down the center of the valley, hugging the flanks of the Caribou Mountains in Idaho. To the east, the Salt Mountains hide the Greys River, running down a deep valley separating the Salt and Wyoming ranges.

At the top of Star Valley is Afton, its largest town and where the Salt grows to true river size. Despite the bucolic nature of its surroundings, public access to the stream is excellent. A dozen brown Game and Fish signs along U.S. 89 direct anglers to the river.

Alpine is nestled on the banks of the Palisades Reservoir at the intersection of U.S. 89 and U.S. 26.

The backwaters of the long, narrow lake flooded the confluence of the Salt, Greys, and Snake in 1959. Below its dam in Idaho's Swan Valley, the Snake's name changes to the South Fork; in Wyoming, it was once called the Lewis Fork. About 60 miles downstream it merges with the famous Henry's Fork, or North Fork. The confluence is the official origin of the Snake.

Salt River

The Salt River's meandering passage through its pastoral valley between Afton and Alpine extends for about 30 miles and presents its best fishing options.

From its rise in the Salt River Range south of Smoot to Afton the river runs through private lands. Irrigation diversions diminish its flows during summer. Just below Afton, three spring creeks—Swift, Crow, and Stump—converge to give birth to the river again.

The creeks are excellent fisheries but they pass through private lands, and permission is required to fish them, except at their mouths. There are two key public access sites below Afton at their confluence with the Salt. From there down, state and county roads branch off of U.S. 89 to 10 more well-marked public access sites on the river.

Key wading and bank fishing sites are in the pasturelands near Afton and behind Etna at the bottom of the valley. Some wading options also are located above and below The Narrows, near Silver Stream Lodge. But for most of its course the river twists and turns through willow-choked channels and deeply undercut bends with a current too strong to wade. The river is usually most productive to anglers fishing from small boats, rafts, or canoes.

The Salt holds a few rainbows and brookies, but its prime attractions are Snake River finespotted cutthroat and brown trout in the 10- to 16-inch range. It offers chances to net a trophy brown year-round, but opportunities improve progressively during the late fall spawning run out of Palisades Reservoir.

The larger browns are generally found in the Salt below the small town of Thayne, but the migrants disperse throughout the river. Extensive drawdown of the reservoir in dry years also makes the last couple miles of the river accessible to anglers who cross its mud flats to meet the browns at the head of their spawning run.

The lower Salt River has undercut banks.

Some browns linger in the river into March. To protect them, the river upstream from the WYO 238 bridge is closed to fishing in November and December. Ardent brown hunters return after New Year's Day to continue their pursuit on mild winter days or in early spring.

From the County Road 125 bridge at Thayne, upstream to Silver Stream Lodge, the trout limit is 4 per day or in possession, only 1 over 18 inches. Trout between 11 and 18 inches must be released. Fishing is permitted with flies and lures only.

Spring runoff occurs sooner and clears earlier on the Salt than other western Wyoming rivers. In normal years it begins to wane by late May or early June, and the river fishes well from July into autumn.

The exceptionally wet years of 1996 and 1997 threw the schedule out of whack, and the river ran strong and high most of these seasons, making float-fishing an especially good choice for this beguiling little river. Few elect to take this option, however, and float-fishers often have the river to themselves.

Look for caddis, golden stones, and willowflies in June and July on the Salt. A prime pattern in late summer is a grasshopper, as well as other large attractors. Generic mayflies and small attractor patterns are effective year-round since matching a hatch is not a big concern. Beadhead nymphs and emergers work in exploring cutbank bends and deeper pools and runs.

Trophy brown hunters switch to big-bad-and-ugly nymphs and streamers in late fall, but just as often give them a try in all seasons.

Stream Facts: Salt River

Season
- Upstream from the WYO 238 bridge, river is closed to fishing in November and December.

Regulations
- From the County Road 125 bridge at Thayne upstream to Silver Stream Lodge, the trout limit is 4 per day or in possession, only 1 over 18 inches. Trout between 11 and 18 inches must be released. Fishing is permitted with flies and lures only.

Trout
- Snake River finespotted cutthroat and brown trout in the 10- to 16-inch range, as well as a few rainbows and brook trout. A late fall brown spawning run out of Palisades Reservoir brings up larger fish.

Miles
- Mile 9: U.S. 89 below Salt Pass
- Mile 15: Smoot
- Mile 25: Confluence of Crow Creek
- Mile 30: Auburn Bridge
- Mile 35: WYO 238 Bridge
- Mile 50: Freedom Bridge
- Mile 57: Etna Bridge
- Mile 67: McCoy Creek Road
- Mile 68: Palisades Reservoir

Character
- Mountain meadow stream flowing through a broad pastoral valley lined by hay fields and pastures. River is small but swift and strong, with many of its channels thickly lined by willows and brush, which makes wading unsafe. Best suited for float-fishing in small boat or canoe except at access sites in open pastures.

Flows
- Spring runoff occurs sooner and clears earlier on the Salt than on other western Wyoming rivers. In normal years it begins to wane by late May or early June, and the river fishes well from July into autumn.

Access
- Swift Creek: parking; 3 miles of bank and stream access.
- Grover: parking, boat launch; 4 miles of bank and stream access.
- WYO 238 Bridge: parking, boat launch; 1.5 miles of bank and stream access.
- The Narrows (Silver Stream Lodge): parking; 2 miles of bank and stream access.

Brown trout are prime targets on the Salt River.

- The Narrows (lower U.S. 89 bridge): parking, boat launch; 2 miles of bank and stream access.
- County Road 126: parking, camping; .5 miles of bank and stream access. Boats and canoes must be portaged around diversion dam; another dam just downstream on side channel.
- Freedom (WYO 239 bridge): parking; 1.5 miles of bank and stream access.
- Etna (County Road 109): parking, boat launch; 2.5 miles of bank and stream access.
- Etna (County Road 108): parking; 2.5 miles of bank and stream access.
- Jeep Trail: parking, boat takeout; 2 miles of bank and stream access.
- McCoy Creek Road: bank and stream access to Wildlife Management Area.
- Palisades Mud Flats: bank and stream access at mouth of river in fall.

Camping
- Bridger Teton National Forest

SALT RIVER MAJOR HATCHES

Insect	A	M	J	J	A	S	O	N	Time	Flies
Golden Stone			▓	▓					A	**Dry:** Golden Stone, Bird's Stone, Orange Stimulator #6–10; **Wet:** Bitch Creek Nymph, Girdlebug, Woolly Bugger #4–12
Little Yellow Stone (Willow Fly)				▓					A/E	Yellow Sally, Blonde Humpy, Willow Fly, Yellow Stimulator, Yellow Wulff #10–14
Caddis					▓	▓			M/D	**Dry:** Elk Hair Caddis, Yellow or Royal Humpy, Renegade #10–16; **Wet:** Beadhead Prince Nymph, Squirrel Tail, Soft-hackles #10–16
Pale Morning Dun				▓	▓				A/E	**Dry:** PMD, Para-PMD, Rusty Spinner, Light Cahill #14–18; **Wet:** Hare's Ear Nymph, Pheasant Tail #14–16
Terrestrials				▓	▓	▓			M/A	Joe's Hopper, Madam X, Turk's Tarantula, Chernobyl Ant #8–14; Foam Beetle, Disc O'Beetle, Dave's Cricket #14–16; Ants #14–18

HATCH TIME CODE: M = morning; A = afternoon; E = evening; D = dark; SF = spinner fall; // = continuation through periods.

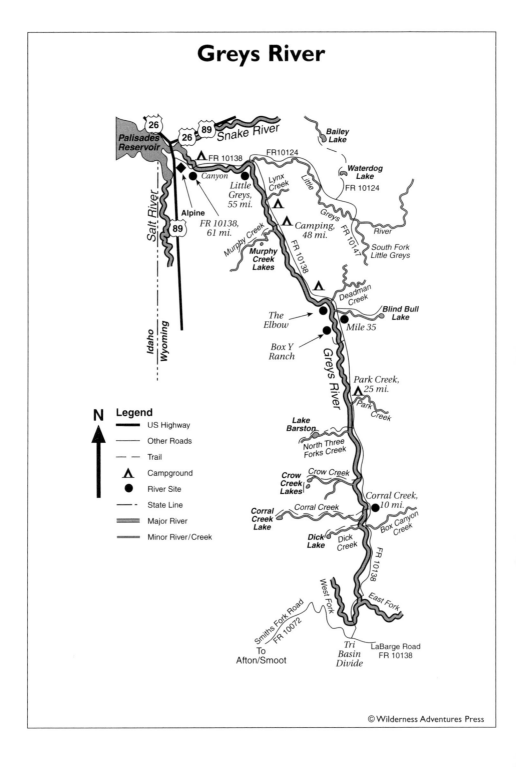

Greys River

Greys River

Tucked into the scenic high mountain valley dividing the Salt and Wyoming ranges, the Greys River gambols down its narrow rocky course to join the Snake River at Alpine.

The Greys is a favorite weekend hideout for Star Valley residents, but its secret charms are rarely explored by flyfishers speeding past its mouth to better known waters. A rarity in a state where no trespassing signs abound, the river's 60-mile run is entirely through a national forest. Only two 1-mile sections at the Box Y Guest Ranch are on private land along the gravel road hugging the stream.

The well-maintained Bridger-Teton National Forest road begins at Alpine and offers easy access to the lower Greys and Little Greys Rivers. In rainy weather, the steeper section near the Greys' source presents slippery driving.

The Greys hosts Snake River finespotted cutthroat in the 8- to 16-inch range, with some larger trout in deeper pools. The lower river is stocked with hatchery trout near campgrounds. Above Murphy Creek, it is managed as a wild trout fishery.

There is a 2 cutthroat limit, only 1 over 16 inches, from Murphy Creek upstream to Corral Creek. Cutthroat between 11 and 16 inches must be released, and fishing is permitted with flies or lures only on this stretch.

The river is easily waded after spring runoff in its braided meadow runs and shallow riffles, but pocket waters in its canyons require serious rock scrambling to reach them. Its variety of fishing waters invites getaways for family fishing parties or neophyte flyfishers who want to hone their skills in relative solitude. It is close enough to Jackson for pleasant day trips, but a half dozen campgrounds tempt anglers into longer stays.

The Greys rises in the Salt Mountains east of Smoot and flows down its narrow, forested valley in strings of riffles and runs, with intermittent logjams, pocket waters, cutbank meanders, and some deep holes. Several canyon runs hold low drops and churning rapids. It grows in strength from a multitude of small creeks along its passage and picks up the Little Greys River 8 miles east of Alpine.

The Little Greys is a small carbon copy of the main river. Most of its trout are smaller, but they hit high-floating attractor patterns with abandon. The deep pools and cutbank bends of a meandering run through its upper meadows can be explored for larger fish.

Spring runoff on the Greys begins to subside in mid-June and usually clears by July, and the river fishes best in late summer and early fall. The autumn blaze of frostbitten cottonwoods contrasted against the deep greens of fir and pine draws local residents to it valley just for the drive. But the fishing is serene and even less crowded as other passersby head for the hills in pursuit of mule deer and elk. The river bottoms are critical wintering grounds for the region's elk herds.

Around the Fourth of July, giant stoneflies buzzing about offer the river's most exciting fishing. Large stone nymphs and woolly buggers can be used to explore its waters in advance of the hatch. Sofa Pillows, salmonflies, and large attractors draw top water action when the adults enter their egg laying cycle.

Braided channels on a meadow run of the lower Greys River.

Hatches of little yellow stones, or willowflies, coincide with the stoneflies and continue past July. Caddis are prolific spring to fall, and sporadic hatches of pale morning duns and gray drakes are the most visible mayflies through summer. Callibaetis also flutter about quiet backwaters of the river's meadow run. Small grasshoppers start to appear in mid-July and are a prime pattern in late August into September.

But matching hatches is not a big concern on the Greys. Bushy, high riding attractor patterns, like elk hair caddis, humpies, stimulators, and Wulffs, consistently produce trout. A basic set of generic mayflies, like Adams, light Cahills, and slate-winged Coachmans, perform in most cases. But it always pays to pack a fishing vest with a selection of PMDs and BWOs on any mountain stream. Grasshopper patterns and attractors like Turk's tarantula, Madam Xs, double humpies, and Chernobyl ants need not be as large as patterns associated with bigger waters like the Snake.

There is plenty of elbowroom to keep exploring if action is slow in one spot or another.

Another aspect of the Greys' enchantment is an opportunity to see the birth and evolution of a mountain trout stream. At its source on the north slope of the Tri Basin Divide, a sign at the merger of its East and West Forks declares, "Watch Me Grow."

Those who accept the invitation embark on one of the most scenic loop trips in western Wyoming. At the top of the loop is another unique aspect of this backwater corner of the state, a cutthroat trout crossroads.

The Greys River originates in the Salt Mountains.

From Alpine, drive south on U.S. 89 though the pastoral beauty of Star Valley to the Salt River Pass, 5 miles south of Smoot, and turn left into the mountains. The Smiths Fork road at the pass continues east to LaBarge Meadows. En route the gravel road crosses the tiny Smiths Fork River and forks north and south at LaBarge Creek. Take the north fork to cross the low pass over Tri Basin Divide to reach the Greys.

The divide between the Salt and Wyoming mountain ranges marks the point where the three streams set their courses for three of the West's basins. The Greys flows north to the Snake, the largest tributary of the Columbia. LaBarge Creek flows to the Green River, the headwaters of the Colorado. The Smith's Fork merges with the Bear River, the source of the Great Salt Lake in Utah's Great Basin.

Each drainage harbors a cutthroat subspecies unique to its basin. Flyfishers cruising its streams have a chance at scoring a hat trick or at least a double-hitter to help complete a Cutt-Slam. Wyoming Game and Fish awards a Cutt Slam certificate to anglers who catch four of the state's principal cutthroat subspecies: Yellowstone, Snake River, Bonneville, and Colorado River cutthroat. The Greys holds Snake River finespotted cutthroat. Bonneville cutthroat are in the Smiths Fork, and Colorado River cutthroat are in LaBarge Creek.

Before embarking for the divide, obtain a copy of the Bridger-Teton National Forest's map for the Big Piney, Greys River, and Kemmerer Rangers Districts at the district offices in Afton or Jackson.

The road down the steep canyon at the top of the Greys is a bit bumpy, but it becomes smoother as the valley broadens and the river grows. Its cascading trickle picks up feeder streams for 8 miles to Smith Creek, where it blossoms into a genuine river. From here to its mouth are innumerable enticements to stop and fish.

As the river grows, watch the trout grow . The quarry will range from pan-sized offerings in the higher waters to secretive old timers lurking in its deep meadow pools, plunge holes, and pocket waters of its lower canyons. In between is a healthy variety of 10- to 16-inch Snake River cutthroat.

While the river is compelling enough, a host of small mountain lakes dot the mountain ranges funneling it to the Snake. Many are at the end of 3- to 5-mile hikes or two-wheel tracks that require 4-wheel-drive vehicles with high clearance.

Along the Salt Range, several of the better alpine lakes at the top of the drainage are the Corral Creek Lakes, Crow Creek Lakes, and Lake Barstow. Two-thirds of the way down the river, the Murphy Creek Lakes are above a popular campground in the valley.

Above the Little Greys in the Wyoming Range are Waterdog Lake and Bailey Lake.

The trout in the alpine ponds are often eager because few anglers take the time and effort to pursue them. Several Star Valley outfitters and guest ranches offer horseback trips into the secluded high country of the Salt and Wyoming Mountains.

Stream Facts: Greys River

Season
- Year-round.

Regulations
- There is a 2 cutthroat limit, only 1 over 16 inches, from Murphy Creek upstream to Corral Creek. Cutthroat between 11 and 16 inches must be released, and fishing is permitted with flies or lures only on this stretch.

Trout
- Snake River finespotted cutthroat in the 8- to 16-inch range, with some larger trout in deeper pools. The lower river is stocked with hatchery trout near campgrounds. Above Murphy Creek, it is managed as a wild trout fishery

Miles
- Mile 0: Confluence of East and West Forks below Tri-Basin Divide
- Mile 8: Spring Creek
- Mile 25: Forest Park campground
- Mile 30: Box Y Guest Ranch
- Mile 40: Moose Flat campground
- Mile 48: Murphy Creek campground
- Mile 55: Confluence of Little Greys River
- Mile 60: Bridge campground
- Mile 65: Confluence with Snake at Alpine

Character
- River flows down its narrow, forested valley in strings of riffles and runs, with intermittent logjams, pocketwater, cutbank meanders, and some deep holes. Several canyon runs hold low drops and churning rapids. It grows in strength from a multitude of small creeks along its passage and picks up the Little Greys River 8 miles east of Alpine.

Flows
- Spring runoff begins to subside in mid-June and usually clears by July. The river fishes best in late summer and early fall.

Access
- Bridger-Teton National Forest road follows entire length.

Camping
- Bridger-Teton National Forest

GREYS RIVER MAJOR HATCHES

Insect	A	M	J	J	A	S	O	N	Time	Flies
Stonefly			■						A	**Dry:** Sofa Pillow, Salmonfly, Turk's Tarantula #4–8; **Wet:** Black Rubberlegs, Bitch Creek Nymph, Woolly Bugger #6–10
Little Yellow Stone (Willow Fly)				■					A/E	Yellow Sally, Blonde Humpy, Yellow Stimulator, Yellow Wulff #10–14
Caddis		■	■	■	■	■	■		M/D	**Dry:** Elk Hair Caddis, Yellow or Royal Humpy, Goddard Caddis, Renegade #10–14; **Wet:** Beadhead Prince Nymph, Peacock Emerger, Soft-hackles #10–12
Pale Morning Dun			■	■	■	■			A/E	**Dry:** PMD, Light Cahill #14–16; **Wet:** Hare's Ear Nymph, Pheasant Tail #12–16
Gray Drake					■				A/E	Adams, Gray Wulff, Royal Humpy #10–12
Callibaetis					■				A	Para-Adams, Sparkle Dun, Crystal Spinner #10–12
Terrestrials				■	■	■	■		M/A	Joe's Hopper, Madam X, Turk's Tarantula, Chernobyl Ant #6–14; Dave's Cricket #14; Ants #14–16

HATCH TIME CODE: M = morning; A = afternoon; E = evening; D = dark; SF = spinner fall; // = continuation through periods.

Western Wyoming Hub Cities
Jackson
Elevation–6,208   Population–4,700

Jackson is the best-known summer and ski resort in Wyoming and, perhaps, the West. Jackson Hole is the home of the Grand Teton National Park and fabulous Snake River. Jackson also is the southern gateway to Yellowstone National Park. In addition to Jackson Hole waters many local outfitters and guides offer trips to Pinedale's Green River, Swan Valley's Salt and Greys Rivers, Yellowstone's lakes and streams, the Teton Wilderness, and the Wind River Mountains.

Jackson's zip code is 83001.

Accommodations
Alpine Motel, 70 South Jean / 307-739-3200 / 18 units / Pets allowed / $
Anglers Inn, 265 North Millward / 307-733-3682 / 28 units / $$
Anvil Motel, 240 North Glenwood / 307-733-3668 / 26 units / $
Lodge at Jackson Hole, 80 Scott Lane / 307-739-9703 / 154 units / $$–$$$
Cowboy Village Resort, 120 South Flat Creek Dr / 307-733-3121 / 82 units / $$–$$$
Days Inn of Jackson Hole, PO Box 2986, Jackson, WY 83001-2986 / 307-733-0033 / 91 units / $$–$$$
Elk Refuge Inn, North Hwy 89 / 307-733-3582 / $ / 22 units
Flat Creek Motel, 1935 North Hwy 89, PO Box 20013 / 307-733-1447 / $$ / 46 units / pets allowed
Jackson Hole Lodge, 420 West Broadway / 307-733-2992 / $$ / 26 units
Motel 6, 1370 West Broadway / 307-733-1620 / $ / 155 units / pets allowed
Snow King Resort, 400 East Snow King Avenue / 307-733-5200 / $$$ / 250 units / Pets allowed
Split Creek Ranch, north of Jackson / 307-733-7522 / $$ / 8 units
Super 8 Motel, 750 South Hwy 89 / 307-733-6833 / $$ / 97 units
The Alpine House, 285 North Glenwood / 307-739-1570
The Virginian Lodge, 750 West Broadway / 307-733-2792 / $$–$$$ / 158 units / Pets allowed
The Wort Hotel, Broadway & Glenwood / 307-733-2190 / $$$ / 60 units
Wagon Wheel Village, 435 North Cache / 307-733-2357 / $$ / 97 units
Wyoming Inn of Jackson, 930 West Broadway, Jackson, WY 83001-9405 / 307-734-0035 / $$$ / 73 units / pets allowed
Teton View Bed and Breakfast, PO Box 652, Wilson, WY 83014-0652 / 307-733-7954 / $ / 18 units / pets allowed
Spring Creek Resort, 1800 Spirit Dance Road / 307-733-8833
Hoback River Resort, Hwy 89 & 189 S / 307-733-5129 / $–$$ / 16 units

CAMPGROUNDS AND RV PARKS

Wagon Wheel Campground, 479 North Cache Drive / 307-733-4588 /
    May 1–October 1 / 36 RV sites / Full services
KOA Kampgrounds, 2780 North Moose Wilson Road / 307-733-5354 /
    April 12–October 6 / 57 RV and 30 tent sites / Full services
Lazy J Corral, 10755 South Hwy 189 / 307-733-1554 / May 1–October 1 / 24 RV
    sites / Full services
Snake River Park, 6705 South Hwy 89 / 307-733-7078 / June 15–September 15
    / 24 RV sites
Virginian RV Park, 750 West Broadway / 307-733-7189 / May 1–October 5 /
    105 RV sites / Full services
Astoria Mineral Hot Springs, (south of Hoback) 12500 South Hwy 89 /
    307-733-2659 / May 15–September 1 / 50 RV and 32 tent sites / Full services
Flagg Ranch, South Entrance of Yellowstone Park; Moran, WY 83013 /
    307-543-2861 / May 15–October 1 / 170 RV sites / Full services

RESTAURANTS

Gun Barrel Steakhouse, 862 West Broadway / 307-733-3287
Nani's, 240 North Glenwood Street #229 / 307-733-3888
Smokey's, 740 West Broadway / 307-739-1861
Granary, 1800 Spirit Dance Road / 307-733-8833
Jedediah's, 135 East Broadway / 307-733-5671
Range Restaurant, 225 North Cache Drive / 307-733-5481
Acadian House, 170 North Millward Street / 307-739-1269
Sugarfoot Cafe, 145 North Glenwood / 307-733-9148
Atrium Restaurant, 400 East Snow King Avenue / 307-733-5200
Stiegler's Restaurant & Bar, Teton Village Road / 307-733-1071
Louie's Steak & Seafood, 175 North Center / 307-733-6803
Rising Sage Cafe, 2820 Rungius Road / 307-733-8649
Billy's Giant Hamburgers, 55 North Cache Street / 307-733-3279
Horse Creek Station, 9800 Hwy 89 South / 307-733-0810
Snake River Grill, 84 East Broadway / 307-733-0557
Blue Moon Diner, 802 West Broadway / 307-733-1102
Mountain Country Wagon Train, 820 Cache Creek Road / 307-733-5386

VETERINARIANS

Animal Care Clinic, 415 East Pearl Avenue / 307-733-5590
Jackson Hole Veterinary Clinic, 2950 South Big Trail Drive / 307-733-4279

OUTFITTERS

Jack Dennis Outdoor Shop, 50 East Broadway / 307-733-3270
Fort Jackson Fishing Expeditions, 315 West Broadway / 307-733-2583
Bressler Outfitters, 485 West Broadway / 307-733-6934

High Country Flies, 185 North Center Street / 307-733-7210
Joe Allen's Scenic Fishing, 225 North Millward / 307-733-2400
Camp Creek Inn Fishing, 12330 South Hwy 191 / 307-733-3099
Teton Boating, P.O. Box 1553 / 307-733-2703
Spike Camp Sports, 852 West Broadway / 307-733-4406
Orvis of Jackson, 485 West Broadway Street / 307-733-5407
Reel Women, 2450 Shooting Iron Road, Jackson, WY 83001 or Box 289, Victor, ID
    83455 / 307-733-6390 / 208-787-2657
Westbank Anglers, 3670 North Moose Wilson Road, Teton Village, WY 83025 /
    307-733-6483
Flagg Ranch, South Entrance of Yellowstone Park; Moran, WY 83013 /
    307-543-2861
Fish Creek Ranch, P.O. Box 40, Wilson, WY 83014 / 307-733-3166
Triangle X Float Trips, Grand Teton National Park, Moose, WY 83012 /
    307-733-5500
Hanna Outfitting, P.O. Box 3832, Jackson WY 83001-3832 / 307-733-5065
Turpin Meadows Ranch, P.O. Box 379 Buffalo Valley, Moran WY 83013-0379 /
    307-543-2496, 800-743-2496
Coy's Wilderness Float/Fishing Trips, Horse Creek Station P.O. Box 3356; Jackson,
    WY 83001-3356 / 307-733-6726 or 800-368-0957
Crescent H Ranch, 1027 S. Fall Creek Road. P.O. Box 730, Wilson WY 83014-0730 /
    307-733-3674
Mangis Guide Service, P.O. Box 3165, Jackson WY 83001-3165 / 307-733-8553
Mill Iron Ranch, Horse Creek Road, P.O. Box 951, Jackson WY 83001-0951 /
    307-733-6390
John Henry Lee Outfitters, Box 8368 Jackson, WY 83001 / 307-733-944,
    800-3-JACKSON

FLY SHOPS AND SPORTING GOODS

Orvis of Jackson, 485 West Broadway Street / 307-733-5407
High Country Flies, 185 North Center Street / 307-733-7210
Jack Dennis Outdoor Shop, 50 East Broadway / 307-733-3270
Westbank Anglers, 3670 North Moose Wilson Road, Teton Village, WY 83025 /
    307-733-6483
Gart Sports, 455 West Broadway / 307-733-4449
Outdoor Sport Center, 1390 West Broadway / 307-733-4859
Rendezvous River Sports, 1035 West Broadway / 307-733-2471

AUTO RENTAL AND REPAIR

Alamo Rent A Car, 1250 East Airport Road / 307-733-0671
Thrifty Car Rental, 220 North Millward Street / 307-739-9300
Hertz Rent A Car, 1250 East Airport Road / 307-733-2272
Budget Rent A Car, 1250 East Airport Road / 307-733-2206

Ugly Duckling Rent-A-Car, 1075 South Hwy 89 / 307-733-3040
Rent-A-Wreck, 1050 South Hwy 89 / 307-733-5014
Browns Towing & Repairs, 4040 Pub Place / 307-733-6237
Jackson Hole Motors, 920 West Broadway / 307-733-2351
Chevron—Jackson Hole, 890 West Broadway / 307-733-7602

Air Service
Jackson Hole Airport / 307-733-7682 / Services include Delta Airlines,
American Airlines, and United Airlines/Charter services

Medical
St John's Hospital, 625 East Broadway Street / 307-733-3636

For More Information
Jackson Hole Chamber of Commerce
Box E
Jackson, WY 83001
307-733-3316 or 307-733-5585

Star Valley
Alpine to Afton
Elevation–6,000   Population–2,000

Star Valley, known as the "Little Switzerland of America," is a pastoral valley
dotted with dairy farms and small hamlets surrounded by rugged mountains on the
Wyoming–Idaho border. The Salt River flows down the center of the valley and to
the east the Greys River divides the Salt and Wyoming mountain ranges. At the top of
Star Valley is the resort town of Afton, and at the bottom is Alpine on the banks of the
Palisades Reservoir. The huge lake extending into Idaho flooded the confluence of
the Salt, Greys, and Snake Rivers. Be sure to visit Thayne's cheese factory and the
Intermittent Spring at Afton.

Accommodations
Hi-Country Inn, US Hwy 89, Afton, WY 83110 / 307-886-3856 / 30 units / Pets
allowed / $
Lazy B Motel, 219 Washington, Afton, WY 83110 / 307-886-3187 / 25 units / $
Mountain Inn Motel, U South Hwy 89, Afton, WY 83110 / 307-886-3156 / 20
units / Pets allowed / $
The Corral Motel, 161 Washington, Afton, WY 83110 / 307-886-5424 / 15 units /
Pets allowed / $
Alpen Haus Hotel, Alpine, WY 83110 / 307-654-7545 / 44 units / Pets allowed /
$$
Alpine Inn, Alpine, WY 83128 / 307-654-7644 / 10 units /$

Best Western, Hwy 89 & 26, Alpine, WY 83128 / 307-654-7561 / 26 units / Pets allowed / $
Lakeside Motel, Alpine, WY 83128 / 307-654-7507 / 11 units / Pets allowed / $
The Nordic Inn, Alpine, WY 83128 / 307-654-7556 / 11 units / $$
Silver Stream Lodge & Restaurant, Hwy 89, Thayne, WY 83127 / 307-883-2440 / 12 units / $

CAMPGROUNDS AND RV PARKS
Flat Creek RV Park, south of Thayne, WY 83127
Cottonwood Creek Campground, Smoot, WY 83126 / 307-886-5565
Burton Springs Trout Ranch, 1515 Kennington Burton Road, Afton, WY 83110 / 307-886-3517

RESTAURANTS
Homestead Restaurant, 84506 Highway 89 South, Afton, WY 83110 / 307-886-5558
Golden Spur Cafe, 484 Washington, Afton, WY 83110 / 307-886-9890
Red Baron Drive-In, 838 Washington, Afton, WY 83110 / 307-886-3745
Noodles Restaurant, Highway 89, Afton, WY 83110 / 307-886-3341
Silver Stream Lodge, State Highway 89 North, Thayne, WY 83127 / 307-883-2440
Elkhorn Family Restaurant, 465 Washington Street, Afton, WY 83110 / 307-886-3080
Bertrand's, Alpine, WY 83128 / 307-654-7508
Brenthoven's Restaurant, 1 Colonial Lane, Alpine, WY 83128 / 307-654-7556
Buffalo Station Restaurant, US Highway 89, Alpine, WY 83128 / 307-654-7578
Bette's Coffee Shop, US Highway 89, Alpine, WY 83128 / 307-654-7536
Gunnar's Pizza, US Highway 89, Alpine, WY 83128 / 307-654-7778
Best Western Inn, Highway 89 & 26, Alpine, WY 83128 / 307-654-7561
Thayne Cheese Factory, Thayne, WY 83127

VETERINARIANS
Star Valley Animal Care, 270 Madison Street, Afton, WY 83110 / 307-886-5572
All Creatures Great & Small, Highway 89, Afton, WY 83110 / 307-886-3005

OUTFITTERS
Box Y Guest Ranch, Rt. 1, Afton, WY 83110 / 307-886-5459
Jensen Hunting Camps, Rt. 1, Afton, WY 83110 / 307-886-3401
Bar Diamond Outfitters, Box 15, Thayne, WY 83127 / 307-883-2526 or 883-2386
Peterson's Hunting Camps, Box 1166, Afton, WY 83110 / 307-886-9693
The Tackle Box, Alpine, WY 83128 / 307-654-7762
Wolf Mountain Outfitters, Rt. 1, Afton, WY 83110 / 307-886-9317
Jenkins Hunting Camps, Box 172, Freedom, WY 83120 / 307-883-2649 or 883-2340
Forest Dell Guest Ranch, Smoot, WY 83126 / 307-886-5665

Burton Springs Trout Ranch, 1515 Kennington Burton Road, Afton, WY 83110 / 307-886-3517

Yellowstone Outfitters, Box 1156, Afton, WY 83110; 800-447-4711

FLY SHOPS AND SPORTING GOODS

Lone Pine Sports, 550 Washington Street, Afton, WY 83110 / 307-886-9581

Al's Sport'N Shop, 848 South Washington, Afton, WY 83110 / 307-886-3981

B G's Alpine Merc, Highway 26, Alpine, WY 83128 / 307-654-7509

Pea Pod, 117556 US Highway 89, Alpine, WY 83128 / 307-654-7694

Hitching Rail, 320 North Main Street, Thayne, WY 83127 / 307-883-2302

AUTO RENTAL AND REPAIR

Rob's Auto Service, North Highway 89, Afton, WY 83110 / 307-886-3244

Turner Automotive Repair, 700 South Washington Street, Afton, WY 83110 / 307-886-3644

Alpine Service & Repair, Greys River Road, Alpine, WY 83110 / 307-654-7515

AIR SERVICE

Nearest airline services are Jackson and Idaho Falls, ID

MEDICAL

Star Valley Hospital, 110 Hospital Lane, Afton, WY 83110 / 307-886-3841

FOR MORE INFORMATION

Afton–Star Valley Chamber of Commerce
498 Washington / P.O. Box 1097
Afton, WY 83110
307-886-5659

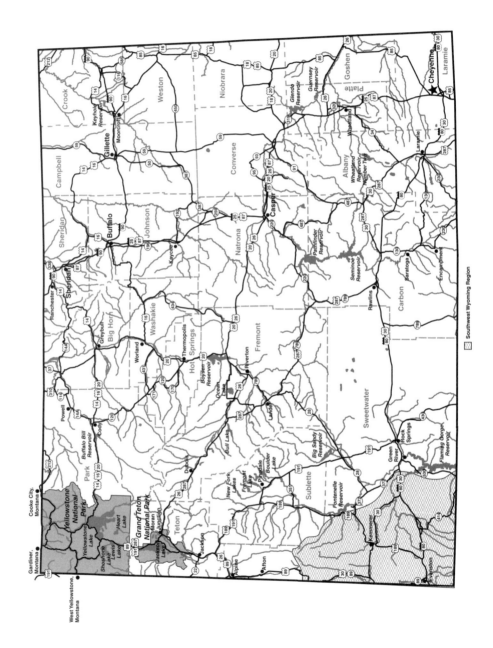

Southwest Wyoming Region

Southwest Wyoming
Tri Basin Divide

Wyoming's southwest corner presents another example of its complex geology. Geologists view it as a vast reserve of fossil fuels awaiting the next boom in oil exploration. Flyfishers often don't see it at all as they speed along Interstate 80 and take exits heading north to the Green, Snake, Yellowstone, and other renowned rivers of western Wyoming.

But a look above the desolate, arid landscape presents several interesting prospects for fly casters. If you like to explore quiet backcountry streams, pause and examine the highlands. A parting of the waters occurs on the mountains to the north that splits the region into three basins. Mountain tributaries flowing from humble beginnings eventually end up in the Pacific Ocean via the Snake and Colorado Rivers and Utah's enclosed Great Basin via the Bear River.

The Tri Basin's streams are home to three of Wyoming's five subspecies of native trout—Colorado River cutthroat in the Green River drainage, Bonneville cutthroat in the Bear River drainage, and Snake River finespotted cutthroat in the Snake's drainage.

The best fishing for these native trout is in the southern tip of Bridger-Teton National Forest. It won't be a big fish quest, but it will be fun. Excellent fishing for nonnative rainbow and brown trout is found in the Hams Fork River and Lake Viva Naughton above Kemmerer. However, the region's largest river, the Bear, presents a very limited fishing option due to its passage through private ranches and farms.

The region is rich in pioneer and geological history. Interesting side trips include Fort Bridger Historical Site and Fossil Butte National Monument. The two principal towns in this very sparsely populated area are Evanston and Kemmerer.

It is a good idea to replenish supplies and top off gas tanks before going into the backcountry. While a web of gravel roads laces the region's interior, there are no services. Some routes to public fishing waters involve round trips of up to 100 miles. Several one way routes to the next town are even longer.

Northern entrances to the Tri Basin divide are reached by driving south from Afton to the Salt River Pass on U.S. 89 or taking the 60-mile forest road up the Greys River to its source. A 40-mile gravel road from the east parallels LaBarge Creek, northwest of the village of LaBarge on U.S. 189.

Cutthroat Crossroads

Matching the hatch to catch 9-inch cutthroat was the last thing I expected when I invited myself to a creel census on LaBarge Creek. While diminutive trout were to be expected in the high mountain stream, it was the novelty of a new breed of cutthroat that drew me to the Green River tributary.

Rare gems, Colorado River cutthroat are among the most colorful members of its far-ranging clan. Blue-green parr marks march down pale lemon yellow flanks,

Tri Basin Divide

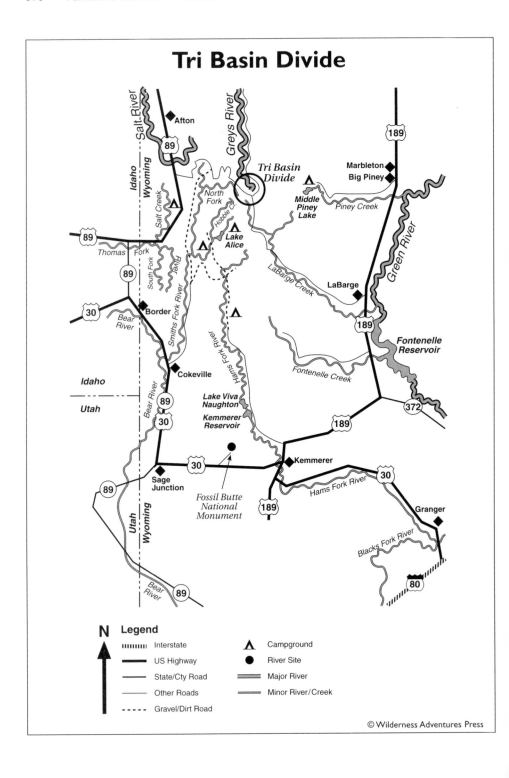

N

Legend

ⅲⅲⅲⅲ	Interstate	▲	Campground
—	US Highway	●	River Site
—	State/Cty Road	▬	Major River
—	Other Roads	▬	Minor River/Creek
----	Gravel/Dirt Road		

© Wilderness Adventures Press

speckled by a sprinkling of black spots which concentrate towards the tail. Delicate paired fins are salmon orange. Gill plates dusted with rouge and orange-red slash marks under the jaws are characteristic of the breed.

Flurries of small western green drakes were enticing the toy fish to rise. A quick baker's dozen hammered the lone No. 10 olive Flav pattern still left in my overstuffed vest. One even pushed the 12-inch mark and presented a reasonable tussle. Several sassy brook trout and a catapulting cutthroat-rainbow hybrid also attacked the fly before it became a tooth-torn sodden mess that refused to float. Later, a No. 14 parachute hopper redeemed my faith in cutthroat intellect.

My partner in the stream survey was Dave Nolte, Trout Unlimited's coordinator for the Bureau of Land Management's Bring Back the Natives program. We had traded trout tales twice before, but this time we got to fish together. The first day, his personal concoction—a gray-bodied deer-hair humpy—saved our team from undue embarrassment by the creek's fussy cutthroat. But the hard-hitting brook trout still in the stream were a mixed blessing.

The annual LaBarge Creek creel census is the fun part of a labor intensive stream restoration project called the Green River Rendezvous for Conservation. All the participants harbor a soft spot for cutthroat. Many journey from as far away as Illinois to volunteer assistance.

It is the brainchild of Ed Michael, president of the Chicago-based Oak Brook Trout Unlimited chapter. A native of Casper, he has long been concerned about the "plight of the interior cutthroat and decided to do something about it.

"One summer I drove all over the Green River Drainage trying to find a viable spot for Colorado River cutthroat recovery," he reminisced. "I liked the LaBarge because it has a long run (through 38 miles of national forest) before it enters private lands. It also had a previous management agreement between TU and state and federal agencies."

Getting Chicago flyfishers to sign on for the project was easy, Michael said. "Obviously, the Illinois chapter doesn't have its own trout stream. We all saw this as an opportunity to make a contribution."

Restoration efforts have been directed at eliminating nonnative species and reestablishing genetic purity of the native trout. It's hoped the smaller creeks will become cutthroat feeder streams to the upper LaBarge.

Working in tandem with Wyoming TU chapters, Wyoming Game and Fish, BLM and the U.S. Forest Service, the volunteers' first job in 1993 was to replace a migration barrier on Rock Creek and repair fencing to keep cattle out of its riparian area. Similar work continues, but perhaps the most intensive task through the years is electroshocking and handpicking nonnative brook and rainbow trout from tributaries like Clear Creek.

"Colorado River cutthroat trout now occupy less than 1 percent of their historic range," said Mike Stone, assistant director of Wyoming Game and Fish. "The department is aggressively attempting to restore this sensitive subspecies and avoid listing" it as an endangered or threatened species.

The Tri Basin Divide.

The state's recovery programs for Colorado River cutthroat and the even rarer Bonneville cutthroat stress habitat protection and improvement, including rehabilitation of streams by removal of nonnative trout and hatchery stocking to expand and upgrade genetic purity of existing populations. Stricter regulations limit fishing harvest in key waters.

An education program initiated in 1996 attempts to encourage further public support by promoting appreciation of all the state's native trout. It awards a Cutt Slam certificate to anglers who score a four-bagger, or grand slam, of the Yellowstone, Snake River finespotted, Bonneville, and Colorado River subspecies. The westslope cutthroat wasn't included in the grand slam because its Wyoming population is confined to Cougar and Specimen Creeks in Yellowstone National Park.

LaBarge Creek is one of three streams flowing off the Tri Basin Divide between the Salt and Wyoming mountain ranges, southeast of Afton and northwest of the village of LaBarge. The other two are the Smiths Fork of the Bear River and the Greys River, a tributary of the Snake. All three flow to a different basin—LaBarge Creek to the Colorado Basin and the southern Pacific, Smith's Fork to the Great Basin and the Great Salt Lake, and Greys River to the Columbia Basin and the northern Pacific. Each harbors a cutthroat subspecies unique to its basin.

Flyfishers cruising Tri Basin's streams have a chance at scoring a hat trick or at least a double-hitter to help complete a Cutt Slam. Before embarking, obtain a copy of the Bridger-Teton National Forest's map for the Big Piney, Greys River, and Kemmerer Ranger Districts.

LaBarge Creek

The headwaters of LaBarge Creek skirt the southern foothills of the Wyoming Mountain Range and meander across a sprawling mountain meadow carpeted with dazzling bouquets of wildflowers in midsummer. It then turns southeast on its descent down a narrow forested valley to the sagebrush desert above its merger with the Green River.

There are more than 20 miles of public access to the creek along the national forest road that begins 20 miles west of LaBarge on U.S. 189. At LaBarge Meadows below the Tri Basin Divide, the gravel forest road forks in two directions. The north fork parallels the Greys River for 60 miles to Alpine. The 20-mile west fork skims the North Fork of the Smiths Fork en route to Salt River Pass on U.S. 89, south of Afton and north of Cokeville.

LaBarge Creek has good fishing for cutthroat and decreasing numbers of brookies and rainbows in the 8- to 12-inch range. Big Fall Creek, its first tributary just inside the forest boundary west of LaBarge, has a strong population of larger rainbows. South LaBarge Creek also has some bigger fish than the mother stream due to hybridization between cutthroat and rainbows.

Special regulations on the LaBarge and its tributaries limit cutthroat harvest to one per day or in possession.

LaBarge Creek stair steps down its narrow valley in a series of riffles and runs, cutbank pools, braided channels and brushy meandering flats. Several twisting runs behind the foothills offer chances to get away from roadside traffic.

Fish in remote mountain streams are not overly selective, so a collection of generic mayfly and caddis patterns, as well as standard attractors, generally work.

"Fishing the correct life stage can be critical, however," noted Ed Michael, president of Chicago's Oak Brook Trout Unlimited chapter. "The trout on LaBarge Creek are fussy enough to refuse adult caddis when they are really concentrating on the emerging insect."

It is a long way back to a fly shop so it helps to come prepared. Generic dry flies should include Adams, size 12 to 20; renegades, 12 to 16; red, royal, and yellow humpies, 10 to 18; gray and royal Wulffs, 12 to 18; and elk hair caddis, 12 to 18. For matching hatches, also pack baetis or BWOs, 14 to 22; pale morning duns, 16 to 18; rusty spinners, 14 to 18; green drakes, Flavs, and western slate-wing olives, 12 to 16; grays drakes and callibaetis, 12 to 16; and tricos and black-and-whites, 18 to 22. For terrestrials, pack ants and beetles, 14 to 16, and grasshoppers, 8 to 12.

Wet flies can include caddis pupa, emergers, and soft-hackles, 14 to 18; Prince, hare's ear, and pheasant tail nymphs, 10 to 20; black, olive, and brown woolly buggers, Zug bugs, black rubberlegs, girdlebugs, Bitch Creek nymphs, and Montana stones, 2 to 8. Small muddler minnows, 4 to 8, and other streamers also are useful.

Short lightweight rods and hip boots work well on small mountain streams and meadow runs. But even if you decide to wade wet, it is best to wear wading boots with felt soles rather than tennis shoes. Also wear polarized sunglasses so you can watch where you are going. The clarity of high mountain streams makes it difficult

The upper, wooded section of LaBarge Creek.

to gauge water depth. Avoid going in over your hips in swift channels or at the tops of deep pools.

The LaBarge's easy access and ample elbow room make it a good family fishing destination and an excellent stream for newcomers who can hone their fly casting skills. There are no developed campgrounds, but camping is permitted throughout the forest.

HAMS FORK RIVER

North of Kemmerer is a three-star complex presenting some of the best fishing in western Wyoming. Many anglers are just starting to hear about the Hams Fork River and its two impoundments, the Kemmerer City Reservoir and Lake Viva Naughton.

The river has strong populations of 10- to 14-inch rainbows and browns, with excellent prospects for fish exceeding 20 inches. The reservoirs fish well for 14- to 18-inch rainbows, and with recent good water years they are producing fish well over 20 inches.

Lake Viva Naughton is a 7,000-acre reservoir popular with deep-water boat fishermen. Fly casters can work the shallows from shore in spring or fall, or float tube near inlet streams by hiking to the west bank. There is no road to the west side of the lake. Parking, supplies, a cafe and a campground are available at the Lake Viva Naughton Marina on the north end of the reservoir.

The 130-acre Kemmerer City Reservoir is managed as a trophy fishery. There is a 13- to 20-inch slot limit and a 2-trout creel limit. Fishing is permitted only with flies or lure, and no motorized boats are allowed. Because its banks are weedy, float-tubers do best.

Public access is good on the lower Hams Fork along WYO 233. A 4-mile easement obtained by Wyoming Game and Fish in 1996 now grants access to 8 miles of streambank on the Hams Fork downstream from the city reservoir.

Access is restricted to a half mile below Naughton Dam on perhaps the most popular stretch of the river. However, by paying $10 on the honor system, the landowner permits fishing on another 2 miles down to the city reservoir. This is also a special regulation section. Trout between 13 and 20 inches must be released, and only 1 may exceed 20 inches in the 2-fish bag and possession limit. Fishing is restricted to flies and lures, and this section and portions of the lower river and several tributaries are closed to fishing April 1 to June 30. Check fishing regulations for landmarks.

The brush is thick in the narrow run between the reservoirs, and the fish are tough to reach. But trophy trout exceeding 20 inches lurk in the deeper pools. In fall, a streamer or woolly bugger with a beadhead nymph dropper 8 to 10 inches behind it can be especially effective. Through the spring and summer the fish may be exasperatingly selective, so it pays to bring a good assortment of flies.

The river below the city reservoir opens up and flows through a broad pastoral valley. It descends in a series of riffles and runs, pools and cutbanks. It breaks into two channels part way down its meadow run and then rejoins in a large pool bordered by swampy banks.

The lower river is fairly easy to wade, and there's plenty of elbowroom to cast. Its flows are crystal clear, so long delicate leaders are required. Medium-sized stonefly nymphs are effective year-round, along with small nymphs and emergers. Caddis are the predominant dry fly hatch, but also watch for sporadic mayfly activity and midges. As it is a meadow stream, hoppers and other terrestrials can be effective through late summer.

The Hams Fork also can be fished in Kemmerer at its city park and in the Bridger-Teton Forest, about 15 miles north of town.

The upper Hams Fork is a small mountain stream with long meadow runs. It has good fishing for 8- to 12-inch rainbows, browns and brookies. Spawning rainbows run upstream from Lake Viva Naughton in spring and linger into early summer.

The road paralleling the upper Hams Fork is another route into Hobble Creek and Lake Alice's Bonneville cutthroat.

Bear River

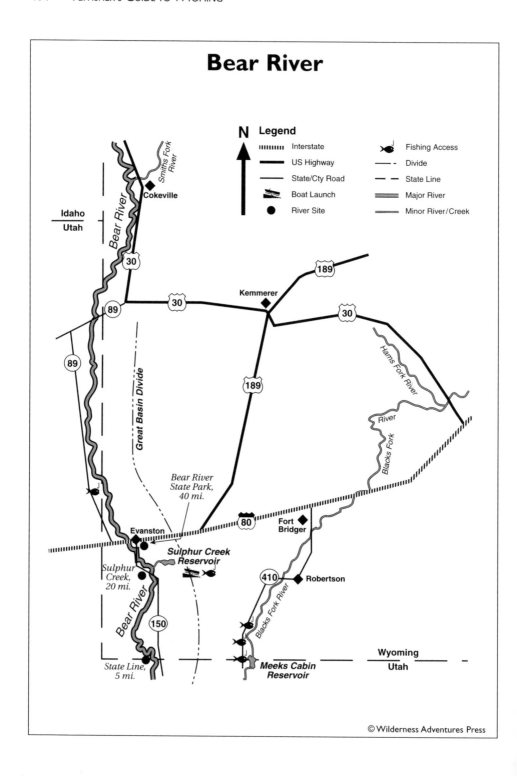

BEAR RIVER

On its 45-mile flirtation with Wyoming, the Bear River crosses the Utah border 35 miles south of Evanston and temporarily returns to its home state about 5 miles north of town. It dips briefly back into Wyoming north of the U.S. 30/89 intersection at Border and departs the state for good near Cokeville on its big loop through Idaho and down into Utah to the Great Salt Lake.

The only good fishing on the river is at Evanston, with public access in town and at Bear River State Park, and downstream at the Woodruff Narrows Reservoir. Upstream from Evanston, fishing is very marginal due to loss of habitat, plus it flows entirely through farm and ranch land with no public access. The same conditions occur along its Cokeville run.

Stream restoration work at Evanston has improved the river's one bright spot in recent years. This section is rated as good fishing for 12- to 16-inch Bonneville cutthroat, rainbows and browns, with some fish going larger.

From Bear River State Park and downstream through Evanston the trout limit is 2 per day or in possession. Only 1 may exceed 20 inches.

Bear River Tributaries

Smiths Fork

The Smiths Fork barely graduates to river size on its 40-mile course from the southern foothills of the Salt Mountains to its merger with the Bear River at Cokeville on U.S. 89/30.

On its upper passage through the forest and Bureau of Land Management rangelands it fishes like a small mountain stream similar to LaBarge Creek. The big difference is that the 6- to 12-inch trout are Bonneville cutthroat.

The bottom 15 miles of the Smiths Fork take on characteristics of a small river as they wind through ranch and farm country. The trout are larger in the lower river—10- to 18-inch cutthroat and browns—but landowner permission is required to fish it.

Special regulations on all tributaries of the Bear River, including the Smiths Fork, require the release of any cutthroat less than 10 inches. Fishing is permitted with flies or lures only.

The scenic forest road from Salt River Pass to LaBarge Meadows skirts the top 5 or 6 miles of the river and provides easy access. However, the Dry Fork Road that follows the remainder of the river when it turns south is very primitive. It is not recommended for sedans or compact cars. It also swings away from the Smiths Fork where it splits into two channels at the Dry Fork. A paved road follows the river upstream from Cokeville for about 12 miles, but the BLM road above it quickly deteriorates into a primitive road on its route to the Dry Fork. A BLM map is recommended for travel in this section.

At the end of the paved road from Cokeville is the turnoff to the Hams Fork Road. It is a rough gravel road that leads to the upper Hams Fork River and Hobble Creek, a tributary of the Smiths Fork. Hobble Creek has excellent late summer fishing for 10- to 12-inch Bonneville cutthroat, plus small brookies and browns.

The outlet of the largest alpine lake in this region, 210-acre Lake Alice, flows into Hobble Creek. Created by a landslide long ago, it is the only lake in Wyoming with Bonneville cutthroat. It is a 1-mile hike upstream from the Hobble Creek Campground, close enough to pack a float tube. It is rated as excellent fishing for 8- to 15-inch fish, but all cutthroat less than 10 inches must be released. Lake Alice's upstream tributaries are closed to fishing from April 1 through June 30.

Thomas Fork River

Midway between Afton and Cokeville on U.S. 89, the tiny Thomas Fork River and dainty Salt Creek merge just before the Thomas Fork enters Idaho and joins the Bear River downstream. There is good road access to the Thomas Fork upstream from a general store and motel at the border, as well as upstream in the forest. Salt Creek flows entirely through national forest along the highway's narrow valley.

Both offer pleasant stopovers on the way home or en route to Afton's Salt River or Jackson's Snake River. Again, Bonneville cutthroat are the quarry. The Thomas Fork is rated as good fishing for 10- to 17-inch cutthroat.

Cutt Slam: Father and Daughter Score First Award

A father-daughter flyfishing team from Casper scored the state's first Cutt Slam in August 1996. The Game and Fish Department award is given to anglers who catch four subspecies of cutthroat trout in Wyoming.

Bill Mixer and his daughter, MacKenzie, spent their summer vacation on four different waterways to catch, photograph, and release Yellowstone, Snake River finespotted, Colorado River, and Bonneville cutthroat.

The program requires each subspecies to be caught in its native waters. So the Mixers went from Casper to Big Piney, south around the Wyoming Mountain Range to Cokeville, and then north to Jackson and Yellowstone National Park to tally their feat.

"My daughter and I try and take a week-long flyfishing excursion every summer," Mixer said. "After I read about the program in Wyoming Wildlife, I decided we'd dedicate this summer's trip to catching all the state's cutthroat, and it worked out great."

Mixer and his 10-year-old daughter hooked all their fish on terrestrial fly patterns. Tricking a trout with a dry fly is old hat to MacKenzie, because she's been flyfishing since she was six. The Cutt Slam pursuit produced the first Colorado River and Bonneville cutthroats of her dad's 20-year flyfishing career. "We discovered some intriguing country in pursuit of these subspecies (Colorado River and Bonneville), and I plan to go back there fishing," said Mixer, director of Casper College's Environmental Training Center. "I think the program certainly accomplishes the Game and Fish's goal of promoting appreciation and understanding of cutthroat habitat."

A year later, Petr Axamit of Liberec, Czech Republic, became the first foreigner to score a Cutt Slam. Owner of a small travel agency providing fishing services for foreigners in the Czech Republic, Axamit said he was impressed with the "very high standard of basic ecological education and thinking" in Wyoming. "One of the smartest ideas of how to involve people into nature conservation is the Cutthroat Trout Grand Slam," he said. "In this non-competitive contest, you will get a lot of new knowledge in a very interesting form if you have to try fishing in four different areas."

Axamit was in Jackson in September 1997 to participate in the World Flyfishing Championship. "I wanted to meet my fishing friends again and visit Grand Teton and Yellowstone National Parks and the Wild West. I made new business contacts and was able to fish in unspoiled country, especially for cutthroat trout," he said.

"Once an angler catches all four subspecies, we send them a color certificate featuring the four subspecies as a pat on the back, recognizing their accomplishment," said Remmick, Green River fisheries supervisor. "We had 12 anglers complete the Slam before Petr, and to have someone from another country qualify adds another dimension to the purpose of the program," said Remmick.

For more information about the Cutt Slam program, write to the Information Section, Wyoming Game and Fish Department, 5400 Bishop Blvd, Cheyenne, WY 82006.

Colorado River cutthroat.

SOUTHWEST HUB CITIES
Evanston
Elevation–6,748   Population–10,900

Evanston started as a railroad town in the 1870s. It is also on the Oregon Trail which parallels present day Interstate 80 and remains an important stopover for travelers going east and west. The town's largest population growth occurred in the 1980s when oil reserves in the Overthrust Belt were developed during the period's energy crisis. Its growth has stabilized since the boom.

Evanston's zip code is 82930.

ACCOMMODATIONS
Alexander Motel, 248 Bear River Drive, Evanston, WY 82930-2803 / 307-789-2346 / 19 units / Pets allowed / $

Bear River Inn & Truck Stop, 261 US Hwy 30 E & I-80 / 307-789-0791 / 91 units / Pets allowed / $

Best Western Dunmar Inn, West Entrance Harrison Drive, Evanston, WY 82930 / 307-789-3770 / 166 units / Pets allowed / $$

Evanston Inn, 247 Bear River Drive, Evanston, WY 82930-2801 / 307-789-6212 / 160 units / $

Hillcrest Motel, 1725 West Lincoln Hwy / 307-789-1111 / 40 units / Pets allowed / $

CAMPGROUNDS AND RV PARKS
Phillips RV Trailer Park, 225 Bear River Drive / 307-789-3805 / March 15 to November 11 / 56 RV and 3 tent sites / Full-service

Sunset RV Park, 196 Bear River Drive / 307-789-3763 / March 15 to November 11 / 62 RV and 6 tent sites / Full-service

RESTAURANTS
Lotty's Family Restaurant, 1925 Harrison Drive / 307-789-9660

Legal Tender Restaurant, 1601 Harrison Drive / 307-789-3770

New Garden Cafe, 333 Front Street / 307-789-1256

El Rancho Grande Restaurant, 528 County Road / 307-789-9642

Quarter Pole, 1920 Harrison Drive / 307-789-9530

Grazia's, 123 10th Street / 307-789-8720

VETERINARIANS
Bear River Veterinary Clinic, 619 Almy Road 107 / 307-789-5230

MJB Animal Clinic, 2301 Wasatch Road / 307-789-4289

FLY SHOPS AND SPORTING GOODS
Bear River Gun & Pawn, 1037 Front Street / 307-789-0830

AUTO RENTAL AND REPAIR
Affordable Used Car Rental, 101 Bear River Drive / 307-789-3096
Grandma's Tires of Evanston, 217 Bear River Drive / 307-789-8632
Amoco, 1901 Harrison Drive / 307-789-9330
Flying J Travel Plaza, 1920 Harrison Drive / 307-789-9129

AIR SERVICE
No airline services.

MEDICAL
IHC Evanston Hospital, 190 Arrowhead Drive / 307-789-3636

FOR MORE INFORMATION
Evanston Chamber of Commerce
36 10th Street
Evanston, WY 82931
307-789-2757

Kemmerer and Diamondville
Elevation–6,972   Population 3,500

Kemmerer and its sister city, Diamondville, are mining communities that also experienced a boom during the energy crisis of the 1980s. Kemmerer is the home of the JC Penney department stores. The "mother store" is still open for business on the corner of the town square. Fossil Butte National Monument is west of town and north of U.S. 30.

ACCOMMODATIONS
Antler's Motel, 419 Coral Street, Kemmerer, WY 83101-3298 / 307-877-4461 /
    58 units; pets allowed / $
Burnett's New Motel, 1326 Central Avenue, Kemmerer, WY 83101-3598 /
    307-877-4471
Fossil Butte Motel, 1424 Central Avenue, Kemmerer, WY 83101-3599 /
    307-877-3996 / 13 units; pets allowed / $
Lake Viva Naughton Marina, WYO 233, 10 miles north of Kemmerer / 307-877-9669
    / 34 units; pets allowed / $

CAMPGROUNDS AND RV PARKS
Riverside RV Park, 216 Spinel Street, Kemmerer, WY 83101 / 307-877-3416 /
    May 1 to Oct. 15 / 30 RV sites / full services

Lake Viva Naughton Marina, WYO 233, 10 miles north of Kemmerer /
307-877-9669 / Year-round / 35 RV and 100 tent sites / Full services

RESTAURANTS
Lake Viva Naughton Marina, WYO 233, 10 miles north of Kemmerer /
307-877-9669
Polar King Drive-In, U.S. 189, Kemmerer, WY 83101 / 307-877-9448
Tom's Place, 1433 Central Avenue, Kemmerer, WY 83101 / 307-877-9412
Sagebrush Sue's, 801 South Main Street, Kemmerer, WY 83101 / 307-877-4007
Luigi's, 915 Susie, Diamondville, WY 83116 / 307-877-6221

VETERINARIANS
Western Veterinary Service, 1702 Antelope Street, Kemmerer, WY 83101 /
307-877-3445

FLY SHOPS AND SPORTING GOODS
Capellen Sporting Goods, N Highway 189, Kemmerer, WY 83101 / 307-877-9231
Van Beacham's Solitary Angler, Kemmerer, WY / Booking agent: Los Rios Anglers,
Box 4006, 226C Paseo Del Norte, Taos, NM 87571, 505-758-2798 or 800-748-1707
The Fontenelle Store, Fontenelle Dam, RR1, Kemmerer, WY 83101 / 307-877-4844

AUTO RENTAL AND REPAIR
Frontier Ford Mercury, 12 Lincoln Street, Diamondville, WY 83116 / 307-877-6966
/ Car rental
Auto Inn Repair, 414 Aspen Avenue, Kemmerer, WY 83101 / 307-877-3380
Don's Service & Supply, 1005 Pine Avenue, Kemmerer, WY 83101 / 307-877-4526

AIR SERVICE
No airline services.

MEDICAL
South Lincoln Medical Center, Moose & Onyx, Kemmerer, WY 83101 /
307-877-4401

FOR MORE INFORMATION
Kemmerer Chamber of Commerce
800 Pine Avenue
Kemmerer, WY 83101
307-877-9761

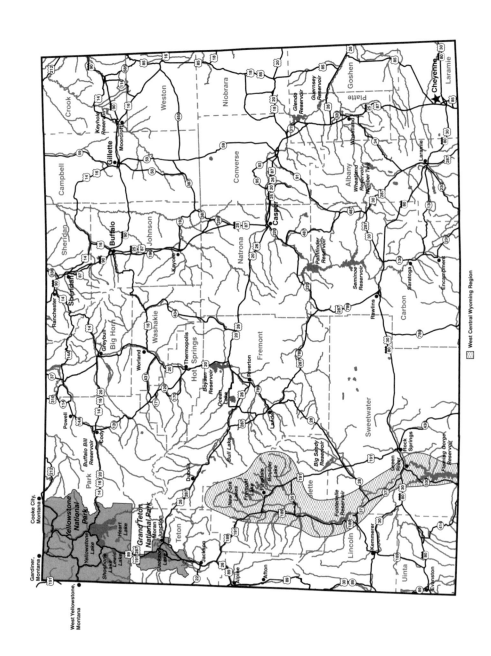

West Central Wyoming
Big Sky Rendezvous Country

One of the most famous landmarks in North American history, the Green River hosted the annual rendezvous of fur traders, mountain men, and Indian tribes a score of times between 1825 and 1840.

The period is fondly remembered as the last completely wild and free days of the West. Pinedale commemorates its history at the Museum of the Mountain Men. The Green River Rendezvous, centered on the second Sunday of July, is a subdued, family-oriented party compared to the riotous summer flings of the early 1800s.

A resort town nestled on the western shoulders of the Wind River Mountains, Pinedale is a flyfishing paradise surrounded by unrivaled alpine scenery. Far off the beaten path, it boasts that its main street has no stoplight. In another era, it was further from a railroad than any other U.S. town. Today, it is the most removed from an interstate highway—I-80, which is 115 miles south at the town of Green River.

The Green and New Fork Rivers present some of the best early summer fishing in western Wyoming since they're usually the first in the area to clear. Late summer and autumn fishing is serene and uncrowded. The region's Finger Lakes at the base of the Wind River Range are popular drive-in fisheries. Trailheads at most of these glacial lakes tempt visitors from around the world to hike up to more than 650 trout-filled alpine lakes dotting the majestic ramparts of the Bridger Wilderness.

The Green River collects the snowfed tributaries of the Wind River and Wyoming mountain ranges on a 2,100-mile journey to the Gulf of California and the Pacific Ocean via the Colorado River.

The town of Green River is the principal service center for the lower river below Fontenelle Reservoir and the huge Flaming Gorge Reservoir that extends past the Utah border. Fishing is great right through the center of town, too.

The best route connecting the dots between Green River and Pinedale follows the river. To go north from Green River turn at the WYO 372 exit on I-80. The state highway intersects with U.S. 189 at Fontenelle, and U.S. 189 meets U.S. 191 at Daniel Junction, 10 miles west of Pinedale.

GREEN RIVER

From snowfed trickles flowing off the west slopes of the Wind River Mountains, the Green River flows 700 miles to join the Colorado River and continue its 2,100-mile journey to the Gulf of California and the Pacific Ocean.

Wyoming's second longest river is considered by many to be the headwaters of the Colorado. However, when 16th-century Spanish explorers discovered the Green's lower canyon, they were unaware of the vastness of the West's interior. It was named Rio Verde because its flows were clearer than the muddy reds of the Little Colorado and Colorado. In the 19th century, the Green was a favorite site for the annual Mountain Men Rendezvous—riotous summer parties and fur trading conclaves. Some of the revelers called it the Spanish River, and others used the Crow Indians' name, *Seeds-ka-dee*, which means sage grouse.

By any name, the Green ranks as a top-notch flyfishing stream in a remote, picturesque basin where more antelope than people still roam.

The Green ran wild and free until 1963 when the Fontenelle Dam trapped its flows midway down its 300-mile passage through Wyoming. A year later the dam at Dutch John, Utah, inundated the scenic Flaming Gorge for nearly 90 miles to the outskirts of Green River City.

Flaming Gorge is a deep-water fishery for monster lake trout and trophy browns. It set a world record for brown trout in 1977 and bested its own record in 1982. The smaller Fontenelle Reservoir is an unheralded fishery for good-sized rainbows and browns.

While 150 miles of the river still flow free, an advisory council recommended in the late 1990s that more impoundments be created on the Green or its tributaries to keep Wyoming's Colorado River apportionment within the state. One proposal would place a small dam on lower Green River Lake. The so-called excess water would be diverted into the North Platte River drainage to bolster industrial development in eastern Wyoming. How far the plan will go and what effect it will have on the Green's fishery remains uncertain.

For flyfishers, the river's special charms are prolific mayfly and caddis hatches and eager wild trout, including the native Colorado River cutthroat. There also is excellent nymph and streamer fishing for large rainbows and browns.

The most popular reach is from Green River Lakes to Daniel Junction, west of Pinedale. Fishing is best in late summer and fall. The tailwater fishery below Fontenelle, down through the Seedskadee National Wildlife Refuge, gains increased recognition annually. It has good spring and fall fishing, but summer flows may be erratic because of the dam.

Substantial public access is available along state and federal lands on much of the upper river. Hardest to get onto are private property stretches below the Bridger-Teton National Forest boundary and between Daniel Junction and the confluence of the New Fork River. There are several public access sites between the New Fork and

Green River
Green River Lakes to Daniel Junction

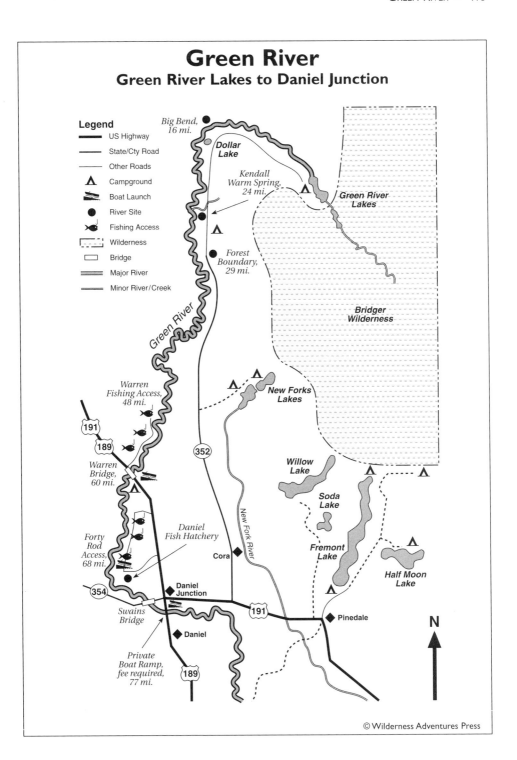

Legend

▬▬▬	US Highway
───	State/Cty Road
───	Other Roads
⛰	Campground
🛶	Boat Launch
●	River Site
✕	Fishing Access
⬚	Wilderness
▭	Bridge
≈≈≈	Major River
───	Minor River/Creek

Big Bend, 16 mi.

Dollar Lake

Kendall Warm Spring, 24 mi.

Green River Lakes

Forest Boundary, 29 mi.

Green River

Bridger Wilderness

Warren Fishing Access, 48 mi.

191

189

New Forks Lakes

352

Warren Bridge, 60 mi.

Willow Lake

Soda Lake

Forty Rod Access, 68 mi.

New Fork River

Daniel Fish Hatchery

Cora

Fremont Lake

Half Moon Lake

354

Daniel Junction

191

Pinedale

Swains Bridge

Daniel

Private Boat Ramp, fee required, 77 mi.

189

N

© Wilderness Adventures Press

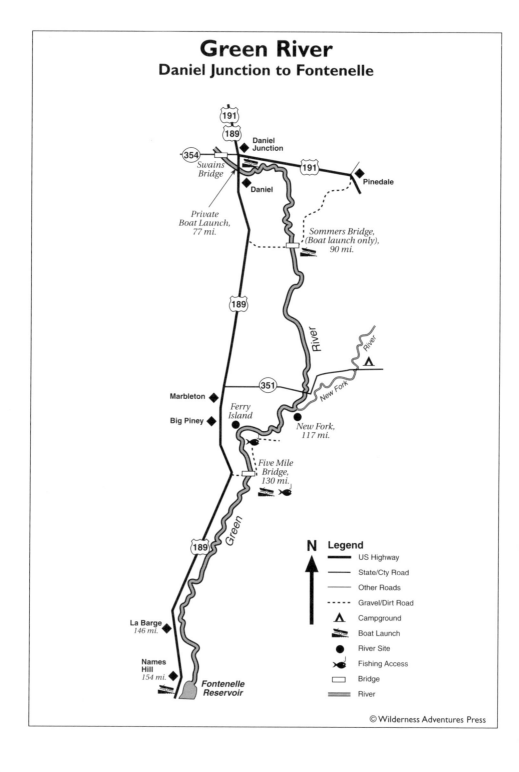

Green River
Daniel Junction to Fontenelle

191
189
Daniel
Junction
354
*Swains
Bridge*
191
Pinedale
*Private
Boat Launch,
77 mi.*
Daniel
*Sommers Bridge,
(Boat launch only),
90 mi.*
189
River
River
351
New Fork
Marbleton
*Ferry
Island*
Big Piney
New Fork,
117 mi.
*Five Mile
Bridge,
130 mi.*
Green
189
N
Legend
————— US Highway
———— State/Cty Road
——— Other Roads
- - - - - Gravel/Dirt Road
Λ Campground
Boat Launch
● River Site
Fishing Access
▭ Bridge
═══ River
La Barge
146 mi.
Names
Hill
154 mi.
**Fontenelle
Reservoir**

© Wilderness Adventures Press

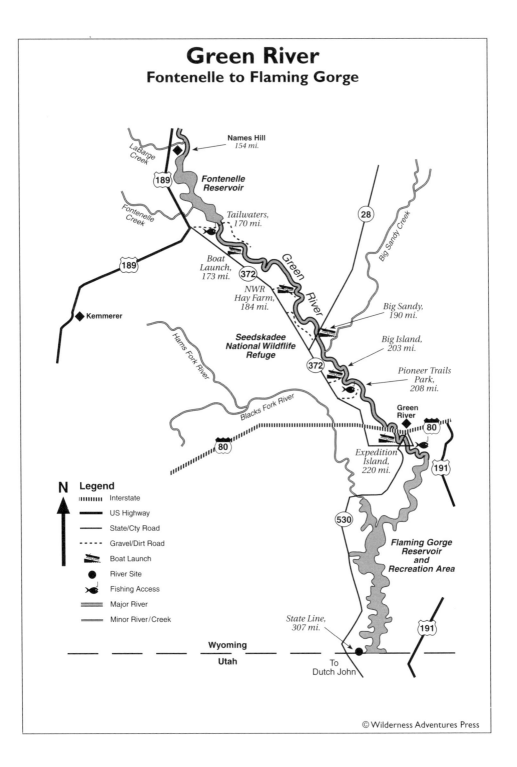

Green River
Fontenelle to Flaming Gorge

Names Hill
154 mi.

LaBarge Creek

189

Fontenelle Reservoir

Fontenelle Creek

Tailwaters,
170 mi.

Boat Launch,
173 mi.

372

189

NWR Hay Farm,
184 mi.

Kemmerer

Green River

28

Big Sandy Creek

Big Sandy,
190 mi.

Seedskadee National Wildlife Refuge

Hams Fork River

Big Island,
203 mi.

372

Pioneer Trails Park,
208 mi.

Blacks Fork River

Green River

80

80

191

Expedition Island,
220 mi.

530

Flaming Gorge Reservoir and Recreation Area

Legend

N

⁍⁍⁍⁍⁍	Interstate
——	US Highway
—	State/Cty Road
- - - -	Gravel/Dirt Road
⌁	Boat Launch
●	River Site
⤢	Fishing Access
▬	Major River
—	Minor River/Creek

State Line,
307 mi.

191

Wyoming

Utah

To Dutch John

© Wilderness Adventures Press

Fontenelle Reservoir. From the dam down through the desert and including the town of Green River, public access is good.

Where there is bank access, wading is relatively easy, but the Green has many long meandering runs, braided channels, and deep pools that are covered best in a float boat or fishing raft. While it is a great river for beginner and intermediate flyfishers, it presents ample technical challenges to test the mettle of advanced anglers. And the alpine horizons surrounding this beautiful river are spectacular.

The resort town of Pinedale on U.S. 191 is the principal service center for the upper Green River, and its attractions are strong enough to draw day visitors from Jackson. Fly shops in both towns keep track of the river's hatches and offer guided float-fishing trips. Shuttle services for those who want to float their own boats, rafts, or canoes can be arranged in Pinedale.

The town of Green River on I-80 is the main service center for the lower river, and its attractions are strong enough to draw the attention of Evanston. Fly shops and outfitters in both towns provide equipment and offer guided trips. Shuttle services can be arranged through The Fontenelle Store at the dam.

Upper Green River

Square Top Mountain's reflection in Green River Lakes is the most photographed scene in the Wind River Range. The picture is almost reward enough for the long bumpy drive to the source of the Green River.

Small brook trout and whitefish are prevalent in the outlet, but as the river increases in width and strength, its trout grow in size and variety. The upper Green River, down through Daniel Junction to Fontenelle Reservoir, has an abundant population of rainbows from 10 to 16 inches, with good possibilities of catching trophies exceeding 20 inches. Browns in the 14- to 18-inch range are routinely netted, and lunkers over 20 inches await dedicated fly casters. Enhanced efforts to return Colorado River cutthroat to the river has resulted in increases in number and size of the native trout.

Green River Lakes are 50 miles northwest of Pinedale at the fringe of the Bridger Wilderness in the Wind River Mountains. The turnoff from U.S. 191 to WYO 352 is 6 miles west of town. The state road is paved for 25 miles to the Bridger-Teton National Forest boundary, where a rough gravel road continues north 20 miles to Green River Lakes Campground.

Exiting the big lake, the river carves a 12-mile loop to the northwest before cutting almost due south through a high plains valley dotted with sagebrush, bunch grass, and wildflowers. Clumps of willows line the riparian zone. Tributaries like Roaring, Moose, and Tosi Creeks feed its flows as the valley opens wider and the river twists and turns in broader sweeps. About 20 miles below the lakes is Kendall Warm Springs, home of the Kendall dace, a minnow species found only in the spring's thermal waters. The Green meanders another 10 miles to the forest service line and enters farm and ranch country. At this point, four mountain ranges are in view: the Winds to the east, the Gros Ventre to the west, the Absaroka to the northwest, and the Wyomings to the southeast.

Outfitter camp above Warren Bridge on the Green River.

There is full public access in the national forest run. After spring runoff subsides, it is fairly easy to wade, except in pools, along undercut banks, and in some swift, deep glides. Short riffles and rock garden runs offer pocket water fishing, and small islands and gravel bars occasionally divide the channel.

This stretch also can be floated in a canoe or raft, but there are several rocky Class II and III stretches in the first 10 miles that inexperienced canoeists need to scout or portage around. Below Moose Creek it is mostly a Class I float to the forest boundary, except for a few rocky runs like the one at Kendall Warm Springs. The next public pullout is 15 miles below the forest at the top BLM access sites north of Warren Bridge on U.S. 191. A drive-in boat ramp at the bridge is another 12 miles.

A slot limit is included in a special regulation section from Kendall Warm Springs downstream to the upper boundary of the Warren Bridge access area. All trout between 10 and 20 inches must be released, and fishing is permitted with flies and lures only. The trout limit is 2 per day or in possession, with only 1 over 20 inches.

Runoff peaks around 2,000 cubic feet per second in mid-June and falls slowly through July as the river wanes to around 750 cfs by the end of the month. The Green clears earlier and is more fishable in July than other larger rivers in the area, like the Snake. But late fall flows below 250 cfs may be too low to float some sections between the lakes and Warren Bridge.

A golden stonefly hatch coincides with the spring flood in June. It produces sporadic top water action, but golden stone nymphs and woolly buggers are effective producers year-round. Early caddis and baetis hatches may provide some pre-runoff action.

July is the prime time to fish this beautiful river when a prolific gray drake hatch kicks off the season. The giant mayfly sometimes lingers as late as September, along with little yellow stones, or willow flies. Large gray Wulffs or Adams, and yellow Sallies, blonde humpies, or yellow stimulators are critical patterns in a fly caster's arsenal. Caddis also remain important throughout the summer, along with pale morning duns starting in mid-July and tricos in mid-August. The best bets to pound up fish during the dog days of summer are grasshoppers, beetles, Turk's tarantulas, stimulators, humpies, and attractor patterns.

Small nymphs and emergers can be tied as dropper flies on larger dry flies to increase chances for strikes. Hammering the banks with large nymphs, woolly buggers, and streamers, and drifting or stripping them through pools and undercuts is effective for the river's larger trout. They are the flies of choice during fall spawning runs of browns.

Surrounded by so many mountain ranges, the long valley of the Green Basin often becomes a giant wind tunnel. The wind may pick up heavily in late morning and blow hard through the afternoon. Get to the river early to find more time to fish comfortably, or catch evening hatches or spinner falls during calmer periods at twilight. A 9-foot, 5- or 6-weight rod works best on the Green.

Developed campgrounds are available at Green River Lakes and just north of the forest boundary at Whiskey Grove. Undeveloped campsites are found at pullouts along the forest road. A BLM campground is located at Warren Bridge.

In recent years, grizzly bears have expanded their range into the upper Green River valley and Wind River Mountains. Keep a clean camp and store all food and cooking utensils in locked vehicles, or hang them from a rope suspended between two trees. A fed bear is a dead bear, as was the case for two grizzlies in 1997.

Warren Bridge to Daniel Bridge

This is the most popular float on the upper Green River. It also has excellent access for wading anglers above Warren Bridge and near the Daniel Fish Hatchery.

North of the bridge, 12 access spurs along a gravel BLM road dip down the west cliff of a small canyon to the river. The river's pace is brisker along this 12-mile run as it stairsteps down shallow, rocky runs with great pocketwater and riffle fishing for browns and rainbows and a few cutthroat. A good day float is to put in at Site 10 and drift down to the bridge. Boaters need to watch for a few Class II rock garden runs and shoot the "Vs" on several low-head irrigation diversions.

Below Warren Bridge the river enters private property, and float-fishers need to stay aware of Wyoming's strict laws against trespass. Riverbanks and the streambed belong to property owners. It is not permitted to get out of a watercraft, put down an anchor, or make any contact with the land or streambed outside public access areas

Lower Forty Rod Access on the Green River.

without landowner permission. "Some of the landowners patrol their water to insure that anglers are abiding by these rules," said a spokesman for Westbank Anglers in Jackson. "But don't let these restrictions keep you away from these stretches. Every year someone catches a fish here that is measured in pounds, not inches."

Three public access sites are located upstream of the Daniel Hatchery in the area known as Forty Rod Flat. To reach it, turn west at the hatchery sign on U.S. 191, 4 miles south of Warren Bridge and 2 miles north of Daniel Junction. The junction, 10 mile miles west of Pinedale, is the intersection of U.S. 191 and U.S. 189. Continue north past the hatchery to reach the public fishing parking lots.

Wade fishing is permitted at the Forty Rod access sites. Be sure to check maps and posted rules at each site before entering the river. A public boat ramp is on the east bank at the lowest site nearest the hatchery, 8 miles downstream of Warren Bridge.

The next boat launch is 9 miles downstream at a private ramp on the north bank above the Daniel Bridge on U.S. 189. A $15 permit to use it must be obtained at Stanley's Junction Food Mart at the highway intersection.

There is a slot limit and flies and lures only restriction from the bottom of Forty Rod Flat downstream to Swain's Bridge on WYO 354, a mile upstream of the Daniel

Bridge. All trout 10 to 20 inches must be released. The trout limit is 2 per day or in possession, only 1 over 20 inches.

The river's course down this stretch meanders through the sagebrush desert in broad sweeps, deep pools, and long glides along undercut banks. There are several rocky runs, a series of riffles and pools, and some channels around small islands. Float-fishers need to keep an eye out for snags and low-head irrigation diversions protruding into the channel.

Hatches may occur earlier here than on the headwaters run because the river warms sooner. It fishes well through late summer and into autumn during the brown spawning run. John Ross at the Two Rivers Emporium in Pinedale tracks hatches and river conditions. Shuttle services or guided trips can be arranged through Ross and other fly shops in town.

Daniel Bridge to Fontenelle Reservoir

The 35-mile run through private lands between Daniel Bridge and the WYO 351 bridge, northeast of Big Piney, has only one public boat launch site. Float times are long because the river's flows are slow and it braids into numerous channels. Logjams and diversion dams may cause problems, and barbed wire fences may be encountered on the lower end.

The only pullout is about 10 miles below U.S. 189 at Sommer's Bridge, a BLM site also known as Trapper's Point. From there it is 25 miles to the WYO 351 bridge, 2 miles north of the confluence of the New Fork River. There are no bank access points to stop to wade fish or camp without landowner permission, which is difficult to obtain.

First-timers who float this reach need to scout the location of the Sommer's Bridge boat ramp ahead of time, especially if a vehicle shuttle is arranged. Before embarking, discuss your itinerary or arrange shuttle services or a guided trip with Pinedale fly shops. The 25-mile float between Sommer's Bridge and the WYO 351 bridge should not be considered without permission to camp overnight on ranch land.

Numerous islands, gravel bars, and side channels continue to braid the river on its final 40-mile run to Fontenelle Reservoir.

In addition to the WY 351 launch site in the Big Piney area, there are Wyoming Game and Fish bank ramps at Five Mile Bridge below town and the Ferry Island area a few miles north of the bridge. Both provide wade-fishing access, but a vehicle with high clearance is needed to follow the east bank to Ferry Island. The float between WYO 351 and Five Mile is 15 miles.

Below Five Mile Bridge, U.S. 189 parallels the river. The next access site and ramp is 15 miles downstream at the Whelan Bridge above LaBarge. Another 10 miles below is the pullout at Names Hill Historic Site, also on the highway and just above the slack waters of the reservoir.

From Swains' Bridge to Fontenelle Reservoir, the limit on trout is 3 per day or in possession, with only 1 over 20 inches. Kokanee salmon also run upstream from the reservoir to spawn in the Green and New Fork in late summer.

Stream Facts: Upper Green River

Season
- Year-round.

Regulations
- Slot limit from Kendall Warm Springs downstream to the upper boundary of the Warren Bridge access area. All trout between 10 and 20 inches must be released, and fishing is permitted with flies and lures only. The trout limit is 2 per day or in possession, with only 1 over 20 inches.
- Slot limit and flies and lures only restriction from the bottom of Forty Rod Flat downstream to Swain's Bridge on WYO 354, a mile upstream of Daniel Bridge. All trout 10 to 20 inches must be released. The trout limit is 2 per day or in possession, only 1 over 20 inches.
- From Swains' Bridge to Fontenelle Reservoir, the limit on trout is 3 per day or in possession, with only 1 over 20 inches.

Trout
- Rainbows from 10 to 16 inches, with a good number exceeding 20 inches. Browns are in the 14- to 18-inch range and a fair number of lunkers over 20 inches. Colorado River cutthroat are increasing in number and size. Brook trout and whitefish are also present.

Miles
- Mile 5: Green River Lakes outlet
- Mile 16: Big Bend
- Mile 24: Kendall Warm Springs
- Mile 26.5: Whiskey Grove Campground
- Mile 29: National forest boundary
- Mile 50: Top of Warren Bridge access area
- Mile 62: Warren Bridge on U.S. 191
- Mile 70: Forty Rod Flat boat ramp
- Mile 79: Daniel Bridge on U.S. 189
- Mile 89: Summer's Bridge at Trapper's Point
- Mile 115: WYO 351 bridge
- Mile 117: Confluence of New Fork River
- Mile 130: Five Mile Bridge, south of Big Piney
- Mile 146: Whalen Bridge at LaBarge
- Mile 154: Names Hill Historic Site
- Mile 157: Fontenelle Reservoir

Character
- A shallow, medium-sized river flowing through a high plains sagebrush desert in a series of broad meanders, riffles and pools, rock garden runs, deeper pools and glides, and increasing number of islands and channels as it progresses deeper into the valley. Relatively easy to wade where permitted but better covered in a float boat or raft.

Flows
- Runoff peaks around 2,000 cubic feet per second in mid-June and falls slowly through July as the river wanes to around 750 cfs. Late fall flows below 250 cfs may be too low to float some sections between the lakes and Warren Bridge.

Access
- Bridger-Teton National Forest
- Warren Bridge BLM lands above U.S. 191
- Forty Rod Flats above Daniel Hatchery
- Five Mile Bridge and Ferry Island southeast of Big Piney
- LaBarge
- Names Hill Historic Site on U.S. 189

Camping
- Bridger-Teton National Forest
- Warren Bridge BLM access area
- Forty Rod Flat access area
- Pinedale

Lower Green River

The Green River below Fontenelle Dam is a largely undiscovered gem flowing through a remote high plains wilderness. Snowcapped peaks of the Wind River Range thrust against the northeast horizon, and the lush riparian habitat of the Seedskadee National Wildlife Refuge is an oasis in the arid sagebrush desert

A fertile tailwater fishery, the 30-mile run down through the refuge to the confluence of the Big Sandy River boasts prolific caddis and mayfly hatches, plus numerous scuds, leeches, and aquatic worms flushed out of the reservoir. Plump, hard-fighting cutthroat and rainbows, 10 to 18 inches, are routinely netted through summer, along with a fair number over 20 inches. Some brown trout reside in the upper river, and starting in late September fall spawning migrations bring up schools of huge browns from Flaming Gorge Reservoir, 45 miles downstream. Trout 3 to 5 pounds are often recorded.

The first mile below the dam to Weeping Rocks Campground is closed to fishing from October 7 through November 7 to protect browns on their redds. Also, from the CCC Bridge, 4.5 miles below the dam, downstream to the Big Sandy the limit is 1 trout over 20 inches per day or in possession. All trout less than 20 inches must be released. Fishing is permitted with flies and lures only.

Caddis and mayfly hatches mimic those of the upper Green, with similar choices for dry flies, nymphs, and emergers. To fish the tailwaters year-round, also carry orange and brown scuds, San Juan worms, damsel nymphs, and black and olive leeches. They can be fished alone and are very effective dropper flies on larger dry and wet patterns, along with beadheads, small nymphs and emergers, and midge pupae.

In autumn, glow bugs and sparkle eggs are prime patterns, along with the standard fare for big browns—in or out of spawning mode—large nymphs, rubberlegs, woolly buggers, and streamers. A popular local pattern is JJ's special, a large yellow-brown nymph with white rubber legs similar to the Bitch Creek nymph.

Baetis and midge hatches are common throughout the seasons. Golden stoneflies hatch from mid-June through July, and are overlapped by the little yellow stones, or willow flies. Blizzard hatches of caddis and mayflies—pale morning duns after mid-July and tricos after August—sometimes occur simultaneously and continue into September. A strong tiny fall baetis hatch lasts through October.

Top water action is best in mornings and evenings, while most large trout hooked during the day are caught on nymphs. Prospecting with terrestrials such as hoppers, beetles, and ants, and large attractors such as Wulffs, Trudes, humpies, and stimulators also draws fish to the top in late summer.

Mosquitoes can be a problem in spring, and midsummer is often hot, dry, and dusty. Early fall is serene and uncrowded, but the price of late season brown hunts is cold, wet, and nasty weather. The winds blow eternally in southern Wyoming, so short, lightweight rods are not good options.

Mike Marble at the Fontenelle Store in the village below the dam keeps track of hatches and river conditions. Boat rentals and shuttle services are provided by the store. There are three campgrounds below the dam and one at Fontenelle Creek on the west bank of the reservoir. Camping is not permitted on Seedskadee National Wildlife Refuge.

The river is paralleled by WYO 372 between Fontenelle and Green River. Public access is excellent for both bank anglers and float-fishers below the dam and through the wildlife refuge down to Big Sandy, where the Green enters a checkerboard of public and private lands. Below Big Sandy there are three key bank access and launch sites in the desert run to the town of Green River. Fishing is encouraged right through town along an extensive system of nature trails and parks.

The lower Green is a swift, shallow stream well suited for float boats, rafts, and canoes. There is no white water, but summer flows can be erratic because of dam releases. Due to its fluctuations, unattended watercraft should be tied securely or pulled above the water line. Vehicles left at drop off points should not be parked in low areas near the river. Wade-fishers should avoid treacherous currents during high flows and exercise caution during periods of fluctuation.

Generally, spring runoff releases peak near the end of May at around 6,000 cubic feet per second and gradually decrease through June and July, reaching below 2,000 cfs by August. In 1997, however, releases reached 13,000 cfs, and high flows continued into October. Still, most years the river fishes well in late summer and fall.

The first boat ramp is at the CCC Bridge, 4.5 miles below the dam. A popular float is from the bridge to the Hay Field boat ramp, 11 miles downstream, on the wildlife refuge. Six other sites north of refuge headquarters offer areas to wade fish or bank launch canoes or rafts. The first boat ramp downstream of refuge headquarters is the WYO 28 bridge, 8 miles below the Hay Field site. The beauty of this stretch is that float-fishers can stop to wade fish promising waters with impunity. Below the refuge anglers need to stay aware of Wyoming's laws against trespass on private property.

Roads in the refuge are good along the west bank. However, 4-wheel-drive vehicles with high clearance are needed for a rough gravel road paralleling the east bank that is reached via the Farson Cutoff Road.

Below the WY0 28 bridge distances to bank access and launch sites are 13 miles to Big Island, 3 miles to Pioneer Trails Park, and 10 miles to the Rolling Green Country Club, west of Green River. In town there are boat ramps at Expedition Island and Stratton Myers Park and bank access at numerous sites along the greenbelt.

Expedition Island is where John Wesley Powell embarked in 1869 on his journey down the canyon of the last unknown river in North America. Today, the inundated Flaming Gorge is the largest reservoir in Wyoming.

Flaming Gorge

Completion of the dam at Dutch John, Utah, in 1964 inundated the scenic Flaming Gorge for nearly 90 miles to the outskirts of Green River.

The lake is famous for the beautiful red rock mountains rising above the canyon and for its trophy lake trout, up to 40 pounds. It produces more lake trout over

*Nora Harris
of Butte, Montana,
with a brown trout
on the lower Green River.*

20 pounds than any other fishery in the world, states John Baughman, Wyoming Game and Fish director and former fisheries director.

Flaming Gorge also gained a lot of attention in the 1970s for its monster brown trout. It set a world record in 1977 and bested its own record in 1982 with a 25.8-pound trophy. The pace has slowed since then, but the lake still produces a lot of browns from 2 to 10 pounds, according to Baughman.

The lake also holds 14- to 18-inch rainbow and kokanee salmon, and 9- to 11-inch smallmouth bass.

A deepwater fishery, the lake draws little attention from flyfishers. It produces best by trolling lures along the shore or using downriggers in the deep channels.

There are several fishing restrictions on Flaming Gorge, so check current regulations before setting out. Also, a $10 Flaming Gorge Reciprocity Stamp is required to fish both sides of the state line. The stamp was reauthorized in 1996 and allows anglers with a Wyoming or Utah fishing license to fish the reservoir in both states. The stamp is available at license agents in southwest Wyoming. It does not permit anglers to creel a limit in both states, but just to fish the reservoir in either state in pursuit of one limit.

Access to the lake is good along WYO 530, which parallels the west rim of the canyon. The other road south to Dutch John is U.S. 191. It makes a wide loop to the east around Flaming Gorge and offers very little access to the lake. South of Dutch John is Vernal, on I-40, and Dinosaur National Monument.

The superb tailwater fishery on the Green from Dutch John to Browns Park in Colorado ranks it as one of the best flyfishing rivers of the West.

Fontenelle Reservoir

The smaller Fontenelle Reservoir is an unheralded fishery for good-sized rainbows and browns and is much more flyfisher friendly.

When full, the 7,000-acre reservoir extends almost 20 miles upstream toward LaBarge. Water levels fluctuate radically, however, as the reservoir fills and drains.

It is a consistent producer of rainbows and browns in the 12- to 24-inch range and occasionally gives up a 10-pound brown. The lake also holds cutthroat and kokanee salmon.

Fontenelle fishes best after ice-out in spring, continuing into June or mid-July. It picks up again in fall when water temperatures drop. Shore anglers and float-tubers can work over spawning rainbows in spring and browns in late fall at the mouth of Fontenelle Creek. Float-tubers also do well along the west cliffs between the creek and the dam, as well as the bays and points along the east bank.

The only developed boat ramp is at the Fontenelle Creek campground and recreation site on U.S. 189. Float-tubers and anglers in small boats or canoes need to keep an eye on the weather. Gale force winds can spring up quickly.

Care also should be taken when walking along the cliffs. The chalky rock is loose and crumbly.

Stream Facts: Lower Green River

Season
- Year-round.

Regulations
- First mile below Fontenelle Dam to Weeping Rocks Campground is closed to fishing October 7 through November 7 to protect spawning brown trout.
- From CCC Bridge, 4.5 miles below the dam, downstream to the Big Sandy River, the limit is 1 trout over 20 inches per day or in possession. All trout less than 20 inches must be released. Fishing is permitted with flies and lures only.

Trout
- Cutthroat and rainbows range from 10 to 18 inches, with a fair number over 20 inches. Some brown trout reside in the upper river, and fall spawning migrations bring up schools of huge browns from the lower river and Flaming Gorge Reservoir. Trout of 3 to 5 pounds are often recorded.

Miles
- Mile 170: Fontenelle Dam
- Mile 174.5: CCC Bridge boat ramp
- Mile 185: Hay Field boat ramp in Seedskadee National Wildlire Refuge
- Mile 193: WYO 28 boat ramp
- Mile 200: Big Sandy River confluence
- Mile 203: Big Island access
- Mile 207: Pioneer Trails Park
- Mile 217: I-80 bridge
- Mile 220: Expedition Island
- Mile 227: Scott Botton Nature Park
- Mile 232: Flaming Gorge
- Mile 307: State line

Character
- Swift shallow river flowing through an arid sagebrush desert in long meanders with undercut banks and pools, riffles and runs, and braided channels. Flows below dam fluctuate through summer from dam releases. Fishes best in late summer and fall.

Flows
- Most years spring runoff releases peak near the end of May at around 6,000 cfs and gradually decrease through June and July to below 2,000 cfs by August. In 1997, releases reached 13,000 cfs, and high flows continued into October.

Access
- Fontenelle Dam
- Seedskadee National Wildlife Refuge
- WYO 28 bridge
- Big Island
- Pioneer Trails Park
- I-80 bridge
- Green River nature trails and parks

Camping
- Two developed and one undeveloped campground below Fontenelle Creek.
- Developed campground at Fontenelle Creek recreation site on reservoir.

GREEN RIVER MAJOR HATCHES

Insect	M	A	M	J	J	A	S	O	N	Time	Flies
Golden Stone				▮	▮					A	**Dry:** Golden Stone, Yellow or Orange Stimulator, Yellow or Red Double Humpy #2–10; **Wet:** Bitch Creek Nymph, JJ's Special, Girdlebug, Black Rubberlegs, Black or Olive Woolly Buggers #2–10; Halfback Nymph #8–14
Little Yellow Stone (Willow Fly)				▮	▮					M/A	Yellow Sallies, Willow Fly, Blonde Humpy, Yellow Stimulator #10–14
Caddis					▮	▮				M/D	**Dry:** Tan or Olive Elk Hair Caddis, Yellow or Royal Humpies, Tent-wing Caddis, Goddard Caddis #10–16; **Wet:** Beadhead Emergers, Peacock Emerger, Soft-hackles, Platte River Special, Prince Nymph #10–16
Pale Morning Dun					▮					A/D	**Dry:** PMD, Light Cahill, Rusty Spinner, Sparkle Dun, PMD Cripple #14–18; **Wet:** Beadhead Hare's Ear Nymph, Pheasant Tail #14–18
Gray Drake					▮					M/E	**Dry:** Adams, Wulff, Gray Wulff, Para-Adams, Adams Hair Wing #10–12; **Wet:** Hare's Ear Nymph #10–12
Trico						▮				M/A	**Dry:** Trico, Black and White, Trico Spinner, Lite-Brite Trico #18–20; Para-Adams #20; **Wet:** Pheasant Tail Nymph #18–22
Baetis			▮	▮		▮	▮	▮		A/E	**Dry:** Blue-winged Olive, Para-BWO, Blue Dun, Olive Sparkle Dun, Para-Adams #14–18; Tiny BWO, Blue Dun #18–22; **Wet:** Pheasant Tail, Baetis Emerger #16–18
Midge	▮	▮					▮	▮		A/E	**Dry:** Griffith's Gnat, Black and White Midge, Palomino Midge #18–22; **Wet:** Blood Midge Pupa, Brassie, Midge Pupa #18–22
Terrestrials					▮	▮				A	Joe's Hopper, Dave's Hopper, Parachute Hopper, Turk's Tarantula, Madam X #8–14; Foam Beetle, Disc O'Beetle, Dave's Cricket #14–18; Black Ant, Rusty Ant #14–18

HATCH TIME CODE: M = morning; A = afternoon; E = evening; D = dark; SF = spinner fall; // = continuation through periods.

NEW FORK RIVER

The New Fork inscribes an S-shaped loop around Pinedale to join the Green River. It intersects only two paved highways on its 65-mile meander through the rolling sagebrush desert southwest of the Wind River Mountains.

When local guides and outfitters hang the "Gone Fishing" sign on the doorknob and hook up the boat trailer, it's a safe bet they're headed for this hidden tributary. And, while the parlance of tourism is often subtle, Jack Dennis of Jackson pulls no punches on this one. The New Fork is where Dennis, the guru of western Wyoming flyfishing, goes to escape the world.

Dennis advertises it as "a small, intimate stream with undercut banks and numerous brush piles which provide excellent cover for German Brown Trout. This river has the best population of 14- to 19-inch trout in Wyoming."

Good chances for 24-inch browns keep fly casters twitching in anticipation, and the river annually produces a few 6- or 7-pound trophies. Also present for a day's entertainment are lesser numbers of rainbows that grow to hefty proportions. And, apparently, there are a few cutthroat-rainbow hybrids.

A batch of photos on a counter at the Two Rivers Emporium fly shop in Pinedale radiates with the toothy grins of flyfishers fondling hook-jawed browns or plump rainbows. The one with the most radiant smile draws a double take. The youth in the picture is clutching a 23-inch cutt-bow.

Perhaps another surprise to some anglers is what appears to be hundreds of red bandanas fluttering in the river in autumn. The New Fork turns red when kokanee salmon start spawning in September. Temporary residents into October, they run upstream from Fontenelle Reservoir on the Green River.

Browns spawn in fall, too, and draw the most attention from fly casters. It is one of the few times they are relatively easy to catch, but outfitters and guides for the New Fork advocate catch-and-release in all seasons.

Still, for all the superlatives showered on the New Fork, there are two caveats newcomers should keep in mind: The river is tough to get onto because it passes almost entirely through private lands. It is hard to fish because of its character and the wary nature of brown trout. Most guides note that it is a challenge for beginners, but they stress it presents valuable learning experiences for intermediate and advanced fly casters.

Float-fishing is essentially the only option. The one wade-fishing access area is very difficult to negotiate. First-timers should seriously consider a guided trip on the bottom 30-mile run of the river. Those setting out on their own, or arranging vehicle shuttles, need to check with Pinedale fly shops on current river conditions and get advice on channel routes.

The New Fork rises as a small mountain stream in the Bridger Wilderness above New Fork Lakes. A half-mile below the lower lake, 15 miles northwest of Pinedale, the river turns south and enters private lands. It gains little in size until it picks up the flows of Duck Creek, 2 miles west of Pinedale, and Pine Creek, just south of town.

New Fork River

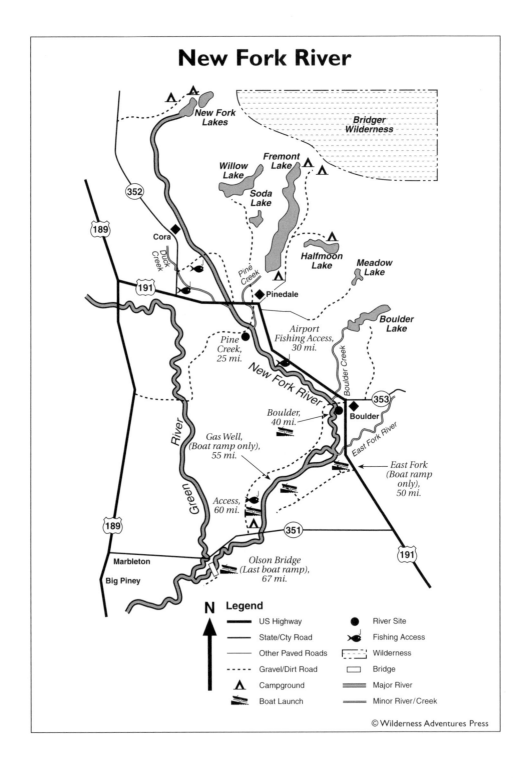

© Wilderness Adventures Press

The river continues to collect tributaries on a 15-mile meandering swing to the east through the valley below Pinedale. At the Boulder Bridge on U.S. 191, the New Fork abruptly turns south. About five miles downstream it picks up the East Fork, its largest tributary, and curves southwest in a 25-mile meandering run to its merger with the Green River.

The New Fork flows slower and deeper than the Green in long curving cutbank glides, deep runs and pools and numerous willow-lined channels with undercut banks. Throughout the river there are thick brushy logjams, and barbed wire fences may cross some braided channels. The broad floodplain is lined with lush ranks of cottonwoods and a few marshy oxbow sloughs.

Spring runoff peaks around 3,000 cubic feet per second in mid-June and drops sharply through July, reaching about 750 cfs in August. Fall flows are 500 cfs or less.

The New Fork is well suited for canoes and small float boats, such as the South Fork skiff. The upper river can be floated from Pinedale to Boulder in early summer, but it usually is too low by late August. The upstream launch site is about 5 miles northwest of Pinedale, just above the confluence with Duck Creek.

Most float trips start at the Boulder Bridge landing, 12 miles southeast of Pinedale on U.S. 191. There are four landing sites downstream. Missing the last one means a 12-mile float on the Green River to the next public landing.

A few miles below Boulder the river divides into two forks which break into a series of brush-lined channels with narrow bends that eventually join again near the East Fork. Keep bearing left to reach the first landing on the east bank just below the East Fork. Also bear left at another fork to reach the next landing on the east bank, 5 miles downstream at the Gas Wells. Large natural gas storage tanks mark the site.

To leave vehicles at either boat landing, drive 5 miles south from Boulder and turn right on County Road 23-106, a well maintained gravel road. The turnoff to the East Fork is about a mile west of U.S. 191. The Gas Wells are another 5 miles. The county road continues southwest to WYO 351. A boat landing, 5 miles downstream of the Gas Wells, is located at a BLM campground on the west bank at the WYO 351 bridge.

The last pullout is on the southeast bank at Olson Bridge on WYO 351, about 7 miles below the BLM campground and 3 miles above the confluence with the Green.

There are two special regulation sections on the lower river:

- From the Mesa Road Bridge, 2 miles south of Pinedale, downstream to the upper boundary of the Boulder Bridge boat ramp, the limit on trout, salmon, and grayling is 2 fish per day or in possession. Only 1 trout may exceed 20 inches. All trout between 10 and 20 inches must be returned to the water immediately. Fishing is permitted with flies and lures only.
- From the upstream boundary of the Boulder Bridge boat ramp downstream to the Green River confluence, the limit on trout is 3 per day or in possession. Only 1 trout may exceed 20 inches.

Kokanee that stay below the Boulder Bridge are included in general regulations aggregate limits.

East Fork boat landing on the New Fork River.

The wade-fishing access site is behind the Wenz Airport, about 5 miles east of Pinedale on U.S. 191. The turnoff onto a rough two-track road is at a Game and Fish sign near Pole Creek. Vehicles with 4-wheel-drive and high clearance are required because of the steep grade down to the floodplain and deep ruts in the road.

Marshy willow-choked flats, undercut banks, deep pools, and thick logjams mark the river at this point. Take care when wading as well as when walking the brush-lined banks. Be careful to stay within the boundaries of the state lands section.

Hatches on the New Fork are about the same as those on the Green River. Caddis, yellow Sallies, humpies, and Wulff or Trude attractors are important patterns through the season and the river has a gray drake hatch that rivals the Green's. Late summer top water action is good with grasshoppers, Turk's tarantulas, Madam Xs, and stimulators. Tie small nymphs or emergers as droppers on large dries for better chances for strikes.

Woolly buggers, Yuk bugs, and Kiwi muddlers are local favorites for stalking big browns with large wet flies. Other streamers can include white, yellow, or black marabou muddlers, light and dark spruce flies, and Matukas. Large nymphs can include black rubberlegs, Montana stones, halfbacks, girdlebugs, and leeches.

A 9-foot 7-weight rod works best to punch streamers and large nymphs into the banks, and floating lines are easier to mend or roll cast than sinking lines. Use split shot to get nymphs down when drifting them through holes. Use heavy tippets to handle big fish and free flies from snags. But don't sacrifice a rod for a fly. When snagged, point the rod straight at the fly and pull the line with your free hand, not the rod.

The New Fork clears in July and fishes well from midsummer through fall. The added attraction of autumn is the brown spawning season, cooler days and no mosquitoes, which can be fierce in summer.

Duck Creek

Brown trout disciples intent on another challenge find it in Duck Creek. The springfed tributary of the New Fork meanders through a marshy meadow west of Pinedale

It is one of the few spring creeks in Wyoming with public access and offers tricky fishing for 12- to 18-inch browns. It also holds pan-sized brookies. The parking lot on U.S. 191 is about 2 miles west of town.

The creek follows a narrow undercut channel that braids into a few smaller runnels on its serpentine course across the grassy flat dotted with clumps of stunted willows and a few potholes.

Fly casters can stalk the creek in hopes of matching a caddis or mayfly hatch, but when in doubt, small hoppers, ants, and beetles are reliable patterns for rising trout. Small nymphs and streamers also are good for prospecting.

Action is best at dusk or on heavily overcast days. Browns tend to feed primarily in late afternoon and early evening as twilight wanes.

Duck Creek is a popular fishery due to its proximity to Pinedale. It is often less crowded in midweek.

Stream Facts: New Fork River

Season
- Above the New Fork Lakes, the river is closed from September 1 through April 30.

Regulations
- From the Mesa Road bridge, 2 miles south of Pinedale, downstream to the upper boundary of the Boulder Bridge boat ramp, the limit on trout, salmon, and grayling is 2 fish per day or in possession. Only 1 trout may exceed 20 inches. All trout between 10 and 20 inches must be returned to the water immediately. Fishing is permitted with flies and lures only.
- From the upstream boundary of the Boulder Bridge boat ramp downstream to the Green River confluence, the limit on trout is 3 per day or in possession. Only 1 trout may exceed 20 inches.

Trout
- Strong population of 14- to 19-inch brown trout, with good chances for 24-inchers. Lesser numbers of rainbows in the 12- to 20-inch range.

Miles
- Mile 5: New Fork Lakes outlet
- Mile 23: Duck Creek confluence
- Mile 25: Pine Creek confluence
- Mile 30: Airport access area
- Mile 38: Boulder Bridge boat ramp
- Mile 45: East Fork boat landing
- Mile 50: Gas Wells boat landing
- Mile 55: WYO 351 boat landing
- Mile 62: Olson Bridge boat landing
- Mile 65: Green River confluence

Character
- A slow, deep river flowing through arid high plains in long curving cutbank glides, deep runs and pools, thick brushy logjams, and numerous willow-lined channels with undercut banks. Barbed wire fences may cross some channels. The broad floodplain is thickly lined with cottonwoods and a few marshy oxbow sloughs.

Flows
- Spring runoff peaks around 3,000 cubic feet per second in mid-June and drops sharply through July to about 750 cfs in August. Fall flows are 500 cfs or less.

Access
- New Fork Lakes outlet
- Upper boat landing, 2 miles above Duck Creek confluence
- Airport access area
- Boulder Bridge boat ramp
- East Fork boat landing
- Gas Wells boat landing
- WYO 351 boat landing
- Olson Bridge boat landing
- Green River confluence

Camping
- Bridger-Teton National Forest
- BLM campground at WYO 352 bridge
- Pinedale

NEW FORK RIVER MAJOR HATCHES

Insect	M	A	M	J	J	A	S	O	N	Time	Flies
Golden Stone				▮	▮					A	**Dry:** Golden Stone, Yellow or Orange Stimulator; Yellow or Red Double Humpy #2–10; **Wet:** Bitch Creek Nymph, JJ's Special, Girdlebug, Black Rubberlegs, Black or Olive Woolly Buggers #2–10; Halfback Nymph #8–14
Little Yellow Stone (Willow Fly)				▮						M/A	Yellow Sallies, Willow Fly, Blonde Humpy, Yellow Stimulator #10–14
Caddis						▮	▮			M/D	**Dry:** Tan or Olive Elk Hair Caddis, Yellow or Royal Humpies, Tent-wing Caddis, Goddard Caddis #10–16; **Wet:** Beadhead Emergers, Peacock Emerger, Soft-hackles, Platte River Special, Prince Nymph #10–16
Pale Morning Dun				▮	▮					A/D	**Dry:** PMD, Light Cahill, Rusty Spinner, Sparkle Dun, PMD Cripple #14–18; **Wet:** Beadhead Hare's Ear Nymph, Pheasant Tail #14–18
Gray Drake				▮	▮					A/E	**Dry:** Adams, Wulff, Gray Wulff, Para-Adams, Adams Hair Wing #10–12; **Wet:** Hare's Ear Nymph #10–12
Trico						▮				M/A	**Dry:** Trico, Black and White, Trico Spinner, Lite-Brite Trico #18–20; Para-Adams #20; **Wet:** Pheasant Tail Nymph #18–22
Baetis				▮			▮	▮		A/E	**Dry:** Blue-winged Olive, Para-BWO, Blue Dun, Olive Sparkle Dun, Para-Adams #14–18; Tiny BWO, Blue Dun #18–22; **Wet:** Pheasant Tail, Baetis Emerger #16–18
Midge							▮	▮		A/E	**Dry:** Griffith's Gnat, Black and White Midge, Palomino Midge #18–22; **Wet:** Blood Midge Pupa, Brassie, Midge Pupa #18–22
Terrestrials						▮	▮			A	Joe's Hopper, Dave's Hopper, Parachute Hopper, Turk's Tarantula, Madam X #8–14; Foam Beetle, Disc O'Beetle, Dave's Cricket #14–18; Black Ant, Rusty Ant #14–18

HATCH TIME CODE: M = morning; A = afternoon; E = evening; D = dark; SF = spinner fall; // = continuation through periods.

WIND RIVER MOUNTAINS

The jagged snowcapped Wind River Range is the most popular alpine backpacking and flyfishing playground in Wyoming.

Pinedale is the western gateway into the range and has the most hiking trails into its alpine wilderness. Across the Continental Divide, Lander is the eastern gateway to the Winds, and Dubois is the northern entrance.

The massive Wind River Range includes 15 of the state's 16 highest peaks and 40 summits over 13,000 feet. The highest at 13,804 feet is Gannet Peak on the divide. The 400,000-acre Bridger Wilderness above Pinedale has 27 active glaciers, 1,300 alpine lakes with 650 holding trout, 800 miles of trout fishing streams, and nearly 600 miles of trails from nine different entrance points.

Most well-used trails are cleared early in the season, but fallen trees may be encountered on secondary trails. Winter snows generally do not leave the high mountain passes and highest trails until mid-July. Stream flows are high and swift during snowmelt runoff in June and July when some stream crossings can be hazardous. August is the best month to hike the Winds, but check at the Pinedale Ranger Station for up-to-date information.

The weather is usually warm and sunny during the day from June through September. Night temperatures may be as low as 25 degrees Fahrenheit. Sudden rain and occasional snow flurries may occur at any time. During lightning storms it is best to avoid open areas such as meadows, ridges, lone trees, and mountaintops. Find safer shelter in dense stands of trees or boulder fields.

Mosquitoes, deerflies, and horseflies are plentiful most of the summer, so don't forget insect repellent.

Roads to all trailheads, except Elkhart Park, are rough dirt. During inclement weather, all trailheads except Elkhart Park may be inaccessible.

Historically, the Bridger Wilderness had no fish in most of its lakes. Stocking programs during the 1920s and 1930s were successful, and today a majority of the range's lakes and streams hold cutthroat, brook, rainbow, golden, brown, and lake trout. There are grayling in Meadow Lake and whitefish in many streams.

More than 300 alpine lakes were stocked with trout in the 1930s from 5-gallon milk cans packed in on mules led by Finis Mitchell. A Rock Springs railroad man, Mitchell and his wife, Emma, opened a summer fishing camp in the Big Sandy area east of Pinedale to eke out an existence during the Great Depression. By 1937, Mitchell boasted of stocking 2.5 million fingerlings in 314 lakes in his beloved mountains. He also hooked adult cutthroat and lake trout in lower lakes for transplants in higher lakes.

Mitchell's guidebook, *Wind River Trails*, is a classic in alpine hiking and fishing literature. It's a great read, but since he pioneered many of the range's trails, Mitchell tends to encourage bushwhacking cross-country. A newer guide with good hiking suggestions is *Walking the Winds*, by Rebecca Woods, which details the current status of trout species in the 2.25 million-acre mountain range's thousands of lakes.

Two publications, the "Pinedale Ranger District Recreation Opportunity Guide" and the "Bridger Wilderness, Pinedale Ranger District," are available at the U.S. Forest

Service office in town. Commercial topographic hiking maps and guides for the Wind River Range published by Earthwalk Press are available at most sporting goods stores.

Wyoming Fish and Game also offers a brochure, "Bridger Wilderness—A Guidebook to Fishing Lakes." Obtain a copy at its Pinedale office, 117 South Sublette Avenue, or call 307-367-4353.

Alpine Fishing Paradise

A loop of deep glacial lakes stretches along the shoulders of the Wind Rivers like a string of pearls. Seven of the ten lakes are named the Finger Lakes after a similar collection of picturesque lakes in upstate New York. Roads to the mountain range end at the lower lakes where trails to the alpine lakes begin.

Developed campgrounds at six of the lakes can serve as bases for day hikes into the wilderness or stopovers for anglers who fish the lower lakes. There are separate parking lots for hikers and horse riders who head straight to the mountains.

Several of the trailheads are used heavily by hikers, and alpine lakes along their trails are fished hard. Others receive moderate or low use and offer hikers more solitude. But the general rule of thumb is that the higher you hike the better the fishing.

Here's a look at the glacial lakes and their trailheads:

Fremont Lake—5 miles north of Pinedale, the 5000-acre Fremont Lake is the largest in the region and the most commercialized. There is a resort and some summer homes along the lake. It contains large lake trout and medium-sized rainbows and has been planted with kokanee salmon. At the top of the Fremont Lake Road is the Elkhart Park Trailhead. It starts at 9,100 feet and is one of the most highly used entrances into the wilderness.

Half Moon Lake—8 miles northeast of Pinedale on the Fremont Lake Road, the 920-acre Half Moon Lake also has a resort as well as summer home development. It holds moderate-sized lake trout and rainbows. Trails from the lake into the mountains start at 7,500 feet and receive low use.

Willow Lake—12 miles northwest of Pinedale, the 1,600-acre Willow Lake has good fishing for moderate-size lake trout and rainbows, and has been planted with kokanee. Trails from Willow Lake start at 7,600 feet and receive low use.

Soda Lake—7 miles northwest of Pinedale on the Willow Lake Road is a popular float tubing lake. The 312-acre lake has a strong population of 12- to 16-inch brown trout, with some fish going 2 to 5 pounds. It also holds brook trout. The lake is closed to fishing from October 1 through May 9. No motorized boats are permitted. There are no trailheads to the mountains from the lake.

New Fork Lakes—20 miles northwest of Pinedale on the Cora Road, the lower New Fork Lake is 700 acres and the upper lake is 300 acres. Both lakes hold large lake trout and moderate-sized rainbows, as well as established populations of kokanee in the 11- to 14-inch range. New Fork River above the lakes is closed from September 1 through April 30. Trails up the river start at 7,800 feet and receive medium use.

Green River Lakes—50 miles northwest of Pinedale Road, the Green River Lakes are the source of the Green River. The lower lake is 453 acres and the upper lake is 155

Square Top Mountain above the channel between the Green River Lakes.

acres. Both lakes hold big lake trout and medium-sized rainbows. Lake trout between 16 and 20 inches must be released. Brook trout and whitefish also are present in the lake. At 8,000 feet, this is top of the Highline Trail that extends 80 miles south along the Wind River Range. It is a popular area for day hikes and backcountry excursions, and receives very high use.

Meadow Lake—About 10 miles east of Pinedale, the 115-acre Meadow Lake is the grayling capital of Wyoming. The fish range from 12 to 18 inches, and the lake offers perhaps the best grayling fishing in the Lower 48 States. It is the state's brood source for grayling eggs. Meadow Creek and that portion of Meadow Lake east of Game and Fish Department markers are closed from April 1 through June 30. There is no developed campground at the lake, but camping is permitted in the forest. Trails into the mountains start at 7,600 feet and receive low use.

Burnt Lake—10 miles east of Pinedale, the 815-acre Burnt Lake has good fishing for moderate-sized lake trout and rainbow. There is no developed campground at the lake, but camping is permitted in the forest. Trails into the mountains start at 7,600 feet and receive low use.

Boulder Lake—25 miles southeast of Pinedale, the 1,400-acre Boulder Lake contains lake trout and medium-sized rainbows and has been planted with kokanee salmon. Trails into the wilderness start at 7,300 feet and receive medium use.

Generally, lakes below 10,500 feet hold cutthroat, rainbow or brook trout. Some may contain more that one species and some only one. Fish sizes vary with the lakes, but brook trout lakes tend to have stunted populations.

The Wind River Range also has the most golden trout lakes outside their native range in California. These beautiful fish top the wish list of many flyfishers heading into the high country, but their pursuit is not a casual endeavor. Most of the lakes with bigger fish are above 10,500 feet, so being physically fit is a prerequisite to stalking golden trout.

Wyoming is looking for a new source of golden trout eggs because a wild brood stock in Surprise Lake near Pinedale was lost following a forest fire. In 1996 and 1997, biologists attempted to collect eggs from the Cooper Lakes in the Absaroka Mountains, but heavy winter snows and ice delayed the spawns and hindered collection efforts. If conditions at the Copper Lakes don't improve, the department may have to look for another source.

California has banned export of golden trout eggs, but the state has been negotiating with them, said Mike Stone, Wyoming Game and Fish's assistant director. "Some Wind River lakes may suffer from missing the stocking rotation," said Stone. "We can get away with it once, but we want to get back to a two- to three-year rotation."

Equipment and fly patterns recommended for fishing alpine lakes and small mountain streams in the Big Horn and Beartooth Mountains are effective in the Wind River Range.

Fly shops in Pinedale can offer recommendations on which lakes are fishing best and offer suggestions on loop hikes. They also can arrange guided horseback trips with outfitters. Some outfitters pack in equipment and supplies to a designated campsite for backpackers who want to hike on their own.

WEST CENTRAL HUB CITIES
Pinedale
Elevation—7,175 • Population—1,180

Nestled on the western shoulders of the Wind River Mountains, Pinedale is a small resort town in the center of an outdoor recreation paradise and a service community to a sprawling ranch and farmland. It is the western gateway for drives to the Wind Rivers' "Finger Lakes" and hikes to hundreds of alpine lakes in the Bridger Teton Wilderness. The Green and New Fork Rivers are favorite playgrounds of flyfishers today as they were for mountain men of the 19th century.

Pinedale's zip code is 82941.

ACCOMMODATIONS
Best Western Pinedale Inn, 864 West Pine / 307-367-6869
Branding Iron B & B, 141 Ehman Lane 144 / 307-367-2146
Camp O' the Pines Motel, 38 North Fremont Avenue / 307-367-4536 / 14 units / Pets allowed / $
Half Moon Motel, 46 North Sublette Avenue / 307-367-2851 / 19 units / Pets allowed / $$
Log Cabin Motel, 49 East Magnolia / 307-367-4579 / 11 units, pets allowed / $$
Rivera Lodge, 442 West Marilyn / 307-367-2424 / 8 units, pets allowed / $$
Wagon Wheel Motel, 407 South Pine / 307-367-2871 / 15 units / Pets allowed / $$
Window on the Winds B & B, 10151 Hwy 191 / 307-367-2600
Green River Guest Ranch, 2000 Highway 352, Cora, WY 82925 / 307-367-2314

CAMPGROUNDS AND RV PARKS
Lakeside Lodge Resort & Marina, 99 Fremont Lake / 307-367-2221 / May 15 to November 1 / 20 RV and 6 tent sites / Full services
Pinedale Campground, 208 South Jackson Avenue / 307-367-4555 / May 25 to October 15 / 24 RV and 36 tent sites / Full services
Wind River View Campground, 8889 Hwy 191, Boulder 82923 / 307-537-5453 / May 15 to September 30 / 22 RV sites, full services

RESTAURANTS
Fremont Peak Restaurant, 20 West Pine Street / 307-367-2259
Patio Grill & Dining Room, 35 West Pine Street / 307-367-4611
McGregor's Pub, 21 North Franklin Avenue / 307-367-4443
Stockman's Steak Pub, 117 West Pine Street / 307-367-4563
Timbers Restaurant, 1033 West Pine Street / 307-367-6600
Sweet Tooth Saloon, 44 West Pine / 307-367-4724
Sue's Bread Box, 423 West Pine Street / 307-367-2150
Lakeside Lodge Resort & Marina, 99 Fremont Lake / 307-367-2221

VETERINARIANS
Animal Clinic—Pinedale, 43 South Madison Avenue / 307-367-4752

OUTFITTERS
Two Rivers Emporium Fly Fishing Shop, Pine Street, P.O. Box 1218 /
    800-329-4353
Half Moon Lake Guest Ranch, Box 983 / 307-367-6373
Daniel Float Co., 21 County Rd 208, P.O. Box 12, Daniel, WY 83115 / 307-859-8409
Green River Outfitters, Box 727 / 307-367-2416
Boulder Lake Lodge, Box 1100-RR / 307-537 5400
The Fishing Guide, P.O. Box 555 / 307-367-4760

FLY SHOPS AND SPORTING GOODS
Two Rivers Emporium Fly Fishing Shop, Pine Street, P.O. Box 1218, Pinedale, WY
    82941 / 307-367-4131 or 800-329-4353
Country Lane Groceries & Gas, 1168 Hwy 191 / 307-367-6354
Great Outdoor Shop, 332 West Pine Street / 307-367-2440
Wind River Sporting Goods, 234 East Pine Street / 307-367-2419
Coast To Coast Store, 641 West Pine Street / 307-367-2116

AUTO RENTAL AND REPAIR
Randall's Repair, 118 South Maybell Avenue / 307-367-4857
Tire Store, 327 South Pine Street / 307-367-2893
L K Repair, 211 East Pine / 307-367-2211

AIR SERVICE
Nearest commercial service is in Jackson.

MEDICAL
Pinedale Medical Clinic, 619 East Hennick Street / 307-367-4133

FOR MORE INFORMATION
Pinedale Area Chamber of Commerce
32 East Pine Street / P. O. Box 176
Pinedale, WY 82941
307-367-2242

Green River
Elevation—6,100 • Population—14,000

Green River began as a western terminus of the railroad and today is a convenient stopover or transition point for travelers on I-80. It was here in 1869 that John Wesley Powell embarked on his journey down the canyon of the last unknown river in North America. Today, the city is the gateway to the inundated Flaming Gorge, the largest reservoir in Wyoming. A deep-water fishery, it harbors monster brown and lake trout. The city also is the gateway to the Green's tailwater fishery below Fontenelle Reservoir that's becoming a newfound destination for flyfishers. Fishing is good right in town along an extensive green belt and parks system.

Green River's zip code is 82935.

Accommodations
Coachman Inn Motel, 470 East Flaming Gorge Way, Green River, WY 82935-4328 / 307-875-3681 / 18 units, pets allowed / $
Desmond Motel, 140 North 7th West St, Green River, WY 82935-4015 / 307-875-3701 / 22 units, pets allowed / $
Flaming Gorge Motel, 316 East Flaming Gorge Way, Green River, WY 82935-4326 / 307-875-4190 / 17 units, pets allowed / $
Super 8 Motel, 280 West Flaming Gorge Way, Green River, WY 82935-4105 / 307-875-9330 / 38 units, pets allowed / $
Sweet Dreams Inn, 1420 Uinta Drive, Green River, WY 82935-5046 / 307-875-7554 / 30 units / $–$$
Walker's Motel, 680 West Railroad Avenue, Green River, WY 82935-4158 / 307-875-3567 / 6 units, pets allowed / $
Western Motel, 890 West Flaming Gorge Way, Green River, WY 82935-4002 / 307-875-2840 / 31 units, pets allowed / $

Campgrounds and RV Parks
Tex's Travel Camp, U.S. 30 West, HC 2 Box 101, Green River, WY 82935 / 307-875-2630 / May 1 to Oct. 1 / 49 RV and 23 tent sites / Full services

Restaurants
Rooster's Perch, 375 Uinta Drive / 307-875-9052
Other Place, 1410 Uinta Drive / 307-875-2695
Embers Family Restaurant, 95 East Railroad Avenue / 307-875-9983
Trudel's Gast Haus, 520 Wilkes Drive / 307-875-8040
Rita's Fine Mexican Food, 520 Wilkes Drive # 10 / 307-875-5503
China Garden, 190 5th Street / 307-875-3259
Red Feather Inn, 211 East Flaming Gorge Way / 307-875-6625

VETERINARIANS
Animal Clinic of Green River, 460 East 2nd South Street / 307-875-9827
Castle Rock Kennels, 1720 Uinta Drive / 307-875-7188

OUTFITTERS
Highland Desert Flies, 218 Uinta Drive / 307-875-2358
The Fontenelle Store, Fontenelle Dam, RR 1, Kemmerer, WY 83101 /
  307-877-4844
Bob's Outdoor Adventures, 221 10th St, Evanston, WY 82930 / 307-789-1017
Van Beacham's Solitary Angler, Kemmerer, WY / Booking agent: Los Rios
  Anglers, Box 4006, 226C Paseo Del Pueblo Norte, Taos, NM 87571, 505-758-2798
  or 800-748-1707

FLY SHOPS AND SPORTING GOODS
Highland Desert Flies, 218 Uinta Drive / 307-875-2358
Wind River Sporting Goods, 420 Uinta Drive / 307-875-4075
Payless Drug & Liquor-Sporting, 50 East Flaming Gorge Way / 307-875-2435
Green River Bait Distributors, 115 South 4th East Street / 307-875-2973
The Fontenelle Store, Fontenelle Dam, RR 1, Kemmerer, WY 83101 / 307-877-4844
Bob's Outdoor Adventures, 221 10th St, Evanston, WY 82930 / 307-789-1017
Pamida, 1105 Budger Drive / 307-875-5244

AUTO RENTAL AND REPAIR
AAA Emergency Service—Norberg's, 75 Uinta Drive / 307-875-3575
Green River 24-hour Towing, 420 Railroad Avenue / 307-875-8118
Darren's Towing & Repair, 321 East Flaming Gorge Way / 307-875-9000

AIR SERVICE
Nearest commercial service is Rock Springs.

MEDICAL
Pine Ridge At Lander Valley, 96 North 1st East Street / 307-875-4424

FOR MORE INFORMATION
Green River Chamber of Commerce
1450 Uinta Drive
Green River, WY 82935
307-875-5711

Wyoming Game Fish
CUTTHROAT TROUT: NATIVE SONS OF THE WEST

The favorite trout of dry fly purists, the cutthroat's lusty rises to fur-and-feather imitations gladden the hearts of novice and expert flyfishers.

Its fight is usually below water and stubborn as it uses stream flows to its advantage, sometimes even rolling with the current and twisting the line around itself. But it is often a short-lived fight if your terminal tackle is not too delicate and you are not forced to prolong it.

The most cutthroat-rich state in the West, Wyoming once had six subspecies. It still has five. Most common are Yellowstone cutthroat and Snake River finespotted cutthroat, followed by a remnant population of westslope cutthroat and pocket populations of Bonneville cutthroat and Colorado River cutthroat. The sixth species, the greenback cutthroat, no longer exists in Wyoming's stretch of the South Fork of the Platte River, although it still populates other Colorado streams.

Anglers who like to pursue these native sons of the Intermountain West can participate in a program called the Cutt Slam. It is a four-bagger grand slam similar to the pursuit practiced by mountain and desert sheep hunters. Cutt Slam recognizes anglers who catch four of the state's cutthroat subspecies: Yellowstone, Snake River, Bonneville, and Colorado River.

The westslope cutthroat is not included in the Cutt Slam because it is present in only two streams in Yellowstone National Park. Anglers who want to find it for their own personal records should head for Cougar Creek, a tributary of the Madison River, or Specimen Creek, a tributary of the Gallatin River.

A geological crossroads, Wyoming's cutthroat are native to four of its principal basins.

Pursue Yellowstone cutthroat in the headwaters of the Missouri River drainage. Key locations include the Yellowstone River, Yellowstone Lake and tributaries, and the watersheds of the Clark's Fork of the Yellowstone, Big Horn, Little Big Horn, and Shoshone Rivers.

Snake River finespotted cutthroat are native to the upper Snake River drainage, including the watersheds of the Hoback, Salt, Greys, and Gros Ventre Rivers, Jackson Lake, and Palisades Reservoir.

Colorado River cutthroat are found in the Green River drainage. Creeks and tributaries in the Pinedale District include Tosi, Rock, Gypsum, Horse, Cottonwood, North Piney, South Piney, and LaBarge. Green River District watersheds include the Hams Fork, Little Snake, Blacks Fork, and Smiths Fork Rivers, and Fontenelle Creek.

Bonneville cutthroat, also called Utah or Bear Lake cutthroat, are native to the Bear River drainage in southwestern Wyoming. Key locations include the Smiths Fork River, including Hobble Creek and Lake Alice; Thomas Fork River, including Salt Creek, and Woodruff and Sulfur Creek Reservoirs.

"The most challenging of the four is likely to be the Bonneville cutthroat," states Al Langston, a Game and Fish spokesman. "The Colorado River cutthroat, which is found in western tributaries of the Green River and at the headwaters of the Little Snake River in the Sierra Madre Range south of Rawlins, may also demand some special effort. The Yellowstone and Snake River cutthroat are common in much of their native range in northwestern Wyoming."

To qualify for an illustrated Cutt Slam certificate, anglers must catch each of the four species in its native range in Wyoming. But the department isn't trying to promote harvest of the trout. It also stresses that this is not a competition. Anglers can pursue the fish at their own rate of interest.

The department will accept color photographs as proof of capture. It also wants information on where and when the fish were caught to add to its data on each species. "The state may have populations of these trout that haven't yet been discovered, and, with luck, known populations may be moving into new habitat," Langston said.

The Cutt Slam is the brainchild of Ron Remmick, a fisheries biologist in the Pinedale District. "We wanted to encourage anglers to learn about Wyoming's cutthroat trout," Remmick said. "At the same time, we hope they'll develop an appreciation for the habitat needs these fish have and the management programs necessary to maintain them."

Remmick said Game and Fish is working on recovery programs for Bonneville and Colorado River cutthroat. There also have been longstanding management programs for Snake River and Yellowstone cutthroat. Brood stocks of all four species are maintained at key hatcheries.

"Each subspecies presents its own management problems," Langston said. "Game and Fish hopes that participation in the Cutt Slam will make anglers more aware of the unique role cutthroat play in Wyoming fisheries management."

Anglers interested in scoring a Cutt Slam can obtain participation forms and copies of distribution listings at district offices. To obtain the illustrated certificate when the grand slam is completed, the form has to be returned with photographs for verification by a biologist.

Until other species were introduced in the late 1800s, the cutthroat was the only trout in much of the vast interior of the West, from the western slopes of the Sierras in California, up through Utah, Idaho, and Montana, and south to northern Mexico. The rainbow, the other native trout of the West, was historically a Pacific slope fish.

Originally, the cutthroat and rainbow were considered to be descendants of the Atlantic salmon, *Salmo salar*. Taxonomy specialists agreed in 1990 that western trout are more closely related to the Pacific salmon. Descendants of this genus are described as *Oncorhynchus*, which means " hooked snout."

Ironically, the taxonomists only recently caught up with the 1804–1806 Corps of Discovery. Meriwether Lewis first recorded the cutthroat for science in 1805 in western Montana. The men of the Lewis and Clark Expedition and later mountain men referred to the fish as the "trout salmon" because of its rich, orange flesh. The

Yellowstone or interior cutthroat is now known by biologists as *Oncorhynchus clarki bouvieri*. The westslope cutthroat's scientific name, *Oncorhynchus clarki lewisi*, honors both captains sent west by President Jefferson to discover a route to the Pacific Ocean.

The Yellowstone cutthroat is a beautiful fish, with rouge-colored gill plates, a rose wash running across its golden flanks, and fins tinted with a translucent salmon-orange. Hundreds of round, black spots are sprinkled across it back, with somewhat larger and more heavily concentrated spots on its tail. Its name and fame come from the bright orange-red slashes on the bottom of its jaw. It is the ancestral parent stock of all the many interior subspecies that evolved in the Intermountain West.

It is evident the Yellowstone cutthroat once had a much broader historical range. Its taxonomic placement is based on the scientific species description made by a U.S. Army officer in 1882 from fish taken from Waha Lake, a now isolated basin in northern Idaho. After Shoshone Falls formed a barrier in the Snake River 50,000 years ago, the rainbow apparently replaced Yellowstone cutthroat in the lower Snake drainage.

During the last Ice Age, it made it across the Continental Divide to the Yellowstone drainage at 8,200-foot Two Ocean Pass north of Jackson. From the pass, Atlantic Creek flows northeast to join the Yellowstone River and Pacific Creek flows southwest to join the Snake River.

Evolving separately, or staying behind, was the Snake River finespotted cutthroat, *Oncorhynchus clarki species*. It is the predominant trout on the Pacific side of the mountains in western Wyoming. The Yellowstone cutthroat also inhabits some Idaho waters but its realm of dominance is in the park on the Atlantic side of the divide.

Although it is not officially recognized as a separate subspecies, the Snake River finespotted is unique in its ability to coexist with a species of its same genus. Its spotting pattern is heavier and has many smaller spots than the Yellowstone cutthroat. Many consider it less gullible and a stronger fighter than its cousin. Wyoming Game and Fish's fish stocking program supplements Snake River finespotted cutthroat populations in some tributaries of the Snake. It also has been transplanted to other Wyoming waters.

Healthy Yellowstone cutthroat populations in the park and improving numbers of Snake River finespotted cutthroat in Jackson Hole are largely the success of special regulations to restrict harvest.

Studies show anglers can easily over-exploit the cutthroat. Even with light fishing pressure, up to half the legal-sized cutthroat in a stream are often caught. But Idaho State University studies in Yellowstone show the fish are amazingly hearty. Cutthroat on the upper Yellowstone are caught and released an average of 9.7 times during the river's short fishing season from mid-July to mid-October.

For this reason, the fish responds well to special regulations, such as size or bag limits, or catch-and-release restrictions. Yellowstone Lake's cutthroat population rebounded to historic proportions following tougher regulations in the park.

Wyoming's other cutthroat species were imperiled through indiscriminant stocking of nonnative species, particularly rainbow trout, and habitat loss—a story repeated throughout the West. While steps are being taken to restock streams and eliminate or reduce hybridization, the threat may occur forever.

The threat of hybridization and competition from other species is unfortunate. As the native trout that evolved in these waters, cutthroat grow at a better rate in a shorter period of time than their introduced brethren, including rainbow, brown, brook, and lake trout. Under wild trout management, cutthroat provide fish of remarkable size for the angler in all but the smallest streams. It's been known to live to 11 years of age, although 6 or 7 is more common.

Cutthroat evolved to spawn on the spring floods common to the Northern Rockies. For this reason, some key tributaries with major spawning runs in Yellowstone are off limits to anglers during the earlier part of the fishing season. A similar ban extends to late summer on the spring creeks in Grand Teton National Park.

Twelve to 17 inches is the average size of Yellowstone cutthroat in the park, with some growing to more than 20 inches and weighing 5 or 6 pounds. But in some lakes outside the park, the fish may exceed 20 pounds. Snake River finespotted cutthroat have a greater size potential since they are more piscivorous. They also are considered to be stronger fighters when hooked.

Cutthroat are most active in water temperatures between 50 and 65 degrees Fahrenheit. They can be found in both fast and slack water, although they are less fond of exceptionally fast waters than rainbows. Like all trout, they take advantage of whatever structural protection a stream provides, from overhanging, willow-lined banks to midstream boulders, logjams, streambed depressions, and deep pools at the base of riffles.

Never pass a logjam or a bankside feeding lane protected by an overhanging tree without working it closely. Riffles also are prime feeding grounds of cutthroat and provide prodigious action, especially at the lip of a deep pool.

Its reputation for eagerly rising to a dry fly remains paramount in most fly-fishers' minds. Larger cutthroat will hit a stonefly or hopper pattern with slashing strikes rivaling the ferocity of rainbows or browns. Casting to the feeding frenzy on the lip of a riffle during a heavy caddis or mayfly hatch can bring a host of fish between 8 and 20 inches to the net. At the same time, a hit during selective, sipping rises to tiny mayflies will startle the angler who hooks a lunker lurking beneath the still waters.

A standard set of dry flies to attract cutthroat should include elk hair caddis, stimulators, yellow sallies, humpies, Adams, pale morning dun, blue-winged olive, light Cahill, and parachute hare's ear. Nymph and emerger patterns for each of these can be equally effective, especially on riffles. Effective sizes for both dry and wet caddis and mayfly patterns can range from No. 10 to 16 in spring and early summer. By late fall, you may have to go as small as No. 18 and 22.

When all else fails, or on big or heavy waters, you can always fall back on standard attractor flies like the renegade, royal Wulff, royal coachman, royal Trude, Goddard caddis, or irresistible.

Cutthroat also succumb to the usual assortment of small streamers, muddlers, weighted nymphs, woolly buggers, super renegades, and rubberlegged patterns. Sizes 8 to 14 generally work best.

Cutthroat can be the least shy of the trout family. Occasionally, you can get amazingly close to feeding fish. On some streams, they may even be right underfoot, feeding on nymphs your boots stir up from the gravel.

But never underestimate the cutthroat. It is not a brown trout with a lobotomy, as some would disparage this remarkable fish. It can be easy to catch, and it can be exactingly selective as it keys in on a specific mayfly or caddis hatch with the resolute intensity of one of its so-called educated brethren.

Either way, it is a joy to catch or to behold.

Cutthroat Trout Identification

Yellowstone Cutthroat Trout (*Oncorhynchus clarki bouvieri*)

Orange-red slash marks on bottom of jaw are source of its name, and a characteristic common to all cutthroat. The body coloration of Yellowstone species ranges from silver-gray to olive-green back, with yellow-brown flanks, orange-tinted fins, and reddish gill-plates. Spots are spaced out on the body, large and round, and are more closely grouped toward the tail, which is slightly forked. Spotting is less dense than on rainbows, particularly on the tail. A pale crimson wash along the flanks is often bright red during spawning.

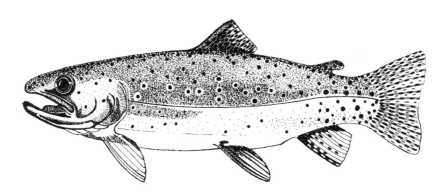

Yellowstone Cutthroat Trout (Oncorhynchus clarki bouvieri)

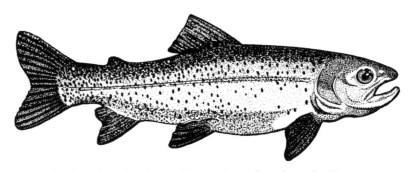

Snake River Cutthroat Trout (Oncorhynchus clarki ssp.)

Snake River Finespotted Cutthroat Trout (*Oncorhynchus clarki ssp.*)
The Snake River finespotted is similar to the Yellowstone cutthroat in body conformation and coloration. Its profuse spotting pattern is more similar to coastal species than interior cutthroat. Its many small spots concentrate toward the tail and extend below midline. The tail and lower fins are sometimes darker orange.

Bonneville Cutthroat Trout (*Oncorhynchus clarki utah*)
Characteristics and coloration are similar to the Yellowstone cutthroat, although its hues are lighter and tend toward silvery white on the belly. Black spots across the back and tail are larger, fewer, and more spaced out; parr marks may be present along midline.

Colorado River Cutthroat Trout (*Oncorhynchus clarki pleuriticus*)
Characteristics and coloration are similar to Yellowstone cutthroat, although the hues are much richer and more brilliant than the Yellowstone or Bonneville species. A small number of large black spots are more spaced out across the back and on the tail. Oval parr marks on flanks remain distinctive even on adults.

Westslope Cutthroat Trout (*Oncorhynchus clarki lewisi*)
The coloration of westslope cutthroat is richer than the Yellowstone cutthroat, with many small, irregularly shaped black spots across the back, concentrating on the tail and rarely extending below midline. It is generally steel gray on the flanks with an olive back and white belly. Gill plates are dusky red, and a pale crimson swath extends along the flanks; the belly may be bright red during spring spawning season. An oval parr mark is also seen along midline.

RAINBOW TROUT: MIGHTY LEAPERS

The most exciting fighter of the trout family, the rainbow always pulls something from its bag of tricks, from cartwheeling leaps to reel-sizzling runs to repeated dashes away from the net.

Colorado River Cutthroat Trout (Oncorhynchus clarki pleuriticus)

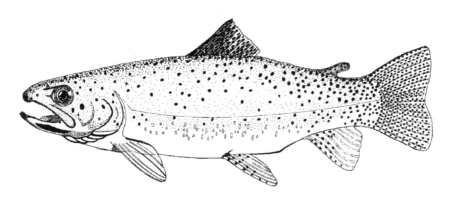

Westslope Cutthroat Trout (Oncorhynchus clarki lewisi)

In waters containing other trout species, there's no doubt in an angler's mind when a rainbow is on the end of the line. A rainbow never hesitates in its frenzied quest for freedom. It often leaps more than once in its desperate panic to throw the hook. Even small fish offer a strong and agile fight. Large fish hooked on light tackle or a delicate leader tippet leave the angler one option—give the fish its head and hope the line is long enough for the first run. Your prayers won't always be answered, even on the second or third run. A rainbow rarely comes to the net willingly.

Anglers should use the heaviest terminal tackle conditions permit to make the fight as short as possible and not unduly tire out the fish. Always use a good-sized, soft-meshed net so you aren't inclined to manhandle the fish in attempting to land it.

The feisty rainbow's acrobatic leaps and speckled, multihued beauty—described by a whimsical writer of the past as "sheened like a Kang Shi porcelain vase"—make it one of the most popular game fish in the world. A native of coastal drainages of the northern Pacific, it has been transplanted throughout North America, Europe, and South America.

It gets its name from the crimson to pinkish red band along the midline of its flanks. This reddish band may be absent in lake dwellers, which are generally more silver in appearance. It is marked across its head, back, and upper flanks with many small, irregular black spots that are concentrated most heavily on its squarish tail.

The rainbow trout, *Oncorhynchus mykiss*, was reclassified as part of the western salmon genus, *Oncorhynchus*, in 1990. Its former classification was with the Atlantic salmon genus, *Salmo*. Its former species name, *gairdneri irideus*, was replaced with *mykiss* because the Japanese description of the rainbow predated descriptions made in the western United States in the early 1800s.

The rainbow has been stocked in rivers and streams around the world. It is the principal hatchery-bred fish in Wyoming, but the modern trend toward wild fish management continues to gain acceptance. It is exhibiting promising results. A number of streams where past rainbow plantings have taken hold are producing remarkable fish under wild trout, quality management or trophy management policies. No new plantings are made in these waters, and harvest is strictly limited.

Shifting hatchery rainbow plantings away from wild trout populations to designated "put-and-take" streams and reservoirs is a policy of appeasement. It helps spread out angling pressure by offering enhanced opportunities to the general public for the waters "negated" by the stricter regulations on wild trout streams.

Discontinuing hatchery plants in restricted management streams is a biological decision, too. The disruptive, negative effects of hatchery rainbows on wild populations are well documented. It is a bit like dumping the cast from "West Side Story" into the serenity of a classical ballet.

Generally, in streams where wild fish predominate or on lakes and reservoirs with good holdover potential for hatchery fish, the average rainbow is 12 to 16 inches, with the potential in nutrient-rich waters for fish over 24 inches. In trophy lakes, a rare rainbow can reach 20 pounds. Landlocked monsters approaching this size take on the appearance of a potbellied pig, unlike the streamlined, typical rainbow characteristics maintained by necessity by the steelhead.

The rainbow is a spring spawner, like the cutthroat, which leads to hybridization when the species coexist. The rainbow, however, reaches sexual maturity earlier, at ages 2 or 3 years. In hatcheries, they often spawn at 1 year of age. The life span of the rainbow is fairly short; few live beyond 5 or 6 years of age.

Rainbow waters can be fast or slow, but chances are it will be found in faster moving and more turbulent waters than the choices made by cutthroat or browns. Larger fish are found in the prime holding areas favored by all trout, like overhanging banks, obvious feeding lanes or sheer lines, in front of or behind midstream structures, or at the head of deep pools. While more active in morning or evening, they will move far up into a riffle even at high noon during a prime hatch, using the moving water as cover. Dark, cloudy days will set the fish on the prowl at any hour. The heaviest mayfly hatches regularly occur on these types of days, too.

The rainbow is most active in waters 45 to 75 degrees Fahrenheit. Peak activity is in waters around 60 degrees.

It is a highly aggressive fish and will vigorously defend a feeding territory, especially against other salmonids of the same size.

Its food is anything it can catch and swallow. All sizes of rainbows depend heavily on aquatic and terrestrial insects. Larger fish prey on smaller fish, too, and are known to take small mammals like mice or meadow voles. While opportunistic, larger rainbows tend to be very selective and key in on a particular food source, especially during a multihatch of mayflies or caddisflies. They also may concentrate on a particular stage of a hatch, keying on the nymph, emerger or adult flying form, or, later, the dead, spinner form. Lake dwellers tend to be more piscivorous.

The selective feeding nature of large rainbows requires more patience and skill by a flyfisher. For those willing to be patient, it boils down to approach and presentation. Approach a feeding fish slowly and quietly to present a fly into its feeding lane. The key is a short-as-possible cast and a drag-free float through that lane. Most rainbows will not move to intercept a fly outside their feeding paths, so keep trying to put your fly right on the mark. Often, presentation is more critical than a perfect hatch match. If a fish shows an interest, present the fly again immediately. If your first choice doesn't work, rest the fish and try a different pattern. Above all, don't let your expectations cloud your appreciation of the challenge. A day on the stream is valuable, no matter how many fish you net.

Of course, all bets are off during major fly hatches like the salmonfly or western green drake. These "Big Macs" of the aquatic insect world bring up trout of all sizes. Wariness is abandoned. This also applies during prime grasshopper activity.

The standard set of dry flies to attract rainbows is much the same as for cutthroat, but, again, presentation is the more important factor. It should include elk hair caddis, stimulators, yellow sallies, humpies, Adams, pale morning dun, bluewinged olive, light Cahill, and parachute hare's ear. Nymph and emerger patterns for each of these can be equally effective, especially on riffles. Effective sizes for both dry and wet caddis and mayfly patterns can range from No. 10 to 16 in spring and early summer. By late fall, you may have to go as small as No. 18 and 22. Micropatterns of midges, callibaetis, and tricos also produce amazing results when that's the action on a particular stream. Sometimes small terrestrial patterns, such as ants and beetles, work best, even during an aquatic insect hatch.

Standard attractor flies like the renegade, royal Wulff, royal coachman, royal Trude, Goddard caddis or irresistible work as well, particularly in faster waters.

Larger streamers, muddlers, weighted nymphs, woolly buggers, super renegades, and rubberlegged patterns can be very effective for rainbows. Waders fish them deep, dredging the bottom; floatboaters pound the banks. Leech, dragonfly nymphs, woolly bugger, and freshwater shrimp patterns are effective in lakes. Sizes can range from No. 2 to 14.

Nine times out of 10, a rainbow will hook itself. Just hang on when a fly scores.

Rainbow Trout Identification

Rainbow Trout (*Oncorhynchus mykiss*)

Its common name comes from the broad swath of crimson to pinkish red usually seen along the midline of its flanks. Reddish band may be absent in lake dwellers, which are generally more silver in total appearance. River rainbow coloration ranges from olive to greenish-blue on the back, with white to silver on the belly. It is marked with many irregularly shaped black spots on the head, back, and tail, and extending below midline.

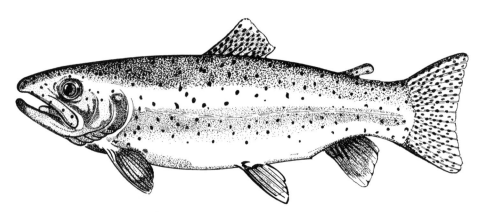

Rainbow Trout (Oncorhynchus mykiss)

GOLDEN TROUT: ALPINE BEAUTIES

Its species name eloquently defines the native haunts of the golden trout—*Oncorhynchus aguabonita*.

The Kern River drainage of California's Sierra Nevada Range harbors a host of *aguas bonita*. Beautiful waters—alpine lakes—complement and reflect the scenic splendors of the golden trout's acceptance of new homes in Wyoming's Wind River, Big Horn, Snowy, Absaroka, and Beartooth mountain ranges.

Golden trout first reached the Wind River in the 1930s in 5-gallon milk cans packed in by mules led by Finis Mitchell. A Rock Springs railroad man, Mitchell and his wife, Emma, opened a summer fishing camp in the Big Sandy area east of Pinedale to eke out an existence during the Great Depression. By 1937, Mitchell boasted of stocking 314 lakes in his beloved mountains. Along with golden trout, the 2.5 million fingerlings transported in sloshing milk cans included cutthroat, brook, rainbow, and brown trout. He also hooked lake trout and cutthroat for transplant to higher lakes.

The 12,482-foot Mitchell Peak was named for the "Man o' the Mountains."

His guidebook, *Wind River Trails*, is a classic in alpine hiking and fishing literature. It's a great read, but since he pioneered many of the range's trails, Mitchell tends to encourage bushwhacking cross-country.

A safer bet for newcomers entering these lofty heights is to pack a copy of *Walking the Winds* by Rebecca Woods and a set of topographical maps. Woods' guide also details the current status of trout species in the thousands of lakes that dot the 2.25-million acre mountain range.

Golden trout top the wish list of many flyfishers, but their pursuit is not a casual endeavor. Most of the lakes with bigger fish are 10,000 feet or higher, so being physically fit is a prerequisite to stalking golden trout. Windows of opportunity are short because ice-out at these elevations typically isn't until mid-July; in addition, goldens are notoriously difficult to catch. Hide-and-seek techniques and delicate presentations of tiny flies common to lowland spring creeks are the norm—only there are no weeds to hide behind, just ice-scoured rocks.

Zooplankton is the principal food of golden trout in high lakes, plus occasional windborne insects and midge hatches. Dry fly action usually is very limited. The most effective patterns are small nymphs and emergers, like caddis pupa, hare's ear, pheasant tail, soft-hackle, prince, and beadheads, sizes 10 to 14; scuds, 12 to 18, and midge dries and pupa, 18 to 20. Still, some lucky fly casters come upon goldens in lake tributaries during their spawning runs that aggressively hammer virtually any fly, including larger nymphs such as woolly worms and streamers.

Wyoming Game and Fish reports most golden trout seldom exceed 14 inches. Backpackers who get off the beaten path, far above timberline, report catches of 16- to 20-inch goldens. The Wind River's Cook Lake produced the world record, 11.25 pounds, in 1948.

A double-dare-you ad posted on the internet by a western Wyoming fishing guide sort of sums up why it has stood so long. "To go with me, you need to be in top physical condition and be able to backpack 15 miles per day in rugged, trailless country at elevations above 11,000 feet. I use no horses," he declaimed. "You'll also need to have nearly unlimited patience and be willing to fish in all weather conditions. And if you expect gourmet food and endless humorous stories around the campfire at night, this trip is not for you."

If you are that "rare one in 100,000 fisherman who truly wants to catch a monster golden trout," he'll take you, alone, for $800 a day. His recommendation for such an adventure is a minimum of 10 days.

More than a hundred lakes are managed for goldens by Game and Fish. But a new source of eggs is needed because a wild brood stock in Surprise Lake near Pinedale was lost in a forest fire. In 1996 and 1997, biologists attempted to collect eggs from the Copper Lakes in the Absarokas, but heavy winter snows and ice delayed the spawns and hindered collection efforts.

If conditions at the Copper Lakes don't improve, the department may have to look for another source. And that may be difficult to find. California long ago banned export of golden trout eggs, said Ron McKnight, Region 2 fisheries manager in Cody. Meanwhile, some golden trout lakes have not been stocked for several years, McKnight said.

Golden Trout Identification

Golden trout (*Oncorhynchus aguabonita*)

It has a silvery-green back with yellow-gold flanks, marked by oval parr marks along the lateral line. Black spots are strongly concentrated toward the tail; no spots appear on the front of the body, unlike on rainbows. It is distinguished from the cutthroat by white tips on the anal and pelvic fins.

BROWN TROUT: CRAFTY BRUTES

The brown trout's well-deserved reputation for wariness demands a dedicated effort on the part of anglers seeking one of these crafty brutes.

While most flyfishers pursue browns with large, heavy nymphs or streamers, they rise well to a dry fly when big flies like stoneflies or hoppers are present or a midge, mayfly, or caddis hatch is heavy enough to be profitable.

When hooked, its run is long and deep, although it will jump, especially in shallow-water runs or on riffles. It fights the hook with a bullheaded tenacity that can strip line from a singing reel more than once.

The brown's scientific name, *Salmo trutta*, declares it as the "true trout." It was first introduced into Wyoming at Yellowstone's Lewis and Shoshone Lakes in 1889 from stocks originating in Scotland and Germany. Many anglers commonly refer to it as a German brown.

Its basic coloration is an overall golden brown, with the back ranging from dark- to greenish-brown, and its sides and belly range from light tan to lemon-yellow or white. The back and flanks are marked with many large black or brown spots. The few red spots on the lower flanks are surrounded by light blue-gray halos. There are very few or no spots on its squarish tail.

Longer-lived than North American species, browns have been known to grow to sizes exceeding 30 pounds in the United States and up to 40 pounds in Europe. A previous U.S. record, 33 pounds, came from the Flaming Gorge Reservoir on the Green River on the southwestern Wyoming–northeastern Utah border.

The older the fish, the bigger and more wary it becomes. Browns normally grow about 4 to 6 inches a year the first three years. Growth then slows to about 2 inches a year, but browns have been know to live up to 15 years. Still, depending on environmental variables such as water temperature and available food, size can range widely. Average fish on some streams may range from 10 to 12 inches and up to 2 pounds, which is still a respectable fish. On others, lunkers over 25 inches and weighing 5 to 10 pounds may be common.

The preferred habitat of the brown is large rivers and lakes at lower elevations, although it can grow to remarkable size in small streams with adequate cover or deep pools. It is generally thought the brown is able to accept warmer waters than North American species, but the brown's most active periods mirror those of the rainbow. It is active in waters ranging from 45 to 70 degrees Fahrenheit, with activity peaking at 60 degrees. Cold water, in fact, spurs the brown's autumn spawning runs. Late October through December are the times trophy hunters most heavily flog the waters.

Browns first spawn at 3 or 4 years of age. They can spawn in lakes in shallow waters, but most move up into tributary streams. In rivers, browns are known to make long upstream runs to tributaries, but they will also spawn in shallow waters of their resident streams. In rivers with dams halting their upstream runs, they will go to extraordinary lengths to spawn, even to the extent of turning over cobble-sized rocks to create their redds.

A large spawning male can be distinguished from a female by its hooked lower jaw. This morphological adaptation is called a kype.

Browns rarely hybridize with brook trout, which also spawn in fall. It has, however, happened. One case was reported in California on a tributary to Lake Tahoe. The hybrids are called "tiger fish" and are sterile.

The typical realm of larger browns can be summed up in a single phrase: "Under the cover of darkness."

Small browns can be found in most waters common to other trout species. Larger fish prefer quieter waters than cutthroat or rainbows, and they are more likely to hole up in areas where they feel safest and don't have to expend undue energy to feed.

By day, they hide out in the darker cover provided by deep pools, overhanging banks, and bankside or midstream structures such as logjams and large boulders. The other essential element of a good brown hiding place is that it has a steady supply of food streaming into it or close by.

A big brown will lay claim to the same prime spot for years. When it succumbs to old age or an angler, another large brown fills the vacancy.

Older browns are nocturnal feeders, as well as being very active during early morning or evening hours and on heavily overcast days. At these times, they'll move out of the deeper waters of lakes and cruise the shallows or come out of their streamside haunts on feeding excursions.

An angler planning to linger into the night should scout out the area first, or only attempt it on well-known home waters. He needs to know the obstacles to avoid when casting to things that go plunk in the night and, for his own safety, to prevent getting into a precarious situation.

Browns are known for their piscivorous nature, which contributes to their ability to obtain massive body weight. They even eat their own kind, but they also feed on a large variety of other organisms, including aquatic and terrestrial insects, mollusks and crawfish.

To entice them from their deeper hiding places, a lot of anglers resort to the chuck-and-duck technique of casting large nymphs to large trout. These heavy patterns in sizes 2 to 6 include large stonefly nymphs, woolly buggers, Zug Bugs, and super renegades. They are bounced off the bottom or drifted just above it. Also effective in similar sizes are streamers such as marabou or bullethead muddlers, zonkers, and spruce flies that imitate sculpin or other baitfish.

Both styles of wet flies can be used to pound the banks, too, by both drift boat and wading anglers. The same goes for large, buggy styles of dry fly patterns. In either case, hit the places with the thickest cover the hardest.

Stonefly hatches bring large browns up just like other trout in spring. In midsummer, a hopper bounced off a grassy bank or tossed up under an overhanging tree can be deadly. Smaller dry flies, including large drakes, caddis patterns, and stimulators in No. 10 to No. 14 occasionally bring up a good-sized fish if floated directly through a feeding lane. Browns will move the least of all the trout to intercept a fly. Still, under the right conditions, they will move up into a riffle to grub for nymphs or take emergers. And when there's a carpet hatch, they will slurp down huge quantities of microflies, such as midges, tricos, and callibaetis. Western anglers pursuing these cruisers call them gulpers and revel in the experience of taking a 20- to 25-inch fish on a No. 20 or 22 hook.

Whether you use wet or dry patterns, you can expect to lose more than a few if you are getting them into the haunts where large browns reside. That is one of the costs of going after these hiders. Also expect to spend more time on the water. Studies show that for every five rainbow or brook trout taken, one brown is caught.

It is sometimes easier to tie into one during the fall spawning season, but some anglers frown on this practice because the fish are more vulnerable at this time, and their redds can be damaged by waders. Other trophy hunters attempt to intercept large browns in long, deep runs on their upstream migrations and in the tailwaters of dams blocking spawning runs. Autumn weather plays a major role in this pursuit. You can encounter conditions commonly associated with steelhead fishing, when days of spitting rain or snow prove to be the most rewarding.

Any time of the year, a brown in the net is a flyfisher's reward earned the hard way.

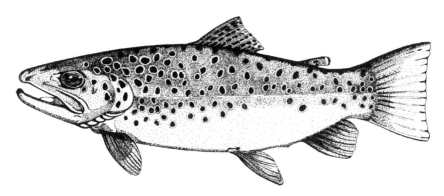

Brown Trout (Salmo trutta)

Brown Trout Identification

Brown Trout (*Salmo trutta*)

The coloration is generally golden brown; the back is dark- to greenish-brown, with the sides and belly ranging from light brown to lemon yellow. Spaced out, large black or brown spots are mixed with a few red spots on the sides. These spots have light blue-gray halos. The adipose fin usually has an orange border. Very few or no spots can be seen on its squarish tail.

Brook Trout: High Country Brawlers

The flamboyant brook trout is the painted porcelain doll of the trout world. A beautiful fish, it is almost birdlike in the brilliance of its colors.

Brookies offer stubborn, scrappy fights, with leaps rivaling the rainbow's, and frantic, line-tugging runs.

Native to East Coast and Canadian waters, the brook trout, *Salvelinus fontinalis*, is actually a char, like the lake trout, bull trout, Dolly Varden, and Arctic char. Both trout and char belong to the same family, *Salmonidae*. The main difference between the two is that char have light spots on dark backgrounds and trout have dark spots on light backgrounds. Both prefer cold water environments, but char seek out the coldest.

Introduced into the West in the 1880s, the brook trout is a resident of pure, cold waters of headwater mountain streams and alpine lakes. To find brookies in Wyoming, head for the high country.

Unfortunately, its eastern reputation as a scrappy fighter is lost to most Western anglers because it tends to overpopulate the waters it occurs in, which stunts its growth. The short growing seasons of alpine lakes also contribute to its diminutive size. But many high country hikers don't mind. They love to catch pan-size brookies because they are excellent table fare, often rated as the best among the trout species.

Take advantage of it, as Wyoming provides anglers a very generous harvest limit on small brook trout.

Average size in most western waters is 8 to 12 inches, although its potential is much greater. Brook trout sometimes take up residence in lower lakes, reservoirs, and beaver ponds, where they may grow to a substantial size and provide a tussle worthy of their renown as excellent game fish. A 2- or 3-pounder taken from one of these waters is considered a good-sized fish.

The brook trout's most distinctive markings are white and black edges on the fronts of its lower fins. It is dark green or blue-black on its back, fading to white on the belly. Numerous wavy wormlike lines, or vermiculations, cover its back and dorsal fin. Scattered red spots surrounded by blue halos are seen on its flanks. The belly and lower fins of a spawning male are brilliant red in autumn.

Brook trout reach sexual maturity in 2 or 3 years. Their life span ranges from 6 to 10 years, although a fish over 5 is rare. It is a fall spawner and breeds in both streams and lakes.

The brook hybridizes with other trout species and its introduction into the West, along with habitat loss and pollution, are the main contributors to the demise of the native bull trout throughout much of its former range.

There is at least one record in California of brook trout naturally crossbreeding with the fall-spawning brown trout, an introduced European species. The two also are crossbred in hatcheries. The hybrids are called "tiger trout," due to their yellowish coloration marked with dark, wavy stripes. Some states, like Wyoming, also cross brook trout with lake trout in hatcheries for introduction into a few lakes. These hybrids are called "splake."

The brook trout is the classic coldwater fish. Anglers who like to fish small waters can do well seeking it out in the churning pocket waters and small pools of Wyoming's cascading mountain streams. In quieter waters, it can be found lurking under overhanging stream banks and under logjams. Beaver pond and lake haunts include the edges of weedbeds near deep pools and along bushy banks. As the summer heats up, they often hang out in the cooler water at the mouths of tributary streams or spring inflows.

Rarely found in waters with prolonged temperatures above 65 degrees Fahrenheit, it is most active in waters ranging from 45 to 65 degrees. Activity peaks at 58 degrees.

Its primary food base is aquatic insects and other small aquatic invertebrates, but it also attacks terrestrial insects with abandon. Larger brook trout eat small fish, including their own kind.

In fast waters, high-floating buggy patterns, such as the Goddard caddis or humpy, and easily seen attractor patterns, such as the royal Wulff or royal Trude, work best. Standard nymphs can include the gold-ribbed hare's ear and caddis emergers. The new beadhead patterns eliminate the bother of dealing with split shot. Streamers also can be effective in streams and lakes. Leech and freshwater shrimp patterns, dragonfly nymphs, and woolly buggers are good producers in lakes and ponds.

Some consider the brook trout only slightly less gullible than the cutthroat. On small streams or alpine lakes where populations are profuse, brookies offer a good chance for young anglers to practice their flyfishing skills.

At times, brook trout can be overexploited like the cutthroat, particularly by hot-spotting anglers going after big fish in a lake or pond. Most often, though, larger fish are more cautious, usually active only in the early morning or evening hours or on heavily overcast days. On quiet waters, such as smooth flowing streams and beaver ponds, they should be approached slowly and quietly, using available cover.

Many flyfishers like to pursue brook trout with light tackle, like a 2-weight rod or one of the smaller backpacking models. A substantial brookie taken on one of these is a true challenge.

Large or small, a brook trout in the hand is a portrait of beauty taken in a picture-postcard setting.

Brook Trout Identification

Brook Trout (*Salvelinus fontinalis*)

The most distinctive markings are the white and black edges on the fronts of lower fins; it also has wavy or wormlike markings on its back and scattered red spots surrounded by blue halos on its flanks. It is dark green or blue-black on the back to white on the belly. In fall, the belly and lower fins turn brilliant red in spawning males. The tail is square.

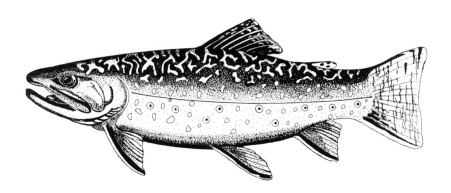

Brook Trout (Salvelinus fontinalis)

LAKE TROUT: WOLVES OF THE DEEP

Wyoming's largest game fish, the lake trout, tipped the scales at 50 pounds and set the state record in both Jackson Lake and Flaming Gorge.

Native to the Northeast, the Great Lakes area and Canadian waters, the lake trout, *Salvelinus namaychush*, is a char like the brook trout. Its overall coloration is gray, and it has no colored spots like the brook trout. The lake trout's tail is deeply forked; the brook trout's is square.

Lake trout planted in Yellowstone Park's Lewis Lake in 1889 are the Bear Island strain from the northwest shore of Lake Michigan. They then migrated to Shoshone and to Heart Lakes. Eventually they made their way down the Snake River to Jackson Lake, and since then they have been stocked in numerous Wyoming waters. In 1994, lakers were discovered in Yellowstone Lake, the progeny of an illegal introduction that may have occurred in the 1970s.

Also called Mackinaw, lake trout inhabit large, deep lakes, but occasionally they are washed through dams or over waterfalls into the rivers below. They are very sensitive to warm temperatures and in summer may go as deep as 300 feet to find cool water. They spawn in fall over rocky shoals in lakes rather than in moving water like other trout.

Once it reaches 20 inches, a lake trout's diet is almost exclusively fish, including other trout, chubs, suckers, whitefish, and kokanee.

Flyfishers get their best shot at lakers in shallow waters after ice-out on lakes in spring and again in fall when cool weather reduces shoreline water temperatures. Lakers also follow spawning rainbow and brown trout out of lakes into streams like the Miracle Mile above Pathfinder Reservoir on the North Platte River and the Lewis River in the park. Large nymphs, streamers, woolly buggers, and egg patterns are the most effective flies.

Wyoming crossbreeds brook trout with lake trout in hatcheries for introduction into a few lakes. Called "splake," these sterile hybrids grow faster than their parents. They also cause less damage if they get into waters where lakers are unwanted—like Yellowstone Lake.

Illegal introduction of lake trout in the lake has caused great dismay because the predator could seriously harm the foremost inland cutthroat sport fishery in North America. In addition to destruction of the lake's fishery, a lake trout takeover would ravage the fabled fishery in the Yellowstone River between the lake and Upper Falls. The threat is real since it is credited with virtually eliminating cutthroat from Jackson Lake.

War has been declared, but escalating numbers and increased sizes of lake trout captured in four years of gillnetting terrify Yellowstone's guardians. In 1997, almost 1,050 were netted by biologists or hooked by anglers. Of perhaps greatest concern is growing evidence that there are more older lake trout in the lake than previously estimated. The largest laker caught in 1996 was a 21-pound female. Stomach analyses show they are feeding almost exclusively on the lake's native Yellowstone cutthroat trout despite the presence of four other prey species.

Anglers are required by the park to kill all lake trout taken from Yellowstone Lake and Heart Lake. On other park waters, as well as elsewhere in Wyoming, regulations for harvest are still in place.

Growth potential for lake trout in Yellowstone Lake is phenomenal, considering the histories of the other lakes. Unofficial trophy fish records from the three range from 50 pounds in Heart Lake to 40 pounds in Shoshone Lake and 30 pounds in Lewis Lake.

The record angler catch was a 63-pound, 51.5-inch lake trout from Lake Superior in 1952. The largest one ever netted was a 121-pound gargantuan from a Canadian lake.

Ironically, eggs collected in Lewis Lake have been used to establish brood stocks to return lake trout to Lake Michigan.

Lake Trout Identification

Lake Trout (*Salvelinus namaychush*)

Colors are dark gray or gray-green on the head and upper flanks, slightly gray to white on the belly. Irregularly shaped gray spots are found on the back, sides, dorsal fin, and tail. There are no pink or blue spots. White borders on the fins are less distinct than on brook trout. The tail is deeply forked.

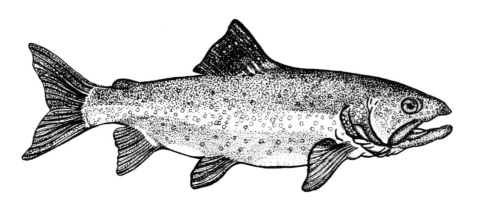

Lake Trout (Salvelinus namaychush)

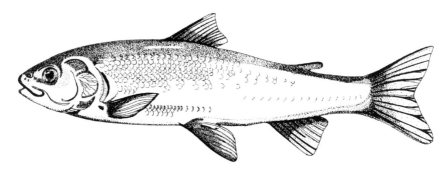

Mountain Whitefish (Prosopium williamsoni)

MOUNTAIN WHITEFISH: UNHERALDED GAME FISH

The whitefish gets little respect from flyfishers on trout-rich waters. There is almost a social stigma against taking one, but it is an excellent food species. Fishing for whitefish is most popular in winter, when they are more active than trout.

Part of the scorn for whitefish is a presumption that it competes with trout. In fact, the two species evolved to occupy separate niches in a shared habitat. There is no biological evidence that high whitefish numbers harm trout populations.

While it is in the same family as trout, salmon, and char, Salmonidae, the whitefish's silvery body is slender and almost round in cross-section. It has a small head and tiny mouth, with a slightly overhanging snout. Its scales are large and coarse. Like its cousins, it has an adipose fin.

The most common species in the Northern Rockies, the mountain whitefish, *Prosopium williamsoni*, prefers clear, cool streams. It is also found in some lakes. The Lewis and Clark Expedition first recorded the species for science.

A similar species is the rare arctic grayling, *Thymallus arcticus*, whose trademark is its huge, colorful sail-like dorsal fin.

Mountain whitefish average 10 to 12 inches, but on nutrient-rich streams, 18- to 20-inch fish are relatively common.

Whitefish hang out in deep pools and shallow, slow-water runs. They feed actively in riffles on mayfly nymphs and caddis larvae. Surface feeding on adult insects occurs most often toward evening.

Among the best wet flies for whitefish are small green-colored nymphs, caddis larvae, and emergers. Beadhead patterns are very effective. Perhaps because of their small mouths, many whitefish fail to take a dry fly when they strike. These misses can be frustrating, but they are also a sign that actively rising fish aren't trout.

Whitefish spawn in late fall and remain active through the winter. Midge patterns can be productive at this time.

Whitefish Identification

Mountain Whitefish (*Prosopium williamsoni*)

The color is light grayish blue on the back, silver on the sides, and dull white on the belly. Scales are large, and it has a small mouth without teeth. The body is almost round in cross-section. (A similar species, the Arctic grayling, *Thymallus arcticus*, has a large dorsal fin, sail-like and colorful. Dark spots are on a silvery body.)

ARCTIC GRAYLING: SILVERY SAILFISH

The first trademark of the arctic grayling, *Thymallus arcticus*, is its huge, colorful sail-like dorsal fin. Its second is a characteristic leap to take floating flies on the returning dive into the water.

The grayling is a popular game fish, both because of its beauty and its rarity.

A native of Wyoming in Yellowstone National Park's Madison drainage, it was exterminated by the early 1900s due to introduction of nonnative species, primarily brook trout. It was reintroduced to the park in 1921 and then transplanted to other Wyoming waters.

Meadow Lake, southeast of Pinedale, is the state's principal grayling fishery and source of its eggs for transplants. Grebe Lake in the park was for many years its hatchery source for grayling after reintroduction of the Montana subspecies. Both Wyoming and Yellowstone have shared grayling eggs with other states and Canadian provinces. The park is attempting to reestablish fluvial, or river-running, grayling in tributaries of the Madison River.

It spawns in spring by migrating into tributaries or outlets of lakes. After high water years, Grebe Lake grayling often show up in the Gibbon and Madison Rivers. It is also present in Wolf and Cascade Lakes in the park.

Though they are coldwater fish, grayling generally do best in shallow mountain lakes with longer growing seasons than in alpine lakes. They sometimes become stunted from overpopulation. The Wyoming record is a 2.4-pounder from Meadow Lake, where larger grayling run from 12 to 18 inches. The Arctic subspecies grows much larger.

Grayling, while suckers for small dry flies, particularly terrestrial patterns like ants and beetles, rise eagerly to most any small dry fly or attractor pattern. And they take small nymphs with even more abandon.

Grayling in Yellowstone are catch-and-release. Wyoming permits inclusion of grayling in its aggregate trout bag limit. Think twice; it's almost too easy to catch one of these relics of the past. Their distinctive lavender sheen quickly fades, and it's not the same fish in a creel.

Arctic Grayling (Thymallus arcticus)

Grayling Identification

Arctic Grayling (*Thymallus arcticus*)

The dorsal fin is large, sail-like, and colorful. Dark spots are on the front half with purple-silver sides; scales are more pronounced than on trout. The mouth is trout-like. The adipose fin is very small and slender. The forked tail has rounded tips. (A similar species, the mountain whitefish, *Prosopium williamsoni*, has a small pointed mouth, small dorsal fin, and large rounded adipose fin.)

Help Prevent Whirling Disease Spread

by Lucy Diggins

Preliminary evidence of fisheries surveys suggests distribution of the whirling disease parasite, or spore, is expanding in Wyoming. Whirling disease is blamed for the reduction or elimination of some rainbow trout populations in Colorado and Montana.

Whirling disease affects trout and salmon. The disease is caused by a microscopic parasite known as *Myxobolus cerebralis*. This water-borne spore attacks cartilage tissue of the fish head and spine. The water-borne parasite may not directly kill trout, but fish heavily infested can become deformed and have black tails. Fish can also exhibit a characteristically erratic tail-chasing or whirling behavior.

The disease parasite has a two-host life cycle involving trout and a common bottom-dwelling tubifex worm. When infected trout die, spores are released and then ingested by the tubifex. Inside the worm's gut, the spores incubate and multiply rapidly. A single tubifex worm can harbor up to 1,000 mature "actinosporean," the infectious stage of whirling disease. Mature triactinomyxon spores are released. Healthy trout are infected by contact with the spores or by eating infected tubifex worms.

Whirling disease spores are hardy, resisting freezing and drought and remaining viable for decades. There is documentation of spores living in dried mud for up to 30 years.

Young fish are at the greatest risk because the parasite attacks their soft cartilage, causing nerve damage, skeletal deformities and sometimes death. Older fish are more resistant to infection. Unfortunately, these fish remain carriers of the parasite.

Whirling disease occurs in Europe and probably originated there. Native brown trout may have developed a natural resistance to the parasite through co-evolution. However, these fish still carry and transmit the spores.

The disease is thought to have been introduced into the United States in the late 1950s via processed fish shipments to Pennsylvania. It spread throughout the Northeast, and in 1965 was documented in California. The disease spread to Oregon by 1986 and to Idaho by 1987, where it became endemic to steelhead spawning grounds of the upper Salmon River system. Also in 1987, an infected Idaho commercial hatchery unknowingly transmitted whirling disease to a private aquaculture operation in Colorado. Within a year, the disease was identified at two state hatcheries, nine private commercial fish hatcheries, and 11 of 15 coldwater river drainages in Colorado.

Whirling disease spores were first detected in Wyoming in 1988 in rainbow and brown trout collected from private farm ponds and adjacent streams and lakes in southeast Wyoming. Currently, 22 states have reported incidents of the disease. The Wyoming Game and Fish Department's fish pathologist, Dave Money, says salmonids from 13 waters, which are part of three major drainage systems in

Wyoming (North Platte, South Platte, and the Snake River), now test positive for the whirling disease parasite. "*Myxobolus cerebralis* has now been identified in adult and juvenile rainbow and brown trout from the upper 65 miles of the North Platte River and in several of its tributaries," says Money. "Currently, no clinical signs of whirling disease have been observed in fish collected from this system. The parasite has not yet been detected in any of the reservoirs (Seminoe, Pathfinder, or Alcova) on the North Platte River drainage."

Rainbow trout (1988) and brook trout (1996) collected from tributaries of the South Platte River system tested positive for *Myxobolus cerebralis*. However, no fish population declines linked to whirling disease have been reported in this area. All trout populations have natural cycles (highs and lows), and, so far, whirling disease has not been implicated in any of these cycles. Money says the presence of the organism in brook trout examined from one stream in the South Platte River system is in about 20 percent of catchable-sized fish. No obvious clinical sign of the disease has been observed in examined fish of either species.

The most recent discovery of whirling disease in Wyoming occurred in 1996 in portions of the Salt River within the Snake River drainage. The Salt River heads in the Salt River Range and flows northwest into Palisades Reservoir and the Snake River. Game and Fish fish biologists detected the parasite in adult rainbow trout, Snake River cutthroat, rainbow/cutthroat hybrids and juvenile mountain whitefish collected from the upper sections of the Salt River.

Money says clinical signs of whirling disease are present in about 10 percent of the examined rainbows of catchable size from an upper section of the Salt River. Thus far, Jackson fisheries biologists have not seen any evidence of population declines in the Salt River system, nor have they received any reports from anglers of morbid or dead fish.

Laboratory spore counts indicate that wild trout collected from Wyoming waters show an obvious pattern of species infectivity, in descending order — rainbow, mountain whitefish, rainbow/cutthroat hybrids, brook, brown and Snake River cutthroat. Money believes this pattern of infectivity may be a reflection of the actual susceptibility of wild trout populations in river environments. "Whether this pattern is due to immunological factors or may be a behavioral adaptation of the fish is yet to be determined," he says.

To date, whirling disease has had little, if any, impact in Wyoming. There have been no fish population crashes in any Wyoming waters where the spores of *Myxobolus cerebralis* have been found. Mature healthy fish continue to thrive, but the occurrence of the parasite is increasing.

Game and Fish biologists continue to monitor wild and domestic fish populations statewide, and disease surveys are conducted annually. There is no known treatment for infected fish in the wild.

Sheridan fisheries biologist Bill Bradshaw reports that whirling disease has not been detected in Sheridan region waters. "At least in the Little Big Horn, Tongue,

Middle Fork Powder, and Bull Creek, it hasn't. We'd really prefer not to have it show up in the region, but other than education, there really is little we can do to prevent it."

Green River fisheries biologist Bill Wengert says no fish in the Green, Bear, or Little Snake River drainages have tested positive for whirling disease spores.

"Certainly we are concerned about the disease and the chance it could accidentally be transported into our waters from out-of-state boaters," Wengert says. "We're worried about bass anglers using live wells on boats coming from known whirling disease drainages in Colorado, Utah, and Idaho. If it does show up in Flaming Gorge Reservoir, we will probably see it manifested in whitefish populations first."

Game and Fish has tried to control or slow the spread of the pathogen by authorizing only disease-free fish to be stocked in Wyoming waters from all private and public hatcheries. And the Colorado Division of Wildlife has agreed not to stock any fish known to be carriers of the pathogen in any waters directly connected to the Laramie or North Platte River drainages that flow into Wyoming.

In some contaminated waters, stocking of susceptible rainbow trout could be replaced by stocking larger, more resistant brown trout. Lake and brown trout hybrids, such as tiger trout and splake, may be evaluated and tested for their resistance to the disease.

Here are a few tips to help anglers slow the spread of whirling disease in Wyoming:

- Clean all equipment, including boats, trailers, boots, and float tubes of mud before leaving the river or lake.
- Do not transport any river or lake water in coolers, buckets, boats, or live wells from one river basin to another.
- Disinfect equipment at home with a 1 percent solution of chlorine bleach to destroy the parasite.
- Don't transport live fish between bodies of water. This practice could spread the disease and is strictly illegal.
- Don't dispose of fish heads, skeletons, or entrails in any body of water. Fish parts should be disposed of in the garbage or by burning.

How will whirling disease affect Wyoming's fisheries? Game and Fish fisheries management coordinator Bob Wiley says the agency does not know what the future holds. "The message is clear. The Game and Fish and Wyoming anglers and recreationalists must do everything possible to prevent the spread of the pathogen," Wiley says. "Wyoming's fish culture system has been and remains free of the whirling disease pathogen. That status is cherished. Many states are not so fortunate."

Rainbows vs. Walleyes

Wyoming Department of Game and Fish

In the upper North Platte reservoirs this is a given: walleye eat trout. But at what size is a rainbow trout walleye-proof? That question is important to Wyoming Game and Fish Department fisheries biologists who have an important goal of helping anglers get a better return on the stocked trout their licenses purchase.

Dan Yule, Game and Fish reservoir research biologist in Casper, coordinated an experiment to examine the vulnerability of different sized trout to walleye predation. With the help of two Colorado State University professors and others, small ponds were stocked with trout and walleye. Each pond received five walleye measuring either 13 to 15 inches, 15 to 17 inches or 19 to 21 inches and 50 5-,7-, or 9-inch hatchery rainbows. Control ponds received trout and no walleye to serve as a yard stick of how many trout were lost to birds and natural mortality. After 10 days the researchers drained the ponds to discover some pretty clear-cut results.

"We learned 5-inch trout are very vulnerable to all the walleye size classes, including the 13- to 15-inchers," Yule said. "On the other hand, 9-inch trout are difficult for even a 21-inch walleye to eat." The 7-inch rainbows were readily eaten by the largest walleye-size class but were difficult for the 15- to 17-inch walleye to ingest.

"We're confident these experiments give us a pretty clear picture of what trout sizes can be eaten by walleye," said Yule, who earned an American Fisheries Society award for his research. "Particularly because the predators have a profound advantage because the ponds had no place for trout to hide and the walleye had nothing else to eat."

The research has now been taken to the wild with Wyoming Game and Fish stocking Alcova and Pathfinder Reservoirs with 7- and 9-inch rainbows. "Since Alcova is dominated by walleye bigger than 20 inches, we expect 9-inch trout to return to anglers better than 7-inch trout," Yule said. "We should see an excellent return of 7-inch trout in Pathfinder where few walleye exceed 16 inches.'

He adds the advantage of planting smaller sizes is that more can be raised in the limited Game and Fish hatchery space.

Equipment Check List and Travel Tips

When setting off on a fishing trip, make your travel list and check it twice. Nothing ruins a vacation more than forgetting to bring a key piece of equipment. Be paranoid; check off your rods, reels, and fishing vest a third time.

Come prepared for inclement weather and be physically fit to handle high-elevation trekking.

Summer Equipment Check List

____ Selection of rods and reels, such as a 7- or 6-weight, 8½- or 9-foot graphite rod and a 4- or 5-weight, 8½- or 9-foot graphite rod. For alpine hiking trips, a 3- or 4-piece backpack rod is recommended. Optional: Extra reel spool(s) equipped with shooting-head floating line or sinking line.

____ Fishing vest or fanny pack to hold tackle.

____ Forceps to remove hooks from fish; line nippers or fingernail clippers to trim leader tippets, trim flies.

____ Selection of tapered leaders and tippet material, 2X to 6X; selection of sinking tips.

____ Selection of standard aquatic insect fly patterns, wet and dry, like pale morning duns, blue-winged olives, elk hair caddis, parachute Adams; beadhead hare's ear, pheasant tail, and Prince nymphs; PMD and caddis emergers; muddler minnows, Zonkers, and woolly worms. Attractor patterns can include renegades, humpies, stimulators, and royal Wulffs. Terrestrial patterns should include grasshoppers, beetles, and ants. Inquire locally for specialized patterns or seasonally appropriate dry flies, emergers and nymphs.

____ Fly floatant.

____ Nontoxic split shot.

____ Fishing net.

____ Stocking foot chest waders and wading shoes.

____ Wading staff if you plan to wade rocky or swift waters.

____ Polarized sunglasses.

____ Stout fishing hat to protect neck and ears.

____ Lightweight rain jacket.

____ Wool or fleece sweater, windbreaker jacket, fingerless gloves for cool mornings and evenings.

____ Water bottle or canteen.

___ Sunscreen lotion.

___ Insect repellent.

___ Camera, extra film, and batteries.

Fall and Winter Equipment Check List

In addition to the above, pack the following:

___ Neoprene chest waders.

___ Extra warm clothing to wear in layers.

___ Warm hat or wool ski cap that covers ears.

___ Neoprene gloves, wool gloves.

___ Heavy wool socks and polypropylene foot liners.

___ Cigarette lighter in waterproof pouch to start fire.

___ High-energy snacks to munch on.

___ Full change of clothing in vehicle in case you get wet.

___ Parka and down vest for campwear, gloves or mittens.

TRAVEL TIPS

Flyfishers embarking for Wyoming via commercial airlines should plan on transfers at one or more service hubs, some with layovers. Plan accordingly and protect your equipment.

Pack rods in aluminum or plastic rod holders or a rod-holder caddy, securely sealed and clearly labeled with name and home address. Make sure flight destination tags are firmly attached.

Better yet, try to carry onto the plane all the rods and reels you can. A good option is to have a travel rod that breaks down into 3 or 4 pieces. It may be more difficult to carry on a two-piece rod, but some airlines permit it. Stuff your basic equipment and bare essentials into a duffel bag for the second carry-on piece of luggage.

Never ship cameras or telephoto lenses as cargo in recognizable photography equipment containers. If you don't plan to take them as carry-on luggage, stuff them into your suitcases.

Travel light; don't be a clotheshorse. Your fishing equipment is most important.

Be in Shape

Wyoming is high, wide, and handsome, its rivers big and powerful. Be prepared for their physical challenges.

Coastal visitors should remember that as soon as the plane lands you're already almost a mile above sea level. Your next destination is often higher.

Don't overextend yourself wading or boating, appreciate the volume of the bigger rivers. One cubic foot per second of water, the standard measurement of flow, is roughly equivalent to one foot of water continually flooding a football field. A football field is flat and rock-free. Wyoming rivers are not, and their waters are almost always frigid. Below some dams, flows can change radically without advance notice.

Hiring a Guide

If you have to ask how much it costs, you can't afford it. Wrong.

This could be the best investment for a successful vacation. A good guide improves the gamble when taking a first venture into new waters or jumping into a drainage for a whirlwind tour. Inexperienced flyfishers benefit the most, but even experts savor the rapport that can develop between pro and client.

Wyoming does not require fishing guides to work for licensed outfitters, but most do. Contact outfitters or fly shops for information or reservations. Ask for references.

Costs have held reasonably steady. Floatboat trips for one or two range from $200 to $350 per day, lunch included. A full-day float is a better deal than the price of a half-day. An even better deal, with more personal one-on-one exchanges and lessons, is a guided wading tour of a stream. Three or five anglers can take advantage of this option. Sign on for a split day and you can fish the best parts of the day, morning and dusk.

Package deals that include fishing, lodging and meals may exceed $1,000 per day. Outfitters that don't have resorts often help arrange accommodations and other travel needs such as airport shuttles.

But first you have to get on board. Most outfitters are booked solid during the busiest parts of the summer or during key hatches. Plan trips in advance and call early for reservations. Plan on making a deposit, but determine what period of advance notice of cancellation or acts of nature qualify for a refund.

Some outfitters have staffs large enough for drop-in traffic. This can be a hit or miss proposition. Again, call ahead. Cancellations reopen opportunities to connect.

Be reasonable and plan to have fun. Don't expect guides or outfitters to overcome current natural conditions if things go sour.

Tip your guide. He's an independent contractor who carries his own load, including equipment and flies, although he works for an outfitter. An offer to pay for a drink or dinner after an 8- to 12-hour day doesn't cut it.

Again, have fun. That's the single guarantee of any venture into the boondocks.

Basic Dry Flies
Traditional Patterns Endure Tests of Time

"I need another one of those green peacock flies with the brown and white hackles," my brother-in-law insisted.

It was John Braastad's first Western flyfishing adventure. He fidgeted impatiently as concentric circles pockmarked the quiet backwater where our canoe was beached. But, with trout rising all around, I was slow to respond to his plea. He waded over and thrust his hand in my face to catch my attention.

The half dozen Renegades I added to his meager fly pattern collection at the boat launch would, I thought, last the day. They were lost to the river's feisty rainbows before we had floated even halfway to our pull-out. He was eager to try another one of my dwindling supply of the dry fly attractor pattern.

Eventually, with encouragement to set the hook delicately and let the rainbow run on their panic-filled escape flights, John landed one. He was ecstatic. The conversion of a usually super-stoic Minnesotan from bait fisherman to fly caster was worth a picture for the scrapbook.

A decade after that trial-and-error day, John returned in 1995. This time he packed his own flies. Many were tied at his bench, and he was eager to see them fulfill the dream-filled nights of Minnesota's interminable winters. So, a conversation on a high-flowing Yellowstone cutthroat stream was decidedly different.

First off, John discounted my advice to tie on a Yellow Sally—even as I landed an 18-inch cutthroat. A No. 14 should work best, I recommended. But, as I was too busy to notice while playing a second cutthroat, John disappeared.

"Typical Scandinavian," I muttered.

John soon redeemed himself. He trotted upstream five minutes later, his net bulging with his own cutthroat. The 22-inch beauty had him scrambling for the camera in his backpack.

"What did you catch him on?"

"A No. 16 dark-brown elk hair caddis. I saw him rising at the end of the run and, then, when he took it, he got into the fast water and I had to go downstream with him. Almost lost him," John replied breathlessly. He was hard pressed to say which amazed him more, the size of the cutthroat or the size of the fly he used to catch it. Either way, the photo probably will fuel fireside stories for generations of Minnesota winters.

As we stood there discussing the phenomenon of catching large trout on small flies, you could tell by our outfits that we were flyfishers. An assortment of doodads and thingamajigs to make it easier to clip lines, make flies float, and catch and release fish dangled from our fishing vests like ornaments on Christmas trees. Neoprene waders, wide brimmed hats and polarized sunglasses completed our uniforms.

More telling were the many bulging pockets on our vests. No dedicated flyfisher's vest is complete without 10 to 30 boxes capable of holding several hundred flies.

Many also pack containers in their car trunks filled with additional fly boxes. Truly rabid flyfishers pack fly tying vices and materials.

This obsession with being prepared for all situations makes fly shop cash registers sing the Star Spangled Banner year-round. For those who tie their own flies, numerous magazine articles send them scurrying to their fly tying benches.

But what if you are only recently learning to wet a line, or just want to have fun without all the hassle? For newcomers and fun seekers, alike, it's a good idea to stick to traditional fly patterns. There's a lot to be said for tradition.

Sure, spring creeks and other selectively feeding trout situations present challenges requiring more finesse in fly selection. Don't worry; you'll evolve to that plateau. On less demanding waters, fly pattern anxiety is unnecessary. Newcomers can perform reasonably well with tried-and-true patterns. Catching a trout on a No. 14 Old Fashion attractor pattern is just as much fun as catching one on a No. 22 High Tech modern concoction.

Interestingly, several of the best traditional dry fly patterns can be fished wet, too, or using a combination of the two. Also, while many generic dry flies originated in the East, Upper Midwest, or on the West Coast, they perform very effectively in the Intermountain West.

Common aquatic choices are generalized imitations of mayflies, caddisflies, and stoneflies. Terrestrial imitations include grasshoppers, ants, beetles, and crickets.

With those options in mind, consider the following as a quick course in Basic Dry Fly Patterns 101:

Dry Fly Attractor Patterns

Attractor patterns that float like corks are steadfast producers on the pocket waters of the West's fast-flowing, cascading mountain streams. When in doubt (or if there is no obvious mayfly or caddis hatch), start with a high-riding attractor pattern. These patterns are not intended to represent any single species of aquatic insect. Instead, their colors and characteristics mimic the essential ingredients of mayflies and caddis, as well as those of some terrestrial insects. Stepped down a size or two, the same flies perform admirably on quiet waters, especially during masking hatches of more than one species.

Mayfly attractor patterns rely on glossy colors to mimic key strike factors presumed to attract fish. More numerous in number, variety and down-to-earth colors are the prolific caddisfly families and the smaller species of the stonefly families. Most caddis attractor patterns employ simple tufts of hair for wings and earth tone body materials. Still, vivid colors cannot be denied a role, and some caddis attractors rival mayfly versions.

Colorful Attractors

The Renegade is a classic dry fly attractor that replicates key characteristics of caddisflies. Hackle wraps at the front and back make it float better than a cork. Its peacock body is the main ingredient of numerous other productive attractor patterns.

The white hackle in front gives it visibility; the brown hackle at the rear provides natural stimulation for fish strikes.

The Renegade's greatest charm is that it often saves the day for novices and pros alike. Play it safe. Don't go afield without a selection in sizes ranging from No. 10 to No. 18.

The royal Wulff is perhaps the best-known and most popular mayfly attractor pattern. Its principal asset, for both fly casters and fish, is the addition of red. The fly's peacock body is divided in the middle with wraps of scarlet. Its divided, white calf-tail wings are visible to even the most myopic of anglers. Sizes can range from No. 6 to No. 20.

Since it is more mayfly-like in appearance, the royal Wulff is often the preferred attractor pattern of most fly casters. An excellent substitute is the Coachman Trude. Its white calf-tail wing is slanted back at a 45-degree angle. Also, many Idaho anglers are partial to it because the Trude series originated at the old Trude Ranch in Island Park.

All these patterns can be fished underwater. Large royal Wulffs and Trudes are fished wet as streamers, or minnow imitations. Renegades, and color variations on its theme, are fished wet in all sizes to imitate mayfly and stonefly nymphs.

Caddisfly Attractors

The elk hair caddis is the ultimate dry fly attractor pattern, especially since its many variations represent such a great number of choices in productive patterns. Caddisfly species far exceed the ever-popular mayfly species. Minor differences between caddisflies, willow flies, and small stoneflies boggle the minds of flyfishers and biologists.

Yet the basic shape and dimensions of the elk hair caddis—a simple tent-like hair wing flared at a 45-degree angle over a thinly wrapped body—fits the bill for the legions it imitates. Adding wraps of hackle over the body or in front of the wing are personal choices. They're not necessary, but they don't hurt. Body color sometimes adds to the success ratio, although wing color and hook size are often the deciding factors. Also, wing hair selection is not limited to different colors of elk hair. Many productive patterns employ color and texture variations in the hair of deer, moose and antelope.

An assortment of basic elk hair caddis patterns is perhaps the one guarantee to success anywhere on mountain streams and lakes, West or East, Midwest or Southwest. Adding a few modern variations—like the stimulator series—certainly ups the ante for a good day. Size selections range from No. 10 to No. 22. Patterns on the same theme, in size No. 8 and larger, mimic stoneflies, or salmonflies, and golden stones.

An equal rival of the elk hair pattern as a caddis attractor is the humpy. This uniquely Western pattern also gained fame as the goofus bug, but don't be turned off by either name. The fly's ability to pop back to the surface after being submerged makes it as unsinkable as the West's best known Titanic survivor, Molly Brown.

The humpy's great flotation qualities are derived from the best feature of both mayfly and caddis patterns. Elk or deer hair is drawn humpback-style over a full body and flared or divided as wings. In front and behind the wings, thick wraps of dry fly quality hackle further guarantee a high-riding fly.

Hands down, the premier producer among humpies is the yellow humpy, mainly because it is also a handy substitute for a small grasshopper. But hair and body colors can be mixed to create numerous variations of the humpy. The royal humpy, of course, incorporates a red body and white calf-tail wings to increase visibility. Small humpy sizes are the same as for elk hair caddis. Similarly, large double humpy patterns are intended to simulate stoneflies or golden stones.

Generic Mayfly Attractors

Although outnumbered by caddis species, the popularity of mayflies prevails among dry fly anglers. Generic patterns developed to meet this demand, like the Adams and light Cahill, rely more on size and shape than color. Both have the classic silhouette of mayfly patterns, but their bodies and hackle colors are generalized or muted. Sizes for both run the gamut from No. 10 to No. 22.

Of the two, the Adams is definitely the single fly pattern no fly caster should leave home without, in a full complement of sizes. Its gray body, grizzly hackle-tip wings, and grizzly and brown hackles perform under all light conditions on streams or lakes. Match the size, and you'll usually match the hatch with this versatile pattern. This is especially true on overcast days when overlapping mayfly hatches often occur. Better yet, the Adams is a prime prospecting fly for testing slipstreams, foam lines, and eddies when action is slow. On lakes it is a handy substitute for both callibaetis and caddis hatches.

Also, the para-Adams is establishing high standards for the many water-hugging parachute styles acquiring growing popularity. The parachute concept was developed by wrapping a fly's hackle around the base of its wings (or a stub) parallel to the water.

The light Cahill is another generic mayfly pattern that often saves the day when prospecting on new waters or fishing less demanding streams. Its light cream body, wood duck wings, and ginger tail and hackle mimic characteristics of pale morning duns, sulfurs and other light-colored species.

While the light Cahill usually isn't tied as a parachute pattern, a good substitute in this style is the recently developed parachute hare's ear. The natural, soft tans of this new pattern ensure its future representation among the traditional patterns. The same goes for its companion pattern, the parachute olive hare's ear.

Prime Terrestrial Patterns

A distinct advantage of terrestrial dry fly patterns is that they play to the opportunistic nature of fish. Grasshoppers, ants, beetles and crickets are out of their element when they land on water. They are extremely vulnerable. Trout know this, and few can resist an opportunity to gobble one.

When prospecting for trout, a grasshopper pattern is one of the most effective options in an angler's arsenal. It produces an adrenaline rush exceeded only by savage strikes on stoneflies. The bonus is the extended season of the grasshopper, compared to the short duration and sometimes fickle timing of stonefly hatches.

Most years, grasshopper patterns are productive from late July to October. They'll produce even after the first frost because the fish are still tuned into these juicy morsels. The best grasshopper prospecting time is late afternoon. If it's windy, all the better.

Patterns come in many colors and styles. Yellow predominates for body dubbing, although green and brown work, depending on the stream. Closed-seal foam bodies of newer patterns are good low-riding floaters. Most patterns have turkey tail or primary wing feathers as the fly's wings. Pheasant tails are another good source of wing material. The head is usually clipped deer or elk hair, but the drawn back, bullet-head style is effective, too.

Most often, size is more critical than color. Choices range from No. 2 to No. 14. Patterns that have stood the test of time include the flared-wing, clipped deer hair head of the Joe's Hopper or Letort Hopper for fast waters and the more realistic Dave Whitlock's Hopper or Henry's Fork Hopper for slow waters. And, again, several new parachute patterns are attracting a lot of attention, from both anglers and fish.

Many anglers also routinely carry a selection of ant patterns, No. 16 to No. 20, for quiet spells on streams, or when they give up trying to match the hatch for a super-selective trout. But anglers packing the right stuff when a swarm of flying ants descends on a stream will think they died and went to heaven.

However, generally more productive as a secondary terrestrial pattern is a small black beetle. Patterns tied with black foam float better and are more durable than older versions tied with deer hair. A few wraps of grizzly around the neck should be clipped at the bottom so the fly floats snug to the water. Sizes can range from No. 12 to No. 16.

The Disc O'Beetle, a newly developed pattern, offers a simple solution to determining the size and shape of foam beetles. Cut the foam in the shape of a circle with a diameter the length of the hook shank. Then place the disc on top of the hook shank, fold it down and tie it off about one-fourth the way back from the head. The pattern also calls for a peacock body, and either short thin legs or a clipped-bottom hackle wing. Harrison Steeves, inventor of the pattern, notes that foam sheets come in many colors in addition to black. Simple but effective, the Disc O'Beetle may be destined for ranking as a traditional pattern. After all, while there's a lot to be said for tradition, necessity is the mother of invention.

Food for Thought
Aquatic Insect Prey of Trout

I was standing on the boardwalk of a little western resort town a few years ago when I overheard two women behind me discussing the slogan on the back of my T-shirt. Its words of wisdom circled a large colorful drawing of a royal Wulff.

"The way to a man's heart is through his fly," the first woman read aloud.

Her companion chuckled. "Isn't that the truth."

They laughed again, and one of them tapped me on the shoulder. "I like your T-shirt," she declared.

The double entendre is intended to draw a chuckle. Some also might assert the message is that the many colorful fur, feather, chenille and wool imitations, tied in newer and better patterns each year, catch more flyfishers than trout. But the record is clear. The way to a trout's heart is through a well-presented fly.

The dry-fly fisher's task is determining what's the Blue Plate Special of the day. Most know, though, that 90 percent of a trout's daily grub is consumed underwater. A working knowledge about the life histories and habitats of aquatic insects can add significantly to bringing more fish to the net.

Aquatic insect forms are available to trout in two basic groups, depending on how they metamorphose after their eggs hatch. Caddisflies and midges, which have a complete metamorphosis, are food sources for trout as larvae, pupae, and adult flying insects. Mayflies, stoneflies and dragonflies have an incomplete metamorphosis and are fed on by trout as nymphs and adults.

Each type of insect is in a biological classification known as an order. An order is divided into families, genera and species. Aquatic insects of most interest to Northern Rocky Mountain flyfishers include:

EPHEMEROPTERA / MAYFLIES

Adult mayflies rest with their large wings in an upright position and their long, slender bodies curved in a graceful arc, front to back. When floating on water they look like miniature sailboats. They usually are quiet and docile on the water, rarely fluttering except for emergers that failed to shuck their nymphal casings. Mating swarms can be very busy and thick. The adults are literally ephemeral. Few species live longer than a day.

The newly emerged adult is known as a subimago, or dun. Large mayflies are called drakes. The body color is dull, nonreflective, and the wings are dark or grayish. After molting into the imago, or reproductive form, the body color is bright, and the wings are clear or transparent. Spent females that have completed laying eggs fall to the water with outspread wings and are called spinners.

Nymphs can live one to three years underwater, although a few species have two or three generations in a single season. The nymphs go through growth stages, called instars, where they shuck their exoskeletons each time they outgrow them. As they approach the emerger stage, the dark wing pad on the back of the thorax becomes more prominent.

The four categories of nymphs—swimmers, crawlers, clingers, and burrowers—reflect their habitats and habits. When it is time to emerge into adults, the nymphs of most species float or swim to the surface as they shuck their exoskeleton and unfold their wings. Most fly off immediately. On cold or rainy days their float on the water can be more prolonged. The nymphs of a few species crawl ashore or up the stems of aquatic vegetation to emerge.

Trout will grub for nymphs in their hiding places, move up into riffles to snatch nymphs or emergers or wait in their feeding lanes to snare dislodged nymphs. Emergers and floating adults are taken as they pass down a feeding lane, flow over the lip of a riffle, or are swirled together in the backwaters of an eddy. When a multiple hatch occurs, trout will often key on a single species—and not always the larger one.

Characteristics of mayfly species are reflected by the colors and other descriptive terms assigned to their common names and popular dry fly patterns.

Major mayfly hatches in the Intermountain West include:

Siphlonuridae

This family has only one major genus in Wyoming, and in most of the West. A large fly, the gray drake is somewhat rare but very important on streams where it occurs. Key hatches begin in late summer and go into fall.

Siphlonurus / Gray Drake

Habitat: Swimming nymphs prefer quiet pools and slack waters in streams, and the edges and shallow waters of lakes and ponds. Nymphs find food and shelter in weed beds and around stems of aquatic vegetation. They emerge by crawling up stems of plants or onto logs.

Nymphs: Gray drake, black drake, No. 10 to 14.

Hatch/dry flies:

Siphlonurus occidentalis—Gray drake dun, gray drake spinner, gray Wulff, Adams, No. 10 to 12; mid-July to mid-October.

Baetidae

One of the most abundant and hardy families in the West, its many important species guarantee blue-ribbon action. Carpet hatches of blue-winged olive (BWO) are common. Baetis hatches overlap through fishing season, from early spring into late fall.

Baetis / Blue-winged Olives

Habitat: Swimming nymphs prefer flowing waters. They are mostly found in shallow riffles but are also in rapids and eddies. They feed and find shelter in crevices and rock cobble of a streambed, sometimes in weed beds. They emerge by floating or swimming to surface to shed nymphal casing. Present adults downstream and across.

Nymphs: Soft-hackle and emerger patterns tied sparsely in olive, brown-olive or tan, No. 14 to 24.

Hatches/dry flies:

Baetis tricaudatus—Blue-winged olive, iron blue quill and Adams; late March through mid-May, No. 16 or 18, and October through November, No. 18 to 22.

Baetis bicaudatus—Tiny blue-winged olive, No. 22 or 24; July through August.

Baetis parvus—Tiny brown dun and tiny blue quill, No. 20 or 22; mid-July through October.

Pseudocloeon edmundsi—Tiny blue-winged olive, No. 22 or 24; mid-July through October.

Callibaetis / Speckle-winged Dun

Habitat: A very important species on lakes, ponds and reservoirs; it is also found in slow, quiet waters of some mountain streams and spring creeks. Sporadic hatches occur throughout the season, spring to autumn, but emergers and spinners offer most action. Swimming nymphs find food and shelter in weed beds, stands of aquatic vegetation, and in the debris of stream and lakebeds. Nymphs are very active prior to emergence and rise swiftly to the surface.

Nymphs: Callibaetis nymph, Sheep Creek Special and gold-ribbed hare's ear, No. 12 to 18. Sizes become smaller as season progresses; usually weighted and fished as rising emergers.

Hatches/dry flies:

Callibaetis coloradensis—Speckled dun, speckled spinner, speckled biot spinner, No. 14 or 16, also light Cahill, comparadun or parachute Adams; mid-July to mid-August.

Callibaetis nigritus—Speckled spinner, No. 14 or 16; July through September.

Ephemerellidae

This family offers perhaps the two most productive patterns on western streams. Tiny pale morning duns (PMD) are a class act throughout the summer, and giant green drakes elicit exciting early season action.

Drunella / Green Drakes

Habitat: This genus marks the beginning of the season on key streams like the Encampment and Green Rivers for anglers who seek big fish on big flies. Crawling nymphs are poor swimmers and prefer to find food and hide in haunts of streams with weedy, silty bottoms. Emergers are very vulnerable as they crawl to quiet waters or haphazardly rise slowly to the surface. Adults are equally vulnerable because of long floats after emerging.

Nymphs: Charles Brooks' Ida Mae, western green drake nymph, lead-wing olive nymph, Zug Bug, No. 8 to 10.

Hatches/dry flies:

Drunella grandis—Western green drake, green drake paradrake, green drake Wulff, green drake comparadun, extended body drake, great red spinner, No. 8 to 12; late June to mid-July.

Drunella flavilinea—Flavs, small western drake, slate-winged olive, parachute olive hare's ear, No. 14 to 16; July.

Drunella coloradensis—Slate-winged olive, parachute olive hare's ear, No. 14 to 16; August.

Ephemerella / Pale Morning Dun

Habitat: Crawling nymphs are poor swimmers and prefer to find food and hide in haunts of streams with weedy, silty bottoms. Emergers are very vulnerable as they crawl to quiet waters or haphazardly rise slowly to the surface. Small size of adults requires downstream or down and across presentations.

Nymphs: Pale morning dun nymph, hare's ear, yellow soft-hackle partridge, No. 16 to 20.

Hatches/dry flies:

Ephemerella infrequens—Pale morning dun, hair wing dun, comparadun PMD, parachute PMD, rusty spinner, No. 14 to 18; June and early July.

Ephemerella inermis—Pale morning dun, hair wing dun, comparadun PMD, parachute PMD, No. 16 to 20; July through September.

Ephemeridae

The principal fly in this family is the brown drake, a large, slow water species that may overlap with the green drake hatch on some streams. It usually hatches in early summer at night.

Ephemera / Brown Drake

Habitat: Nymphs burrow into silty sand bottoms of streams and lakes and feed at night. The hatch occurs at twilight or at night, with the emerger rapidly rising to the surface.

Nymphs: Brown drake nymph, No. 10 to 12.

Hatch/dry flies:

Ephemera simulans—Brown drake, brown drake parachute, brown drake spinner, No. 10 to 12; mid-June to early July.

Leptophlebiidae

The principal fly in this family is the mahogany dun, a tiny, fast water species with a relatively long season. Late summer hatches are common.

Paraleptophlebia / Mahogany Dun

Habitat: Crawling nymphs prefer flowing waters, like fast riffles; they hide and feed in debris and gravel of the streambed. Poor swimmers, they move to quieter waters prior to emerging.

Nymphs: Charles Brooks' floating natant nylon nymph, hare's ear nymph, No. 14 to 18.

Hatch/dry flies:

Paraleptophlebia bicornuta—Mahogany dun, mahogany spinner, No. 16 or 18; late August through September.

Tricorythodidae

The very tiny flies of this family are a major feeding source for selective trout, mostly on streams but also on some lakes. Late summer hatches are common.

Tricorythodes / White-winged Black

Habitat: Nymphs prefer slow waters of streams and hide in bottom debris. Floating emerger and dun patterns work, but spent female spinners are most vulnerable to slurping trout.

Nymphs: Poxy-white-black nymphs, black or olive midge pupa, pheasant tail nymph, No. 20 to 24.

Hatch/dry flies:

Tricorythodes minutus—White-wing black, parachute Trico, black or olive midges, Griffith's gnat, Trico spinner, No. 20 to 24; August into September.

Heptageniidae

Common to fast mountain streams, the species of this family prefers clear, cold water. The midsummer hatch continues into fall.

Eperous / Pink Albert

Habitat: Nymphs cling to the substrate of tumbling riffles and fast runs. Emergers and floating duns are most vulnerable to quick-acting trout.

Nymphs: Soft-hackle patterns and hare's ear nymph, No. 10 to 16.

Hatch/dry flies:

Eperous albertea—Pink Albert Cahill, Pink Lady, cream dun, No. 14 to 16; July to September.

TRICHOPTERA / CADDISFLIES

Few anglers bother to learn the Latin names of caddisflies. Almost none have common names, although on many streams they are more prolific than mayflies. Popular caddis patterns are impressionistic but take tons of trout. Larval patterns are effective year-round because caddis are so common. Emerger patterns generally are more productive during a hatch than dry flies. A dry fly plays best when females return to deposit their eggs. But a dry fly is a good attractor pattern in spring and summer because caddis are on the water throughout their adult stage.

The two pairs of wings of the caddisfly slant back over the body in a tent-like position when it is resting. In the air, caddis have an erratic, bouncing flight pattern. On the water, they often continue fluttering or swimming about. Their wings are not transparent, and coloration tends toward earth tones in shades of tan, brown, gray, or black. The body color can match the wings or be in shades of green or yellow. Adult caddisflies may live one to two weeks.

In the larval stage, most caddis live in cases built from small grains of sand, sticks, strands of vegetation, or a combination of materials. Some live in a free-swimming form or construct a silken retreat with a web.

Caddis hibernate a week or more during pupation, like caterpillars, as they change into winged adults in their cases. When the transformation is complete, the pupae shuck their casings as they soar to the surface in a dash to freedom. Most adults fly off as soon as they hit the surface.

Trout chasing caddis emergers often rocket fully out of the water in their pursuit. Their next best shot at caddis is when the females return to deposit their eggs. It is a busy affair, with lots of buzzing wings and swimming about, although a few dive straight to the bottom. With all that activity, trout hit caddis hard. Fishing strategies should follow suit.

The two most common families in the West are *Brachycentridae*, dark-gray and dark-brown caddis with wood-case larvae, and *Rhyacophilidae*, green caddis with free swimming larvae.

The most effective dry fly to cover the bases is the elk hair caddis in No. 12 to 20 with green, tan, brown or gray bodies. Other popular patterns include Colorado king, Goddard caddis, humpies, Henryville Special, Hemingway caddis, bucktail caddis and stimulators.

Larval and pupa patterns in No. 10 to 18 can include the peacock herl caddis and latex caddis, or soft-hackle patterns like the green partridge, Charles Brooks' little green caddis and little gray caddis and Moss' caddis emerger.

Plecoptera / Stoneflies

These prehistoric monsters of the aquatic insect world incite slashing, explosive rises by trophy trout during early season hatches. But for wet flyfishers, the 2- to 3-inch nymphs of the largest species, *Pteronarcys californica*, are a standard pattern year-round.

The "salmonfly" feeding frenzy often peaks around the Fourth of July in the Yellowstone River's canyon. But nature doesn't always make it easy. Local weather or spring runoff conditions can speed up or slow a hatch dramatically. Elsewhere in the state, hatches can be very sporadic, and nymph patterns often perform better than dry flies.

Stoneflies look a lot like giant caddisflies, although their two pairs of heavily veined wings lie flat over their backs. Their flight is helicopter-like, with the long body hanging below the whirling wings. Nymphs follow the same life history as mayflies and live underwater one to four years. All species are found in swift, rocky waters rich in oxygen.

Members of the *P. californica* species were dubbed salmonflies because of the bright orange highlights on dark brown bodies of nymphs and adult flying insects. A smaller species, the golden stonefly, *Acroneuria pacifica*, is highlighted by golden yellow markings on its light brown body. Golden stones hatch toward the end of a salmonfly hatch. They also come in a wider variety of sizes and can be an effective dry fly pattern for a longer duration.

Stoneflies do not emerge in midstream. The nymphs crawl across the streambed to water's edge, climb a rock or bush and shuck their shells as they metamorphose into short-lived, airborne insects.

The key to fishing salmonflies is staying at the front of the hatch as it moves upstream, usually about 5 miles a day. The point at which only a few flying insects or nymph casings can be found determines a hatch's head. The best bet here is to cast nymphs toward the shoreline from a boat or parallel to it when wading.

Behind the vanguard of the emerging nymphs, dry flies come into play. Late afternoon flights of salmonflies occur when egg-laying females ride the up-swells of hot air flowing up the canyons cut by the rivers. The large, black egg sacs are deposited like bombs in rocky, fast-water stretches of the stream to begin the cycle anew. Many females fall exhausted onto the water, and the bugs are often blown off streamside bushes by high winds.

There are hundreds of patterns, ranging from super realistic to plain buggy looking impressions, and new ones are being created annually. Check with local fly tackle shops on what's hot.

A variety of salmonflies, No. 2 to 8, is highly recommended. Golden stone patterns range from No. 8 to 14. Popular dry flies include the sofa pillow, Bird's stonefly, golden stonefly, large yellow or orange stimulators, and double humpies. One of the latest inventions is the Rainy's salmonfly, tied with a Rainy float foam body. Traditional nymph patterns include the Charles Brooks stone, tied in the round, Box Canyon stone, Montana stone, Bitch Creek Special, orange or black girdlebug, black rubber-legs, super renegade, and woolly bugger.

Small caddis-like insects on the water with wings resting flat over orange or yellow bodies are small species of brown or golden stoneflies. These are often called little yellow stoneflies, willowflies, or yellow Sallies, after the *Isogenus* species. Smaller yellow or orange stimulators and yellow Sally or willow fly patterns are very effective, along with humpies, bucktail caddis, and yellow elk hair caddis, No. 10 to 14.

Willowfly hatches may overlap salmonfly and golden stone hatches, and typically last through July into August.

DIPTERA / TRUE FLIES

Midges and mosquitoes are the two families in this order of most interest to fly-fishers.

Chironomidae / Midges

Midges can be a dry-fly fisher's best friend in winter and early spring on streams open year-round. Float-tubers often count on chironomid emergers to ensure a good day on lakes and ponds.

Midge larva and pupa patterns are tied very sparsely with green, olive, light olive, tan, brown, or black dubbing on No. 18 to 28 hooks. Peacock or ostrich herl are used on the thorax of pupa patterns.

Flying midge patterns are tied very sparsely in colors to match a variety of hatches with only two or three turns of the same colored hackle for wings, No. 14 to 26. The Griffith's gnat, tied with a grizzly hackle palmered over a peacock herl body, No. 18 to 28, represents a clump of midges on the water.

Culicidae / Mosquitoes

This is the one fly every one can identify.

Both larva and pupa patterns are tied to float in the surface film. Stripped hackle stems or peacock herls are used for the thin body, in No. 14 to 18. The mosquito dry fly and Adams also work in No. 14 to 18.

ODONATA / DRAGONFLIES

Dragonfly and damselfly hatches on lakes and ponds can rival the excitement of stonefly hatches on mountain streams. But even without a hatch, damsel nymphs, Charles Brooks' Assam dragon, woolly worms, crystal buggers and Carey's Special, No. 4 to 12, should be part of a stillwater flyfisher's arsenal year-round.

Green damsel nymphs, No. 8 to 12, and woolly buggers and crystal buggers, No. 8 to 10, are popular patterns on prairie lakes during the damselfly hatch from late June to mid-July.

Long-bodied dry flies also are available at some fly tackle shops.

Catch and Release Tips

All anglers can help make future fishing better by releasing wild trout. Flies with only one barbless hook make release of fish easier.

Catch and release fish following these procedures:

- Use the strongest terminal tackle conditions permit to make the landing battle as short as possible.
- Land fish using a net with fine, soft mesh.
- Wet hands before touching the fish. Do not squeeze it.
- Do not touch the gills or hold the fish by its gill covers.
- If possible, leave the fish in the water while removing the hook. Use of needle-nose pliers or medical forceps is recommended. Work quickly but gently.
- If the hook cannot be easily removed, cut the leader. The hook will rust out rapidly.
- Do not toss the fish back into the water or shake it off the hook by suspending it in mid-air. Turn over the mouth of net to let it escape, or lean over the side of boat to slide it gently into the water.
- If the fish is exhausted, hold it in a swimming position in the water and move gently back and forth to force water through its gills. Maintain a light grip on the tail until it pulls itself out of your hands and swims off on its own.
- Avoid excessive and unnecessary handling of the fish, especially when taking photographs.

Wyoming Fishing Regulations

Fishing is permitted year-round 24 hours a day in any of the waters in Wyoming except as specifically prescribed for some particular area, stream or lake. Check the current regulations pamphlet.

Daily Creel and Possession for Trout
- Trout, salmon, grayling in combination: 6—only 1 fish may exceed 20 inches.
- Brook trout 8 inches or less: 10, in addition to the general creel limit on trout.
- Whitefish: 50

License Fees
A resident license fee is $15 for season or $3 per day. A license for a youth between 14 and 19 years of age is $3. A $5 conservation stamp is also required on all but one-day licenses. No license is required for those under age 14.

Tourist fishing license fees are $65 for a season or $6 per day. The fee for out-of-state youth between 14 and 19 is $15 for season or $10 for 10 days. A $5 conservation stamp is also required on all but one-day licenses.

Additional Information
Wyoming Game and Fish Department
Information Section
5400 Bishop Blvd
Cheyenne, WY 82006
307-777-7014, 800-842-1934 (toll-free in-state only)

Grand Teton National Park
General Information and Regulations

Grand Teton National Park
P.O. Drawer 170
Moose, WY 83012
307-739-3300
Visitor Information: 307-739-3399

Fees
* The entrance fee is $20 per car, good for both Grand Teton and Yellowstone National Parks; $12 per night per site camping fee. Fees are also charged for watercraft.

Season
* The park is open every day; visitor centers are closed on Christmas Day.

Campgrounds
Reservations through AMFac Parks & Resorts: 307-344-7311
* Gros Ventre Campground, open late April to early October
* Jenny Lake Campground, open late May to late September, fills by 8AM
* Signal Mountain Campground, open early May to mid-October, fills by 10AM
* Colter Bay Campground, open late May to late September
* Lizard Creek Campground, open early June to early September

Lodging and Reservations
* Jackson Lake Lodge, Jenny Lake Lodge, and Colter Bay Village: contact Grand Teton Lodge Co., Box 240, Moran, WY 83013 / Reservations: 307-543-2855 or 800-628-9988 / Nonreservation calls: 307-543-2811
* Flagg Ranch, Box 187, Moran, WY 83013, 800-443-2311
* Signal Mountain Lodge Co., Box 50, Moran, WY 83013, 307-543-2831
* Dornan's Spur Ranch Cabins, Box 39, Moose, WY 83012, 307-733-2415

Backcountry Camping Permits
* Overnight stays in the backcountry require a free backcountry permit available at the Moose or Colter Bay Visitor Centers and the Jenny Lake Ranger Station. Reservations may be made for backcountry campsites between January 1 and May 15, or up to 30 days ahead of your first night's stay. For information or copy of permit application call 307-739-3309 or 739-3397, or write Permits Office in care of the above address.
* River and backcountry permit information (recorded): 307-739-3602

Fishing
- A Wyoming fishing license is required for fishing in the park, and regulations are set by the Wyoming Game and Fish Department. Licenses may be purchased in fishing tackle stores in Jackson, Dornan's, and at park marinas.

Boating
- Permits required for motorized and nonmotorized watercraft are available at visitor centers and ranger stations. Nonmotorized boat fees are $5 for a week permit or $10 for an annual permit. Motorized boat fees are $10 for a week permit and $20 for an annual permit.

Additional Information
Jackson Hole Chamber of Commerce
Box E
Jackson, Wyoming 83001
307-733-3316 or 307-733-5585

Yellowstone National Park
General Information and Regulations

Yellowstone National Park
Visitor's Service
P.O. Box 168
Yellowstone National Park, WY 82190-0168
307-344-7381; 307-344-2386

Operating Hours, Seasons
- **Summer:** Season runs from mid-April to late October. Once a road/entrance opens, it is open 24 hours. (Exceptions: road construction and weather-caused restrictions.)
- **Winter:** Season runs from mid-December to mid-March. The road from the North Entrance at Gardiner, MT, to the Northeast Entrance and Cooke City, MT, is open to wheeled vehicle use year round.

Entrance Fees
- The entrance fee is $20 for a private, noncommercial vehicle; $15 for each visitor over 16 years of age entering by snowmobile or motorcycle; or $10 for each visitor over 16 years of age entering by foot, bike, ski, etc. This fee provides the visitor with a 7-day entrance permit for both Yellowstone and Grand Teton National Parks. Remember to keep your admission receipt in order to re-enter the parks.
- **Annual Area Pass:** A $40 Annual pass for Yellowstone and Grand Teton National Parks is available. It is valid for one year from the date of purchase.
- **Golden Access Passport:** This lifetime passport is available to citizens or permanent residents of the United States, regardless of age, who have been medically determined to be blind or permanently disabled.
- **Golden Age Passport:** This lifetime passport is for U.S. citizens or permanent residents 62 years of age or older. A one-time fee of $10 is charged.
- **Golden Eagle Passport:** This $50 passport is valid for one year from the date of purchase.

Reservations / Permits
- Campground/Lodging/Dining Reservations are strongly recommended for all concession operated facilities. Reservations should be made as far in advance as possible.
- For reservation information, call 307-344-7311
- Or write to: AmFac Parks & Resorts, P.O. Box 165, Yellowstone National Park, WY 82190

Medical Services

Yellowstone Park Medical Services provides facilities at these locations in the park:
* Mammoth Clinic is open year-round. Hours are typically from 8:30AM to 5:00PM. Call 307-344-7965
* Lake Hospital is open from mid-May to mid-September; 307-242-7241
* Old Faithful Clinic is open from early May to mid-October; 307-545-7325
* Emergency medical services are provided by on-duty park rangers. Call 911 in case of an emergency.
* Medical Services in Yellowstone are provided by West Park Hospital, 707 Sheridan Avenue, Cody, WY 82414; 307-527-7501 or 800-654-9447

Chambers of Commerce near Yellowstone National Park

* Big Sky, MT: 800-943-4111
* Billings, MT: 406-245-4111
* Bozeman, MT: 406-586-5421
* Cooke City/Silver Gate, MT: 406-838-2272
* Gardiner, MT: 406-848-7971
* Livingston, MT: 406-222-0850
* Red Lodge, MT: 406-446-1718
* West Yellowstone, MT: 406-646-7701
* Cody, WY: 307-587-2297
* Dubois, WY: 307-455-2556
* East Yellowstone–Wapiti Valley, WY: 307-587-9595
* Jackson, WY: 307-733-3316
* Idaho Falls, ID: 208-523-1010
* Eastern Idaho Visitor Information Center, Idaho Falls, ID: 800-634-3246

Yellowstone Fishing Regulations

* **Fees:** Price of a fishing permit in Yellowstone National Park is $10 for a 10-day permit (16 years of age or older) and $20 for a season permit. Children 12 to 15 continue to fish free but need a permit of their own. Children 11 or younger do not need a permit when supervised by an adult.
* **Lake Trout:** In Yellowstone Lake, as well as Heart Lake, all nonnative lake trout caught must be killed. Captured lake trout must be kept intact and presented for inspection at a visitor's center or park ranger's office. An angler may keep his catch after inspection by park biologists. The 2-fish limit, any size, still applies for lake trout caught in Lewis and Shoshone lakes.
* **Cutthroat Trout:** The catch-and-release rule for native Yellowstone cutthroat applies for all park waters downstream from Yellowstone Lake, including the Soda Butte Creek drainage and the upper Lamar River drainage. All netted cutthroat must be released immediately, except in Yellowstone Lake and upstream tributaries, where there is a 2-fish under 13 inches limit.

- **Rainbow Trout:** Daily creel limit on nonnative rainbow is 2 fish any size, except for four rivers. Rainbows are catch-and-release on the Bechler, Madison, Firehole and its tributaries, and Gibbon below its waterfall.
- **Brook Trout:** Daily creel limit for nonnative brook trout is 5 fish any size, except for Richard's Pond, Fawn Lake, and Blacktail Ponds where the limit is 5 brook trout under 13 inches.
- **Brown Trout:** Daily creel limit on nonnative brown trout in the Madison, Firehole and its tributaries, and the Gibbon below its waterfall is 2 fish less than 13 inches. A 2-fish limit any size on browns applies in other park waters, except for the catch-and-release rule on the Lewis River below its waterfall to Lewis Canyon.
- The fishing season in Yellowstone National Park is open each day from 5AM to 10PM. It begins on the Saturday of Memorial Day weekend and continues through the first Sunday in November, with a few exceptions. Key waters with later opening dates include Yellowstone Lake, which doesn't open until June 15, and Yellowstone River, from the park's south boundary to the upper falls, which doesn't open until July 15.
- Be sure to sign your fishing permit and read all the park's regulations before fishing. For example, a rule to remember is that Yellowstone implemented a non-toxic fishing program in 1994. Fishing tackle, such as lead split-shot or sinkers, weighted jigs (lead molded to a hook), and soft lead-weighted ribbon for flyfishing nymphs is no longer allowed. Only nontoxic alternatives are permitted for these types of fishing tackle to prevent lead poisoning of waterfowl.
- For more information, contact the Chief Ranger's Office, P.O. Box 168, Yellowstone National Park, WY 82190.

Boating in Yellowstone
- A permit is required for all vessels (motorized and nonmotorized, including floattubes) and must be obtained in person at any of the following locations: South Entrance, Lewis Lake Campground, Grant Village Visitor Center, Bridge Bay Ranger Station, and Lake Ranger Station. At Canyon and Mammoth Visitor Centers, only nonmotorized boating permits are available. The fee is $20 (annual) or $10 (7 day) for motorized vessels and $10 (annual) or $5 (7 day) for nonmotorized vessels. A Coast Guard approved wearable personal flotation device is required for each person boating.
- Grand Teton National Park's boat permit will be honored as a one-time, 7-day permit or can be applied toward a Yellowstone annual permit.
- All vessels are prohibited on park rivers and streams except the channel between Lewis and Shoshone lakes, where only hand-propelled vessels are permitted.
- Outboards and rowboats may be rented (first come, first served) from AmFac Parks & Resorts at Bridge Bay Marina on Yellowstone Lake. AmFac also provides guided fishing boats that may be reserved in advance by calling 307-344-7311. Other commercial businesses are permitted to offer guided services for canoeing, kayaking, and motorized boating.

Advance Reservations for Backcountry Campsites

- Although permits must be obtained in person no more than 48 hours in advance, backcountry campsites may be reserved in advance. Requests for reservations must be submitted by mail or in person. They cannot be made over the phone or by fax. Reservations are booked on a first come, first served basis. A confirmation notice, not a permit, is given or mailed to the camper. This confirmation notice must then be converted to the actual permit not more than 48 hours in advance of the first camping date. Details are provided on the confirmation notice. The reservation fee is $15, regardless of the number of nights out or the number of people involved. The fee is not refundable. To receive the forms to make an advance reservation, write to: National Park Service, Attention: Backcountry Office, P.O. Box 168, Yellowstone National Park, WY 82190. Or you may call 307-344-2160 or 307-344-2163 to request forms.
- **Permits and Reservations Made Less than 48 Hours in Advance:** Because only a portion of the approximately 300 backcountry campsites are available for advance reservations, you may choose to wait until you arrive in the park to reserve your site(s) and obtain your permit. The $15 fee applies only to reservations made more than 48 hours in advance of the start of your trip.
- **Where to Get Your Permit:** During the summer season (June–August), permits are available 7 days a week between 8AM and 4:30PM at the following locations:
  - Bechler Ranger Station
  - Canyon Ranger Station/Visitor Center
  - Grant Village Visitor Center
  - Lake Ranger Station
  - Mammoth Ranger Station/Visitor Center
  - Old Faithful Ranger Station
  - South Entrance Ranger Station
  - Tower Ranger Station
  - West Entrance Ranger Station

Licensed Outfitters Serving Yellowstone

The table below lists fishing guides permitted to operate in Yellowstone.

Arrick's Fishing Flies
Arrick Swanson
P.O. Box 873
West Yellowstone, MT 59758
406-646-7290

Blue Ribbon Flies
Craig Mathews
P.O. Box 1037
West Yellowstone, MT 59758
406-646-9365

Blue Ribbon Fishing Tours
Dale Siegle
209 Blue Heron Drive
Livingston, MT 59047
406-222-7714

Boyne U.S.A.
John Kircher
P.O. Box 160001
Big Sky, MT 59716
406-995-5000

Bressler Outfitters, Inc.
Joe Bressler
P.O. Box 766
Wilson, WY 83014
307-733-6934

Bud Lilly's Trout Shop
Jim Criner
P.O. Box 698
West Yellowstone, MT 59758
406-646-7801

Camp Creek Inn
Sam Coutts
Star Route, Box 45-B
Jackson, WY 83001
307-733-3099

Coy's Wilderness Float Trips
Thomas Coy
P.O. Box 3356
Jackson, WY 83001
307-733-6726

Eagle Creek Outfitters
Chuck Tuchschmidt
322 1/2 Lindley Place
Bozeman, MT 59715
406-586-3157

East Slope Anglers
Brad Parsch
P.O. Box 160249
Big Sky, MT 59716
406-995-4369

Experience Montana
Allen Schallenberger
53 Elser Lane
Sheridan, MT 59749
406-842-5134

Far and Away Adventures/
  Paddle Yellowstone
Steve Lentz
P.O. Box 54
Sun Valley, ID 83353
208-726-8888

Fatboy Fishing
A.J. DeRosa
P.O. Box 121
Wilson, WY 83014
307-733-3061

Firehole Ranch
Stan Klassen
P.O. Box 360
Jackson, WY 83001
307-733-7669

Gallatin River Guides
Steve French
P.O. Box 160212
Big Sky, MT 59716
406-995-2290

Gary Evans Madison River Guides
Gary Evans
P.O. Box 1456
Ennis, MT 59729
406-682-4802

Greater Yellowstone Flyfishers
Robert & Chad Olsen
8471 Lupine Lane
Bozeman, MT 59715
406-586-2489

Grub Steak Expeditions
Bob Richard
P.O. Box 1013
Cody, WY 82414
307-527-6316

Hatch Finders
Dean Reiner
120 South M Street
Livingston, MT 59047
406-222-0989

Hawkridge Outfitters
Howard Bethel
8000 Trail Creek Road
Bozeman, MT 59715
406-585-9608

Headwaters Guide Service
Robert Cunningham
P.O. Box 311
Gallatin Gateway, MT 59730
406-763-4761

Henry's Fork Anglers, Inc.
Michael Lawson
P.O. Box 487
St. Anthony, ID 83445
208-558-7525

High Country Outfitters
Carman Rizzotto
158 Bridger Hollow Road
Pray, MT 59065
406-333-4763

Hyde Outfitters
Messrs. Sessions and Hyde
1520 Pancheri
Idaho Falls, ID 83402
208-529-4343

Jacklin's, Inc.
Bob Jacklin
P.O. Box 310
West Yellowstone, MT 59758
406-646-7336

John Henry Lee Outfitters, Inc.
John Henry Lee
P.O. Box 8368
Jackson, WY 83001
307-733-9441

Lee Watson Outfitter
Lee Watson
1254 Highway 89 North
Livingston, MT 59047
406-686-4669

Lost River Outfitters
Scott Schnebly
P.O. Box 3445
Ketchum, ID 83340
208-726-1706

Lund Outfitters
Kurt Lund
P.O. Box 3459
Jackson, WY 83001
307-733-0261

Madison River Outfitters
Brad Richey
P.O. Box 398, 117 Canyon
West Yellowstone, MT 59758
406-646-9644

Montana Flyfishing Adventures
Patrick Bannon
P.O. Box 64
Deer Lodge, MT 59722
406-846-0002

Montana Outdoor Adventures, Inc.
Randy Cain
2201 Milwaukee Road
Bozeman, MT 59715
406-586-8524

Montana's Master Angler
Tom Travis
P.O. Box 1320
Livingston, MT 59047
406-222-2273

Outpost Wilderness
David Appleton
P.O. Box 7
Lake George, CO 80827
719-748-3080

Overland Travel, Inc.
Tom Costley
P.O. Box 31
Williamstown, MA 01267
413-458-9672

Parks' Fly Shop
Richard Parks
P.O. Box 196
Gardiner, MT 59030
406-848-7314

Reel Adventures
Dean Jones
1692 Wallace Pate Drive
Georgetown, SC 29440
803-527-2982

Rendezvous Outfitters
H. A. Moore
P.O. Box 447
Gardiner, MT 59030
406-848-7967

Rivermeadows, Inc.
Edward Ingold
P.O. Box 347
Wilson, WY 83014
307-733-9263

Running River Fly Guide
Stuart Howard
113 West Villard
Bozeman, MT 59715
406-586-1758

Sleepy Hollow Lodge
Larry Miller
P.O. Box 1080
West Yellowstone, MT 59758
406-646-7707

Snake River Fishing Trips
Bruce James
P.O. Box 3369
Jackson, WY 83001
307-733-3270

Snake River Kayak and Canoe School
Donald Perkins
P.O. Box 3482
Jackson, WY 83002
307-733-3127

Stillwaters Outfitting
Lee Scherer
3234 Reimers Park
Billings, MT 59102
406-652-8111

Sun Raven Guide Service
Katherine Howe
73 Chicory Road
Livingston, MT 59047
406-333-4454

Sun Valley Trekking Co.
Robert Jonas
P.O. Box 2200
Sun Valley, ID 83353
208-788-9585

Teton Troutfitters
Scott Hocking
P.O. Box 536
Wilson, WY 83014
307-733-5362

The Lone Mountain Ranch, Inc.
Robert L. Schaap
P.O. Box 160069
Big Sky, MT 59716
406-995-4644

The River's Edge
David Corcoran
2012 North 7th Ave.
Bozeman, MT 59715
406-586-5373

Three Rivers Ranch
Ms. Lonnie Lee Allen
P.O. Box 856, Warm River
Ashton, ID 83420
208-652-3750

Tom Miner Lodge
John Keenan
P.O. 1060
Emigrant, MT 59027
406-848-7525

Triangle X Ranch
Harold Turner
Moose, WY 83012
307-733-2183

Westbank Anglers
Reynolds Pomeroy
P.O. Box 523
Teton Village, WY 83025
307-733-6483

Wild Trout Outfitters
J.D. Bingman
P.O. Box 160003
Big Sky, MT 59716
406-995-4895

Wilderness Inquiry
Greg Lais
1313 5th Street SE, Suite 117
Minneapolis MN 55414
612-379-3858

Williams Guide Service
Don Williams
P.O. Box 2
Livingston, MT 59047
406-222-1386

Yellowstone Angler
George Anderson
Highway 89 South
Livingston, MT 59047
406-222-7130

Yellowstone Association
Pat Cole
P.O. Box 117
Yellowstone NP, WY 82190
307-344-2293

Yellowstone Outfitters
Jim Hubbard
Route 1, Box 662
Emigrant, MT 59027
406-848-7755

Yellowstone/Glacier Adventures
Steve Braun
P.O. Box 165
Bozeman, MT 59771
406-585-9041

Important Phone Numbers

Tourist Information
- Wyoming Division of Tourism, I-25 at College Drive, Cheyenne, WY 82002-0660 / 307-777-7777; Fax: 307-777-6904
- Travel information: 800-225-5996
- Web Site Homepage URL: http://commerce.state.wy.us/tourism/index.htm
- Wyoming Outfitters Association, Box 2284, Cody, WY 82414 / 307-527-7453
- Wyoming Board of Outfitters and Professional Guides, 1750 Westland Road, Cheyenne, WY 82001 / 307-777-5323

Wyoming Game and Fish Department
(Note: 800 numbers are for in-state calls only.)
- **Information Section,** 5400 Bishop Blvd., Cheyenne, WY 82006 / 307-777-7014, 800-842-1934
- **Region 1 Fisheries Supervisor,** 360 N. Cache, Jackson, WY 83001 / 307-733-2321, 800-423-4113
- **Pinedale Fisheries Supervisor,** 117 S. Sublette Avenue, Pinedale, WY 82941 / 307-367-4353, 800-452-9107
- **Region 2 Fisheries Supervisor,** 2820 Hwy 120, Cody, WY 82414 / 307-527-7125, 800-654-1178
- **Region 3 Fisheries Supervisor,** 700 Valley View Drive, Sheridan, WY 82801 / 307-672-7418, 800-331-9834
- **Region 4 Fisheries Supervisor,** 351 Castle, Green River, WY 82935 / 307-875-3223, 800-843-8096
- **Region 5 Fisheries Supervisor,** 528 S. Adams, Laramie, WY 82070 / 307-745-4046, 800-843-2352
- **Region 6 Fisheries Supervisor,** 260 Buena Vista, Lander, WY 82520 / 307-332-2688, 800-654-7862
- **Region 7 Fisheries Supervisor,** 3030 Energy Lane, Suite 100, Casper, WY 82604 / 307-473-3400, 800-233-8544

U.S. Forest Service
- **Bridger-Teton National Forest,** 350 N. Cache Street, P.O. Box 1888, Jackson, WY 83001 / 307-733-2752
- **Bighorn National Forest,** 1969 S. Sheridan Avenue, Sheridan, WY 82801/ 307-672-0751
- **Shoshone National Forest,** 808 Meadow Lane, Cody, WY 82414 / 307-527-6241
- **Medicine Bow National Forest,** 2468 Jackson Street, Laramie, WY 82070 / 307-745-2300

Bureau of Land Management

- **Bureau of Land Management, Wyoming State Office,** 5353 Yellowstone Road, P.O. Box 1828, Cheyenne, WY 82003 / 307-722-2334
- **Casper BLM District Office,** 1701 East E Street, Casper, WY 82601-2167 / 307-261-7600
- **Rawlins BLM District Office,** 1300 N. Third, Rawlins, WY 82301 / 307-328-4200 or 307-328-4256
- **Rock Springs BLM District Office,** 280 Highway 191 North, Rock Springs, WY 82901 / 307-382-5350

Wind River Indian Reservation

- **Shoshone and Arapahoe Tribes Game and Fish Department,** Wind River Indian Reservation, P.O. Box 217, Fort Washakie, WY 82514 / 307-332-7207

Index

A

Absaroka Mountains   110, 112, 143–144,
151–152, 166, 175, 200, 213, 223, 310,
326, 441
Absaroka-Beartooth Wilderness   129, 135,
159, 324
Afton, WY   340, 377, 386, 392–394, 397,
400–401, 406
Alcova Reservoir   14, 33–34, 39
Alder Lake   315
Allen, Joe   346, 391
Alpine, WY   340, 377, 383, 385, 387, 392–394,
401
Alum Creek   202, 204, 207
American Fisheries Society   180, 473
Amfac Resorts   497, 499, 501
Amsden WMA   63, 70
Anderson, George   325, 506
Andrews, Chip   144, 153, 159
Annenburg, Moe   89
Apollinaris Springs   318
Arapahoe Tribes   104, 107, 508
Arctic grayling, description of   467–468
Arizona Creek   365
Arizona Lake   365
Arnica Creek   179, 298, 302
Ash Mountain Creek   287–288
Ashton Dam   43
Astoria Hot Springs   390
Atlantic Basin   200
Atlantic Creek   200, 206, 339, 341, 367, 449
Axamit, Petr   407

B

Back, Howard   259
Bacon Rind Creek   265, 267, 319
Baetis/Baetidae, description of,   486–487
Bailey Lake   386
Bailey, Dan   324–325
Barns Holes   240–241, 244
Barrows, Sue   328
Basin Creek Lake   320
Bass Lake   115
Battle Park   81
Bauer, Diane   328
Baughman, John   14, 27, 427
Beach Springs   316

Beacham, Van   411, 445
Bear Creek   111
Bear Island   303–304, 464
Bear Lake   362, 447
Bear River   385, 397, 400, 404–406, 409–410,
447
Bear River State Park   405
Beartooth Mountains   127, 151, 165, 221,
225, 441
Beartooth Pass   165, 168
Beartooth Plateau   151, 163, 169
Beartooth, The   164
Beartooth Wilderness   127, 162–165, 324
Beaver Creek   213, 310, 312–313
Beaver Meadows   240–242, 244
Beaverdam Creek   298
Bechler Basin   190
Bechler Meadows   176, 191, 271, 282–283,
285, 321
Bechler Ranger Station   281, 283, 502
Bechler River   171, 176, 178, 187, 190,
280–288, 321
   Ferris Fork   283–285
   Gregg Fork   283–285
   Phillips Fork   283–285, 323, 409
Behnke, Robert   341
Belgrade, MT   328
Belle Fourche River   90
Benson, Brian   46
Bergman, Ray   8
Bessemer Bend   34–35, 38
Bessemer Bend Bridge   34–35, 38
Beula Lake   271, 281, 287–288, 321
Big Bend   33, 241, 324, 423
Big Fall Creek   401
Big Horn Basin   83–84, 127, 140, 143–144
Big Horn Canyon National Recreation Area
101
Big Horn Lake   102
Big Horn Mountains   53, 61, 63, 66, 68–70,
74–75, 77–78, 80–85, 92, 94–95, 97, 101,
112, 127, 143
Big Horn River   42, 56, 68–70, 73–78, 81–85,
92–95, 97, 99–103, 107, 121–122, 124,
140, 143–144, 147, 160, 167–168, 200,
267, 341, 441, 457, 507
Big Island   426, 429
Big Piney, WY   386, 400, 407, 422–424

Big Sandy, WY   426, 438, 457
Big Sandy River   425, 429
Big Sky, MT   163, 213, 323, 326, 413, 500, 502–503, 506
Bighorn National Forest   61, 69–70, 78, 81–82, 507
Billings, MT   200, 500, 505
Birrer, Steve   147
Biscuit Basin   250, 252–253
Black Canyon   193, 200, 205–208
Black Hills   61, 89
Black Hills National Forest   89
Black Sands Geyser Basin   247, 250, 254, 319
Blacks Fork   447
Blacktail Deer Creek   205, 207
Blacktail Ponds   187–188, 317, 501
Blacktail Spring Creek   373
Blue-winged olive, description of,   486–487
Boating permits   294, 314, 363, 498, 501
Boating regulations   294
Boiling River (Gardner River)   229, 233
Bonneville cutthroat trout   405, 447–448, 452
Booth, David C.   179
Boulder Creek   176
Boulder Lake   440, 443
Bourke, Lt. John   73
Box Canyon   63, 70, 287, 491
Box Creek   365
Boysen Reservoir   98–99, 101–102, 107–108, 113, 115, 121
Boysen State Park   98, 102, 108, 121
Bozeman Trail   61, 78
Bozeman, John   328
Bozeman, MT   61, 74, 78, 93, 186, 237, 257, 324, 327–329, 500, 503–506
Braastad, John   479
Bradley Lakes   362
Bradshaw, Bill   470
Brenkerfoff, Dick   147
Bridger Lake   367
Bridger, Jim   111, 247, 339
Bridger-Teton National Forest   104, 274, 278, 281, 285, 288, 339, 348, 351, 354, 364, 369, 380, 383, 386–387, 397, 400, 403, 414, 418, 424, 436, 507
Bridger–Teton Wilderness   442
Brook trout, description of,   461–463
Brooks Lake   112, 124
Brooks, Charles   213, 237, 241, 249, 266, 487, 489–492
Brown drake, description of,   488
Brown trout, description of,   458–461

Brush Creek   21, 56
Buck Lakes   317
Buffalo Bill (see Cody, William)
Buffalo Bill Reservoir   129, 134–135, 140
Buffalo Bill State Park   134–135
Buffalo Creek   84–85
Buffalo Ford   201, 203–204, 332, 335
Buffalo Fork River   206, 340, 350–351, 353, 367
  North Fork of   206, 367
Buffalo Fork Valley   365
Bull Creek   66–67, 70, 470–471
Bull Lake   110
Bull Lake Creeks   110
Bureau of Land Management   1, 7, 9, 21, 399, 405, 508
Bureau of Reclamation   347
Burgess Junction   61, 63, 66, 69, 77, 84, 94
Burnett   410
Burnt Lake   440

C

Cabin Creek   139
Cable Car Run   239–241, 244
Cache Creek   213, 215, 218, 390
Cache Lake   229
Caddisfly, description of,   489–490
Cain, Randy   504
Calf Creek   281
Calfee Creek   187, 213, 215, 218
Calhoun, Darren   101
Calhoun, Pete   107
Callibaetis, description of,   487
Campanula Creeks   243
Canyon Creek   61, 81, 83–84, 184–185
Caribou Mountains   377
Carrington Island   298, 300
Carter, President Jimmy   175, 223
Cascade Canyon   361
Cascade Corner   171, 280–281, 323
Cascade Creek   316
Cascade Lake   316
Cascade Lakes   180, 185, 467
Casper, WY   5, 14, 27, 30, 33–36, 38, 41, 44, 53–55, 399, 407, 473, 507–508
Cassidy, Butch   57, 61, 84
Catch–and–release   8, 11, 51, 61, 67, 70, 78, 145, 181–182, 186–189, 202, 213, 218, 229, 233, 239, 244, 249, 253, 257, 261, 263, 267, 281, 283, 285, 296–297, 321, 431, 449, 467, 500–501
Catlin, David E.   328

Cave Falls   271, 281, 283, 285, 287–288
Chastain, Debora   55
Cheyenne, WY   10, 17, 27, 47, 50, 59, 73–74, 408, 507–508
Chief Joseph   145, 151, 157, 165, 168, 193
Chironomidae, description of,   492
Chittenden, Hiram   193
Christian Ponds   359
Christina Lake   118
Clark, William   277
Clark's Fork of the Yellowstone River   127, 150–158, 165–166, 168, 193, 447
Clay Butte   165
Clear Creek   81, 92, 297, 315, 399
Clearwater Creek   134
Cleveland, President Grover   213
Cloud Peak Wilderness   61, 77, 81–82, 92
Cody, William (Buffalo Bill)   127, 166
Cody, WY   61, 112, 120, 127, 130, 133, 135, 139–140, 142–145, 147, 149, 151–153, 157, 159–160, 165–168, 171, 175, 193, 322, 458, 500, 503, 507
Coleman, Stu   300
Colonnade Falls   283, 285
Colorado Basin   400
Colorado River cutthroat trout, description of,   447–448, 452
Colter Bay   339, 357, 497
Colter Pass   151, 168
Colter, John   110, 339
Columbia Basin   400
Columbia River   44, 180
Conkle, Ed   167
Conner Battlefield   63
Cook Lake   457
Cook, Charles   291
Cook, Gary   328
Cooke City, MT   151–152, 157, 165, 168–169, 171–172, 193, 207, 213, 218, 221–222, 225–226, 316, 322, 326, 499–500
Cooper Cove   50
Cooper Lakes   441
Copper Lakes   159, 441, 458
Corbett Dam   142
Corps of Discovery   448
Corral Creek   159, 383, 386–387
Corral Creek Lakes   386
Corwin Springs   202
Cottonwood Creek   351, 362, 373, 393
Cottonwood Creeks   205
Cougar Creek   184–185, 191, 242, 447
Court, Frank   168

Crandall Creek   152, 156, 159
Crazy Creek   163, 165
Crazy Horse   73, 78
Crazy Mountain Ranges   324
Crazy Woman Creek   81
Crook, General George   73–74
Crow Creek Lakes   386
Crow Indians   74, 113, 414
Cruikshank, Matthew   130
Crystal Creek   369–370
Crystal Reservoir   50
Cub Creek   297
Culex Basin   252
Culicidae, description of,   492
Curt Gowdy State Park   50
Custer, George Armstrong   73
Cutthroat Trout Grand Slam   385, 400, 407–408, 447–448
Cutthroat trout, description of   447–452
    Bonneville   405, 447–448, 452
    Colorado River   447–448, 452
    Snake River finespotted   447–450, 452
    Westslope   447, 452
    Yellowstone   447–451

D

Damselfly, description of,   492
Daniel, WY   413–416, 418, 420–424, 443
Daniel Junction, WY   413–416, 418, 421
Dead Indian Creek   152, 159
Death Canyon   362
Deer Creek   139, 205, 207
Deer Lodge, MT   504
Dees, Jason   66–67
DeLacey Creek   309, 321
Dennis, Jack   390–391, 431
Denver, CO   27, 47, 66, 168
Devils Tower National Monument   61, 90
Diamond Lake   49
Diamondville, WY   410–411
Dickinson Park   118
Diggins, Lucy   469
Dinwoody Creek   110
Dinwoody Lake   110
Diptera, description of,   492
Divide Lake   263, 265
Doyle Creek   81
Dragonfly, description of,   492
Drunella, description of,   487–488
Dry Creek   78
Dry Fork   405
Duck Creek   242–243, 431, 433, 435–436

Du Noir Access   109, 111
Du Noir Creek   110
Dubois, WY   97, 99, 104, 108, 110–112, 115,
    119, 124–125, 438, 500
Duck Creek   243
Duck Lake   179, 302
Dunraven Pass   335

E

E. K. Wilkins State Park   29, 34–35, 38–39
Eagle Creek   134, 503
Eagle Lake   90
East Fork Madison River   257
East Fork River   433–434, 346
East Fork South Tongue   69, 77
East Fork Wind River   104, 108, 110–111
East Fork Yellowstone River   213
East Newton Lake   144
Eleanor Lake   314
Elk Creek   324
Elk Fork Creek   133–134
Elk Meadow   241, 244
Elk Park   216, 257–258, 261, 375
Elk Tongue Creek   225
Elkhart Park   438–439
Elkhorn Creek   78
Emigrant, MT   326, 506
Encampment River   6–13, 21, 51, 55
Encampment River Wilderness Area   7
Encampment, WY   5–13, 21–22, 51, 55–57,
    74, 487
Ennis, MT   503
Enos Lake   365
Entrance Falls   7, 9–10
Eperous, description of,   489
Ephemera, description of,   488
Ephemerella, description of,   488
Ephemerellidae, description of,   487–488
Ephemeridae, description of,   488
Ephemeroptera, description of,   485–489
Erickson, Jon   347
Evans, John   193
Evanston, WY   397, 405, 409–410, 418,
    445
Excelsior Geyser Crater   247
Expedition Island   426, 429

F

Fairy Falls   319
Fall Creek   373, 391, 401
Fall River Basin   287, 320
Fall River   280, 283, 287–290

Fan Creek   265
Fawn Lake   187–188, 318, 501
Fawn Pass   233, 265, 318
Federation of Fly Fishers   184
Fern Lake   316
Ferris Fork Bechler River   283–285
Ferry Island   422, 424
Fiddlers Lake   118
Finger Lakes   413, 439, 442
Finley, Mike, YNP Superintendent   184
Firehole Canyon   239
Firehole Cascade   251, 253
Firehole Falls   247, 252–253
Firehole River   179, 187, 236–237, 247–255,
    319
First Meadow, Slough Creek   174–175,
    223–226, 317
Fish Creek   21, 221, 373, 391
Fish Lake   282, 287–288, 302
Fishhawk Creek   133–134
Fishing Bridge   109, 172, 181–182, 193,
    202–204, 207–208, 294, 297, 314–315
Fishing Cone   182–183
Fitzpatrick Wilderness   111, 124
Fitzpatrick, Tom   111
Flagg Ranch   271, 274, 277–278, 281–282,
    285, 287–288, 306, 321, 350–351, 357,
    390–391, 497
Flaming Gorge   413, 425–426, 429, 444, 459,
    471
Flat Creek   340, 352, 373–375, 389, 393
Floating Island   317
Folsom, David   291
Fontenelle Creek   426, 428–429, 447
Fontenelle Reservoir   414, 418
Foote Bridge   21, 23–24
Fort Phil Kearny State Historic Site   78, 92
Forty Rod Flat   421, 423–424
Fossil Butte National Monument   397, 410
Fountain Flats   251–252, 319
Franke, Mary Anne   180
Freedom, WY   8, 291, 379–380, 393, 453,
    490
Fremont Canyon   33, 35
Fremont Lake   439, 442
Fremont, John C.   33
French Creek   21
Frye Lake   118

G

Gallatin Gateway, MT   328, 504
Gallatin Lake   265, 267

Gallatin Mountains   229, 263, 265, 319–320
Gallatin National Forest   218, 226, 241, 245, 254, 267
Gallatin River   185, 236–237, 263–269, 319–320, 447, 503
Gallatin, Albert   239, 263
Gardiner, MT   168, 171–172, 189, 193, 199–200, 202, 207, 229, 233–234, 326–327, 499–500, 505
Gardner Canyon   229, 231–232
Gardner Meadows   191, 229, 231, 233, 318, 333
Gardner River   177, 191, 229–235, 333
Gelatt Lake   47, 49
Geronimo   74
Gibbon Falls   187, 257, 260–261
Gibbon Meadows   257–259, 261
Gibbon River   179, 187, 236–237, 256–262, 318–319, 333
Gibbon, Frank   257
Gibbon, John   74
Gibson Meadows   281
Glacier National Park   200
Glen Creek   232–233
Glendo Reservoir   30–31
Glenn Creek   179, 318, 320
Gneiss Creek   243
Golden trout, description of,   457–458
Goose Lake   179, 251–253, 319
Gould, Charlie   86
Grand Canyon of the Yellowstone   171, 176, 191, 193, 196–197, 200, 204–205, 207, 291, 351
Grand Teton National Park   1, 110, 193, 271, 294, 339, 341, 348–349, 352–354, 356–363, 373, 389, 391, 450, 497, 501
Grand Tetons   358
Granite Creek   340, 370
Granite Springs Reservoir   50
Grant Village   172, 315
Grassy Lake Reservoir   287
Gravel Creek Fork   364
Gravel Lake   364
Gray drake, description of,   486
Grayling (see arctic grayling)
Grayling Creek   242–243
Gray Reef Dam   34, 38
Great Basin   385, 397, 400
Grebe Lake   179–180, 191, 237, 244, 257–258, 261, 316, 318–319, 467
Green Basin   420
Green drake, description of,   487–488

Green River   140, 333, 385, 389, 397–399, 401, 408, 413–434, 436, 442–445, 447–448, 459, 471
Green River Lakes   333, 414, 439–440
Green River, WY   413, 417–418, 426, 442–445, 507
Gregg Fork Bechler River   283–285
Gresswell, Robert   180, 298
Grey Reef Dam   34, 38–39
Greybull, WY   61, 69, 84, 101, 143, 145, 167
Greybull River   143, 145
Greys River   377, 382–388, 392, 394, 397, 400–401
Grinnell Creek   133
Grizzly Lake   318
Gros Ventre Mountains   369
Gros Ventre River   340, 364–365, 368–369
Gros Ventre Wilderness Area   370

H

Haines, Aubrey   190
Half Moon Lake   439, 443
Hamilton Dome   122
Hams Fork River   397, 402–403, 405
Hawks Rest   367
Hayden Valley   200, 202, 207
Haystack Mountains   32
Healy Reservoir   91
Heart Lake Geyser Basin   310
Heart Lake   271, 293, 310–313
Heart River   176, 271, 273–274, 311
Hebgen Lake   237, 239, 242–244, 252, 257, 322
Hellroaring Creek   207
Heptageniidae, description of,   489
Hering Lake   287, 321
Hewitt, Edward   176
Hidden Falls   361
High Desert Lakes   127, 144–150, 166
High Lake   319
Hoback Junction   370
Hoback River   340, 369–372, 389
Hobble Creek   403, 405–406, 447
Hog Creek   9–10
Hog Park Creek   10
Hog Park Recreation Area   10, 12
Hog Park Reservoir   9–11
Hogan Reservoir   145
Hoodoo Basin   215
Hoppin River   257
Horseshoe Lakes   163
Hot Springs State Park   98, 101, 121

Hughes Basin   129
Huston Park   51

I

I. O. O. F. Lodge Camp   9
Ice Lake   319
Icebox Canyon   221
Idaho Falls, ID   46, 147, 149, 281, 324, 394, 500, 504
Indian Creek   172, 191, 229, 231–232, 234
Indian Lake   282
Indian Pond   314
Iris Falls   285
Iron Spring Creek   247, 250
Ishawooa Creek   139
Island Lake   165, 317, 323
Island Park, ID   323–324, 481

J

Jack Creek   143
Jacklin, Bob   185, 188, 504
Jackson Game and Fish Office   348
Jackson Hole   110, 171, 200, 206, 247, 271, 312, 339–341, 347, 354, 357, 359, 369–370, 372–373, 389–390, 392, 449, 498
Jackson Lake   347, 353, 359
Jackson, David   339
Jackson, WY   52, 110, 125, 139, 171, 193, 200, 206, 247, 271, 273–274, 281, 285, 288, 303, 312, 333, 339–344, 346–354, 357, 359, 361, 364–365, 367, 369–370, 372–373, 375, 383, 386, 389–392, 394, 406–407, 418, 421, 431, 442–443, 447, 449, 464, 470, 497–498, 500, 503–505, 507
Jakeys Fork   110–111
Jefferson, President Thomas   239, 263
Jenny Lake   357–358, 361–362, 497
Joffe Lake   191, 229, 233, 318
John D. Rockefeller Memorial Parkway   281, 358
Johnson County Cattle War   61
Jordan, David Starr   178
Jordan, Ryan   186
Junction Pool   215, 218
June Creek   166

K

Kaeding, Lynn   247, 294, 302
Kaycee, WY   61, 84, 87–88, 92–93
Kelley, Tim   17

Kemmerer, WY   386, 397, 400, 402–403, 410–411, 445
Kemmerer City Reservoir   402–403
Kendall Warm Springs   418–419, 423
Kepler Cascade   252
Kern River   457
Kerns Wildlife Management Area   78
Ketchum, ID   504
Keyhole State Park   90
Kids-only waters   229, 375
Kiefling, John   347
Knowles Falls   200, 204, 207
Kortes Reservoir   38

L

LaBarge Creek   385–386, 397, 399–402, 405
LaBarge Meadows   385, 401, 405
Lake Alice   403, 406, 447
Lake Alsop   49
Lake Angeline   81
Lake Barstow   386
Lake Butte Drive   206, 297
Lake Cameahwait   115
Lake DeSmet   61, 90
Lake George   505
Lake Hattie   47, 49
Lake Michigan   179, 303–304, 464–465
Lake Solitude   81, 359
Lake Superior   301, 465
Lake Tahoe   459
Lake trout
   description of   464–465
   in Yellowstone National Park   182–189, 294–297
Lake Village   172
Lake Viva Naughton   397, 402–403, 410–411
Lamar Basin   213
Lamar Canyon   213, 217
Lamar River   168, 176, 187–188, 191, 197–198, 200, 205–208, 213–221, 500
Lamar Valley   168, 193, 213, 215, 218, 326
Lamar, Lucius   213
Lander Loop Road   117
Lander, WY   36, 97–98, 104, 110–113, 115–120, 122–124, 438, 445, 507
Lane, Scott   389
Langford, Nathaniel   291
Langston, Al   448
Laramie Plains   5, 47–52, 57
Laramie River   5, 48, 50–51
Laramie, WY   5, 17–18, 46–52, 57–59, 83, 471, 507

Lava Creek   229, 231
Lawson, Mike   324
Leazenby Lake   49
LeHardy Rapids   160
Leigh Canyon   361
Leigh Lake   359, 361–362
Lemm, Doug   36
Leptophlebiidae, description of,   488–489
Lewis Canyon   276–278, 501
Lewis Falls   278, 307
Lewis Fork of the Snake   377
Lewis Lake   172, 179, 271, 273–278, 291,
   293–294, 300–310, 315, 464–465, 501
Lewis River   187, 271, 275–279, 293,
   304–306, 309, 464, 501
Lewis, Dan   36
Lewis, Meriwether   239, 276, 448
Lilly, Bud   322, 503
Little Bighorn River   73, 76, 78, 447, 470
Little Firehole River   247, 250, 252–253
Little Goose Creek   73
Little Greys River   383–384, 387
Little Lamar River   215
Little Laramie River   51
Little Moose Lake   163
Little Popo Agie   113, 115–116, 118–119
Little Snake River   10–11, 448, 471
Little Wind River   110
Livingston, MT   190, 193, 200, 277, 324–327,
   500, 502, 504–506
Loch Leven   304
Long Lakes   163
Louis Lake   117–118, 123
Lovell, WY   61, 69, 97, 101, 145, 167
Lower Falls   173, 200
Lower Geyser Basin   179, 247
Lower Jade Lakes   112
Lower Slide Lake   364–365, 369
Lower Sunlight Creek   159
Lower Tensleep Creek   83
Luce Reservoir   145
Lunch Counter Rapids   350
Lusby Access   38

M

Maclean, Norman   266
Madison Basin   237, 239
Madison, President James   237
Madison Junction   172, 237, 242, 244–245,
   252–254, 257, 261
Madison Lake   247, 253
Madison Mountain Range   237

Madison River   176, 179, 187–188, 236–246,
   252, 257, 261, 307, 319, 322, 337, 447,
   467, 503–504
Mahogany dun, description of,   488–489
Mahoney, Dan   186, 296, 300
Mammoth, Mammoth Hot Springs   172,
   193
Mammoth Beaver Ponds   317
Marble, Mike   425
Mariposa Lake   271, 274, 320
Matthews, Cheryl   302
Matthews, Chip   130
Mayfly, description of,   485–489
McBride Lake   160, 317
McClane, Albert   175, 202
McDonald, Leland   151, 160
McKnight, Ron   159, 163, 458
McPhee, John   47
Meadow Creek   440
Meadow Lake   438, 440, 467
Meadowlark Lake   82–83, 92
Medicine Bow National Forest   7, 12, 18, 21,
   25, 51–52, 55, 57, 507
Medicine Bow National Forest Snowy Range
   Area   52
Medicine Bow Range   47, 51
Medicine Lodge Creek   84
Medicine Lodge State Archaeological Site
   84
Meeboer Lake   49
Meeteetse, WY   143, 145
Michael, Ed   399, 401
Middle Fork Popo Agie River   117, 119
Middle Fork Powder River   84–88, 92
Middle Geyser Basin   251
Midge, description of,   492
Midway Geyser Basin   247, 253
Miller Creeks   215
Minnetaree Indians   193, 200
Miracle Mile, Lower North Platte River   5,
   14, 21, 27, 32–34, 38, 41–43, 45–46, 53,
   464
Missouri River   14, 190, 193, 237, 263, 447
Mist Creek   215, 218
Mitchell, Finis   438, 457
Mixer, Bill   407
Money, Dave   469
Monster Lake   142, 144–145, 147–149, 167,
   414
Montgomery, M. R.   202
Moody, Dave   139
Moose Creek   225, 276, 308, 418–419

Moose Flat   387
Moose Lake   163
Moose Landing   348, 353
Moose Pond   359
Moose, WY, GTNP   206, 343–344, 348–349, 353, 357, 359, 362, 267, 390–391, 497, 506
Moran Junction   351, 364–365
Mosquito, description of,   492
Mountain Ash Creek   287–288
Mountain whitefish, description of,   466–467
Muddy Creek   165
Muddy Guard Reservoirs   90–91
Murphy Creek Lakes   386

N

Names Hill Historic Site   422–424
National Bighorn Sheep Interpretive Center   124
National Elk Refuge   340, 369, 373, 375
National Park Service   177–179, 181–184, 186, 307, 310, 312–313, 351, 359, 502
Native Fish Restoration Plan   182
Never Summer Mountains   50
New Fork Lakes   439
New Fork River   413–414, 422–423, 430–437, 439
Newton Creek   130, 135
Nez Perce Creek   247, 251–254
Nez Perce Indians   257
Nolte, Dave   399
Norris   172, 177, 233–234, 237, 257–258, 260–261, 316, 318–319, 329
Norris Geyser Basin   177, 237, 257–258, 261
North Fork Buffalo River   206, 367
North Fork Shoshone River   127–137
North Gate Canyon   17–18, 21, 25
North Platte Reservoirs   33, 473
North Platte River   5, 7, 12, 14–46, 50, 55, 83, 414, 464, 470–471
North Tongue River   66–68, 70
Northern Arapahoe Indian Tribes   104
Northern Big Horns Lakes   77
Northern Range   213, 221, 231–232
Nowlin Creek   375
Nowood River   84

O

Obsidian Creeks   231, 233
Ocean Lake   115
Odonata, description of,   492
Ojo Caliente   251–252, 254

Old Faithful   172, 247, 250, 253
Olsen, Chad   503
Oregon Trail   14, 33, 36, 409
Osprey Falls   229, 231, 233
Outlaw Cave   84–85, 87–88
Outlaw Cave Canyon   84, 88
Outlaw Trail   61
Outlet Lake   201, 207, 261, 278, 312, 319–320
Ouzel Creek   283, 285
Owl Creek Mountains   104, 107, 109

P

Pacific Creek   200, 206, 316, 339–341, 346, 349–350, 353, 364, 367, 449
Paint Rock Creek   84, 160
Pale morning dun, description of,   488
Palisades Reservoir   340–341, 348, 353, 377, 379, 392, 447, 470
Panther Creek   233
Paraleptophlebia, description of,   488–489
Parker, Jack   50, 147, 149
Parks, Gary   302
Parks, Richard   189, 505
Pathfinder Reservoir   27, 33, 35–36, 38, 41, 464
Pebble Creek   172, 187, 213, 218, 221–223, 226, 316
Pedro Mountains   33
Pelican Creek   298, 316, 351
Peterson, William   291
Phelps Lake   362
Phillips Fork Bechler River   283–285, 323, 409
Pick Bridge   21–22, 44
Pierce, Steve   302, 314
Pine Creek   431, 436
Pinedale, WY   104, 111, 115, 139, 159, 333, 389, 413–414, 418, 421–422, 424, 431, 433–436, 438–443, 447–448, 457–458, 467, 507
Pink Albert, description of,   489
Plains Indian Museum   166
Platte River
   North   5, 7, 12, 14–46, 50, 55, 83, 414, 464, 470–471
   South   14, 447, 470
Platte River Wilderness Area   17
Plecoptera, description of,   490–491
PMD (see pale morning dun)
Pocket Lake   187, 304, 308, 321
Pole Creek   434
Polecat Creek   352

Pollard, Russ   293
Popo Agie Falls   118
Popo Agie River   113–119, 122
    Middle Fork   117, 119
    North Fork   119
Popo Agie Wilderness   111–112, 114–115,
    118–119
Powder River   61, 82, 84–88, 92
    Middle Fork   84–88, 92
Powell, John Wesley   426, 444
Powell, WY   142, 426, 444
Prune Creek   69–70
Pryor Mountains   101

R

Ragged Falls   285
Rainbow Falls   288
Rainbow trout, description of,   452–456, 473
Rainey Lakes   316
Ranchester, WY   63, 70, 101
Ranger Lake   294, 315, 321, 497, 501–502
Rasmussen, Ted   147
Rawlins, WY   22, 32, 56–57, 448, 508
Red Canyon   116
Red Creek   273
Red Mountains   271
Red Rock Lakes National Wildlife Refuge
    185
Reef Creek   156
Reese Creek   173
Remmick, Ron   448
Rexburg, ID   324
Ribbon Lake   316
Riddle Lake   315
Ring Lake   112
Rio Verde (see also Green River)   414
Risch, Jim   301
Riverton, WY   104, 108, 113, 122, 124–125
Robertson, Philip W.   166
Robinder, Rod   41
Robinson Dam   101
Roches Jaunes, Rocks Yellow   193
Rock Canyon   200
Rock Creek   84, 160, 399
Rock Point   297
Rock Springs, WY   438, 445, 457, 508
Rocky Ford   283, 285
Roosevelt, President Theodore   127, 166
Rose, Jeremy   145
Rosebud Creek   73
Ross, John   422
Routt National Forest   18

Russell, Osborne   213

S

Salt Creek   406, 447
Salt Lake   168, 385, 400, 405
Salt Mountains   377, 383, 385–286, 405, 470
Salt River   376–381, 385, 392, 397, 401,
    405–406, 470
Sand Creek   61, 89
Saratoga Lake   21, 25
Saratoga, WY   5, 7, 14, 17, 19, 21–25, 33,
    55–57
Savage Run Wilderness Area   18
Sawmill Lakes   77
Sawmill Pond   359
Sawtooth Mountains   151
Schneider, Bill   165
Schwiebert, Ernest   249
Scott Botton Nature Park   429
Second Meadow, Slough Creek   224–225
Sedge Creek   178
Seedskadee National Wildlife Refuge   414,
    425–426, 429
Seminoe Mountains   32, 41
Seminoe Reservoir   5, 27
Seminoe State Park   32
Sentinel Creek   251, 253
Shaky Lake   317
Sharpe, F. Phillip   302
Sheep Creek   63, 70, 134, 487
Sheep Gulch   351, 353
Sheepeater Canyon   229, 231, 233
Sheepeater Cliffs   233
Shell Creek   61, 84
Shell Creek Canyon   61, 84
Sheridan Creek   110
Sheridan Lake   320
Sheridan, Philip   76
Sheridan, WY   61, 63, 68–69, 73, 75–78, 82,
    94–95, 101, 110, 166–168, 310–311, 320,
    470, 500, 503, 507
Shoshone Creek   309
Shoshone Falls   181, 341, 449
Shoshone Lake   176, 179, 187, 190, 271, 275,
    278, 293, 301, 303–304, 307–309, 321, 465
Shoshone National Forest   36, 104, 110, 112,
    115, 118, 120, 127, 130, 135, 139, 143,
    152, 156–157, 159, 166, 507
Shoshone River   127–141, 166
    North Fork   128–137
    South Fork   138–140
Sibley Lake   77

Sierra Madre Mountains   14, 55
Sierra Nevada Range   448, 457
Silver Corde Cascade   204
Silver Creek   323
Silver Gate, MT   168–169, 500
Silvertip Creeks   129
Sinclair, WY   22, 24, 32, 41
Sinks Canyon   98, 116–117, 122
Sinks Canyon State Park   98, 116–117, 122
Sioux Indian   78, 92
Sioux Indian Wars   78
Siphlonuridae, description of,   486
Sitting Bull   73
Six Mile Gap, North Platte River   17–20, 24
Slide Lakes   318
Slough Creek   172, 174–175, 191, 213, 215,
   218, 223–228, 317
Smith Creek   386
Smith, Donald   325
Smiths Fork River   385–386, 400, 405, 447
Smoot, WY   377, 379, 383, 385, 393
Snake River   10–11, 107, 145, 178, 181, 188,
   190–191, 270–274, 277–278, 303, 306,
   309–310, 313, 320, 333–334, 336,
   339–357, 359, 369–373, 377, 379, 383,
   386–387, 389–390, 397, 400, 406–407,
   447–450, 452, 464, 470–471, 505
   Lewis Fork   377
Snake River Basin   191, 271
Snake River finespotted cutthroat trout,
   description of,   447–450, 452
Snowy Mountain Range   5, 14, 18, 21, 47,
   50–52, 55, 57–59
Snyder Lake   163
Soda Butte   214, 220–221
Soda Butte Creek   168, 187–189, 191–193,
   213–215, 218–222, 225, 500
Soda Lake   364, 439
Sodergreen Lake   49
Solfatara Creek   258
Solfatara Plateau   258
Solution Creek   315
South Fork Shoshone River   138–140
South Park, WY (Jackson Hole)   98, 350, 352,
   354, 373, 393
South Pass, WY   14, 33, 36, 97, 117–119, 320
South Pine, WY   442–443
South Piney Creek   78–79
South Platte River   14, 447, 470
South Tongue River   66, 69–70
Southern Big Horns Gateway   80–81, 83–84
Spanish River   414

Specimen Creek   265, 267, 320, 447
Speckle-winged dun, description of,   484
Sportsman Lake   265, 319–320
Squaw Lake   314
Staples, Bruce   307, 309–311, 313
Star Valley   339–340, 377, 383, 385–386,
   392–394
Steadham, George   166
Steamboat Springs, CO   11
Stone, Mike   67, 89, 160, 399, 441
Stonefly, description of,   490–491
Story, WY   78–79, 92–94
Straight Creek   318
String Lake   361–363
Strong, W. F.   176
Sulfur Creek Reservoirs   447
Sulphur Cauldron   202, 204, 207
Sunlight Basin   151, 159, 166, 193
Sunlight Creek   152, 156–157, 159
Sunshine Reservoirs   145
Surprise Creeks   310, 312
Surprise Lake   159, 441, 458
Swamp Lake   159
Swan Lake   232, 359
Swan Valley   377, 389
Sweetwater Creek   134
Sweetwater Gap   36, 118
Sweetwater River   14, 33, 36–37
Swift Creek   379
Sylvan Lake   315

T

Taggart Lake   351
Tall Grass River   113
Targhee National Forest   281, 283, 285, 288
Tensleep Creek   61, 82–84
Terrace Falls   288
Teton Mountains   282, 339, 341, 358–359,
   361–362
Teton Village, WY   390–391, 506
Teton Wilderness Area   271, 281, 364–365
Thayne, WY   377–379, 392–394
Thermopolis, WY   97–99, 101–102, 104, 108,
   121–122
Third Meadow, Slough Creek   224–225
Thomas Fork River   406, 447
Thompson, David   193
Thornberry, Matt   43, 45
Thornberry, Rob   41, 43, 45–46
Thorofare Creek   206–207, 340
Three Forks, MT   36, 81, 190, 237, 239, 263,
   266

Tice, Lloyd   166
Tillery Lake   282
Tongue River   61–74, 76, 78, 81, 84, 94
   North Tongue   66–68, 70
   South Tongue   66, 69–70
Tongue River Canyon   70, 78, 94
Toppings Lakes   364
Torrey Lake   112
Tosi Creeks   418
Tower Creek   205, 207
Tower Falls   172, 205
Tower Junction   172, 193, 200, 205, 221
Trail Creek   206–207, 233, 297, 315–317,
   320–321, 364, 504
Trail Lake   112, 265, 271, 273, 288, 310,
   315–316, 319–321, 367
Trapper Lake   362
Treasure Island   15–16, 19–22, 24
Treese, Reggie   99
Tri Basin Divide   384–385, 387, 397–400
Trichoptera, description of,   489–490
Tricorythodes, description of,   489
Tricorythodidae, description of,   489
Trout (*see* brook trout, brown trout, cutthroat
   trout, golden trout, and lake trout)
Trout Unlimited   347, 399, 401
Turpin Meadows   206, 367, 391
Twin Buttes Lake   49
Twin Lakes   77, 163
Two Ocean Pass   200, 206, 339, 341, 367,
   449

U

U. S. Fish and Wildlife Service   89, 104,
   180–181, 185, 191, 247, 299
U. S. Fish Commission   178–179, 302
U. S. Forest Service   66, 82, 298, 399, 507
U. S. Geological Survey   287, 348, 367
Union Falls   283, 287
Upper Geyser Basin   237, 247, 249, 253
Upper Slide Lake   364, 369

V

Vanhoff, Randall   259
Varley, John   179, 185, 191
Victor, WY   391
Virginia Cascade   257–258, 261, 318
Virginia Meadows   258, 261

W

Wade, Tim   130, 142, 155, 159, 175
Waha Lake   449

Walinchus, Rod   14
Walleye   14, 24, 34, 44, 90, 98, 113, 473
Wapiti Ranger Station   127, 129, 134
Wapiti Valley   127, 129, 166, 193, 500
Warm Springs   55, 124, 418–419, 423
Warren Bridge   419–421, 423–424
Washakie Wilderness Area   127
Washburn Expedition   291
Waterdog Lake   386
Wedding of the Waters   97, 99, 101–102,
   107–108, 121
Wengert, Bill   471
West Newton Lake   145
West Pass Creek   78
Westslope cutthroat trout, description of,
   447, 452
West Tensleep Creek   83
West Tensleep Lake   81, 83
West Thumb Geyser Basin   183
West Yellowstone, MT   53, 166–167, 171,
   176, 185, 188, 237, 240, 242–243, 245,
   254, 261, 265, 267, 281, 322–324, 500,
   502–505
Whirling Disease   8, 130, 179, 469–471
Whiskey Mountain Wildlife Management
   Area   111–112
White Lakes   316
White-winged black, description of,   489
Whitlock, Dave   483
Whittlesey, Lee   293
Wichers, Bill   42
Widrig, Jim   17
Wiley, Bob   471
Willow Lake   439
Willow Park Reservoir   81
Willwood Dam   142
Wilson, WY   345, 347–350, 352–353, 359,
   372, 389–391, 503, 505–506
Wind River   33, 36, 97–99, 101, 104–113,
   115–116, 118–119, 121–125, 339, 389,
   413–414, 418, 420, 425, 431, 438–443,
   445, 457, 508
Wind River Canyon   97, 99, 101, 104,
   107–108, 121–122
Wind River Headwaters   110
Wind River Indian Reservation   97, 104–105,
   107, 110–111, 115, 118, 122, 508
Wind River Lake   110, 115
Wind River Mountains   110, 420, 438, 441
Wind River Roadless Area   115
Wind Rivers Divide   110
Winegar Wilderness Area   281

Wister, Owen   176
Witch Creek   310–311
Wolf Lake   258, 261, 319
Wood River   143
Woodruff Narrows Reservoir   405
Woods Landing   51, 58
Woods, Rebecca   112, 119, 438, 457
Worland, WY   61, 83, 101
Worthen Reservoir   118
Wyoming Dinosaur Center   121
Wyoming Division of Tourism   507
Wyoming Fishing Regulations   495
Wyoming Game and Fish Department, Information and Regions   507
Wyoming Mountain Range   370, 386, 401, 407

Y

Yekel, Steve   145, 151
Yellowstone cutthroat trout, description of, 447–451
Yellowstone Delta   193, 202, 207–208, 320
Yellowstone Falls   302

Yellowstone Lake   171–191, 193, 195–196, 200–202, 207–208, 278, 291–303, 307, 314–315, 367, 447, 449, 464–465, 500–501
Yellowstone National Park   1, 104, 110, 127, 129, 135, 147, 151, 160, 163, 166, 168–331, 335, 347, 353, 357, 389–391, 400, 407, 447, 464, 467, 499–502, 506
   General Information   499
Yellowstone River   73, 83, 110, 150–153, 155–157, 160, 171, 173, 176–177, 179, 181–182, 184, 186–213, 223, 229, 233, 273, 277, 291, 293–294, 297, 315, 317, 321, 324, 326, 331–332, 337, 339–341, 366–367, 447–451, 464, 490, 501
   Clark's Fork   127, 150–158, 165–166, 168, 193, 447
Yellowstone Timberland Reserve   127
Yellowtail Dam   101–102
Yule, Dan   473

Z

Zapatas   167

NOTES

NOTES

NOTES

NOTES

WILDERNESS ADVENTURES GUIDE SERIES

If you would like to order additional copies of this book or our other Wilderness Adventures Press guidebooks, please fill out the order form below or call **800-925-3339** or **fax 800-390-7558.** Visit our website for a listing of over 2500 sporting books — the largest online: **www.wildadv.com**

Mail to: Wilderness Adventures Press, 45 Buckskin Road
                     Belgrade, MT 59714

☐ **Please send me your quarterly catalog on hunting and fishing books.**

Ship to:
Name _____

Address _____

City _____State_____ Zip_____

Home Phone_____Work Phone_____

Payment: ☐ Check   ☐ Visa   ☐ Mastercard   ☐ Discover   ☐ American Express

Card Number _____ Expiration Date_____

Signature_____

Qty	Title of Book and Author	Price	Total
	Flyfisher's Guide to Colorado	$26.95	
	Flyfisher's Guide to Idaho	$26.95	
	Flyfisher's Guide to Montana	$26.95	
	Flyfisher's Guide to Northern California	$26.95	
	Flyfisher's Guide to Wyoming	$26.95	
	Flyfisher's Guide to Washington	$26.95	
	Flyfisher's Guide to Oregon	$26.95	
	Flyfisher's Guide to Northern New England	$26.95	
	Total Order + shipping & handling		

**Shipping and handling: $4.00 for first book,
$2.50 per additional book, up to $11.50 maximum**